The British Isles

Varieties of English 1

The British Isles

Edited by
Bernd Kortmann and Clive Upton

Mouton de Gruyter · Berlin · New York

Mouton de Gruyter (formerly Mouton, The Hague)
is a Division of Walter de Gruyter GmbH & Co. KG, Berlin.

♾ Printed on acid-free paper which falls within the guidelines of the ANSI to ensure permanence and durability.

Library of Congress Cataloging-in-Publication Data

The British Isles / edited by Bernd Kortmann, Clive Upton.
p. cm. – (Varieties of English ; 1)
Includes bibliographical references and indexes.
ISBN 978-3-11-019635-1 (pbk. : alk. paper)
1. English language – Dialects – Great Britain. 2. English language – Variation – Great Britain. I. Kortmann, Bernd, 1960– II. Upton, Clive, 1946–
PE1711.B65 2008
427–dc22
2007045291

Bibliographic information published by the Deutsche Nationalbibliothek

The Deutsche Nationalbibliothek lists this publication in the Deutsche Nationalbibliografie; detailed bibliographic data are available in the Internet at http://dnb.d-nb.de.

ISBN 978-3-11-019635-1

Cover design: Martin Zech, Bremen.
Imagery provided by Google Earth/TerraMetrics, NASA.
Typesetting: Dörlemann Satz GmbH & Co. KG, Lemförde.
Printing and binding: AZ Druck und Datentechnik GmbH, Kempten (Allgäu).
Printed in Germany.

Contents

Phonology

Morphology and Syntax

Contents of volume 2

Phonology

Morphology and Syntax

Contents of volume 3

Phonology

Morphology and Syntax

Contents of volume 4

Phonology

Morphology and Syntax

Abbreviations

AAVE	African American Vernacular English
AbE/C/P	(Australian) Aboriginal English / Creole / Pidgin
AfBahE	Afro-Bahamian English
AfkE	Afrikaans English
AmE	American English
AnBahE	Anglo-Bahamian English
AppE	Appalachian English
AusE/VE/C	Australian English/Vernacular English/Creoles
BahE	Bahamian English
Baj	Bajan (Barbadian Creole)
BelC	Belizean Creole
BIE	Bay Islands English (Honduras)
BrC	British Creole
BrE	British English (= EngE + ScE + WelE)
ButlE	Butler English (India)
CajE	Cajun English
CAmC	Central American Creoles (Belize, Miskito, Limón, etc.)
CamP/E	Cameroon Pidgin/English
CanE	Canadian English
CarE	Caribbean English
Car(E)C	Caribbean (English-lexicon) Creoles
CFE	Cape Flats English
ChcE	Chicano English
ChnP	Chinese Pidgin English
CollAmE	Colloquial American English
CollSgE	Colloquial Singapore English
EAfE	East African English
EMarC	Eastern Maroon Creole
EngE	English English
EModE	Early Modern English
ME	Middle English
OE	Old English
ESM	English in Singapore and Malaysia
FijE	Fiji English
GhE/P	Ghanaian English/Pidgin
GuyC	Guyanese Creole
HawC	Hawaii Creole

HKE	Hong Kong English
IndE	Indian English, Anglo-Indian
InlNE	Inland Northern (American) English
IrE	Irish English
JamC/E	Jamaican Creole / English
KenE	Kenyan English
KPE	Kru Pidgin English
LibC/E	Liberian Creole/English
LibSE	Liberian Settler English
LibVE	Liberian Vernacular English
LimC	Limonese Creole (Costa Rica)
LonVE	London Vernacular English
LnkE	Lankan English
MalE	Malaysian English
NEngE	New England English
NfldE	Newfoundland English
NigP/E	Nigerian Pidgin / English
NZE	New Zealand English
NYCE	New York City English
OzE	Ozarks English
PakE	Pakistani English
PanC	Panamanian Creole
PhilE	Philadelphia English
PhlE	Philippines English
RP	Received Pronunciation
SAfE	South African English
BlSAfE	Black South African English
CoSAfE	Coloured South African English
InSAfE	Indian South African English
WhSAfE	White South African English
SAmE	Southern American English
SAsE	South Asian English
SEAmE	South Eastern American English enclave dialects
ScE	Scottish English, Scots
ScStE	Scottish Standard English
SgE	Singapore English
SLVE	St. Lucian Vernacular English
SolP	Solomon Islands Pidgin
StAmE	Standard American English
StAusCE	Standard Australian Colloquial English

StAusFE	Standard Australian Formal English
StBrE	Standard British English
StE	Standard English
StGhE	Standard Ghanaian English
StHE	St. Helena English
StIndE	Standard Indian English
StJamE	Standard Jamaican English
SurC	Suriname Creoles
TanE	Tanzanian English
TobC	Tobagonian Creole
Trad-RP	Traditional Received Pronunciation
TrnC	Trinidadian Creole
T&TC	Trinidadian & mesolectal Tobagonian Creoles
TP	Tok Pisin, New Guinea Pidgin, Neomelanesian
WAfE/P	West African English/Pidgin
WelE	Welsh English
WMwE	Western and Midwestern American English
ZamE	Zambian English

More abbreviations

ESL	English as Second Language
EFL	English as Foreign Language
EIL	English as International Language
ENL	English as Native Language
L1	First Language
L2	Second Language
P/C	Pidgins and Creoles

List of features: Phonology and phonetics

Edgar W. Schneider

Please indicate whether or to what extent the following features / variants occur in the variety that you have discussed by inserting A, B or C in the left-most column as follows:

A occurs normally / is widespread
B occurs sometimes / occasionally, with some speakers / groups, in some environments
C does not normally occur.

If you have covered more than one variety, please give your set of responses for each of them, or give a summary assessment for a group of related varieties as specified.

Elements in parentheses (../..) are optional; ">" suggests a direction of movement.

Please note that the variants suggested for a single item (e.g. lexical set) are meant to be relatively exhaustive but not necessarily mutually exclusive.

Phonetic realization: vowels (lexical sets)

1. KIT [ɪ]
2. KIT raised / fronted, > [i]
3. KIT centralized, > [ə]
4. KIT with offglide, e.g. [ɪə/iə]
5. DRESS half-close [e]
6. DRESS raised, > [i]
7. DRESS half-open [ɛ]
8. DRESS backed, > [ʌ/ɐ]
9. DRESS with centralizing offglide, e.g. [eə]
10. DRESS with rising offglide, e.g. [eɪ]
11. TRAP [æ]
12. TRAP raised, > [ɛ/e]
13. TRAP lowered, > [a]
14. TRAP with offglide, e.g. [æə/æɛ/æɪ/ɛə]
15. LOT rounded, e.g. [ɒ]
16. LOT back unrounded, e.g. [ɑ]

17. LOT front unrounded, e.g. [a]
18. LOT with offglide, e.g. [ɒə]
19. STRUT [ʌ]
20. STRUT high back, > [ʊ]
21. STRUT central [ə/ɐ]
22. STRUT backed, > [ɔ]
23. FOOT [ʊ]
24. FOOT tensed [u]
25. FOOT back, lower, e.g. [ʌ]
26. BATH half-open front [æ]
27. BATH low front [a]
28. BATH low back [ɑ]
29. BATH long
30. BATH with offglide, e.g. [æə/æɪ/ɛə]
31. CLOTH rounded [ɔ/ɒ]
32. CLOTH back unrounded [ɑ]
33. CLOTH front unrounded [a]
34. NURSE central [ɜː/ɚ]
35. NURSE raised / fronted / rounded, e.g. [ø]
36. NURSE mid front [ɛ/e(r)]
37. NURSE [ʌ(r)] (possibly lexically conditioned, e.g. WORD)
38. NURSE backed, e.g. [o/ɔ]
39. NURSE diphthongal, e.g. [əɪ/ɔɪ]
40. FLEECE [iː]
41. FLEECE with centralizing offglide, e.g. [iə]
42. FLEECE with mid/central onset and upglide, e.g. [əɪ/ei]
43. FLEECE with high onset and upglide, e.g. [ɪi]
44. FLEECE shortened, e.g. [i/ɪ]
45. FACE upgliding diphthong with half-close onset, e.g. [eɪ]
46. FACE upgliding diphthong with half-open or lower onset, e.g. [ɛɪ/æɪ]
47. FACE upgliding diphthong with low / backed onset, e.g. [a(ː)ɪ/ʌɪ]
48. FACE upgliding diphthong with central onset, e.g. [əɪ]
49. FACE monophthong, e.g. [eː]
50. FACE ingliding diphthong, e.g. [ɪə/ɪɛ]
51. PALM low back [ɑ(ː)]
52. PALM low front [a(ː)]
53. PALM with offglide, e.g. [ɑə/ɒə]
54. THOUGHT [ɔ(ː)]
55. THOUGHT low [aː/ɑː]
56. THOUGHT with offglide, e.g. [ɔə/ʊə]

57. GOAT with central onset, e.g. [əʊ/əʉ]
58. GOAT with back rounded onset, e.g. [oʊ/ou]
59. GOAT with low or back unrounded onset, e.g. [a(:)u/aʉ/ʌʊ/ʌʉ]
60. GOAT with relatively high back onset [ʊu]
61. GOAT ingliding, e.g. [ʊə/uɔ/ua]
62. GOAT monophthongal, e.g. [o(:)]
63. GOOSE [u:]
64. GOOSE fronted, > [ʉ(:)]
65. GOOSE gliding, e.g. [ʊu/ɪu/ə(:)ʉ]
66. PRICE upgliding diphthong, e.g. [aɪ/ɑɪ/ʌɪ]
67. PRICE monophthong [a:] before voiced C
68. PRICE monophthong [a:] in all environments
69. PRICE with raised / central onset, e.g. [əɪ/ɜɪ]
70. PRICE with backed onset, e.g. [ɔ(:)ɪ/ɒɪ]
71. PRICE with mid-front offglide, e.g. [ae/aɛ]
72. CHOICE [ɔɪ]
73. CHOICE with low onset [ɒɪ]
74. CHOICE with central onset [əɪ/əi]
75. MOUTH [aʊ/ɑʊ]
76. MOUTH with raised and backed onset, e.g. [ʌu/ɔʊ]
77. MOUTH with raised onset [əʊ] only before voiceless C
78. MOUTH with raised onset [əʊ] in all environments
79. MOUTH with fronted onset, e.g. [æʉ/æʊ/æo/ɛo]
80. MOUTH low monophthong, e.g. [a:]
81. MOUTH mid/high back monophthong, e.g. [o:]
82. NEAR [ɪə(r)]
83. NEAR without offglide, e.g. [ɪr]
84. NEAR with tensed / raised onset, e.g. [i(:)ə]
85. NEAR with half-closed onset [e(:/ə/r)/ea]
86. NEAR with half-open onset [ɛ(:/ə/r)]
87. NEAR high-front to low glide, e.g. [ia]
88. SQUARE with half-open onset [ɛə]
89. SQUARE with half-closed onset [eə/ea]
90. SQUARE with high front onset [ɪə]
91. SQUARE with relatively open onset, possibly rising [æə/æɪ]
92. SQUARE half-closed monophthong, [e(:/r)]
93. SQUARE half-open monophthong, [ɛ(:/r)]
94. START low back unrounded, e.g. [ɑ(:/r)]
95. START central, e.g. [ɐ(:/r)]
96. START low front, e.g. [a(:/r)]

97. START front, raised, e.g. [æ(:/r)]
98. START with offglide, e.g. [ɑə/ɒə)]
99. NORTH half-open monophthong [ɔ(:/r)]
100. NORTH half-closed monophthong [o(:/r)]
101. NORTH [ɒ]
102. NORTH with offglide, e.g. [ɒə/oa]
103. FORCE half-open monophthong [ɔ(:/r)]
104. FORCE half-closed monophthong [o(:/r)]
105. FORCE ingliding, e.g. [ɔə(r)/oə(r)/oa]
106. FORCE with upglide, e.g.[oʊ(r)]
107. CURE [ʊə/ʊr]
108. CURE with tensed / raised onset, e.g. [u(:)ə/ur]
109. CURE lowered monophthong, e.g. [o:/ɔ:]
110. CURE with upglide, e.g. [oʊ(r)]
111. CURE low offglide, e.g. [ua/oa(r)]
112. happY relatively centralized, e.g. [ɪ]
113. happY central, e.g. [ə]
114. happY tensed / relatively high front, e.g. [i(:)]
115. happY mid front, e.g. [e/ɛ]
116. lettER [ə]
117. lettER (relatively) open, e.g. [a/ʌ]
118. horsES central [ə]
119. horsES high front [ɪ]
120. commA [ə]
121. commA (relatively) open, e.g. [a/ʌ]

Distribution: vowels

122. homophony of KIT and FLEECE
123. homophony of TRAP and BATH
124. homophony of *Mary* and *merry*
125. homophony of *Mary*, *merry* and *marry*
126. homophony of TRAP and DRESS before /l/
127. merger of KIT and DRESS before nasals (*pin* = *pen*)
128. homophony of DRESS and FACE
129. homophony of FOOT and GOOSE
130. homophony of LOT and THOUGHT
131. homophony of LOT and STRUT
132. homophony of NEAR and SQUARE

133. vowels nasalized before nasal consonants
134. vowel harmony / cross-syllable assimilation phenomena in some words
135. vowels short unless before /r/, voiced fricative, or in open syllable (SVLR)
136. commA/lettER (etc.): [ɑ/ɛ/i/ɔ/u], reflecting spelling

Phonetic realization and distribution: consonants

137. P/T/K-: weak or no aspiration of word-initial stops
138. -T-: lenisation / flapping / voicing of intervocalic /t/ (*writer* = *rider*)
139. -T: realization of word-final or intervocalic /t/ as glottal stop
140. K-: palatalization of velar stop word-initially: e.g. kj-/gj-in *can't/ garden*
141. B-: word-initial *bw-* for b-: e.g. *bw-* in *boy*
142. S-/F-: voiceless initial fricatives voiced: [z-/v-]
143. TH-: realization of word-initial voiced TH as stop, e.g. *dis*, 'this'
144. TH-: realization of word-initial voiceless TH as stop, e.g. *ting, 'thing'*
145. TH-: realization of word-initial voiced TH as affricate [dð]
146. TH-: realization of word-initial voiceless TH as affricate [tθ]
147. WH-: velar fricative onset retained, i.e. *which* is not homophonous with *witch*
148. CH: voiceless velar fricative [χ/x] exists
149. h-deletion (word-initial), e.g., *'eart* 'heart*'*
150. h-insertion (word-initial), e.g. *haxe* 'axe'
151. L-: palatal (clear) variant in syllable onsets
152. L-: velar variant in syllable onsets
153. –L: palatal variant in syllable codas
154. "jod"-dropping: no /j/ after alveolars before /u:/, e.g. in *news*, *tune*
155. deletion of word-initial /h/ in /hj-/ clusters, e.g. in *human*, *huge*
156. labialization of word-central voiced -TH-, e.g. [-v-] in *brother*
157. labialization of word-final / word-central voiceless –TH, e.g. [-f] in *mouth*, *nothing*
158. intervocalic /-v-/ > [b], e.g. in *river*
159. W: substitution of labiodental fricative /v/ for semi-vowel /w/
160. word-final consonant cluster deletion, monomorphemic
161. word-final consonant cluster deletion, bimorphemic
162. deletion of word-final single consonants
163. simplification of word-initial consonant clusters, e.g. in *splash*, *square*
164. non-rhotic (no postvocalic –r)

165. rhotic (postvocalic –r realized)
166. phonetic realization of /r/ as velar retroflex constriction
167. phonetic realization of /r/ as alveolar flap
168. phonetic realization of /r/ as apical trill
169. /r/ uvular
170. intrusive –r–, e.g. *idea*-r-*is*
171. post-vocalic –l vocalized
172. neutralization / confusion of liquids /l/ and /r/ in some words
173. realization of velar nasals with stop: -NG > [-ŋg]
174. velarization of some word-final nasals, e.g. /-ŋ/ in *down*

Prosodic features and intonation

175. deletion of word-initial unstressed syllables, e.g. *'bout, 'cept*
176. stress not infrequently shifted from first to later syllable, e.g. *indiˈcate, holiˈday*
177. (relatively) syllable-timed rather than stress-timed
178. HRT (High-Rising Terminal) contour: rise at end of statement
179. tone distinctions exist

List of features: Morphology and Syntax

Bernd Kortmann

The features in the catalogue are numbered from 1 to 76 (for easy reference in later parts of the chapter) and provided with the short definitions and illustrations. They include all usual suspects known from survey articles on grammatical properties of (individual groups of) non-standard varieties of English, with a slight bias towards features observed in L1 varieties. The 76 features fall into 11 groups corresponding to the following broad areas of morphosyntax: pronouns, noun phrase, tense and aspect, modal verbs, verb morphology, adverbs, negation, agreement, relativization, complementation, discourse organization and word order.

Pronouns, pronoun exchange, pronominal gender

1. *them* instead of demonstrative *those* (e.g. *in them days, one of them things*)
2. *me* instead of possessive *my* (e.g. *He's me brother, I've lost me bike*)
3. special forms or phrases for the second person plural pronoun (e.g. *youse, y'all, aay', yufela, you ... together, all of you, you ones/'uns, you guys, you people*)
4. regularized reflexives-paradigm (e.g. *hisself, theirselves/theirself*)
5. object pronoun forms serving as base for reflexives (e.g. *meself*)
6. lack of number distinction in reflexives (e.g. plural *-self*)
7. *she/her* used for inanimate referents (e.g. *She was burning good* [about a house])
8. generic *he/his* for all genders (e.g. *My car, he's broken*)
9. *myself/meself* in a non-reflexive function (e.g. *my/me husband and myself*)
10. *me* instead of *I* in coordinate subjects (e.g. *Me and my brother/My brother and me were late for school*)
11. non-standard use of *us* (e.g. *Us George was a nice one, We like us town, Show us* 'me' *them boots, Us kids used to pinch the sweets like hell, Us'll do it*)
12. non-coordinated subject pronoun forms in object function (e.g. *You did get he out of bed in the middle of the night*)
13. non-coordinated object pronoun forms in subject function (e.g. *Us say 'er's dry*)

Noun phrase

14. absence of plural marking after measure nouns (e.g. *four pound, five year*)
15. group plurals (e.g. *That President has two Secretary of States*)
16. group genitives (e.g. *The man I met's girlfriend is a real beauty*)
17. irregular use of articles (e.g. *Take them to market, I had nice garden, about a three fields, I had the toothache*)
18. postnominal *for*-phrases to express possession (e.g. *The house for me*)
19. double comparatives and superlatives (e.g. *That is so much more easier to follow*)
20. regularized comparison strategies (e.g. in *He is the regularest kind a guy I know, in one of the most pretty sunsets*)

Verb phrase: Tense & aspect

21. wider range of uses of the Progressive (e.g. *I'm liking this, What are you wanting?*)
22. habitual *be* (e.g. *He be sick*)
23. habitual *do* (e.g. *He does catch fish pretty*)
24. non-standard habitual markers other than *be* and *do*
25. levelling of difference between Present Perfect and Simple Past (e.g. *Were you ever in London?, Some of us have been to New York years ago*)
26. *be* as perfect auxiliary (e.g. *They're not left school yet*)
27. *do* as a tense and aspect marker (e.g. *This man what do own this*)
28. completive/perfect *done* (e.g. *He done go fishing, You don ate what I has sent you?*)
29. past tense/anterior marker *been* (e.g. *I been cut the bread*)
30. loosening of sequence of tense rule (e.g. *I noticed the van I came in*)
31. *would* in if-clauses (e.g. *If I'd be you, ...*)
32. *was sat/stood* with progressive meaning (e.g. *when you're stood* 'are standing' *there you can see the flames*)
33. *after*-Perfect (e.g. *She's after selling the boat*)

Verb phrase: Modal verbs

34. double modals (e.g. *I tell you what we might should do*)
35. epistemic *mustn't* ('can't, it is concluded that… not'; e.g. *This mustn't be true*)

Verb phrase: Verb morphology

36. levelling of preterite and past participle verb forms: regularization of irregular verb paradigms (e.g. *catch-catched-catched*)
37. levelling of preterite and past participle verb forms: unmarked forms (frequent with e.g. *give* and *run*)
38. levelling of preterite and past partiple verb forms: past form replacing the participle (e.g. *He had went*)
39. levelling of preterite and past partiple verb forms: participle replacing the past form (e.g. *He gone to Mary*)
40. zero past tense forms of regular verbs (e.g. *I walk* for *I walked*)
41. *a*-prefixing on *ing*-forms (e.g. *They wasn't a-doin' nothin' wrong*)

Adverbs

42. adverbs (other than degree modifiers) have same form as adjectives (e.g. *Come quick!*)
43. degree modifier adverbs lack *-ly* (e.g. *That's real good*)

Negation

44. multiple negation / negative concord (e.g. *He won't do no harm*)
45. *ain't* as the negated form of *be* (e.g. *They're all in there, ain't they?*)
46. *ain't* as the negated form of *have* (e.g. *I ain't had a look at them yet*)
47. *ain't* as generic negator before a main verb (e.g. *Something I ain't know about*)
48. invariant *don't* for all persons in the present tense (e.g. *He don't like me*)
49. *never* as preverbal past tense negator (e.g. *He never came* [= he didn't come])
50. *no* as preverbal negator (e.g. *me no iit brekfus*)
51. *was–weren't* split (e.g. *The boys was interested, but Mary weren't*)
52. invariant non-concord tags, (e.g. *innit/in't it/isn't* in *They had them in their hair, innit?)*

Agreement

53. invariant present tense forms due to zero marking for the third person singular (e.g. *So he show up and say, What's up?*)
54. invariant present tense forms due to generalization of third person *-s* to all persons (e.g. *I sees the house*)
55. existential/presentational *there's, there is, there was* with plural subjects (e.g. *There's two men waiting in the hall*)
56. variant forms of dummy subjects in existential clauses (e.g. *they, it,* or zero for *there*)
57. deletion of *be* (e.g. *She ___ smart*)
58. deletion of auxiliary *have* (e.g. *I ___ eaten my lunch)*
59. *was/were* generalization (e.g. *You were hungry but he were thirsty*, or: *You was hungry but he was thirsty*)
60. Northern Subject Rule (e.g. *I sing* [vs. **I sings*], *Birds sings, I sing and dances*)

Relativization

61. relative particle *what* (e.g. *This is the man what painted my house*)
62. relative particle *that* or *what* in non-restrictive contexts (e.g. *My daughter, that/what lives in London,…*)
63. relative particle *as* (e.g. *He was a chap as got a living anyhow*)
64. relative particle *at* (e.g. *This is the man at painted my house*)
65. use of analytic *that his/that's, what his/what's, at's, as'* instead of *whose* (e.g. *The man what's wife has died*)
66. gapping or zero-relativization in subject position (e.g. *The man ___ lives there is a nice chap*)
67. resumptive / shadow pronouns (e.g. *This is the house which I painted it yesterday*)

Complementation

68. *say*-based complementizers
69. inverted word order in indirect questions (e.g. *I'm wondering what are you gonna do*)
70. unsplit *for to* in infinitival purpose clauses (e.g. *We always had gutters in the winter time for to drain the water away*)

71. *as what / than what* in comparative clauses (e.g. *It's harder than what you think it is*)
72. serial verbs (e.g. *give* meaning 'to, for', as in *Karibuk giv mi*, 'Give the book to me')

Discourse organization and word order

73. lack of inversion / lack of auxiliaries in *wh*-questions (e.g. *What you doing?*)
74. lack of inversion in main clause *yes/no* questions (e.g. *You get the point?*)
75. *like* as a focussing device (e.g. *How did you get away with that like? Like for one round five quid, that was like three quid, like two-fifty each*)
76. *like* as a quotative particle (e.g. *And she was like "What do you mean?"*)

General introduction

Bernd Kortmann and Edgar W. Schneider

This book, together with its three companion volumes on other world regions, derives from the *Handbook of Varieties of English*, edited by Kortmann, Schneider et al. (2004). To make the material compiled in the *Handbook* more easily accessible and affordable, especially to student pockets, it has been decided to regroup the articles in such a way that all descriptive papers on any of the seven major anglophone world regions distinguished there are put together in a set of four paperback volumes, and accompanied by the CD-ROM which covers data and sources from all around the world. In this brief introduction we are briefly revisiting and summarizing the major design features of the *Handbook* and its contributions, i.e. information which, by implication, also characterizes the articles in the present volume.

The all-important design feature of the *Handbook* and of these offspring paperbacks is its focus on structure and on the solid description and documentation of data. The volumes, together with the CD-ROM, provide comprehensive up-to-date accounts of the salient phonological and grammatical properties of the varieties of English around the world. Reliable structural information in a somewhat standardized format and presented in an accessible way is a necessary prerequisite for any kind of study of language varieties, independent of the theoretical framework used for analysis. It is especially important for comparative studies of the phonological and morphosyntactic patterns across varieties of English, and the inclusion of this kind of data in typological studies (e.g. in the spirit of Kortmann 2004).

Of course, all of this structural information can be and has to be put in perspective by the conditions of uses of these varieties, i.e. their sociohistorical backgrounds, their current sociolinguistic settings (not infrequently in multilingual societies), and their associated political dimensions (like issues of norm-setting, language policies, and pedagogical applications). Ultimately, all of the varieties under discussion here, certainly so the ones spoken outside of England but in a sense, looking way back in time, even the English dialects themselves, are products of colonization processes, predominantly the European colonial expansion in the modern age. A number of highly interesting questions, linguistically and culturally, might be asked in this context, including the central issue of why all of this has happened, whether there is an underlying scheme that has continued to drive and motivate the evolution of new varieties of English (Schneider 2003, 2007). These linguistic and sociohistorical background issues will be briefly addressed in the regional introductions and in some of the individual chapters, but it should be made clear that it is the issue of structural description and comparison which is at the heart of this project.

The chapters in the four paperbacks are geared towards documenting and mapping the structural variation among (spontaneously spoken) non-standard varieties of English. Standard English is of course that variety, or set of closely related varieties, which enjoys the highest social prestige. It serves as a reference system and target norm in formal situations, in the language used by people taking on a public persona (including, for example, anchorpersons in the news media), and as a model in the teaching of English worldwide. Here, however, it is treated as is commonplace in modern descriptive linguistics, i.e. as a variety on a par with all other (regional, social, ethnic, or contact) varieties of English. Clearly, in terms of its structural properties it is not inherently superior to any of the non-standard varieties. Besides, the very notion of "Standard English" itself obviously refers to an abstraction. On the written level, it is under discussion to what extent a "common core" or a putatively homogeneous variety called "International English" actually exists: there is some degree of uniformity across the major national varieties, but once one looks into details of expression and preferences, there are also considerable differences. On the spoken level, there are reference accents like, for example, Received Pronunciation for British English, but their definition also builds upon abstractions from real individuals' performance. Thus, in the present context especially the grammar of (written) Standard English figures as no more than an implicit standard of comparison, in the sense that all chapters focus upon those phenomena in a given variety which are (more or less strikingly) different from this standard (these being perceived as not, note again, in any sense deficient or inferior to it).

The articles in this collection cover all main national standard varieties, distinctive regional, ethnic, and social varieties, major contact varieties (pidgins and creoles), as well as major varieties of English as a Second Language. The inclusion of second-language varieties and, especially, English-based pidgins and creoles may come as a surprise to some readers. Normally these varieties are addressed from different perspectives (such as, for example, language policy, language pedagogy, linguistic attitudes, language and identity (construction), substrate vs. superstrate influence), each standing in its own research tradition. Here they are primarily discussed from the point of view of their structural properties.

This will make possible comparisons with structural properties of, for example, other varieties of English spoken in the same region, or second-language or contact varieties in other parts of the English-speaking world. At the same time the availability of solid structural descriptions may open new perspectives for a fruitful interaction between the different research traditions within which second-language and contact varieties are studied. The boundaries of what is considered and accepted as "varieties of English" has thus been drawn fairly widely. In accepting English-oriented pidgins and creoles in the present context, we adopt a trend of recent research to consider them as contact varieties closely related to, possibly to be categorized as varieties of, their respective superstrate languages (e.g. Mufwene 2001). Creoles, and also some pidgins, in many regions vary along a continuum from acrolectal forms, relatively close to English and used by the higher sociolinguistic strata in formal contexts, to basilects, "deep" varieties maximally different from English. Most of our contributions focus upon the mesolects, the middle ranges which in most creole-speaking societies are used most widely.

For other varieties, too, it may be asked why or why not they have been selected for inclusion in this collection. Among the considerations that led to the present selection, the following figured most prominently: amount and quality of existing data and research documentation for the individual varieties, intensity of ongoing research activities, availability of authors, and space constraints (leading, for example, to the exclusion of strictly local accents and dialects). More information on the selection of varieties will be given in the regional introductions.

While in the *Handbook* there is one volume each for phonology and grammar (i.e. morphology and syntax), this set of paperbacks has been arranged by the major world regions relevant for the discussion of varieties of English: the British Isles; the Americas and the Caribbean; Africa, South and Southeast Asia; and the Pacific and Australasia. Each of the volumes comprises all articles on the respective regions, both on phonology and on grammar, together with the regional introductions, which include accounts of the histories, the cultural and sociolinguistic situations, and the most important data sources for the relevant locations, ethnic groups and varieties, and the regional synopses, in which the editors summarize the most striking properties of the varieties of English spoken in the respective world regions. Global synopses offering the most noteworthy findings and tendencies on phonological and morphosyntactic variation in English from a global perspective are available in the two hardcover Handbooks and in the electronic online version. In addition, there is a list of "General references", all of them exclusively book publications, which are either globally relevant or central for for individual world regions.

What emerges from the synopses is that many of the features described for individual varieties or sets of varieties in this Handbook are not unique to these (sets of) varieties. This is true both for morphology and syntax and for phonology.

As a matter of fact, quite a number of morphosyntactic features described as salient properties of individual varieties may strike the reader as typical of other varieties, too, possibly even of the grammar of spoken English, in general. In a similar vein, it turns out that certain phonological processes (like the monophthongization of certain diphthongs, the fronting, backing or merging of some vowels, and some consonantal substitutions or suprasegmental processes) can be documented in quite a number of fairly disparate language varieties – not surprisingly, perhaps, given shared underlying principles like constraints of articulatory space or tendencies towards simplification and the reduction of contrasts.

The distributions of selected individual features, both morphosyntactic and phonological, across varieties world-wide is visualized by the interactive world maps on the accompanying CD-ROM. The lists of these features, which are also referred to in some contributions, especially the regional synopses, are appended to this introduction. On these maps, each of a set of selected features, for almost all of the varieties under discussion, is categorized as occurring regularly (marked as "A" and colour-coded in red), occasionally or only in certain specified environments (marked as "B" and represented by a yellow circle) or practically not at all ("C", black). These innovative maps, which are accompanied by statistical distribution data on the spread of selected variants, provide the reader with an immediate visual representation of regional distribution and diffusion patterns. Further information on the nature of the multimedia material accompanying these books is available on the CD itself. It includes audio samples of free conversations (some of them transcribed), a standard reading passage, and recordings of the spoken "lexical sets" which define and illustrate vocalic variation (Wells 1982).

The chapters are descriptive survey articles providing state-of-the-art reports on major issues in current research, with a common core in order to make the collection an interesting and useful tool especially from a comparative, i.e. cross-dialectal and cross-linguistic, point of view. All chapters aim primarily at a qualitative rather than quantitative perspective, i.e. whether or not a given feature occurs is more important than its frequency. Of course, for varieties where research has focused upon documenting frequency relationships between variants of variables, some information on relevant quantitative tendencies has been provided. Depending upon the research coverage in a given world region (which varies widely from one continent to another), some contributions build upon existing sociolinguistic, dialectological, or structural research; a small number of other chapters make systematic use of available computerized corpora; and in some cases and for some regions the chapters in this compilation provide the first-ever systematic qualitative survey of the phonological and grammatical properties of English as spoken there.

For almost all varieties of English covered there are companion chapters in the phonology and morphosyntax parts of each paperback volume. In these cases it is in the phonology chapter that the reader will find a concise introductory section on the historical and cultural background as well as the current sociolinguistic situation of the relevant variety or set of varieties spoken at this location.

In order to ensure a certain degree of comparability, the authors were given a set of core issues that they were asked to address (provided something interesting can be said about them in the respective variety). For the phonology chapters, this set included the following items:

- phonological systems
- phonetic realization(s) and (phonotactic) distributions of a selection of phonemes (to be selected according to salience in the variety in question)
- specific phonological processes at work in the relevant variety
- lexical distribution
- prosodic features (stress, rhythm)
- intonation patterns
- observations/generalizations on the basis of lexical sets à la Wells (1982) and Foulkes/Docherty (1999), a standard reading passage and/or samples of free conversation.

It is worth noting that for some of the contributions, notably the chapters on pidgins and creoles, the lexical sets were not sufficient or suitable to describe the variability found. In such cases authors were encouraged to expand the set of target words, or replace one of the items. The reading passage was also adjusted or substituted by some authors, for instance because it was felt to be culturally inappropriate.

This is the corresponding set for the morphology and syntax chapters:

- tense – aspect – modality systems
- auxiliaries
- negation
- relativization
- complementation
- other subordination phenomena (notably adverbial subordination)
- agreement
- noun phrase structure
- pronominal systems
- word order (and information structure: especially focus/topicalizing constructions)

- selected salient features of the morphological paradigms of, for example, auxiliaries and pronouns

Lexical variation was not our primary concern, given that it fails to lend itself to the systematic generalization and comparability that we are interested in in this project. However, authors were offered the opportunity to comment on highly salient features of the vocabulary of any given variety (briefly and within the overall space constraints) if this was considered rewarding. The reader may find such information on distinctive properties of the respective vocabularies in the morphology and syntax chapters. Especially for a student readership, short sets of exercises and study questions have been added at the end of all chapters in the four paperback volumes.

In the interest of combining guidance for readers, efficiency, and space constraints, but also the goal of comprehensiveness, bibliographic references are systematically divided between three different types of reference lists. As was stated above, in each paperback a "General references" list can be found which compiles a relatively large number of books which, taken together, are central to the field of world-wide varieties of English – "classic" publications, collective volumes, particularly important publications, and so on. It is understood that in the individual contributions all authors may refer to titles from this list without these being repeated in their respective source lists. Each of the individual chapters ends with a list of "Selected references" comprising, on average, only 15–20 references – including the most pertinent ones on the respective variety (or closely related varieties) beyond any others possibly included in the General references list, and possibly others cited in the respective article. In other words, the Selected references do not repeat any of the titles cited in the list of General references. Thirdly, a "Comprehensive bibliography", with further publications specifically on the phonology and morphosyntax of each of the varieties covered, for which no space limitations were imposed, is available on the CD-ROM. The idea behind this limitation of the number of references allowed to go with each article was to free the texts of too much technical apparatus and thus to increase their reader-friendliness for a target audience of non-specialists while at the same time combining basic guidance to the most important literature (in the General References list) with the possibility of providing comprehensive coverage of the writings available on any given region (in the Bibliographies on the CD-ROM). It must be noted, however, that at times this rule imposed limitations upon possible source credits allowed in the discussions, because to make the books self-contained authors were allowed to refer to titles from the General and the Select References lists only. In other words, it is possible that articles touch upon material drawn from publications listed in the CD-ROM bibliographies without explicit credit, although every effort has been made to avoid this.

A publication project as huge as this one would have been impossible, indeed impossible even to think of, without the support of a great number of people devoted to their profession and to the subject of this Handbook. The editors would like thank the members of their editorial teams in Freiburg, Regensburg, and Cape Town. We are also much indebted to Elizabeth Traugott, for all the thought, support and feedback she gave to this project right from the very beginning of the planning stage, and to Jürgen Handke, who produced the rich audio-visual multimedia support on the CD. Furthermore, we have always benefitted from the support and interest invested into this project by Anke Beck and the people at Mouton de Gruyter. Finally, and most importantly, of course, the editors would like to thank the contributors and informants for having conformed to the rigid guidelines, deadlines and time frames that we set them for the various stages of (re)writing their chapters and providing the input material for the CD-ROM.

This collection truly represents an impressive product of scholarly collaboration of people from all around the globe. Right until the end it has been an exciting and wonderful experience for the editors (as well as, we would like to think, for the authors) to bring all these scholars and their work together, and we believe that this shows in the quality of the chapters and the material presented on the CD-ROM. We hope that, like the *Handbook*, it will be enjoyed, appreciated and esteemed by its readers, and treasured as the reference work and research tool it was designed as for anyone interested in and fascinated by variation in English!

References

Kortmann, Bernd (ed.)
2004 *Dialectology meets Typology: Dialect Grammar from a Cross-Linguistic Perspective.* Berlin/New York: Mouton de Gruyter.

Kortmann, Bernd, and Edgar W. Schneider, with Kate Burridge, Rajend Mesthrie, and Clive Upton (eds.)
2004 *A Handbook of Varieties of English.* Vol. 1: *Phonology*. Vol. 2: *Morphology and Syntax*. Berlin/New York: Mouton de Gruyter.

Schneider, Edgar W.
2003 "The dynamics of New Englishes: From identity construction to dialect birth." *Language* 79: 233-281.

Schneider, Edgar W.
2007 *Postcolonial English: Varieties Around the World.* Cambridge: Cambridge University Press.

General references

The following is a list of general reference works relevant across the world regions covered in the Handbook and for individual of these world regions. The list consists exclusively of book publications. Those monographs, dictionaries and collective volumes in the list which are referred to in the chapters of the four paperbacks will not be separately listed in the selected references at the end of the individual chapters.

Aceto, Michael and Jeffrey Williams (eds.)
2003 *Contact Englishes of the Eastern Caribbean.* (Varieties of English around the World, General Series 30.) Amsterdam/Philadelphia: Benjamins.

Aitken, Jack and Tom McArthur (eds.)
1979 *The Languages of Scotland.* Edinburgh: Chambers.

Algeo, John
2006 *British or American English? A Handbook of Word and Grammar Patterns.* Cambridge: Cambridge University Press.

Algeo, John (ed.)
2001 *The Cambridge History of the English Language, Volume VI: English in North America.* Cambridge: Cambridge University Press.

Allen, Harold B.
1973–1976 *Linguistic Atlas of the Upper Midwest.* 3 Volumes. Minneapolis: University of Minnesota Press.

Allen, Harold B. and Gary Underwood (eds.)
1971 *Readings in American Dialectology.* New York: Appleton-Century Crofts.

Allen, Harold B. and Michael D. Linn (eds.)
1997 *Dialects and Language Variation.* New York: Academic Press.

Alleyne, Mervyn C.
1980 *Comparative Afro-American: An Historical-Comparative Study of English-Based Afro-American Dialects of the New World.* (Linguistica Extranea 11.) Ann Arbor: Karoma.

Allsopp, Richard (ed.)
1996 *Dictionary of Caribbean English Usage.* Oxford: Oxford University Press.

Anderson, Peter M.
1987 *A Structural Atlas of the English Dialects.* London: Croom Helm.

Anderwald, Lieselotte
2002 *Negation in Non-standard British English: Gaps, Regularizations, Asymmetries.* (Routledge Studies in Germanic Linguistics 8.) London/New York: Routledge.

Atwood, E. Bagby
1953 *A Survey of Verb Forms in the Eastern United States.* (Studies in American English 2.) Ann Arbor: University of Michigan Press.

Avis, Walter S., Charles Crate, Patrick Drysdale, Douglas Leechman and Matthew H. Scargill
1967 *A Dictionary of Canadianisms on Historical Principles*. Toronto: Gage.

Bailey, Beryl Loftman
1966 *Jamaican Creole Syntax*. Cambridge: Cambridge University Press.

Bailey, Richard W. and Jay L. Robinson
1973 *Varieties of Present-Day English.* New York: Macmillan.

Bailey, Richard W. and Manfred Görlach (eds.)
1982 *English as a World Language*. Ann Arbor: University of Michigan Press.

Bailey, Guy, Natalie Maynor and Patricia Cukor-Avila (eds.)
1991 *The Emergence of Black English: Text and Commentary*. (Creole Language Library 8.) Amsterdam/Philadelphia: Benjamins.

Baker, Philip and Adrienne Bruyn (eds.)
1998 *St. Kitts and the Atlantic Creoles: The Texts of Samuel Augustus Mathews in Perspective*. (Westminster Creolistics Series 4). London: University of Westminster Press.

Bamgbose, Ayo, Ayo Banjo and Andrew Thomas (eds.)
1997 *New Englishes – A West African Perspective*. Trenton, NJ: Africa World Press.

Baugh, John
1983 *Black Street Speech: Its History, Structure, and Survival*. Austin: University of Texas Press.

Baumgardner, Robert J.
1996 *South Asian English: Structure, Use, and Users*. Urbana, IL: University of Illinois Press.

Bell, Allan and Koenrad Kuiper (eds.)
2000 *New Zealand English*. (Varieties of English around the World, General Series 25.) Amsterdam/Philadelphia: Benjamins and Wellington: Victoria University Press.

Bernstein, Cynthia, Thomas Nunnally and Robin Sabino (eds.)
1997 *Language Variety in the South Revisited.* Tuscaloosa: University of Alabama Press.

Bickerton, Derek
1975 *Dynamics of a Creole System*. Cambridge: Cambridge University Press.
1981 *Roots of Language*. Ann Arbor: Karoma.

Blair, David and Peter Collins (eds.)
2001 *English in Australia.* (Varieties of English around the World, General Series 26.) Amsterdam/Philadelphia: Benjamins.

Bliss, Alan J.
1979 *Spoken English in Ireland 1600–1740*. Dublin: Dolmen Press.

Bolton, Kingsley
2003 *Chinese Englishes. A Sociolinguistic History.* Cambridge: Cambridge Univeristy Press.

Bolton, Kinglsey and Braj B. Kachru (eds.)
2006 *World Englishes: critical concept in linguistics.* 6 vols. London: Routledge.

Bolton, Kingsley (ed.)
2002 *Hong Kong English: Autonomy and Creativity*. Hong Kong: Hong Kong University Press.

Britain, David (ed.)
2007 *Language in the British Isles*. Cambridge: Cambridge University Press.

Burchfield, Robert (ed.)
1994 *The Cambridge History of the English Language, Volume V: English in Britain and Overseas: Origins and Development*. Cambridge: Cambridge University Press.

Carrington, Lawrence D., Dennis Craig and Ramon Todd Dandare (eds.)
1983 *Studies in Caribbean Language. Papers Presented at the 3rd Biennial Conference of the Society for Caribbean Linguistics Held in Aruba, Netherlands Antilles from 16–20 Sept 1980*. St. Augustine, Trinidad: Society for Caribbean Linguistics.

Carver, Craig M.
1987 *American Regional Dialects: A Word Geography*. Ann Arbor: University of Michigan Press.

Cassidy, Frederic G.
1961 *Jamaica Talk: 300 Years of the English Language in Jamaica*. London: Macmillan.

Cassidy, Frederic G. (ed.)
1985–2002 *Dictionary of American Regional English*. 4 Volumes to date. Cambridge, MA/London: The Belknap Press of Harvard University Press.

Cassidy, Frederic G. and Robert B. LePage (eds.)
1967 *Dictionary of Jamaican English*. Cambridge: Cambridge University Press.

Chambers, J.K.
2003 *Sociolinguistic Theory: Linguistic Variation and its Social Significance*. 2nd edition. (Language in Society 22.) Oxford: Blackwell.

Chambers, J.K. and Peter Trudgill
1998 *Dialectology*. 2nd edition. (Cambridge Textbooks in Linguistics.) Cambridge: Cambridge University Press.

Chambers, J.K. (ed.)
1975 *Canadian English: Origins and Structures*. Toronto: Methuen.

Chambers, J.K., Peter Trudgill and Natalie Schilling-Estes (eds.)
2002 *The Handbook of Language Variation and Change*. (Blackwell Handbooks in Linguistics.) Malden, MA: Blackwell.

Cheshire, Jenny L. (ed.)
1991 *English Around the World: Sociolinguistic Perspectives*. Cambridge: Cambridge University Press.

Cheshire, Jenny L. and Dieter Stein (eds.)
1997 *Taming the Vernacular: From Dialect to Written Standard Language*. Harlow: Longman.

Christian, Donna, Nanjo Dube and Walt Wolfram
1988 *Variation and Change in Geographically Isolated Communities: Appalachian English and Ozark English.* (American Dialect Society 74.) Tuscaloosa: University of Alabama Press.

Christie, Pauline, Lawrence Carrington, Barbara Lalla and Velma Pollard (eds.)
1998 *Studies in Caribbean Language II. Papers from the Ninth Biennial Conference of the SCL, 1992.* St. Augustine, Trinidad: Society for Caribbean Linguistics.

Clarke, Sandra (ed.)
1993 *Focus on Canada.* (Varieties of English around the World, General Series 11.) Amsterdam/Philadelphia: Benjamins.

Collins, Peter and David Blair (eds.)
1989 *Australian English: the Language of a New Society.* St. Lucia: University of Queensland Press.

Corbett, John, J. Derrick McClure and Jane Stuart-Smith (eds.)
2003 *The Edinburgh Companion to Scots.* Edinburgh: Edinburgh University Press.

Crystal, David
2003 *The Cambridge Encyclopedia of the English Language.* 2nd edition. Cambridge: Cambridge University Press.

D'Costa, Jean and Barbara Lalla
1989 *Voices in Exile: Jamaican Texts of the 18th and 19th Centuries.* Tuscaloosa/ London: University of Alabama Press.

Davis, Lawrence M.
1983 *English Dialectology: An Introduction.* University, Alabama: University of Alabama Press.

Day, Richard R. (ed.)
1980 *Issues in English Creoles: Papers from the 1975 Hawaii Conference.* (Varieties of English around the World, General Series 2.) Heidelberg: Groos.

De Klerk, Vivian (ed.)
1996 *Focus on South Africa.* (Varieties of English around the World, General Series 15.) Amsterdam/Philadelphia: Benjamins.

De Wolf, Gaelan Dodds
1992 *Social and Regional Factors in Canadian English. Study of Phonological Variables and Grammatical Items in Ottawa and Vancouver.* Toronto: Canadian Scholar's Press.

DeCamp, David and Ian F. Hancock (eds.)
1974 *Pidgins and Creoles: Current Trends and Prospects.* Washington, D.C.: Georgetown University Press.

Devonish, Hubert
1989 *Talking in Tones: A Study of Tone in Afro-European Creole Languages.* London/Barbados: Karia Press and Caribbean Academic Publications.

Eckert, Penelope (ed.)
1991 *New Ways of Analyzing Sound Change.* (Qualitative Analyses of Linguistic Structure 5.) New York/San Diego: Academic Press.

Edwards, Viv
1986 *Language in a Black Community.* (Multilingual Matters 24.) Clevedon: Multilingual Matters.

Edwards, Walter F. and Donald Winford (ed.)
1991 *Verb Phrase Patterns in Black English and Creole.* Detroit: Wayne State University.

Ellis, Alexander J.
1869–1889 *On Early English Pronunciation.* 5 Volumes. London: Trübner.

Fasold, Ralph W.
1972 *Tense Marking in Black English: A Linguistic and Social Analysis.* (Urban Language Series 8.) Arlington, VA: Center for Applied Linguistics.

Fasold, Ralph W. and Roger W. Shuy (eds.)
1970 *Teaching Standard English in the Inner City.* (Urban Language Series 6.) Washington, D.C.: Center for Applied Linguistics.
1975 *Analyzing Variation in Language. Papers from the Second Colloquium on New Ways of Analyzing Variation.* Washington, D.C.: Georgetown University Press.

Ferguson, Charles and Shirley Brice Heat (eds.)
1981 *Language in the USA.* Cambridge: Cambridge University Press.

Filppula, Markku
1999 *The Grammar of Irish English: Language in Hibernian Style.* (Routledge Studies in Germanic Linguistics 5.) London/New York: Routledge.

Foley, Joseph A. (ed.)
1988 *New Englishes – The Case of Singapore.* Singapore: Singapore University Press.

Foley, Joseph A., Thiru Kandiah, Bao Zhiming, Anthea F. Gupta, Lubna Alasgoff, Ho Chee Lick, Lionel Wee, Ismail S. Talib and Wendy Bokhurst-Heng
1998 *English in New Cultural Contexts: Reflections from Singapore.* Singapore: Oxford University Press.

Foulkes, Paul and Gerard Docherty (eds.)
1999 *Urban Voices: Accent Studies in the British Isles.* London: Arnold.

Francis, W. Nelson
1958 *The Structure of American English.* New York: Ronald Press.

Frazer, Timothy C. (ed.)
1993 *'Heartland' English: Variation and Transition in the American Midwest.* Tuscaloosa: University of Alabama Press.

García, Ofelia and Ricardo Otheguy (eds.)
1989 *English across Cultures, Cultures across English: A Reader in Cross-Cultural Communication.* (Contributions to the Sociology of Language 53.) Berlin/New York: Mouton de Gruyter.

Gilbert, Glenn (ed.)
1987 *Pidgin and Creole Languages: Essays in Memory of John E. Reinecke.* Honolulu: University of Hawaii Press.

Gordon, Elizabeth and Tony Deverson
1998 *New Zealand English and English in New Zealand.* Auckland: New House Publishers.
Gordon, Matthew J.
2001 *Small-Town Values and Big-City Vowels: A Study of the Northern Cities Shift in Michigan.* (Publication of the American Dialect Society 84.) Durham: Duke University Press.
Görlach, Manfred (ed.)
1985 *Focus on Scotland.* (Varieties of English around the World, General Series 5.) Amsterdam/Philadelphia: Benjamins.
Görlach, Manfred and John A. Holm (eds.)
1986 *Focus on the Caribbean.* (Varieties of English around the World, General Series 8.) Amsterdam/Philadelphia: Benjamins.
Green, Lisa
2002 *African American English: A Linguistic Introduction.* Cambridge: Cambridge University Press.
Guy, Gregory, John Baugh, Crawford Feagin and Deborah Schiffrin (eds.)
1996 *Towards a Social Science of Language, Volume 1: Variation and Change in Language and Society.* Amsterdam/Philadelphia: Benjamins.
1997 *Towards a Social Science of Language, Volume 2: Social Interaction and Discourse Structures.* Amsterdam/Philadelphia: Benjamins.
Hackert, Stephanie
2004 *Urban Bahamian Creole. System and Variation.* Amsterdam/Philadelphia: Benjamins.
Hancock, Ian F., Morris Goodman, Bernd Heine and Edgar Polomé (eds.)
1979 *Readings in Creole Studies.* Ghent: Story-Scientia.
Hewitt, Roger
1986 *White Talk, Black Talk: Inter-Racial Friendship and Communication amongst Adolescents.* Cambridge: Cambridge University Press.
Hickey, Raymond
2004 *The Legacy of Colonial English: Transported Dialects.* Cambridge: Cambridge University Press.
2005 *The Sound Atlas of Irish English.* Berlin/New York: Mouton de Gruyter.
Holm, John A.
1988
–1989 *Pidgins and Creoles.* 2 Volumes. Cambridge: Cambridge University Press.
2000 *An Introduction to Pidgins and Creoles.* Cambridge: Cambridge University Press.
Holm, John A. and Peter Patrick
forthcoming *Comparative Creole Syntax: Parallel Outlines of 18 Creole Grammars.* London: Battlebridge.
Holm, John A. (ed.)
1983 *Central American English.* (Varieties of English around the World, Text Series 2.) Heidelberg: Groos.

Huber, Magnus and Mikael Parkvall (eds.)
1999 *Spreading the Word: The Issue of Diffusion among the Atlantic Creoles*. London: University of Westminster Press.
Hughes, Arthur and Peter Trudgill
1996 *English Accents and Dialects: An Introduction to Social and Regional Varieties of English in the British Isles*. 3rd edition. London: Arnold.
Hymes, Dell H. (ed.)
1971 *Pidginization and Creolization of Languages: Proceedings of a Conference, Held at the University of the West Indies Mona, Jamaica, April 1968*. Cambridge: Cambridge University Press.
James, Winford and Valerie Youssef
2002 *The Languages of Tobago. Genesis, Structure and Perspectives*. St. Augustine, Trinidad: University of the West Indies.
Jones, Charles (ed.)
1997 *The Edinburgh History of the Scots Language*. Edinburgh: Edinburgh University Press.
Kachru, Braj B.
1983 *The Indianization of English: The English Language in India*. Delhi: Oxford University Press.
Kachru, Braj B. (ed.)
1982 *The Other Tongue: English Across Cultures*. Urbana: University of Illinois Press.
Kachru, Braj B. (ed.)
2005 *Asian Englishes. Beyond the Canon:* Hong Kong: Hong Kong University Press.
Kachru, Braj B., Yamuna Kachru and Cecil L. Nelson (eds.)
2006 *The Handbook of World Englishes*. Oxford: Blackwell.
Kachru, Yamuna and Cecil L. Nelson
2006 *World Englishes in Asian Contexts*. Hong Kong: Hong Kong University Press.
Kautzsch, Alexander
2002 *The Historical Evolution of Earlier African American English. An Empirical Comparison of Early Sources*. (Topics in English Linguistics 38.) Berlin/New York: Mouton de Gruyter.
Keesing, Roger M.
1988 *Melanesian Pidgin and the Oceanic Substrate*. Stanford: Stanford University Press.
Kirk, John M. and Dónall P. Ó Baoill
2001 *Language Links: The Languages of Scotland and Ireland*. Belfast: Cló Olscoill na Banríona [Queen's University Press].
Kirk, John M., Stewart Sanderson and John D.A. Widdowson (eds.)
1985 *Studies in Linguistic Geography: The Dialects of English in Britain and Ireland*. London et al.: Croom Helm.
Kortmann, Bernd, Tanja Herrmann, Lukas Pietsch and Susanne Wagner
2005 *A Comparative Grammar of British English Dialects: Agreement, Gender, Relative Clauses*. Berlin/New York: Mouton de Gruyter.

Kortmann, Bernd (ed.)
2004 *Dialectology Meets Typology: Dialect Grammar from a Cross-Linguistic Perspective.* Berlin/New York: Mouton de Gruyter.

Krapp, George P.
1925 *The English Language in America.* 2 Volumes. New York: Century.

Kretzschmar, William A. and Edgar W. Schneider
1996 *Introduction to Quantitative Analysis of Linguistic Survey Data: An Atlas by the Numbers.* (Empirical Linguistics Series.) Thousand Oaks, CA: Sage.

Kretzschmar, William A., Virginia G. McDavid, Theodore K. Lerud and Ellen Johnson (eds.)
1993 *Handbook of the Linguistic Atlas of the Middle and South Atlantic States.* Chicago: University of Chicago Press.

Kurath, Hans
1949 *A Word Geography of the Eastern United States.* Ann Arbor: University of Michigan Press.

Kurath, Hans and Raven I. McDavid, Jr.
1961 *The Pronunciation of English in the Atlantic States. Based upon the Collections of the Linguistic Atlas.* (Studies in American English 3.) Ann Arbor: University of Michigan Press.

Kurath, Hans (ed.)
1939–1943 *Linguistic Atlas of New England.* Providence: Brown University Press.

Labov, William
1966 *The Social Stratification of English in New York City.* (Urban Language Series 1.) Washington, D.C.: Center for Applied Linguistics.
1972a *Language in the Inner City: Studies in the Black English Vernacular.* (Conduct and Communication 3.) Philadelphia: University of Pennsylvania Press.
1972b *Sociolinguistic Patterns.* (Conduct and Communication 4.) Philadelphia: University of Pennsylvania Press.
1980 *Locating Language in Time and Space.* (Quantitative Analyses of Linguistic Structure.) New York: Academic Press.
1994 *Principles of Linguistic Change, Volume 1: Internal Factors.* (Language in Society 20.) Oxford/Malden, MA: Blackwell.
2001 *Principles of Linguistic Change, Volume 2: Social Factors.* (Language in Society 29.) Oxford/Malden, MA: Blackwell.

Labov, William, Richard Steiner and Malcah Yaeger
1972 *A Quantitative Study of Sound Change in Progress: Report on National Science Foundation Contract NSF-GS-3278 University of Pennsylvania.* Philadelphia: University of Pennsylvania Regional Survey.

Labov, William, Sharon Ash and Charles Boberg
2006 *Atlas of North American English: Phonetics, Phonology and Sound Change.* (Topics in English Linguistics 41.) Berlin/New York: Mouton de Gruyter.

Lalla, Barbara and Jean D'Costa
1990 *Language in Exile: Three Hundred Years of Jamaican Creole*. Tuscaloosa: University of Alabama Press.
Lanehart, Sonja L. (ed.)
2001 *Sociocultural and Historical Contexts of African American English*. (Varieties of English around the World, General Series 27.) Amsterdam/ Philadelphia: Benjamins.
Leitner, Gerhard
2004a *Australia's Many Voices. Australian English – The National Language*. Berlin/New York: Mouton de Gruyter.
2004b *Australia's Many Voices. Ethnic Englishes, Indigenous and Migrant Languages. Policy and Education*. Berlin/New York: Mouton de Gruyter.
LePage, Robert B. and Andrée Tabouret-Keller
1985 *Acts of Identity: Creole-based Approaches to Language and Ethnicity*. Cambridge: Cambridge University Press.
Lim, Lisa (ed.)
2004 *Singapore English. A Grammatical Description*. Amsterdam/Philadelphia: Benjamins.
Lindquist, Hans, Maria Estling, Staffan Klintborg and Magnus Levin (eds.)
1998 *The Major Varieties of English: Papers from MAVEN 97, Växjö 20–22 November 1997*. (Acta Wexionensia: Humaniora; 1.) Växjö: Växjo University.
Matthews, William
1938 *Cockney Past and Present: A Short History of the Dialect of London*. London: Routledge.
McArthur, Tom
1992 *The Oxford Companion to the English Language*. Oxford: Oxford University Press.
2002 *Oxford Guide to World English*. Oxford: Oxford University Press.
McMillan, James B. and Michel B. Montgomery
1989 *Annotated Bibliography of Southern American English*. Tuscaloosa/ London: University of Alabama Press.
McWhorter, John H. (ed.)
2000 *Language Change and Language Contact in Pidgins and Creoles*. (Creole Language Library 21.) Amsterdam/Philadelphia: Benjamins.
Mehrotra, Raja Ram
1998 *Indian English – Text and Interpretation*. (Varieties of English around the World, Text Series 7.) Amsterdam/Philadelphia: Benjamins.
Melchers, Gunnel and Philip Shaw
2003 *World Englishes*. London: Arnold.
Mencken, Henry
1963 *The American Language: An Inquiry into the Development of English in the United States. With the Assistance of David W. Maurer*. New York: Knopf.

Mesthrie, Rajend (ed.)
1995 *Language and Social History: Studies in South African Sociolinguistics*. Cape Town: David Philip.
2002 *Language in South Africa*. Cambridge: Cambridge University Press.
Milroy, James
1981 *Regional Accents of English: Belfast*. Belfast: Blackstaff.
Milroy, James and Lesley Milroy (eds.)
1993 *Real English: The Grammar of English Dialects in the British Isles*. (Real Language Series.) London: Longman.
Montgomery, Michael B. and Guy Bailey (eds.)
1986 *Language Variety in the South: Perspectives in Black and White*. University, AL: University of Alabama Press.
Montgomery, Michael B. and Thomas Nunnally (eds.)
1998 *From the Gulf States and Beyond. The Legacy of Lee Pederson and LAGS*. Tuscaloosa, AL/London: University of Alabama Press.
Mufwene, Salikoko S.
2001 *The Ecology of Language Evolution*. (Cambridge Approaches to Language Contact.) Cambridge: Cambridge University Press.
Mufwene, Salikoko S., Guy Bailey, John Baugh and John R. Rickford (eds.)
1998 *African-American English. Structure, History and Use*. London: Routledge.
Mufwene, Salikoko S. (ed.)
1993 *Africanisms in Afro-American Language Varieties*. Athens: University of Georgia Press.
Mühleisen, Susanne
2002 *Creole Discourse: Exploring Prestige Formation and Change across Caribbean English-Lexicon Creoles*. (Creole Language Library 24.) Amsterdam/Philadelphia: Benjamins.
Mühlhäusler, Peter
1997 *Pidgin and Creole Linguistics*. (Westminster Creolistic Series 3.) London: University of Westminster Press.
Murray, Thomas and Beth Lee Simon (eds.)
2006 *Language Variation and Change in the American Midland: A New Look at "Heartland" English*. Amsterdam/Philadelphia: Benjamins.
Muysken, Pieter and Norval Smith (eds.)
1986 *Substrata versus Universals in Creole Genesis. Papers from the Amsterdam Creole Workshop, April 1985*. (Creole Language Library 1.) Amsterdam/Philadelphia: Benjamins.
Myers-Scotton, Carol
2002 *Contact Linguistics: Bilingual Encounters and Grammatical Outcomes*. (Oxford Linguistics.) Oxford: Oxford University Press.
Nagle, Stephen J. and Sara L. Sanders (eds.)
2003 *English in the Southern United States*. (Studies in English Language.) Cambridge: Cambridge University Press.

Neumann-Holzschuh, Ingrid and Edgar W. Schneider (eds.)
2000 *Degrees of Restructuring in Creole Languages*. (Creole Language Library 22.) Amsterdam/Philadelphia: Benjamins.

Nihalani, Paroo, Priya Hosali and Ray K. Tongue
1989 *Indian and British English: A Handbook of Usage and Pronunciation.* (Oxford India Paperbacks.) Delhi: Oxford University Press.

Noss, Richard B. (ed.)
1984 *An Overview of Language Issues in South-East Asia: 1950–1980.* Singapore: Oxford University Press.

Orton, Harold (ed.)
1962 –1971 *Survey of English Dialects: The Basic Material.* 4 Volumes. Leeds: Arnold.

Orton, Harold, Stewart Sanderson and John Widdowson (eds.)
1978 *The Linguistic Atlas of England.* London: Croom Helm.

Parasher, S.V.
1991 *Indian English: Functions and Form.* (Sell-series in English Language and Literature 19.) New Delhi: Bahri.

Parkvall, Mikael
2000 *Out of Africa: African Influences in Atlantic Creoles*. London: Battlebridge.

Patrick, Peter L.
1999 *Urban Jamaican Creole: Variation in the Mesolect*. (Varieties of English around the World, General Series 17.) Amsterdam/Philadelphia: Benjamins.

Pederson, Lee (ed.)
1986 –1992 *The Linguistic Atlas of the Gulf States*. 7 Volumes. Athens, GA: University of Georgia Press.

Plag, Ingo (ed.)
2003 *Phonology and Morphology of Creole Languages*. (Linguistische Arbeiten 478.) Tübingen: Niemeyer.

Platt, John, Mian Lian Ho and Heidi Weber
1983 *Singapore and Malaysia*. (Varieties of English around the World, Text Series 4.) Amsterdam/Philadelphia: Benjamins.
1984 *The New Englishes*. London: Routledge and Kegan Paul.

Poplack, Shana and Sali Tagliamonte
2001 *African American English in the Diaspora*. (Language in Society 30.) Oxford/Malden, MA: Blackwell.

Poplack, Shana (ed.)
2000 *The English History of African American English.* (Language in Society 28.) Oxford/Malden, MA: Blackwell.

Preston, Dennis R. (ed.)
1993 *American Dialect Research: An Anthology Celebrating the 100th Anniversary of the American Dialect Society*. (Centennial Series of the American Dialect Society.) Amsterdam/Philadelphia: Benjamins.

Rampton, Ben
1995 *Crossing: Language and Ethnicity among Adolescents*. (Real Language Series.) London: Longman.
Rickford, John R.
1987 *Dimensions of a Creole Continuum: History, Texts, and Linguistics Analysis of Guyanese Creole*. Stanford: Stanford University Press.
1999 *African American Vernacular English: Features, Evolution, Educational Implications*. (Language in Society 26.) Oxford/Malden, MA: Blackwell.
Rickford, John R. and Suzanne Romaine (eds.)
1999 *Creole Genesis, Attitudes and Discourse*: *Studies Celebrating Charlene J. Sato*. (Creole Language Library 20.) Amsterdam/Philadelphia: Benjamins.
Roberts, Peter A.
1988 *West Indians and their Language*. Cambridge: Cambridge University Press.
Romaine, Suzanne
1988 *Pidgin and Creole Languages*. (Longman Linguistics Library.) London/New York: Longman.
Schmied, Josef J.
1991 *English in Africa: An Introduction*. (Longman Linguistics Library.) London: Longman.
Schneider, Edgar W.
1989 *American Earlier Black English. Morphological and Syntactical Variables*. Tuscaloosa, AL/London: University of Alabama Press.
Schneider, Edgar W. (ed.)
1996 *Focus on the USA*. (Varieties of English around the World, General Series 16.) Amsterdam/Philadelphia: Benjamins.
1997a *Englishes Around the World, Volume 1: General Studies, British Isles, North America: Studies in Honour of Manfred Görlach*. (Varieties of English around the World, General Series 18.) Amsterdam/Philadelphia: Benjamins.
1997b *Englishes Around the World, Volume 2: Caribbean, Africa, Asia, Australasia. Studies in Honour of Manfred Görlach*. (Varieties of English around the World, General Series 19.) Amsterdam/Philadelphia: Benjamins.
2007 *Postcolonial English*. Cambridge: Cambridge University Press.
Sebba, Mark
1993 *London Jamaican: Language Systems in Interaction*. (Real Language Series.) London: Longman.
1997 *Contact Languages – Pidgins and Creoles*. (Modern Linguistics Series.) London: Macmillan.
Singh, Ishtla
2000 *Pidgins and Creoles – An Introduction*. London: Arnold.
Singler, John V. (ed.)
1990 *Pidgin and Creole Tense-Mood-Aspect Systems*. (Creole Language Library 6.) Amsterdam/Philadelphia: Benjamins.

Spears, Arthur K. and Donald Winford (eds.)
1997 *The Structure and Status of Pidgins and Creoles. Including Selected Papers from the Meetings of the Society for Pidgin and Creole Linguistics.* (Creole Language Library 19.) Amsterdam/Philadelphia: Benjamins.

Spencer, John (ed.)
1971 *The English Language in West Africa.* (English Language Series.) London: Longman.

Thomas, Erik R.
2001 *An Acoustic Analysis of Vowel Variation in New World English.* (Publication of the American Dialect Society 85.) Durham: Duke University Press.

Thomason, Sarah G.
2001 *Contact Languages.* Edinburgh: University of Edinburgh Press.

Thomason, Sarah G. and Terrence Kaufman
1988 *Language Contact, Creolization and Genetic Linguistics.* Berkeley: University of California Press.

Tristram, Hildegard, L.C. (ed.)
1998 *The Celtic Englishes.* (Anglistische Forschungen 247.) Heidelberg: Winter.
2000 *The Celtic Englishes II.* (Anglistische Forschungen 286.) Heidelberg: Winter.
2003 *The Celtic Englishes III.* (Anglistische Forschungen 324.) Heidelberg: Winter.

Trudgill, Peter
1974 *The Social Differentiation of English in Norwich.* (Cambridge Studies in Linguistics 13.) Cambridge: Cambridge University Press.
1986 *Dialects in Contact.* (Language in Society 10.) Oxford: Blackwell.
1999 *The Dialects of England.* 2nd edition. Oxford: Blackwell. also: *The Dialects of England.* 2nd edition. Oxford: Blackwell.

Trudgill, Peter and Jean Hannah
2002 *International English: A Guide to Varieties of Standard English.* 4th edition. London: Arnold.
1994 *International English: A Guide to Varieties of Standard English.* 3rd edition. London: Arnold.
1985 *International English: A Guide to Varieties of Standard English.* 2nd edition. London: Arnold.
1982 *International English: A Guide to Varieties of Standard English.* London: Arnold.

Trudgill, Peter (ed.)
1978 *Sociolinguistic Patterns in British English.* London: Arnold.
1984 *Language in the British Isles.* Cambridge: Cambridge University Press.

Trudgill, Peter and J.K. Chambers (eds.)
1991 *Dialects of English: Studies in Grammatical Variation.* (Longman Linguistics Library.) London/New York: Longman.

Upton, Clive, David Parry and John D.A. Widdowson
1994 *Survey of English Dialects: The Dictionary and Grammar.* London: Routledge.

Viereck, Wolfgang (ed.)
1985 *Focus on England and Wales*. (Varieties of English around the World, General Series 4.) Amsterdam/Philadelphia: Benjamins.

Wakelin, Martyn
1981 *English Dialects: An Introduction*. London: Athlone Press.

Wakelin, Martyn F. (ed.)
1972 *Patterns in the Folk Speech of the British Isles. With a Foreword by Harold Orton*. London: Athlone Press.

Watts, Richard and Peter Trudgill (eds.)
2002 *Alternative Histories of English*. London: Routledge.

Wells, John C.
1982 *Accents of English*. 3 Volumes. Cambridge: Cambridge University Press.

Williamson, Juanita and Virginia M. Burke (eds.)
1971 *A Various Language. Perspectives on American Dialects*. New York: Holt, Rinehart and Winston.

Winer, Lise
1993 *Trinidad and Tobago*. (Varieties of English around the World, Text Series 6.) Amsterdam/Philadelphia: Benjamins.

Winford, Donald
1993 *Predication in Carribean English Creoles*. (Creole Language Library 10.) Amsterdam/Philadelphia: Benjamins.
2003 *An Introduction to Contact Linguistics*. (Language in Society 33.) Malden/Oxford/Melbourne: Blackwell.

Wolfram, Walt
1969 *A Sociolinguistic Description of Detroit Negro Speech*. (Urban Language Series 5.) Washington, D.C.: Center for Applied Linguistics.

Wolfram, Walt and Ralph W. Fasold
1974 *The Study of Social Dialects in American English*. Englewood Cliffs, NJ: Prentice Hall.

Wolfram, Walt and Donna Christian
1976 *Appalachian Speech*. Arlington, VA: Center for Applied Linguistics.

Wolfram, Walt and Natalie Schilling-Estes
2005 *American English: Dialects and Variation*. (Language in Society 25.) 2nd ed. Malden, MA/Oxford: Blackwell.

Wolfram, Walt, Kirk Hazen and Natalie Schilling-Estes
1999 *Dialect Change and Maintenance on the Outer Banks*. (Publication of the American Dialect Society 81.) Tuscaloosa, AL/London: University of Alabama Press.

Wolfram, Walt and Erik R. Thomas
2002 *The Development of African American English*. (Language in Society 31.) Oxford/Malden, MA: Blackwell.

Wolfram, Walt and Ben Wards (eds.)
2006 *American Voices: How Dialects Differ from Coast to Coast*. Oxford: Blackwell

Wright, Joseph
1898
–1905 *The English Dialect Dictionary*. Oxford: Clarendon Press.
1905 *The English Dialect Grammar*. Oxford: Frowde.

Introduction: varieties of English in the British Isles

Bernd Kortmann and Clive Upton

1. A note on geopolitical terminology

'The British Isles' is a geographical term which refers to the two large islands that contain the mainlands of Scotland, Northern Ireland, the Irish Republic, Wales, and England, together with a large number of other, smaller islands that are part of the territories of these countries: one island (the Isle of Man) and one archipelago (the Channel Islands) have a significant degree of autonomy within the state which encompasses the bulk of the British Isles, the United Kingdom. 'The United Kingdom of Great Britain and Northern Ireland' (the UK) is a state that encompasses Scotland, Wales, England, Man, and the Channel Islands, together with the northernmost part of the island of Ireland. If Northern Ireland is omitted entirely from a description, the designation of the area described is properly 'Great Britain'. 'Ireland' properly designates the whole of the island of Ireland (though popularly it is used to refer to the *state* of Ireland, that is the Republic of Ireland, which occupies the central, southern, and north-western parts).

2. The coverage of British Isles accents and dialects

In this volume major accent and dialect distinctions in the British Isles are represented in chapters covering Scotland, Wales, Ireland, Northern England, and Southern England. Other chapters cover the distinctive accents and dialects of somewhat less extensive areas: Orkney and Shetland, the Channel Islands, the eastern England region of East Anglia, and the very major conurbation and administrative area of the English West Midlands. Variation *within* each of these areas is, of course, discussed in the relevant chapters: in particular, Northern and Southern Irish are distinguished, as is the speech of southwest and southeast England, where major differences apply. It is expected that the reader might concentrate on particular chapters or smaller sections to gain in-depth knowledge of a particular variety or group of closely-related varieties or, especially by referring to the sound charts, to obtain an overview of wider overall variation or of variation relating to specific linguistic variables.

Whilst Received Pronunciation (RP) is specifically presented as a supra-regional accent model frequently used in the teaching of English worldwide and for purposes of wide communication, its description plays only a very minor part in the analysis of the regional varieties, each of which is described in its own terms rather than in any sense as divergent from an externally-imposed norm. For reasons spelt out in the General Introduction, Standard English grammar is not explicitly discussed as a separate entity.

3. The concept of the 'dialect area'

The linguistic varieties of the UK and Ireland presented in this volume are discussed along geographical lines. This arrangement by region is convenient in terms of structure, and is helpful to the user who wishes to understand regional differences, or who needs to concentrate on the variety or group of varieties found in one particular region. But it is also potentially misleading, since the impression might be gained that UK and Irish varieties are tidily to be separated from each other, with one being spoken by a fixed, geographically identifiable group of people quite distinct from another group using another quite different set of speech-forms.

Nothing could be further from the truth. Far from there being regional cut-off points for ways of speaking, i.e. boundaries where, for example, one accent ceases to be heard and another takes its place, accents and dialects blend subtly and imperceptibly into one another. Rather than the hearer detecting the presence or absence of features as they move about a country or region, particularly at a local level it is a matter of 'more or less', of features being heard with greater or lesser frequency as features most characteristic of one region are left behind, to be replaced with greater intensity by others associated with a region being approached.

Nor should we think that all speakers in one place use the same set of features with the same level of intensity, if they use them at all. It is to be expected that some speakers, those who sound most local to a particular place, will fairly consistently exhibit a set of features which most closely conform to a characteristic local way of speaking, and it is these which form a central part of the local accent and dialect descriptions given in the chapters that follow. However, very many speakers will not be consistent in their use of these features, being variably more or less regional in different situations or under different social promptings (e.g. the social status of addresser and addressee, and the degree of familiarity between them), even within the same discourse (e.g. depending on the topic). It is important to note immediately that such variation is not random: speakers do not drift between, towards, or away from markedly regional pronunciations on a whim. Rather, it has been shown in numerous studies that such movement patterns correlate with such social phenomena as age, gender, socio-economic status, ethnicity and local affiliations of both speaker and hearer, and can result in short-term, but also long-term, language change.

The acceptance of the absence of tight boundaries for phonological and grammatical features, and the acknowledgement of speakers in any one place being socially heterogeneous and, moreover, inconsistent in their speech lead to the inevitable conclusion that the concept of the 'dialect area' as a fixed, tidy entity is ultimately a myth. In terms of pronunciation, what we are faced with, in place of a certain number of accents, is in reality a continuum: accents shade one into another as individual speakers espouse features drawn from a range of accents to which they have access and that are indicative not just of their regional connections but also of their social needs and aspirations. The same is true for grammatical usage, and for lexical choice.

4. The distinction between 'traditional' and 'modern' dialects

Another often-used notion in dialectology we would like to question is the separation of dialects into two distinct categories, the 'Traditional' and the 'Modern'. This artificially tidy categorisation is not only questionable given the fact of constant language change. It is even more debatable in the light of the fact that, as will be explained below, much of our knowledge of recent distributions of dialect features over wide sweeps of territory in the British Isles continues to be based on surveys now considered to have focused on the 'traditional', in the sense that their target was the essentially rural speech of comparatively static communities. (No community is ever wholly static or isolated, of course: there will always be incomers and external contacts, however few these might be in particular communities at certain times.) Nevertheless, the bipartite distinction does have some undoubted merit as an idealisation: it reminds us that urbanisation and geographical and social mobility have resulted in some accelerated and often quite dramatic changes in speech in recent years, as is made clear in the following chapters. Perhaps it reminds us, too, that language should be seen in its continuous historical (diachronic) as well as its 'snapshot-in-time' (synchronic) dimension, that there was a 'then' to contrast with the 'now'. However, we would be wrong to suppose that there is a straightforward, clear-cut distinction between the way English was spoken in the rural communities of half a century ago and as it is in the towns and cities of today, or that change is happening to language now as it has not happened before. Across time there are periods of comparatively rapid and of slower alteration in speech, but language is *constantly* changing. (And, indeed, the mechanisms of language change occupy the research attention of very many dialectologists today, just as ascertaining the facts of its progress absorbed the efforts of dialect researchers of previous generations.) Furthermore, since human society is in essence the same as it was in the past, a greater understanding of the facts of and reasons for that change today informs our understanding of developments both in the past and into the future.

5. Historical and cultural elements in the formation of British accents

Varieties of English around the world are all derived from one ancestral rootstock (variously called Anglo-Saxon or Old English). In part at least, the distinctive sounds and grammatical properties of each are tied to developments in the history of the language, these sometimes dating back many centuries. It is in the UK and Ireland, and in England in particular, however, that this matter of pedigree is most significant. This fact is unsurprising. English is, after all, at bottom the product of England and southern Scotland, born of a fusion of West Germanic dialects brought from mainland Europe to the islands of Britain in the fifth and sixth centuries AD, and perhaps even earlier. Fusing over the centuries with elements of Celtic, Norse, and French, and subject to sundry other influences as a result of the islands' complex history of trade and conquest, the language in its homeland has had time and motive both to preserve ancient forms and to fragment to a degree unknown elsewhere in the English-speaking world.

Thus, constant echoes of earlier phonology and grammar are to be heard in the British regional varieties discussed in this volume. They are very clearly evident where contrasts appear between regional accents and the convenient touchstone accent of RP, which is itself an evolving accent but one which, as a model for pronunciation of British English, does not go back before the nineteenth century. The STRUT/PUT merger of the English North and North Midlands, i.e. the vowel in words like *strut* and *hut* being the same as in *put*, is Anglo-Saxon, for example. So are long monophthongs where RP and some other accents have diphthongs. So too, among many other features, are the 'Velar Nasal Plus' feature (as in the pronunciation /sɪŋg/ of *sing* or /ˈsɪŋgə/ of *singer* [Wells 1982: 365]) of the English north-west Midlands, and the rhoticity (i.e. the pronunciation of /r/ following a vowel, as in *star* or *start*) characteristic of Scotland, Ireland, south-west England, parts of Lancashire and the Northeast, as too of North America of course. Corresponding grammatical features from earlier periods of English include multiple negation (or negative concord), as in *She couldn't say nothing about them*, and personal pronoun forms like *thou* and *thee*.

The length of time over which English has been evolving in the small area that is the British Isles accounts in large part for the complex variation in its present-day dialects. To this must be added the region's ethnic and political mix, both now and in the past. There are, of course, two sovereign states represented, the United Kingdom and the Republic of Ireland. The United Kingdom in turn comprises the nations of England, Scotland, Wales, and Northern Ireland, and matters of national as well as of narrower regional identity come into play when espousal of features of language are concerned. In the present, Wales especially, and Scotland and Ireland to lesser extents, see the interaction of English with Celtic languages. In the past, this interaction with Celtic has been most influential in the north and west of the region, as has that with Norse in Ireland, in northern Scotland and the Orkney and Shetland Isles, and in northwest and eastern England. The economic and political dominance exerted on Britain by London and the southeast of England has also inevitably shaped accents: not itself a regional accent, RP nevertheless has an essentially southeastern phonemic structure and phonetic bias; such processes as the Great Vowel Shift have acted to shape modern phonology more consistently and more completely in the south of England than elsewhere. All of this cultural and historical complexity, as it affects language, is rehearsed in the various chapters that follow, and each in consequence has its own unique perspective.

6. Dialect surveys

Although they are neither very recent nor focused upon the accents of major centres of population, a small group of major regional dialect surveys are heavily drawn upon in the writing of the following chapters, as they must inevitably be by anyone commenting on variation in the speech of the British Isles. Foremost among these, for England, is the *Survey of English Dialects* (*SED*). This essentially rural survey from the mid-twentieth century continues to be drawn upon for information because of its detailed coverage, its reliability (given the constraints under which it operated) and the accessibility of its information: it is fair to say that no reliable statements can be made about the widespread distribution of linguistic features within England without reference to its findings, since there exists no more recent country-wide comprehensive evidence. The SED is paralleled by its contemporary in Scotland, the *Linguistic Survey of Scotland*, in Wales by the *Survey of Anglo-Welsh Dialects*, and in Ireland by the *Tape-recorded Survey of Hiberno-English Speech*. The last two surveys were in some large measure directly inspired by the SED, under whose founder, Harold Orton, some of their founder-workers had trained.

Recently, however, whilst there have been some comparatively large-scale efforts at data-gathering (see especially the *Survey of British Dialect Grammar* [Cheshire/Edwards/Whittle 1993], the *Freiburg English Dialect Corpus* [Kortmann 2003, Kortmann and Wagner 2005], and the *Sound Atlas of Irish English* [Hickey 2005 and this volume]), the reader will notice that, with the notable exception of the latter, even these have not been on the scale of earlier surveys. This has not, however, been accidental or the result of academic indolence on the part of the linguistic community. Rather, recent concentration on social variation in speech, in order to better understand the mechanisms of language change, has resulted in focus being on small(er) areas and fewer locations in which diverse populations can be studied in close detail: the wide sweeps of variation that were the object of earlier research do not speak to the considerations of motivation for language use, and for language variation, which are a preoccupation of today's dialectologists. (In this regard, there have been a number of seminal works which have been drawn upon in the present volume, such as Foulkes and Docherty's *Urban Voices* [1999] and Milroy and Milroy's *Real English* [1993].) Beyond the larger survey materials, therefore, the authors have drawn upon a wide range of materials which result from their own and others' intensive study of the localised speech of their respective areas.

7. The chapters on phonology

Melchers' focus is on distinctions between the phonology of Orkney ("Orcadian") and Shetland, and also between their divergence from and correspondence to the accents of mainland Scotland. Amongst those accents, Stuart-Smith identifies a continuum corresponding to a phonological range available to very many in Scotland, whose speech ranges seamlessly between Scottish Standard English and Scots: as regards the latter, on grounds of population density and the existence of detailed research data, she concentrates on the Urban Scots of the 'Central Belt' around Edinburgh and (especially) Glasgow. In a chapter which, concerning its northern data, relates very closely to that of Scotland, Hickey describes a complex of accents in which a north-south split provides a basic structure. He identifies a supraregional Southern accent and three regional southern varieties, distinguishing these from Northern varieties. He includes discussion of the complex terminology associated with northern variation, and three urban accents, those of Dublin, Belfast, and Derry. As Hickey's chapter treats the admixture of English, Irish and Scots influences on the Irish English accents, so Penhallurick's is concerned with the interface of English and Welsh in the phonology of Wales. Welsh sounds in English, the effects of long-established cultural links with the English Midlands and Southwest, and the existence of English as a Foreign Language for Welsh speakers are shown to be factors in the creation of the Principality's distinctive English accents.

Directly across the border from Wales, Clark's West Midlands is the second largest conurbation of England and the UK, home to the two distinct if closely-related accents of Birmingham and the Black Country. Concentration in this chapter is on the Black Country on the one hand and on the wider West Midland conurbation on the other, with the various accents discussed as both distinctive and as collectively a Northern English variety. In a discussion of the Northern accents of England proper, Beal identifies pan-northern accent features, whilst pointing also to more locally distinctive characteristics, most especially though not exclusively those of the Northeast ('Geordie') and Liverpool ('Scouse'). Altendorf and Watt, in their chapter on the phonology of southern England, divide their area firmly into east and west (the non-rhotic and rhotic areas respectively), and describe the distinctive characteristics of the accents of these areas quite separately. Whilst they regard East Anglia as part of the South they do not venture specifically into this region: features of the East Anglian accents, and their relation to those of surrounding areas to the south, west, and north, are the subject of Trudgill's chapter. Concluding the chapters which deal with the accents associated with specific geographical regions, Ramisch concentrates on the Channel Islands, where interaction with Channel Island (Norman) French and mainland immigrant English have both had an impact on distinctively local English pronunciation.

Descriptions of two non-regional accents round off the discussion of accents of the British Isles. The first is that of British Creole, an ethnic variety which, in Patrick's words, 'is the product of dialect contact between West Indian migrants … and vernacular varieties of urban English'. The second is Received Pronunciation (authored by Upton), an accent that is in essence unmarked for place and so attracts none of the (sometimes adverse) social judgements which regional accents attract, and that is, in consequence, frequently used in broadcasting and as a language-teaching model.

8. The chapters on morphology and syntax

With the exception of the West Midlands and the Channel Islands, all regional and ethnic (British Creole) varieties in the British Isles discussed in the phonology part have a companion chapter in the morphosyntax part. In all morphosyntax chapters the features described are distinctive of the relevant varieties, but in the vast majority of cases not to be understood as unique to these varieties (cf. also the General Introduction). Another property the majority of these chapters share is that they provide qualitative, only exceptionally quantitative, accounts based on large digitized and/or computerized corpora of spontaneous non-standard present-day speech.

The first two chapters complement each other. The one by Melchers on Orkney and Shetland is geared towards highlighting morphosyntactic features which are distinctive of the Northern Isles especially due to their Scandinavian substratum. The Scandinavian features are particularly pronounced at the Broad Scots end of the dialect continuum. Especially for the Central Lowlands (Edinburgh and East Lothian), this is also the focus of Miller's chapter on Scottish English. Southern Irish English, but also varieties of Ulster and Ulster Scots stand at the centre of Filppula's chapter on Irish English. Especially the morphosyntax of Irish English varieties shows an interesting mix of features which, due to one or a combination of the following four factors, have affected the development of Irish English: retention of features from earlier periods of English, dialect contact with other varieties spoken in the British Isles, substratal influence from the indigenous Celtic language (Irish), and universal features we associate with varieties resulting from rapid, large-scale second-language acquisition. The second and third of these features also figure prominently in Penhallurick's account of the morphosyntax of Welsh English: the influences of Welsh, and of the regional dialects spoken in the neighbouring counties of England.

Beal provides a survey of features found in the grammars of varieties spoken in the North of England, the vast majority of which are restricted to particular regions or cities. This variation in the morphology and syntax reflects the diverse histories of the different parts and urban centres of the North: in the far north, the shared history with Scotland and the continuing migration from central Scotland to Tyneside; the large-scale medieval Scandinavian settlements in an area stretching from the Northwest (Cumbria) south-east down to East Anglia, the so-called "Scandinavian belt" (including, for example, all of Yorkshire); in the large cities like Liverpool, Newcastle, and Manchester, high Irish immigration since the 19th century.

Three chapters are concerned with the morphology and syntax of non-standard varieties spoken in the southern parts of England. Trudgill deals with East

Anglia, Wagner with the Southwest (traditionally known as the West Country), and Anderwald with the Southeast (London and the neighbouring counties, the so-called Home Counties). East Anglia and the Southwest have been well-established dialect areas since medieval times, especially the Southwest still boasting not only a unique mix of morphosyntactic features but also individual morphosyntactic properties which are truly unique to this area. The Southeast, by contrast, is a relatively young and, at least with regard to grammar, surprisingly underresearched area in modern dialect research. Here most morphosyntactic features seem to be representative of non-standard speech in present-day England in general. Anderwald's survey is based, among other things, on quantitative analyses of the British National Corpus (BNC), the Bergen Corpus of London Teenage Language (COLT) and the Freiburg English Dialect Corpus (FRED), and provides a solid basis for studies wanting to explore the extent to which the Southeast may be responsible for the (partly ongoing) spread of the relevant morphosyntactic features in the British Isles.

The chapter on the Southeast is also useful background reading against which to judge Sebba's observations on British Creole, since the conversational data Sebba has analyzed are all taken from British-born Caribbean adolescents living in London. This contact variety displays a fascinating degree of syntactic variability which cannot be explained by a continuum model, as known from pidgin and creole studies, alone. What additionally needs to be factored in is, for example, the existence of (especially Jamaican) creole- and standard-like variants for many linguistic forms, and the fact that (for a variety of reasons) speakers often mix Creole and English English forms.

References

Cheshire, Jenny, Viv Edwards and Pamela Whittle
1993 Non-standard English and dialect levelling. In: Milroy and Milroy (eds.), 53–96.

Foulkes, Paul and Gerard Docherty (eds.)
1999 *Urban Voices: Accent Studies in the British Isles.* London: Arnold.

Hickey, Raymond
2005 *A Sound Atlas of Irish English.* Berlin/New York: Mouton de Gruyter.

Kortmann, Bernd
2003 Comparative English dialect grammar: A typological approach. In: Ignacio M. Palacios, María José López Couso, Patricia Fra and Elena Seoane (eds.), *Fifty Years of English Studies in Spain (1952:2002). A Commemorative Volume,* 65–83. Santiago de Compostela: University of Santiago.

Kortmann, Bernd and Susanne Wagner
2005 The Freiburg English Dialect Project and Corpus. In: Bernd Kortmann, Tanja Herrmann, Lukas Pietsch and Susanne Wagner, *A Comparative Grammar of British English Dialects: Agreement, Gender, Relative Clauses,* 1–20. Berlin/New York: Mouton de Gruyter.

Milroy, John and Lesley Milroy (eds.)
1993 *Real English. The Grammar of English Dialects in the British Isles.* London/New York: Longman.

Orton, Harold (ed.)
1962–1971 *Survey of English Dialects: The Basic Material.* 4 vols. Leeds: E.J. Arnold.

Phonology

English spoken in Orkney and Shetland: phonology

Gunnel Melchers

1. General background

Orkney and Shetland, known as "the Northern Isles", are indeed the most northerly units of land in the British Isles. The lighthouse of Muckle Flugga, at a latitude of 61°, is the northernmost point of Shetland as well as of the whole of Britain, and Orkney is as far north as Bristol Bay in Alaska. Lerwick, the capital of Shetland, is equidistant from Aberdeen in Scotland, Bergen in Norway, and Tórshavn in the Faroe Islands.

The Shetland archipelago has a total area of 1,468 sq. km (to be compared with Orkney's 976 sq. km) and consists of well over 100 islands, 15 of which are inhabited. In Shetland as well as Orkney the largest island is simply known as Mainland. Otherwise the names of the islands in both archipelagos can all be traced back to Norn, the Scandinavian variety once spoken in the area, e.g. Whalsay and Foula in Shetland, Westray and Egilsay in Orkney.

There are many similarities between Orkney and Shetland with regard to topography, history, population structure, culture and language but also some characteristic differences. Arable land, for example, amounts to a mere 3% of the total area in Shetland, whereas it is almost 40% in Orkney. It used to be said that the typical Shetlander is a fisherman who occasionally does a bit of farming, while the Orkneyman is a farmer who occasionally devotes himself to fishing. Other differences have to do with the fact that Orkney is much closer to the Scottish mainland (the southernmost point of South Ronaldsay is only about a mile north of Caithness). This is, among other things, reflected in language in that the Orkney dialect is less distinct from mainland Scots/Scottish English.

In spite of their peripheral location, Orkney and Shetland should not be seen as isolated communities, neither in the past nor today. The islands have always been at the crossroads of shipping and trade, and have been subjected to different kinds of immigration and impulses from various peoples: the Norse settlers first arriving in the 9th century, the Scots gradually taking over from the early Middle Ages onwards, and the Dutch and German tradesmen in the Hansa period. The Northern Isles today are modern British societies, with excellent educational establishments and a highly developed infrastructure. While traditional local industries live on, such as the production of cheese and whisky in Orkney, yarn and knitwear in Shetland, the last few decades have seen major changes in population growth, occupation and life styles as a result of the activities related to North Sea oil. The real boom took place in the 1970s in connection with the construction work, but the population level is fairly stable and there is less unemployment than in Scotland as a whole. Shetland now has a population of about 23,000 (to be compared with 17,000 in the mid-sixties) and Orkney about 20,000.

Considering social stratification, Shetland and Orkney make the impression of being more egalitarian than most other regions in Britain. Erving Goffman, the renowned American social anthropologist, who did fieldwork for his Ph.D. thesis as a "participant observer" on Unst, Shetland's northernmost island, was impressed by the general classlessness of the society. More than half of the working population work in services; the second largest category is self-employed, which could stand for running a spinning mill as well as home-based knitting. It is not uncommon for an individual to be employed in widely different spheres, as in the case of a Fair Islander who until recently (1) ran the local post office, (2) was a member of the crew of "The Good Shepherd" connecting Fair Isle with Shetland Mainland, (3) was the local butcher, (4) taught traditional fiddle music at the school, and (5) looked after hundreds of sheep. With regard to gender as a sociolinguistic factor, results from recent linguistic work suggest that it is not significant either. Orten (1991: 65) reports similar observations from Orkney.

In the 10th century Orkney and Shetland were invaded and settled by Vikings, probably coming from South West Norway, as described in the *Orkneyinga Saga*, *Landnámabok* and *Historia Norvegiae*. It is claimed that they defeated the Picts, who are believed to have been the indigenous inhabitants of the area but have left few traces. It is no coincidence that the name of the Icelandic saga documenting the early history of the Northern Isles is derived from Orkney – that is where the heart of the Viking earldom lay and other Scandinavian settlements such as Shetland and Caithness were seen from an Orkney perspective.

Orkney and Shetland remained all-Scandinavian, with a native language variety known as Norn, the first Germanic language to be spoken on the islands, until well into the 14th century, when the Scots began to come in, making the Scottish element in the joint earldom the dominant cultural influence extending northwards into the islands. In 1379 a Scotsman was appointed Earl of Orkney, which included the sovereignty of Shetland, and about a century later the islands became part of Scotland. A serious plea for reunion with Norway was put forward as late as 1905, in connection with the Sweden-Norway separation, but the islands have remained under Scottish and British rule. It should be pointed out, however, that the links with Scandinavia, especially Norway, were never broken, as so remarkably demonstrated through the support given to the Norwegian resistance movement during World War II ("the Shetland Bus"). The Scandinavian heritage is an integral part of Orkney and Shetland identity.

2. The linguistic background

Norn was the dominant language in Orkney and Shetland for at least 500 years, but a natural consequence of the political changes beginning in the late Middle Ages was a gradual shift from Norn to Scots. Owing to the scarcity of written sources we have neither a complete documentation of the structure of the Norn language nor of the rate and character of the process of change. There is an ongoing, heated debate considering the actual demise of Norn (Barnes vs. Rendboe), where a group of "Nornomaniacs" (cf. Waugh 1996) argue that it lived on at least until the end of the 19th century in Shetland. What real evidence there is, however, suggests that in both Orkney and Shetland it died out no later than the second half of the 18th century.

Today, the traditional dialects as spoken in the Northern Isles must be described as varieties of Scots, yet with a substantial component of Scandinavian, manifested above all in the lexicon but also in phonology and, to a lesser extent, in grammar. These varieties are often referred to as "Insular Scots", recognized as one of the four main dialect divisions of Lowland Scots (cf. Grant and Murison 1931–1976; Johnston 1997).

Orkney and Shetland can be characterized as bidialectal speech communities with access to a choice of two discrete, definable forms of speech: one a form of standard, basically Standard Scottish English, and the other what Wells (1982) calls traditional-dialect. Orcadians and Shetlanders are generally aware of commanding two distinct varieties and they have names for these, e.g. "English" vs. "Shetland" or "Orcadian". Admittedly, age-related differences have been observed: on the one hand young people are losing some of the traditional-dialect indexicals, on the other they often state explicitly that they do not wish to adapt to outsiders and tend to be scathing about islanders who do. It would, however, be difficult to find truly monolingual speakers of the traditional dialect today.

As some of the recordings will reveal, the "either-or" scenario is probably not quite categorical, especially not with regard to phonology. In fact, there may well be something of a continuum, where certain traditional-dialect features are stable, such as the palatalization of dental plosives, whereas others vary with the speaker, the situation, and the topic, such as th-stopping. The following account of Orkney and Shetland phonology is not restricted to one end of the continuum and includes some observations on the considerable regional variation found in the Northern Isles. The presentation should be viewed as a complement to the full-length description of Scots/Scottish English in this volume (cf. the contributions by Stuart-Smith, this volume, and Miller, this volume); in other words, it focuses on features where Orkney and Shetland accents differ from other accents in Scotland.

3. Research and data

There exists as yet no definitive description of the present-day phonology of the Northern Isles. A number of young scholars, however, are currently researching topics such as the Shetland vowel system, aspects of quantity in Orkney and Shetland speech, and dialect levelling in young speakers. The final results from this research, which tends to focus on realizations of Standard (Scottish) English rather than traditional dialect, are unfortunately not yet available at the time of writing this text.

The only existing full-length work on Orkney dialect as spoken in the 20th century is Marwick's *The Orkney Norn* (1929). Confusingly, Marwick uses the term Norn both for the all-Scandinavian language once spoken on the islands and for contemporary Orkney dialect. His work is mainly a dictionary of the dialect but with a brief introduction to grammar and phonology and with phonetic transcriptions of all headwords. As the title suggests, it has a marked Scandinavian and historical bias, particularly apparent in the phonology, which takes the Old Norse sound system as its starting-point, simply listing its modern reflections in Orkney. Although contemporary evidence suggests that Marwick's data are characterized by a touch of "Nornomania" and that he had preconceived notions of "correct" answers from his informants, his work is clearly of great importance for the present study. As a phonetician he seems very competent, and fairly narrow distinctions, such as [o] vs. [ɔ] have been noted in individual entries.

Shetland dialect as spoken at the end of the 19th century was carefully documented in the Faroese scholar Jakob Jakobsen's monumental *An Etymological Dictionary of the Norn Language in Shetland* (1928–1932). As the title suggests, it, too, has a clear Scandinavian bias but provides information about the language variety as a whole, including phonology (pre-structural, naturally). Jakobsen, who was a trained philologist in the German school, notes very fine distinctions indeed, to the degree that he has been accused of practising "phonetics run riot" (cf. Waugh 1996: 6). Some of his headwords have up to twenty-five different realizations, but there is no indication of a systematic account of vowels and consonants. This does not mean that he should be ignored in a study of Shetland phonology.

The phonological section of *The Linguistic Survey of Scotland* (LSS) (cf. Mather and Speitel 1986), which above all was designed to elicit vowel systems, included a number of localities in the Northern Isles (thirteen in Orkney, ten in Shetland). John C. Catford, who was instrumental in setting up the survey, took the view that Shetland phonology was unique among Scottish accents in its rich vowel system, palatalization of final /d/, /n/, and /l/, certain consonant mergers and characteristic syllable structure. Before the actual launching of the LSS, Catford found it necessary to do some pilot fieldwork in Shetland, "a phonological reconnaissance", which resulted in a special Shetland section in the questionnaire, e.g. eliciting Scandinavian-based words expected to be realized with [ø], such as *brööl* 'moo'. There was no similar highlighting of Orkney. Catford (1957: 75) assesses Shetland dialect in general as having a "somewhat archaic character", suggesting that its vowel system may be similar to Scots as spoken in the metropolitan area of Scotland in the 16th–17th centuries. Interestingly, aspects of Shetland verbal usage can also be characterized as archaic (cf. Melchers, this volume).

A recent excellent study of Insular Scots, i.e. Orcadian and 'Shetlandic', based on data from LSS and considering Catford's preliminary analyses of vowel systems, can be extracted from Paul Johnston's chapter on regional variation for the *Edinburgh History of the Scots Language* (Johnston 1997).

The only existing account of a particular Insular Scots accent is Elise Orten's *The Kirkwall Accent* (Orten 1991), an M.A. thesis submitted at the University of Bergen, claiming to be "based on the London School of phonology", but not making use of the Wells lexical sets.

An interesting source of information is John Tait's article on Shetland vowels (Tait 2000). Tait, a native Shetlander, first began taking an interest in Shetland phonology for the purpose of creating a workable writing system. He takes a critical view of the LSS material and introduces the concept of "soft mutation", i.e. the raising of certain vowels before certain consonants, which "provides, along with vowel length, a framework for looking at Shetlandic vowel phonology as a whole" (Tait 2000: 88; cf. section 4.1. below).

With the help of instrumental analysis, van Leyden (2002) has investigated vowel and consonant duration in Orkney and Shetland dialects, taking Catford's impressionistic observations as her starting-point. Whereas her Shetland data suggested a Scandinavian-like pattern, Orkney showed more affinity with Standard Scottish English.

In addition to the research described above, this presentation draws on material collected for a project entitled *The Scandinavian Element in Shetland Dialect*, directed by the present writer. The material consists of tape-recordings eliciting phonological as well as lexical and attitudinal aspects. In addition, a great deal of material recorded for the purpose of oral history has been placed at my disposal by the Orkney and Shetland Archives. This is particularly useful since the interviewers are mostly dialect speakers themselves, which means that the informants do not tend to adapt their language.

For the purpose of this publication, recordings were made in Shetland and Orkney during the summer of 2002. Regrettably, however, the presentation will still have a marked "Shetland bias", since considerably more data and information is available on the most northerly part of the Insular Scots region.

4. Orkney and Shetland phonology

With the exception of the table showing the realizations of lexical sets, this presentation is not explicitly organized according to region; in other words, there are no specific Orkney and Shetland sections but the two speech communities are discussed jointly in connections with the various phonetic and phonological issues. Any known differences are of course indicated.

Orkney and Shetland may be small speech communities, but they are both characterized by considerable regional variation, not least evident from the LSS data. In his introduction, Jakobsen (1928–1932) claims that there are nine main dialect areas in Shetland, which, in turn, consist of several sub-areas; Fetlar, for example, which has an area of 39 sq. kilometres, is said to have several dialects, without further specification. In my opinion, such claims must be taken with a pinch of salt and may simply reflect idiosyncrasies.

The local accents mostly singled out as "deviant" by Shetlanders today are spoken in Whalsay and Out Skerries, two close-knit fishing communities east of Shetland Mainland. This view is corroborated by linguistic research, including my own fieldwork. Surprisingly, these particular localities were not investigated by LSS although they are mentioned in Catford's pilot study (Catford 1957). In Orkney, the northernmost islands (Westray and North Ronaldsay) are held to be different, showing for example traces of palatalized consonants as regularly found in Shetland.

Some established regional variation is accounted for here, e.g. the front-back variation of PALM and START and the realization of initial <wh> as [ʍ] or [kw], but the bulk of the data refers to Orkney and Shetland accents in general, as commonly heard in the "capitals", Kirkwall and Lerwick.

4.1. Phonological systems

A traditional phonological inventory of Shetland and Orkney vowels will, naturally, categorize them as Scots/Scottish English (cf. Stuart-Smith, this volume). In his pilot study for the LSS, Catford (1957) argues that most accents in Shetland (along with Angus and parts of Perthshire and Kincardineshire, which is plausible from a demographic point of view) display the maximal Scots vowel system of twelve monophthongs and at least two diphthongs. The twelve-vowel system typically makes a distinction between e.g. *bread* and *bred*, *sale* and *sell*, where the latter in the pair is considerably more open.

Johnston, who is alone in having made a phonemic inventory of the LSS data, does not dispute Catford's claims, but draws attention to a series of changes in Shetland and Orkney accents that he calls "the Insular Clockwise Vowel Shift, from the direction in which the nuclei move from the point of view of a conventional vowel chart" (Johnston 1997: 449).

This shift implies that Older Scots /a/ is reflected as [æ], /ɛ/ as [e] or [ei], /ɑː/ as [aː ~ æː], /ɔ/ and /ɔː/ to [ɒ] or [ɒː]. Further information from Johnston's detailed inventory is included in the presentation of lexical sets below.

Tait (2000), also a discussion of LSS data and to some extent a critique of Johnston's analysis, emphasizes the importance of "soft mutation" (his own term), by which he means qualitative changes in a number of Shetland vowels before certain consonants, predictable according to phonetic environment. He refers to allophones occurring typically before voiceless consonants as "hard" and those which occur typically before voiced consonants as "soft". The BATH vowel, for example, is raised from /a/ to /æ/ before /d/. Tait views these systematic changes, in part, as an alternative and an addition to the concept of a clockwise vowel shift. He summarizes his analysis in a vowel table, which lists as many as fifteen contrastive vowel phonemes, six of which have length as "potentially contrastive". Tait's interesting vowel analysis is further considered in the presentation of lexical sets.

In her traditional study of Orkney phonology, Orten (1991) identifies twelve vowel phonemes in the accent of her main informant: nine monophthongs and three diphthongs, viz. /i/, /ɪ/, /e/, /ɛ/, /a/, /ɔ/, /o/, /ʉ/, /ʌ/, /aɪ/, /au/, /ɔɪ/. A general finding by Orten is that the Kirkwall accent is heavily influenced by Standard Scottish English (StScE).

No attempt is made here to identify the number of contrastive vowel phonemes in Shetland or Orkney, however. As should be apparent from the above, such an inventory is very problematic, among other things for the following reasons:

- the wide span of the available speech continuum, from StScE to broad, traditional dialect on a Norse substratum;
- the considerable regional variation within the island communities;
- the striking effect of the phonetic environment as demonstrated by Tait

In connection with the last-mentioned point, a further complication is of course the effects of the Scottish Vowel Length Rule (SVLR). This rule is described in the main chapter on Scottish English (see Stuart-Smith, this volume). As shown by van Leyden (2002), the SVLR is fairly strictly applied in Shetland dialect today, but less so in Orkney, which she ascribes to the influence of "Standard English". The main research question for van Leyden, however, was to test the claim first made by Catford (cf. section 3) that Shetland dialect retains a Scandinavian-like syllable structure, in that stressed monosyllables, when closed by a consonant, contain either a short vowel followed by a long consonant (VC:), as in *back* [bak:], or a long vowel followed by a short consonant (V:C), as in *baulk* [ba:k]. The results of the study, relying on instrumental analysis, basically confirmed this claim, also showing that it was particularly valid for traditional-dialect lexical items. The Orkney data, however, show that there "this particular relic of Norn has apparently been lost because of the strong influence of mainland Scots dialects" (van Leyden 2002: 15).

Catford (1957: 73) points out that most of the Scandinavian-based features in Shetland phonology have to do with consonants. He ascribes it to the fact that the Norn speakers "had a smaller 'repertoire' of consonants than the incomers, and failed to acquire some of the essential consonantal distinctions of Scots". In addition to the existence of long consonants (geminates), there are, indeed, other interesting systematic characteristics. In Shetland as well as Orkney (though not mentioned in Orten 1991), there is a categorical palato-alveolar affricate merger to the effect that a word pair such as *gin* and *chin* is homophonous, realized as /tʃɪn/.

Another feature affecting the phonemic inventory is th-stopping, occasionally found in Orkney dialect, but categorical in Shetland accents, unless adapted to outsiders, i.e. towards the StScE end of the continuum. The familiar form of address, for example, is represented as *thu* or *thoo* in Orkney dialect writing, but as *du* in Shetland. Th-stopping has also taken place in mainland Scandinavia, but after the end of Viking rule in the Northern Isles. Hence it might be due to an independent innovation and/or to the never-ceasing close contact with Norway.

The realization of initial <wh> as in *wheel* and <kn> as in *knee* also deserves mention in this context. In Shetland, initial <wh> is usually [ʍ], but in some regions, notably the west side of Shetland mainland, the outlying islands of Foula and Papa Stour and some pockets on the east side, it is realized as [kw], even in lexical items such as *whisky* and *whole*. Hypercorrections are common in these accents, e.g. [hwin] for *queen*. Similar realizations are believed to have existed in Orkney, but there is no evidence in present-day speech (Marwick 1929). Initial /kn/ clusters are recessive in Shetland, but can still be heard in the speech of some older speakers realized as a voiceless velar nasal followed by [n]. A better-known variant, very lexically restricted, is characterized by enforced articulation of [k], sometimes followed by an epenthetic vowel. In dialect writing, this variant is often represented as *k-n* as in *k-nee*. This pronunciation is something of a stereotype and is particularly well known from an old phrase, denoting the simple Shetland fare in the old days, *kale and knockit corn*, where the force of alliteration obviously plays a part as well.

In Orkney, retroflex, "Scandinavian-like" realizations of /r/ + /s/ as [ʂ] in final position are the rule rather than the exception, i.e. in words such as *force*, *nurse*, *incomers*, *tours*.

4.2. Vowels

4.2.1. Lexical sets

Variation in quantity is not indicated in the following table.

	Orkney	**Shetland**
KIT	ɪ ~ ï ~ ë ~ ɛ̈	ï ~ ë ~ ɛ̈ ~ ɤ̈
DRESS	ɛ	ɛ
TRAP	a	a
LOT	ɔ	ɔ ~ ɒ
STRUT	ʌ ~ ɔ̈	ɔ̈ ~ ʊ̈ ~ ʌ
FOOT	ʊ ~ u	u
BATH	a	a ~ ɑ
CLOTH	ɔ	ɔ ~ ɑ
NURSE	ɔ̈	ɔ ~ ɔ̈
FLEECE	i	i
FACE	eɪ	eɪ ~ e
PALM	ɑ	a ~ ɑ
THOUGHT	ɔ ~ ʌ̈ʊ	ɔ
GOAT	ɔ	o
GOAL	o ~ ɔ	o

	Orkney	Shetland
GOOSE	u ~ ʉ	u ~ ø
PRICE	aɪ ~ ɛɪ	aɪ ~ ɜɪ
CHOICE	ɔɪ	ɔɪ
MOUTH	əʊ ~ u	ʌü ~ u
NEAR	iə	iə
SQUARE	e ~ ɛ	e ~ ɛ
START	ɑ ~ a	a ~ ɑ
NORTH	ɒ ~ ɔ	ɒ ~ ɔ
FORCE	ɔ	ɔ ~ o
CURE	uə	uə
HAPPY	i	i
LETTER	ə	e
HORSES	ɪ	ə
COMMA	ə ~ a	ɐ

4.2.2. *Further comments relating to the lexical sets*

KIT

This vowel is always short, but displays considerable qualitative variation, most of which is not exclusive to Insular Scots. The last allophone in the Shetland column is, however. It is found before labials and velars. A piece of evidence of its use before the velar nasal is the following cross-dialectal miscomprehension as experienced in a Shetland knitting course by the present writer: The local teacher asked one of the participants, a lady from Lancashire working on a pair of gloves, whether she had trouble with her *fingers*, which was perceived as *fungus*.

DRESS

is usually half-long and often fully-long. Before /d/ and /n/ which are dental in Shetland, it is commonly realized as an upgliding vowel [ɛɪ]. This is probably what some lay observers have in mind when they talk about "palatalized" consonants.

TRAP

There are raised variants in Fair Isle and some Orcadian accents. Before certain consonants, on the other hand, notably the cluster /nd/, the realization is generally [ɑː], so-called HAND darkening (Johnston 1997: 485).

STRUT
tends to be rounded, especially in Shetland.

NURSE
As in Scots generally, there is no NURSE merger.

PALM AND START
vary regionally. The use of a back vowel may signal locality as well as influence from Standard varieties.

GOOSE
In traditional Shetland dialect, a great number of words in this set have an [ø] vowel. It is popularly believed to be a preserved Norn feature, and is indeed typically found in Scandinavian-based vocabulary, such as *tröni* 'pig's snout', and *löf* 'palm of the hand', but also in more modern words, such as *curious*, *poor* (with a lowered variant [œ] before the /r/).

The use of these vowels is recessive.

PRICE
varies according to phonetic environment in quality (cf. the table) as well as quantity.

MOUTH
varies along the dialect continuum, i.e. the monophthong is a regular feature of the traditional dialects.

SQUARE
is very distinctive in Fair Isle and Whalsay, realized as [ɔɪ].

NORTH AND FORCE
are clearly distinctive in the speech of many Shetlanders and Orcadians.

4.3. Consonants – some additional remarks

Consonants that are alveolar in English English, e.g. /d/, /t/, /n/, are generally dental in Shetland accents and /ʃ/, too, is fronted. /l/ is clear. In fact, the articulatory setting in Shetland speech is generally fronted, as shown by some palatograms made for the project investigating the Scandinavian element in Shetland dialect (cf. section 3 above).

In restricted areas (Whalsay and Out Skerries in Shetland, North Ronaldsay in Orkney), /k/ and /g/ before front vowels are palatalized/affricated: *cake* [tçeək], *skerries* [ˈstçɛːrɪs]. During my fieldwork in Whalsay in the early 1980s, a lady told me that unless her grandchildren pronounced *cake* in the proper "Whalsa" way, they would not get a piece! Some recent data collections suggest that this feature is now recessive.

4.4. A note on prosody

Neither Shetland nor Orkney intonation has been researched. It is popularly believed that the accents have a Scandinavian ring about them. Yet, impressionistically, there seems to be nothing remarkable about the Shetland tone of voice.

A difference between Shetland and Orkney, however, is the unmistakable intonation of the latter. It is often held to be Scandinavian in character, but seems, in fact, to be more similar to Welsh English. Orcadians themselves confirm that they are often taken for Welshmen. Yet the romantic ("Nornomaniac"?) view lives on, as the following quote by the Orcadian poet Edwin Muir nicely illustrates:

> The men spoke for the most part in a slow deliberate voice, but some of the women could rattle on at a great rate in the soft sing-song lilt of the islands, which has remained unchanged for a thousand years.

Exercises and study questions

1. Identify some characteristic differences between Orkney and Shetland accents.
2. How can Orkney and Shetland accents be distinguished from other varieties in Scotland?
3. Has the peripheral location of Orkney and Shetland contributed to the distinctiveness of their accents? Give reasons for your answer.
4. Listen to the recordings on the CD-ROM and try to find vowel and consonant realizations not described in the text.
5. In what other varieties of English does TH STOPPING occur? How does it affect the phonemic inventory?
6. How can it be explained that a small speech community like Shetland displays considerable regional variation in language?

Selected references

Please consult the General references for titles mentioned in the text but not included in the references below. For a full bibliography see the accompanying CD-ROM.

Catford, John C.
1957 Shetland Dialect. *Shetland Folk Book* 3: 71–76.

Grant, William and David Murison (eds.)
1931–1976 *The Scottish National Dictionary*, 10 Volumes. Edinburgh: Scottish National Dictionary Association.

Jakobsen, Jakob
1928–32 *An Etymological Dictionary of the Norn Language in Shetland*, 2 Volumes. Copenhagen: Vilhelm Prior.

Johnston, Paul
1997 Regional Variation. In: Jones (ed.), 433–513.

Marwick, Hugh
1929 *The Orkney Norn*. Oxford: Oxford University Press.

Mather, James Y. and Hans H. Speitel (eds.)
1986 *The Linguistic Atlas of Scotland. Scots Section, Volume III: Phonology*. London: Croom Helm.

Orten, Elise
1991 The Kirkwall accent. M.A. thesis, Department of English, University of Bergen.

Tait, John M.
2000 Some characteristics of the Shetlandic vowel system. *Scottish Language* 19: 83–99.

van Leyden, Klaske
2002 The relationship between vowel and consonant duration in Orkney and Shetland dialects. *Phonetica* 59: 1–19.

Waugh, Doreen J. (ed.)
1996 *Shetland's Northern Links. Language and History*. Edinburgh: Scottish Society for Northern Studies.

Scottish English: phonology*

Jane Stuart-Smith

1. Introduction

Defining the term 'Scottish English' is difficult. There is considerable debate about the position and appropriate terminology for the varieties which are spoken in Scotland and which ultimately share a common historical derivation from Old English. Here I follow Aitken (e.g. 1979, 1984) and describe Scottish English as a bipolar linguistic continuum, with broad Scots at one end and Scottish Standard English at the other. Scots is generally, but not always, spoken by the working classes, while Scottish Standard English is typical of educated middle class speakers. Following Aitken's model, speakers of Scottish English either switch discretely between points on the continuum (style/dialect-switching), which is more common in rural varieties, or drift up and down the continuum (style/dialect-drifting), which is more characteristic of the urban dialects of cities such as Edinburgh and Glasgow. Throughout Scotland, Scots is increasingly becoming limited to certain domains, for example, amongst family and friends, while more formal occasions tend to invoke Scottish Standard English. Of course the boundaries between Scots and Scottish Standard English, and English English, spoken by a small percentage of the population, are not discrete, but fuzzy and overlapping.

Scottish Standard English, taken here as Standard English spoken with a Scottish accent, is a possible variety for many speakers across Scotland, depending on social context. There are only slight regional differences in Scottish Standard English across the country. Scots is also widely available to speakers in the appropriate context. The *Scottish National Dictionary* recognizes four main dialect divisions of Scots whose names reflect their geographical distribution across Scotland: Mid or Central Scots, Southern or Border Scots, Northern Scots, and Insular Scots. Alongside spoken Scots, there also exists a literary variety, Lallans (literally 'Lowlands'), but this is rarely spoken and thus not discussed here. Northern Scots, particularly the variety spoken in the North East, is often called the Doric. Urban Scots spoken in the cities of Glasgow and Edinburgh and across the Central Belt, is historically derived from forms of Central Scots.

The Scottish English continuum is the result of dialect contact and language change over many centuries. A brief account follows (for more details, see for example Jones 1997; Corbett, McClure, and Stuart-Smith 2003). Before the Anglian invasions during the seventh century AD, Scotland was predominately Celtic-speaking. The invaders introduced a northern variety of Anglo-Saxon ('Anglian') into south-east Scotland. A century and a half later, the southern borders of Scotland were invaded again by the Vikings, who also separately reached the far north of the country. At the time of the Norman Conquest, most people in Scotland spoke a form of Celtic. Anglian was spoken in the south-east, and Norse was used in the far north and possibly in the western borders. Political developments in England and Scotland during the twelfth century led to an influx of northern English speakers into Scotland. The twelfth to the fourteenth centuries saw the gradual development of a particular variety of English in Lowland Scotland which we recognize as Scots, but which was known as 'Inglis' (Gaelic was called 'Erse' or 'Irish'). By the fifteenth century Scots was noted as distinct from contemporary forms of southern English English. Despite the early Anglian settlement, the main historical basis of Scots was probably the language of northern English settlers from 1100 onwards, which was considerably influenced by Norse after the long period of Scandinavian occupation of the north of England. Prolonged contact with Norman French also contributed to its distinct character. Before the first large-scale literary work in Scots, Barbour's *Brus* (1375), preliterary Scots is only scantily attested, e.g. in place names and glosses. In 1398 the Scottish Parliament moved from Latin to Scots as the language of record, and until the Union of the Crowns (1603), Scots flourished as a literary and spoken language. Thereafter, with increasing English influence, particularly after the Act of Union of the English and Scottish parliaments in 1707, the use of literary Scots declined beyond specific literary genres (e.g. comedy, satire) and gave way to Standard Southern English, which is today the written standard. The eighteenth century also saw the development of Scottish Standard English in the emergence of a variety of Standard English spoken with a refined Scottish accent, typically by the middle classes whose reference for prestige were Southern English accents of England. While literary Scots declined, spoken Scots remained vigorous, at least in rural areas and among the burgeoning working classes. Despite ongoing dialect change and levelling of Scots towards Scottish Standard English, this linguistic situation still persists, although with the additional qualification of Scots as either 'good', i.e. traditional and rural, or 'bad', i.e. degenerate and urban (cf. Aitken 1984: 529).

It is probably fair to say that a good proportion of the population of Scotland, now estimated at 5,062,011 according to the 2001 census (GROS 2003), are potential speakers of Scottish Standard English. There are no official estimates or census statistics for the number of Scots speakers in Scotland, although

Scots is now counted as a 'language' by the European Bureau for Lesser-Used Languages. Defining the number of speakers of Scots in Scotland is extremely difficult, and cannot be easily resolved by asking speakers (Murdoch 1995; Maté 1996; for discussion, see Macafee 1997: 515–518). The problem is created and exacerbated by a number of interrelated factors:

1. the difficulty of recognizing Scots as a variety which is linguistically distinct from Scottish Standard English (for both linguists and native speakers);
2. the broad range of communicative competence in Scots found in speakers across Scotland;
3. the unresolved difficulty of determining whether Scots is an autonomous language;
4. the negative attitudes held towards Urban Scots, which is often regarded as a degenerate form of speech synonymous with slang (e.g. Macafee 1994);
5. the ongoing process of dialect levelling towards English throughout Scotland

Two recent studies (Murdoch 1995; Maté 1996) have attempted to survey the number of Scots speakers, and at the same time (Maté 1996) to evaluate the feasibility of assessing Scots-speaking population through a survey tool such as a Census question. The number of self-professed Scots speakers was relatively low in both sample surveys (57% in Murdoch, 30% in Maté). In both cases, older working-class speakers were more likely to classify themselves as speaking Scots. The conclusions of Maté's research, sponsored by the General Register Office For Scotland, state that the "inclusion of such a Census question would undoubtedly raise the profile of Scots" (1996: 2), but at the same time do not argue strongly for the Census as the optimal tool for estimating Scots speakers:

> Adequate estimates of the numbers of people who assess themselves as Scots speakers can be obtained from sample surveys much more cheaply than from a Census [...] A more precise assessment of genuine Scots language ability would require a more in-depth interview survey and may involve asking various questions about the language used in different situations. Such an approach would be inappropriate for a Census. (Maté 1996: 2)

The 2001 Census did not include a Scots language question.

It is possible to provide a very gross estimate of Urban Scots speakers by using Census data which refer to the population of the Central Belt. Of the total population of the Central Belt, 3,088,938, 66% are assigned to classes 3–8 of the socio-economic classification index used to compile the Census. If we guess that people assigned to these classes may in some domains and to differing degrees be more likely to use Scots than those in classes 1–2, on the grounds that Scots is likely to be continued in the lower middle and working classes (including those who have never worked or who are long-term unemployed), we could suggest that potentially this proportion has access to Urban Scots in some form. The population of the Central Belt makes up approximately two-thirds of the population of Scotland, and hence those classified as class 3–8 in that area make up 40% of the total population. People assigned to classes 3–8 in Scotland as a whole gives 67%, which might be very roughly indicative of a potential for Scots across the country, though this is much less certain.

Beside the varieties of English origin which make up the Scottish English continuum, there are also other languages spoken in Scotland whose influence on Scottish English is known to a greater or lesser extent. Scottish Gaelic was once widespread across Scotland, particularly in the Western Isles and Highlands of Scotland. The proportion of speakers bilingual in Gaelic and English living in Scotland is now estimated at 58,652 (1.2% of the population; a slightly higher figure reported comprehension of Gaelic: 93,282, 1.84%). These figures are a slight reduction from those registered in 1991 (65,978, 1.3%). The English spoken in these areas, and also in small Gaelic/English bilingual enclaves in the cities, such as in Partick in Glasgow, has particular phonetic and phonological characteristics, for example the realization of /l/ as clear in all environments (e.g. Johnston 1997: 510), or the use of voiceless /s, ʃ, tʃ/ where voiced /z, ʒ, dʒ/ are expected, or the retroflex fricative [ʂ] as the outcome of /rs/ in words like *force*, some of which are due to Gaelic influence (see for example Wells 1982: 412–414).

Another small subset of the population of Scotland are recorded in the Census as belonging to an ethnic minority. The number of people defined as 'Pakistani/ Indian/Bangladeshi/Chinese/other Asian/Black-African/Black-Caribbean/ Black-Other/Mixed/Other' make up 2% of the total population of the country, and 5.45% of the population of Glasgow (GROS 2003). As Verma (1995: 120) has pointed out, this substantial ethnic minority population also has linguistic implications, leading to "the recent emergence of a bilingual, and culturally and linguistically diverse, population in schools, where for historical reasons monolingualism was the norm". His analysis of data for ESL provision for the Lothian region reveal 54 languages other than English in primary schools, and 37 in secondary schools, with overall Punjabi and Chinese (Hakka/Cantonese and Mandarin) as most common. The extent of influence of South Asian languages such as Punjabi, on Scottish English and particularly Urban Scots, has not yet been investigated, but my own informal observations suggest that younger members of these communities do show distinctive features, particularly in the realization of FACE and GOAT as closer monophthongs (even with expected breaking), some retraction in the articulation of /t, d/ which are often fronter in Scottish English, and characteristic patterns of intonation (higher nuclear tones) and voice quality (more nasalization and tenser phonation).

Reviews of Scottish English phonology, such as that of Wells (1982: 393), typically concentrate on Scottish Standard English (ScStE), and for good reasons. After all, one could assume that Scots is a language distinct from English and hence not within the scope of any discussion of 'English' in Scotland. Certainly, Scots phonology is largely defined through a rather different lexical distribution resulting from differing historical developments in Scots (Wells 1982: 396). However, at the same time, excluding Scots means effectively excluding description of the possible phonological range of a very large number of speakers for whom Scots is a seamless part of their linguistic repertoire (see, e.g. Wells 1982: 395). Certainly any sociolinguistic analysis of urban Scottish English which includes phonetic or phonological variables and which includes working-class or lower middle class (or even middle-middle class) speakers is going to encounter Scots in some form. This will be most overt in lexical alternations such as *hame* /e/ for *home*, usually ScStE /o/. It will be less clear for those vowels whose lexical incidence is largely the same, such as Glaswegian KIT/BIT, and where socially-stratified variation occurs along a continuum correlating with social class (e.g. Macaulay 1977). However, close analysis of such data often reveals particular patterns of variants which may occur in working-class speakers that make more sense if we can acknowledge them as ongoing developments within and from Scots. Vowels and consonants may appear to be 'the same' in Scottish Standard English and Scots, but the patterns of variation may be rather different, and these differences may correlate with linguistic heritage (Stuart-Smith 2003). Of course this explanation makes it sound as if ScStE and Scots are distinct linguistic entities and the difficulty is that of course they are not. Nevertheless the blurred observable socio-phonetic continua do seem to show focussing about two poles, or at least about one which is 'ScStE-like' and another which owes much, but certainly not everything, to what I call Scots here (see Stuart-Smith 2003: 117). Another motivation for including some discussion of Scots is provided by recent results of variation and change in Scottish English. For it is the speech of working-class youngsters which is showing the most vigorous innovation and change, and hence it seems that Urban Scots is undergoing the most far-reaching changes.

Thus I take the view here that Scottish English must refer to the entire continuum, not simply to Scottish Standard English, and Scots is therefore included in my discussion. However, I too must choose an uneasy compromise in what material may or may not be included, since there is not space here to outline the phonology of Scottish Standard English and Scots in their entirety. Given that around two-thirds of Scottish English speakers inhabit the 'Central Belt', which loosely refers to the cities of Glasgow and Edinburgh and the relatively small strip of land which lies between and about them, and because much recent phonetic and phonological research has been carried out on these accents, the material in this chapter is biased towards these accents and especially Glaswegian. 'Scots' here generally refers to continuations of Central Scots found in contemporary Urban Scots. For an outline of historical developments in Scots see Macafee (2003), for the most comprehensive discussion of regional differences in Scots phonology, see Johnston (1997). Macafee (1997) provides a full review of sociolinguistic results, many of which are phonological.

2. Phonological system

I have already argued that Scottish English is a bipolar continuum, and thus to describe the phonology of this continuum we need, at least descriptively, to refer to the phonologies of the two ends, Scottish Standard English and Scots. Both systems share inventories of vowels and consonants, but differ in lexical incidence, that is in the way that they are distributed across the lexicon. This results from the different historical developments of the two varieties. In fact, for the majority of the lexicon, lexical incidence largely overlaps, so we can recognise common or shared vowels, e.g. KIT/BIT, or consonants, e.g. /l/, which differ only in having distinctive (and sometimes overlapping) realizations in Scottish Standard English and Scots. Those speakers who have access to the Scots end of the continuum may also use particular Scots realizations for certain words, e.g. /ʉ/ for /ʌʉ/ in *house*, and so have a distinct system of Scots lexical incidence. Recent research based on recorded interviews and conversations reveals that the actual number of words involved in Scots incidence is small, and their overall frequency is low (Stuart-Smith 2003), though the actual frequency may be higher in unobserved vernacular speech. Using the Scots variant is strongly marked both for speaker and hearer in the Scottish context.

This division into Scottish Standard English and Scots systems inevitably presents an over-simplistic picture when we look at Scottish English speech. There are certainly speakers who use Scottish Standard English more or less exclusively. But there are far more who have access to Scottish Standard English, but who also have access to Scots, and who drift between the two, and this is especially common of those living in the Central Belt. What this means in practice is that there is a large number of Scottish English speakers, of working-class background, either still working class or recently moved into the middle classes, who may use distinctive Scots variants for most words, but who may alternate to a Scots variant for a smaller set of Scots words. Describing the phonological behaviour of these speakers, who seem to use systematically an alternating system of vowels and some consonants, presents quite a challenge to phoneticians, phonologists and sociolinguists (Stuart-Smith 2003).

The phonetic and phonological description that follows owes much to previous work which is difficult to supersede and where many more details and extensive further bibliography may be found. Relevant works include Abercrombie (1979), Aitken (1979, 1984), Johnston (1997) and Macafee (1997). Particularly useful studies for Edinburgh, and for Glasgow, which is the accent used as the example for the tables and generally for comments unless noted, include Chirrey (1999), Johnston (1985), Macafee (1983, 1994), Macaulay (1977), Johnston and Speitel (1983), Romaine (1978) and Stuart-Smith (1999, 2003). The source of my comments on Glaswegian largely derive from analysis of a corpus of Glaswegian collected in 1997 by me with the help of Claire Timmins, a Scottish fieldworker and researcher.

3. Vowels

The vowels of Scottish English are: /i, ɪ, e, ɛ, a, o, ɔ, ʉ, ʌ, əi, ae, oe, ʌʉ/. Describing these vowels is complicated by the fact that they show two distinct but intersecting systems of lexical incidence typical of Scottish Standard English and Scots, which cannot be captured by using Wells' (1982) lexical sets alone (e.g. Macafee 2003: 139). The picture is further complicated by Scots showing some regional differences for certain vowels. I therefore use three tables to illustrate the vowels of Scottish English. Table 1 shows the phonetic realizations of the vowels of Scottish Standard English together with variants typical of Urban Scots found in Glasgow, which is similar in many, but not all respects, to that of Edinburgh and across the Central Belt (e.g. Macafee 1994: 23–24). Table 2 gives the view from Scots, by showing Scots lexical incidence (after Johnston 1997). The column in the middle reflects the 'system' that is found in most Urban Scots speakers in Glasgow, that is certain vowels whose categories, if not realizations, are largely 'shared' across Scots and Scottish Standard English, and others which may alternate. Table 3 gives a very broad overview of regional variation in Scots across Central, Southern and Northern dialects according to Scots lexical incidence, which may be translated by detailed reference to Johnston (1997: 453–499); further details cannot be given here. All the tables emphasize phonetic realization, although inevitably the symbols are also used to represent phonemic categories, as in Table 2. After some deliberation I have chosen in general to use narrower transcriptions on the grounds that broader (and more abstract) symbols provoke impressions which may be potentially misleading phonetically and phonologically (see Foulkes and Docherty 1999: 12–13). This leads to the less usual representation of Scots BIT with /ɛ̈/ as opposed to /ɪ/, and following from this BET with /ɛ̞/.

Table 1. The vowels of Scottish English (example from Glasgow) – the view from Scottish Standard English (ScStE); after Stuart-Smith (1999: 206).

	ScStE	**Urban Scots**		**ScStE**	**Urban Scots**
KIT	ɪ ~ ë	ɛ̈ ~ ë ~ ʌ ~ ɪ	CHOICE	ɔe	ɔe
DRESS	ɛ	ɛ̞	MOUTH	ʌʉ̠	ʉ ~ ʌʉ
TRAP	a	a̠	NEAR	i	i
LOT	ɔ̞	o ~ ɔ	SQUARE	e	e ~ ɛ̞
STRUT	ʌ	ʌ̈	START	a	ɛ̞ ~ a̠
FOOT	ʉ̠	ɛ̈ ~ ʉ ~ ʏ	NORTH	ɔ̞	o ~ ɔ
BATH	a	a̠	FORCE	o	o
CLOTH	ɔ̞	o ~ ɔ	CURE	jʉ̠	jʉ
FLEECE	i	i	HEAD	ɛ	i ~ ɛ̞
FACE	e	e	AFTER	a	ɛ̞ ~ a̠
PALM	a	a̠	NEVER	ɛ ~ ɛ̈	ɛ̈ ~ ë ~ ɪ
THOUGHT	ɔ̞	ɔ	STAY	e	əi ~ e
GOAT	o	o	STONE	o	e ~ o
GOOSE	ʉ̠	ʉ ~ ʏ	STAND	a	ɔ̞ ~ a̠
BIRTH	ɪ	ɛ̈ ~ ʌ̈	OFF	ɔ̞	a̠ ~ ɔ
BERTH	ɛ	ɛ̞ ~ ɛ̈	DO	ʉ	e ~ ʉ
NURSE	ʌ	ʌ̈ ~ ɛ̈	happY	e	e ~ ɛ̈
PRICE	ʌi	əi	lettER	ɪ ~ ʌ	ʌ̈
PRIZE	ae	ae	commA	ʌ	ʌ̈

Table 2. The vowels of Scottish English (example from Glasgow) – the view from Scots; after Stuart-Smith (2003: 116). ↔ indicates alternation.

	Urban Scots	**Urban Scots (in practice)**	**ScStE**
MEET	i	i	i
BEAT	i	i	i
(DEAD)	i	i ↔ ɛ̝	ɛ
MATE	e	e	e
(BOTH)	e	e ↔ o	o
BAIT	e	e	e
PAY	əi	əi ↔ e	e
BOOT	ɛ̈	ɛ̈ ↔ ʉ	ʉ̠
DO	e	e ↔ ʉ	ʉ̠
BIT	ɛ̈	ɛ̈	ɪ
BET	ɛ̝	ɛ̝	ɛ
OUT	ʉ	ʉ ↔ ʌʉ	ʌʉ̠
COAT	o	o	o
COT	o	o ↔ ɔ	ɔ̝
OFF	a̠	a̠ ↔ ɔ	ɔ̝
CAT	a̠	a̠	a
(LONG)	a̠	a̠ ↔ ɔ	ɔ̝
(WASH)	a̠	a̠ ↔ ɔ	ɔ̝
HAND	ɔ	ɔ ↔ a̠	a
START	ɛ̝	ɛ̝ ↔ a̠	a
CAUGHT	ɔ	ɔ	ɔ̝
(SNOW)	ɔ	ɔ ↔ o	o
CUT	ʌ̈	ʌ̈	ʌ
(PULL)	ʌ̈	ʌ̈ ↔ ʉ	ʉ̠
NEW/DEW	jʉ	jʉ	jʉ̠
BITE	əi	əi	əi
TRY	ae	ae	ae
EYE	i	i ↔ ae	ae
LOIN	əi	əi ↔ oe	oe
VOICE	oe	oe	oe
LOUP 'jump'	ʌʉ	ʌʉ	(ʌʉ)

Table 3. Outline of main regional variants for Scots vowels. For locations of variants, see Johnston (1997), whose descriptions are the source of this table.

	Central Scots	**Southern Scots**	**Northern Scots**
MEET	i	i	i, ɪi
TREE	i	ɛi	i, ɪi
BEAT	i	i	e, ɛi, i
MATE	e	e	e, i
BAIT	e	e	e
BOOT	ɛ̈	ɛ̈	i, e
DO	e	e	iː, ɪi, eː
BIT	ɛ̈	ɛ̈	ɛ̈, ɪ, ɜ
BET	ɛ̞	æ, a	e ~ ɛ
OUT	ʉ	ʉ	u, ü, ʉ
COW	ʉ, ʌʉ	ʌʉ	ʊu, u
COAT	o	o	o, ou
COT	o	o	ɔ, ɒ
CAT	a, ɑ, ɒ	ɒ, ɑ, a	ɑ, ɒ, ɔ, a
CAUGHT	ɔ	ɑ, ɒ, ɔ	ɑ, ɒ, ɔ, a
CUT	ʌ	ʌ	ʌ, ɐ, ɜ, ɔ
NEW	jʉ	jʉ, iu, iʉ	jʉ, ju
DEW	jʉ	jʉ	ju
BITE	əi, ɛ̈i	əi, ɛ̈i	ʌi, ɛi, əi
TRY	ae	ae, ɐe	ɑe, ae ~ ɐe
LOIN	əi, ɛ̈i	oe	ʌi, ɛi, əi
VOICE	oe	oe	ʌi, ɛi, əi, oe, ɒi
LOUP 'jump'	əʉ, ʌʉ, ʌu	əʉ	ɛʏ, əu, əʉ

Rhoticity

The retention of underlying post-vocalic /r/ means that in comparison to many other English accents, Scottish English in general does not show phonemic centring diphthongs in words such as *near*, *hair*. However, the selection and realization of vowels before /r/ varies considerably. In Scottish Standard English, in words such as *fir*, *fern* and *fur*, some speakers will show one vowel /ɪ/ or

/ʌ/, others two /ɛ, ʌ/, and still others all three /ɪ, ɛ, ʌ/. It is also possible to hear the realization [ə] in some types of ScStE (Johnston 1997: 470). There are also differences in the back vowel used before /r/ in NORTH and FORCE (for more discussion, see Wells 1982: 407–408; Macafee 2004). In Scots it is common to find vowel breaking in the form of epenthetic schwa emerging before /r/ (and /n, l/) after most high vowels (e.g. MEET, MATE, COAT); see Johnston (1997: 455).

Vowel length

An important aspect of Scottish vowels is vowel length. The Scottish Vowel Length Rule (SVLR, also called 'Aitken's Law') refers to the phenomenon whereby vowels are phonetically long in certain environments: before voiced fricatives, before /r/, and before a boundary, including a morpheme boundary. Thus the vowels in *breathe*, *beer*, *bee*, and *agreed* are longer than in *brief*, *bead*, and *greed*. In diphthongs, e.g. PRICE/PRIZE (BITE/TRY), the SVLR manifests itself in quantity and quality differences which may be phonemic in Scots, e.g. *aye* [ae], *ay* [əi]. In the refined accents of ScStE, such as 'Kelvinside' (Glasgow) and 'Morningside' (Edinburgh), these diphthongs can be merged stereotypically as [ae] and show a raised first vowel followed by a reduced second vowel (Johnston 1985: 39, 1997: 493). The SVLR still operates in most varieties of Scots and in Scottish English in general, though it appears to be receding in some middle-class speakers in Edinburgh and in children of English-born parents (Jones 2002: 78). Recent accounts of the SVLR based on durational data conclude that the monophthongs /i, ʉ/ and the diphthong /ai/ alone are subject to the SVLR.

KIT

The usual realization of this vowel in ScStE is [ɪ], though it is often more open [ë]. Corresponding to KIT is Scots BIT which is generally in the region of [ɛ̈] but in certain contexts, e.g. after labials, as in *milk*, *fill*, may be substantially lowered and retracted and even merged with CUT (Johnston 1997: 468). A sociophonetic continuum stretches between KIT/BIT, such that the realization shows clear differences according to class. This has been investigated in Edinburgh (Johnston and Speitel 1983) and Glasgow in the 1970s (Macaulay 1977) and again in the 1990s (Stuart-Smith 1999: 207). In all cases lower-class speakers used lower and more retracted variants than those of higher-class speakers. In a recent study by Viktoria Eremeeva and myself, acoustic data from male Glaswegian speakers show middle-class men using the highest vowels, but middle-class boys using the frontest variants, but lower, at the same height as working-class speakers. Interestingly, in spontaneous speech working-class boys are not as retracted as working-class men, suggesting a move away from stereotypically retracted localized variants for this vowel. Though not part of our analysis, we also noticed that [ɛ̈] was usual even in contexts where CUT would be expected in these speakers.

DRESS

The ScStE vowel is closer than that of RP, and in Scots corresponding BET is closer still, represented here as [ɛ̝]; see Johnston (1997: 472).

NEVER

Abercrombie (1979: 74) discusses the possibility of a 'third' phoneme between /ɪ/ and /ɛ/ for Scottish Standard English, occurring in a few words such as *never*, *seven*, *heaven*, *devil*, which he transcribes with /ɛ̈/, and which may be restricted to certain regions such as the West of Scotland, the Borders, and Edinburgh. My own experience from teaching Scottish students confirms /ɛ̈/ for some speakers but with no obvious areal distribution and a good deal of individual variation (cf. Wells 1982: 404). In Scots the equivalent vowel is BIT or BET (Johnston 1997: 471).

TRAP/PALM/BATH

Scottish Standard English usually shows a single vowel for TRAP and PALM, and the same for BATH, represented here as /a/, though Abercrombie (1979: 75–76) observes that "quite a lot of people, particularly in Edinburgh" do have two vowels but with slightly different lexical incidence, giving rise to /ɑ/ in e.g. *value*, *salmon*. The corresponding Scots vowel is CAT, whose realization tends to be more retracted in Glasgow (Macaulay 1977; Stuart-Smith 1999: 208) and even more so in Edinburgh (Johnston and Speitel 1983). Macaulay (1997) again found social stratification in the realization of /a/, with fronter variants in higher class speakers and backer ones in lower class speakers. Some of Macaulay's Class I speakers showed the very front [æ] which is stereotypical of the speech of the middle-class 'Kelvinside'/'Morningside' areas (Wells 1982: 403), where it is said that "'*sex* is what the coal comes in' and '*rates* are large rodents akin to mice'" (Johnston 1985: 37). As in Macaulay's data, the working-class pronunciation in the 1997 Glasgow data was more retracted than that of middle-class informants, though with some unexpected alignment of allophonic variation with English English lexical incidence such that fronter allophones were found in e.g. *cap* [kap] and backer ones in e.g. *car* [ka̠ɾ̥] (Stuart-Smith 1999: 209).

LOT/CLOTH/THOUGHT

Again, Scottish Standard English usually shows one vowel here, transcribed /ɔ̞/, but some speakers may have a distinction between LOT and THOUGHT, with again a slightly different lexical incidence such that e.g. *lorry* would select /ɔ̞/ rather than expected English English /ɒ/ (Abercrombie 1979: 76). Abercrombie observes that an /ɒ ~ ɔ/ contrast assumes an /a ~ ɑ/ contrast. In Urban Scots COT and CAUGHT are distinct but with different realizations, [o] and [ɔ] respectively (Johnston 1997: 490).

GOOSE/FOOT

According to Wells (1982: 401), "from a diagnostic point of view, the most important characteristic of the Scottish vowel system is its lack [...] of a phoneme /ʊ/". The vowels of these two sets are together realized as a high, usually rounded, vowel which is central or even front, transcribed here as [ʉ]. As for LOT/THOUGHT and TRAP/PALM, ScStE speakers may show two vowels here, but this is less usual and presumes the other contrasts (Abercrombie 1979: 76–77). The corresponding Scots vowel is OUT, whose realization tends to be fronter (on Scots OUT-fronting, see Johnston 1997: 475), and can even be unrounded to [ɪ]. (GOOSE and FOOT correspond to the Scots set BOOT and so select the vowel of BIT, though lexical 'bleeding' leading to replacement with ScStE /ʉ/ is gradually progressing: Johnston 1997: 466). As with KIT/BIT and TRAP,BATH,PALM/CAT, there is sociolinguistic variation in the realization of GOOSE,FOOT/OUT. Macaulay (1977) reported backer variants in higher class speakers and fronter variants in lower class informants.

FACE/GOAT

The vowels of these sets tend to be monophthongs, though some Scottish Standard English speakers, such as the rather unusual-sounding Scottish-English-speaking BBC Scotland newscasters, will sometimes use diphthongs similar to Southern English English (Macafee 1983: 35). The Scots monophthongs in MATE/BAIT and COAT/COT can be realized as closer vowels. Apart from phonetic breaking before /r/ (and sometimes /n, l/) in working-class speakers in the 1997 Glasgow corpus, there was very little evidence for a diphthongal realization of these vowels in any speakers.

SQUARE

In the Urban Scots of Glasgow, /er/ from all sources, including MORE/MATE and POOR/BOOT, may be lowered to BET, perhaps as a result of Irish/Ulster influence. Macafee's (1994: 225) analysis of her Glaswegian sample showed weak support for this as a particularly Catholic feature.

Scots OUT

The selection of the Scots vowel /ʉ/ in a word like *house* (OUT) tends to correlate with social stratification, such that middle-class speakers will avoid Scots variants and working-class speakers will use them to differing degrees depending on the alternating vowel and even the word involved. Though Macafee (1994) has analysed the results for 11 alternating vowels in her sample of Glaswegian, the Scots alternation which has received the most attention is that of OUT (see e.g. Macaulay 1977; Johnston and Speitel 1983; Stuart-Smith 2003). The results of these studies confirm that: (i) the Scots form is characteristic of working-class speech; (ii) few lexical items occur in these data (only 12 in the 1997 Glasgow corpus); (iii) speakers always show some alternation (sole use of Scots /ʉ/ is not attested); and (iv) that the alternation appears to be stable over the past 30 years (in Glaswegian at least). This last finding is interesting as it demonstrates that some features of Scots phonology are vigorous.

4. Consonants

The consonants of Scottish English are:
/p, b, t, d, k, g, f, θ, v, ð, s, z, ʃ, ʒ, x, ʍ, h, tʃ, dʒ, r, l, m, n, ŋ, w/. As for the vowels, alternations arise from Scots lexical incidence, but fewer consonants are involved: /v ~ ∅/, e.g. *give/gie*; /θ ~ ∅/, e.g. *with/wi'*; /nd ~ n/, e.g. *stand/staun*; /t ~ d/, e.g. *bastard/bastart*; /l ~ V/, e.g. *football/fitbaw*.

We now have a substantial body of information about the realisation of consonants in Urban Scots, largely as a result of recent work on Glaswegian (e.g. Stuart-Smith 2003), but also arising from other studies (see e.g. the summaries in Johnston 1997 and Macafee 1997). To date 11 consonant variables have been considered in detail from the 1997 Glasgow corpus: t, th, dh, s, x, hw, l, r-realisation, postvocalic r, k, w. In what follows, I restrict my discussion mainly to Scottish English of the Central Belt; for details for regional variation, particularly in Scots, see Johnston (1997).

Stops

Stops are generally reported to be less aspirated in Scottish Standard English (e.g. Wells 1982: 409) and the same is said for Scots, though Johnston (1997: 505) notes that aspiration is creeping into the dialects of the Central Belt. My auditory impressions from the Glasgow data are also that all speakers are less aspirated than typical Southern English English, but this has yet to be investigated acoustically (a recent student project with two informants showed consistently shorter duration of aspiration for a working-class speaker as opposed to a middle-class speaker for /t, p, k/). The place of articulation for /t, d/ can be alveolar or dental, with dental articulations reported for Scots (Wells 1982: 409; Johnston 1997: 505). In Glasgow all speakers showed degrees of advanced tongue tip/blade, indicating a fronted or dental articulation for /t, d/ (and /l, n/); see Stuart-Smith (1999: 216). I deal with /t/-glottalling in the next section, but note here that glottalling of /p/ and /k/ is also reported for Glaswegian, as are ejective realizations of emphatic utterance final stops. See Johnston 1997: 501 for regional variation in glottalling and preglottalization in Scots.

/t/

/t/-glottalling, the realisation of non-initial /t/ with a glottal stop in words such as *butter* and *bottle*, is a stereotype of Glasgow speech and Urban Scots more generally (cf. e.g. Johnston and Speitel 1983; Macafee 1994: 27, 1997; Johnston 1997: 500). It is even spreading into Scots as a general Scottish feature (Johnston 1997: 501). In Glasgow, /t/-glottalling is clearly evidenced in Macaulay's data with the lower classes using glottals extensively (90% for Class III). An analysis of the 1997 Glasgow data revealed similar patterns, and a cautious real-time comparison across the two suggested some increase among working-class speakers, especially girls (though with the already high numbers in 1973 there was little room for manoeuvre).

Perhaps more interesting were the qualitative patterns of /t/-glottalling which were found from a close analysis of my 1997 corpus. In other accents of English /t/-glottalling is a feature which seems to correlate with social class on a continuum, with higher class speakers using few glottals and lower classes using more. On the face of it a similar impression can be gained from looking at Scottish English, and certainly this is how it looks for the 1973 and 1997 results. However, when I analysed the patterning of glottals in working-class speakers and middle-class speakers according to phonetic environment, comparing the usage in prepausal position (e.g. *but*) compared with word-final prevocalic (e.g. *a lot of*) and intervocalic position (e.g. *water*), a striking difference in patterning emerged. When all instances where [t] was used (exceptions to /t/-glottalling) were considered, it became clear that /t/-glottalling is the norm for working-class speakers, and we could even say obligatory for working-class adolescents. All exceptions are clearly motivated. Middle-class speakers however show a different pattern. For them [t] is the norm, and /t/-glottalling optional. That these distributions amounted to systematic patterning was shown when speakers tried to shift socially through /t/-glottalling. Movement sociolinguistically seems to require a systematic shift which neither middle- nor working-class speakers achieved successfully. Middle-class children moving 'down' approximated the working-class pattern but were not entirely successful, retaining traces of typical middle-class patterning. Working-class adults trying to move 'up' approximated their middle-class peers intervocalically, but again retained working-class patterns in the categorical use of glottals before a pause. Thus successful style-shifting along the Scottish English continuum requires more than simply increasing or reducing the number of glottals used, and demonstrates the continuation of different constraints inherited from Scots and Scottish Standard English respectively. Variants other than released [t] or glottals were less usual.

/x, ʍ/

/x, ʍ/ are not generally found in southern accents of English English and RP (Wells 1982: 408). However, the extent to which these categories are intact for some speakers of Urban Scots is doubtful. Macafee's (1983: 32) observation of [k] and [w] as possible realisations in localized Glasgow speech was confirmed for the speech of the working class speakers in 1997, especially the adolescents, for whom [k] and [w] are the majority forms. Johnston (1997: 507) reports [w] for [ʍ] in Edinburgh, and a recent study of the speech of the new town Livingston, which lies between Edinburgh and Glasgow, found [k] but not [w] (Jones 2002: 57). [x] and [ʍ], which we might expect to be characteristic of Urban Scots, are generally maintained in Scottish Standard English. (In Northern Scots [ʍ] has been replaced by [f], see Wells 1982: 397–398; Johnston 1997: 507).

/θ, ð/

In Scottish Standard English /θ, ð/ are realized as voiceless dental fricatives. In Urban Scots /θ/ has the traditional variant [h], in e.g. *think*, *something*, which may also be completely deleted in e.g. *think*, *both*, and a possible retroflex or alveolo-palatal fricative or [ɹ̥] in the initial cluster /θr/, in e.g. *three* (Wells 1982: 410; Macafee 1983: 33). Macafee (1983: 34) noted sporadic instances of /f/ for /θ/ in Glasgow. By the time of the collection of the 1997 Glasgow corpus [f] had emerged as a variable but frequent variant in the speech of working-class adolescents (Stuart-Smith 1999: 209). Interestingly [f] is added to the existing Scots variants to form a constellation of 'non-standard' variants for /θ/ such that in spontaneous speech [θ] accounts for less than a third of the overall variation in these speakers.

The traditional Urban Scots variant for /ð/, particularly in intervocalic position, is the tap [ɾ], in e.g. *brother*, though complete elision is also common, in e.g. the tag, *an(d th)at* (Wells 1982: 410; Johnston 1997: 508). Again the working-class adolescents in the 1997 Glasgow sample showed [v] for /ð/ in words such as *smooth*; [v] joins the traditional Scots variants to extend the array of possible 'non-standard' variation, though unlike /θ/ this makes up a much smaller proportion of the variation (under 20%).

Stopping of /θ, ð/ occurs occasionally in Scots in Glasgow (Johnston 1997: 506) where it may be due to Irish/Ulster influence.

/s, z/

Urban Scots is commonly noted as having a distinctive articulation of /s, z/, which has been described as apico-alveolar (e.g. Johnston 1997: 509). Auditory and acoustic analyses of the 1997 Glasgow corpus suggest that the traditional Scots articulation is also governed by gender.

/h/ and /j/

/h/-dropping is not generally reported for Scottish English (Wells 1982: 412). It is only rarely apparent in e.g. enclitic *him*, *her*. Similarly, yod-dropping appears to function much as Wells states, i.e. after [l] and commonly after [s], with only sporadic instances elsewhere. Clusters with yod, such as [tj] in *nature*, which have undergone coalescence to [tʃ] in Standard English are still retained by some speakers (Wells 1982: 412; Macafee 1983: 32–33). In Urban Scots /hj/ in e.g. *Hugh*, *human* can be realized as [ç] or [ʃ]; see Johnston (1997: 509).

/r/

Scottish Standard English is generally rhotic (Wells 1982: 10–11); in the 1997 Glasgow data articulated /r/ made up around 90% of all variants for postvocalic /r/ in middle-class speakers (Stuart-Smith 2003: 128–129.). In Urban Scots /r/-vocalization is becoming increasingly common (Johnston 1997: 511). Romaine (1978) reported loss of postvocalic /r/ in the speech of working-class children in Edinburgh, where she also noted gendered distribution of variants, with girls showing more approximants and boys showing more r-lessness. The analysis of postvocalic /r/ in the Glasgow data confirmed Macafee's (1983: 32) comments in the discovery of extensive /r/-vocalization in working-class adolescents (Stuart-Smith 2003). Two 'vowel' variant categories were set up: vowels with audible secondary velarization/pharyngealization (cf. Johnston 1997: 511), and 'plain' vowels with no audible secondary articulation. Interestingly, there appears to be subtle conditioning according to gender in the use of these variants: girls overall tended to vocalize more, and to favour plain vowels, especially in contexts such as before a consonant, e.g. *card* or unstressed prepausal, e.g. *better;* boys used both plain and velarized variants before a consonant, but preferred velarized vowels in words like *better* (Stuart-Smith 2003: 126–135).

The phonetic realization of /r/ is variable. Wells states that trills are unusual, and certainly I have rarely heard them amongst Scottish English students.

More usual are approximants, post-alveolar [ɹ] and retroflex [ɻ], and alveolar taps [ɾ], which vary according to position in the word, phonetic environment, and sociolinguistic factors. Scots is usually said to favour taps, though Johnston (1997: 510) notes that [ɹ], more typical of Scottish Standard English, is encroaching. My analysis of the realization of /r/ in the Glasgow data showed that all variants were present in all speakers, with differences in distributional patterns and tendencies. Taps emerged as more common in working-class speakers (especially men) but only in read speech; retroflex approximants were more common in middle-class speakers. There was a slight tendency for the working-class adolescents, who produced a high proportion of vocalized variants, to use taps for articulated /r/.

/l/

Across the Scottish English continuum, the secondary articulation of /l/ tends to be dark in all positions in the word (Wells 1982: 11; Johnston 1997: 510). Exceptional use of clear /l/ is sometimes found in Highland English and occasionally in Scottish Standard English with a distribution similar to that of English English (Macafee 1983: 33). In the 1997 Glasgow data velarized, and velarized and pharyngealized secondary articulations were heard.

/l/-vocalization was a historical process in Scots, yielding common forms such as *a'* 'all' (Macafee 1983: 38). More recently, /l/-vocalization of the kind usually found in southern English, to a high back vowel [ɤ] or [o] (Wells 1982: 258) was reported in Glaswegian (Macafee 1983: 34), and confirmed by subsequent analysis, especially for working class adolescents.

5. Suprasegmentals

In describing vowels and consonants, the preceding description has emphasized segments, perhaps at the expense of obscuring recurring traits which may occur in groups of speakers and which may arise from shared features of the longer domain phenomenon of voice quality. However, there are certainly links between a number of features noted above for Glaswegian and features of voice quality in the same data. For example, /r/-vocalization to a vowel with secondary velarization with some pharyngealization in working-class speakers fits well with my earlier observation of raised and backed tongue body with possible retracted tongue root for the same speakers (Stuart-Smith 1999: 215).

Apart from the work of Brown and colleagues on Edinburgh intonation (e.g. Brown, Currie, and Kenworthy 1980), there has been surprisingly little research on intonation in Scottish English. Cruttenden (1997: 136) notes that for accents of Scotland other than those found in Glasgow, statements and questions will invariably show "a sequence of falling tones". The main difference between the speech of Edinburgh and Glasgow is in terminating mid-to-low-falls in Edinburgh (e.g. Brown, Currie, and Kenworthy 1980) but a tendency towards high rising patterns in Glasgow (e.g. Macafee 1983: 36; Stuart-Smith 1999: 211). The extent to which these continue patterns from earlier forms of Scots is not known, though Northern Irish influence may be invoked to some extent to explain distinctive Glaswegian patterns (Macafee 1983: 37; on Irish English influence more generally, see Cruttenden 1997: 133). It seems unlikely that Glasgow's 'high rise' is linked to the apparently rapid spread of high-rising terminal intonation patterns in southern accents of English English (see Cruttenden 1997: 129).

Even less has been said about rhythm in Scottish English, bar Abercrombie's (1979: 67) comments that disyllabic words such as *table* are often pronounced with a short first syllable and long second syllable. This is also my impression when teaching rhythm to Scottish English students. Abercrombie also makes the observation that syllabification in Scottish Standard English tends to favour open syllables, so that a phrase like *St Andrews* will be syllabified into [sn̩ tan̤ drʉz].

6. Major issues in current research

Good summaries of previous phonetic, phonological and sociolinguistic research on Scottish English may be found in Aitken (1984) and Macafee (1997). The most recent fundamental research into the phonetics and phonology of Scottish English has been carried out by James Scobbie (Queen Margaret University College, Edinburgh), who is concentrating on empirical investigation of the Scottish Vowel Length Rule using articulatory and acoustic phonetic analysis (e.g. Scobbie, Hewlett and Turk 1999), but who is also working on other aspects of Scottish English, such as the voicing contrast as reflected in Voice Onset Time (VOT) systems in Shetlandic. Closely related to Scobbie's work is that of Ben Matthews who looked at the acquisition of the Scottish Vowel Length Rule in Edinburgh children. The reader is referred to the full bibliography on the CD-ROM for the relevant studies mentioned in this section.

Much other current research on the phonology of Scottish English is concerned with the interrelation of accent and user. Dominic Watt (Aberdeen) is developing research on accent and identity, looking specifically at phonetic and phonological features of Scottish English on the Scottish/English Border, as illustrated by the inhabitants of Berwick upon Tweed. Attitudes and accent change have been investigated recently by Karen Torrance (2002). She tracked the relationship between incoming diffusing features such as /th/-fronting in Glaswegian and attitudes of speakers using such features towards different regional accents of English. Her complex results show that attitudes seem to relate to language use for certain speakers only, thus highlighting the role of the individual in this process. Call centres, outlets of companies which conduct their business with customers using the telephone, have flourished in the Central Belt of Scotland. Features of Scottish English in call centre interaction is thus an obvious but neglected area of research which formed the focus of Suzy Orr's (2003) study. She found some evidence of accommodation in Glaswegian agents to their callers.

Phonological variation and change in the Scottish English of Glasgow is the subject of my own research with colleagues Claire Timmins, Eleanor Lawson and Viktoria Eremeeva (e.g. Stuart-Smith 2003), which tackles some of the issues raised above and others including sound change in Glaswegian, real time change in Glaswegian, social factors and sound change, mobility and dialect contact in Glaswegian, and acoustic analysis in sociolinguistic investigation. Most of my work has concentrated on consonant change, but Eremeeva (2002) started the work of analysing vowels in the 1997 corpus. The first phase of the work, which took 11 consonants and considered them both singly and together, has identified innovation and change led by working-class adolescents, with few indications of gendered distribution. What emerges from these results is the extent to which Urban Scots is developing as a dynamic mixture of vigorous local and non-local features. Exactly how and why the dialect is changing in these ways remains the subject of further research.

* I am very grateful to the Leverhulme Trust for supporting the data analysis with a research grant (F/179/AX) and the AHRB for supporting its writing up with a research leave grant. Thanks are due to Claire Timmins who acted as researcher on the Leverhulme project, and to Wolf-Gerrit Fruh who compiled the Census statistics. I am grateful to Clive Upton for his editing, and to Caroline Macafee, Claire Timmins, Suzy Orr, and Dom Watt who commented on an earlier draft. All errors and opinions remain my own.

Exercises and study questions

1. What is meant by the 'Scottish English continuum'? What does this mean for the sound system of Scottish English? Provide examples to support your answer from the tables and the lexical set.
2. To what extent does the free passage show 'drifting' up and down the Scottish English continuum in terms of phonology? Identify the phonological features that you think demonstrate drifting, and suggest some reasons for this.
3. Scottish English is usually thought to show the consonant phonemes /x/ and /ʍ/. What can you say about the realization of these sounds in the sound samples provided? Can you suggest any reasons for the variation that you find?
4. List the innovations in consonant pronunciation that have been identified recently for Scottish English. Listen to the sound samples. To what extent can you find evidence for these innovations in these speakers? Explain your findings.
5. What is the 'Scottish Vowel Length Rule'?
6. The vowels /ɪ a ʉ/ have been shown to vary according to social class. What can you say about the variation in the realization of these vowels in the speakers in the sound samples?
7. Listen to the free passage, thinking particularly about the intonational (pitch) patterns that occur in declarative sentences in the two speakers. To what extent do speakers from the West Coast of Scotland show evidence for a High Rising Tone in this environment?

Selected references

Please consult the General references for titles mentioned in the text but not included in the references below. For a full bibliography see the accompanying CD-ROM.

Abercrombie, David
1979 The accents of standard English in Scotland. In: Aitken and McArthur (eds.), 68–84.

Aitken, Jack
1979 Scottish speech: a historical view with special reference to the Standard English of Scotland. In: Aitken and McArthur (eds.), 85–118.

Aitken, Jack
1984 Scots and English in Scotland. In: Trudgill (ed.), 517–532.

Brown, Gillian, Karen Currie and Joanne Kenworthy
1980 *Questions of Intonation*. London: Croom Helm.

Chirrey, Deborah
1999 Edinburgh: descriptive material. In: Foulkes and Docherty (eds.), 223–229.

Cruttenden, Alan
1997 *Intonation*. Cambridge: Cambridge University Press.

GROS
2003 *Census 2001 Scotland*. General Register Office for Scotland.

Johnston, Paul
1985 The rise and fall of the Morningside/Kelvinside accent. In: Görlach (ed.), 37–56.

Johnston, Paul
1997 Regional variation. In: Jones (ed.), 433–513.

Johnston, Paul and Hans Speitel
1983 A sociolinguistic investigation of Edinburgh speech. Final Report to the ESRC.

Jones, Charles
2002 *The English Language in Scotland: An Introduction to Scots*. East Linton: Tuckwell.

Macafee, Caroline
1983 *Glasgow*. Amsterdam/Philadelphia: Benjamins.
1994 *Traditional Dialect in the Modern World: A Glasgow Case Study*. Frankfurt am Main: Lang.
1997 Ongoing change in modern Scots: the social dimension. In: Jones (ed.), 514–548.
2003 The phonology of older Scots. In: Corbett, McClure and Stuart-Smith (eds.), 138–169.
2004 Scots and Scottish English. In: Hickey (ed.).

Macaulay, Ronald
1977 *Language, Social Class and Education: A Glasgow Study*. Edinburgh: Edinburgh University Press.

Maté, Ian
1996 *Scots Language: A Report on the Scots Language Research Carried out by the General Register Office for Scotland in 1996*. Edinburgh: General Register Office.

Murdoch, Steve
1995 *Language Politics in Scotland*. Aberdeen: Aiberdeen Univairsitie Scots Leid Quorum.

Romaine, Suzanne
1978 Postvocalic /r/ in Scottish English: sound change in progress? In: Trudgill (ed.), 144–157.

Scobbie, James, Nigel Hewlett and Alice Turk
1999 Standard English in Edinburgh and Glasgow: the Scottish vowel length rule revealed. In: Foulkes and Docherty (eds.), 230–245.

Stuart-Smith, Jane
1999 Glasgow: accent and voice quality. In: Foulkes and Docherty (eds.), 203–222.

Stuart-Smith, Jane
2003 The phonology of modern urban Scots. In: Corbett, McClure and Stuart-Smith (eds.), 110–137.

Torrance, Karen
2002 Attitudes and language change in Glaswegian. M.A. thesis, University of Glasgow.

Verma, Mahendra
1995 Ethnic minority languages in Scotland: a sociolinguistic appraisal. *Scottish Language* 14/15: 118–133.

Irish English: phonology

Raymond Hickey

1. Introduction

The English language was introduced to Ireland with the coming of the Anglo-Normans from West Wales in the late 12th century. Among the settlers were English speakers who coexisted with the Norman French in Ireland, settling down in the towns of the east coast of Ireland and providing the cells out of which the English-speaking population of Ireland was later to emerge. Since the late 12th century, the fate of English has been closely linked with that of the Irish language which it came largely to replace in the late modern period. In addition, the interaction of existing forms of English with the Scots imported in the early 17th century in the north of the country led to the linguistic separation of Ulster, the most northerly province, from the rest of the country. This state of affairs provides the rationale for the division of English in Ireland into two broad groups as reflected by divisions in the current chapter. For the many varieties of English on the island of Ireland there are different designations.

Anglo-Irish is an established term in the literature to refer to works written in English by authors born in Ireland and is also used in politics. The difficulty with the term is its occurrence in these other spheres. Within the context of other varieties, Canadian English, for instance, the term is still used to refer to English in Ireland.

Hiberno-English is a learned term which is derived from the Latin term *Hibernia* 'Ireland'. The term enjoyed a certain currency in the 1970s and 1980s but in the 1990s many authors ceased to employ it, as it often needs explanation to a non-Irish audience or readership. However, not all authors share this opinion, see for example Dolan (1998) who uses the term Hiberno-English.

Irish English is the simplest and most convenient term. It has the advantage that it is parallel to the designations for other varieties, e.g. American, Australian, Welsh English and can be further differentiated where necessary. Throughout the present chapter this term will be used.

In the north of the country terms are used which reflect historical origins, e.g. *Ulster Scots* for the English stemming from the initial Lowland Scots settlers, *Mid-Ulster English* for geographically central varieties which are largely of northern English provenance. There is much discussion of the status of Ulster Scots as a possible separate language and similarly the status of Scots is debated. A discussion of this issue is, however, well beyond the brief of the current chapter.

Contact English is found occasionally to refer globally to varieties spoken in areas where Irish is also spoken (in Donegal, Connemara and Kerry, see maps at end of chapter).

1.1. Historical background

The most cursory glance at the history of Irish English reveals that it is divided into two periods. The first period starts in the late 12th century with the arrival of the first English-speaking settlers and finishes around 1600 when the second period opens. The main event which justifies this periodisation is the renewed and vigorous planting of English in Ireland at the beginning of the 17th century. One must first understand that during the first period the Old English, as this group is called in the Irish context, came increasingly under the influence of the Irish. The Anglo-Normans who were the military leaders during the initial settlement had been completely absorbed by the Irish by the end of the 15th century. The progressive Gaelicisation led the English to attempt planting the Irish countryside in order to reinforce the English presence there. This was by and large a failure and it was only with James I that successful planting of (Lowland Scottish and English) settlers in the north of the country tipped the linguistic balance in favour of English in the north. During the seventeenth century (after the Cromwellian campaigns at the middle of the century) new forms of English were brought to Ireland: Scots in the north and West/North Midland varieties in the south (where there had been a predominantly West Midland and south-west input in the first period). Although there was renewed Anglicisation, on the east coast, in Dublin and other locations down to Waterford in the south-east, there is a definite continuation of south-west English features which stem from the imported varieties of the first period. This fact underlies a distinctive east coast dialect area.

1.1.1. The medieval period

The documentary record of medieval Irish English is confined for all intents and purposes to the collection of 16 poems of Irish provenance in BM Harley 913 which are known collectively as the *Kildare Poems* (Heuser 1904; Lucas 1995) after one of the poems in which the author identifies himself as from the county of Kildare to the south-west of Dublin. The collection probably dates from the early 14th century. The language of these poems is of a general west Midland to southern English character. Many of the idiosyncratic features can be traced to Irish influence (see discussion in Hickey 1993). It is a moot point whether the *Kildare Poems* were written by native speakers of Irish using English as a H-language in a diglossic situation or whether indeed the set was written by one or more individuals. Apart from the *Kildare Poems*, medieval Irish English is attested in a number of verse fragments and in city records from Dublin and Waterford, comments on which can be found in Henry (1958).

1.1.2. The early and late modern period

At the end of the 16th century attestations of Irish English begin to appear which are deliberate representations of the variety of the time. These are frequently in the guise of literary parody of the Irish by English authors (Bliss 1979). The value of these written representations of Irish English for reconstructing the language of the time has been much questioned and it is true that little if any detail can be extracted from these sources. In addition most of the satirical pieces were written by Englishmen so that one is dealing with an external perception of Irish English at the time. Satirical writings are not the only source of Irish English, however. There are some writers, especially in the 19th century, who seriously attempt to indicate vernacular speech of their time, such as Maria Edgeworth in her novel *Castle Rackrent* (1801).

1.2. Language shift in early modern Ireland

Literary parodies do not reveal anything about the then relationship of Irish to English, the spread of English and the regional input from England. There were no censuses before 1851 which gave data on speakers of Irish and English. Adams (1965) is a useful attempt to nonetheless produce a linguistic cartography of Ireland at the beginning of the early modern period. The upshot of this situation is that there is no reliable data on the language shift which began in earnest in the early 17th century and which had been all but completed by the late 19th century.

It is clear that the Irish learned English from other Irish who already knew some, perhaps through contact with those urban Irish who were English speakers, especially on the east coast and through contact with the English planters and their employees. This fact had consequences for the nature of Irish English. Bliss (1977) pointed out that this fact is responsible for both the common malapropisms and the unconventional word stress found in Irish English. However, the stress pattern in verbs with final long vowels, e.g. *distribute* [dɪstrɪˈbjuːt], *educate* [edju'ke:t], can also be due to English input, particularly as late stress is a feature of southern Irish, not of the west and north, and so influence due to contact with Irish could only be posited for the south of Ireland.

Another point concerning the language shift in Ireland is that it was relatively long, spanning at least three centuries from 1600 to 1900 for most of the country. The scenario for language shift is one where lexical transfer into English is unlikely, or at least unlikely to become established in any nascent supraregional variety of English in Ireland. Such dictionaries as Ó Muirithe (1996) and to a lesser extent Dolan (1998) seem to reveal a large number of Irish loans in present-day Irish English. But the question of currency is the key issue here: there is a great difference between the vocabulary of an older agricultural generation (which is frequently reflected in the entries in these dictionaries) and a younger urban one.

In phonology and syntax the matter is quite different. Speakers who learn a language as adults retain the pronunciation of their native language and have difficulty with segments which are unknown to them. A simple case of this would be the substitution of English dental fricatives by stops (dental or sometimes alveolar, depending on region) in Irish English. A more subtle case would be the lenition of stops in Irish English, e.g. *cat* [kæṱ], which, while systemically completely different from lenition in Irish, could be the result of a phonological directive applied by the Irish learning English to lenite elements in positions of maximal sonority.

1.2.1. Contact Irish English

In present-day Ireland there are only a few small remaining enclaves scattered along the western seaboard where Irish is still spoken as a native language in a situation of unbroken historical continuity. Apart from this there is an increasing number of language enthusiasts who speak Irish as a second language and attempt to keep the language alive by using it as much as they can, frequently in an urban environment which is completely English-speaking. In principle, the rural setting just mentioned should be the one in which the language shift scenario of previous centuries (Hickey 1995) is replicated, thus enabling linguists to view the process of language contact and transfer in vivo. Despite this fact there are few studies of contact Irish English today although the Irish language in contact areas has repeatedly been the subject of investigation, e.g. Stenson (1991). This study was carried out on seven informants from the north west of Ireland (Co. Donegal) to see what kinds of /l/ sounds they showed in English. To this end their Irish was investigated. This variety of Irish shows three types of /l/-sounds: a velarised [ɫ], a palatalised [ʎ] and a (lenited) neutral [l]. It turned out that the speakers used the last sound as the realisation of English /l/ in all positions (bar before /j/ as in *million* /mɪljən/ = [mɪʎən]) which tallies with the realisation of /l/ in the rest of the country where this was decided a century or two ago.

1.3. Supraregionalisation

It is obvious from English loanwords in Irish that early Irish English had not progressed through the major long vowel shift in England, e.g. Irish *bacús* 'bakehouse' shows unshifted /aː/ and /uː/. The play *Captain Thomas Stukeley* (1596/1605), the first widespread representation of Irish English in literary parody, consistently uses <*oo*> for words with /au/ from Middle English /uː/, e.g. *toon* for *town*. Furthermore, comments from Thomas Sheridan in the late 18th century (Sheridan 1781) show that Middle English /aː/, as in *patron*, still had not shifted, nor had Middle English /ɛː/ as in *meat*. But present-day Irish English shows little or no trace of these unshifted vowels. The reason is not that the shift took place in Irish English some time in the 19th century but that the unshifted forms were replaced by mainstream English pronunciations due to a process which I have labelled *supraregionalisation*. The essence of this process is the replacement of salient features of a variety by more standard ones, frequently from an extranational norm, as with southern British English vis à vis Irish English. The motivation for this move is to render a variety less locally bound, more acceptable to a wider community, hence the term supra-regionalisation.

1.4. Vernacularisation

The story of supraregionalisation does not end with the disappearance of strongly local features. There is another pathway which such features can take. This is the relegation to vernacular varieties. Take the instance of Middle English /ɛː/ as in *beat* /bɛːt/. This pronunciation is now confined to strongly local varieties where supraregionalisation has not taken place. Furthermore, non-local speakers can style-shift downwards to achieve a vernacular effect. Another example of this would be the use of *youse* or *yez* for the second person plural (also found in other Anglophone areas such as Tyneside). This is shunned by non-local speakers but can be employed when deliberately switching to a vernacular mode.

The process of vernacularisation has in some instances led to a lexical split. Consider the reflex of velarised [ɫ] before [d] in Irish English: this led to the diphthong [au] as in the words *old* [aul] and *bold* [baul] with the common postsonorant stop deletion. These forms are available alongside /o:ld/ and /bo:ld/ to non-local speakers but the meanings are somewhat different as the original forms with [au] have gained additional meaning components: [aul] 'old + affectionate attachment', e.g. *His [aul] car has finally given up the ghost*, [baul] 'daring + sneaking admiration', e.g. *The [baul] Charlie is back on top again.*

2. Varieties of Southern Irish English

It is obvious that linguistically, as well as politically, Ireland is divided into two broad sections, the north and the south. The former consists of the six counties presently within the state of Northern Ireland and of the large county of Donegal which is part of the Republic of Ireland. The north has a complex linguistic landscape of its own with at least two major historical varieties: Ulster Scots, the speech of those directly derived from the original Lowland Scots settlers, and Mid-Ulster English, the speech of those descendants of English settlers to central parts of Ulster. In addition there is the sociolinguistically complex capital, Belfast. Co. Donegal by and large goes with the rest of Ulster in sharing key features of English in the province and also of the varieties of Irish used there.

The north of the country is quite distinct from the south, accents of northerners being immediately recognisable to southerners. A dividing line can be drawn roughly between Sligo, just south of Co. Donegal, and Dundalk on the east coast immediately below the border with Northern Ireland (Ó Baoill 1991). North of this line the accents are distinctly Ulster-like. South of this line the northern features rapidly give way to southern values. The term *line* here might imply a clearly delimited boundary, perhaps *zone* might be more accurate, as border counties such as Monaghan, Cavan or Louth show mixed accents which have adopted features from both northern and southern types.

The transition can be clearly seen moving down the east coast: Dundalk has a northern flavour to its speech but this is more or less lost by the time one reaches Drogheda travelling southwards. However, the recordings of *A Sound Atlas of Irish English* show that key features of northern Irish English, such as mid front vowel breaking, as in *save* [seːəv], and /u/-fronting, as in *boot* [bʉt], extend quite far down the east coast, indeed in the case of the latter almost to the border of Co. Dublin.

Table 1. Northern features which occur in the transition zone from south to north

Use of interdental fricatives for dental stops in the south
Use of a fronted allophone of /u:/ and /u/, i.e. [ʉ(:)]
A reduction in the vowel length distinctions
Use of a retroflex [ɻ] in syllable-final position
Greater pitch range between stressed and unstressed syllables
Greater allophony of /æ/, e.g. raised variants in a velar environment *bag* [bɛg] and a retracted realisation in a nasal environment *family* [ˈfɑmli]
Recessive occurrence of glides after velars and before front vowels as in *Cavan* [ˈkjævən] (a border county)

2.1. The East Coast

The east of the country stretches from the town of Drogheda somewhat north of Dublin down to Waterford in the south-east and includes such towns as Carlow, Kilkenny, New Ross, Wexford. This is the area which was first settled by the English from the late 12th century onwards and it is roughly coterminous with that which was encompassed by the *Pale*, the region of English influence in the late medieval ages, at its greatest extension. The original input from south-west England did in fact survive in altered form until the beginning of the 19th century in the archaic dialect of Forth and Bargy which was recorded by a few glossary compilers before it finally ceased to exist.

Table 2. East band features from Dundalk down to Waterford (including Dublin)

Fortition of dental fricatives to alveolar stops (also south), e.g. *think* [tɪŋk]
Lack of low vowel lengthening before voiceless fricatives (not Dublin), e.g. *path* [pat]
Front onset of /au/, e.g. *town* [tæʊn], [tɛʊn]
Centralised onset of /ai/ (also south), e.g. *quite* [kwəɪt]
Breaking of long high vowels (especially Dublin), e.g. *clean* [klijən]
Fortition of alveolar sibilants in pre-nasal position, e.g. *isnt* [ɪdn̩t]
No lowering of early modern /u/ (only Dublin), e.g. *done* [dʊn]
Glottalisation of lenited /t/, e.g. *foot* [fʊt] → [fʊt̞] → [fʊʔ] → [fʊh]

2.2. The South and West

This is a large region, from Co. Cork up to Co. Mayo, and was that in which Irish survived longest. As rule of thumb one can say that Irish receded from east to west. Furthermore, in this western and southern half of the country there is no survival of English from the first period with the possible exception of very small pockets in the major cities Cork, Limerick and Galway. Hence the English which developed here was that of the early modern period which arose through uncontrolled adult second language acquisition on the part of the rural inhabitants who represented the vast majority of speakers. Furthermore, the regional English input of the early modern period was of a largely West Midlands character.

The south and the west can also be distinguished from each other, at least on phonological grounds. The major segmental feature is the raising of /ɛ/ to /ɪ/ before nasals in the south and southwest. This phenomenon is not spectacular in itself and is found in many varieties of English, most notably in the Lower South of the United States. But a consideration of the history of Irish English shows that this raising was of a more general type previously. If one looks at the many literary satires which contain Irish English, for instance in the collection by Alan Bliss (1979) or in *A Corpus of Irish English* (Hickey 2003), then one sees that formerly the raising occurred in non-nasal environments as well, e.g. *divil*, *togithir*, (from Dion Boucicault's play *Arragh na Pogue*, 1864). What would appear to have happened in late 19th-century and/or early 20th-century Irish English is that the raising came to be restricted to environments in which it was phonetically natural, i.e. before nasals as these often trigger vowel raising due to their formant structure. This would mean that the situation in the south and south-west of Ireland (roughly the counties of Cork and Kerry) is a remnant of a much wider occurrence of /ɛ/ to /ɪ/ raising.

A suprasegmental feature of the south, especially of the city of Cork, is the large intonational range characterised by a noticeable drop in pitch on stressed syllables. This intonational pattern is shared by Cork Irish, in the remnants which are still extant, so that this prosodic feature can be viewed as an areal feature of the south/south-west. The city of Cork also has a very open realisation of the vowels in the LOT and THOUGHT lexical sets which is seen in (often stereotypical) pronunciations of the city's name, [kaɹk].

A distinctive feature of the west is the use of dental stops in the THINK-THIS lexical sets. In vernacular varieties in the east and south, alveolar stops are employed here. In the history of Irish English one can assume that Irish speakers switching to English would have used the nearest equivalent to English /θ, ð/, i.e. the coronal stops of Irish. These stops were alveolar in the east and south, but dental in the west so that speakers used /t̪, d̪/ as equivalents to the English dental fricatives in their second language English. This dental pronunciation of the west has become that of the supraregional variety of Irish English, itself deriving from usage in Dublin and spreading then throughout the country. But in vernacular Dublin English the realisation of dental fricatives has been as alveolar stops so it is not clear how vernacular speakers in Dublin came to use dental stops. One view is that they picked this articulation up from the many immigrants into Dublin in the latter half of the 19th century, because it (i) allowed them to dissociate themselves phonetically from vernacular speakers in the city and (ii) permitted a reversal of homophony in the words *thinker* and *tinker*.

2.3. The Midlands

The centre of Ireland is a flat expanse bordered by the hills and mountains which occupy the coastal regions of the country. In general the term *Midlands* is used in Ireland to describe an area west of Co. Dublin as far as the Shannon and including its western shore linking up with east Clare, Galway and Mayo and on a north-south axis delimited by the border with Northern Ireland in the north and to the south by a line running roughly from Limerick across to Dublin. In this sense, Midlands actually refers to the north-central part of Ireland. Its extension to the south is limited and does not stretch far down into Co. Tipperary. The counties which are regarded as typically part of the Midlands are Westmeath, Longford, Offaly, Laois along with west Kildare and Meath, south Roscommon and north Tipperary. The main town in the Midlands is Athlone, situated on the Shannon about half way on its north-south course.

To the north, the Midlands show the transitional features of the north-south divide (Ó Baoill 1991) such as /u/-fronting, the use of dental fricatives for stops in the THINK-THIS lexical set or a retroflex [ɻ] for the more general, traditional velarised [ɹ] of the south. The single most obvious feature of the Midlands is the shift of /tj/ to /k/ in intervocalic position as in *fortune* ['fɔrku:n], already mentioned in the 19th century. Other features are shared by adjoining varieties.

Table 3. Phonological features of the South, West and Midlands of Ireland

South and west from Cork through Limerick up to Galway and Sligo
/ɛ/ to /ɪ/ before nasals
Tense, raised articulation of /æ/ (also east)
Considerable intonational range (only south, south-west)

Table 3. (continued) Phonological features of the South, West and Midlands of Ireland

West
Dental stop realisation in THINK-THIS lexical sets
Low central onset for /ai/ and /au/, e.g. *quite* [kwaɪt], *town* [taʊn]
Midlands
Shift of /tj/ to /k/ in word-internal position, e.g. *fortune* ['fɔrku:n]

3. Varieties of Northern Irish English

Any treatment of English in Ireland must take special account of the situation in Ulster. The reason for this lies in the settlement history of this province which led to the introduction of Scots and forms of northern English which were, and still definitely are, distinctive from all varieties of English in the south of the country. There has also been, as in the south, interaction between forms of English and Irish which has added a further dimension to the linguistic complexity in the north. A common means of alluding to the northern part of the island of Ireland is by the historical name *Ulster* which covers the entire north of Ireland.

3.1. Terminology

Similarly to the south, any discussion of English in the north must begin with a consideration of terminology as there are many and frequently contradictory usages found in treatments of language in Ulster.

Ulster English: 1) A cover term for various forms of English used in Northern Ireland. 2) A specific reference to English brought to Ulster from the north-west Midlands of England (Adams 1958: 61) and separate from the Scots element in the province. Because Ulster Scots (see section 3.2) is found in the peripheral counties of Ulster (Donegal, Derry, Antrim and Down), the label *Mid-Ulster English* (Harris 1984) is sometimes used to refer to general forms of English in Northern Ireland which are not derived from Scots.

Ulster Scots: This refers to a continuation of the Scots language brought to Ireland chiefly in the 17th century onwards. Some tens of thousands of Scots arrived in the first half of this century and were mainly from the West-Mid and South-West Lowlands. Ulster Scots today still shows many features typical of the most characteristic form of English in Scotland, Scots.

Northern Irish English: This subsumes all kinds of English in the north of the country, i.e. in all the nine countries of the province of Ulster, and is used in the present chapter.

3.2. Ulster Scots

Of all the varieties of English taken to Ireland since the 17th century, Ulster Scots is the only one which has retained a distinct profile and which can be unambiguously linked to the present-day varieties to which it is immediately related: Scots in western Scotland. Undoubtedly, Ulster Scots, especially in its rural forms, is quite separate from other varieties of English in the north of Ireland, let alone the south. Its highly divergent nature has meant that much debate has taken place concerning its status as a language or a dialect.

The regions where Ulster Scots is spoken are nowadays no longer contiguous. This would seem to imply a reduction of the previous geographical distribution. The areas where it is still found do, however, represent historical regions of settlement. There are three of these located on the northern periphery from north-west to north-east, hence the term *Coastal Crescent* or *Northern Crescent* (see maps at end of article).

3.2.1. Delimiting Ulster Scots

A treatment of Ulster Scots must start with differentiating between conservative Ulster Scots (*braid*, i.e. broad, Ulster Scots, which has its base in rural areas of Ulster) and more standard forms which are spoken chiefly in urban centres, parallel to the established distinction in Scotland between Lowland Scots and Scottish Standard English (Harris 1984: 119). An essential feature of standard Ulster Scots is that most words with non-standard Scots vowel values have re-allocated values which are nearer to those in general Ulster English. The following list illustrates vowel values and some consonantal features which are indicative of conservative Ulster Scots; the yardstick of reference is Older Scots (Older Scots), up to 1700, i.e. before the emigration to Ulster began.

Table 4. Features of conservative Ulster Scots

Retention of Older Scots *ū* (not shifted to /au/) *cow* /kʉː/, *hoos* /hʉs/
A low, unrounded back vowel for Older Scots *o*, *soft* /saːft/, *top* /tɑːp/
Older Scots *ei* merges with /i/ and not /ai/ [əɪ, ɑe], *die* /diː/
Older Scots *ō* has a fronted, unrounded reflex, *blood* /blɪd/

Table 4. (*continued*) Features of conservative Ulster Scots

Fronting and raising of Old English *ā*, *home* /he:m/
Little raising of above vowel after labio-velars, *two* /twɔ:/
Lowering of /ɪ/ to /ɛ/, *thick* /θɛk/
No raising of Middle English /ɛ:/ to /i:/, *beat* /bet/, *meat* /met/
Raising of Older Scots /a/ especially before /r/, *farm* /fɛ:rm/
Distinct open and close mid back vowels, *horse* /hɔ:rs/, *hoarse* /ho:rs/
Distinction between short vowels before /r/, *term* /tɛrm/, *burn* /bʌrn/
No rounding of /a/ after /w/, *swan* /swan/
Retention of distinction between /w/ and /ʍ/, *whale* /ʍe:l/, *wale* /we:l/
Retention of syllable-final /x/, *bought* /bɔ:xt/
Vocalisation of word-final /l/ [ɫ], *full* /fʉ:/, *wall* /wɔ:/

The shifts of vowel values in Ulster Scots when compared to southern British English have led to a re-alignment of vowel space. This can best be indicated diagrammatically as follows. The first shift one should note is that of Middle English /o:/ to a front vowel, with or without rounding, i.e. Older Scots /ɪ, ø/. In Ulster Scots this vowel appears as /ɪ/.

Table 5. Ulster Scots vowel shifts

/ɪ/	←	/o:/	*loom* /lɪm/
/æ/	←	/ɪ/	*limb* /læm/
/ɑ:/	←	/æ/	*lamb* /lɑ:m/

3.3. Contrasting northern and southern Irish English

In the following sections those features in which varieties in Ulster (both Ulster Scots and general Ulster English) differ from those south of the province will be discussed. In a number of instances it is necessary to distinguish the two main groups within Ulster. The yardstick for the south is the supraregional standard which ultimately is derived from middle-class Dublin English of the early and mid 20th century.

Equivalents of dental fricatives

In the entire area of Ulster the <u>TH</u>IN and <u>TH</u>IS lexical sets show fricatives. The only exception to this are areas of contact with Irish (in County Donegal) where one finds [t̪] and [d̪] because of the transfer from Irish of the realisations of /t/ and /d/ in the latter language.

Table 6. The <u>TH</u>IN and <u>TH</u>IS lexical sets

	Ulster	**Supraregional Southern**
thick	[θɛk]	[t̪ɪk]
that	[ðat]	[d̪æṱ]
lather	[lɑː(ð)əɹ]	[laːd̪əɹ]
brother	[brʌər]	[brʌd̪əɹ]

Dentalisation of alveolar stops before /r/

This is a phonetic process whereby an alveolar stop, typically /t/, is shifted forward to a dental point of articulation when it is followed by an unstressed rhotic schwa. The /r/ is realised as a tap or slight trill due to the position of the tongue parallel to the escaping airstream (Bernoulli effect) and is frequently voiceless.

Table 7. Dentalisation of alveolar stops before /r/

	Ulster and Conservative Vernacular Southern
water	[wɑːt̪ər]
better	[bɛt̪ər]

Allophones of alveolar plosives

The fricativisation of /t/ and often /d/ intervocalically and word-finally before a pause is not generally to be found in the north – nor in other varieties of English, bar the Irish section of Newfoundland – and thus gains the status of a defining feature of southern Irish English.

Table 8. Allophones of alveolar plosives

	Ulster	**Supraregional Southern**
bat	[bat]	[bæṱ]
bead	[bid]	[biḓ]

The palatalisation of velar plosives
A conspicuous feature of generalised Ulster English is the palatalisation of /g/ and /k/ to /kj/ and /gj/ respectively. This palatalisation is only to be found before low vowels. It would appear to be an English and not a Scots feature and is attested in 18th-century mainland English although it was later lost.

Table 9. The palatalisation of velar plosives

	Ulster	**Supraregional Southern**
cat	[kjat]	[kæṱ]
gap	[gjap]	[gæp]

Off-glides
When mid front vowels occur in stressed position, they tend to develop off-glides. This is particularly clear before a following consonant.

Table 10. Off-glides

	Ulster	**Supraregional Southern**
save	[seːəv]	[seːv]
bait	[beːət]	[beːṱ]

Unstressed vowels
In unstressed positions southern Irish English frequently has the high vowel [i], i.e. without any centralisation to [ɪ], so-called happY-tensing. Ulster English tends to lower an unstressed /i/ to a value approaching /e/.

Table 11. Unstressed vowels

	Ulster	**Supraregional Southern**
tricky	[trĕke]	[trɪki]
happy	[hɑpe]	[hæpi]

Vowel quantity
In Ulster, in strong contradistinction to the South, vowel quantity is often non-distinctive. High and mid vowels, which are elsewhere either long or short, appear phonetically half-long.

Table 12. Vowel quantity

	Ulster	Supraregional Southern
full	[fʉl]	[fʊl]
fool	[fʉl]	[fuːl]

4. Interpreting features of Irish English

In the history of Irish English studies, the pendulum of opinion concerning the role of contact in the genesis of these forms of English has swung back and forth. Initially writers like Joyce, P. L. Henry and, to a lesser extent, Hogan assumed that every feature which had a parallel in Irish was of Irish origin. This stance has been labelled the *substratist* position and came under heavy fire in the mid 1980's most noticeably in John Harris' (1984) influential article. The *retentionist* standpoint, which saw the input varieties of English in early modern Ireland as the source of features hitherto accounted for by contact, came into vogue and was represented by various scholars. But in the 1990's the pendulum moved more to the centre with the gradual acceptance of contact as a source of specific features in Irish English (Hickey 1995), not for ideological reasons, as often previously, but due to a better understanding of the mechanisms of language transfer and language shift, not least due to authors on Irish English, such as Markku Filppula, taking on board the ideas of other linguists examining contact in general, expressed most clearly in the seminal monograph, Thomason and Kaufman (1988). Convergence became the new standard wisdom with contact and retention occupying places of equal standing in the history of Irish English. The following table offers suggestions for sources of key phonological features of Irish English.

Table 13. Phonological features and their possible sources

Phonological feature	Possible source
Dental/alveolar stops for fricatives	Transfer of nearest Irish equivalent, coronal stops
Intervocalic and pre-pausal lenition of /t/	Lenition as a phonological directive from Irish
Alveolar /l/ in all positions	Use of non-velar, non-palatal [l] from Irish
Retention of [ʍ] for <*wh*>	Convergence of input with Irish /f/ [ɸ]

Table 13. (continued) Phonological features and their possible sources

Phonological feature	Possible source
Retention of syllable-final /r/	Convergence of English input and Irish
Distinction of short vowels before /r/, e.g. *term* [tɛɹm] and *turn* [tʌɹn]	Convergence of English input and Irish
Epenthesis in heavy clusters in syllable codas, *film* [fɪləm]	Areal feature of both Irish and English in Ireland
/u/-fronting in the north, e.g. *boot* [bʉt]	Areal feature of both Irish and English in Ulster
Lowering of short front vowels, e.g. *bit* [bet]	Input to Ulster from Scotland
Use of retroflex /r/ in Ulster	Input to Ulster from Scotland

4.1. Ireland as a linguistic area

Table 13 contains features which are traits of vernacular varieties throughout the entire island. When treating features of Irish English, a holistic view can be useful, that is, rather than stress differences, one could examine the features common to most or all varieties and indeed go a step further and compare these to parallel structures in Irish. This approach is largely typological and sees Ireland (north and south) as a linguistic area. Not all of these are strongly diagnostic of Ireland as a linguistic area; they are also found in forms of English in England, quite apart from Anglophone varieties overseas. One should also mention that the non-existence of features across the entire country has led to negative definers for Irish English arising. For instance /r/-lessness and/or /h/-dropping are definite signs that a speaker is not Irish.

5. Urban English in Ireland

5.1. English in Dublin

The English language has been spoken in Dublin since the late 12th century. English never died out in the capital and there are some features of vernacular Dublin English which can be traced to the first period. The records of Dublin English are slight and consist before 1600 mainly of municipal records which here and there betray the kind of English which must have been spoken in the city (Henry 1958). For a historical background to present-day speech one must look to the elocutionist Thomas Sheridan (the father of the playwright Richard Brinsley Sheridan) who in 1781 published *A Rhetorical Grammar of the English Language* with an appendix in which he commented on the English used by middle class Dubliners, the "gentlemen of Ireland" in his words, which he regarded as worthy of censure on his part. When discussing consonants, Sheridan remarks on "the thickening (of) the sounds of *d* and *t* in certain situations". Here he is probably referring to the realisation of dental fricatives as alveolar plosives as found in vernacular forms of Dublin English today. There is no hint in Sheridan of anything like a distinction between dental and alveolar plosive realisations, which is an essential marker of local versus non-local speech today.

Table 14. Dental versus alveolar stops in Dublin English

Local Dublin	Non-local Dublin
thank, *tank* [tæŋk]	*thank* [t̪æŋk], *tank* [tæŋk]

5.1.2. Varieties of Dublin English

Any discussion of English in Dublin necessitates a few basic divisions into types. For the present contribution a twofold division, with a further subdivision, is employed. The first group of speakers consists of those who use the inherited popular form of English in the capital. The term *local* is intended to capture this and to emphasise that these speakers are those who show strongest identification with traditional conservative Dublin life of which the popular accent is very much a part. The reverse of this is *non-local* which refers to sections of the metropolitan population who do not wish a narrow, restrictive identification with popular Dublin culture. This group then subdivides into a larger, more general section, *mainstream*, and a currently smaller group which vigorously rejects a confining association with low-prestige Dublin. For want of a better term, this group is labelled *fashionable*.

Table 15. Varieties of Dublin English

Forms of English in present-day Dublin	
1) *local* Dublin English	
2) *non-local* Dublin English	a) *mainstream* Dublin English
	b) *fashionable* Dublin English

A central issue in contemporary Dublin English is the set of vowel shifts which represent the most recent phonological innovation in Irish English (see section 5.1.4 for details). This is not surprising as Dublin is a typical location for language change given the following features: Firstly, the city has expanded greatly in population in the last three or four decades. The increase in population has been due both to internal growth and migration into the city from the rest of the country. Secondly, it has undergone an economic boom in the last 15 years or so, reflected in its position as an important financial centre and a location for many computer firms which run their European operations from Dublin. The increase in wealth and international position has meant that many young people aspire to an urban sophistication which is divorced from strongly local Dublin life. For this reason the developments in fashionable Dublin English diverge from those in local Dublin English, indeed can be interpreted as a reaction to it. This type of linguistic behaviour can be termed *local dissociation* as it is motivated by the desire of speakers to hive themselves off from vernacular forms of a variety spoken in their immediate surroundings.

5.1.3. Features of local Dublin English

Vowel breaking

Long high vowels are realised as two syllables with a hiatus between the two when they occur in closed syllables. The hiatus element is [j] with front vowels and [w] with back vowels, *clean* [klijən], *fool* [fuwəl]. The disyllabification of long high vowels extends to diphthongs which have a high ending point as can be seen in the following realisations: *time* [təjəm], *pound* [pɛwən]. Among the further prominent vocalic characteristics of Dublin English are the following: (a) Fronting of /au/, e.g. *down* [dɛʊn] - [deʊn], (b) Lengthening of historically short vowels before /r/, e.g. *circle* [sɛːkl̩], *first* [fʊːs(t)], (c) Retention of early modern English short /ʊ/, e.g. *Dublin* [dʊblən].

Cluster simplification

Stops after fricatives or sonorants are liable to deletion. Intermediate registers may have a glottal stop as a trace of the stop in question: *pound* [peʊn(ʔ)], *last* [læːs(ʔ)].

Fortition of dental fricatives:

It is safe to assume that the realisation of the first sound in the THOUGHT lexical set in popular Dublin English as an alveolar plosive [t] is not a recent phenomenon. Hogan (1927: 71–72) notes that it is found in the seventeenth century plays (assuming that *t*, *d* represent [t, d]) and furthermore in the Dublin City

Records (from the first period, i.e. before the 17th century, see above) where the third person singular ending *-th* appears as *-t*.

T-lenition

The clearest phonetic feature of southern Irish English is the realisation of /t/ as a fricative with identical characteristics of the stop, i.e. an apico-alveolar fricative in weak positions. Extensions include the lenition of /t/ in a weak position beyond the initial stage of apico-alveolar fricative to /r/ then to /h/ with final deletion as in the following instance.

Table 16. T-lenition

Cline of t-lenition in Dublin English						
/t/	[t̺]	→	[ɹ] →	[h]	→	ø
water	[wɑːt̺ɚ]		[wɑːɹɚ]	[wɑːhɚ]		[wɑːɚ]

As mentioned above, the THIN and THIS lexical sets show alveolar stops rather than the dental stops of supraregional Irish English.

5.1.4. *Recent developments*

As mentioned in section 5.1.2., the major instance of language change in present-day Ireland is undoubtedly the shift in pronunciation of Dublin English. To understand the workings of this shift one must realise that in the course of the 1980s and 1990s the city of Dublin, as the capital of the Republic of Ireland, underwent an unprecedented expansion in population size and in relative prosperity with a great increase in international connections to and from the metropolis. The immigrants to the city, who arrived there chiefly to avail of the job opportunities resulting from the economic boom, formed a group of socially mobile, weak-tie speakers and their section of the city's population has been a key locus for language change. The change which arose in the last two decades of the 20th century was reactive in nature: fashionable speakers began to move away in their speech from their perception of popular Dublin English, a classic case of dissociation in an urban setting.

The variable /ai/ in Irish English

A conservative pronunciation of /ai/ in Dublin is maintained in lower-class speech as [əɪ] whereas the supraregional variety of the south has for /ai/ a diphthong which has a low mid or low front starting point, i.e., either [aɪ] or [æi]. For fashionable Dubliners the [aɪ, æɪ] pronunciations sufficiently delimit them from local Dublin English. But increasingly a back starting point came to be used with this diphthong. This retracted starting point is particularly noticeable before /r/ so that the name of the country is realised as [ɑɪɹlənd] rather than [aɪɹlənd].

General shift of low vowels
The vowel shift in Dublin English is not just confined to the realisation of /ai/. Other vowels in the area of this diphthong are affected, particularly the diphthong in the CHOICE lexical set and the low and mid vowels in the LOT and THOUGHT sets which usually have a lower realisation than in Britain (or unrounded in the case of the LOT vowel): *boy* /ɔɪ/ → [bɒɪ], *pot* /ɒ/ → [pɒṱ] - [pɑṱ], *law* /ɔː/ → [lɒː]. These realisations show that the change has the characteristics of a chain shift, that is, it affects several segments by a process of retraction and raising in phonological vowel space. This can be seen from the following tables which summarise the various vowel developments.

Table 17. Summary of the present-day Dublin Vowel Shift

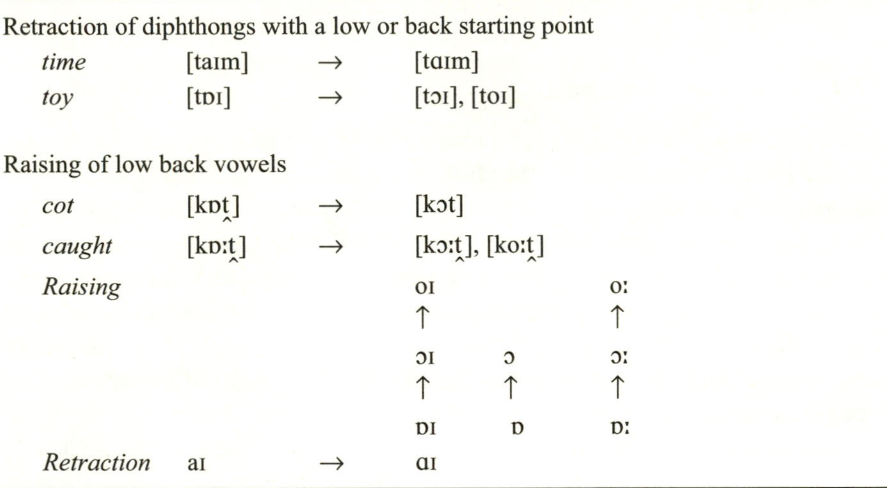

Retraction of diphthongs with a low or back starting point					
time	[taɪm]	→	[tɑɪm]		
toy	[tɒɪ]	→	[tɔɪ], [toɪ]		
Raising of low back vowels					
cot	[kɒṱ]	→	[kɔt]		
caught	[kɒːṱ]	→	[kɔːṱ], [koːṱ]		
Raising			oɪ		oː
			↑		↑
			ɔɪ	ɔ	ɔː
			↑	↑	↑
			ɒɪ	ɒ	ɒː
Retraction	aɪ	→	ɑɪ		

5.1.5. The spread of fashionable Dublin speech

Because of the status of Dublin, non-vernacular speech of the capital acts as a de facto standard for the rest of the south when speakers, outside of Dublin, are seeking a non-local, generally acceptable form of Irish English. This has also meant, for instance, that the retroflex [ɻ] used by fashionable speakers in Dublin is spreading out of the capital, especially with younger urbanites from different parts of the country. Various features of fashionable Dublin English, both vocalic and consonantal, are spreading rapidly, especially among the younger female population. For the following discussion, this speech is labelled the *New Pronunciation*, the capital letters deliberately suggesting a bundle of features which are adopted as a group by innovative speakers.

Apart from vowels, the New Pronunciation of southern Irish English involves above all the realisation of liquids /l/ and /r/. Other segments do not seem to be affected by the shift in pronunciation. Specifically, the complex area of coronal segments has not been altered to any significant extent. In addition to /ai/-retraction and back vowel raising, discussed above, one can note the following features:

/au/-fronting

In Dublin English, and indeed in traditional east-coast varieties of Irish English in general, the vowel in the MOUTH lexical set has a front starting point, either [æ] or [ɛ]. A realisation as [au] is more conservative in Dublin, and in rural areas it is traditionally typical of the south-west and west of Ireland, but is being replaced by the fronted realisation in the speech of the younger generation.

SOFT-lengthening

Here one is again dealing with a traditional feature of Dublin English. The vowel of the LOT lexical set, when it occurs before a voiceless fricative, is lengthened. This in its turn is in keeping with the general Early Modern English lengthening of /aː/ before such fricatives and is seen in words like *staff*, *pass*, *path* in southern British English (Wells 1982: 203–206). In conservative mainstream Irish English SOFT-lengthening (to use a cover term with a typical word involving this lengthening) is not found, but again because it is present in fashionable Dublin English, it is spreading to the rest of the country.

/r/-retroflexion

Traditionally, the realisation of /r/ in southern Irish English is as a velarised alveolar continuant, a pronunciation found in western and south-western varieties of Irish to this day. Thus, it can be assumed that this type of /r/ resulted in Irish English from transfer of the Irish realisation of the same phoneme. In Northern Ireland, a retroflex /r/ is to be found, a parallel with Scotland, which may well have been the source for this realisation. In current fashionable Dublin English a retroflex /r/ is also to be found, though definitely independently of the occurrence in Northern Ireland, as varieties of English there have played no role in the shaping of the speech of fashionable urbanites in Dublin. Dissociation from the traditional velarised realisation is most likely the reason for the retroflex [ɻ] which has become so widespread throughout Ireland among younger female speakers. A slightly raised /aː/ ([æː], [ɛː] co-occurs with the retroflexion of the /r/ so that one has pronunciations like [kæːɻd] for *card*.

/l/-velarisation
Traditionally, Irish English has an alveolar [l] in all syllable positions. However, the recordings for young female speakers in *A Sound Atlas of Irish English* (see below) overwhelmingly show a definite velarisation of /l/ in this position, e.g. *field* [fiːəɫd]. The development of [ɫ], or its adoption from other accents of English, could be seen as a reaction to the traditional alveolar [l] so long a prominent feature of Irish accents.

Apart from the features described above there are others which play a minor role in the sound profile of the New Pronunciation. One obvious feature of local Dublin English which has avoided stigma and hence is found in fashionable speech in the city is the loss of /hw/ [ʍ] in words like *whale* and *while* and which leads to mergers of pairs like *which* and *witch*. Traditionally, the occurrence of [ʍ] in all words beginning with *wh* is a prominent feature of Irish English, but if the New Pronunciation establishes itself as the new supraregional form of English in the next generation then this will no longer be the case.

5.2. English in Belfast

The area of contemporary Belfast is characterised by a conurbation which stretches along the north shore of Belfast Lough at least to Newtownabbey in County Antrim and on the south shore at least to Holywood in County Down. Along the Lagan Valley the city stretches to the south-west at least to Lisburn with a motorway to the triad of towns Lurgan, Craigavon, Portadown to the south of Lough Neagh. The Lagan Valley is the hinterland of Belfast and there is a similarity between accents in the city and those in its hinterland to the south-west. In general, one can say that Lagan Valley speech is similar to the accents in West Belfast. The east of the city shows greater similarity with accents from rural North Down, an originally Scots area of settlement, as opposed to Lagan Valley which was settled largely by people from England.

5.2.1. Sources of Belfast English

The English spoken in Belfast is an amalgam of features which come from the two main English communities in Ulster with independent traits only found in the capital city. The following is a list of features which can be clearly attributed to one of the two main English-language sources in Ulster (Milroy 1981: 25–26).

Table 18. Ulster Anglo-Irish features in Belfast English (after Milroy 1981)

Feature
Palatalisation of /k, g/ before /a/, /kjat/ for *cat*
Dentalisation of /t, d/ before /r/, /bɛt̪ə / for *better*
Lowering and unrounding of /ɒ/, /pɑt/ for *pot*
ME /ɛː/ realised as a mid-vowel, /bɛːt/ for *beat*
/ʊ/ for /ʌ/ in *but*, *luck*, etc.
Lowering of /ɛ/ to /æ/, *set* /sæt/
The use of /au/ before /l/ in monosyllables, /aul/ for *old*, also a feature of Lowland Scots.
Raising of /æ/ to /ɛ/ before velars, /bɛk, bɛg/ for *back*, *bag*
Raising of /æ/ to /ɛ/ after /k/ and (residually) /g/ /kɛp, kɛsl̩/ for *cap*, *castle*
Short realisations of high vowels, /bit, bʉt/ for *beet*, *boot*
Lowering and sometimes centralisation of /ɪ/, /bɛt, sɛns/ or /bʌt, sʌns/ for *bit*, *sense*

The sociolinguistic developments in Belfast English, which were described in ground-breaking studies by James and Lesley Milroy in terms of social networks in the 1970s and early 1980s, are outside the scope of the present study, for appropriate references, consult the relevant section of Hickey (2002).

Mention should also be made of the distinct intonational patterns in northern Irish English. In her study, Rahilly (1997) notes a general predominance of rises in intonation in Belfast which contrast explicitly with falls in the south of Britain. Indeed the high numbers of rising nuclei and level tails in tone sequences are regarded as typical of the Anglo-Irish group of dialects rather than the British group. Rahilly concludes that the primary cue to prominence in Belfast is a high pitch, but with much less movement than with nuclei in Received Pronunciation.

5.3. English in Derry

The city of Derry has a population of over 95,000 (1991 census) and is ethnically over 70% Catholic as opposed to Belfast which has a majority Protestant population. The designation Londonderry is a variant preferred by both Ulster Protestants and British commentators and goes back to a renaming of the city when

London companies were commissioned with the task of transporting English settlers there at the beginning of the 17th century. The city's name is an Anglicisation of Irish *doire* 'oak-grove', a common name, or element of name, in the north and south of the country.

There is a large degree of segregation in terms of residence for the two communities: east of the River Foyle, which divides the city, are found Protestants and west of the river is almost exclusively Catholic. The segregation increased greatly in the last 30 years because of the sectarian violence.

The only research on the English of Derry city is that of McCafferty (see McCafferty 2001 as a representative example of his work), apart from one study of intonation in Derry. The city has a special status within Northern Ireland as it is on the one hand the second largest and on the other the only major city with a Catholic majority. It is understandable that it would receive innovations which arise in Belfast but also that the Catholic majority in the city might well show an inherent resistance to these. A number of changes are recorded for Derry which are listed in the following.

Table 19. Four major linguistic changes in Derry English

(1) A gradual replacement of [ʌ] with [ʉ] (standard Northern Irish English [NIE]) which has been on-going in Ulster and Scotland for some time.

(2) A widespread vernacular innovation originating in the east of Northern Ireland which sees older [ɪ] replaced by [iə] in the FACE class and both of these alternating with standard [e].

(3) A vernacular innovation that appears to have originated in the east in the last hundred years by which intervocalic [ð] is dropped giving a null variant.

(4) A localised Derry English vernacular innovation which realises the same intervocalic [ð] as a lateral [l].

Variable	Standard NIE	Older General DE	Recent Local DE	Lexical set
(ʌ)	[ʉ]	[ʌ]	[ʉ]	PULL
(e)	[e]	[ɪ]	[iə]	FACE
(ð)	[ð]	0	[l]	MOTHER

McCafferty (2001) maintains that there is a tendency for the SQUARE and NURSE lexical sets to merge, a feature spreading from the east of Northern Ireland and typical of the Protestant middle class. For this group a lack of quantity distinction with the NORTH and FORCE lexical set is also found. The shift of older [ɪ] to [ɪə] in the FACE class is taken to be characteristic of younger

Protestants. Protestant changes are in general incoming innovations which are spreading from eastern Northern Ireland, i.e. from the Belfast conurbation. In this case the changes for the Protestants in Derry have arisen through a process of supraregionalisation of Belfast innovations. The only leading change among the Catholics in Derry is the shift of intervocalic [ð] to a lateral [l]. The Protestants in Derry have no vernacular innovations of their own.

Table 20. Changes in Derry English according to ethnicity

Ethnic group				**Source**
Protestants	[oːr]	→	[ɔːr]	Eastern Northern Ireland
	[ɛr]	→	[əːr]	---
	[e, ɪ]	→	[iə]	---
Catholics	[- ð -]	→	[- l -]	Local to Derry city

6. Lexical sets for the phonological description of Irish English

Tables 21 and 22 use the lexical sets as originally introduced by John Wells in the early 1980s. Certain adaptions and extensions of Wells' original set are necessary for the correct description of Irish English, for instance the PRICE vowel can have a different realisation before voiceless and voiced consonants. In addition the NORTH and FORCE sets must be kept separate, though increasingly with supraregional speakers in the south, a distinction is not made between the vowels in each of these words.

The five columns in each table correspond to the five sound samples which accompany this chapter.

6.1. Vocalic sets

Table 21. Lexical sets and representative values in Irish English (vowels)

Lexical set	**Rural Northern**	**Popular Dublin**	**Fashionable Dublin**	**Rural South-West/West**	**Supraregional Southern**
KIT	e	ɪ	ɪ	ɪ	ɪ
DRESS	ɛ˔	ɛ	ɛ	ɛ	ɛ
TRAP	a	æ	æ	æ	æ

Table 21. (continued) Lexical sets and representative values in Irish English (vowels)

Lexical set	Rural Northern	Popular Dublin	Fashionable Dublin	Rural South-West/West	Supraregional Southern
LOT	ɒ	a	ɔ	a	ɑ
STRUT	ʌ	ʊ	ʌ	ʌ̈	ʌ̈
FOOT	ʉ	ʊ	ʊ	ʊ	ʊ
FLEECE	iː	ɨʲə	iː	iː	iː
FACE	eːə	eː	eː	eː	eː
BATH	ɑ(ː)	æː	aː	aː	aː
THOUGHT	ɔ(ː)	aː	ɔː, oː	ɑː	ɒː
SOFT	ɔ(ː)	aː	ɔː	ɑ	ɒ
GOOSE	ʉ(ː)	ʉʲə	uː	uː	uː
PRICE	ɛɪ	əɪ	ɑɪ	æɪ	aɪ
PRIDE	ɛɪ, aɪ	əɪ	ɑɪ	æɪ	ɑɪ
MOUTH	ɛʉ	ɛʊ	ɛʊ	aʊ	aʊ
CHOICE	ɔɪ	aɪ	ɔɪ, oɪ	ɑɪ	ɒɪ
GOAT	ɔʊ, oː	ʌɔ	əʊ	oː	əʊ, oʊ
NEAR	i(ː)ɻ	iː(ɹ)	iːɻ	iːɹ	iːɹ
SQUARE	ə(ː)ɻ	ɛː (ɹ)	eːɻ, øːɻ	eːɹ	eːɹ
START	ɑ(ː)ɻ	æː (ɹ)	ɑːɻ	aːɹ	ɑːɹ
NORTH	ɔ(ː)ɻ	aː (ɹ)	ɒːɻ, ɔːɻ	ɑːɹ	ɒːɹ
FORCE	o(ː)ɻ	ɒː (ɹ)	ɔːɻ, oːɻ	ɔːɹ	oːɹ
CURE	u(ː)ɻ	ʉʲə (ɹ)	uːɻ,	uːɹ	uːɹ
NURSE	ə(ː)ɻ	ʊː (ɹ)	ɚːɻ, øːɻ	ɚːɹ	ɚːɹ
COMMA	ə	ə, ɐ	ə	ə	ə
LETTER	əɻ	ə (ɹ)	əɻ	əɹ	əɹ
HAPPY	ɪ, e	i	i	i	i
DANCE	æ, ɑ	æː	aː, (ɑː)	æː, aː	aː
PATH	ɑ	æː	aː, (ɑː)	æː, aː	aː

Remarks

1) The vowel values which are associated with the now unfashionable Dublin 4 accent are not shared entirely by younger fashionable Dublin English speak-

ers. In particular the retraction of /aː/, and raising of the rhotacised version /ɒːɻ/, is avoided so that the earlier pronunciation of *Dart* as [dɔːɻt / doːɻt] is regarded as "uncool".

2) The vowel transcribed as [ʌ̈] is a variant which is somewhat more centralised than the corresponding [ʌ] vowel found in supraregional varieties.
3) The realisation [øːɻ] in the SQUARE lexical set can be interpreted as a deliberate reaction to the very open, unrounded realisation of population Dublin English, [eː(ɹ̝)].
4) Popular Dublin English is weakly rhotic and early conservative forms of this variety are often entirely non-rhotic.
5) There is a complex distribution of low vowels in northern Irish English. Basically one can say that a front and raised vowel is found before velars and a retracted variant before labials and nasals, giving pronunciations like *bag* [bɛ˕g] and *family* [ˈfɑmlɪ].

6.2. Consonantal sets

Wells' lexical sets were designed to deal with the vowel distinctions found in Received Pronunciation. They do not handle consonants. For that reason new sets are necessary for the current discussion. A number of key words have been chosen and the consonant which is at issue in each case is underlined as can be seen from Table 22.

Table 22. Lexical sets and representative values in Irish English (consonants)

Lexical set	**Rural Northern**	**Popular Dublin**	**Fashionable Dublin**	**Rural South-West/West**	**Supraregional Southern**
THIN	θ	t	t̪	t	t̪
BREATHE	ð	d	d̥	d	d̪
TWO	t	t	t, tˢ	t	t
WATER	ɾ, ʔ, Ø	ʔ h	ɾṱ	ṱ	ɾ, ṱ
GET	t˺, ʔ	h, Ø	ṱ	ṱ	ṱ
FEEL	Ø	l, ɫ	ɫ	l	l, ɫ
SORE	ɻ	ɹ̝, Ø	ɻ	ɹ̝	ɹ̝, ɻ
WET	w	w	w	w	w
WHICH	w	ʍ	w	ʍ	ʍ, w

Remarks

1) The distinction between dental and alveolar stops is sociolinguistically significant in Ireland. All speakers can hear this difference clearly and the use of alveolar for dental stops in the THIN and THIS lexical sets is highly stigmatised.
2) Fashionable Dublin English speakers may have a slight afflication of syllable-initial /t-/, as in *two* [t^{s}uː].
3) The allophony of syllable-coda and intersyllabic /t/ is quite complicated. With conservative supraregional speakers the apico-alveolar fricative [ṱ] is found. With younger supraregional speakers a flap occurs. In popular Dublin English the lenition of /t/ continues through a glottal stop to /h/ and frequently to zero, especially in word-final position. In many forms of northern Irish English, final alveolar stops may be unreleased.
4) The merger of [w] and [ʍ] is increasingly frequent with supraregional speakers so that word pairs like *which* and *witch* now consist of homophones.
5) It is merely a coincidence that fashionable Dublin English shares a flap and a retroflex /r/ with northern Irish English.

7. Data sources for Irish English phonology

In the recent history of Irish English studies there have been two incomplete surveys of English in Ireland. The first was initiated by P. L. Henry and preliminary findings were published in 1958 (see Henry 1958). Nothing more was heard of the project, but the material presented is of value for the study of Irish English up to that date.

The second survey is called *The Tape-Recorded Survey of Hiberno-English Speech* and was supervised by Michael Barry, then of the English Department at Queen's University, Belfast. A large amount of material was collected, particularly for the north and approximately 50% of this material, which by a fortunate circumstance was given to the present author in the mid 1980s, has been digitised and is available as two CDs from the present author. The material comes with a software interface to examine the data of the survey which in this form consists of some 80 files (approximately 22 hours of recording). The survey includes both wordlists and free speech.

The Irish English Resource Centre is a website dedicated to all matters pertaining to academic research into Irish English. It is maintained by the present author at the following address: http://www.uni-essen.de/IERC. The resource centre as it stands contains much information on past and current research on Irish English, an online history and overview of Irish English, summaries of issues in the field, biosketches of scholars, details of various corpora and data collections, links to related sites, etc. Importantly, it contains much bibliographical information of use to interested scholars and students. The website is updated regularly with new information as this becomes available. It is intended as a primary source for up-to-date data on topical research into Irish English which can be used liberally by scholars and students alike.

A Sound Atlas of Irish English (Hickey 2005) is a set of over 1,500 recordings of Irish English from the entire country covering urban and rural informants with an age spread from under 10 to over 80 (both genders). A supplied software interface allows end-users to view the recordings in a tree divided by province and county and then listen to individual recordings. The recordings can also be sorted by county, age, gender and rural versus urban speakers. Five of these recordings are available on the accompanying CD-ROM.

Exercises and study questions

1. What historical demographical movements led to distinctive forms of English arising in the north and the south of Ireland? In this context discuss the role of language contact and language shift in the genesis of English in Ireland.

2. List the main distinctions between forms of English in the North and in the South of Ireland. Describe the main differences between vowel and consonants, and mention some processes which are operative in both areas.
(compare the first three sound files with each other)

3. Describe the main changes which are occurring in Southern Irish English at the present. What shifts can one observe? Do they form a pattern in phonological space? If you think there is a sociolinguistic motivation for these, then outline them briefly.
(contrast sound files three and four)

4. What is meant by supraregional speech in the Irish context? Describe some of the main features to be found in this speech in the south of Ireland.
(consult sound file five)

5. What do you understand by a shibboleth? Mention a few of those which you can discern for forms of English in both the north and the south of Ireland.

6. What is lenition and what phonological framework can best be employed to describe it adequately? Give examples from southern Irish English. (consult sound files three and four for audio examples)

Selected references

Please consult the General references for titles mentioned in the text but not included in the references below. For a full bibliography see the accompanying CD-ROM.

Adams, George Brendan

1958 The emergence of Ulster as a distinct dialect area. *Ulster Folklife* 4: 61–73.

1965 Materials for a language map of 17th century Ireland. *Ulster Dialect Archive Bulletin* 4: 15–30.

Bliss, Alan J.

1976 The English language in early modern Ireland. In: Terry W. Moody, Francis X. Martin and Francis J. Byrne (eds.), *Early Modern Ireland, 1534-1691*, 546–560. Oxford: Clarendon.

1977 The emergence of modern English dialects in Ireland. In: Diarmaid Ó Muirithe (ed.), *The English Language in Ireland*, 7–19. Dublin/Cork: Mercier Press.

Dolan, Terence P.

1998 *A Dictionary of Hiberno-English. The Irish Use of English*. Dublin: Gill and Macmillan.

Harris, John

1984 Syntactic variation and dialect divergence. *Journal of Linguistics* 20: 303–327.

Henry, Patrick Leo

1958 A linguistic survey of Ireland. Preliminary report. *Norsk Tidsskrift for Sprogvidenskap [Lochlann, A Review of Celtic Studies]* Supplement 5: 49–208.

Heuser, Wilhelm

1904 *Die Kildare-Gedichte. Die ältesten mittelenglischen Denkmäler in anglo-irischer Überlieferung*. Bonn: Hanstein.

Hickey, Raymond

1993 The beginnings of Irish English. *Folia Linguistica Historica* 14: 213–238.

1995 An assessment of language contact in the development of Irish English. In: Jacek Fisiak (ed.), *Linguistic Change under Contact Conditions*, 109–130. Berlin/New York: Mouton de Gruyter.

1999 Dublin English: Current changes and their motivation. In: Foulkes and Docherty (eds.), 265–281.

2002 *A Source Book for Irish English*. Amsterdam/Philadelphia: Benjamins.
2003 *Corpus Presenter. Processing Software for Language Analysis*. Including *A Corpus of Irish English*. Amsterdam/Philadelphia: Benjamins.

Hogan, James Jeremiah
1927 *The English Language in Ireland*. Dublin: Educational Company of Ireland.

Lucas, Angela (ed.)
1995 *Anglo-Irish Poems of the Middle Ages*. Dublin: Columba Press.

McCafferty, Kevin
2001 *Ethnicity and Language Change. English in (London)Derry, Northern Ireland*. Amsterdam/Philadelphia: Benjamins.

Moody, Theodore W., Francis X. Martin and Francis J. Byrne (eds)
1976 *A New History of Ireland, Volume III: Early Modern Ireland (1534–1691)*. Oxford: Clarendon Press.

Ní Chasaide, Ailbhe
1979 Laterals in Gaoth-Dobhair Irish and Hiberno-English. In: Donall Ó Baoill (ed.), *Papers in Celtic Phonology*, 54–78. Coleraine: New University of Ulster.

Ó Baoill, Dónall
1991 Contact phenomena in the phonology of Irish and English in Ireland. In: P. Sture Ureland and George Broderick (eds.), *Language Contact in the British Isles. Proceedings of the Eighth International Symposium on Language Contact in Europe*, 581–595. Tübingen: Niemeyer.

Ó Muirithe, Diarmuid
1996 *Dictionary of Anglo-Irish. Words and Phrases from Irish*. Dublin: Four Courts Press.

Rahilly, Joan
1997 Aspects of prosody in Hiberno-English: the case of Belfast. In: Jeffrey L. Kallen (ed.), *Focus on Ireland*, 109–132. Amsterdam/Philadelphia: Benjamins.

Sheridan, Thomas
1781 *A Rhetorical Grammar of the English Language Calculated Solely for the Purpose of Teaching Propriety of Pronunciation and Justness of Delivery, in that Tongue*. Dublin: Price.

Stenson, Nancy
1991 Code-switching vs. borrowing in modern Irish. In: P. Sture Ureland and George Broderick (eds.), *Language Contact in the British Isles. Proceedings of the Eighth International Symposium on Language Contact in Europe*, 559–579. Tübingen: Niemeyer.

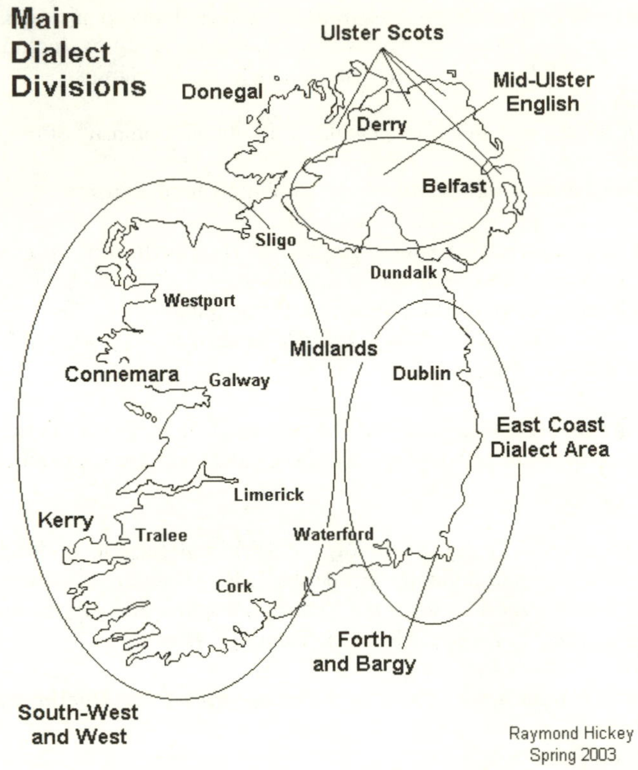

Map of chief dialectal divisions in Ireland

Comments The south of Ireland can be divided into two broad dialect regions. The first and oldest is the east coast dialect area which stretches from Waterford up to beyond Dublin, probably as far as Dundalk in its original extension before 1600.

The second area is that of the south-west and west and is the part of the country which was latest to engage in the language shift from Irish to English. Indeed for a few small pockets on the western seaboard, in Kerry, Connemara and Donegal, the Irish language has not died out yet.

In the centre and north-central part of the country there is a diffuse and dialectally indeterminate Midlands region which extends from southern Offaly and Laois up to Cavan and south Leitrim.

Between Sligo in the west and Dundalk in the east there is a broad transitional band which shows a mixture of southern and northern features (see discussions above).

The north of Ireland consists of the counties of Ulster and can be divided into a large central region, that of Mid-Ulster English, and a 'Coastal Crescent' running from Co. Down, south-east of Belfast, up to Antrim in the extreme north-east, through Co. Derry and across to the north-east of Donegal (but excluding the city of Derry). This area is that of strongest Scottish settlement and hence it represents Ulster Scots in its most original form (there are also some other smaller areas, such as north Co. Armagh). In the west of Donegal, contact forms of Ulster English are spoken.

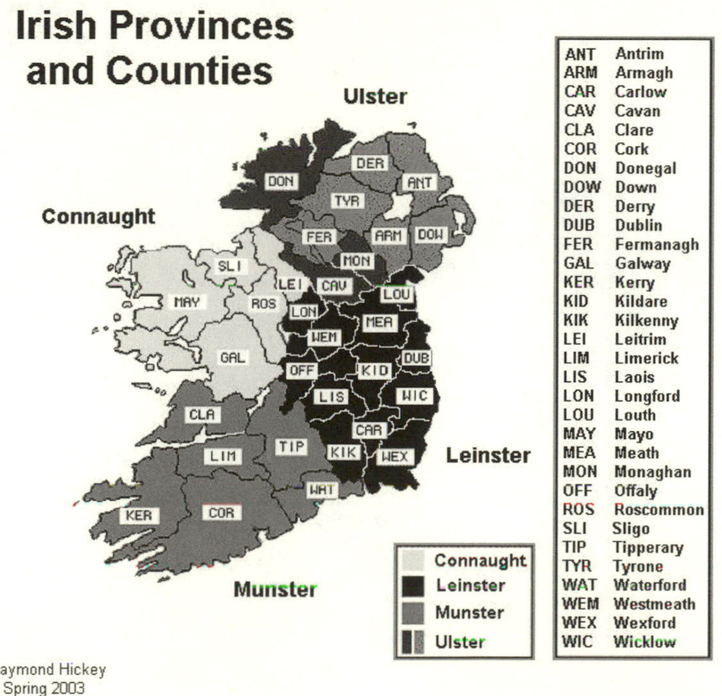

Map of provinces and counties in Ireland

There are thirty two counties in present-day Ireland distributed in somewhat uneven fashion across four provinces. The counties vary in size, Cork and Galway being the largest, Louth and Carlow the smallest. The population of counties depends on whether they contain large towns or cities. Some counties, like Leitrim and Clare do not, while other have an associated town or city, e.g. Limerick, Cork, Wexford, etc.

The province of Ulster contains nine counties, six of which are within the borders of Northern Ireland, formed on the partition of Ireland in 1921. There is a limited presence of Ulster Scots speech outside of Northern Ireland, in the Lagan district of north-west Donegal. Features of northern speech spread much further southwards than previously thought as attested by *A Sound Atlas of Irish English* (see remarks above).

Welsh English: phonology

Robert Penhallurick

1. Cultural and socio-historical background

The longer-standing language of Wales is Welsh, belonging to the Celtic branch of the Indo-European family. In pre-Roman times, Celtic speakers were dispersed over most of western Europe, but during the age of the Roman Empire Celtic appears to have been pushed to the peripheries, with two branches developing: Goidelic or Q Celtic, and Brittonic or P Celtic, to which Welsh belongs. The arrival of Angles, Saxons and other Germanic-speaking tribes in Britain from the fifth century onwards exerted a pressure on Welsh which continues to the present day. Celtic speakers were driven into the area now known as Wales, thereafter to be subject to a long process of anglicization. At the end of the eighth century AD, a physical boundary was constructed to mark the political separation of the nascent England and Wales, in the shape of Offa's Dyke, a linear earthwork running north/south for some 130 kilometres from the River Dee to the Severn Estuary. It was constructed by Offa, king of Mercia, to indicate the western boundary of his territory. Aitchison and Carter (2000: 24) point out that whilst the construction of Offa's Dyke should not be understood as marking a firm divide between Welsh and English speakers, it does serve "as a base line from which to chart the slow and complex westward retreat of the Welsh language", or to put it another way, the inexorable advance of English to all parts of Wales.

The first major incursions of English came in the wake of the Norman invasion of Wales, which began towards the end of the eleventh century AD. The Normans established strongholds through the north and south, and English speakers arrived in numbers. The areas most affected were the lower-lying borders with England, and substantial parts of south Wales, with perhaps the most interesting developments occurring in the Gower Peninsula and south Pembrokeshire. Here, dialects of Welsh English influenced by the south-west of England existed from the twelfth century onwards, brought about it seems by population movement across the Bristol Channel from Somerset and Devon.

Anglicization down the centuries was aided by events which boosted the status of English and lowered that of Welsh. Under the Acts of Union of 1536–

1543, English was made the sole language of government and law in Wales. Aitchison and Carter (2000: 27) state that although this "formally abstracted a domain of use from Welsh which had effectively been lost long before", it also meant that "[i]f Welsh were not to be used in a significant formal context then it meant, too, that its use in informal contexts would diminish". They add:

> Inevitably, if the Welsh gentry wished to participate in public life then that participation would be in English and the language of polite society, if such it can be called, would also be English. There followed the conviction that Welsh was the language of the barbarous past, English the language of the civilized future. (Aitchison and Carter 2000: 27)

Aitchison and Carter here probably borrow from the (at least in Wales) well-known editorial of *The Times* of 8 September 1866 which argued that the "antiquated and semi-barbarous" Welsh language, together with ignorance of the English language, was responsible for the exclusion of the Welsh people "from the civilization, the improvement and the material prosperity of their English neighbours". Certainly, higher prestige (further enhanced by the education system during the second half of the nineteenth century and first half of the twentieth especially) and increasing incoming speaker numbers (from the Industrial Revolution onwards) helped establish English as a language of the whole of Wales by the second half of the twentieth century. Census statistics show large increases in the numbers of monolingual and bilingual English speakers in Wales during the twentieth century, and the extinction of monolingual Welsh speakers.

However, none of this has led to the demise of the Welsh language. Even in the areas subject to the earliest anglicization, Welsh-speaking persisted for centuries, and although its traditional geographical heartlands continue to shrink, up until the end of the twentieth century Welsh remained the first language in much of rural Wales (in the north-west, west midlands and south-west). The concerted attempt in recent decades to promote the use of Welsh, in particular through expanding the availability of Welsh-medium education, has apparently led to positive news for the language's supporters in the most recent statistics, but arguably what lies ahead for Welsh is a process of 'Latinization', in which its use becomes restricted to a decreasing number of social domains as its traditional regional dialects decline.

These regional dialects in particular have had the greatest influence overall on the special character of English in Wales. As noted in Penhallurick (1993: 33), there are notable differences between the traditional Welsh dialects of north and south Wales, in phonology, lexis and grammar. These differences are mirrored to a degree, more so in pronunciation, in spoken English. Thus it is possible to talk of two main types of Welsh English, one centred in the north-west, the other in the mid-south. In these main northern and southern sub-varieties, non-standard features tend to be derived from Welsh-language influence. But there are other determining factors, such as influence from the neighbouring non-standard dialects (rural and urban) of England, particularly but not exclusively in the border areas, south Pembrokeshire and Gower.

As for the term *Welsh English*, it has not been the universal label of choice. At the outset of the only national survey of spoken English in Wales, David Parry chose the term *Anglo-Welsh* for the varieties used by elderly English-speaking Welsh people. In addition, *Welsh English* has the potential to arouse nationalist sensibilities. As Coupland and Thomas (1989: 2) noted:

> the language question in Wales is sufficiently highly charged that some might infer that even to pay analytic attention to English in Wales, or 'Welsh English' [...] represents an ideological position, perhaps even a form of capitulation, or collusion with the forces threatening the Welsh language.

My view, briefly, is that English is a thoroughly established language of Wales, a language used by and belonging to the Welsh people – not that they have sole ownership of it, of course. My only anxiety over using the umbrella *Welsh English* could apply equally to other similar labels: that it masks diversity (that is, of English in Wales) and connections (between English inside and English outside Wales).

2. The phonological system

The most comprehensive collection of Welsh English data is in the archives of the *Survey of Anglo-Welsh Dialects* (henceforth SAWD) at the Department of English, University of Wales Swansea. Under the directorship of David Parry, material was collected in rural areas of Wales between 1968 and 1982 (cf. Parry 1977–1979, 1999), and in urban areas between 1985 and 1987. SAWD is the chief source of the present chapter, which aims to provide an overview of Welsh English phonology, focussing on traditional, rural Welsh English. Use will be made, in particular, of the analysis and description attempted in David Parry's *A Grammar and Glossary of the Conservative Anglo-Welsh Dialects of Rural Wales* (1999). Parry (1999) attempts a general phonemicization for Welsh English based on the rural data, drawn from the 60-plus age-group, which can be presented as follows:

Short vowels: /ɪ ɛ a ʌ ɔ ʊ/
Long vowels: /iː eː ɛː œː aː ɔː oː uː/
Diphthongs: /ɪu ai au ɔi oə iə/
Unstressed vowels: /i ə ɪ/
Consonants: /p b t d k g f v θ ð ɬ s z ʃ ʒ x h tʃ dʒ m n ŋ l w j r/

Table 1 maps this broad phonemicization against the lexical set. STAY and SNOW are included for comparison with FACE and GOAT respectively, and highlight a tricky area in the phonemicization. In Table 1, the vowels for STAY and SNOW are not given phonemic status, in order to remain consistent with the system above. However, discussion of alternative analyses and the status of the vowels in FACE/STAY and GOAT/SNOW can be found in section 2.1. below.

The remainder of the chapter discusses the phonological system in detail, including realizations of the vowel phonemes and significant regional variations (under headings from the lexical set), followed by a description of noteworthy consonantal and prosodic features.

Table 1. Traditional rural Welsh English vowels

KIT	ɪ
DRESS	ɛ
TRAP	a
LOT	ɔ
STRUT	ʌ
ONE	ʌ ~ ɔ
FOOT	ʊ
BATH	a ~ aː
CLOTH	ɔ
NURSE	œː
FLEECE	iː
FACE	eː
STAY	[ei]
GOAT	oː
SNOW	[ou]
PALM	aː
THOUGHT	ɔː

Table 1. (continued)	Traditional rural Welsh English vowels
GOOSE	uː
PRICE	ai
CHOICE	ɔ
MOUTH	au
SQUARE	ɛː
START	aː
NORTH	ɔː
FORCE	ɔː
BOAR	oə
CURE	(ɪ)uwə
POWER	auwə
FIRE	aijə
NEAR	iə
EARS	œː ~ iə
TUESDAY	ɪu
happY	iː
lettER	ə ~ ʌ
horsES	ɪ
commA	ə ~ ʌ

2.1. Stressed vowels

KIT
The realization of KIT words throughout Wales is [ɪ].

DRESS
Similarly, the realization of DRESS is [ɛ].

TRAP
Through most of Wales the realization of TRAP is [a], but in mid Wales, where the county of Powys borders with the English counties of Shropshire and Hereford, a raised [æ] or even [ɛ] is recorded. A long [aː] is also recorded very sporadically.

LOT

The chief realization in LOT words is [ɔ], though [ɒ] is also recorded frequently, more so in the north than in the south. Some words which have the LOT vowel in RP but an <a> in their spelling, such as *quarry*, *wash*, and *wasps*, may have [a ~ æ] in Welsh English. Such forms are recorded in all regions. In Welsh-speaking areas they might be spelling pronunciations influenced by Welsh-language conventions (orthographic <wa> is pronounced [wa] in Welsh), but such [a ~ æ] vowels were also recorded widely by the Survey of English Dialects.

STRUT

In STRUT there is a marked tendency to a vowel raised and centralized compared with RP /ʌ/, even to the extent that [ə] is a common variant. There is also variation in unstressed syllables between [ʌ] and [ə]. Wells (1982: 380) speaks of the "STRUT-Schwa Merger" in Welsh English, that is to say, the lack of phonemic distinction between /ʌ/ and /ə/. Parry (1999: 15) opts for /ʌ/ as the phonemic designation for STRUT vowels (rather than /ə/), which can be justified on grounds of frequency of occurrence, but he adds the rider that [ʌ] in his STRUT group is "most commonly a raised and centralized Cardinal Vowel 14". The Welsh language has no /ʌ/ phoneme, but it does have /ə/, and this may be behind both the centralizing tendency in STRUT and the blurring or even erasing of distinction between /ʌ/ and /ə/ (cf. also section 2.2. below on unstressed vowels). In addition, it should be noted that occasionally the realization of the STRUT vowel strays into [a] territory, as recorded in Parry (1999: 15) in *butter*, *furrow*, *uncle*. These instances are few and are mainly restricted to the north and mid Wales border with England.

Also, [ʊ] can occur in STRUT words, and is recorded, interestingly, in the north-east corner and the south-west corner. The north-east occurrences can be readily explained by the presence of the well-known northern English [ʊ] in STRUT in neighbouring Cheshire. The south-west occurrences, mainly in south Pembrokeshire, an area subject to anglicizing influences since the twelfth century, are more mysterious. One could presume that they result from historical connections with south-west England, but as Parry (1999: 18) points out, there is only a small amount of evidence of [ʊ] in STRUT words in the traditional accents of Cornwall, Devon and Somerset.

ONE

Wells (1982: 362) notes that *one* and other words (for example, *none*, *nothing*), which have /ʌ/ in RP and an <o> in their spelling, have /ɒ/ as their stressed vowel across a wide band of the mid-north of England. Similarly, in Wales ONE words sometimes fall in with the LOT group, though more frequently they belong with STRUT. ONE with [ɔ ~ ɒ] is associated with the traditional Welsh-speaking areas of north and west Wales, where it may result from Welsh-influenced spelling pronunciation, and also with the north and mid border with England and the long-anglicized areas of south Pembrokeshire and the Gower Peninsula, to where it may have travelled from the accents of the north-west, west and south-west of England.

As with STRUT, [ʊ] can occur in ONE words. The details in Parry (1999: 18) indicate that [ʊ] occurs less frequently in ONE than in STRUT, but as with STRUT there is an association with the north-east and south-west corners of Wales.

FOOT

By far the most widespread realization of FOOT words is [ʊ]. Very rarely, in the north, unrounded [ɤ] is recorded. There are also instances of 'hypercorrect' [ʌ] in FOOT words, recorded in Parry (1999: 16) in the north-west, eastern mid Wales, and the south-west. The instances that occur in Welsh-speaking areas, in the north-west and south-west, are all of FOOT words with orthographic <u> (*bull*, *butcher*, *put*), and these might conceivably be spelling pronunciations. The instances elsewhere (eastern mid Wales, the south-west corner) might in most cases be linked with traditional [ʌ]-forms in west and south-west of England accents.

BATH

In BATH words there is competition between the short forms [a ~ æ] and long forms [aː ~ æː ~ ɑː], with [a] the most common realization, occurring in all regions. Of the long realizations, [aː] is also fairly common, whilst [ɑː] is less so, though it too is not regionally restricted. Wells states that "[t]he situation in the BATH words is not altogether clear" (1982: 387), and the same could be said now that SAWD material for the whole of rural Wales has been made available. Nevertheless, Parry's (1999: 214) phonemic map for *chaff* shows /a/ dominating, with a few instances of /aː/ in the mid- and south-eastern border areas. His phonetic map for *draught* (Parry 1999: 217) shows a similar distribution of [a] and [aː], with one significant difference: an area dominated by [aː] in the north-west corner of Wales. The general picture (as Wells concluded) seems to be of confrontation between a non-standard short /a/ and a standard-influenced long /aː/, with the short vowel more than holding its own. However, whilst it is clearly sensible to differentiate between two phonemes here (a short and a long), this is one of those areas in Welsh English phonology where there is fluidity, as indicated also by the sporadic occurrence of the long vowel in TRAP words. On the other hand, it is likely that variation between the short and long forms can be correlated to some extent with register and social class.

CLOTH

Parry (1999: 24–25) shows a scattering of long [ɔː] realizations in CLOTH words, the majority in mid-Wales, but overall the pattern is similar to LOT, with [ɔ] the main realization, and [ɒ] common also.

NURSE

A realization of NURSE identified with the southern region of Welsh English is the long, rounded, centralized-front, half-open [œː]. There is no ready explanation for this realization, although it may mark an intermediate stage between Welsh English stressed /ə/ + /r/ and RP (the NURSE group is one of several subject to rhoticity in Welsh English – see /r/ in section 3 below). Parry (1999: 21) shows that this realization is not exclusive to the south, but occurs throughout Wales. However, its main competitor, /əː/, which is also widespread, is notably absent from the mid-south-east (that is, the Rhondda Valleys), the area associated in the public mind with [œː].

FLEECE

The dominant realization is [iː], though [iə], that is, realizations with a glide to the centre, are recorded (Parry 1999: 32), mainly in more strongly Welsh-speaking regions in mid-Wales.

FACE/STAY and GOAT/SNOW

The regional patterning of two characteristic sounds of Welsh English, the long monophthongs [eː] and [oː], is complex. They occur in both the main northern and southern areas in words such as *bacon*, *break*, *great*, *make* (FACE) and *coal*, *road*, *spoke*, *toe* (GOAT) respectively. In these cases, the monophthongs can be regarded as phonemic, but overall their distribution is complicated by their occurrence also in words such as *clay*, *drain*, *weigh*, *whey* (STAY) and *cold*, *shoulder*, *snow* (SNOW). In STAY and SNOW, it is difficult to argue that the monophthongs are phonemic, for in these groups diphthongs, [ei] and [ou], are more likely. In addition, diphthongal forms can occur in FACE and GOAT. Table 2 summarizes the situation for the whole of Wales, outlining the competition between monophthongs and diphthongs in FACE, STAY, GOAT, and SNOW.

[eː] occurs most commonly in FACE, being dominant (in these words) in the north and south, and in the northern peripheries. [ei] in FACE is dominant only in the southern peripheries. In STAY, however, the diphthong is prevalent throughout the south, whilst the monophthong is dominant in the north. The sequence is the same for the [oː] – [ou] pair: the monophthong is dominant in GOAT everywhere but the southern peripheries, and in SNOW the diphthong dominates in the south, the monophthong in the north.

Table 2. Regional distribution of FACE/STAY and GOAT/SNOW vowels (table lists only regions where one variant dominates)

	[eː]	[ei]	[oː]	[ou]
FACE	north, south, northern peripheries	southern peripheries	----	----
STAY	north	south, southern peripheries	----	----
GOAT	----	----	north, south, northern peripheries	southern peripheries
SNOW	----	----	north	south, southern peripheries

A number of processes have produced this pattern. Firstly, the Welsh language has no diphthongs of the /ei/ and /ou/ types, and the Welsh monophthongs /eː/ and /oː/ have exerted an influence in Welsh English over words which have /eɪ/ and /oʊ/ in RP. Running counter to this are spelling pronunciations affecting STAY and SNOW, leading to the diphthongal forms, the general rules being: spellings with <ai>, <ay>, <ei>, <ey> encourage [ei], and spellings with <ou>, <ow> encourage [ou], with <ol> spellings falling in with SNOW rather than GOAT. Furthermore, there has been influence from neighbouring accents of English English: [eː] and [oː] have been reinforced in the north of Wales by the influence of monophthongs occurring in the north-west of England; [ei] and [ou] have been supported by the diphthongs of the west and south-west of England, as well as those of RP, of course.

It is worth emphasizing that Table 2 simplifies a fluid situation. For example, the accents of particular localities or even individuals exhibit register-sensitive movement between monophthongal and diphthongal types, especially in the FACE and GOAT groups. Table 2 also simplifies the overall regional pattern: we can note here, for example, that neither monophthong nor diphthong dominates in STAY and SNOW in the northern peripheries.

PALM

There is some evidence from SAWD that PALM words are subject to the same competition between short [a] and long [aː] that occurs in BATH and, to a lesser extent, in TRAP. Parry's phonetic map for *calf* (1999: 216), for example, shows a sizeable area in Carmarthenshire and north Pembrokeshire dominated by the short realization. However, through the rest of Wales a long vowel dominates and, furthermore, across mid Wales and in the area surrounding Swansea this long vowel is a back [ɑː]. The short forms recorded for *calf* are probably not typical of PALM words, in which the main contest is between non-standard front [aː] and RP-style back [ɑː].

THOUGHT

The dominant realization in THOUGHT words is [ɔː], with, however, a significant sprinkling of r-coloured versions recorded (Parry 1999: 25) along the south-eastern border and in south Pembrokeshire, perhaps under the influence of west of England accents. For example, the Survey of English Dialects records r-colouring in *saw-dust*, *slaughter*, *straw* in Shropshire and Warwickshire.

GOOSE

The dominant realization in GOOSE is [uː], although short [ʊ] is also recorded in certain words, especially *tooth*. Parry's map of *tooth* (1999: 229) shows the short form covering the majority of Wales, with the exception of most of the north and a pocket in the south-west corner. In other GOOSE words used by Parry (*goose*, *hoof*, *root*, *stool*), the short form is more sporadic.

PRICE, CHOICE, MOUSE

Common to these three groups is a very close final element in the diphthong: [i] in PRICE and CHOICE, [u] in MOUSE. The first element in PRICE and MOUSE tends also to be very open: [a]. There is, however, a major counter-tendency in PRICE and MOUSE, that is, for a central [ə] to be used as the first element. Indeed, Wells (1982: 385) talks tentatively of the possibility of a phonemic distinction between [ai] and [əi], and between [au] and [əu], although this does seem unlikely. SAWD data shows a pretty clear regional distribution, with [əɪ] and [əu] restricted to the main southern, especially south-eastern, areas. Tench's (1989: 141) view is that this variation in PRICE and MOUTH diphthongs tells us something about the chronology of English spoken in Wales: diphthongs with central first elements indicate areas where English was spoken relatively early, while diphthongs with open first elements indicate the more recent arrival of English.

SQUARE, START, NORTH, FORCE, BOAR

The main point of interest in each of these groups is rhoticity, to which all are subject. An outline of types of rhoticity and their regional distribution is given in section 3 below. However, whilst the situation varies from word to word, it is non-rhotic forms that have the upper hand in terms of frequency of occurrence.

Also worth noting in START is competition between front [aː] forms and back [ɑː] forms, with front realizations dominating in SAWD data. Parry's (1999: 215) phonetic map for *arm* shows only pockets of back realizations in the south-west and mid borders (cf. BATH in section 2.1. above).

There is a notable tendency also for a raised [oː] realization to occur in BOAR words.

CURE, POWER, FIRE

Of interest in these groups is their tendency to be firmly disyllabic, with /w/ separating the syllables in CURE and POWER, and /j/ separating them in FIRE. The first syllable in CURE tends towards the /ɪu/ found in TUESDAY; the first syllable in POWER exhibits the variation between [au] and [əu] found in MOUTH; and the first syllable in FIRE falls in with the division between [ai] and [əi] found in PRICE. In their final syllable, all three tend towards an [ʌ] realization (cf. section 2.2. below).

NEAR, EARS

Two points to note here: a sporadic rhoticity (r-colouring) in both groups in south Pembrokeshire, Gower, and the borders; and a strong tendency for EARS to have an initial /j/ followed either by [œː] (as in NURSE, above) or [əː]. This latter feature, especially as [jœː], is prevalent throughout south Wales except for pockets in the west.

TUESDAY

In TUESDAY words we find a Welsh English phoneme, /ɪu/. This phoneme is recorded in the overwhelming majority of SAWD localities. It is found also in the CURE group. As both Parry (1999: 28) and Walters (2003: 76) note, it is likely that there are two separate sources for this /ɪu/: one is influence from Welsh-language /ɪu/ (represented in ordinary orthography by <iw>), which probably lies behind /ɪu/ in Welsh English in most regions; the other is influence from similar diphthongs occurring in west of England accents, which probably lies behind the forms recorded in the south-east border regions.

2.2. Unstressed vowels

Walters (2003: 74), referring to Rhondda Valleys English (south Wales), reports that "the vowel in the final unstressed syllables of *butter*, *sofa* etc. is characteristically lengthened and with a fuller quality than normally ascribed to schwa", which he attributes to Welsh-language influence, "which has a single central vowel and in which final unstressed syllables are said never to be reduced to schwa". The data in Parry (1999: 34–35) corroborates this to some extent: [ʌ] is shown as a widespread realization in the lettER group, but occurring in most other parts of Wales as well as in the south-east. Its chief competitors are [ɚ] and [ɛ ~ ɛʳ], which occur chiefly in the long-anglicized areas of south Pembrokeshire, Gower, and the borders. However, we should remember that the "single central vowel" of Welsh is actually schwa, and in the STRUT group above (section 2.1.) there is a considerable trend towards a central vowel. Thus whilst both STRUT and lettER exhibit variation between [ʌ] and [ə] types, in STRUT the movement is towards schwa, in lettER the movement is away from schwa.

Also worth noting is the widespread tendency in happY for the final unstressed vowel to be very close and, according to Parry (1999: 36), long.

2.3. Pharyngalization

Just as, for example, [œː] in NURSE is particularly associated with southern Welsh English in popular opinion, so too is a certain 'throatiness' associated with northern Welsh English. This 'throatiness' is actually pharyngalization, that is, contraction of the pharyngeal arches. Jones (1984: 57) has noted that pharyngalization affects the articulation of the two high central vowels of northern Welsh, but Penhallurick (1991) records it with many Welsh English vowels in the traditional Welsh-speaking areas of west and central north Wales (Anglesey, Gwynedd, Conwy and Denbighshire). In Penhallurick (1991: 34–95), the only unaffected Welsh English vowels are the most open ones. [ɫ] tends also to be pharyngalized in northern Welsh English, as mentioned in section 3 below.

3. Consonants

Strong aspiration of /p, t, k/

In north Wales, strong aspiration (which sometimes approaches affrication) affects the voiceless plosives /p, t, k/, particularly in word-initial and word-final positions. This strong aspiration is exceptionally prominent in the north, but

Parry (1999: 37–38) notes that throughout Wales each voiceless plosive "normally has strong aspiration in initial stressed position, and often finally before a pause".

Dental /t, d, n/

In mid Wales and especially in the north (where they are the norm), dental realizations of /t, d, n/ occur. In the Welsh language, /t, d, n/ tend to have dental realizations in northern accents, and presumably Welsh-derived sound-substitution lies behind dental /t, d, n/ in northern Welsh English. Such dental realizations are infrequent elsewhere in Welsh English.

Unvoicing of /d/ and /z/

Parry (1999: 37) records the very occasional use of [t] finally in *cold, second*, which he links to certain English loanwords in Welsh in which final /ld/ becomes /lt/, and final /nd/ becomes /nt/ (for example, *golt* "gold", *diamwnt* "diamond").

Also, in traditional Welsh-speaking regions in the north-west and west-to-south-west, there is a considerable tendency to use [s] for RP /z/ in word-medial and word-final positions, for example, in *thousand*, and *cheese*. This again can be explained by influence from the Welsh language, which has no /z/, although the phoneme can occur in loanwords from English.

Should these cases of 'unvoicing' in Welsh English, when compared with RP phonology, be treated as phonemic substitution (/t/ for /d/, and /s/ for /z/), or as variant realizations (of /d/, and /z/)? The decision is not altogether straightforward. Given the evident phonotactic constraints, the latter analysis is perhaps tidier. However, the apparent underlying cause (originating in the Welsh language) is phonemic.

Initial fricative voicing

Parry (1999: 39) records the use of initial /v/ where RP has initial /f/ in *first, four, furrow* in south-eastern Powys, Monmouthshire, south Pembrokeshire and in south Gower. He also records one instance of /ð/ for /θ/ in *third* in west Powys (Parry 1999: 40). Such Initial Fricative Voicing, as Wells (1982: 343) calls it, is associated with west-country accents of England, where traditionally it can affect /f, θ, s, ʃ/. Penhallurick (1994: 145–148) provides evidence of voicing of initial /f, s/ in the southern half of the Gower Peninsula from the seventeenth century to the late twentieth century, though by the 1980s it was very much a relic feature in Gower English. Where it occurs, or has occurred, in Welsh English, Initial Fricative Voicing is no doubt due to longstanding influence from west English English.

/ɬ, x/

These two fricatives belong to the sound system of the Welsh language, in which they are represented orthographically by <ll> and <ch> respectively. Excepting place-names, they each have a very limited occurrence in traditional Welsh English, in loanwords from Welsh, such as *cawellt* 'wicker basket' and *crochon* 'bread-basket'.

/l/

The detail of the distribution of clear [l] and dark [ɫ] in Welsh English is rather intricate, but the data from SAWD permits the following summary. In the south and midlands of Wales, [l] dominates in all phonetic environments. In the north, particularly in Gwynedd, [ɫ] dominates in all positions. The peripheral, historically anglicized regions follow RP, with [l] before a vowel, and [ɫ] before a consonant or pause. This Welsh English pattern is influenced by the Welsh language, in which /l/ is clear in southern Welsh and noticeably dark in northern Welsh, where it is accompanied by strong pharyngalization. Thus /l/ provides two of the popular diagnostics of Welsh English: dark, pharyngalized [ɫ] in all positions for the main northern variety, and clear [l] in all positions for the main southern variety.

Dropping of initial /w/

Initial /w/ is foreign to Welsh as an unmutated form (several consonants in Welsh are subject to mutation rules in word-initial position), and influence from this may lie behind the occasional dropping of initial /w/ in traditional Welsh English, particularly in words with a following back, close, rounded stressed vowel, such as *woman*, *wool*. Parry (1999: 40–41) records zero-/w/ initially in these words scattered through north, mid and south Wales, though forms with initial /w/ are dominant overall.

/r/

The Welsh language has two *r* phonemes: a voiced alveolar rolled /r/, which is sometimes realized as a flap [ɾ] and sometimes, particularly in the Bala area, north Wales, as a uvular rolled [ʀ] or uvular fricative [ʁ]; and a voiceless alveolar rolled /r̥/ (<rh> in ordinary orthography). Welsh /r̥/ impacts little on Welsh English, but rolled [r] realizations occur often in the spoken English of north and south Wales, excepting the border areas, and the Gower Peninsula and south Pembrokeshire, where an approximant [ɹ] dominates. There is also a high frequency of flapped [ɾ] in Welsh English, particularly in traditional Welsh-speaking areas, and this can be interpreted as further evidence of Welsh influence on Welsh English /r/. Uvular realizations of Welsh English /r/ are confined to the north, where they are rare and possibly usually idiolectal.

Orthographic *r* is always articulated in the Welsh language, in all word-positions, and this practice is carried over at times into Welsh English, resulting in post-vocalic /r/ word-medially and word-finally in the north and the south, this rhoticity being centred in the traditional Welsh-speaking areas in the west half of Wales. This Welsh-influenced rhoticity in NURSE, SQUARE, START, NORTH, FORCE, BOAR sometimes leads to a short vowel followed by /r/ (Parry 1999: 14–17), such as: /ʌr/ in *first*, *third*, *work* in western mid Wales; /ɛr/ in *heard* (a spelling pronunciation) and in *chair*, *mare*, *pears* in pockets in the west; /ar ~ ɑr/ in *arm*, *farmer*, *farthing* in the west; /ɔr/ in *forks*, *morning* and in *boar*, *four* a few times in north, mid and west Wales. Occasionally the short vowel minus following /r/ is recorded. Rhotic forms with long vowels are common in NURSE, SQUARE, START, NORTH, FORCE, BOAR, with the general pattern as follows: long vowel followed by /r/ (that is, forms influenced by the Welsh pronunciation convention of always articulating orthographic *r*), widespread in the western half of Wales; long r-coloured vowel without a following /r/ (that is, forms influenced by west of England accents), occurring in the mid- and south-eastern border areas, and in south Pembrokeshire and the Gower Peninsula.

Lengthened consonants

The consonants /p, b, t, d, k, g, v, θ, s, ʃ, tʃ, m, n, ŋ, l/ are all recorded by Parry (1999: 37–40) as being subject to lengthened duration of pronunciation in Welsh English, when located in word-medial position. Parry records these lengthened forms in most parts of Wales. In the Welsh language, medial consonants tend to be long, especially between vowels when the preceding vowel is stressed. The most likely cause for these lengthened consonants in Welsh English is therefore once again influence from Welsh. However, it should be noted that SAWD data shows lengthening affecting medial consonants when followed by a consonant as well as when followed by a vowel (for example, [mː] in *thimble*). Furthermore, many instances occur in the more anglicized regions of Wales.

4. Prosody

Wells (1982: 392) notes: “Popular English views about Welsh accents include the claim that they have a ‘sing-song’ or lilting intonation”, a characteristic associated particularly with the industrial valleys of south Wales. Comparatively little has been published on Welsh English intonation, but studies have been carried out since Wells's *Accents of English*. Tench (1989: 140), on the English of Abercrave in the Swansea Valley, notes "the high degree of pitch movement on an unaccented post-tonic syllable" and "the high degree of pitch independence of unaccented syllables in pre-tonic position", features which, says Tench, lie behind the sing-song claim. The detailed analysis in Walters (2003: 81–84), which draws on his substantial 1999 study, describes striking pitch movement in the pronunciation of Rhondda Valleys English (for example, the tendency for pitch to rise from the stressed syllable), which Walters connects with influence from Welsh-language intonation patterns.

Exercises and study questions

1. What are the major differences between the northern and southern speakers in the pronunciation of vowels?
2. What are the major differences between the northern and southern speakers in the pronunciation of consonants?
3. Which speakers in the audio samples exhibit rhoticity? What kind of rhoticity is exhibited?
4. What evidence is there of Welsh-language influence in the audio samples?
5. Compared with the Welsh language and Standard English, varieties of Welsh English possess low overt prestige. Can this situation be changed, and, if so, how?
6. The character of the varieties of Welsh English (for example, northern, southern, borders, south Pembrokeshire, Gower) can tell us much about how and when English arrived in the regions of Wales. Outline an inventory of varieties of Welsh English and assess their relationship with the history of anglicization.

Selected references

Please consult the General references for titles mentioned in the text but not included in the references below. For a full bibliography see the accompanying CD-ROM.

Aitchison, John and Harold Carter
2000 *Language, Economy and Society: The Changing Fortunes of the Welsh Language in the Twentieth Century*. Cardiff: University of Wales Press.

Coupland, Nikolas and Alan R. Thomas
1989 Introduction: social and linguistic perspectives on English in Wales. In: Nikolas Coupland and Alan R. Thomas (eds.), *English in Wales: Diversity, Conflict and Change*, 1–16. Clevedon/Philadelphia: Multilingual Matters.

Jones, Glyn E.
1984 The distinctive vowels and consonants of Welsh. In: Martin J. Ball and Glyn E. Jones (eds.), *Welsh Phonology: Selected Readings*, 40–64. Cardiff: University of Wales Press.

Parry, David (ed.)
1977–1979 *The Survey of Anglo-Welsh Dialects*, 2 Volumes. Swansea: privately published.
1999 *A Grammar and Glossary of the Conservative Anglo-Welsh Dialects of Rural Wales*. Sheffield: National Centre for English Cultural Tradition.

Penhallurick, Robert J.
1991 *The Anglo-Welsh Dialects of North Wales: A Survey of Conservative Rural Spoken English in the Counties of Gwynedd and Clwyd*. Frankfurt am Main: Lang.
1993 Welsh English: a national language? *Dialectologia et Geolinguistica* 1: 28–46.
1994 *Gowerland and its Language: A History of the English Speech of the Gower Peninsula, South Wales*. Frankfurt am Main: Lang.

Tench, Paul
1989 The pronunciation of English in Abercrave. In: Nikolas Coupland and Alan R. Thomas (eds.), *English in Wales: Diversity, Conflict and Change*, 130–141. Clevedon /Philadelphia: Multilingual Matters.

Walters, J. Roderick
2003 "Celtic English": influences on a South Wales valleys accent. *English World-Wide* 24: 63–87.

English dialects in the North of England: phonology

Joan Beal

1. Introduction

1.1. Defining "the North of England"

The North of England is a region whose boundaries have been defined in a number of different ways by laypersons, members of the tourist industry and linguists. Wales (2002), using the methodology of perceptual dialectology, demonstrates that undergraduate students in a British university vary widely in their perceptions of the geographical boundaries of the North. Typically, when asked to draw a line on a map of Britain, students resident in the South of England would place this line much further South than those resident in the North or Midlands. Expressions such as "North of Watford Gap" testify to the perceptions of southerners in this "austrocentric" nation (Wales 2002: 46). Historically, we might think of the North as the area covered by the Anglo-Saxon kingdom of Northumbria, stretching from the Humber to the Firth, with Sheffield marking its southernmost point on the border with Mercia. This area would include the modern counties of Northumberland, Cumbria, Tyne and Wear, Teesside, Humberside, Yorkshire, Merseyside, Greater Manchester and Lancashire, but exclude Cheshire, Derbyshire, Nottinghamshire and Lincolnshire. Tourist maps tend to agree with this definition: the National Trust handbook has Merseyside and Lancashire in the North-west, but Cheshire in the central area; the route maps in *Country Walking* magazine place Cheshire in the "Heart of England", Lincolnshire in the "East of England" and Derbyshire alongside Nottinghamshire in the East Midlands. Confirming this last location, a film released in the cinema in summer, 2002, is set in Nottingham and entitled *Once upon a time in the Midlands*.

Dialectologists have attempted to define the North in purely linguistic terms. Whilst these more objective judgements do not show the same range of divergence as the students in Wales's (2000) study, there are differences, particularly apparent when we contrast accounts of "traditional" dialects with those of "modern" ones. Ellis (1869–1889) divided England into six major dialect areas, on the basis of ten isoglosses. His area V, the northern division, covers "the entire North and East Ridings with some of the West Riding of Yorkshire, northern Lancashire, most of Cumberland and Northumberland, all Westmorland and Durham" (Ihalainen 1994: 245). Ellis's divisions are based on four phonological criteria: the pronunciation of words like *some*, the pronunciation of *r*, the pronunciation of the definite article and the pronunciation of words like *house*. His northern division excludes the southern parts of Lancashire and Yorkshire, and the far North of Northumberland and Cumbria (these latter belonging to area VI, "the lowland division"). Wakelin (1983) divides the traditional dialects of England into four regions, roughly corresponding to the dialect areas of Middle English: North, West Midlands, East Midlands and South-west. Wakelin's northern region reaches slightly further South than Ellis's, with its southern boundary stretching from the Humber to the Ribble. The *SED* likewise follows the divisions of Middle English dialects. The *Basic Materials* are divided into four volumes: the northern counties and Man; the West Midlands; the East Midlands and the South. The northern Counties covered in volume I are Cumberland, Westmorland, Northumberland, Durham, Lancashire and Yorkshire. By using county boundaries to delimit the regions covered by their volumes, Orton (1962–1971) thus brings the territory covered by "the North" further south than either Ellis or Wakelin to coincide with Anglo-Saxon Northumbria. Although Orton and his fellow *SED* researchers seem to have organised their volumes in this way for administrative convenience rather than as a theoretical statement, as Wales (2002: 48) points out, their "northern Counties" division does accord with popular perceptions, especially those of northerners. Wales herself follows the *SED*'s example in her cultural history of northern English (Wales 2002: 48). Most recently, Trudgill (1999) divides the traditional dialect areas of England into three regions: North, central and South. Trudgill's criteria are the pronunciation of *long* as /laŋ/ vs. /lɒŋ/, *night* as /niːt/ vs. /nait/, *blind* as /blɪnd/ vs. /blaind/, *land* as /land/ vs. /lɒnd/, *arm* as /arm/ vs. ɑːm/, *hill* as /hɪl/ vs. /ɪl/, *seven* as /sɛvən/ vs. /zɛvən/, and *bat* as /bat/ vs. /bæt/. Trudgill's northern region is subdivided into the Lower North and Northumbria, with Lancashire in the western central and South Yorkshire in the eastern central regions. Trudgill's definition of the North is thus closer to Ellis's, with Northumberland separated from the rest of the North, and Lancashire and South Yorkshire outside the North altogether.

Trudgill uses a different set of criteria to classify modern dialects, of which he writes:

> In Britain, they are particularly associated with those areas of the country from which Standard English originally came – the southeast of England; with most urban areas; with places which have become English-speaking only relatively recently, such as the Scottish Highlands, much of Wales, and western Cornwall; with the speech of younger people; and with middle- and upper-class speakers everywhere. (Trudgill 1999: 6).

These criteria are: the vowel in *but* /bʊt/ vs. /bʌt/, the pronunciation of *arm* as /arm/ vs. /ɑːm/, the pronunciation of *singer* as /siŋə/ vs. /siŋgə/, the pronunciation of *few as* /fjuː/ vs. /fuː/, the pronunciation of *ee* in *coffee* as /ɪ/ vs. /iː/, the pronunciation of *gate* as /geːt/ vs. /geit/ and the pronunciation of *l* in *milk* [mɪlk] vs. [mɪɫk]. On the basis of these criteria, Trudgill divides the modern dialects into two major areas, North and South, with the North subdivided into northern and central. Merseyside is here classified along with the West Midlands and Northwest Midlands as part of the West central group, on the basis of having /siŋgə/ for *singer*. The northern division is then further subdivided into the Northeast (from the Tees to the Tweed) and the Lower North (Humberside, central Lancashire and the central North). The single criterion for the major division between North and South here is the vowel in *but*, pronounced /bʊt/ to the North of a line running from the Wash just south of Birmingham to the Welsh border and /bʌt/ South of this line.

Wells likewise uses this feature as one of the main criteria for dividing English accents into northern and southern types:

> We cross from the south to the linguistic north at the point where we pass the northern limits (in broad local accents) of the FOOT-STRUT split and of BATH broadening. In a northern accent, then, *put* and *putt* are typically homophones, [pʊt], while *gas* and *glass* rhyme perfectly, [gas, glas]. (Wells 1982: 349)

Like Trudgill, Wells (1982) notes that the North, so defined, also includes "most of the midlands. It includes, for example, the Birmingham-Wolverhampton conurbation, Leicester and Peterborough" Wells (1982: 349). He then goes on to subdivide the North into the Midlands, the middle North and the far North. The geographical areas covered by these subdivisions are similar to those in Trudgill (1999), except that, for Wells, Liverpool is in the middle North rather than the Midlands.

The accounts of linguists thus differ according to the type of dialect classified (traditional vs. modern) and the range of linguistic criteria used in classification. They do, however, all agree on a core area which is indisputably northern, an area roughly corresponding to the territory of the Anglo-Saxon kingdom of Northumbria, south of the present-day border with Scotland. It is acknowledged that the far North, or the North-east from Tees to Tweed, has dialects which are markedly different from those of the lower or middle North. Whilst acknowledging that, according to the criteria selected by Wells, the Midlands share certain highly salient characteristics with the North, in this chapter I shall define "the North of England" as coterminous with that of Anglo-Saxon Northumbria, i.e. stretching from Berwick-upon-Tweed and Carlisle in the North, to Sheffield in the South, and including Merseyside and all of pre-1972

Lancashire (thus Warrington and Widnes, which are now in Cheshire), and all of Yorkshire and Humberside. This area is coterminous with the six northern counties of the *SED*, and is also the area covered in Wales's (2002) cultural history of northern English.

1.2. A brief history of northern English

The origins of northern English can be traced to the language of the first settlements of northern Germanic tribes in what was to become the Anglo-Saxon kingdom of Northumbria. However, as Wales (2002: 47) points out, the Romans had already divided Britain into *Britannia superior* (south of the Mersey-Wash line); *Britannia Inferior*, north of this line; and *Britannia Barbara*, north of Hadrian's Wall. Thus, even before English was spoken in this country, the threefold cultural division of South, North and far North was recognised. What can further be established is that Britain had been invaded by Germanic tribes before the end of the 5th century, and that by the 9th century, written records show clear dialectal differences between texts written in the North and South of what is now England. Versions of Caedmon's hymn, which is found in Bede's *History of the English Church and People*, exist in both West Saxon and Northumbrian dialects. Both these versions were written in the 9th century, when Bede's *Ecclesiastical History* was translated from Latin. Differences between the two texts include West Saxon <ea> for Northumbrian <a>, and West Saxon <eo> for Northumbrian <e> suggesting that the West Saxon had diphthongs where Northumbrian had monophthongs in words such as *bearn/barn* ('child', cf. present-day northern *bairn*) and *heofon/hefon* ('heaven') (see Freeborn 1998: 32–33 for a full transcription of these two versions).

Opinion is divided as to whether these dialectal differences in Old English have their origins in the different tribal dialects of the Angles in the North and the Saxons in the South, or whether they evolved in the 200 years between the first settlements and the first written records. Certainly, by the 8th century, the geographical distribution of the dialects of Old English coincided with some of the political boundaries of the Heptarchy, but even at this early stage, the differences between northern and southern dialects were the most distinctive, with Northumbrian and Mercian more similar to each other than to the dialects of East Anglia, Wessex or Kent.

Texts from the Middle English period provide evidence both of a number of differences between northern, midland and southern dialects of English, and of a growing awareness of these distinctions on the part of writers. By the 14th century, there is clear evidence that northern dialects were becoming stigmatised, at least in the eyes (or ears) of southerners. Perhaps the most frequently-quoted example of this is John of Trevisa's (1380) translation of Higden's *Polychronicon*, in which Trevisa inserts the following comment:

> Al the longage of the Northumbres, and speciallich at York, is so scharp, slitting and frotyng and unshape, that we southerne men may that longage unnethe understonde. I trowe that that is bycause that they beeth nigh to straunge men and aliens that speketh strongeliche (cited in Freeborn 1998: 259).

Notable here is the characterisation of northern English as both harsh and unintelligible to "we southerne men", an in-group whose superiority is assumed. However, the superiority of the South did not go unchallenged: in the Second Shepherd's Play of the Townley Cycle (Wakefield), the sheep-stealer Mak disguises himself as a court official in order to trick the locals. His attempt is received with ridicule, as he is told 'let be thy southern tooth and set in it a turd'. Thus the stereotypes of the condescending southerner and the proudly defiant Yorkshireman are already established by the end of the 14th century.

Some of the dialectal differences between northern and southern dialects of Middle English are apparent in versions of the *Cursor Mundi*, originally written in the North towards the end of the 13th century, but copied by a southern scribe in the 14th century. The southern scribe makes several changes which provide evidence of dialectal differences. One clear North-South distinction is that between <a> spellings in the North and <o> spellings in the South for words like *know*, *none* and *hold*. As the modern spellings show, the <o> spelling has prevailed in Standard English, but survival of pronunciations with /e:/ in Scots provide evidence for an earlier /a/ or /a:/ which is retained in the North, but rounded to /o/ in southern dialects. This change seems to have happened at least by the 12th century, for texts from this period show the same pattern of <a> spellings in the North (and Midlands) but <o> in the South (Examples can be found in Freeborn 1998: 116).

Many of the differences between northern and southern dialects of Middle English can be attributed to the greater influence of Scandinavian languages in the North. The first recorded landing of Viking invaders was the raid on Lindisfarne in 793, but sustained contact between English- and Scandinavian-speaking people did not occur until the second half of the 9th century, when the great armies of the Vikings settled in East Anglia, the eastern part of Mercia, and southern Northumbria. Along with those of the Norwegians who sailed from Ireland to the North-west of England, these settlements make up the 'Scandinavian Belt' crossing England diagonally from Cumbria to Lincolnshire, in which the greatest concentration of Scandinavian features in English dialects is still found. In the Middle English period, northern dialects of English were characterised by Scandinavian features such as the pronouns *they*, *their*, *them*, as well as the levelling of inflections which has been attributed to language contact. These morphological features were to be adopted into the Standard English which developed in 15th century London, and so are no longer recognised as northern. As Wales (2002: 45) points out, no comprehensive history of northern English has ever been written: typically, histories of English confine their accounts of northern dialects to an enumeration of the characteristics of Middle English dialects and the contributions of northern dialects to the 15th century standard. References to northern English after 1500 tend to consist largely of quoting the derogatory remarks of southerners as proof that only Standard English mattered in the modern period. Perhaps the most frequently-quoted extract is the following, from Puttenham's *Art of English Poesie*, where the author says of the would-be poet:

> …neither shall he take the termes of Northern-men, such as they use in dayly talke, whether they be noblemen or gentlemen, or of their best clarkes all is a matter: nor in effect any speach used beyond the river of Trent, though no man can deny but that theirs is the purer English Saxon at this day, yet it is not so Courtly nor so currant as our Southerne English is, no more is the far Westerne mans speach: ye shall therefore take the vsuall speach of the Court, and that of London and the shires lying about London within lx myles, and not much aboue. (1589, cited in Freeborn 1998: 307).

Representations of northern English in 16th-century literature emphasise the outlandishness of these dialects to Londoners' ears. In William Bullein's *Dialogue both Pleasant and Pitifull* (1578), the character Mendicus is quite literally the beggar at the gates of London. His Northumbrian dialect is noticed at once by the lady of the house, who remarks: "What doest thou here in this Countrie? me thinke thou art a Scot by thy tongue." Mendicu's speech is one of the few 16th-century representations of Northumbrian dialect, characterised by the use of <o> for <a> in words such as *mare* for *more* and *sarie* for *sorry*, as well as a number of words which would have been familiar to Londoners from the Border Ballads sung in the streets: *limmer* 'scoundrel', *fellon* 'brave', *deadlie feede* (the blood feud of the North Marches). Other words, such as *barnes* 'children' and *ne* 'no', are still used in Northumberland today. Bullein had spent several years in Tynemouth, and so had had the opportunity to observe the Northumbrian dialect first-hand. His representation of the dialect seems accurate, but the effect in the play is to reinforce the stereotype of the uncivilised northerner.

The quote from Puttenham suggests that the acceptable model for literary English was that of an area within a 60-mile radius of London, and that the English spoken north of the Trent was singled out, along with that of the Southwest, as particularly outlandish, albeit northern English is acknowledged to be 'purer'. This double-edged attitude towards northern English was to persist throughout the modern period. John Ray's *Collection of English Words not generally used* (1674) shows an antiquarian interest in northern dialect, and even Dr Johnson acknowledged that, having "many words…commonly of the genuine Teutonic race…the northern speech is…not barbarous but obsolete" (1755). On the other hand, 18th century grammarians and elocutionists catered for readers who were anxious to rid themselves of the stigma of provincialism in an increasingly London-centric society. John Walker's *Critical Pronouncing Dictionary* (1791), after outlining his "Rules for the Natives of Scotland, Ireland and London for avoiding their respective peculiarities", makes the following remark about "those at a considerable distance from the capital":

> If the short sound of the letter *u* in *trunk*, *sunk*, &c. differ from the sound of that letter in the northern parts of England, where thay sound it like the *u* in *bull*, and nearly as if the words were written *troonk*, *soonk*, &c. *it necessarily follows that every word where the second sound of that letter occurs must by these provincials be mispronounced.* (Walker 1791: xii, my emphasis)

Walker's remarks here show a clear judgement that any dialect diverging from the polite usage of London (not that of the Cockneys, who are the "inhabitants of London" intended to benefit from Walker's rules) is simply wrong, and must be corrected with the help of the *Critical Pronouncing Dictionary*. A by-product of this is that Walker, along with other 18th-century authors such as Thomas Sheridan, William Kenrick and the northerner John Kirkby, give us detailed information about northern pronunciation in the 18th century, if only in order to proscribe it. The feature described by Walker in the quote above is of course one of the most salient markers of northern English pronunciation to this day: the lack of what Wells (1982: 196) terms the "FOOT-STRUT split" (see 2.1.1. below for a further discussion of this feature). Other features of northern pronunciation particularly singled out for censure in the 18th century include the *Northumbrian burr*, first noticed by Defoe, who wrote:

> I must not quit *Northumberland* without taking notice, that the Natives of this Country, of the ancient original Race or Families, are distinguished by a *Shibboleth* upon their Tongues in pronouncing the Letter *R*, which they cannot utter without a hollow Jarring in the Throat, by which they are as plainly known, as a foreigner is in pronouncing the *Th*: this they call the *Northumberland R*, or *Wharle*; and the Natives value themselves upon that Imperfection, because, forsooth, it shews the Antiquity of their Blood. (Defoe, Daniel. 1724–1727. *A Tour Thro' the Whole Island of Great Britain*. Volume 3. London, 232–233)

Although Defoe calls this an "imperfection", he acknowledges that the Northumbrians themselves take pride in this feature, possibly alluding to the folk-belief that it arose from copying a speech impediment of local hero Harry 'Hotspur' Percy, heir to the Duke of Northumberland. 18th-century authors, in condemning northern dialects, provide us with a good deal of information about the characteristic features of these dialects at the time (see 3.4.2. below for further discussion of the Northumbrian burr).

The 19th century saw the rise of the large industrial towns and cities of the North, and a corresponding awakening of working-class consciousness and regional pride. This found its expression in various forms of dialect writing: almanacs, poetry, dialogues and music-hall songs and recitations. At the same time, the new discipline of philology gives rise to scholarly accounts of northern dialects such as Joseph Wright's (1892) *Grammar of the Dialect of Windhill* and numerous dialect glossaries such as Richard Heslop's *Northumberland Words* (1892). By the end of the 19th century, universal primary education was perceived as a threat to the survival of traditional dialects: Heslop expresses his concern that "the tendency to assimilate the form of the dialect with the current English of the schools is increasing", but the construction which he uses to illustrate this point, *Me and my marrow was ganning to work*, is still in use today.

Similar concerns about the viability of English dialects have been expressed throughout the 20th century, and continue into the 21st. The *SED*, which began in the 1950's, set out with the intention of recording "traditional vernacular, genuine and old", before such dialects were irretrievably lost due to the effects of urbanisation, mobility and the BBC. Echoes of these concerns can be found in accounts of dialect levelling at the turn of the millennium, both in scholarly texts such as the papers in Foulkes and Docherty (1999) and in popular accounts of the spread of Estuary English (see also Altendorf and Watt, this volume). It is certainly the case that traditional dialects are being replaced by more modern, urban vernaculars, and that, within certain regions, the dialect of influential towns and cities is spreading (see Newbrook [1986, 1999] and Llamas [2000] for accounts of the influence of Liverpool and Newcastle on their respective hinterlands). But even where there is clear evidence of levelling in the North, this seems to be in the direction of a regional, or pan-northern, rather than a national model, so that we can confidently expect northern dialects to remain distinctive for some time yet.

1.3. Differences between dialects in the North of England

According to Wells (1982), "local differences in dialect and accent as one moves from valley to valley or from village to village are sharper in the north than in any other part of England, and become sharper the further north one goes" (Wells 1982: 351). In the light of recent studies which provide evidence of levelling in the North of England (discussed in 1.2 above), this may seem too bold a statement. Nevertheless, it is certainly the case that, even with regard to modern dialects, more features differentiate northern dialects from each other than are common to all of them. Even in areas where levelling occurs, new shibboleths are emerging to represent perceived differences between speakers living as little as 10 miles apart (cf. Beal [2000a] for an account of differences between 'Geordie' [Newcastle] and 'Mackem' [Sunderland]).

Whilst all northern dialects share certain phonological features, notably the short /a/ in BATH and 'unsplit' /u/ in FOOT/ STRUT, others differentiate dialects within the North. Some of these distinctions are not strictly geographical, except insofar as they distinguish the more traditional speakers in rural areas from their urban neighbours. Even in the most remote corners of England today, young people attend high school and carry out leisure pursuits in larger towns and cities, so speakers of traditional dialects are likely to be older as well as rural. An example of a distinctive feature of traditional dialect can be found in the North-east, where increasingly only traditional dialect speakers have the Northumbrian burr /ʁ/. However, other North-eastern features, such as /h/- retention, would be common to all speakers in this area, at least north of the Wear.

Other features distinguish dialect areas within the North from each other. In Trudgill's account (1999: 65–75), the area which I have defined as the North in 1.1. above includes six dialect areas: Northeast, lower North, central Lancashire, Merseyside, Humberside and Northwest Midlands (the last of these includes Manchester). These divisions are arrived at on the basis of five phonological criteria: /h/-dropping/retention, monophthong versus diphthong in FACE, velar nasal plus in SING, rhoticity versus non-rhoticity, and the final vowel of happY. As we shall see in the next section, whilst these features do serve to distinguish the major dialect divisions in the North of England, they are not the only features which are salient.

2. Vowels and diphthongs

KIT	ɪ	FLEECE	iː ~ i ~ ei	NEAR	iə ~iɐ
DRESS	ɛ	FACE	eː ~ ei ~ iə	SQUARE	ɛː ~ ɛə ~ɜː
TRAP	a	PALM	aː ~ ɑː ~ ɒː	START	aː ~ ɑː ~ ɒː
LOT	ɒ	THOUGHT	ɔː ~ ɒː ~ aː	NORTH	ɔː ~ ɒː~ ːʊə
STRUT	ʊ ~ ə	GOAT	oː ~ oʊ ~ ʊə ~ ɵː	FORCE	ɔː ~ ɒː ~ ʊə
FOOT	ʊ ~ ə	GOOSE	uː ~ ʊu	CURE	jɔː ~ jʊə ~ jʊɐ
BATH	a	PRICE	ai ~ ɑː ~ ɛi ~iː	happY	ɪ ~ ɛ ~ i
CLOTH	ɒ	CHOICE	ɔɪ ~ ɒɪ	lettER	ə ~ ɒ ~ ɐ
NURSE	ɜː~ɛː~øː~ɔː	MOUTH	aʊ ~ aː ~ ɛu ~ uː	horsES	ɪ ~ ə
				CommA	ə ~ ɑ ~ ɐ

2.1. FOOT and STRUT

One of the most salient markers of northern English pronunciation, and the only one which involves a difference between dialects of the North (and Midlands) and those of the South as far as their phonemic inventories are concerned, is the lack of what Wells (1982: 132) terms the "FOOT–STRUT split" everywhere in England north of Birmingham. This split is of relatively recent origin, and is the result of unrounding of the Middle English short /ʊ/ in certain environments. By the middle of the eighteenth century the 'unsplit' /ʊ/ was already recognised as a northern characteristic. The Cumbrian John Kirkby remarked in 1746 that his "seventh vowel", found in *skull*, *gun*, *supper*, *figure*, *nature*, "is scarce known to the Inhabitants of the North, who always use the short sound of the eighth vowel instead of it." (quoted in Bergström 1955: 71) (Kirkby's "eighth vowel" is long in *too*, *woo*, *Food*, etc., short in *good*, *stood*, *Foot*, etc. and so most likely to be /ʊ/ ~ /uː/) This suggests that 18th century northerners pronounced /ʊ/ where southerners had /ʌ/, but William Kenrick (1773: 36) indicates otherwise in his *New Dictionary of the English Language*.

> It is further observable of this sound, that the people of Ireland, Yorkshire, and many other provincials mistake its use; applying it to words which in London are pronounced with the **u** full… as *bull*, *wool*, *put*, *push*, all of which they pronounce as the inhabitants of the Metropolis do *trull*, *blood*, *rut*, *rush*. Thus the ingenious Mr. Ward of Beverley, has given us in his grammar the words *put*, *thus* and *rub* as having one quality of sound.

Thus both Kirkby and Kenrick (as well as Walker, see 1.2. above) attest to the lack of any FOOT–STRUT split as a salient feature of northern speech in the 18th century, but whilst Kirkby suggests that the unsplit northern phoneme is /ʊ/, Kenrick's account indicates that it is more like /ʌ/. In fact, both types of pronunciation exist in the North England today. Wells (1982: 132) writes that "relatively open, STRUT–like qualities may be encountered as hypercorrections in FOOT words, as [ʃʌgə]" whilst Watt and Milroy (1999: 28) note that in Newcastle "STRUT/FOOT may be heard as [ə], among middle-class speakers, particularly females." Kenrick's "Mr Ward of Beverly" could well have been describing a similarly hypercorrect or middle class pronunciation in his grammar. Quite apart from these hypercorrect pronunciations, realisations of the FOOT–STRUT vowel vary from [ʊ] in the lower North and central Lancashire to something more like [ɣ] in Tyneside and Northumberland.

Distribution of /uː/ and /ʊ/ across the FOOT and GOOSE sets also varies within and between northern dialects. Except in Tyneside and Northumberland, older speakers throughout the North have /uː/ in some FOOT words, notably *cook*, *brook*, *hook*. These words, along with such as *stood*, *good*, *foot* etc. would have had a long vowel until the 17th century. 17th century evidence shows that pronunciation of these words was very variable, with /ʌ/, /ʊ/ and /uː/ all attested for the same words. In the case of words in which the vowel is followed by /k/, this shortening has simply taken much longer to affect certain northern dialects, but the short vowel is now spreading. There are also some words in which pronunciation varies idiosyncratically: in Tyneside, both /fʊd/ and /fuːd/ can be heard, but the distribution seems to be idiolectal rather than regional, and *soot* is likewise highly variable.

2.2. BATH

Although /ɑː/ exists as a contrastive phoneme in northern English dialects, its distribution is more restricted than in the South. In the North, this vowel is notably absent from the BATH set. This feature and the unsplit FOOT–STRUT vowel are the two most salient markers of northern English, but the vowel in BATH words is the more stable and salient of the two. Wells (1982: 354) puts this point elegantly: "there are many educated northerners who would not be caught dead doing something so vulgar as to pronounce STRUT words with [ʊ], but who would feel it to be a denial of their identity as northerners to say BATH words with anything other than short [a]". Like the FOOT–STRUT split, lengthening of an earlier short vowel /a/ in BATH words dates from the 17th century. The history of these words is very complex, but the lengthening certainly seems to have been a southern innovation, which was, in fact, stigmatised as a Cockneyism until well into the 19th century. Today, it is the northern short /a/ which is stigmatised, popularly described as a flat vowel, but as Wells's quote suggests, it is a stigma which is worn with pride by the vast majority of northerners. Indeed, in northern universities, students from the South are observed to shorten their pronunciation of the vowel in BATH words, assimilating to the pronunciation of their peers. In some northern varieties, there are lexical exceptions to the rule that BATH words have a short vowel: in Tyneside and Northumberland, *master*, *plaster* and less frequently *disaster* are pronounced with /ɑː/ (phonetically more like [ɒː]), but *faster* with /a/, whilst *master* alone is pronounced with /ɑː/ in other varieties (Lancashire, Sheffield). As with unsplit FOOT–STRUT, the short vowel in BATH words is a feature of all northern English dialects, but is also found throughout the Midlands, at least as far south as Birmingham. Nevertheless, these are the features most often referred to in stereotypes of northern speech, and most often mentioned when subjects are asked to name features of northern dialect. All the features discussed below differentiate dialects in the North of England from each other.

2.3. GOAT and FACE

These lexical sets have monophthongal pronunciations /oː/ and /eː/ respectively in traditional dialects in the lower North, central Lancashire and Humberside, but diphthongal pronunciations in the far North and Merseyside. In Tyneside and Northumberland, traditional dialect speakers have centring diphthongs /uə/ and /iə/ in these words, whilst in Merseyside the corresponding diphthongs are more like RP. In the North-east, there is evidence of levelling in younger and/or middle-class speakers, not towards the closing diphthongs of RP, but to the monophthongal pronunciations found throughout most of the North. Watt and Milroy (1999) report that, in a study of speech recorded in 1994, only the older, working-class males used /ɪə/ in the majority of tokens of FACE vowels. Amongst all other groups, the most frequent variant was /eː/, with /eɪ/ emerging as a minority variant in the speech of young, middle-class males and females. Watt and Milroy suggest that the younger Tynesiders are signalling that they do not wish to identify with the old-fashioned cloth-cap-and-whippet image of their fathers, but still wish to be identified as northerners, so they are assimilating their speech to a pan-northern norm. At the opposite end of the northern dialect region, pronunciations of FACE words vary between older monophthongal /eː/ and the diphthongal /eɪ/ found in Merseyside and the Midlands as well as in RP. In these areas, the monophthongal pronunciations would be the old-fashioned variants, and the diphthongal variants are spreading from urban centres such as Liverpool. Some northern dialects retain traces of an earlier distinction between /ɛɪ/ in e.g. *eight*, *weight* and /eː/ in e.g. *ate*, *wait*. Both Hughes and Trudgill (1996: 89) and Petyt (1985: 119–124) note this distinction in speakers from West Yorkshire. However, the maintenance of a phonemic distinction appears to be recessive in these dialects. Petyt concludes that the influence of RP has led to confusion as to the incidence of these two phonemes, though some speakers retain a distinction between [eɪ] in *wait* and [ɛɪ] in *weight*.

To a certain extent, the variants of GOAT words are parallel to those of FACE: traditional North-eastern dialects have a centring diphthong /uə/, most of the North has a monophthong /oː/, whilst Merseyside has /ou/. Some West Yorkshire speakers maintain a distinction between /oː/ in e.g. *nose* and /ɔu/ in e.g. *knows*, but, as with the parallel distribution of variants in the FACE set, this is recessive (Petyt 1985: 124–132). Whilst Watt and Milroy found an overall preference for the pan-northern monophthongal variant /oː/ in every group of their Tyneside informants except the older working-class males, another conservative variant [ɵː] was used more by young, middle-class males than any other group. Watt and Milroy suggest that, for this group, the adoption of this variant is a "symbolic affirmation of local identity" (Watt and Milroy 1999: 37). A similar fronted variant is found in Humberside and South and West Yorkshire, and has become a stereotypical marker of the dialect of Hull, where humorous texts use semi-phonetic spellings such as *fern curls* for *phone calls*.

2.4. MOUTH

In traditional dialects, especially in the far North (and Scotland), words of this class are pronounced with [uː]. This monophthongal pronunciation is the same as that of Middle English: in the far North, the Great Vowel Shift did not affect the back vowels, so that /uː/ remains unshifted. In traditional dialects, this pronunciation could be found north of the Humber, but this receded in the later 20th century. In Tyneside and Northumberland, it is now used mostly by speakers who are older and/or working-class and/or male, and most speakers would use a diphthongal pronunciation [ɛu] for the majority of words in this set. However, in certain words which are strongly associated with local identity this pronunciation has been lexicalised and reflected in the spelling (Beal 2000a). For example, the spelling *Toon* (pronounced /tuːn/) has traditionally been used by Northumbrians to refer to the City of Newcastle, where they would go for shopping and leisure. *The Toon* is also the local name for *Newcastle United Football Club*, but more recently this spelling has also been adopted by the national press ("Toon must hit back" *Daily Mirror* April 14th 2003). This semi-phonetic spelling and monophthongal pronunciation can also be found in the words *brown* (when referring to Newcastle Brown Ale), *down* and *out*, all of which either refer to local items, or are used in collocation with *town* in phrases such as *down the Town, a night out in the Town.*

In some parts of the middle North, especially South Yorkshire, this set is pronounced /aː/. According to Petyt (1985: 82–91), accounts of the traditional dialects of Bradford, Halifax and Huddersfield suggest that words such as *down, ground, town* had /aː/ in Bradford, /eə/ in Halifax, and that there was variation between /aː/ and /ɛə/ in Huddersfield. Petyt's own investigation (conducted from 1970 to 1971) revealed that the monophthongal pronunciation was recessive, but that a compromise between "traditional" /aː/ and "RP" /au/, in which the diphthong has a lengthened first element "may be among the regional features that persist". (Petyt 1985: 165)

2.5. PRICE

Most words in this set have the diphthong /aɪ/ in the majority of northern English dialects. In Tyneside and Northumberland, the diphthong is a narrower [ɛɪ], whilst in parts of the 'middle North', including West and South Yorkshire, a monophthongal [ɑː], distinct from the monophthongal [aː] variant in *down*, etc., is found in more traditional dialects. In such dialects, *ground* and *grind* would be pronounced [graːnd], [grɑːnd] respectively. As with MOUTH words, Petyt found that a compromise variant comprising a diphthong with a lengthened first element was more common in the speech of his 1970–1971 informants. In words such as *night* or *right*, northern dialects retained the consonant /χ/ when this was vocalised in southern dialects in the 16th century. In dialects which retained this northern pronunciation, the vowel before /χ/ remained short, and so was not shifted to /aɪ/ in the Great Vowel Shift. When northern English dialects later lost this consonant, the preceding vowel was lengthened to /iː/ giving pronunciations such as /niːt, riːt/ for *night*, *right* etc. This is now retained mainly in frequently-used words and phrases. Thus [aːriːt] *alright* is a common greeting between working-class males on Tyneside and [niːt] is similarly used for *night* especially in the expression *the night* ('tonight'), but [lɛit] would be the more usual pronunciation of *light*. Petyt (1985: 164) notes that /iː/ was used in words of this subset by his West Yorkshire informants, but that the compromise diphthong described above was also used in these words.

2.6. SQUARE and NURSE

Whilst in RP SQUARE is pronounced with /ɛː/ and NURSE with the central vowel /əː/, the two sets are merged in certain dialects within the North. In Liverpool, words from either of these sets can be pronounced either as [ɛː] or [ɜː], thus *fur* and *fair* can both be heard as [fɛː] or [ɜː]. The [ɜː] pronunciation in SQUARE words is typical of traditional Lancashire dialects, and so can be heard in e.g. Wigan and Bolton, but is less common in the city of Manchester. Since Liverpool was in the old county of Lancashire, the [ɜː] pronunciation is perhaps a more traditional variant, and is heard in smaller Merseyside towns such as St Helens. However, [ɛː] in NURSE is also found in Hull and Middlesbrough on the East coast, but not north of the Teesside conurbation. More research needs to be carried out on the history of northern dialects of English before we can know whether this distribution is significant. In each locality, the [ɛː] in NURSE acts as a local shibboleth, distinguishing Liverpool from Lancashire, Hull from the rest of Yorkshire, and Teesside from the rest of the North-east.

2.7. NURSE and NORTH

These are merged for older/working-class speakers in Tyneside and Northumberland, where, in traditional dialects the vowel in NURSE words has been retracted to [ɔː]. Påhlsson (1972) explains this retraction as having been caused by "burr-modification", the effect of the following uvular [ʁ], or Northumbrian burr, prior to loss of rhoticity in this dialect (see section 3.4. below for a discussion of rhoticity on northern dialects). This merger is a stereotypical feature of Tyneside and Northumbrian dialects, often referred to in humorous dialect literature (see Beal [2000a]). However, recent research shows that the retracted pronunciation of NURSE is found mostly in the speech of older, male speakers, whilst a front, rounded variant [ø] is found in the speech of younger women in particular (Watt and Milroy 1999).

2.8. happY

The unstressed vowel at the end of words in this set varies between tense and lax realisations in northern dialects. Dialects with what Wells (1982: 255–256) terms "happY-tensing" include those of the North-east, Liverpool and Hull. Elsewhere in the North, lax realisations of this vowel as [ɪ] or [ɛ] are heard. In the happY-tensing areas, the realisation may be [i] or even long [iː]. Perhaps because the tense vowel is found throughout the South and Midlands and in RP, both Hughes and Trudgill (1996: 57) and Wells (1982: 258) describe this as a southern feature, which has spread to certain urban areas in the North. However, a closer examination of 18th century sources reveals that the tense vowel was found both in the North-east and in London, suggesting that this is not such a recent innovation in these dialects (Beal 2000b). In all the northern happY-tensing areas, the lax vowel is a shibboleth of the neighbouring dialects: it marks the difference between Teesside and Yorkshire, Humberside and West Yorkshire, and Liverpool and Lancashire. In every case, it is the lax variant which is stigmatised. For example, young, middle-class women in Sheffield, which is on the border of the North and the Midlands, are increasingly using either a more tense variant or a compromise diphthong [eɪ], perhaps in order to avoid the stigmatised Yorkshire [ɛ].

2.9. lettER

This unstressed vowel has a range of realisations in different northern dialects. Whilst the majority of northern speakers have [ə] in this context, speakers in Manchester and Sheffield have [ɒ], whilst Tynesiders have [ɐ]. In the case of Tyneside, the [ɐ] is also heard as the second element of centering diphthongs in e.g. *here*, and *poor* [hiɐ, puɐ].

3. Consonants

3.1. /ŋ/ in SING

This phoneme is not part of the inventory of dialects in the south-western corner of the North as here defined, i.e. from Liverpool and South Lancashire as far across as Sheffield. Here, [ŋ] is only ever pronounced before a velar consonant, e.g. in *singing* [sɪŋgɪŋg]. Thus [ŋ] in these varieties is an allophonic variant of /n/. Speakers in other parts of the North would often have [ɪn] for the bound morpheme *-ing*, but would have [ɪŋ] elsewhere, thus *singing* would be [sɪŋɪn]. In the areas which retain the velar nasal plus pronunciation, [ɪn] occurs as a less careful, stigmatised variant, whilst [ɪŋg] is perceived as correct, almost certainly because of the spelling. The [ɪn] pronunciation was not perceived as incorrect until the later 18th century, when it began to be proscribed in pronouncing dictionaries. John Rice in his *Introduction to the Art of Reading with Energy and Propriety* (1765) writes that whilst /in/ is "taught in many of Our Grammars" it is "a viscious and indistinct Method of Pronunciation, and ought to be avoided". However, well into the 20th century, this pronunciation was also perceived to be stereotypical of the English aristocracy, whose favourite pastimes were *huntin'*, *shootin'* and *fishin'*. In the words *something* and *anything*, a variant pronunciation [ɪŋk] is heard throughout the North, though in the North-east, the nasal may be dropped altogether to give [sʊmɪk]. These words are not used in traditional northern dialects, where the equivalents would be *summat* and *nowt*, so the [ɪŋk] pronunciation here is perhaps hypercorrect.

3.2. /h/

Pronunciation of initial <h> is socially stratified in most areas of the North, as in most of England. Petyt's study of West Yorkshire (1985: 106) shows that *h-dropping* is near-categorical for working-class males in casual speech style (93% in class V), but that class I males in the same speech style only have 12% h-dropping. The one area of the North in which initial <h> is retained, at least in stressed syllables, is the North-East. Trudgill (1999: 29) shows the isogloss for [hɪl], [ɪl] (*hill*) just north of the Tees, but Beal (2000a) demonstrates that h-dropping is perceived as a salient feature of Sunderland speech within Tyne and Wear. In fact, close examination of the *SED* material shows a set of very loosely bundled isoglosses for individual words, with that for *home* as far north as mid-Northumberland, and those for *house*, *hear* and *hair* following the Tees. Recent studies indicate that the h-dropping isogloss is moving further north, with even younger speakers as far north as Newcastle providing some evidence of this. Given that h-dropping is the most stigmatised feature of non-standard speech in England, this is a surprising development, but in the context of the spread of other pan-northern features such as the monophthongal pronunciation of GOAT and FACE, it is perhaps more understandable. Young north-easterners are converging with their northern peers rather than with RP speakers.

3.3. /t/, /p/, /k/

The voiceless stops are subject to both regional and social variation within the North. Of this set, /t/ is the most variable. It can be realised as /r/, as an affricate [ts], as a glottal [ʔ] or glottalised [ʔt].

Throughout the North, the pronunciation of /t/ as /r/ is found in certain phonological and morphological environments. Usually, this occurs intervocalically before a morpheme boundary, as in *get off* [gɛrɑf] or *put it* [pʊrɪt], or an environment perceived as a morpheme boundary, e.g. *matter* [marə]. According to Watt and Milroy (1999: 29–30), in Newcastle this realisation of /t/ is heard "most often in the speech of older females".

In many urban areas of Britain, and in the North-east of England generally, /t/ can be glottalised. Glottalisation of /p/, /t/ and /k/ is a sociolinguistic variable correlating with age and gender in the North-east. According to Foulkes and Docherty (1999: 54), there are two distinct patterns of what may be loosely termed glottalisation in the speech of Newcastle:

> First, what sounds on auditory analysis to be a plain glottal stop occurs categorically before syllabic /l/ (e.g. in *battle*). The second type of variant presents the auditory impression of a glottal stop reinforcing any of the three voiceless stops /p, t, k/ when they occur between sonorants (e.g. in *happy*, *set off*, *bacon*). These variants are usually labelled 'glottalised'. (Foulkes and Docherty 1999: 54)

The glottal stop pronunciation, especially of /t/, has been observed to be spreading to almost all urban centres in Britain, and is often cited as evidence of the influence of Estuary English (see also Altendorf and Watt, this volume). However, it was first noticed at the turn of the 20th century as occurring in the North of England and in Scotland. In the second half of the 20th century, use of the glottal stop for /t/ has spread to most urban areas of Britain. Indeed, Trudgill describes this as "one of the most dramatic, widespread and rapid changes to have occurred in British English in recent times" (Trudgill 1999: 136). In the North of England, it is found in every urban centre except Liverpool, and even here, Newbrook (1999: 97) notes glottal pronunciation of pre-consonantal and final /t/ in West Wirral. In the North-east, the glottalised [ʔt] pronunciation is more characteristic of traditional Tyneside speech. However, research carried out at the University of Newcastle shows that younger speakers, and especially middle-class females, use [ʔ] in the non-initial prevocalic context (as in *set off*), whilst the glottalised forms tend to be used mainly by older, working-class males. There is thus a pattern of variation correlating with age, gender and social class, suggesting that young, middle-class females are in the vanguard of a change towards a non-localised pronunciation. (See Watt and Milroy [1999]; Docherty and Foulkes [1999] for further discussion of this.) Although this pattern might suggest that the glottalised forms are recessive in Tyneside, Llamas (2000) demonstrates that these variants are being adopted by younger speakers on Teesside, which "suggests that Middlesbrough English is converging with the varieties found further north in Tyneside, Wearside and Durham". (Llamas 2000: 11)

Whilst the glottal stop pronunciation of /t/ is, as reported above, spreading to all urban areas of Britain, glottal and glottalised forms of /p/ and /k/ are confined to the North-east. In Tyneside, glottalised forms of these consonants, as of /t/, are found, though less frequently in the speech of females than males. In Middlesbrough, these glottalised forms are increasingly used by younger speakers, but there is also a trend towards a full glottal stop for /p/ in younger speakers (Llamas 2000: 10).

In Liverpool, /t/, /p/ and /k/ can be affricated in all positions, thus *right*, *time* [raɪts, tsaɪm], *hope*, *pay* [hɛupf, pfaɪ], *work*, *cry* [wɛːkχ, kχraɪ]. In final position, they may be realised as full fricatives [ɸ, s, χ]. Hughes and Trudgill (1996: 93) suggest that this phenomenon may account for the relative lack of glottal forms in this conurbation.

3.4. /r/

The phonetic realisations and distributions of /r/ vary considerably between different northern dialects. In two areas of the North, /r/ was attested in preconsonantal environments in the *SED*. These rhotic areas were found in Lancashire and in Northumberland. In the latter case, there was more r-colouring (in which the articulation of the vowel anticipates the position of the /r/, but the consonant is not fully realized) than full articulation of /r/. In modern dialects, rhoticity is more likely to be found in north Northumberland, which borders (rhotic) Scotland, than further south, and it would certainly not be found in Newcastle. In Lancashire, rhoticity is still found in central Lancashire, including some of the towns within Greater Manchester, but not in the City of Manchester itself, except perhaps in the speech of older people. The dialect of Liverpool was not rhotic even at the time when the *SED* data was collected: this lack of rhoticity has been one of the features distinguishing Liverpool from its Lancashire hinterland, but, increasingly, rhoticity is being lost even in Lancashire.

Where speakers in Lancashire and Northumberland are rhotic, the quality of the /r/ or /r/-colouring is distinct in each area. In Northumberland, the traditional dialect has a uvular /ʁ/, known as the Northumbrian burr. As the quote from Defoe in 1.2. above indicates, this pronunciation has been a source of pride to Northumbrians, many of whom today will perform the burr as a party-trick even though they would not use it in everyday speech. In the 18th century, the burr was heard in Durham and Newcastle as well as Northumberland; however, Påhlsson's (1972) study shows that, even in north Northumberland, the burr is now recessive, confined as it is mainly to the speech of older, working-class males in rural or fishing communities. The influence of the burr remains in the burr-modified vowel of NURSE, as discussed in 2.7. above.

In Lancashire, the /r/ is a retroflex [ɹ], especially in rhotic accents, but in Liverpool and the surrounding areas of Lancashire and Cheshire, the /r/ is a flap [ɾ].

3.5. Clear vs. dark /l/

In RP /l/ has clear [l] and dark [ɫ] allophones, the former occurring intervocalically as in *silly*, the latter pre- and postvocalically, as in *lip*, *film*. In Tyneside and Northumberland, the dark allophone is not used, so that, e.g. *lip*, *film* are pronounced with clear [l]. Where the /l/ occurs before a nasal, an epenthetic vowel is inserted between the /l/ and the nasal, so that *film*, *elm* and the river *Aln* are pronounced [fɪləm, ɛləm, alən]. Conversely, in Lancashire, the dark [ɫ] is used in clear contexts, as in *Lancashire*, *really* [ɫaŋkɪʃə, ɹiəɫɪ].

4. Prosodic and intonational features

Although popular discussions of dialect often refer to the speech of a certain area as sing-song, lilting or monotonous, until very recently there has been relatively little research on the prosodic and intonational features of northern English dialects, except for the discussion of the sociolinguistic patterning of intonational variation in Tyneside English in Pellowe and Jones (1978). However, preliminary results from the *Intonational Variation in English* (IviE) project indicate that "dialect variation is a significant variable in prosodic typology" (Grabe and Post 2002: 346). An intonational pattern known as the *Urban Northern British Rise* occurs in Newcastle (as well as in Belfast and Dublin). In this pattern, there is a rise-plateau intonation in declarative sentences, distinct from the high rising tone heard in Australian and New Zealand English. This intonation is highly salient for Tyneside English, but can also be found in other northern British varieties. Grabe and Post (2002) also found differences between dialects of English with regard to the truncation or compression of falling accents on "very short IP-final words" (Grabe and Post 2002: 345). Whereas speakers in Leeds and Liverpool tended to truncate these patterns, those in Newcastle compressed them. Clearly, there is much work to be done on the study of intonational variation in English dialects, but these findings support the division of northern dialects into middle North and far North discussed in 1.1.

Even less research has been carried out on prosodic variation in English dialects. Here, again, the North-East is distinct from the rest of the North, with a tendency for level stress, or with the main stress on the second element, in compounds. The place name *Stakeford* (in Northumberland) is pronounced with equal stress on each element, whereas a speaker from outside the region would pronounce it /ˈsteɪkfəd/. Likewise, *pitheap*, the Northumbrian word for a colliery spoil heap, is pronounced /ˌpɪʔˈhiːp/.

5. Articulatory setting

We have seen in the sections above that northern English dialects can be differentiated from each other with regard to segmental phonology and intonation. In some cases, though, the distinctive voice of a region, is produced by the articulatory setting. The only full and accessible study of articulatory setting in a northern English dialect is Knowles', description of what he calls the "'Scouse voice', the total undifferentiated characteristic sound of a Liverpudlian" (Knowles 1978: 88). This voice quality is described here and elsewhere (Hughes and Trudgill 1996: 94) as velarization. Knowles describes this in detail as follows:

> In Scouse, the centre of gravity of the tongue is brought backwards and upwards, the pillars of the fauces are narrowed, the pharynx is tightened, and the larynx is displaced upwards. The lower jaw is typically held close to the upper jaw, and this position is maintained even for 'open' vowels. The main auditory effect of this setting is the 'adenoidal' quality of Scouse, which is produced even if the speaker's nasal passages are unobstructed. (Knowles 1978: 89)

Hughes and Trudgill describe this more succinctly as "the accompaniment of other articulations by the raising of the back of the tongue towards the soft palate (as in the production of dark /l/)". (Hughes and Trudgill 1996: 94)

Although the articulatory setting of Liverpool English is very distinctive, it would be interesting to see whether the study of articulatory setting in other northern dialects might indicate typological distinctions parallel to those found for segmental and non-segmental phonology.

Exercises and study questions

1. Are the vowels in STRUT and FOOT pronounced exactly the same by each of the speakers from the North of England?
2. Is the final vowel of happY pronounced differently by the three speakers from the North of England? Is there any variation for any of these speakers between the pronunciation of this vowel in the word lists and the reading passage?
3. For each word beginning with <h> in writing, count how many times each speaker from the North of England pronounces or 'drops' the /h/. Is there a difference between the three speakers and/or for any of these between the word list and the reading passage? Also analyse this for the speaker in the free conversation extract, and compare her use of /h/ with the other Northern speakers.
4. Compare the three speakers from the North of England with regard to the use of 'velar nasal plus'.
5. Can you detect any differences in the intonational patterns of the three speakers from the North of England? If so, try to describe them.
6. What range of pronunciations of /t/ can you hear in the three speakers from the North of England?
7. Compare the three speakers' pronunciations of the vowels/diphthongs in GOAT and FACE.

Selected references

Please consult the General references for titles mentioned in the text but not included in the references below. For a full bibliography see the accompanying CD-ROM.

Beal, Joan

2000a From Geordie Ridley to Viz: popular literature in Tyneside English. *Language and Literature* 9: 343–359.

2000b HappY-tensing: a recent innovation? In: Ricardo Bermudez-Ortero, David Denison, Richard M. Hogg and Christopher B. McCully (eds.), *Generative Theory and Corpus Studies: A Dialogue from 10 ICEHL*, 483–497. Berlin/New York: Mouton de Gruyter.

Bergström, F.
1955 John Kirkby (1746) on English pronunciation. *Studia Neophilologica* 27: 65–104.
Docherty, Gerard and Paul Foulkes
1999 Derby and Newcastle: instrumental phonetics and variationist studies. In: Foulkes and Docherty (eds.), 47–71.
Freeborn, Dennis
1998[2] *From Old English to Standard English*. Houndmills: Macmillan.
Grabe, Esther and Brechtje Post
2002 Intonational Variation in English. In: Bernard Bel and Isabelle Marlin (eds.), *Proceedings of the Speech Prosody 2002 Conference*, 343–346. Aix-en-Provence: Laboratoire Parole et Langage.
Heslop, Richard O.
1892 *Northumberland Words*. London: English Dialect Society.
Ihalainen, Ossi
1994 The dialects of England since 1776. In: Burchfield (ed.), 197–274.
Johnson, Samuel
1755 A Dictionary of the English Language. London: Strahan for Knapton.
Kenrick, William
1773 *A New Dictionary of the English Language*. London: John and Francis Rivington.
Knowles, Gerald
1978 The nature of phonological variables in Scouse. In: Trudgill (ed.), 80–90.
Llamas, Carmen
2000 Middlesbrough English: convergent and divergent trends in a 'part of Britain with no identity'. *Leeds Working Papers in Phonetics and Linguistics* 8: 1–26.
Newbrook, Mark
1986 *Sociolinguistic Reflexes of Dialect Interference in West Wirral*. Bern/ Frankfurt am Main: Lang.
1999 West Wirral: norms, self-reports and usage. In: Foulkes and Docherty (eds.), 90–106.
Påhlsson, Christer
1972 *The Northumbrian Burr*. Lund: Gleerup.
Pellowe, John and Val Jones
1978 On intonational variability in Tyneside speech. In: Trudgill (ed.), 101–121.
Petyt, Malcolm K.
1985 *Dialect and Accent in Industrial West Yorkshire*. Amsterdam/Philadelphia: Benjamins.
Rice, John
1765 *An Introduction to the Art of Reading with Energy and Propriety*. London: Tonson.
Wakelin, Martyn
1983 The stability of English dialect boundaries. *English World-Wide* 4: 1–15.

Wales, Katie
2000 North and South: An English linguistic divide? *English Today: The International Review of the English Language.* 16: 4–15.
2002 'North of Watford'. A cultural history of northern English (from 1700). In: Watts and Trudgill (eds.), 45–66.

Walker, John
1791 *A Critical Pronouncing Dictionary*. London: Robinson.
Watt, Dominic and Lesley Milroy
1999 Patterns of variation in Newcastle vowels. In: Foulkes and Docherty (eds.), 25–46.
Wright, Joseph
1892 *A Grammar of the Dialect of Windhill in the West Riding of Yorkshire.* London: English Dialect Society.

The English West Midlands: phonology*

Urszula Clark

1. Introduction

Today, the term *West Midlands* (WM) is generally used to refer to the conurbation that includes Wolverhampton, Birmingham, Walsall, West Bromwich and Coventry, and can also be used to refer to speech associated with the modern urban area, although the historical Middle English WM dialect covered a much wider area (see Hughes and Trudgill 1996: 85; Wells 1982: 364). Within the modern urban area at least two main dialect types can be identified: those of Birmingham, and those of the Black Country to the west.

The Black Country dialect – currently the focus of a research project, the Black Country Dialect Project (BCDP) at the University of Wolverhampton – is often considered to be particularly distinctive. Wells (1982: 364) explains that the variety is linguistically notable for its retention of traditional dialect forms such as have disappeared from the rest of the Midlands. Chinn and Thorne (2001: 25) define the Black Country dialect as "a working class dialect spoken in the South Staffordshire area of the English Midlands", and similarly note that it has "retained many of its distinctive lexico-grammatical features" (Chinn and Thorne 2001: 30). At the present state of BCDP research, it is as yet unclear how many of these forms may survive in widespread use, in the Black Country at least.

It is also unclear whether and if so to what degree the dialect of the large but geographically distinct city of Coventry may differ from other West Midlands varieties. Therefore, while some data are also available from Cannock (Heath 1980), which is technically just outside the West Midlands administrative area, the term West Midlands will be taken to refer to Birmingham and the wider Black Country, unless explicitly stated otherwise. The wider Black Country here is taken to include Walsall, West Bromwich and Wolverhampton.

According to Todd and Ellis (1992b), the Midland group of Middle English (ME) dialects can be considered to have had clearly defined boundaries: north of the Thames, south of a line from the rivers Humber to Lune, and with the

Pennines subdividing the area into East and West Midlands sub-areas. Brook (1972: 68) maintains that the WM dialect of ME was intermediate between the East Midlands and South-Western dialects, with its southern part most resembling the latter. During the Old English period the region had been part of the Mercian dialect area, but following the Danish wars it came under the West-Saxon-speaking kingdom of Wessex, and it retained a closer connection with Wessex than the South-west, even after the unification of England. The result is that the ME dialect resembles the East Midlands in terms of early dialect characteristics, and the South-west in terms of later ones.

Todd and Ellis (1992b) say some dialectologists consider the ME dialect boundaries as still significant in contemporary dialect research, but others maintain that the post-industrial urban dialects of cities like Birmingham and Wolverhampton now exert greater influence than those of rural areas.

Chinn and Thorne (2001) suggest that Birmingham was clearly within the ME West Midlands dialect area: "Beginning as a place of some importance in 1166 when it first had a market, it was a town that was clearly embedded within its rural hinterland. For centuries it drew most of its people from the surrounding villages" (Chinn and Thorne 2001: 14–19). They cite evidence regarding the origins of 700 people who came to live in Birmingham between 1686 and 1726, to the effect that more than 90% came from within 20 miles of Birmingham; of these, more than 200 had migrated from within Warwickshire and a similar number from Staffordshire; almost 100 came from Worcestershire and some 40 from Shropshire. Of the remainder, about 60 came cumulatively from Leicester, Cheshire, Derbyshire, Lancashire and Middlesex, and another 50 from other parts of Britain. For Chinn and Thorne, it is not surprising that Birmingham speech should have evolved from the dialect of north Warwickshire, south Staffordshire and north-eastern Worcestershire – essentially encompassing the ME West Mercian dialect area. In the 19th century Birmingham attracted people from further afield (including Cornwall, Wales, Scotland, Ireland, Italy and the Jewish pale of settlement in Tsarist Russia), but Chinn and Thorne (2001: 19) maintain that "local migrants continued to form the great majority of newcomers, and as late as 1951, 71% of Birmingham's citizens had been born in Warwickshire".

Biddulph (1986: 1) similarly suggests that the conurbation of the Black Country was populated largely from the surrounding farming counties of Worcestershire, Staffordshire, Warwickshire and Shropshire.

The Black Country is a relatively small area, centring on the major towns of Dudley and Walsall, and probably including Wolverhampton, plus surrounding areas. One reason given for the distinctiveness of the Black Country dialect is its relative geographical isolation. The local area is essentially an

800ft plateau without a major river or Roman road passing through it, so it was only when the Industrial Revolution got into full swing in the 19th century that the area ceased to be relatively isolated from other developments in the country. During the Industrial Revolution, Birmingham, Wolverhampton and Walsall grew into large manufacturing towns, separated from the centre of the plateau by belts of open land which provided raw materials – iron and coal – for the heavy industries of the towns. Today's urban areas were originally small villages which developed with the growing industries, and with the exception of Birmingham these still have relatively small populations. Again with the exception of Birmingham, development in the region was relatively slow and the population remained relatively stable. Until the 1960s, there was no sudden influx of workers, immigrant or otherwise, who might have significantly altered the character of the area. Similarly, there was little out-migration, as the Black Country generally remained prosperous. As a result, there was little alteration in the population, and communities remained close-knit and generally introspective. Consequently, although the dialect is usually classed synchronically as an urban dialect, it has strong links with a recent, rural past and with traditional dialects. Indeed, the *Survey of English Dialects* (*SED*, Orton 1962-1971), a project which concentrates on the traditional dialect typical of rural areas, nevertheless includes the Black Country village of Himley among the Staffordshire localities covered. Data sources comprise:

(1) For the WM dialect generally:
   a. Ongoing work for the BCDP. The corpus used here comprises mainly younger and young middle-class speakers, especially from the Black Country;
   b. Wells (1982);
   c. Lass (1987);
   d. Hughes and Trudgill (1996);
   e. Todd and Ellis (1992a, 1992b);
   f. Material in Chinn and Thorne (2001).

(2) For Black Country specifically:
   a. Mathisen (1999): the most extensive study accessed to date. Based on 30 hours of data from 57 informants, collected in Sandwell (Wednesbury, Tipton and Rowley Regis), 1984;
   b. Painter (1963): Data from three speakers in Rowley Regis, analysed in detail. Note that Painter analyses Black Country in terms of a dialect-specific phonemic system; hence, his citations include both phonemic and phonetic forms;

c. *SED* traditional dialect data for Himley (south Staffordshire), from non-mobile older rural males, collected in the 1960s;
d. Biddulph (1986): a semi-professional analysis of the Black Country dialect writing material in Fletcher (1975). This includes an attempt at phonological analysis based on an interpretation of Fletcher's respelling rules, combined with Birmingham-born Biddulph's own claimed insights into WM accents. The particular variety represented by Fletcher is intended to be that of Bilston;
e. Dialect writing material from the *Black Country Bugle*, the *Walsall Observe*, Chitham (1972), Parsons (1977), Solomon (2000), and various websites on the internet (see full bibliography on the CD-ROM).

(3) For Cannock (south Staffordshire): Heath (1980). Cannock is some nine miles north-east of Wolverhampton, eight miles north-west of Walsall, and according to Heath (1980: 1) "just outside the Black Country".

(4) For Middle English dialects of the West Midlands, Kristensson (1987; analysis based on place-name data).

(5) For etymological analyses: Oxford English Dictionarly (OED).

Caution has to be exercised with the dialect writing material, since it may contain inaccuracies, sometimes due to archaising; that is, such forms often reflect canonical forms for dialect writers, which may in turn reflect traditional dialect forms that are now highly recessive or obsolete in terms of contemporary usage. Some distinctive forms, which may indeed be obsolete or recessive, act fairly clearly as identity markers within the Black Country at least: e.g. [dʒɛd] *dead*, [lɒf] *laugh*, [saft] *soft* 'stupid', [ɪəz] *years*.

2. Vowels

Table 1. Summary of "typical" West Midlands vowels

	BC (Himley) (O/B)	BC (R. Regis) (CP)	BC (S'well) (AM)	Bm (RL)	WM (JW)	WM (BCDP)
KIT	ɪ	ɪ > i	ɪ	ɪ	ɪ	ɪ > ɪ̞
DRESS	ɛ	e > ɛ	ɛ	ɛ	ɛ	ɛ
TRAP	a > æ	a	æ > æː	a	a	a > a̠ > æ
LOT	ɒ > ʊ	ɔ	ɒ > ɔ	ɒ	ɒ	ɒ > ɒ̞
STRUT	ʊ > ɒ	ɒ > ʊ	ɒ > ʊ > ə	ʊ > ɒ	ʊ > ʌ	ʊ > ɤ
ONE						ɒ
FOOT	ʊ	ʊ	ʊ	ʊ	ʊ	ʊ > ɤ
BATH	a	a > ɑː	æ > a	a	a	a > aː > ɒː
CLOTH	ɒ	ɔ(ː)	ɒ > ɔ	–	ɒ	ɒ
NURSE	əː > əːɹ	eə	ə > əː	ɜː	ɜː	ɜː ~ œː
FLEECE	iː > ɪ > ɛɪ	əɪ	iː > ɪi > əi	ɪi	iː	ɪi > əi > iː
FACE	ɛɪ > æɪ	æɪ ~ e	æɪ > ɛɪ	ʌɪ	ʌɪ	ɛɪ ~ æɪ > ʌɪ ~ eɪ
PALM	ɑː	ɑː	ɑː	–	ɑː	ɑː > ɒː
THOUGHT		ɔː	oː	ɔː	ɔː	ɔː
GOAT	oʊ > ʊ	oʊ ~ əu	aʊ ~ ɔʊ	ʌʊ	ʌʊ	ʌʊ > ɛʊ > æʊ
GOOSE	uː > ʊ	uː ~ ɔʊ ~ əu	uː	uː	uː	ʉː > əʉ
NEW						ɪəʉ > ɪu
PRICE	aɪ ~ ɒɪ	ɑɪ	aɪ ~ ɑɪ > ɔɪ	ɒɪ	ɒɪ	ɒɪ > aɪ
CHOICE	ɔɪ > ɒɪ	oɪ	ɔɪ	ɒɪ	ɒɪ	ɔ̞ɪ
MOUTH	aʊ > æʊ	ɛʊ	æʊ ~ ɛʊ	æʊ	æʊ	æʊ > ɛʊ ~ aʊ
NEAR	ɪə > eə	iə	iːə > ɪə	–	–	iə > ɪə > ɛə > eə
SQUARE	ɛ(ɹ)	ɪə > ɛə	ɛː	ɛː	ɛː	ɛə > ɛː ~ əː
START	ɑː > aː	–	ɑː	ɑː	ɑː	ɑː > ɒː
NORTH	ɔː > ɔː(ɹ)	oə	ɔː	–	ɔː	ɔ̞ː
FORCE	ɔː > ɔːə	oə	ʌʊə > ɔː	–	ʌʊə > ɔː	ɔ̞ː
CURE	uːə	uə	uːə > ɔː	–	uːə > ʊə	ʊə

Table 1. (continued) Summary of "typical" West Midlands vowels

	BC (Himley) (O/B)	**BC (R. Regis) (CP)**	**BC (S'well) (AM)**	**Bm (RL)**	**WM (JW)**	**WM (BCDP)**
happY	ɪ	ɪi	ɪi > iː	iː	iː	ɪi > iː
lettER	ə	ə	ə	ə	ə	ə > ɜ
horsES	ɪ	–	ɪ	ɪ	ɪ	ɪ ~ i > ə
commA	ə	ə	ə	ə	ə	ə > ɐ

Key:

Bm	=	Birmingham
BC	=	Black Country
R. Regis	=	Rowley Regis
S'well	=	Sandwell
WM	=	West Midlands
AM	=	Mathisen (1999)
BCDP	=	Black Country Dialect Project
CP	=	Painter (1963)
JW	=	Wells (1982)
O/B	=	Orton and Barry (1998 [1969])
RL	=	Lass (1987)

2.1. The WM dialect as a Northern variety

It is widely recognised that the broader WM dialect, located as it is just on the Northern side of the main North-South dialect isoglosses, has features typical of both Northern and Southern British English accents (see Todd and Ellis 1992b).

As Wells (1982: 349, 353) explains, the main isoglosses dividing North from South are the FOOT-STRUT split and BATH-broadening. Under such a criterion, the linguistic North includes the Midlands, incorporating the Birmingham-Wolverhampton conurbation, i.e., the West Midlands. Wells notes that the local accent of the WM dialect is markedly different from that of the East Midlands, although there is a transitional area including Stoke and Derby.

Trudgill (1999; see also Hughes and Trudgill 1996: 85) provides a fuller list involving nine diagnostic features for British English dialects. In terms of this analysis, the West Midlands:

(1) lacks a FOOT-STRUT distinction (shared with Northern Anglo-English varieties; note "fudged" realisations [Hughes and Trudgill 1996: 55]);

(2) lacks a TRAP-BATH distinction (shared with Northern Anglo-English varieties);

(3) has happY-tensing (shared with Southern Irish, many Northern, and with Anglo-Welsh and Southern accents);

(4) is non-rhotic (like most varieties of British English except those of the South-West, parts of Wales and the North of England, and those of Scotland and Ireland);

(5) distinguishes FOOT from GOOSE and LOT from THOUGHT (like most varieties of British English except Scots);

(6) has /h/-dropping as a normal feature (like most varieties of British English except those of the South-West, Wales, parts of the North of England, Scotland and Ireland);

(7) has *velar nasal plus* – i.e. the possibility of [ŋg] in cases where other varieties have [ŋ] or [n] (occurring in a band stretching from the West Midlands as far as Lancashire, and including the urban vernaculars of the WM dialect, Stoke, Manchester, Liverpool and Sheffield);

(8) retains yod in the NEW subset of GOOSE (like most varieties of British English except those of the East Midlands, South Midlands and East Anglia);

(9) has broad diphthongs for FACE and GOAT (shared with other Midlands varieties, the South-East and East Anglia). As Hughes and Trudgill (1996: 66) note, Southern and Midlands dialects have undergone long mid diphthonging (Wells 1982: 210–211), such that the more southerly an accent is, the wider are its FACE and GOAT diphthongs.

Such an analysis supports the contention that the WM accent evidences features typical of both the Northern and Southern dialect types. Typical Northern features include (1) and (2), whereas more typically Southern features include (3) and (9) (as well as partial PRICE-CHOICE merger, shared with some London accents).

Of the two main North-South isoglosses (for FOOT-STRUT and TRAP-BATH), the former clearly runs to the South of the West Midlands, while the situation for the latter is much less clear. However, it is perhaps significant that the WM dialect also shares features particularly with North-Western varieties, including (7), as well as [uː] in the BOOK subset of GOOSE, and [ɒ] in the ONE subset of STRUT.

Trudgill's (1999: 68) diagnostic test sentence, "Very few cars made it up the long hill", would therefore yield, for the West Midlands generally, something close to the following:

very fyoow cahs meid it oop the longg ill
[ˈvɛɹiː ˈfjuː ˈkʰaːz ˈmɛɪd ɪt ʊp ðə ˈlɒŋg ˈɪl]

For Birmingham (Bm) and the Black Country (BC) specifically (and more precisely), the following broad-accent realisations would probably be typical:

Birmingham:	[ˈvɛɹɪi ˈfjʉː ˈkʰaːz ˈmʌɪd itʰ ʊpʰ ðə ˈlɒŋg ˈɪl]
Black Country:	[ˈvɛɹɪi ˈfɪuː ˈkʰaːz ˈmæɪd itʰ ʊpʰ ðə ˈlʊŋg ˈɤl]

Wells (1982: 363) claims the shifted diphthongs in parts of the WM dialect system resemble London diphthongs, while other parts of the system resemble more typically Northern accents.

Wells (1982: 351–353) notes that in the area that has not undergone the FOOT-STRUT split there is sociolinguistic variation with the prestige norm. In the WM conurbation probably all speakers distinguish STRUT from FOOT, although the distinction is variably realised and sometimes of uncertain incidence. For instance, he notes that Heath's (1980) study of Cannock found that all except the lowest of five socio-economic classes had some kind of opposition. Wells notes that intermediate accents or speech styles may have either a fudge between STRUT and FOOT, such as [ʊ̞ ~ ɤ ~ ʌ̈ ~ ə̞ ~ ə], or hypercorrect avoidance of [ʊ] in FOOT, for example as [ə]. However, Wells notes that short-vowel BATH is retained higher up the social scale than unsplit FOOT-STRUT.

Hughes and Trudgill (1996: 55) also comment on the fudging issue, maintaining that it is especially younger middle-class speakers in the south Midlands who tend to fudge the vowel. The phenomenon is also dealt with in some detail in Upton (1995).

2.2. The WM dialect as a distinctive variety

Gugerell-Scharsach (1992) is an attempt to discover whether the Middle English WM dialect as defined by Moore, Meech and Whitehall (1935) can be traced in the *SED* material. Glauser (1997: 93) notes that Moore, Meech and Whitehall defined their WM dialect with the help of a single phonological feature, ME /o/ before nasals, locating it in a semicircular territory with the Welsh border as its diameter and reaching as far east as Derbyshire and Warwickshire. Glauser further notes that 19th-century evidence in favour of a single WM dialect is scanty, with Wright (1905) showing no east-west divide at all, Bonaparte (1875–1876) setting up an area similar to the ME one, and Ellis (1889) delimiting the WM with the aid of the criterion used by Moore Meech and Whitehall. Glauser says the *SED* still documents TRAP/BATH rounding before nasals in much the same area Moore, Meech and Whitehall did, but notes (1997: 95) that Gugerell-Scharsach finds herself able to identify (partially using phonological data) three main WM dialect areas from the *SED* data, namely a Staffordshire, a Shropshire and a Southern WM dialect. Of these, the dialects of the WM urban conurbation are likely to constitute the latter grouping.

Brook (1972: 68–69) claims that certain phonological features can indeed be taken to be characteristic of a WM (traditional) dialect area, the most important being:

(1) Retention of late ME /ŋg/ as WM [ŋg], where other dialects have [ŋ] (e.g. in *among*, *hang*, *sing*, *tongue*);

(2) Rounding of ME /a/ and /o/ to WM [ɒ] before nasal consonants, where other dialects have [a ~ æ] (the correlation highlighted by Moore, Meech and Whitehall 1935). However, Wakelin notes (1981: 164) that in parts of the WM, with great variation from word to word, [ɒ] occurs in other positions also (e.g. *rat*, *apples*, *latch*); also Brook (1972: 68) points out that OE /a/ before nasals remained /a/ under non-heavy stress);

(3) OE /o/ tended to become ME /u/ before /ŋg/; see LOT below.

Chinn and Thorne (2001: 22) propose that the WM accent once had much more in common with general Northern speech, but has been gradually pulled in the direction of prestige Southern variants (see his data on LOT below).

2.3. Birmingham versus Black Country

According to Gibson (1955, cited in Heath 1980: 87), it is apparent "even to the casual visitor" that the phonetic system of the Black Country differs fundamentally from that of other localities in the neighbourhood of the Black Country – or at least, it was so in the 1950s. However, Heath (1980: 87) considers this an exaggerated claim.

Biddulph (1986: 17) claims (anecdotally) to have noted significant differences between the Black Country (Bilston) dialect as represented by Fletcher (1975), and his own native dialect, that of the Nechells area of Birmingham. Specific differences he proposes would seem to include (at least):

(1) MOUTH: Bilston [aː] versus Nechells [ɛʊ];

(2) TRAP/BATH: Bilston [ɒ] versus Nechells [æ] before nasal consonants;

(3) D: Bilston [dʒ] versus Nechells [d] in *dead*, *death*;

(4) H: Bilston [j] versus Nechells ∅ in *head*;

(5) H: Bilston ∅ versus Nechells [j] in *year*.

2.4. Prosodic features

Wells (1982) points out that many Northern dialects, the WM dialect included, tend not to reduce vowels in unstressed Latinate prefixes (e.g. *con*-, *ex*-) as much as do RP and Southern-based varieties. Such a tendency was indeed noted in the BCDP audio data.

Although relatively little work has so far been done on dialect intonation, Wells (1982: 91) points out that certain British accents (including Birmingham, Liverpool, Newcastle and Glasgow) appear to have some tendency to use rising tones where most other accents have falling tones. Such tendencies are also noted by Biddulph (1986: 3), who suggests that WM speech characteristically has a "peculiar" intonation involving terminal raising in statements, as well as negative verbs (such as <wor> *wasn't*/*weren't*) taking a markedly high tone.

Wells (1982: 93) also points out that the working-class accents of the WM dialect (as well as Liverpool and some New York) characteristically have a velarised voice quality (with the centre of gravity of the tongue backer and higher than for other accents).

2.5. Vowels

KIT

All data sources indicate a characteristic strong tendency towards high realisations for the WM dialect – BCDP [i̞] or even [i]; Wells (1982: 28, 363) and Mathisen (1999: 108) close to [i]; Hughes and Trudgill (1996: 85–86) [ɪ̟]. Chinn and Thorne (2001: 20) note /i/-like realisations as typical of Birmingham in both stressed and unstressed position, e.g. in stressed *lip*, *symbol*, *wo̲men*; also unstressed *wome̲n*, *ladies*, *lettuce*, *private*, *bracelet*, *chocolate*, *necklace*, *harness*. Painter (1963: 30–31) has Black Country /ɪ/, realised as stressed [i̠] and unstressed [ɪ̞], with sporadic stressed [ɛ̈ɪ] and unstressed [ë]. Heath (1980: 87) has [ɪ̞] for Cannock.

Audio and written data also suggest that in the WM dialect generally there is a tendency to lower KIT to [ɤ] or [ə] before /l/ (which typically appears to be dark), e.g. in *will* (as dialect spellings such as Bm <ull>, BC <wool> suggest). That there has been a historical tendency towards backing before /l/ is suggested by Kristensson's (1987: 209) claim that /y/ in forms derived from OE *hyll* 'hill' was retained at least until the ME period in place names in much of the WM area, including Staffordshire, Warwickshire and Shropshire.

DRESS

Most data sources suggest [ɛ], including BCDP and Mathisen (1999: 108). However, Painter (1963: 30–31) records BC /e/, realised as [ë], with sporadic [ɛ] > [e ~ ɛ̝]. Heath (1980: 87) has [ɛ] for Cannock.

Furthermore, the BCDP data indicate that before /l/ (which is typically dark) there is a strong tendency towards lowering and/or breaking (e.g. [weᵊɫ], [wɤɫ], *well*). There is some written evidence for BC lowering to [a], especially before /l/ in <bally> *belly*, <ballies> *bellows*, *belluck* 'to bellow', but also in other environments, e.g. <zad> *zed*, <franzy> *frenzy* 'fretful'. Similar realisations occur in the *SED* data for localities close to Black Country.

Written data also suggest possible [ɪ]-type realisations in some words, e.g. Bm <git> 'get', Bm/BC <bibble> 'pebble'.

TRAP

As noted, the WM dialect, being a Northern accent, generally lacks a TRAP/BATH distinction.

Most data sources suggest a typical realisation [a] (BCDP; Painter 1963: 30), with a tendency in more formal styles to approximate to [æ] (BCDP). Chinn and Thorne (2001: 20) note [a]-like realisations as typical of Bm in e.g. *cat*, *plait*, and Heath (1980: 87) also has [a] for Cannock.

For Sandwell (Black Country), Mathisen (1999: 107) found the TRAP vowel to be fronter than most Northern varieties, closer to [æ] and very short. The older, overlong [æ::] occurred occasionally, even among teenagers.

There is also evidence, although so far mainly only from written, *SED* or informants' anecdotal material, for rounding of TRAP (to [ɒ]) especially before nasals. This may in fact be the only phonological characteristic of the historical WM dialect area (see section 2.2. above), although its relative absence from the interview material may indicate it is now recessive. Pre-nasal examples include: Bm/BC <'ommer/'omber> *hammer*; BC <clomber> *clamber*; Bm/BC <mon> *man*, <donny> *danny* 'hand'; BC <con> *can* (v.), <pon> *pan*, <'ond> *hand*, <sond> *sand*, <stond> *stand*, <caercumstonces> *circumstances*; Bm/BC

<bonk> *bank* 'hillock'; Bm <Bonksmen> *Banksmen* 'Black-Countrymen'; Bm <donky> *danky* 'damp, dank'; BC <ronk> *rank*.

As also noted in section 2.2. above, Wakelin (1977: 96) points out that rounding of ME [a] to WM [ɒ] can occur other than prenasally. Written examples in other environments include: BC <scrobble/scromble> *scrabble/scramble* 'tangle', <opple> *apple*, <thot> *that*, <gobble> *gabble*; Bm/BC <boffle> *baffle* 'hinder; thwart'; BC <motches> *matches*, <sholl> *shall*, <gollopin > *galloping*, <volve> *valve*.

There is written evidence for TRAP-raising in some words, e.g. Bm <ess-hole> *ass-hole*, BC <ketch> *catch*, Bm <ketchpit> *catch-pit*, <reddle> *raddle*, <sleck> *slack* 'small coal'. Many of these forms are evidenced in the *SED* material.

LOT

The BCDP data indicate that the WM dialect typically has [ɒ], with some raising. However, for Sandwell, Mathisen (1999: 108) characterises the LOT vowel as [ɒ > ɔ], and Painter (1963: 30–31) has BC /ɔ/, realised as [ɔ], with sporadic (rare) [ʊ̈]. Heath (1980: 87) has [ɒ] for Cannock.

The [ʊ]-type realisations are particularly interesting. Chinn and Thorne (2001: 21–22, 30) suggest that for Bm speakers, LOT is typically [ɒ ~ ʊ], with [ɒ] especially for younger speakers and [ʊ] especially for WC and/or older speakers. He claims that the latter pronunciation is still largely retained in the Black Country and the more westerly parts of Birmingham; as noted above, he suggests the historically Northern-type WM accent has been influenced by Southern variants. There is indeed evidence (especially written, but some audio) for [ʊ] realisations (especially before nasals, and especially /ŋ/), e.g. Bm <lung> *long*; BC <sung> *song*, <(w)rung> *wrong*, <frum> *from*, <bunnyfire> *bonfire*, <Aynuk> *Enoch*, <wuz> *was*. This alternation would seem to go back to ME times: as noted above, Brook (1972: 69) claims as a defining characteristic of the Middle English WM dialect the tendency for OE /o/_ to become ME /u/ before /ŋg/.

There is written evidence for unrounded realisations in words such as BC <drap> *drop*, <shaps> *shops*; similar failure to round also occurs in some cases of CLOTH (e.g. *soft*, *wasp*) and THOUGHT (e. g. *water*); see below.

STRUT

As noted above, the WM dialect maintains the typically Northern lack of distinction between STRUT and FOOT, with STRUT typically realised as [ʊ]. However, the BCDP data revealed a tendency in more formal styles to produce a more RP-like fudge vowel with [ɤ].

Wells (1982: 363) claims that the Bm FOOT-STRUT opposition is apparently variably neutralised (e.g. as [ɤ]), while Hughes and Trudgill (1996: 55) have WM [ʊ > ə]. Broad WM accents typically have [ʊ], less broad accents [ə]. Chinn and Thorne (2001: 21) indicate that in Bm, STRUT is typically [ʊ], e.g. in *tuck, putt, cud, stud,* while Heath (1980: 87) also has [ʊ] for Cannock.

In the subset ONE, the WM dialect is typical in having [ɒ] (see Hughes and Trudgill 1996: 55; Chinn and Thorne 2001: 21). Wells notes (1982: 362) that there is a difference in lexical incidence from RP and many other accents as regards this subset, in that parts of the North (including Birmingham, Stoke, Liverpool, Manchester and Sheffield) have [ɒ] in *one*; accents in a more restricted area also have this vowel in *once, among, none, nothing*.

However, Mathisen (1999: 108) claims that Sandwell actually has [ɒ] as the most common variant, for all generations, and especially in words where most Northern varieties have [ʊ]. It occurs frequently with the elderly, in all phonetic contexts, and especially before /l/ and /ŋ/_ for younger speakers (as the BCDP data also suggest). Mathisen also notes the appearance of fudge-type, closer variants (occasionally even [ə]), especially in disyllables and quite frequently among teenagers in monitored speech. Painter (1963: 30), too, notes a lower rounded vowel: BC /o/, realised as [o̞].

One salient feature (attested in speech as well as writing) is [ɒ]-type realisations (especially before nasals) in Bm <mom> *mum*; Bm/BC <lommock> *lummox*, <ackidock> *aqueduct*, <bost(in')> *bust*(*ing*), Bm <chock> *chuck* (v.) (note *chuck* may derive from French *chuquer, choquer* 'to knock').

FOOT

Chinn and Thorne's (2001: 21) analysis suggests Bm speakers typically have [ʊ], e.g. *took, put, could, stood.* BCDP data show that FOOT is typically [ʊ]. However, there is some tendency towards (probably hypercorrect) unrounding to [ɤ], particularly for younger speakers. Painter (1963: 30) has BC /ʊ/, realised as [ʊ̞].

Wells (1982: 362) and Hughes and Trudgill (1996: 55) point out that there is a difference of lexical incidence in much of the North in that several words spelt <-ook> (the subset BOOK) have kept their historically long vowel, [uː]. This is evidenced in the BCDP data, although it is recessive, and Wells notes that Birmingham conversely has some shortened vowels in [tʊθ] *tooth*, which is echoed in some of the *SED* data. Heath (1980: 87) has Cannock [ʊ].

BATH

As an essentially Northern accent, the WM dialect generally lacks a TRAP/BATH distinction. According to the BCDP data (and see Hughes and Trudgill

1996: 55), BATH is typically [a]. Some speakers (in more formal registers) may have long realisations. According to Painter (1963: 30) BC has /a/, realised as [a]. Heath (1980: 87) has Cannock [a], while Chinn and Thorne's (2001: 20) analysis similarly suggests that for Bm speakers, BATH is typically [a], e.g. in *fast*, *mask*, *grass*, *bath*, *daft*, *after*, *chance*, *command*. However, he suggests that this is a relatively recent development, since older speakers often produce a long sound similar to Cockney [ɑː].

Mathisen (1999: 108) notes [æ] predominantly for Sandwell, with typically Northern [a] occurring less commonly, perhaps associated especially with older males. Middle-class users (especially females in monitored speech) sometimes use [ɑː].

There is evidence that some speakers (particularly in Birmingham rather than in the Black Country) may have a TRAP-BATH contrast. Chinn and Thorne (2001: 20) provide written evidence for long vowels in Bm <larst> *last* ([aː]? [ɑː]), <cor/cawn't> *can't* ([ɔː]); also <arter> *after* (although compensation for /f/-loss could also be implicated here; see F below). They claim that many working-class Bm speakers vary between a "short and long vowel sound" for *after* <arfter> ([ɑːftə]) and <after> ([aftə]), also <barstud> vs <bastard>. Such a distinction may be what is intended in the spelling BC <aste> *asked*. However, there is also written evidence for a short, rounded realisation ([ɒ]) in <loff(in')> *laugh*(*ing*).

CLOTH

According to the BCDP data, this vowel is typically [ɒ]; Wells (1982: 357) notes that CLOTH is short throughout the North.

Although there is written evidence for long vowels ([ɔː]) in Bm <'orspital/orsepickle> *hospital*, <orf> *off*, there is also written and audio evidence for a more widespread process: unrounding.

A salient example involves the locally distinctive pronunciations of *soft* 'stupid'. Mathisen (1999: 108) notes that many adults in Sandwell have [saft], while older speakers may have [sæft ~ sɛft]. Such pronunciations, indicated by the typical Bm/BC dialect spelling <saft>, are claimed by Chinn and Thorne (2001: 141) to be especially typical of Black Country; these forms may perhaps be compared to Early OE *sēfte*. For failure to round following /w/ (as in *wasp*), see W below. Unrounding may also affect some LOT words; see LOT above.

NURSE

The BCDP data indicate that NURSE is somewhat variable, between [œː ~ ɜː]. Hughes and Trudgill (1996: 55) have WM [œː].

According to Wells (1982: 360–361, 363), Northern accents often have [ɜː], but some western Midland accents (such as Birmingham and Stoke) typically have [ə̣ː ~ ɨ̣ː]. He suggests that merger with SQUARE may variably occur in the WM dialect (probably as [ɜː]). For Sandwell, Mathisen (1999: 108–109) notes that while teenagers and elderly both typically have [ə̣ː], teenage women and middle-class speakers prefer the RP-type [əː]. Some speakers, especially the elderly and working class, have [ə̣]. Heath (1980: 87) has Cannock [ə̣ː].

Painter (1963: 30) has BC /ëə/, realised as [ə̣ə̣]. He notes that speakers using [ëə] for NEAR do not also use the "common free variant" [ëə] for NURSE.

Written evidence (note conventions) suggests a typically non-RP-like pronunciation in various cases. Given that typically the same conventional spellings are used as for (some) FACE, START and THOUGHT words, the intended pronunciation may be in the region of [eə ~ eː], which may in turn represent a merger or near-merger for dialect writers. Examples include:

(1) Bm <Baernegum> *Birmingham*, <taerned> *turned*; Bm/BC <taernip(s)> *turnip(s)*; Bm <Gaertie> *Gertie*; BC <shaerty> *shirty*; Bm <thaerteen> *thirteen*; BC <baerk> *burke*; Bm <waerks> *works*; BC <caercumstonces> *circumstances*; Bm <Aerbut> *Herbert*, <distaerbed> *disturbed*; BC <'aeard> *heard*, Bm <baerd> *bird*, BC <waerd> *word*, <occaerred> *occurred*; <Baertha> *Bertha*, <baerthday> *birthday*, <naerse> *nurse*, <paerse> *purse*, <caerse> *curse*, <faerst> *first*; Bm <thaerst> *thirst*, <naerves> *nerves*, <saervice> *service*, <Waerthingtons> *Worthington's*; BC <paerchase> *purchase*, <chaerch> *church*; Bm <early> *early*; BC <waerld> *world*.

(2) Bm/BC <werk> *work*; Bm <shert> *shirt*; BC <werds> *words*, <tern(ed)> *turn(ed)*.

(3) Bm <Pairsher> *Pershore*.

(4) BC <wourkin> *working*.

There is written evidence for shortened realisations ([ʊ]) before historical /rs/ in BC <fust> *first* (though compare <faerst>), <puss> *purse*, <cuss> *curse* (but compare <caerse>; see also Wells [1982: 356]), <wuss/wussen> *worse*, <wust> *worst* (but compare <wurse>). Written evidence also suggests shortened realisations in Bm/BC <gansey> *guernsey* 'long johns' ([a]) and BC <gel> *girl* ([ɛ]).

FLEECE

The BCDP data confirm that, as in South-East England, there is a definite tendency towards diphthongisation, typically [ɪi]; compare GOOSE. Hughes and Trudgill (1996: 55) have WM [ɜi], while Mathisen (1999: 109) maintains that in Sandwell, diphthongal variants often occur, especially with working-class and elderly speakers. Painter (1963: 30) has BC /əɪ/, realised as [ə̞ɪ], with sporadic unstressed [ɪ ~ ëɪ].

Wells (1982: 357) notes that FLEECE merger has not fully carried through everywhere in the North, so that one can find the historical opposition preserved, especially in traditional dialect, but also in some less broad dialects. For example, a distinction is found in Staffordshire between MEET [ɛɪ] and MEAT [iː]. Wells (1982: 363) notes, for Birmingham, [ɪi ~ əi]. It is possible that some speakers (particularly in Black Country) may retain a distinction between MEET and MEAT.

Chinn and Thorne (2001: 21) maintain that Bm speakers' realisation of FLEECE is typically "closer to an 'ay' sound" ([əi ~ ɪi]), e.g. *need*, *these*, *disease*, *piece*, *receive*, *key*, *quay*, *people*, *machine*. Indeed, there is considerable written evidence for Bm/BC diphthongisation (to [ɪi ~ əi]), possibly representing (partial?) lack of operation of the FLEECE merger (or MEET-MEAT merger). Various spellings are employed, especially representing StE <ea> spellings (i.e. representing Middle English /ɛː/):

<ay>	e.g. Bm <pays> *peas*; Bm <spayk> *speak*; BC <Aynuk> *Enoch*, <kay> *key*; Bm/BC <tay> *tea*; Bm <nayther> *neither*	= StE <e>, <ey>, <ea>
<ai>	e.g. Bm/BC <aive> *heave*, <naither> *neither*, <aither> *either*	= StE <ea>, <ei>
<ae>	e.g. BC <flae> *flea*, <tae> *tea*	= StE <ea>
<aCe>	e.g. Bm <tagious> *tedious*; BC <spake> *speak*, <clane> *clean*, <chate> *cheat*, <stale> *steal*	= StE <ea>

Chinn and Thorne (2001: 138–139) note that many local Birmingham placenames with spellings in <ea> have a FACE-type pronunciation, e.g. (River) <Rea>, <Weaman> (Street). There appears to be a potential shortening (to [ɛ]) before obstruent in BC <chep> *cheap*. Chinn and Thorne also note that short [ɪ] is usual in *week*, *seen*, *been*, a claim supported for Black Country also by written, *SED* and audio evidence (apparently for shortening before an obstruent), but especially involving words with <ee> spellings (i.e. usually derived from ME /eː/).Examples include BC <bi> *be*; Bm/BC <bin> *been*; BC <(tha) bist> (*thou*) *art*; Bm/ BC <sin> *seen*; BC <sid> *seed* 'seen'; BC

<kippin'> *keeping*; Bm/ BC <wi(c)k> *week* (from OE *wice*); BC <wi(c)k> *weak*, <Haysich Brook> *Hayseech Brook*.

Heath (1980: 87) has [ïi] for Cannock.

FACE

This is one of the few variables for which there appears to be a consistent difference between the Black Country and Birmingham conurbations.

As Wells (1982: 210–211) explains, the West Midlands variety has undergone long mid diphthonging, producing diphthongs rather than pure vowels in FACE. It appears from the BCDP data that Birmingham typically has [ʌɪ], much as in South-East England, while the Black Country typically has [æɪ]. In more formal styles, [ɛɪ] occurs in both areas.

According to Wells (1982: 357), the long mid mergers (see also GOAT) were generally carried through in the Midlands, so that distinctions are no longer made between pairs like *mane* and *main*.

Mathisen (1999: 109) maintains that Sandwell speakers typically have [æi], compared to Bm [ʌi]; elderly speakers also have [ɛi], or [ɛ] as in TAKE. Hughes and Trudgill (1996: 55) have WM [æɪ]. Painter (1963: 30) similarly has BC /æɪ/, realised as [äɪ], alternating with /e/, realised as [ë], the latter presumably in the TAKE subset. Chinn and Thorne (2001: 22) maintain that Bm speakers' realisation here is typically "very open, similar to (…) Cockney speakers" ([ʌɪ]), e.g. in *break*, *way*, *waist*, *weight*. However, he notes [ɛ] in various verb forms of the TAKE subset, e.g. *make*, *made*, *take*.

There is evidence for various non-short realisations (quality unclear – possibly [æɪ]). See also NURSE, START, THOUGHT, PALM, where the same written convention may be used:

<aer>	e.g. Bm <taerter> *potato*; BC <aerprun> *apron*, <baerked> *baked*, <baersun> *basin*, <caerke> *cake*, <caerse> *case*, <aerl> *ale*, <paerstin'> *pasting*, <paerpers> *papers*, <thraerpe> *thrape* "a hiding", <waerst> *waste*	= StE <aCe>
<ae>	e.g. BC <naeme> *name*	= StE <aCe>
<air>	e.g. BC <fairce> *face*, <mairt> *mate*, <tairter> *potato*	= StE <aCV>
<aa>	e.g. Bm <baacon> *bacon*, <caake> *cake*	= StE <aCV>
<ay>	e.g. BC <rayn> *rain*, <payn> *pain*, <tayste> *taste*, <Ayli> *Eli* (possibly 'eye-dialect'?)	= StE <ai>; <aCe>, <e>

<er> e.g. BC <wert> *weight*, <nerbours> *neighbours*, <wertin> *waiting* = StE <eigh>, <ai>

There is evidence (written, also audio) for various short-vowel realisations, apparently:

(1) [ɛ] in verb forms in Bm <en't/ennit> *ain't*; Bm/ BC <tek/tekkin'/tekin> *take/taking*; Bm/ BC <mek/mekin/med> *make/making/made* (the TAKE subset).

(2) [ɪ] in Bm <in't/inarf> *ain't/ain't half* (*isn't/isn't half*), <agin> *again*(*st*), <allis> (also Bm/ BC <allus>) *always*. Note especially [ɪ] or [iː] in Bm <causey> *causeway* (as in other dialects, e.g. North-eastern place-name *Causey Arch*).

(3) [a] in Bm/ BC <babby> *baby*.

Heath (1980: 87) has [ɛɪ] for Cannock.

PALM

Data from the BCDP, Hughes and Trudgill (1996: 55) and Mathisen (1999: 109) suggest that the WM dialect typically has [ɑː]; Wells (1982: 360) claims this is typical of the Midland cities. Chinn and Thorne (2001: 23) similarly maintain that Bm speakers' realisation here is typically long ([ɑː]), e.g. *half*, *aunt*, *laugh*, *laughter*.

Painter (1963: 30) has BC /a/, realised as [a], apparently alternating with /ɑː/, realised as [ɑ̟ː].

There is written evidence for a BC pronunciation of (*grand*)*father* possibly in the region of [eə ~ eɪ], with spellings <faerther>, <fai(r)ther> and <grandferther> (as for NURSE and FACE).

THOUGHT

BCDP found that THOUGHT was typically higher than RP, i.e. [ɔ̝ː]. Mathisen (1999: 109) maintains that Sandwell speakers typically have [ɔː], while Painter (1963: 30) has BC /oː/, realised as [o̞ː]. There is written evidence for BC shortening (to [ɒ]) before stops in <brod> *broad*, <ockerd> *awkward* and for BC failure to undergo rounding, along with other processes:

(1) apparently to [aː] in <dahb> *daub*, <aanchboon> *haunchbone*;

(2) in <allus> *always*;

(3) after /w/ in <wairter>, <waerter>; see section 3 below.

GOAT

According to the BCDP data, typically [ʌʊ]. Before /l/, there is a tendency for onset lowering (e.g. GOAL [gæʊɫ]). It is possible that some speakers, particularly in the Black Country, may retain a lack of distinction between NOSE and KNOWS, although according to Wells (1982: 357), the long mid mergers (see also FACE) were generally carried through in the Midlands (typical realisations being [ɔʊ ~ ʌʊ]). Hughes and Trudgill (1996: 55) have WM [ʌʊ], while Mathisen (1999: 109) has [aʊ > ɔʊ] for Sandwell.

Painter (1963: 30) has BC /ɔʊ/, realised as [ɔ̝ʊ], with sporadic [ɐʊ ~ ɐʊ̈], as well as sporadic [ü ~ ɔ̝wə] or (rare) [ëʊ̈], while Chinn and Thorne (2001: 22) maintain that Bm speakers' realisation here is typically "something similar to 'ow'" ([əʉ]), e.g. in *do*, *mood*, *rude*, *group*, *flew*, *shoe*, *juice*, *blue*.

There is some evidence (mostly written, some audio) for lack of a NOSE/KNOWS merger, in the form of /ʊ/-type vowels at least in forms of the verb *go* (e.g. Bm <goo/a-gooin'/gu/guin'/guz>), as well as <'um/um> *home*, <wunnarf> *won't half*, <dun't> *don't*. Chinn and Thorne (2001: 160) claim that the feature also occurs in *home* in Worcestershire and Black Country, although in the latter case <wum> is said to be more frequent.

In fact, the written material may provide evidence for lack of NOSE/KNOWS merger: words especially with StE <oCe> may be respelt as follows (suggesting something like [ʊ ~ uʊ ~ uː]):

<oo>	e.g. Bm/ BC <goo> *go*; BC <boone> *bone*, <wool> *whole*, <Joones> *Jones*	= StE <oC(e)>
<oo>	e.g. BC <coot> *coat*	= StE <oa>
<u>	e.g. Bm <'um> *home*, <gu> *go*, <dun't> *don't*; Bm/ BC <wum> *home*; BC <su> *so*	= StE <oC(e)>

There is also some written evidence for variable [ɔː]-type realisations in Bm/BC <grawt>/<grort> *groat*(*s*) (cf. <grawty/grorty dick>, but also <grawty/greaty pudding>).

Heath (1980: 87) has [ɔ̝ʊ > ɔʊ] for Cannock.

GOOSE

The BCDP data indicate that as in South-East England, there is a definite tendency towards diphthongisation, typically [əʉ]; compare FLEECE. Also as in the South-East, there is some tendency towards fronting, particularly among younger people. In the subset NEW, it appears that Black Country speakers (at least) typically have older [ɪʊ] rather than [juː].

Wells (1982: 359, 363) notes that Northern accents usually have [uː ~ ʊu], but [uː ~ əu] is characteristic of Bm and some other urban dialects. Some speakers retain contrastive [ɪu] in words of the NEW subset, like *blue*, *suit*, although this appears to be quite sharply recessive against the RP-type [uː ~ juː], so that there is a tendency to lose the historical distinction between *threw* and *through*. Traditional-dialect possibilities include [ɛʊ] in parts of Staffordshire and Derbyshire, although Hughes and Trudgill (1996: 55) have WM [ɛu].

Mathisen (1999: 109) notes [uː] generally, but diphthongised variants for older Sandwell speakers, while Painter (1963: 30) has BC /ü/, realised as [u̟ː], alternating with /əʊ/, realised as [ə̟ʊ], with sporadic [ü ~ ə̟wə] or (rare) [ëʊ̈].

There is written evidence for an [ɔː]-type realisation in Bm <chaw> 'chew' (compare, for example, US dialects; OE *cēowan*), for an [aː]-type realisation in WM <mardy> (if this = *moody*; compare other dialects, e.g. Yorkshire <mardy>), and for early shortening to [ɒ] in Bm <goss> (OE *gōs*).

A typical feature of the WM dialect is that of markedly diphthongal realisations in (stressed) *you*-forms. Hughes and Trudgill (1996: 85) characterise a Walsall speaker as having [jau], while Chinn and Thorne (2001: 168) claim that, typically, Bm has <yo> ([jʌʊ]) and BC has <yow> ([jaʊ]). For BC, *you*-forms – including e.g. *you'd*, *you've*, *you'm* (the latter being the contracted form of dialectal *you am*) – are often conventionally represented as <yow/yoe/yo>, <yer>, <ya>. Analysis of usage in Bm/BC dialect writing suggests that <yow/yoe/yo> represent stressed forms like [jaʊ], [jʌʊ], while <yer>/<ya> represents unstressed forms like [jə]. Biddulph (1986: 12) suggests that written forms such as <yow> should be taken to represent [jæw] or [jæww].

Heath (1980: 87) has [ə̟ü] for Cannock.

PRICE

The BCDP evidence suggests that WM PRICE is typically [ɒɪ] but approaches [aɪ] in more formal registers.

Wells (1982: 358, 363) notes that the Midlands rang from most typical [ɑɪ] to [ɒɪ ~ ɔɪ]. PRICE-CHOICE merger may be possible because the [ɒɪ ~ oɪ] opposition is apparently variably neutralisable, often as [ɔɪ] (see CHOICE).

Hughes and Trudgill (1996: 55) have WM [ɔi], while Chinn and Thorne (2001: 22) maintain that speakers with broad Bm accents barely differentiate the vowel sounds in *five* and *noise*. Mathisen (1999: 109) claims [ɔi] occurs "occasional[ly]" in Sandwell, allowing potential merger with CHOICE, while Painter (1963: 30–31) has BC /ɑɪ/, realised as [ɑ̟ɪ], with sporadic unstressed [ɑ̟ː].

Heath (1980: 87) has Cannock [ɑ̈ɪ].

CHOICE

As noted above, PRICE-CHOICE confusion may occur in the WM dialect due to merger under [ɔɪ]. However, there is also written evidence for PRICE-CHOICE confusion as [aɪ], in Bm <chice> *choice*, <nineter> 'mischievous or disobedient boy' (according to Chinn and Thorne [2001: 126] apparently from *anointer*, cf. <nineted> *anointed* (by the devil?); also BC <biled> *boiled*, <spile('t)> *spoil*(*t*).

Heath (1980: 87) has Cannock [ɔ̣ɪ].

MOUTH

The BCDP data suggest that as in South-East England, MOUTH is typically [æʊ] > [ɛʊ], approaching [aʊ] in more formal styles. Wells (1982: 359) notes that MOUTH is generally of the [aʊ]-type in the Midlands, although there is quite a lot of phonetic variation. Bm typically has [æʊ > æə], although realisations like [ɛʊ] are not as common as in the South.

Mathisen (1999: 109–110) notes that Sandwell speakers usually have [æu ~ ɛu], with an occasional [eu] among working-class males. She adds that MOUTH-GOOSE merger may be possible. Painter (1963: 30) has BC /ɛ̈ʊ/, realised as [ɛ̈ʊ], with sporadic [ɛ̈ʊ̈ ~ ɛ̈ː ~ ɛ̈ə ~ ɐː].

There is written evidence for:

(1) monophthongal realisations in Bm/BC <dahn>/<darn> *down*; Bm <rahnd> *round*, <abaht/abart> *about*, <tha> *thou*; BC <ar> *our*;

(2) raised onsets (of [æʊ ~ ɛʊ]-type) in Bm <deawn> *down*, <geawnd> *gown*; BC <aer> *our*;

(3) reduction to schwa when unstressed, in BC <broo 'us> *brew-house*, <glass 'us> *glass-house*.

Heath (1980: 87) has [äʊ] for Cannock.

NEAR

The BCDP data indicate typical [ɪə ~ iə]. Wells (1982: 361) notes that the more conservative Northern accents have disyllabic (but recessive) [iːə].

Mathisen (1999: 110) notes [iə] for all Sandwell speakers, also /iː/ with linking /r/, while Painter (1963: 30–31) has BC /ɪə/, realised as [ɪə], evidencing a (potential) NEAR-SQUARE merger. There is written evidence for an /eə/-type realisation in <nayer> *near*.

Heath (1980: 87) has [ïiə] for Cannock.

SQUARE

The BCDP data indicate that SQUARE typically has [ɛə > ɛː ~ əː]. According to Wells (1982: 361), merger with NURSE may variably occur in the WM dialect (probably as [ɜː]). Where there is no merger, Northern speakers often have monophthongal [ɛː]. Hughes and Trudgill (1996: 55) have WM [œː], evidencing NEAR-SQUARE merger.

Mathisen (1999: 110) holds that most speakers have a monophthong, although some older speakers may have [ɛə], while Painter (1963: 30) has BC /ɪə/, realised as [ɪə], but alternating with /ɛ̈ə/, realised as [ɛ̩ə ~ ɛə]. Again, these can be interpreted as instances of NEAR-SQUARE merger. A similar phenomenon can be observed for onset raising (apparently yielding [ɪə]) in Bm/BC <theer>/<thee'er> *there*, <w(h)eer> *where*, for which there is written evidence.

Heath (1980: 87) has [ɛː] for Cannock.

START

The BCDP data indicate typical [ɑː]. Wells (1982: 360) notes that this is typical of the Midland cities. Hughes and Trudgill (1996: 55) also have WM [ɑː], but Painter (1963: 30) has BC /a/, realised as [a], apparently alternating with /ɑː/, realised as [ɑ̟ː].

Heath (1980: 87) has [ɑ̈ː] for Cannock.

NORTH

The BCDP data indicate typical [ɔ̟ː], although some speakers may retain a NORTH-FORCE distinction (see FORCE). However, Wells (1982: 360) notes that Northern speakers typically have [ɔː], which is being extended to the FORCE set. Painter (1963: 30) has BC /oː/, realised as [o̩ː], alternating with /oə/, realised as [o̩ə], while Heath (1980: 87) has Cannock [ɔ̟ː].

FORCE

The BCDP data indicate typical [ɔ̟ː]. As noted, some speakers may retain a NORTH-FORCE distinction, with FORCE having [ʌʊə] instead. Older speakers of the WM dialect may retain [ʊə ~ oə]. Mathisen (1999: 108) has Sandwell [jaʊ] *your* (see <yow>-forms under GOOSE above) while Painter (1963: 30) has BC /oː/, realised as [o̩ː]. There is written evidence for:

(1) an [ʌuə]-type realisation in Bm <fower> *four* (OE *feower*), BC <yower/yoer/yo're> *your* (versus unstressed <yer/ya>);

(2) raising (to [uː]) in BC <cootin'> *courting*.

Heath (1980: 87) has Cannock [ɔəː].

CURE

The BCDP data indicate that [ɔ̜ː] is typical (especially for younger speakers); [uə] is common for older speakers. Indeed, Wells (1982: 361) notes that the more conservative Northern accents have [uːə] or even [ɪuə], although these are receding in the face of the RP-type [ɔː].

Chinn and Thorne (2001: 22) maintain that Bm speakers' realisation here is typically "similar to 'ooa'" ([uːɐ]), e.g. in *cure*, *endure*, *lure*, *mature*, *poor*, *pure*, *sure*, *tour*. For Mathisen (1999: 110), potential Black Country variants include [juːə ~ jɔː ~ əuːə ~ ʊə ~ ɔː], although Painter (1963: 30–31) has BC /üə/, realised as [u̟ə], with sporadic [ə̞wə].

happY

The BCDP data suggest that this is typically tense and with diphthongisation, i.e. [ɪi > iː]. Wells (1982: 362) notes [iː] in the peripheral North (including Birmingham), and Hughes and Trudgill (1996: 55) also note WM [iː]. However, Painter (1963: 30–31) has BC /əɪ/, realised as [ə̞ɪ], with sporadic unstressed [ɪ ~ ëɪ]; similarly, Chinn and Thorne (2001: 21) maintain that Bm speakers' realisation here is typically "close to 'ay'" ([əi ~ ɪi]), e.g. in *pretty*, *family*, *money*, *gulley*.

lettER

The BCDP data suggest that this is typically [ə], with a marked tendency towards lowering to [ɐ]; /r/ usually reappears in linking positions.

Chinn and Thorne (2001: 20–21) maintain that Bm speakers' realisation here is typically "a"-like ([ɐ]), e.g. in *mother*, *computer*, *water*, *Christopher*, *mitre*, *doctor*, *razor*, *sugar*, *pillar*, *picture*, *mixture*, *sulphur*, *colour*, *amateur*. Hughes and Trudgill (1996: 55) have WM [ə], but for Mathisen (1999: 110) this vowel is often /ɛ/. Painter (1963: 30–31) has BC /ə/, realised as [ə̝ ~ ə̞] (following close/half-close vowel versus open/half-open vowel respectively).

horsES

Hughes and Trudgill (1996: 55) have WM [əz].

commA

The BCDP data indicate that this is typically [ə], with a marked tendency towards lowering to [ɐ]. Painter (1963: 30–31) has BC /ə/, realised as [ə̝ ~ ə̞] (following close/half-close vowel versus open/half-open vowel respectively), while Chinn and Thorne (2001: 20–24) maintain that Bm speakers' realisation here is typically "a"-like ([ɐ]), e.g. in *China*, *dogma*.

3. Consonants

Regarding the Black Country, Painter (1963: 31–2) maintains that:

(1) consonants are slightly labialised before stressed THOUGHT, NORTH, FORCE, LOT and GOAT;

(2) consonants are slightly palatalised before stressed FLEECE or GOOSE;

(3) voiced initial and final consonants are usually fully voiced;

(4) final voiceless stops are ejective;

(5) final voiced stops are fully exploded and fully voiced;

(6) in the case of the *-ing* suffix, BC phrase-final [-ɪn] contrasts with Bm [-ɪŋg];

(7) intervocalic /r/ = [ɾ];

(8) "linking" /r/ is common;

(9) [ɹ] is rare;

(10) BC often evidences the "T-to-R" rule (with /t/ realised as [ɾ] especially in intervocalic environments).

Biddulph (1986: 2, 17–18) claims WM accents have so-called doubled or emphatic consonants (apparently geminate obstruents in medial position) – although so far no instances of such a phenomenon have been noted in the research literature or fieldwork data – as well as some aspiration on final plosives for Bm speakers (see D below). He claims the emphatic consonants are more prevalent in Birmingham than in the Black Country.

N

There is written evidence for the potential realisation of /n/ as [d] in <chimdy> *chimney*.

NG

As noted above, the NG variable provides one major distinguishing factor as regards the WM dialect. As Hughes and Trudgill (1996: 63) explain, most varieties do not, in informal speech, have [ŋ] in <*-ing*>, but rather [n]. However, in a West-Central area of England (including Birmingham, Coventry, Stoke, Manchester, Liverpool and Sheffield, as well as rural counties including Staffordshire and parts of Warwickshire) there is a form [ŋg] for cases showing <ng> in the spelling. Thus, as Wells (1982: 365–366) notes, while most accents of English have a three-term system of nasals, the West Midlands and parts of the (southern) North-West have a two-term system whereby [ŋ] is merely an allophone of /n/. Wells calls this phenomenon velar nasal plus. Most accents (including RP) have [ŋ] in words like *song*, *hang*, *wrong*; but some Northern accents are non-NG-coalescing and so disallow final [ŋ] (at least after stressed vowels).

Chinn and Thorne (2001: 22) go so far as to suggest that while [ŋg] frequently occurs in the speech of younger Birmingham speakers, this pattern may actually be a recent development, as it is "not altogether true" of older speakers. Wells notes that [ŋg] occurs well up the social scale; Heath (1980) found it in all social classes in Cannock, while in the BC [ŋ] has been reported as occurring in unstressed word-final syllables (thus [ˈmoːniŋ] vs. [sɪŋg]). Indeed, although NG is stereotypically realised as [ŋg] in the WM dialect, analysis of the BCDP data makes it clear that there is variation (particularly among younger speakers) between [ŋg] and [n] and [ŋ].

Similarly, for Sandwell, Mathisen (1999: 111) notes word-final [ŋg ~ ŋ] and [ŋg] before a word-initial suffix, but comments that it is subject to considerable stylistic variation, with [ŋg] favoured by teenage women and for monitored speech.

The potential alternation between [n] and [ŋg] in BC is noted also by Biddulph (1986: 12).

PLOSIVES

BCDP data reveal that there may be marked aspiration in syllable-final position for all the plosives.

B, D, G

There is (particularly) written evidence for fortition (following /h/ loss) of the onset of OE *ēa* to [j], [dj] and especially [dʒ] in BC <yed> *head*, <d'yed> *dead*; Bm/BC <jed> *dead*; BC <jeth> *death*. Chinn and Thorne (2001: 106) claim that such forms are today found mainly in BC, but were formerly also widely found in Bm.

There is written evidence for excrescent [d] following /n/ in Bm <aprond/appund/haprond> *apron* (from ME *naperon*), <gownd/geawnd> *gown* (from ME *goune*), <saucepand> *saucepan* (from ME *sauce* + OE *panne*), <drownd-ed> *drowned* (from (Northern)ME *drun*(*e*), *droun*(*e*)). But note the legitimate presence of [d] in <lawnd> *lawn* (from ME *laund*(*e*) 'glade', ultimately from Celtic), <riband> *ribbon* (*ribbon* = variant of *riband* from ME *riband*).

There is written evidence for [ð] rather than /d/ in Bm/BC <blather> *bladder* (compare OE *blǣdre* but Old Norse *bláðra*) and BC <lather> *ladder*. A change of /d/ to /ð/ before /r/ is attested for local ME dialects by Kristensson (1987: 213).

There is written evidence for affrication before a high front segment in Bm <tagious> *tedious* (probably [ˈtʌɪdʒɪs]).

There is some written evidence for final devoicing in Bm <fount> *found*, <olt> *hold*. According to Brook (1972: 69), one of the defining characteristics of the Middle English WM dialect was word-final devoicing of /b d g/ following liquids or nasals, as well as of /d/ in final position in unstressed syllables (e.g. *hadet* 'beheaded').

P

Mathisen (1999: 110) notes that glottalling for P is quite frequent, but less so than for T. There is apparent /p/-voicing in Bm/BC <bibble> *pebble*.

T

Mathisen (1999: 110) identifies [t] as the standard realisation, with T-glottalling frequent for younger speakers but infrequent for the elderly. Tap [ɾ] is considered mainly a male variant.

The BCDP data do indicate that many speakers have such a T-to-R rule (tapping of /t/ in intervocalic position), while T-glottalling occurs especially among younger speakers.

As Wells (1982: 261) notes, T-glottalling is widespread in most of the British Isles. Hughes and Trudgill (1996: 62) certify that this is indeed prevalent among younger urban working-class speakers in the UK. It is therefore not surprising to find this feature in the West Midlands. There is written evidence for word-final T-glottalling (or deletion) in Bm <wha'> *what*, <doan> *don't*, <las' night>, <in' arf> *isn't half*, <ackidock> *aqueduct*.

However, Chinn and Thorne (2001: 23) maintain that there are "relatively few glottal stops [replacing /t/] in Birmingham speech", whether occurring medially (e.g. *daughter*, *cutlery*, *butter*) or finally (e.g. *feet*, *that*).

There is considerable written evidence for the T-to-R rule (noted also by Biddulph 1986: 12), e.g. in Bm <gerra/gerron/a-gerrin'/gerrout/gerraway> *get a/get on/getting/get out/get away*, <gorra/gurra/gorrin/gorrall> *got a/in/all*, <irrin/irrup> *it in/up*, <marrer/marra> *matter*, <birra> *bit of*, <purron> *put on*; BC <gerroff> *get off*, <bur 'e> *but he*, <bur at> *but at*, <ger 'undred> *get hundred*.

There is also written evidence for anticipatory realisation of /t/ as [k] between /ɪ/ and syllabic /l/, as in Bm/BC <lickle> *little* or Bm <orsepickle> *hospital*. Note apparent hypercorrection in BC <pittle> *pickle*, <tittle> *tickle*. Furthermore, there is audio and written evidence for yod-coalescence to /tʃ/ before high front segments, e.g. in Bm <ackchullay> *actually*.

K

Mathisen (1999: 110) notes that glottalling of K is quite frequent, but less so than for T. There is written evidence for [tʃ] rather than /k/ in Bm <reechy> *reeky* 'smoky' (from OE *rēc*,**riec*).

F

There is written evidence for medial and final deletion of /f/ (paralleled for V, see below) in Bm <arter>; BC <airta> *after*. There is written evidence for [g] rather than /f/ in <durgey> 'dwarf; small, diminutive' (note also variation in OE *dweorg* vs *dweorh* 'dwarf').

H

As Wells points out (1982: 371; see also Hughes and Trudgill 1996: 85; Chinn and Thorne 2001: 22), /h/-dropping is prevalent in the vernacular accents of the Midlands and Middle North in initial or medial position. /h/ is especially likely to be canonically deleted in word-initial position (as shown by numerous audio and written examples, and noted also by Biddulph 1986: 3).

The BCDP data suggest that /h/-dropping is near-canonical in the WM dialect, although Mathisen (1999: 110) in Sandwell found it to be typical of teenage and working-class speech.

There is also written evidence for epenthetic (hypercorrect) /h/ in Bm <haprond> *apron*, and for realisation as [w] initially in BC <wum> *home* (also <hum>, <'um>).

GH

There is *SED* and written evidence for cases of ME /x/→ WM [f] in contexts where RP might have different realisations, e.g. Bm <duff> *dough* (from OE *dāg*), <sluff> *slough* 'midden pool' (from OE *slōh*, *slōg*), WM <suff> *sough* 'drain' (compare other dialects; RP *rough*, *tough*, *enough*, *slough* (v.) etc).

V

There is written evidence for deletion of /v/ in medial and final position, possibly in low-stressed or unstressed syllables. This is paralleled for F, see above. Examples include Bm/BC <gi'/gie> *give*; Bm <gin> *given*; WM <ne'er/nare> *never*, <nerrun> *never a one* (compare other dialect or archaic forms like *nary* (*a one*), *ne'er*), BC <o'> *of*, <gimme> *give me*, <atta> *have to*.

TH

For Sandwell, Mathisen (1999: 111) notes [θ ~ ð] for adult speakers, but [f ~ v] for a growing number of teenagers, especially males.

There is written evidence for /θ/-deletion in BC <wi'> *with*, <wie 'er> *with her*, <wi'outen> *without*; for /ð/-stopping in BC <furder> *further* (an archaism, cf. *burthen* ~ *burden*; see D), and for rhoticisation of /ð/ (to a tap, [ɾ]) in Bm/BC <Smerrick> *Smethwick*. A sporadic local change of OE /rð/ to ME /rd/ is noted by Kristensson (1987: 213).

Z

There is written evidence for /z/-deletion (as well as possibly /t/-deletion) in *isn't* in Bm <in' arf> *isn't half*.

W

There is written evidence for /w/-deletion in unstressed initial and medial position in Bm <ull> *will*, <'ud> *would*, <(big) 'uns> (*big*) *ones*, <back'ards> *backwards*, <forrards> *forwards* (compare data from the *OED*: colloquial *can't get any forrader*; maritime usage *forr'ard*), <arse-uppards> *arse-upwards* 'topsy-turvy', <causey> *causeway* (as in other dialects, e.g. North-Eastern place-name *Causey Arch*); also BC <ud/ood> *would*, <udn't> *wouldn't*, <oot> *wouldst* (*thou*).

There is also written and anecdotal evidence of cases of failure to round historical /a/ following /w/ (relating to instances of CLOTH and THOUGHT; see above); sometimes this appears to be accompanied by fronting. Thus, Chitham (1972: 171–172) claims that in BC *wasp* rhymes with *clasp* (presumably as [wasp]); for *wash*, Mathisen (1999: 108) has Sandwell [wæʃ], for which note also BC <wesh> ([wɛʃ]). There is also Bm/BC <wairter>/<waerter> *water*, where presumably raising of historical /aː/ to something like [eə ~ eː] occurred (see also FACE, NURSE, START, PALM, where the same convention may be used). In the cases of fronting, OE (Mercian) second fronting may have been involved (note the derivations of *wash* and *water* in OE *wæscan* and *wæter* respectively).

WH

Wells (1982: 371) notes that historical /hw/ has become /w/ in all English urban accents; certainly the BCDP data reveal no /w/ ~ /hw/ distinction. However, there is written evidence for /hw/-simplification to [w] rather than [h] in BC <wool> *whole* (possibly represents [wʊɫ]).

R

WM accents, like those of the South-East, are non-rhotic (Wells 1982: 360), but have both linking and intrusive /r/. While the *SED* material does show that locations near and within the Black Country (Himley and other areas nearby) were at least partially rhotic until comparatively recently, the current isogloss separating the rhotic South-West from the non-rhotic Midlands (and indeed most of the country) runs some way to the South of the West Midlands conurbation.

Chinn and Thorne (2001: 23) maintain that tapped realisations of /r/ are frequent in Birmingham speech, occurring especially in disyllabic words such as *marry*, *very*, *sorry*, *perhaps*, *all right*, but also in monosyllables such as *bright*, *great*, *cream*. They note that tap production varies considerably between speakers and sociolinguistic contexts.

Mathisen (1999: 110) explains that Sandwell usually has [ɹ], but there are some instances of prevocalic [ɾ]. Linking-R is categorical and intrusive R very frequent.

Y

The West Midlands has some degree of yod-dropping, as the BCDP data reveal (e.g. *new* [nʊu]). Mathisen (1999: 111) also found some instances of yod-dropping in Sandwell, especially with teenagers and especially with *new*. Yod-dropping is also evidenced in Bm <dook> *duke*, <dooks> *dukes* 'fists', BC <noo> *new*, possibly <tewns> *tunes*; also in BC <'ears> *years*. Note also written evidence for (hypercorrect?) yod-insertion in BC <unkyoothe> *uncouth*.

L

According to BCDP, L typically appears to be dark. Mathisen (1999: 111) notes that L is frequently dark in all positions for males, but usually clear for females, with some L-vocalisation among younger speakers. Note Mathisen's (1999: 108) datum for Sandwell: [faʊd] *fold*.

There is written evidence for medial preconsonantal L-vocalisation or loss in Bm <mawkin> *malkin* 'scarecrow' (from pet-name for *Matilda*); Bm/BC <fode> *fold* 'backyard', <ode> *old*; BC <tode> *told*, <code> *cold*, <sode> *sold*, <onny> *any*, <bawk> *ba(u)lk*.

4. Morphophonological processes

The Black Country is noted for its highly contracted negative modal forms, evidenced where possible using Painter's (1963: 32–33) transcriptions, as well as respelling conventions, as follows:

[æɪ]	<ay/ai'>	*ain't* 'am not/isn't/aren't, hasn't/haven't'
[bæɪ]	<bay/bey>	*bain't* 'am not/isn't/aren't'
	<in'>	*isn't*
	<wor(e)>	*wasn't/weren't*
	<doe/doh/dow>	*doesn't/don't*
[dëəsn̩t]	<dursn't>?	*don't*
	<day>	*didn't*
[wɔʊ]	<woh/wo'/woa>	*won't*
[ʃoː]	<share>	*shan't*
[koː]	<cor(e)/caw>	*can't*
[moː]	<mo>	*mustn't*

Note also Mathisen (1999: 108) [kɔː] *can't*, [kɔːɹ ævit] *can't have it*.

Written evidence from Chinn and Thorne (2001: 74, 121) suggests that similar phonological processes may operate in Birmingham (at least in traditional working-class dialect), e.g. <dain't>/<dain> *didn't*. Chinn and Thorne (2001: 121) cite a form <mon't> *mustn't*. This could perhaps be a contraction of *mustn't*, or derived from earlier (ME) *maun* 'must' + *-n't* (Bm <mun>).

There is evidence for the retention of the reflex of the OE form *axian* 'to ask' (rather than OE *ascian*) in <aks> *ask*.

5. Current issues

The English West Midlands dialect is an under-researched area in all its linguistic aspects, which is surprising given its continued widespread use in both speech and writing. Mathisen (1999) found that in Sandwell the exogenous factor T-glottalling was spreading, but the local identity marker [ŋg] was robust and not significantly eroded. Changes seem to be largely brought about by females within the speech community.

Research in progress includes work on language change in the Black Country, attitudes to the Black Country and Birmingham accents, and the relationship between language and identity.

* Project leader, Black Country Dialect Project, University of Wolverhampton. Phonological analysis undertaken with the assistance of Peter Finn, research assistant, BCDP.

Exercises and study questions

1. Listen to the speaker's patterning of NG and of T in the audio sample. What conclusions do you draw regarding local identity versus innovations from further south?

2. What might the speaker's use of fudged STRUT and/or hypercorrect FOOT say about their socio-economic status?

3. Explain the phonological process involved in the change of [n] to [d] in <chimdy> *chimney*.

4. Why might a form such as [ɪnt] for *isn't* be described as 'double-contracted'?

5. Account for the process of development of the distinctive phonological forms of the modal verbs especially in the Black Country, e.g. <day> *didn't*, <cor> *can't*.

6. As noted under GOOSE above, West Midlands speech (WM) typically shows markedly diphthongal realisations in stressed *you*-forms, e.g. [jaʊ]. These forms as well as RP [juː] may be compared with Middle English *yow* ← Old English *ēow*, originally the accusative and dative forms of *gē* "ye". How might the Middle English forms have developed differently to yield the variant forms in WM and RP? Hint: Stress is involved.

Selected references

Please consult the General references for titles mentioned in the text but not included in the references below. For a full bibliography see the accompanying CD-ROM.

Biddulph, Joseph
1986 *A Short Grammar of Black Country.* Pontypridd: Languages Information Centre.

Bonaparte, Prince Louis Lucien
1875–1876 On the dialects of Monmouthshire, Herefordshire, Worcestershire, Gloucestershire, Berkshire, Oxfordshire, South Warwickshire, South Northamptonshire, Buckinghamshire, Hertfordshire, Middlesex and Surrey, with a new classification of the English dialects. *Transactions of the Philological Society*: 570–581.

Brook, George L.
1972 *English Dialects*. London: Deutsch.
Chinn, Carl and Steve Thorne (eds.)
2001 *Proper Brummie: A Dictionary of Birmingham Words and Phrases.* Studley, Warks.: Brewin Books.
Chitham, Edward
1972 *The Black Country.* London: Longman.
Fletcher, Kate
1975 *The Old Testament in the Dialect of the Black Country, Part I: Genesis to Deuteronomy.* Tipton: Black Country Society.
Gibson, P. H.
1955 Studies in the linguistic geography of Staffordshire. M.A. thesis, Department of Linguistics, University of Leeds.
Glauser, Beat
1997 Review of Heide Gugerell-Scharsach. The West Midlands as a dialect area: A phonological, lexical and morphological investigation based on the Survey of English Dialects. *Anglia* 115: 92–97.
Gugerell-Scharsach, Heide
1992 *The West Midlands as a Dialect Area: A Phonological, Lexical and Morphological Investigation Based on the Survey of English Dialects.* München: Awi.
Heath, Christopher D.
1980 *Pronunciation of English in Cannock, Staffordshire: A Socio-Linguistic Survey of an Urban Speech-Community*. Oxford: Blackwell.
Kristensson, Gillis
1987 *A Survey of Middle English Dialects 1290–1350: The West Midlands Counties.* Lund: Lund University Press.
Lass, Roger
1987 *The Shape of English: Structure and History*. London: Dent.
Mathisen, Anne Grethe
1999 Sandwell, West Midlands: Ambiguous perspectives on gender patterns and models of change. In: Foulkes and Docherty (eds.), 107–123.
Moore, Samuel, Sanford B. Meech and Harold Whitehall
1935 *Middle English Dialect Characteristics and Boundaries*. Ann Arbor: University of Michigan Press.
Orton, Harold and Michael Barry
1998 *Survey of English Dialects (B) Basic Material, Volume 2: The West Midlands Counties, Parts 1–2.* 2nd edition. Leeds: Arnold.
Painter, Collin
1963 Black Country speech. *Maître Phonétique* 120: 30–33.
Parsons, Harold (ed.)
1977 *Black Country Stories.* Dudley: Black Country Society.
Solomon, Philip
2000 *Philip Solomon's On-line Dictionary of Black Country Words*. *http://www.philipsolomon.co.uk/page20.html*.

Thorne, Steve
1999 Accent and prejudice: a sociolinguistic survey of evaluative reactions to the Birmingham accent. M.A. thesis, Department of English, University of Birmingham.

Todd, Loreto and Stanley Ellis
1992a The Midlands. In: McArthur (ed.), 660.
1992b Birmingham. In: McArthur (ed.), 130–131.

Upton, Clive
1995 Mixing and fudging in Midland and Southern dialects of England: The *cup* and *foot* vowels. In: Jack Windsor Lewis (ed.), *Studies in General and English Phonetics*, 385–394. London: Routledge.

The dialect of East Anglia: phonology

Peter Trudgill

1. Introduction

1.1. East Anglia

As a modern topographical and cultural term, *East Anglia* refers to an area with no official status. Like similar terms such as "The Midlands" or "The Midwest", the term is widely understood but stands for an area which has no clear boundaries. Most people would agree that the English counties of Norfolk and Suffolk are prototypically East Anglian, although even here the status of the Fenland areas of western Norfolk and northwestern Suffolk is ambiguous: the Fens were for the most part uninhabited until the 17th century, and the cultural orientations of this area are therefore less clear. The main issue, however, has to do with the extent to which the neighbouring counties, notably Cambridgeshire and Essex, are East Anglian or not.

Historically, the Anglo-Saxon kingdom of East Anglia was bordered in the south by the river Stour, and in the west by the Ouse, the Lark and the Kennett, thus leaving the Newmarket and Haverhill areas of Suffolk, from a modern perspective, on the 'wrong' side of the border. The Kingdom later expanded further west, however, up to the River Cam; Anglo-Saxon East Anglia at its greatest extent therefore consisted of the habitable parts of Norfolk and Suffolk plus eastern Cambridgeshire.

East Anglian English has probably always been a distinctive area. Fisiak (2001) discusses its distinctive character in Old English and Middle English times. It has also played an important role in the history of the language. If it is accepted that the English language came into being when West Germanic groups first started to settle in Britain, then East Anglia – just across the North Sea from the coastline of the original West Germanic-speaking area – has a serious claim to be the first place in the world where English was ever spoken. Subsequently, East Anglian English played an important role in the formation of Standard English. East Anglia was one of the most densely populated areas of England for many centuries, and until the Industrial Revolution Norwich was one of the three largest provincial cities in the country. Together with the proximity of East Anglia to London and large-scale migration from the area to London, this meant that a number of features that came to be part of Standard English had their origins in East Anglia. East Anglia also played an important role in the development of colonial Englishes, notably the American English of New England. The *New England short o* clearly has its origins in East Anglian pronunciations such as *home* /hʊm/; and *yod-dropping* (see below) and 'conjunction *do*' (see Trudgill, this volume) were also transmitted to the USA from this area. East Anglian English also formed part of the input for the formation of the Englishes of Australia and New Zealand (see Trudgill 1986; Trudgill et al. 2000). More recently, however, East Anglia, particularly the northern area, has become much more isolated, and its English has retained a number of conservative features.

As a distinctive linguistic area, East Anglia is clearly smaller today than it was two hundred years ago: it has shrunk over the past many decades under the influence of English from the London area. In the 19th century, it would probably have been reasonable to consider parts of Bedfordshire and Hertfordshire as linguistically East Anglian; now it would no longer be so (see Trudgill 1999a). On the other hand, there are still parts of Essex which are linguistically very similar to Norfolk and Suffolk.

Modern linguistic East Anglia consists of a core area together with surrounding transition zones. The core area, as defined by Trudgill (2001), consists of the counties of Norfolk and Suffolk, except for the Fenland areas of western Norfolk and northwestern Suffolk, plus northeastern Essex. The transition zones consist of the Norfolk and Suffolk Fens, together with eastern Cambridgeshire, central Essex, and a small area of northeastern Hertfordshire (see Map 1).

This definition of linguistic East Anglia is based on traditional dialect features (see Wells 1982) as presented in the Survey of English Dialects (SED). As far as Modern Dialects are concerned (see Trudgill 1999b), the transition zones of northeastern Hertfordshire, central Essex and southern Cambridgeshire can no longer be considered East Anglian. Within the core region, urban areas such as Norwich, the largest urban centre in the region, and Ipswich are still solidly East Anglian. Colchester, however, shows much southeastern influence; and the East Anglian character of King's Lynn and Thetford has been somewhat weakened by considerable in-migration from London and elsewhere.

1.2. Phonology

Within the core area of East Anglia, the biggest regional differentiation phonologically is between the north and the south. As indicated in Map 1, the northern area includes Norfolk, with the exception of some of the Fens, as well as the northeastern part of Suffolk as far south, approximately, as Southwold. The southern area includes the rest of Suffolk, and those areas of northeastern Essex which are still East Anglian-speaking. King's Lynn, Norwich, Yarmouth and Lowestoft are thus in the northern area, Ipswich and Colchester in the southern.

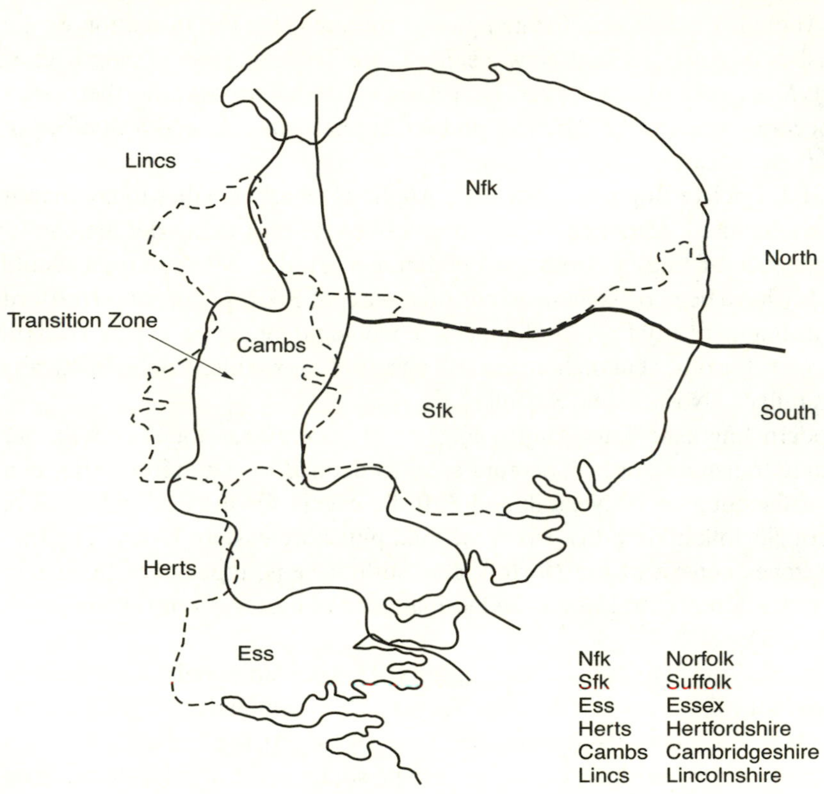

Map 1. East Anglia

2. Vowels

2.1. Short vowels

The system of short, checked vowels in modern East Anglia is the normal south-of-England six vowel system involving the lexical sets of: KIT, DRESS, TRAP, FOOT, STRUT, LOT.

KIT

The phonetic realisation of this vowel in the modern dialect is the same as in RP. Older speakers, however, have a closer realisation nearer to, but not as close as [i].

One of the most interesting features of the older East Anglian dialect short vowel system was that, unlike most other varieties, /ɪ/ did not occur at all in unstressed syllables. Unstressed /ə/ continues to be the norm to this day in words such as *wanted*, *horses*, *David*, *naked*, *hundred*. More striking, however, is the fact that /ə/ was the only vowel which could occur in any unstressed syllable. This was true not only in the case of word-final syllables in words such as *water*, *butter*, which of course also have /ə/ in RP, and in words such as *window*, *barrow*, which are pronounced /wɪndə, bærə/ in very many other forms of English, but also in items such as *very*, *money*, *city* which were /vɛrə, mʌnə, sɪtə/. In the modern dialect, dedialectalisation has taken place in that words from the *very* set are now pronounced with final /ɪ/ by older speakers and /iː/ by younger speakers, as is now usual throughout southern England.

The KIT vowel occurred not only in items such as *pit*, *bid* in the older dialect but also in a number of other words, such as *get*, *yet*, *head*, *again*. There is little predictability as to which items have or had the raised vowel, but in all the words concerned the vowel was followed by /n/, /t/ or /d/.

DRESS

The vowel /ɛ/ in the older dialect was a rather close vowel approaching [e]. During the course of this century, it has gradually opened until it is now much closer to [ɛ]. In Norwich, it is now also very retracted before /l/ and in the most modern accents has merged with /ʌ/ in this context, i.e. *hell* and *hull* are identical (Trudgill 1988).

In older forms of the dialect, /ɛ/ occurred not only in the expected *bet*, *help*, *bed*, etc., but also in a number of items which elsewhere have /æ/, such as *catch*, *have*/*has*/*had*.

In the traditional dialect of northern Norfolk, /ɛ/ has become /æ/ before /v/ and /ð/: *never* /nævə/, *together* /təgæðə/. In the older dialect, *shed* is /ʃʌd/.

TRAP

The vowel /æ/ appears to have undergone a certain amount of phonetic change. For older speakers for whom /ɛ/ was [e], /æ/ was closer to [ɛ], while in the modern dialect it is a good deal more open. In the urban dialect of Norwich it has now also undergone a further change involving diphthongisation in some phonological environments: *back* [bæɛk] (see further Trudgill 1974).

FOOT

The FOOT vowel /ʊ/ was rather more frequent in the older East Anglian dialect than in General English (Wells 1982). Middle English /ɔː/ and /ou/ remain distinct in the northern dialects e.g. *road* /ruːd/, *rowed* /rʌud/ (see further below). However, there has been a strong tendency in East Anglia for the /uː/ descended from Middle English /ɔː/ to be shortened to /ʊ/ in closed syllables. Thus *road* can rhyme with *good*, and we find pronunciations such as in *toad*, *home*, *stone*, *coat* /tʊd, hʊm, stʊn, kʊt/. This shortening does not normally occur before /l/, so *coal* is /kuːl/. The shortening process has clearly been a productive one. Norwich, for example, until the 1960s had a theatre known as *The Hippodrome* /hɪpədrʊm/, and trade names such as Kodachrome can be heard with pronunciations such as /kʊdəkrʊm/. The feature thus survives quite well in modern speech, but a number of words appear to have been changed permanently to the /uː/ set as a result of lexical transfer (see below). Trudgill (1974) showed that 29 different lexemes from this set occurred with /ʊ/.

The vowel /ʊ/ also occurs in *roof*, *proof*, *hoof* and their plurals, e.g. /rʊfs/. It also occurs in middle-class sociolects in *room*, *broom*; working-class sociolects tend to have the GOOSE vowel in these items.

In the older dialect, a number of FOOT words derived from Middle English /oː/ plus shortening followed the same route as *blood* and *flood* and had /ʌ/: *soot*, *roof* /sʌt, rʌf/.

STRUT

There have been clear phonetic developments over the past century in the phonetic realisation of this vowel. It has moved forward from an earlier fully back [ʌ] to a more recent low-central [ɐ], as in much of the south of England. The movement has not been nearly so extensive, however, as the actual fronting which has taken place in London (see Wells 1982: 305). This movement (see Trudgill 1986) started in the south of East Anglia and has gradually spread north, so that the vowel is backer in Norwich than in Ipswich, and backer in Ipswich than in Colchester. The Kings Lynn area has a distinctive closer quality to this vowel around [ə].

LOT

In the southern area, rounded [ɒ] is usual. In the older accents of the northern area unrounded [ɑ] is the norm, but this is gradually being replaced by the rounded vowel in the speech of younger people.

The lexical set associated with this vowel was formerly rather smaller in that, as in most of southern England, the lengthened vowel /ɔː/ was found before the front voiceless fricatives, as in *off*, *cloth*, *lost*. This feature survives to a certain extent, but mostly in working-class speech, and particularly in the word *off*. The word *dog* is also typically /dɔːg/. On the other hand, traditional dialect speakers also have LOT in *un-* and *under* rather than STRUT. *Nothing* also has LOT: /nɑθn/.

NURSE

Older forms of the dialect have an additional vowel in this sub-system. If we examine representations of words from the NURSE set in twentieth-century dialect literature, we find the following (for details of the dialect literature involved, see Trudgill 1996):

Item	**Dialect Spelling**
her	*har*
heard	*hard*
nerves	*narves*
herself	*harself*
service	*sarvice*
earn	*arn*
early	*arly*
concern	*consarn*
sir	*sar*
fur	*far*
daren't	*dussent*
first	*fust, fasst*
worse	*wuss*
church	*chuch, chatch*
purpose	*pappus*
turnip	*tannip*
further	*futher*
hurl	*hull*
turkey	*takkey*
turn	*tann*
hurting	*hatten*
nightshirt	*niteshat*
shirts	*shats*
girl	*gal*

On the subject of words such as these in East Anglian dialects, Forby (1830: 92) wrote:

> To the syllable *ur* (and consequently to *ir* and *or*, which have often the same sound) we give a pronunciation certainly our own.
>
> Ex. *Third word burn curse*
> *Bird curd dirt worse*
>
> It is one which can be neither intelligibly described, nor represented by other letters. It must be heard. Of all legitimate English sounds, it seems to come nearest to *open a* [the vowel of *balm*], or rather to the rapid utterance of the *a* in the word *arrow*, supposing it to be caught before it light on the *r*... *Bahd* has been used to convey our sound of *bird*. Certainly this gets rid of the danger of *r*; but the *h* must as certainly be understood to lengthen the sound of *a*; which is quite inconsistent with our snap-short utterance of the syllable. In short it must be heard.

My own observations of speakers this century suggest that earlier forms of East Anglian English had a checked vowel system consisting of seven vowels. The additional vocalic item, which I represent as /ɐ/, was a vowel somewhat more open than half-open, and slightly front of central, which occurred in the lexical set of *church*, *first*. Dialect literature, as we have seen, generally spells words from the lexical set of *first*, *church* as either as <fust> or <chatch>. The reason for this vacillation between <u> and <a> was that the vowel was in fact phonetically intermediate between /ʌ/ and /æ/. This additional vowel occurred in items descended from Middle English *ur*, *or* and *ir* in closed syllables. Words ending in open syllables, such as *sir* and *fur*, had /aː/, as did items descended from ME *er*, such as *earth* and *her* (as well as items descended from *ar* such as *part*, *cart*, of course). The vowel /ɜː/ did not exist in the dialect until relatively recently.

During the last fifty years, the /ɐ/ vowel has more or less disappeared. In my 1968 study of Norwich (Trudgill 1974), /ɐ/ was recorded a number of times, but the overwhelming majority of words from the relevant lexical set had the originally alien vowel /ɜː/. Only in lower working class speech was /ɐ/ at all common in 1968, and then only 25 percent of potential occurrences had the short vowel even in informal speech. The vowel did not occur at all in my 1983 corpus (Trudgill 1988).

The older checked stressed vowel system of East Anglian English was thus:

/ɪ/ *kit*, *get*	/ʊ/ *foot*, *home*, *roof*
/e/ *dress*, *catch*	/ʌ/ *strut*
/ɛ/ *trap*	/ɑ ~ ɒ/ *top*, *under*

/ɐ/ *church*

The newer short vowel system looks as follows:

/ɪ/ *kit*	/ʊ/ *foot, home, roof*
/ɛ/ *dress, get*	/ɐ/ *strut, under*
/æ/ *trap, catch*	/a ~ ɒ/ *top, off*

2.2. Upgliding diphthongs

Characteristic of all of the upgliding diphthongs, of which there is one more than in most accents of English (see below), is the phonetic characteristic that, unlike in other south-of-England varieties, the second element is most usually a fully close vowel, e.g. the FACE vowel is typically [æi] rather than [æɪ].

FLEECE

The /iː/ vowel is an upgliding diphthong of the type [ɪi], noticeably different from London [əɪ]. The modern accent demonstrates *happy-tensing*, and this vowel therefore also occurs in the modern dialects in the lexical set of *money*, *city*, etc. Unstressed *they* has /iː/ *Are they coming?* /aːðiːkʌmən/ (see also Trudgill, this volume). In the traditional dialect, *mice* was /miːs/, and *deaf* could be /diːf/.

FACE

In the traditional dialects of East Anglia, the Long Mid Mergers have not taken place (Wells 1982: 192–194). The vowel /æi/ in these lects occurs only in items descended from ME /ai/, while items descended from ME /aː/ have /eː/ = [eː ~ ɛː]. Thus pairs such as *days-daze*, *maid-made* are not homophonous. (The /eː/ vowel also occurred in the older dialect in a number of words descended from ME /ɛː/ such as *beans*, *creature* [kɹɛːʔə].) This distinction, which now survives only in the northern area, is currently being lost through a process of transfer of lexical items from /eː/ to /æi/ (Trudgill and Foxcroft 1978). The most local modern pronunciation of /æi/ is [æi], but qualities intermediate between this and RP [eɪ] occur in middle-class speech (see Trudgill 1974).

PRICE

There is considerable variation in the articulation of the /ai/ vowel, as described in detail for Norwich in Trudgill (1974, 1988). The most typical realisation is [ɐi], but younger speakers are increasingly favouring a variant approaching [ɑi] (see further below).

CHOICE

It is still possible to hear from older speakers certain words from this set, notably *boil*, with the PRICE vowel, although this is now very recessive. The vowel /oi/ itself ranges from the most local variant [ʊi] to a less local variant [ɔi], with a whole range of phonetically intermediate variants.

GOOSE

The vowel /ʉː/ is a central diphthong [ʉ̯ʉ] with more lip-rounding on the second element than on the first. Since northern East Anglia demonstrates total yod-dropping (see below), there is in this part of the area complete homophony between pairs of words which have this vowel, such as *dew* = *do*, *Hugh* = *who*, *cute* = *coot*. In northern East Anglia, many words in this set may also occur with the vowel /uː/ (see below).

GOAT

As we saw above, the Long Mid Mergers have not taken place in East Anglia. There are therefore two vowels at this point in the East Anglian vowel system. Paralleling the vestigial distinction in the front vowel system between the sets of *made* and *maid*, corresponding to the distinction between the ME monophthong and diphthong, there is a similar distinction in the back vowel system which, however, is by no means vestigial in the northern part of the area. The distinction is between /uː/ = [ʊu], descended from ME /ɔː/, and /ʌu/ = [ɐu], descended from ME /ou/. Thus pairs such as *moan* ≠ *mown*, *road* ≠ *rowed*, *nose* ≠ *knows*, *sole* ≠ *soul* are not homophonous.

ME /ɔː/ plus /l/ also gives /ʌu/, as in *hold*. Words such as *bowl* and *shoulder* have /au/ in the older dialect, however.

One further complication is that, in modern speech, adverbial *no* has /uː/ while the negative particle *no* has /ʌu/: *No, that's no good* /nʌu, ðæs nuː gʊd/.

There are two additional complications. One is that, as we have already seen, words descended from the ME monophthong may also have /ʊ/, i.e. *road* can be either/rʊd/ or /ruːd/.

Secondly, as was mentioned briefly above, many words from the set of GOOSE which are descended from ME /oː/ may have /uː/ rather than /ʉː/. That is, words such as *boot* may be pronounced either /bʉːt/ or /buːt/. In the latter case, they are of course then homophonous with words such as *boat*. Therefore *rood* may be homophonous either with *rude* or with *road* which, however, will not be homophonous with *rowed*.

It is probable that this alternation in the GOOSE set is the result of lexical transfer, perhaps under the influence of earlier forms of RP, from /ʉː/ to /uː/. Forms in /uː/ are more typical of middle-class than of working-class speech;

and phonological environment can also have some effect: /ʉː/ before /l/ as in *school* has much lower social status than it does before other consonants. Words which in my own lower-middle class Norwich speech have /ʉː/ rather than /uː/ include: *who*, *whose*, *do*, *soon*, *to*, *too*, *two*, *hoot*, *loot*, *root*, *toot*, *soup*, *chose*, *lose*, *loose*, *through*, *shoe*. I have no explanation at all for why, for example, *soon* and *moon* do not rhyme in my speech. There is also considerable individual variation: my mother has /uː/ in *chose* and *root*, for instance, and my late father had /uː/ in *who*. Note that this alternation never occurs in the case of those items such as *rule*, *tune*, *new* etc. which have historical sources other than ME/oː/; these words always have /ʉː/. For very many speakers, then, *rule* and *school* do not rhyme.

In summary:

rowed	/ʌu/
road	/uː/ ~ /ʊ/
rude	/ʉː/
rood	/ʉː/ ~ /uː/

Two modern developments should also be noted. First, the phonetic realisation of /uː/ in the northern area is currently undergoing a rather noticeable change (see below), with younger speakers favouring a fronter first element [ɵu] (see Trudgill 1988; Labov 1994). This is more advanced in Lowestoft, Gorleston and Yarmouth than in Norwich. Secondly, in the southern zone, the *moan: mown* distinction is now very recessive, so that for most speakers /ʌu/ is used in both lexical sets and /uː/ has disappeared. As a consequence, GOOSE words can no longer alternate in their pronunciation.

MOUTH

The most typical realisation of the /æu/ vowel in the northern area is [æʉ], although there is some variation in the quality of the first element, e.g. qualities such as [əʉ] can also be heard. In the south a more typical realisation is [ɛʉ].

2.3. Long monophthongs

NEAR/SQUARE

These two lexical sets are not distinct in northern East Anglian English. The most usual realisation of this single vowel, which I symbolise as /ɛː/, is [ẹ ~ ɛ̣ː]. It is possible that some speakers thus pronounce items such as *fierce* and *face* identically. In the southern area, NEAR is [ɪə], SQUARE is [ɛː].

THOUGHT/NORTH/FORCE
The /ɔː/ vowel has a realisation which is approximately [ɔː] without, however, very much lip-rounding. It occurs in items such as *poor*, *pore*, *paw*. As is typical of more conservative south-of-England varieties, it also occurs frequently in the lexical set of CLOTH.

START/BATH/PALM
In its most local realisation the vowel /aː/ is a very front vowel approaching [aː], but in more middle-class speech more central variants occur. Typical London and RP back variants around [ɑː] are not found. As we saw above, in the older dialect this vowel also occurs in *sir*, *fur*, *earth*, *her*.

NURSE/CURE
It was pointed out before that the vowel /ɜː/ is a relative newcomer into East Anglian English. Its phonetic realisation is perhaps a little closer than in RP [ɜː]. It occurs in all items from the set of NURSE, but it also occurs in words from the CURE set that are descended from ME /iu/ or /eu/ before r, so that *sure* rhymes with *her* (see also below on 'smoothing'). Note also that, because of *yod-dropping* (see section 3), the following are homophones in northern East Anglia: *pure* = *purr*, *cure* = *cur*, *fury* = *furry*.

2.4. Smoothing

We have already noted that earlier ingliding diphthongs have become monophthongs: /ɪə/ > /ɛː/ in *near*, /ɛə/ > /ɛː/ in *square*. This is also true of /ʊə/ > /ɔː/ in *poor*, /ɔə/ > /ɔː/ in *pore*, and (presumably) /ʉə/ > /ɜː/ in *pure*. This development has also occurred in original triphthongs, giving *tower* /taː/ and *fire* /fɑː/ in working-class speech – the vowel /ɑː/ occurs only as a result of smoothing. In middle class speech, however, in which /aː/ is more central, /ɑː/ does not occur, and *tar* and *tower* are homophonous.

This historical process involving lowering before /ə/ and then loss of /ə/ is paralleled by a synchronic phonological process which carries across morpheme and word boundaries, and extends to additional vowels. (In examining the following examples, recall that East Anglia has /ə/ in most unstressed syllables where many other accents have /ɪ/.) The full facts can be summarised as follows:

Vowel + /ə/	Example	Output
/iː/	*seeing*	/sɛːn/
/æi/	*playing*	/plæːn/
/ai/	*trying*	/traːn ~ trɑːn/
/oi/	*annoying*	/ənɔːn/
/ʉː/	*do it*	/dɜːt/
/uː/	*going*	/gɔːn/
/ou/	*know it*	/nɒːt/
/æu/	*allow it*	/əlaːt/

Thus, *do it* is homophonous with *dirt* and *going* rhymes with *lawn*. The vowels /æː/, /ɑː/, /ɒː/ occur only as a result of smoothing. Interestingly, some speakers in Norwich pronounce *towel* as /tɜːl/. Smoothing is most typical of the northern zone of East Anglia, but is currently spreading southwards (Trudgill 1986).

3. Consonants

/p, t, k/

Intervocalic and word-final /p, k/ are most usually glottalised. This is most noticeable in intervocalic position where there is simultaneous oral and glottal closure, with the oral closure then being released inaudibly prior to the audible release of the glottal closure, thus *paper* [pæipʔə], *baker* [bæikʔə].

This also occurs in the case of /t/, as in *later* [læitʔə], but more frequently, especially in the speech of younger people, glottaling occurs: [læiʔə]. East Anglia (see Trudgill 1974) appears to have been one of the centres from which glottaling has diffused geographically in modern English English. Trudgill (1988) showed for Norwich that [ʔ] is the usual realisation of intervocalic and word-final /t/ in casual speech, and that it is now also increasingly diffusing into more formal styles. There is an interesting constraint on the use of [ʔ] and [tʔ] in East Anglian English in that these allophones cannot occur before [ə] if another instance follows. Thus *lit it* has to be [lɪtəʔ] rather than *[lɪʔəʔ].

In /nt/ clusters, the /n/ is frequently deleted if (and only if) the /t/ is realised as glottal stop: *twenty* [twɛʔɪi], *plenty* [plɛʔɪi], *going to* [gɔːʔə].

/d/

Northeastern Norfolk Traditional Dialects had word-final /d/ merged with /t/ in unstressed syllables, e.g. *hundred* /hʌndrət/, *David* /deːvət/.

/kl, gl/
In the older dialect, these clusters could be pronounced /tl, dl/: *clock* [tlɑkʔ], *glove* [dlʌv].

/θr, ʃr/
The older East Anglian dialect had /tr/ from original /θr/ and /sr/ from original /ʃr/. Thus *thread* was pronounced /trɪd/, *threshold* /trɑʃl/; and *shriek* /sri:k/. My own surname appears to be an East Anglian form of *Threadgold.* /tw/ could also occur for original /θw/, as in the placename *Thwaite* /twæit/.

/h/
Traditional Dialects in East Anglia did not have *h-dropping*. Norwich and Ipswich, however, have had h-dropping for many generations. Trudgill (1974) showed that in Norwich in 1968 levels of h-dropping correlated with social class and style, ranging from 0 percent for the Middle Middle Class (the highest social class group) in formal speech to 61 percent for Lower Working Class informants in casual speech. It is interesting that these levels are much lower than in other parts of the country, and that hypercorrect forms do not occur.

/v/
The present-tense verb-form *have* is normally pronounced /hæ ~ hɛ ~ hə ~ ə/, i.e. without a final /v/, unless the next word begins with a vowel: *Have you done it?* /hɛ jə dʌn ət/. This has the consequence that, because of smoothing (see above), some forms involving *to have* and *to be* are homophonous: *we're coming* /wɛ: kʌmən/, *we've done it* /wɛ: dʌn ət/.

In many of the local varieties spoken in the southeast of England in the 18th and 19th centuries, prevocalic /v/ in items like *village* was replaced by /w/. Most reports focus on word-initial /w/ in items such as *village*, *victuals*, *vegetables*, *vermin*. It would seem than that [v] occurred only in non-prevocalic position, i.e. in items such as *love*, with the consequence that [w] and [v] were in complementary distribution and /w/ and /v/ were no longer distinct. Ellis (1889) describes the southeast of 19th century England as the "land of wee" and Wright (1905: 227) says that "initial and medial v has become w in mid-Buckinghamshire, Norfolk, Suffolk, Essex, Kent, east Sussex". Wakelin (1981: 95–96) writes that the SED materials show that: "In parts of southern England, notably East Anglia and the south-east, initial and medial [v] may appear as [w], cf. V.7.19 *vinegar*, IV.9.4 *viper* (under *adder*), V.8.2 *victuals* (under *food*). […] The use of [w] for [v] was a well-known Cockney feature up to the last century."

Wakelin (1984: 79) also says that "Old East Anglian and south-eastern dialect is noted for its pronunciation of initial /v/ as /w/ in, e.g., *vinegar*, *viper*; a very old feature, which was preserved in Cockney up to the last century". The SED materials show spontaneous responses to VIII.3.2 with *very* with initial /w/ in Grimston, North Elmham, Ludham, Reedham, and Pulham St Mary, Norfolk. Norfolk is one of the areas in which this merger lasted longest. The merger is 'remembered' by the local community decades after its actual disappearance: most local people in the area over a certain age 'know' that *village* used to be pronounced *willage* and that *very* used to be pronounced *werra*, but discussions with older Norfolk people suggest that it was in widespread normal unselfconscious use only until the 1920s. We can assume that it died out in the southern part of the East Anglian area even earlier. The fact that modern dialect writers still use the feature is therefore highly noteworthy. For example, Michael Brindred in his local dialect column in the Norwich-based Eastern Daily Press of August 26th, 1998 writes *anniversary* <anniwarsary>.

/l/

/l/ was traditionally clear in all positions in northern rural East Anglian dialects, and this can still be heard from speakers born before 1920, but modern speech now has the same distribution of clear and dark allophones as RP. Vocalisation of /l/ does not occur in the north but is increasingly common in the south of the region.

/r/

East Anglian English is non-rhotic, although the SED did record a few rhotic tokens on the Essex peninsulas.

Intrusive /r/ is the norm in East Anglia. It occurs invariably where the vowels /ɛː, aː, ɔː, ə/ occur before another vowel both across word and morpheme boundaries: *drawing* /drɔːrən/, *draw it* /drɔːrət/. Because of the high level of reduction of unstressed vowels to /ə/ (see above), intrusive /r/ occurs in positions where it would be unusual in other accents: e.g. *Give it to Anne* /gɪv ət tər æn/. Linking /r/ is essentially the same phenomenon and occurs additionally after /ɜː/.

/j/

The northern zone (as well as adjacent areas of Cambridgeshire, Lincolnshire and even parts of Leicestershire and Bedfordshire, see Trudgill 1999a) demonstrates total yod-dropping (Wells 1982). That is, earlier /j/ has gone missing before /ʉː/ not only after /r/, as in *rule*, as in all accents of English; and not only after /l, s, n, t, d, θ/, as in *lute*, *sue*, *news*, *tune*, *duke*, *enthuse*, as in many accents of English; but after all consonants. Pronunciations without /j/ are usual in items such as *music*, *pew*, *beauty*, *few*, *view*, *cue*, *hew*. The word *ewe* now begins with /j/, although this was formerly not the case, and *education* is now /ɛdʒəkæiʃn/ although it was formerly /ɛdəkeːʃn/. The southern part of East Anglia does not have yod-dropping but typically has /ɪʉː/ rather than /jʉː/ in such words.

4. Rhythm and intonation

East Anglian English has a distinctive rhythm. This is due to the fact that stressed syllables tend to be longer than in RP, and unstressed syllables correspondingly shorter. The reduction of unstressed vowels to schwa appears to be part of this same pattern. Indeed, unstressed syllables consisting of schwa may disappear altogether in non-utterance final position, e.g. *forty two* [fɔːʔtʉː]; *what are you on holiday?* [wɑʔ jɑːn hɑːldə]; *half past eight* [haːːpəs æɪʔ]; *have you got any coats?* [hæjə gɑʔnə kʊʔs]; *shall I?* [ʃælə].

Intonation in yes-no questions is also distinctive. Such questions begin on a low level tone followed by high-level tone on the stressed syllable and subsequent syllables:

[wɑʔ jɑːn hɑːldə]

— —

— —

What are you on holiday?

Exercises and study questions

1. Compile a list of those phonological features that appear on your reading of the chapter to be most distinctive of East Anglian speech overall, and that mark it out from other English accents.
2. Within East Anglia, identify those features which support the idea of there being a north-south distinction in the accents of the region.
3. What are the features of East Anglian accents that place them firmly among those of southern England?
4. List as many features of East Anglian accents as possible that are in the process of changing.

5. Study in depth the history of the 'Long Mid Mergers', discussed in the chapter in relation to East Anglian FACE and GOAT vowels.
6. Investigate the 'land of wee' in linguistics and in literature. (The work of Dickens might be particularly fruitful for the latter.)

Selected references

Please consult the General references for titles mentioned in the text but not included in the references below. For a full bibliography see the accompanying CD-ROM.

Fisiak, Jacek
2001 Old East Anglian: a problem in Old English dialectology. In: Fisiak and Trudgill (eds.), 18–38.

Fisiak, Jacek and Peter Trudgill (eds.)
2001 *East Anglian English*. Woodbridge: Boydell and Brewer.

Forby, Robert
1830 *The Vocabulary of East Anglia*. London: J.B. Nichols and Son.

Trudgill, Peter
1988 Norwich revisited: recent changes in an English urban dialect. *English World-Wide* 9: 33–49.

Trudgill, Peter
1996 Two hundred years of dedialectalisation: the East Anglian short vowel system. In: Mats Thelander (ed.), *Samspel och variation*, 469–478. Uppsala: Uppsala Universitet.
1999a Norwich: endogenous and exogenous linguistic change. In: Foulkes and Docherty (eds.), 124–140.
1999b *The Dialects of England*. Second edition. Oxford: Blackwell.
2001 Modern East Anglia as a dialect area. In: Fisiak and Trudgill (eds.), 1–12.

Trudgill, Peter and Tina Foxcroft
1978 On the sociolinguistics of vocalic mergers: Transfer and approximation in East Anglia. In: Trudgill (ed.), 69–79.

Trudgill, Peter, Elizabeth Gordon, Gillian Lewis and Margaret MacLagan
2000 The role of drift in the formation of native-speaker southern hemisphere Englishes: Some New Zealand evidence. *Diachronica: International Journal for Historical Linguistics* 17: 111–138.

Wakelin, Martyn F.
1984 Rural dialects in England. In: Trudgill (ed.), 70–93.

The dialects in the South of England: phonology

Ulrike Altendorf and Dominic Watt

1. Introduction

From a dialectological point of view, the South of England falls into three main dialect areas: the Southeast, centred on the Home Counties area; the Southwest of England, which covers the area known as the "West Country"; and East Anglia, which comprises Norfolk and Suffolk, together with adjacent parts of Essex and Cambridgeshire. This article will focus on two of these three areas: the Southeast and the Southwest.

2. North and South

According to Trudgill in his *The Dialects of England* (1999), the major dialect boundary in England today is the line separating the North from the South. This line also has an acknowledged folk-linguistic status since it is used "informally to divide 'southerners' from 'northerners'" (Trudgill 1999: 80; see also Wales 2002). In linguistic terms, it consists of two major isoglosses marking the northern limit of two historical developments which are referred to by Wells (1982) as the FOOT-STRUT split and as BATH broadening. The FOOT-STRUT split is a sound change by which the Middle English short vowel *u* underwent a split resulting in phonemic contrast between [ʊ] and [ʌ] in words such as *put* and *putt*. The term BATH broadening refers to a historical process by which /a/ preceding a voiceless fricative, a nasal + /s, t/, or syllable-final /r/, was lengthened (e.g. from [baθ] to [baːθ]) in the late 17th century, and then later retracted to [ɑː] (giving [bɑːθ]) sometime in the 19th century. These changes mark the vowel systems of the South but are absent from the North. Local accents in the South therefore tend to have separate phonemes for the vowels in FOOT and STRUT and a long (in popular terminology "broad") vowel /ɑː/ in BATH (although the situation is more complicated in the Southwest; see section 5.5.). Their northern counterparts have the same vowel – /ʊ/ – in both FOOT and STRUT, and a short front ("flat") /a/ vowel in BATH. According to the *Survey of English Dialects* (SED) (see e.g. Chambers and Trudgill 1998, Fig. 8-I; here: Map 1), the FOOT-STRUT isogloss runs from the Severn estuary in the West to the Wash in the East. The BATH isogloss follows a similar path, but at its western end starts somewhat further south, crossing the FOOT-STRUT line in Herefordshire, then continuing to run north of it up to the Wash.

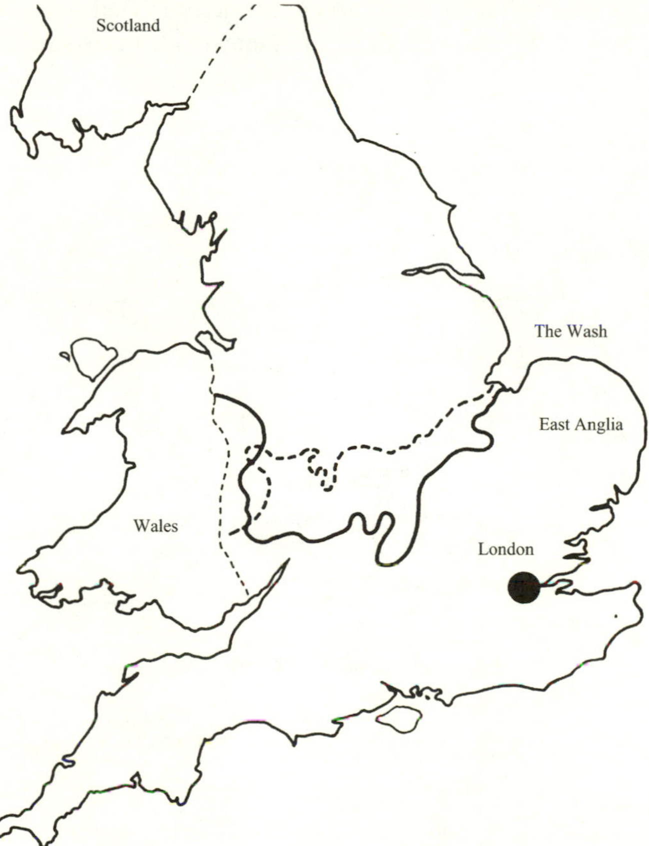

Map 1: England, showing the southern limit of [ʊ] in *some* (solid line) and the short vowel [a] in *chaff* (broken line

3. Southeast and Southwest

The major subdivision of southern accents into Southeastern and Southwestern accents is based on the pronunciation of post-vocalic /r/ in syllable-final pre-pausal and pre-consonantal position, as in *far* or *farmer*. In these positions /r/ is preserved in local accents of the Southwest, whereas it is absent or rapidly disappearing from accents in the Southeast. In the Southeast, rhoticity used to be a characteristic of rural accents in Kent, Sussex and Surrey where it has been recessive for quite a while (see Trudgill 1999: 27, Map 5 and 1999: 55, Map 12; here: Map 2 and Map 3). According to Wells (1982: 341), "traces of variable rhoticity may be found" in Reading, formerly in Berkshire. As Trudgill (1999: 54) puts it, "[e]very year the r-pronouncing area gets smaller".

Map 2. Arm; r = [r] pronounced in *arm* etc.; (r) = some [rs] pronounced

Map 3. Areas where [r] is pronounced in *arm*

4. The Southeast

4.1. The Home Counties Modern Dialect area

The Southeast of England is here loosely equated with the Home Counties, these being the counties adjacent to London: Kent, Surrey, East and West Sussex, Essex, Hertfordshire, Hampshire, Buckinghamshire, Berkshire, and Bedfordshire. In the past, however, the accents of the Home Counties used to belong to very different dialect areas. Trudgill (1999: 44–47) labels these traditional dialect areas the Southeast (Berkshire, north-eastern Hampshire, Sussex, Kent, Surrey), the Central East (parts of Northamptonshire, Cambridgeshire, non-metropolitan Hertfordshire and Essex) and the Eastern Counties (Norfolk, Suffolk, north-eastern Essex) plus London, which was considered a "separate branch of the Eastern dialects" (Trudgill 1999: 46). Note that the Eastern Counties are also referred to as East Anglia (see Wells 1982: 335), an area treated separately in this handbook.

The accents of these areas have been undergoing extensive dialect levelling in recent decades (see e.g. Kerswill 2002). As a result, a considerable part of these different dialect areas are now joined together to form one large modern dialect area, called by Trudgill the "Home Counties Modern Dialect area" (see Trudgill 1999: 65, Map 18; here: Map 4).

> [...] the non-traditional dialect area of London has now expanded enormously to swallow up the old Southeast area, part of East Anglia, most of the eastern Southwest, and most of the Central East, of which now only the South Midlands remain. The new London-based area we call the Home Counties Modern Dialect area. (Trudgill 1999: 80)

The exact degree of linguistic uniformity within this area is still unclear. Research on urban accents in the Southeast (see e.g. Williams and Kerswill 1999; Altendorf 2003) indeed points to an increase in homogeneity, in particular with regard to middle-class accents. However, local and regional accent differences also persist (see also section 4.2.).

4.2. Dialect levelling in the Southeast

The restructuring of the Southeastern dialect area is in large part due to processes of linguistic convergence (e.g. Williams and Kerswill 1999; Kerswill 2002). These processes have, it is argued, been promoted by an increase in geographical mobility in the second half of the 20th century. Mobility and migration have taken place in three different directions:

(1) Trend I: Centrifugal migration:
Londoners have been moving out of the capital since the Second World War, during which time London was the most heavily bombed city in Britain. The Blitz forced millions of families out of their London homes into the country. After the war, and for less dramatic reasons, around one million overspill Londoners were re-housed in municipal re-housing schemes designed to decentralize the metropolitan population. For this purpose, a number of new towns, among them Milton Keynes, Stevenage, Hemel Hempstead, Bracknell and Basildon, were founded within an eighty-kilo-

metre radius of London. In more recent years, young families and old-age pensioners have also often moved out of the city. Young families have been moving into the London suburbs or the neighbouring Home Counties to bring up their children in a safer and more pleasant environment. Old-age pensioners have been moving away to realize, where feasible, the English dream of buying a house by the seaside or a cottage in the country, or for less idealistic motives such as unaffordable London rents and living costs, spiralling crime and alienation. Lately, the increased necessity and willingness to commute has further enhanced the interchange between London and elsewhere.

Map 4. Modern Dialect areas

(2) Trend II: Centripetal migration (Moving to the Southeast and the "North-South divide"):
Since the economic revival of the Thatcher era, employment growth in Southeastern England has outstripped that in the rest of the United Kingdom. The media regularly report on the "North-South divide", a term used to imply stronger economic growth and higher living standards in the South of England than in the North. This economic prosperity has attracted many (work) migrants, mostly to Southeastern areas outside London. The population in these areas has therefore grown at a faster rate than in the rest of the country. Today, about one third of the population of the United Kingdom lives in Southeast England.

(3) Trend III: Internal migration within the Southeast:
As people resident in the Southeast now tend to change their place of work more often than they used to, there has been a resultant increase in the levels of admixture of the population within the region. These processes of mobility have increased face-to-face interaction among speakers of different accents. This kind of communicative situation tends to bring about short-term accommodation among the interlocutors, which in turn can then lead to long-term accommodation, accent convergence and change, providing that attitudinal factors are favourable. In addition, mobility has been shown to weaken network ties and to promote the diffusion of "new" variants. In the Southeast, these processes have been dominated by the "London element". Faced with a choice between a London variant and one associated with a rural or provincial accent, most young speakers have tended to opt for the former. This is likely to be particularly true for those young professionals who have been moving to the Southeast from other parts of Britain. To employ a term coined in the 1980s, a metropolitan accent is higher on "street cred" than a provincial one. This does not mean, however, that local accent features have been completely lost. The dialect survey by Williams and Kerswill (1999), for instance, has shown that there are still qualitative and quantitative differences between the accents of adolescents in the two Southeastern towns of Milton Keynes and Reading.

4.3. London as "innovator"

An important aspect in the linguistic development and folk-linguistic perception of the Southeast is the presence of the capital London within this area. London has a long tradition as a source of linguistic innovation for accents of the surrounding area as well as for RP itself. In recent years, a number of London working-class variants have not only been spreading to areas outside London but also to higher social classes, including the RP-speaking upper and upper middle classes. Wells describes this trend in a series of articles, in one of which he states that "some of the changes … can reasonably be attributed to influence from Cockney – often overtly despised, but covertly imitated" (Wells 1994: 205). This development is currently exciting a high degree of public attention.

Another phenomenon connected with the Southeast of England which is attracting much public attention is the occurrence of variants associated with London English in urban accents as distant from Southeast England as Hull (in east Yorkshire) and Glasgow (in central Scotland). These variants are, in particular, T-glottalling, TH-fronting and labio-dental [ʋ] (for a more detailed discussion of these variants, see section 4.6.). The British media have had a tendency to attribute, in a very simplistic way, the presence of these features in the speech of younger speakers of these accents to the direct influence of metropolitan London English. This, some media observers believe, is linked closely to the popularity throughout the United Kingdom of the London-based television soap opera *EastEnders*, which has for nearly two decades been one of Britain's most popular television programmes. A product of this alleged connection is the label *Jockney* – a blend of *Jock* (a nickname for a Scotsman) and *Cockney* – which has been used by some journalists to describe a new form of Glaswegian dialect borrowing from the television series *EastEnders*. However, in view of (a) the substantial body of evidence which points to the crucial role of face-to-face interaction in the transmission of changes in pronunciation, and (b) the continuing absence of any compelling evidence of the adoption of innovative forms as a direct consequence of television viewing, it is problematic to attribute the occurrence of these variants in accents outside Southeast England to the dissemination of London English in public broadcasting. Furthermore, it does not seem very likely that attitudes toward London English among speakers in cities like Hull and Glasgow are generally favourable (for more detailed discussion, see Foulkes and Docherty 1999: 11; Williams and Kerswill 1999: 161–162). In any case, many of the so-called London variants have long existed in the accents of areas surrounding cities such as Glasgow and Norwich, and appear more likely to have originated from accents of the immediate vicinity than to have spread from London (see e.g. Trudgill [1999]) on the antiquity of T-glottalling in geographically dispersed regions of the British Isles).

4.4. "Estuary English"

The changes described above are often referred to as being characteristic of Estuary English, a term coined by David Rosewarne in 1984. He defines it as follows:

> 'Estuary English' is a variety of modified regional speech. It is a mixture of non-regional and local Southeastern English pronunciation and intonation. If one imagines a continuum with RP and London speech at either end, 'Estuary English' speakers are to be found grouped in the middle ground (Rosewarne 1984: 29).

Since the appearance of Rosewarne's article, Estuary English has been discussed among laypeople and linguists with increasing frequency and unreduced controversy, although linguists have tended to adopt the term as shorthand rather more sceptically than have the general public (see e.g. Przedlacka 2002; Altendorf 2003). Journalists and literary authors make frequent use of the term to label a number of different and divergent trends. For example:

(1) socio-phonetic changes within the accents of Southeastern England in the direction of a supra-local regional accent (see also section 4.1.).

(2) the social spread of London working-class variants into higher social classes, including the advanced version of RP (see also section 4.3.).

(3) the situation-related use of London working-class variants by speakers who are otherwise speakers of RP.

(4) the retention of Southeastern regional accent features by speakers who would otherwise have been expected to become speakers of adoptive RP.

(5) the occurrence of variants which are (rightly or wrongly) associated with Southeastern England in accents in which they were not used before (see also section 4.3.).

The existence of these developments, with the exception of (5), is not disputed by linguists; what they dispute is the practice (a) of subsuming all these developments under the same name, (b) of choosing a new name to describe them, and (c) of choosing the particular name 'Estuary English'. With regard to the choice of name, Trudgill (1999) remarks:

> This [Estuary English] is an inappropriate term which [...] has become widely accepted. It is inappropriate because it suggests that we are talking about a new variety, which we are not; and because it suggests that this is a variety of English confined to the banks of the Thames Estuary, which it is not. (Trudgill (1999: 80)

With regard to choosing a new name, Wells (1997) remarks:

> Estuary English is a new name. But it is not a new phenomenon. It is the continuation of a trend that has been going on for five hundred years or more – the tendency for features of popular London speech to spread out geographically (to other parts of the country) and socially (to higher social classes). (Wells 1997: 47)

Here, Wells touches on one of the central aspects of the Estuary English controversy. To the layperson, the situation has changed in such a way (and/or is brought to his/her attention in such a way) that it is perceived as a new phenomenon requiring a new name. For the linguist, on the other hand, the current linguistic situation is just another phase within a longer historical process which does not merit a distinct designation, at least no more so than any other phase in the development of any particular accent.

4.5. Southeastern phonology: vowels and diphthongs

Table 1 shows the inventory of London vowels and diphthongs on the basis of Wells (1982: 304). For the purposes of comparison, Table 2 gives an overview of the variants used by adolescent speakers from the Southeast of England, including London, in the late 1990s. The forms for Milton Keynes and Reading are taken from Williams and Kerswill (1999: 143), those for London from Tollfree (1999: 165) and, in individual cases, from Altendorf (2003). Altendorf's study covers fewer variables and will only be cited when results do not tally with those reported by Tollfree.

Table 1. London vowels – summary

KIT	ɪ	FLEECE	ɪi	NEAR	iə
DRESS	e	FACE	ʌɪ	SQUARE	eə
TRAP	æ	PALM	ɑː	START	ɑː
LOT	ɒ	THOUGHT	oː, ɔə	NORTH	oː, ɔə
STRUT	ʌ	GOAT	ʌʊ	FORCE	oː, ɔə
FOOT	ʊ	GOAL	ɒʊ	CURE	uə
BATH	ɑː	GOOSE	ʉː	happY	ɪi
CLOTH	ɒ	PRICE	ɑɪ	lettER	ə
NURSE	ɜː	CHOICE	ɔɪ	commA	ə
		MOUTH	æʊ		

happY

Accents in the South of England have undergone happY tensing, a term coined by Wells (1982: 257–258) to describe a historical process by which the short final [ɪ] in happY has been replaced by a closer vowel of the [i(:)] type. There is still uncertainty about the exact phonetic quality of [i(:)] but the general consensus is that it patterns with FLEECE rather than KIT. In addition, London and Southeastern accents have diphthongal happY variants. With regard to these variants, the general socio-phonetic principle is: the more central the starting-point, the more basilectal the variant. The most basilectal variant is [əi] with a fully central starting-point. Suburban working-class speakers and middle-class speakers use a variant with a less central starting point, which we have chosen to transcribe as [ᵊi].

Table 2. The vowels of London, Milton Keynes and Reading – summary

STANDARD LEXICAL SET	**London** (middle class)	**Milton Keynes** (middle class and working class)	**Reading** (middle class and working class)
KIT	ɪ ~ ̈ɪ	ɪ > ɪ̣ ~ ị	ɪ > ɪ̣ ~ ẹ
DRESS	ɛ ~ ɛ̣	ɛ̣ > ẹ	ɛ̣ > ẹ
TRAP	æ	a ~ ạ	a ~ a̠
LOT	ɒ ~ ɒ̈	ɒ̣	ɒ̣ ~ ɑ
STRUT	ɐ ~ ʌ̟	ʌ > ʌ̟ ~ ɐ	ʌ > ʌ̟ ~ ɐ ~ ə̣ː
FOOT	ʊ ~ ʊ̹̈ (Tollfree) ɵ (Altendorf)	ɵ > ʊ̟ ~ ø̠ ~ ʏ	ɵ > ʊ̟ ~ ø̠ ~ ʏ
BATH	ɑː ~ ɑ̟ː ~ ɑ̹ː	ɑː > ɑ̟ː ~ a̠ː	ɑ̟ː > a̠ː
CLOTH	ɒ ~ ɒ̈	ɒ̣	ɒ̣ ~ ɑ
NURSE	ɜː ~ əː	ə̣ː	ə̣ː
FLEECE	iː~ ̈i(ː) (Tollfree) iː ~ ɪi > ᵊi > əi (Altendorf)	ᶦi > ᵊi	iː ~ ᶦi > ᵊi
FACE	eɪ ~ ẹɪ ~ ẹ̈ɪ	ɛi > æɪ ~ ɐɪ ~ ẹɪ	ɛi > æi ~ ẹɪ
PALM	ɑː ~ ɑ̟ ~ ɑ̹	ɑː > ɑ̟ː ~ a̠ː	ɑ̟ː > a̠ː
THOUGHT	ɔː ~ o̟ː	ọː > oʊ̠	ọː > oʊ̠
GOAT	ʌʊ(ʷ) ~ ɤʊ ~ ɤə ~ ə̣ʊ (Tollfree) əʊ ~ ɐʉ > ɐʊ (Altendorf)	əʏ ~ ɐʏ ~ əɪ ~ ɐɪ	əʏ ~ əɪ ~ ə̟ʏ ~ əʊ̟

Table 2. (continued) The vowels of London, Milton Keynes and Reading – summary

STANDARD LEXICAL SET	**London** (middle class)	**Milton Keynes** (middle class and working class)	**Reading** (middle class and working class)
GOAL	ɒʊ(ʷ) ~ ɒɤ ~ a̠ʊ	ʌʊ > ɔ̝ʊ	ʌʊ > ɔ̝ʊ
GOOSE	u̟(ʷ) : ~ ʉː ~ ʉ̝ː (Tollfree) ʉː ~ ʏː > ɨː ~ ɪː (Altendorf)	ʉː ~ ʉ̟ː ~ ʏː ~ yː > ᵊʉ̟ː	ʉː ~ ʉ̟ː ~ ʏː ~ yː > ᵊʉ̟ː
PRICE	aɪ ~ a̠ɪ ~ äɪ	ɑɪ > ɑ̟ɪ ~ ɑː ~ ɔɪ ~ ʌ̟ɪ	ɑɪ ~ ɔɪ ~ ʌ̟ɪ > ɑː
CHOICE	ɔɪ ~ oɪ	ɔ̝ɪ ~ ɔɪ	ɔ̝ɪ ~ ɔɪ
MOUTH	aʊ ~ aɤ (Tollfree) aʊ ~ æʊ (Altendorf)	aʊ > aː ~ ɛː ~ æʊ	aʊ > aː ~ ɛɪ ~ ɛʊ̟
NEAR	ɪː ~ ɪᵊ	e̝ː ~ eə	e̝ː ~ eə
SQUARE	ɛ̝ː(ᵊ) ~ e̝ː(ᵊ)	ɛː ~ ɛ̝ə	ɛː ~ ɛ̝ə
START	ɑː > ɑ̟ː ~ ɑ̹	ɑː > ɑ̟ː ~ a̠ː	ɑ̟ː > a̠ː
NORTH	ɔː ~ o̟ː	o̝ː > oʊ̠	o̝ː > oʊ̠
FORCE	ɔː ~ o̟ː	o̝ː > oʊ̠	o̝ > oʊ̠
CURE	jʉ̝ə ~ jʊ̹ə ~ jɔ̝ː	jo̝ː	jo̝ː
happY	i(ː) (Tollfree) i(ː) > ᵊi (Altendorf)	i̝	i̝
lettER	ə ~ ə̝	ɒː ~ ə̝	ɐ ~ ə̝
horsES	ɪ ~ ɪ̈	ɪ	ɪ
commA	ə ~ ə̝	ɒ̟ː ~ ə̝	ɐ ~ ə̝

FLEECE, FACE, PRICE, CHOICE, GOOSE, GOAT, MOUTH

If described with reference to traditional RP, London and Southeastern long vowels and diphthongs are involved in a diphthong shift which Labov (1994: 170) describes as "the closest replication of the Great Vowel Shift that can take place under the present conditions". In addition, there is social variation within the Southeastern system with working-class variants being even more advanced than their middle-class counterparts (see Table 3).

Note that Wells (1982: 302–303) defines Popular London (PL) as the accent of suburban working-class speakers and Cockney as the accent of the inner-London working class.

Table 3. London Diphthong Shift (adapted from Wells 1982: 308, 310)

RP:	iː	eɪ	aɪ	ɔɪ	ɑʊ	əʊ	uː
	↘	↘	↘	↘	↙	↙	↙
PL:	ɪi	ʌɪ	ɑɪ	ɔ̥ɪ	æʊ	ʌʊ	ʊʉ
	↘	↘	↘	↘	↙	↙	↙
Cockney:	əi	aɪ	ɒɪ	oɪ	æː	a - ʊ	əʉ ~ ʉː

FLEECE
The London and Southeastern FLEECE variant is a diphthong. The general socio-phonetic principle is again: the more central the starting-point, the more basilectal the variant. The most basilectal variant is [əi] with a full central starting-point. Suburban working-class speakers and middle-class speakers use a variant with a less central starting-point, which we transcribe as [ᵊi].
GOOSE
London and Southeastern English have monophthongal and diphthongal GOOSE variants. The occurrence of the monophthongal variants is favoured by preceding /j/ and disfavoured by following dark [ɫ].

In the 1980s, the most common Mainstream RP variant was reported to be a "slight glide" (Gimson 1984: 192) of the [ʊu] type or a more central monophthong of the [y] kind. If the first element of the diphthong was further centralized or the monophthong further fronted, Gimson did not regard the resulting variants as representative of RP but as characteristic of Southeastern English. This principle still applies in the case of the diphthongal GOOSE variants. The general socio-phonetic principle is the same as for happY and FLEECE: the more centralized the first element of the diphthong, the more basilectal the variant. The most basilectal variant is [əu] with a full central starting-point. Suburban working-class and middle-class speakers tend to use a diphthong with a less central starting-point, which we transcribe as [ᵊu].

In the case of the monophthongal GOOSE variants, a new set of variants has emerged. These variants represent the continuation of an already existing trend. The process of fronting has been taken a step further, producing variants ranging between the central variant [ʉː] described above, and a mid-front variant [ʏː], which is, incidentally, also a characteristic of rural Southwestern accents (see section 5.5.). Variation between these two variants is continuous rather than discrete. The same development can be noted in the case of the central unrounded variant [ɨː]. Here fronting can also be more advanced, leading to alternation between [ɨː] and [ɪː]. These variants were found by Altendorf (2003) in London, Colchester and Canterbury and by Williams and Kerswill (1999) in

Milton Keynes and Reading. Williams and Kerswill (1999: 144–145) can trace a change in apparent time. For both towns, they report that elderly speakers still have [ʉː], whereas younger speakers have [ʏː], or even more front [yː] in palatal environments.

GOAT-GOAL split and GOAT

London English and other Southeastern accents are subject to a phoneme split whereby oppositions such as *goal* [gɒʊɫ] and *goat* [gʌʊt] have developed (see Wells 1982: 312–313). Interaction of this alternation with L vocalization has led to the emergence of further contrasts between pairs like *sole-soul* [sɒʊ] and *so-sew* [sʌʊ] (see section 4.6.).

In London and Southeastern varieties the GOAT vowel is diphthongal. The basic socio-phonetic principle is: the more front and open the starting-point, the more basilectal the variant. The most basilectal form is a variant approaching [aʊ] with a full front and open starting-point. Suburban working-class and middle-class speakers use a variant with a less open starting-point in the area of [æ̈ ~ ɐ]. Recently, an additional new set of variants has emerged. The first element is similar to the old mesolectal London GOAT variant [ɐʊ], but the endpoint is different. This element has been considerably advanced and has variable lip rounding resulting in alternation between [ɐʉ] and [ɐɨ]. These new variants were found by Altendorf (2003) in London, Colchester and Canterbury and by Williams and Kerswill (1999) in Milton Keynes and Reading. Williams and Kerswill (1999: 143) report even further fronting of the second element resulting in variants of the [ɐʏ ~ ɐɪ] type. In addition, they have found an extra set of variants in Reading. The Reading adolescents have variants with a more central onset of the [əʏ ~ əɪ] type which they use alongside with the Milton Keynes set.

MOUTH

In London English, MOUTH has diphthongal and monophthongal variants. For the social stratification of London English the general principle is: the weaker the endpoint, the more basilectal the variant. According to Wells (1982: 309), the MOUTH vowel monophthong is a "touchstone for distinguishing between 'true Cockney' and popular London". Only "true Cockney" working-class speakers have a long monophthong of the [æː ~ aː] kind or alternatively a diphthong with a weak second element of the [æə ~ æᵊ] type. Suburban working-class speakers and middle-class speakers have a closing diphthong of the [æʊ] type.

According to the *Survey of English Dialects* (SED), the prevalent variant in most Southeastern accents used to be a variant of the [ɛʊ] type. In the speech of younger speakers, this "provincial" variant was neither found by Altendorf

(2003) in Colchester and Canterbury nor by Williams and Kerswill (1999) in Milton Keynes. Adolescent speakers in these towns use "metropolitan" [æʊ] rather than the older "provincial" form [ɛʊ]. In Milton Keynes and Reading, they even prefer [aʊ]. Williams and Kerswill (1999: 152) comment that this is a case in which levelling in the Southeast has led to a compromise on the RP form rather than the intermediate London variant.

FOOT

Another recent trend in London and Southeastern accents is FOOT fronting. In the 1980s, Gimson (1984: 119) and Wells (1982: 133) agreed that the FOOT vowel showed little variability. The only variability they conceded consisted in the occasional occurrence of "more centralized and/or unrounded" variants (Wells 1982: 133). Wells (1982: 133) described them as characteristic of "innovative or urban speech" in England, Wales and Ireland. In the meantime, this innovative tendency has led to further fronting of the FOOT vowel resulting in variants of the [ü ~ ɵ] type.

Tollfree (1999) has found such variants in London and Altendorf (2003) in London, Colchester and Canterbury. Williams and Kerswill (1999) have found even more front variants of the [ø ~ ʏ] type in Milton Keynes and Reading, these variants being particularly favoured by middle-class speakers. Torgersen (2002) reports on patterns of FOOT fronting in Southeastern English, which reveal effects for speaker age and speaking style, as well as effects for phonological context and lexical item.

4.6. Southeastern phonology: consonants

H

London and Southeastern accents have sociolinguistically variable H dropping (see Tollfree 1999: 172–174). The zero form tends to be avoided by middle-class speakers, except in contexts in which H dropping is "licensed" in virtually all British accents (in unstressed pronouns and verbs such as *his*, *her*, *him*, *have*, *had*, etc.).

TH

London and Southeastern accents have sociolinguistically variable TH fronting (i.e. the use of [f] and [v] for /θ/ and /ð/, respectively). In these accents, TH fronting can apply to /θ/ in all positions (e.g. *think*, *something*, *mouth*) and to /ð/ in non-initial position (e.g. *brother*, *with*). In the case of /ð/ in initial position, /d/ (or ø, as in [ənæʔ] for *and that*) are more likely alternatives (see e.g. Wells 1982: 328; Hughes and Trudgill 1996: 71).

The labio-dental variants have traditionally been socially stigmatized, and therefore tend to be avoided by middle-class speakers. Neither Altendorf (2003) nor Tollfree (1999) found them in the speech of their middle-class informants. However, there are reports that TH fronting is now on the verge of spreading into Southeastern middle-class accents (see e.g. Williams and Kerswill 1999; Kerswill 2002). Williams and Kerswill (1999: 160, Table 8.8) have found instances of TH fronting in male and female middle-class speech in Milton Keynes and male middle-class speech in Reading. In both towns, TH fronting affects sexes and classes in the following order: working-class boys > working-class girls > middle-class boys > middle-class girls. In terms of change in apparent time, this pattern is indicative of a "change from below" in the social sense of the term (see e.g. Trudgill 1974: 95). It has started in male working-class speech and is now working its way "upwards" to female middle-class speakers. At the moment, this development is still at an early stage. Accordingly, labio-dental fricatives in the speech of female middle-class speakers in Milton Keynes (14.3%) and Reading (0%) are infrequent or altogether absent. This could also explain why they do not occur in the London surveys by Altendorf (2003) and Tollfree (1999).

P, T, K

Pre-glottalization and glottal replacement of syllable-final /t/ and (to a lesser extent) /p/ and /k/ are very common in London and the Southeast. Despite its wide geographical dissemination, T glottalling has a tradition of being regarded as a stereotype of London English. Its current spread (at least in the Southeast) is equally ascribed to the "influence of London English, where it is indeed very common" (Wells 1982: 323). In recent years, glottalling – and in particular T glottalling – has increased dramatically in all social classes, styles and phonetic contexts. Social differentiation is, however, retained by differences in frequency and distribution of the glottal variant in different phonetic contexts. The result of this interplay can be seen in Figures 1 and 2, taken from Altendorf (2003). These data show the frequency of T glottaling in two styles of speech produced by schoolchildren drawn from three school types (comprehensive, grammar, and public) and demonstrate marked contextual effects for some speaker groups.

Phonetic constraints affect the occurrence and frequency of the glottal variant in the following order: pre-consonantal position (*Scotland*, *quite nice)* > pre-vocalic across word boundaries (*quite easy*) and pre-pausal position (*Quite!*) > word-internal pre-lateral position (*bottle*) > word-internal intervocalic position (*butter*). Their effect is further enhanced by social and stylistic factors:

(1) Middle-class speakers differ from working-class speakers by avoiding the glottal variant in socially sensitive positions when speaking in more formal styles. They reduce the frequency of the glottal variant in pre-pausal and pre-vocalic positions (as in *Quite!* and *quite easy*), and avoid it completely in the most stigmatized word-internal intervocalic position (as in *butter*).

(2) Upper-middle-class speakers differ from all other social classes in that they avoid the glottal variant in these socially sensitive positions in both styles. They have a markedly lower frequency of pre-pausal and pre-vocalic T glottaling in the most informal style and avoid it almost completely in the more formal reading style. T glottaling in the most stigmatized positions, in pre-lateral and intervocalic position (as in *bottle* and *butter*), does not occur at all for these speakers.

The results for the London upper middle class reported by Altendorf (2003) confirm those of Fabricius (2000). In the results for her young RP speakers, there is no intervocalic T glottaling in any style, and no pre-pausal or pre-vocalic T glottaling in the more formal style. Fabricius also shows that the effect of phonetic context and style is highly significant.

> Examination of the result for environment using the Newman Keuls test for pairwise comparison showed that the consonantal environment was significantly different from the pre-vocalic and the pre-pausal environments ($p<0.02$). The prevocalic and prepausal results were not significantly different from each other. (Fabricius 2000: 140)

It is also interesting to note that T glottaling displays regional variation within Fabricius' group of RP speakers.

> Pre-consonantal glottalling can reasonably be regarded as the 'first wave' of glottalling. The 'second wave' seems to be the prepausal category, which shows a significant difference between the Southeastern category and the 'rest of England' category. As we have seen, London and the Home Counties pattern together on this feature, while the rest of England lags behind. The 'newest' wave of glottalling is evident in the pre-vocalic category, where the London-raised public school speakers use pre-vocalic t-glottalling at a significantly higher rate than speakers from other parts of England in less formal styles of speech. (Fabricius 2000: 134)

R

/r/ is generally realised in Southeastern accents as an alveolar or post-alveolar approximant, [ɹ]. Southeastern accents are non-rhotic, but /r/ is pronounced in post-vocalic position if the following word begins with a vowel (so-called linking /r/, thus ['kʰɑːɹə'lɑːm] *car alarm*, but ['kʰɑː'pʰɑːk] *car park*). Intrusive /r/ is

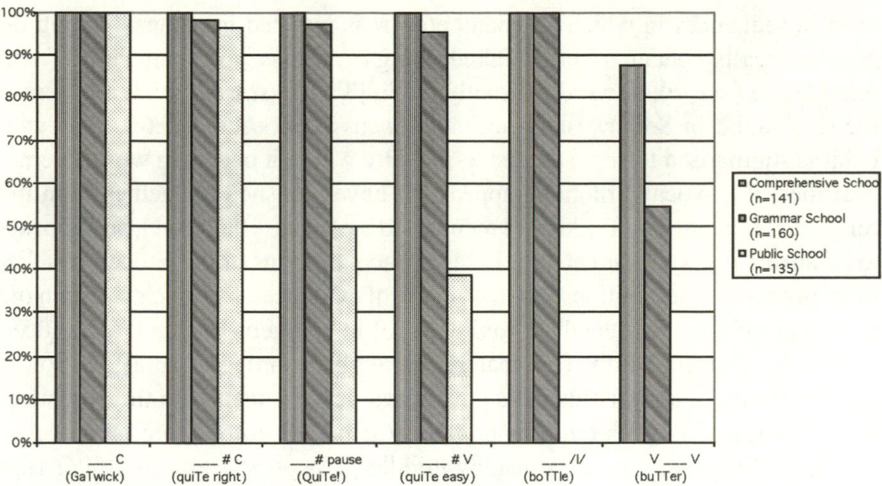

Figure 1. T glottaling by phonetic context and school: London – Interview Style (N=436)

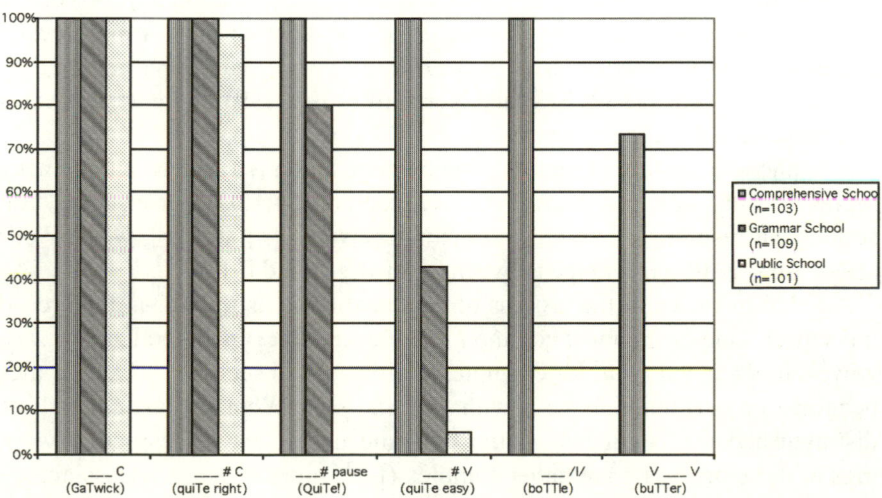

Figure 2. T glottaling by phonetic context and school: London – Reading Style (N=313)

used in sequences in which an epenthetic /r/ is inserted in contexts which do not historically contain /r/: either, like linking /r/, across word-boundaries (as in *pizza* [ɹ] *and pasta*), or word-internally (as in [ˈsɔːɹɪŋ] *sawing*; cf. the hypercorrections found in Southwestern accents, discussed in section 5.6.). The latter habit is stigmatised to some degree, especially where it occurs in word-internal positions. Post-vocalic rhoticity appears to have vanished altogether from the relic area (Reading and Berkshire) mentioned by Wells (1982: 341), and appears to be advancing westward at a fairly rapid pace. In terms of the phonetic quality of /r/ in pre-vocalic positions, there is plentiful evidence of a dramatic rise in the frequency of the labiodental approximant [ʋ] in southern England, and indeed also in parts of the North. This feature, formerly regarded as an affectation, a speech defect, or an infantilism, is now heard very frequently in the accents of a wide range of English cities, and appears generally to be more favoured by young working-class speakers than by middle-class ones. Kerswill (1996: 189) suggests that the increased usage of [ʋ] (and [f, v] for /θ, ð/) among younger speakers represents a failure to eradicate immature pronunciations as a result of an attrition of the stigma attached to these forms.

L

London and Southeastern accents have variable L vocalization in post-vocalic positions (as in *mill*, *milk*), but instances of vocalization of /l/ in pre-vocalic position across word boundaries (as in *roll up*, *peel it*) have been reported by, for example, Wells (1982: 313) and Kerswill (1996: 199) in the local accents of London and Reading respectively.

The phonetic quality of the resulting pronunciation is variable and phonetic representations of it vary a great deal. Gimson (1984: 202), for instance, transcribes the resulting vocoid as alternating between [ö] and [ɤ], while Wells (1995: 263) indicates a range between [ɤ], [o], [ʊ] and [u].

Another intricacy of the process of vocalization is its impact on the preceding vowel. One of the most common allophonic effects is neutralization. The vowels in *meal* and *pool*, for example, are lowered to such an extent that they become (almost) homophonous with *mill* and *pull*. Whether they can still be distinguished by length is a matter of some uncertainty. The precise workings of these processes are rather complex (for a more detailed discussion, see Wells 1982: 314–317).

Another consequence of the process of vocalization might be the rise of new diphthongs consisting of the preceding vowel and the resulting vocalized variant. Like R dropping, L vocalization may lead to a re-organization of the vowel system. According to Wells (1982: 259), it "offers the prospect of eventual phonemic status for new diphthongs such as /ɪʊ/ (*milk*), /ɛʊ/ (*shelf*), etc.".

Like T glottaling, L vocalization is spreading regionally, so far mostly within the Southeast, and socially to higher social classes. In London, Kent and Essex (see Altendorf 2003), it is already very frequent, almost categorical, in the accents of young middle-class speakers.

YOD

London and Southeastern English accents have variable Yod dropping and Yod coalescence. These processes affect initial consonant clusters in stressed syllables consisting of the alveolar stops /t/ and /d/ and a following palatal glide /j/, as in *tune*, *duke*. In addition, Yod dropping can affect syllable initial /n/ plus /j/ (as in [nʊuːz] *news*). Yod coalescence involves the "merging" of /tj/ and /dj/ to [tʃ] and [dʒ] respectively, such that *dune* and *June*, for instance, may be homophonous. In the 1980s, Wells (1982: 331) had already observed that in working-class London English the "older" phenomenon of Yod dropping was faced with competition from Yod coalescence. Whether the same is true for other Southeastern accents has not yet been reported.

5. The Southwest

5.1. The West Country

The West Country is a region with imprecise boundaries. According to Wells (1982: 335–336), three main areas can be identified: The centre of the region is formed by the "cider counties" of Gloucestershire, the former county of Avon, Somerset and Devon. To the East and nearer to London lies "the transitional area of Wessex" (Wells 1982: 335), which comprises Dorset, Wiltshire and Hampshire and parts of Oxfordshire. To the far West, "Cornwall stands somewhat apart" (Wells 1982: 335). This area differs from the two other areas with regard to its distinctive Celtic background and its Cornish language. Cornish became extinct in the late 18th century but has been revived to a small degree in recent decades.

Trudgill (1999: 76–77) agrees with Wells (1982) in dividing the Southwest into three dialect areas. He differs from Wells with regard to the (northern) extension of this area and its internal structure. Trudgill's centre, the Central Southwest, comprises most of the central and eastern regions identified by Wells, i.e. Somerset, the former county of Avon, and parts of Gloucestershire, together with parts of the more eastern counties of Wells' transitional area, i.e. Dorset and Wiltshire, and western districts of Buckinghamshire, Oxfordshire, Berkshire and Hampshire. In addition, Trudgill distinguishes between the Upper and Lower Southwest. The Upper Southwest covers much of Gloucestershire and Worcestershire as well as areas as far north as Herefordshire and

Shropshire up to Shrewsbury. The Lower Southwest is formed by Devon and Cornwall.

Another attempt to establish dialect areas in the Southwest has been proposed by Klemola (1994). Klemola's study is based on cluster analysis making use of *SED* material for 80 variables (25 phonological, 30 morphosyntactic and 25 lexical) in nine Southwestern counties. The results of this study do not coincide completely with the structures proposed by Wells and by Trudgill but show interesting parallels. Klemola (1994: 373) has found a very stable cluster in a region comprising Eastern Cornwall and Devon (cf. Trudgill's Lower Southwest). Typical phonological features of this area at the time of the *SED* fieldwork are initial fricative voicing, /ʏ(:)/ in GOOSE and /d/ in *butter* (see sections 5.5. and 5.6.). The second relatively stable cluster is formed at the eastern end of the region comprising Berkshire, Oxfordshire and eastern parts of Gloucestershire and Hampshire (cf. Wells' transitional area). Typical phonological features of this area are the absence of initial fricative voicing, /u(:)/ in GOOSE and /t/ in *butter*. The internal structure of the "central" areas identified by Klemola is more variable.

5.2. The influence of the Home Counties Modern Dialect Area

The internal structure of the Southwestern group of dialects does not seem to have changed to the same extent as that of the Southeastern group (see sections 4.1. and 4.2.). More recently, however, it has also been reported that parts of the Southwest are changing more markedly and are, moreover, doing so under the influence of the expanding Home Counties Modern Dialect Area. Trudgill (1999: 76) claims that this is true for coastal cities such as Southampton, Portsmouth and Bournemouth. From a geographical point of view, these cities are part of the Central Southwest. From a dialectological point of view, they may not belong to this area any longer. Similar developments can also be observed in the more easterly regions of Oxfordshire and Berkshire.

5.3. The West Country "burr"

Southwestern accents are characterized by post-vocalic rhoticity, a feature known informally as the "West Country burr". Post-vocalic /r/ is retroflex in many Southwestern accents (see section 5.6.). This feature is perceived as particularly pleasing by many speakers from outside the area, but is at the same time one of the major stereotypes responsible for the impression of rusticity also often associated with Southwestern accents. McArthur (1992) describes this image:

Two particular shibboleths are associated with 'yokels' leaning on gates and sucking straws: a strong West Country burr, as in *Arr, that it be* 'Yes, that's so'; voiced initial fricatives, as in *The varmer zeez thik dhreevurrow plough* 'The farmer sees that three-furrow plough'. (McArthur 1992: 1112)

Initial fricative voicing (see section 5.6.) appears to have been stereotyped for several hundred years: it is a feature of the stage accent "Mummerset", a form of which is used by the disguised Edgar in Shakespeare's *King Lear* (see e.g. McArthur 1992: 1112). It is now recessive, and virtually extinct in urban areas and in the speech of the young.

5.4. Bristol /l/

Another stereotype of Southwestern English is Bristol /l/. This term refers to the presence of epenthetic /l/ following word-final /ə/ in words of the lexical set commA (e.g. *America*) and in words that in RP end in [əʊ], such as *window*. Thus *America* is pronounced [ə'mɛɹɪkəl] and *Eva* becomes homophonous with *evil* (Hughes and Trudgill 1996: 78). Bristol /l/ is a stereotype which has become the butt of many jokes (for examples, see Wells 1982: 344; Trudgill 1999: 76). It is, however, confined to the Bristol area, and is not as common as its folk-linguistic status might suggest.

5.5. Southwestern phonology: vowels and diphthongs

Table 4 shows the inventory of Bristol vowels and diphthongs, based on Wells (1982: 348–349).

Table 4. Bristol vowels – summary

KIT	ɪ	FLEECE	i	NEAR	ir [ɪɻ]
DRESS	ɛ	FACE	ɛɪ	SQUARE	ɛɪr [ɛɻ]
TRAP	æ	PALM	a	START	ar [aɻ ~ aʵ]
LOT	ɑ	THOUGHT	ɔ	NORTH	ɔr [ɔɻ ~ ɔʵ]
STRUT	ʌ	GOAT	ɔʊ	FORCE	ɔr
FOOT	ʊ	GOOSE	u*	CURE	ur ~ ɔr
BATH	a	PRICE	ɑɪ	happY	i
CLOTH	ɒ	CHOICE	oɪ	lettER	ər [ɚ]
NURSE	ɜr [ɝ]	MOUTH	aʊ	commA	ə ~ əl

*see also GOOSE below

Vowel Length:
Short vowels in Southwestern accents tend to be lengthened somewhat relative to their counterparts in other English accents. This applies in particular to vowels in monosyllabic lexical items when they occur in phrase-final or in intonationally prominent position: e.g. *trap* [tɹaˑp], *did* [dɪˑd], *top* [tɑˑp] (see Hughes and Trudgill 1996: 78).

STRUT
There is some uncertainty about the phonetic quality of the STRUT vowel in Southwestern accents (see Wells 1982: 48). Wakelin (1986: 23) cites [ə] and [ɐ] for Bristol, [ɪ] in words such as *dozen* and *brother* in some accents of Devon and Cornwall, a range of rounded variants including [ʊ] and [ʏː] in certain areas, and even some diphthongal pronunciations such as [aʊ] and [œʏ] in *dust* and *sludge*.

TRAP
In many Southwestern accents the TRAP vowel is realized as [a]. This realization is typical of rural accents in the region, but it also occurs in urban accents. Bristol and Southampton, however, are reported to have [æ] rather than [a] (Wells 1982: 345; Hughes and Trudgill 1996: 57, 77), as are Somerset and West Cornwall. (Wakelin 1986: 21)

BATH, PALM
The phonetic qualities of the BATH and PALM vowels depend on their phonetic environments, and vary in different areas and localities. The exact phonetic quality and distribution of the Southwestern variants is not fully understood. Wells (1982: 345–346) and Hughes and Trudgill (1996: 57) suggest the following description:

(1) In the standard lexical set of BATH, two vowels are possible: (a) [aˑ] and (b) [æː]. In those accents which have BATH [aˑ] *and* (lengthened) TRAP [aˑ], phonemic contrast is absent or variable. However, neither TRAP [aˑ] nor the TRAP-BATH merger are categorical. According to Wells (1982: 346), Bristol and Southampton, for instance, retain an opposition between TRAP and BATH as in "*gas* [gæs] vs. *grass* [græːs ~ graːs]".
(2) The situation becomes yet more complex when we consider the vowel of the lexical set PALM. Wells (1982: 346) suggests the following rule of thumb: If historical /l/ in words such as *palm* and *calm* is retained, which is the case in some parts of the Southwest, the vowel is probably a back unrounded [ɑ], such that *palm* is pronounced as [pɑɫm]. PALM words

without historical /l/, such as *father*, *bra*, *spa*, *tomato*, *banana*, etc., have the same vowel as that found in BATH items.

FACE and GOAT

Traditional rural accents in Devon and Cornwall have the monophthongal FACE and GOAT variants [eː] and [oː] (see e.g. Wakelin 1986: 27). Wakelin also reports some instances of centring and opening diphthongs (e.g. [eə], [ɪə], [jə]) which appear to be rather like those used in north-eastern England. These pronunciations and the close-mid monophthongs [eː] and [oː] are, however, recessive and appear to be giving way to (closing) diphthongal variants resembling those used in Southeastern England. Such diphthongal variants have fairly open starting points in the vicinity of [ɛ] and [ɔ]. (see Hughes and Trudgill 1996: 64, 109)

PRICE

The quality of the vowel in words of this set is often quite close to that of CHOICE in accents such as RP, although Wells (1982: 347) contends that a PRICE-CHOICE opposition is usually (but not always) maintained by Southwestern speakers. This feature is nonetheless stereotyped to the extent that pseudo-phonetic spellings like *roit* (*right*) and *Vroiday* (*Friday*) are commonly found in attempts to render West Country accents orthographically (see e.g. McArthur 1992: 674). Wakelin describes the first element of the diphthong as being heavily centralized in the eastern part of the region, but as one proceeds westward [æ̈] becomes increasingly common. He also cites monophthongal pronunciations as [æː ~ aː] for Devon (Wakelin 1986: 27–28).

MOUTH

According to Wells (1982: 347–348), typical Southwestern qualities of MOUTH are "perhaps [æʊ] and [ɐʊ]" and [ɛɪ ~ eɪ] in Southwestern areas nearer to London. This vowel and PRICE exhibit what Wells terms "crossover" (1982: 310, 347), whereby the first elements of the diphthongs are the opposite in front-back terms from those found in RP.

GOOSE and FOOT

Rural accents in Devon and parts of Somerset and Cornwall have GOOSE and FOOT fronting (see section 4.5.). Wells (1982: 347) quotes the *Linguistic Atlas of England* (LAE) variants [ʏː] for GOOSE and [ʏ] or [øʏ] for FOOT.

LOT

The LOT vowel is frequently [ɒ], but also [ɑ], as in varieties of US English. Conservative pronunciations featuring [ɔː] in items like *off*, *cross* and *broth* are cited by Wakelin (1986: 23) on the basis of SED responses.

Gradation

In some words, vowels in unstressed syllables retain full vowel quality. *Goodness*, for instance, can be pronounced as ['gʊdnɛs]. (Hughes and Trudgill 1996: 79)

5.6. Southwestern phonology: consonants

Rhoticity:

Most Southwestern accents preserve post-vocalic /r/, which is frequently retroflex in quality (i.e. [ɻ]). Wells (1982: 342), quoting LAE results, reports that the isogloss separating retroflex from post-alveolar /r/ runs from Bristol to Portsmouth. The retroflex areas are thus Hampshire, Wiltshire, Dorset, Somerset, Devon and Cornwall. Full rhoticity occurs in a wide range of social and local accents ranging from the working to the middle class and from rural to urban accents. According to Wells (1982: 341), rhoticity can be found in Bristol, Exeter and (to a lesser extent) in Southampton, but not in Plymouth and Bournemouth.

The exact workings of rhoticity in the Southwest of England are complex and not yet fully understood. According to Wells (1982: 342), rhoticity in the Southwest means R colouring of the preceding vowel. In words of the lexical sets NURSE and lettER, the entire vowel receives R colouring, but for words of the START, NORTH, FORCE, NEAR, SQUARE and CURE sets, it is either the whole vowel or just the endpoint of the diphthong/triphthong which receives R colouring. As with L vocalization, R colouring affects the phonetic quality of the preceding vowel and has led to the rise of new monophthongs and diphthongs. These processes and the theoretical problems that they pose are discussed in Wells (1982: 342–343).

Southwestern middle-class speakers sometimes have a pronunciation where post-vocalic /r/ is not phonetically realized but the effects of rhoticity are still preserved. These speakers have, for instance, a centring diphthong in START words, [stɑət], but not in words such as *spa*, [spɑː ~ spaː] (Wells 1982: 343).

Hyper-rhoticity can also occur, especially in commA words, which then end in /r/. It can also be sporadically heard in items such as *khaki* ['kaːɻki] for which, presumably, Southwestern speakers have mistakenly reconstructed a post-vocalic /r/ on the basis of productions they have heard produced by speakers of non-rhotic accents such as RP (see Wells 1982: 343). Wakelin (1986: 31) lists *path*, *nought*, *idea*, *yellow* and *window* as items recorded with hyper-rhotic pronunciations, and also cites post-vocalic /r/ in words in which metathesis may take place (e.g. 'purty' for *pretty*, 'gurt' for *great*, etc.).

H

As with the Southeastern accents discussed above, Southwestern accents have sociolinguistically variable H dropping. According to Upton, Sanderson, and Widdowson (1987: 104), H dropping occurs in *house* in Cornwall, Devon, western Somerset, northern Wiltshire, and southern Dorset, but does not occur in other areas of the Southwest. According to Wakelin (1986: 31), aspiration may occur before /r/ in word-initial clusters (i.e. /hrV/) in southern Somerset, while in West Somerset and North Devon the aforementioned metathesis of a syllable onset /r/ and its following vowel may result in the pronunciation /hərd/ *red*.

F, TH, S, SH

Southwestern accents traditionally featured initial fricative voicing, a process by which the otherwise voiceless fricatives /f, θ, s, ʃ/ are voiced to [v, ð, z, ʒ] respectively. This feature, which Wakelin (1986: 29) dubs "the [Southwestern] feature *par excellence*", has long been a stereotype of rural West Country accents (see section 5.3.); yet it is highly recessive today.

TH

Southwestern accents, like those of Southeastern England, have sociolinguistically variable TH fronting (for Bristol, see Hughes and Trudgill 1996: 78). Wakelin (1986: 29) reports [f] for /θ/ in *think*, *through* and *mouth* for Bristol, as well as stopped pronunciations of /θ/ and /ð/ as [d] in e.g. *three*, *thistle*, *the*, and *then* (see also Wells 1982: 343). There is, however, something of a lack of recent published research on this variable in accents of the Southwest.

T

Southwestern accents have variable T glottaling in syllable-final pre-pausal and intervocalic position (for Bristol, see Hughes and Trudgill 1996: 78). Wells (1982: 344) gives ['dɝːʔi 'wɔːʔɚ] *dirty water* as an example of the sort of glottalled pronunciation frequently found in Bristol, and cites a study in which it is stated that glottalling of /k/ renders *lot* and *lock* homophonous at [lɒʔ]. In intervocalic position, a widespread alternative to T glottaling is T voicing (see [d]in *butter* in section 5.1.). Wells (1982: 344) reports tapping of /r/ to be "certainly very common" in *butter*, *beautiful*, *hospital* in urban areas of the Southwest. voicing of intervocalic /p/ and /k/ is also said to occur. (see Wells 1982: 344)

Syllabic consonants
Word-final vowel + nasal sequences (as in *button*) are often pronounced as such, rather than as syllabic consonants. In these circumstances, *happen* would be ['hapən] rather than ['hapn̩]. (Hughes and Trudgill 1996: 790)

Exercises and study questions

1. What are the linguistic characteristics used by linguists to separate the dialectological north of England from the dialectological south, and the south-western group of dialects from the south-eastern group of dialects?

2. a) Identify the phonetic contexts in which T Glottalling is reported to be taking place in south-eastern accents today.
   b) Arrange these contexts as an implicational hierarchy based on the following principle: If a speaker has T Glottalling in one phonetic context listed in the hierarchy, he/she tends to have T Glottalling in all the other contexts listed below this context. For more information on the concept of the implicational hierarchy, see Bickerton, D. (1971). "Inherent variability and variable rules." *Foundations of Language* 7, 457-492.

3. As mentioned in section 3.3., there is disagreement among journalists and linguists about the alleged London provenance of variants such as T Glottalling and TH Fronting in urban accents outside the south-east. Collect the arguments and counterarguments put forward by both "camps". Consult additional sources on this topic, e.g. the UCL webpage on Estuary English at <www.phon.ucl.ac.uk/ home/estuary/home.htm >.

4. Discuss the effects of L Vocalization and rhoticity on the linguistic structure of the respective accents.

5. Carry out a small field study into the current urban accents of Southampton, Portsmouth or Bournemouth. Discuss on the basis of your results to which extent and in which way they have changed. Would you go so far as to classify them as belonging to the Home Counties Modern Dialect Area rather than to the Central Southwest?

6. The male South-Eastern English informant (45 yrs.) in the reading passage exhibits variability in terms of rhoticity (presence of non-prevocalic /r/) and in /h/-dropping. Quantify (i) the proportions of /r/-presence vs. absence and (ii) /h/-dropping vs. /h/-realisation by expressing each as a percentage of the number of sites in which these phenomena *could* occur, even if they don't.

7. Discuss the free passage speaker's monophthong and diphthong productions (South-Eastern English), and contrast them with those of RP (for instance, the female speaker [45 yrs.] to be heard in the reading passage).
8. (relates to freepassage.swf) List as many similarities as can you identify between the free passage speaker's accent and those of Ireland.
9. The speech of this young male South-Eastern English informant (13 yrs.) in the reading passage is phonologically different in several respects from that of the older south-eastern speakers on the CD-ROM. Identify at least one consonantal variable and two vocalic variables that serve to distinguish these speakers' productions.
10. Observe the distribution of the glottal stop as a variant of (t) in all informants in the reading passage for south-eastern England. For which speakers is it most frequent? In which phonological environment does it occur most commonly? For the speakers whose speech you have analysed, does the distribution of glottal stop match the pattern described in the chapter *The Dialects of the South of England: Phonology*?

Selected references

Please consult the General references for titles mentioned in the text but not included in the references below. For a full bibliography see the accompanying CD-ROM.

Altendorf, Ulrike
2003 *'Estuary English':Levelling at the interface of RP and Southeastern British English.* Tübingen: Narr.

Fabricius, Anne
2000 T-glottalling between stigma and prestige. Ph.D. dissertation, Copenhagen Business School. <http//www.babel.ruc.dk/~fabri/pdfdocs/Fabricius-2000-PhD-thesis.pdf>

Gimson, Alfred C.
1984 *An Introduction to the Pronunciation of English.* London: Arnold.

Kerswill, Paul
1996 Phonological convergence in dialect contact: evidence from citation forms. *Language Variation and Change* 7: 195–207.
2002 Models of linguistic change and diffusion: new evidence from dialect levelling in British English. *Reading Working Papers in Linguistics* 6: 187–216.

Klemola, Juhani
1994 Dialect areas in the Southwest of England: an exercise in cluster analysis. In: Wolfgang Viereck (ed.), *Verhandlungen des internationalen Dialektologenkongresses, Volume 3: Regional Variation, Colloquial and Standard Languages*, 368–384. Stuttgart: Franz Steiner Verlag.

Przedlacka, Joanna
2002 *Estuary English? A Sociophonetic Study of Teenage Speech in the Home Counties*. Frankfurt am Main: Lang.

Rosewarne, David
1984 Estuary English. *Times Educational Supplement*, 19th October 1984.

Tollfree, Laura
1999 South East London English: discrete versus continuous modelling of consonantal reduction. In: Foulkes and Docherty (eds.), 163–184.

Torgersen, Eivind Nessa
2002 Phonological distribution of the FOOT vowel, /ʊ/, in young people's speech in Southeastern British English. *Reading Working Papers in Linguistics* 6: 25–38.

Wakelin, Martyn F.
1986 *The Southwest of England*. Amsterdam/Philadelphia: Benjamins.

Wales, Katie
2002 'North of Watford Gap': a cultural history of northern English (from 1700). In: Watts and Trudgill (eds.), 45–66.

Wells, John
1994 The cockneyfication of R.P.? In: Gunnel Melchers and Nils-Lennart Johannesson (eds.), *Nonstandard Varieties of Language*, 189–205. Stockholm: Almqvist and Wiksell.

1995 Transcribing Estuary English: a discussion document. *Speech, Hearing and Language* 8: 261–267.

1997 ′What is Estuary English? *English Teaching Professional* 3: 46–47. <www.phon.ucl.ac.uk/home/estuary/whatis.htm>.

Williams, Ann and Paul Kerswill
1999 Dialect levelling: change and continuity in Milton Keynes, Reading and Hull. In: Foulkes and Docherty (eds.), 141–162.

Channel Island English: phonology*

Heinrich Ramisch

1. Introduction

The Channel Islands (Jersey, Guernsey, Alderney and Sark) are regarded as a French-speaking area in traditional dialectology, as can be seen in J. Gilliéron and E. Edmont's *Atlas Linguistique de la France* (1902–1920), and also in the regional dialect atlas for Normandy, *Atlas Linguistique et Ethnographique Normand* (Brasseur 1980–1997). This is certainly justified, because the original language in the islands is a form of Norman French that has been spoken there for centuries. But there can be no doubt that English is the dominant language in the islands today. The number of speakers of Norman French is relatively small and constantly decreasing. Over the last 200 years, English has gained more and more influence and has gradually replaced the local Norman French dialects. Indeed, there are clear indications that they will become extinct within the foreseeable future. A detailed account of the past and present sociolinguistic situation in the Channel Islands can be found in Ramisch (1989: 5–62) and Jones (2001); for the general history of the Channel Islands see in particular Lemprière (1974), Guillot (1975: 24–55) and Syvret and Stevens (1998).

A brief look at Map 1 shows that the Channel Islands are much closer to France than to England. Alderney is just 9 miles away from Cap de la Hague in France, while Jersey is only about 15 miles from the French coast but 90 miles south of England. Therefore, it comes as no real surprise that the native language in the Channel Islands is Norman French rather than English. From a political point of view, however, the islands have been connected with England for a long time. Originally, the islands were part of the Duchy of Normandy, but after the Battle of Hastings in 1066 Duke William II of Normandy (William the Conqueror) became King of England, and the Duchy of Normandy was united with England under one ruler. Thus, 1066 is the date that first associates the Channel Islands with England and the English Crown, and this association has existed ever since. 1066 also provides the background for a longstanding joke. When asking local people whether they think that the Channel Islands belong to England they will tell you that just the opposite is true. They will point out that after all they were on the winning side in the Battle of Hastings and it was they who conquered England. The exceptional political situation of the Channel Islands really arose after the year 1204, when King John (Lackland) lost all his territories on the Continent to King Philippe Auguste of France, but the Channel Islands were *not* conquered by the French. As a result, they became the only part of the former Duchy of Normandy to remain in the possession of the English king, who continued to reign in the islands in his function as Duke of Normandy.

Because of their strategic importance the French repeatedly tried to capture the Channel Islands during the following centuries, but never succeeded. The islands stayed loyal to the English Crown which in turn granted them special privileges and a high degree of autonomy; to this day the islands do not belong to the United Kingdom and are not directly subject to the British Government. They have their own legislative assemblies (called *States*), and their own legal and tax systems, which is in fact the reason why they have become a tax haven and international centres of banking and finance.

After the separation of the Channel Islands from the Norman mainland in 1204, their political links with England at first had no far-reaching consequences (see Guillot 1975: 31–32 and Le Patourel 1937: 35). The native inhabitants, their culture and their language were Norman, keeping them in close contact with their neighbours on the Norman mainland. At a time when distances played a far greater role than today, trade with the outside world mainly took place with Normandy. On the whole, it seems that English influence in the Channel Islands during the Middle Ages was rather limited. However, the situation began to change in the late 18th and early 19th centuries, when larger military units from England were brought to the islands to defend them against the French. It was above all the tradespeople and the inhabitants of the capital towns St. Helier (in Jersey) and St. Peter Port (in Guernsey) who first came into contact with English through the soldiers stationed in the area. Furthermore, English merchants had also settled in these towns, which had developed into international trade centres.

But during the first half of the 19th century the islands were still largely French-speaking. There is an interesting comment from the 1830s by the English travel writer Henry Inglis. He writes in a guidebook:

> [...] there are certain points of interest attached to the Channel Islands, peculiarly their own [...] their native civilized inhabitants, their vicinity to the coast of France, and the general use of the French language. (Inglis 1844: 2)

Talking about Jersey, he makes clear what he means by "French language":

> "The universal language is still a barbarous dialect." (Inglis 1844: 72)

But Inglis also reports on the beginnings of a process of anglicization:

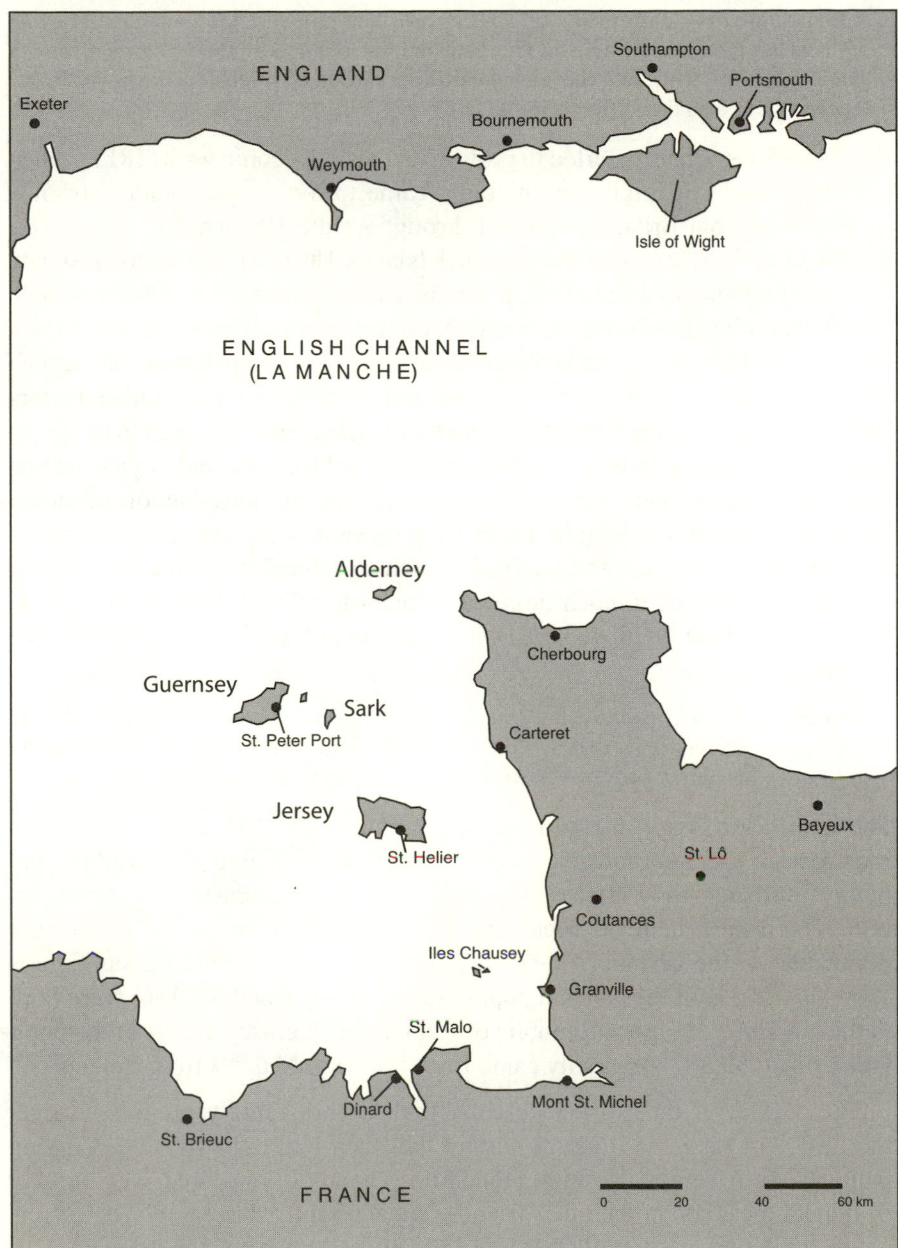

Map 1. The Channel Islands

> Children are now universally taught English; and amongst the young, there is an evident preference of English. The constant intercourse of the tradespeople with the English residents; and the considerable sprinkling of English residents in Jersey society, have also their effect. (Inglis 1844: 73)

English influence really started to grow after the Napoleonic wars (1815), when a larger number of English immigrants came to live in the Channel Islands. Immigration from Britain continued throughout the 19th century. The census figures of 1891 (Census of the Channel Islands 1891: 4) reveal, for instance, that 5,844 people (or 15.5%) of the inhabitants of Guernsey and 8,626 people (or 15.8%) of the inhabitants of Jersey were immigrants from England, Wales, Scotland or Ireland. At the same time, immigration from France was much lower, namely only 2.92% in Guernsey and 10.22% in Jersey. Other factors that contributed to an increased influence of English are to be seen in the growing trade relations with England, the emergence of tourism, and improvements in communication and traffic links. For example, the introduction of steamboats played an important role. From 1824 onwards a regular service between England and the islands was established, which offered new opportunities for commerce and made it much more convenient for British tourists to visit the islands (cf. Tupper 1876: 403). Towards the end of the 19th century a historian comments:

> During the present century the English language has made vast strides both in Guernsey and Jersey, so that it is difficult now to find a native even in the country parishes who cannot converse fairly well in that tongue. (Nicolle 1893: 387)

The influence of English continued to rise during the 20th century. The mass media, such as radio and television, brought English into practically every home. Tourism greatly increased and became a major industry. Moreover, immigration from Britain has been very strong. A high proportion of the present population of the Channel Islands are non-natives. The 2001 census figures show that 33.5% of the resident population of Jersey (total: 87,186) were born in the UK and 2.3% in the Republic of Ireland. In Guernsey 27.4% of the population (total: 59,807) originally came from the UK and 0.7% from Ireland.

The decline of the Norman French dialects has rapidly progressed over the last 100 years, and it seems certain that they will not survive as a living language. In Alderney, Norman French has already disappeared. The number of dialect speakers on the other islands has constantly decreased. The results of the 2001 census show that only 3.3% (2,874 people) of the population in Jersey still claim to be active speakers of Jersey French (see Table 1). About two-thirds of these speakers are in fact aged 60 and above. In Guernsey 1,327 people (2.2% of the total population) stated that they "speak Guernsey French

Table 1. Languages spoken in Jersey (Census of Jersey 2001: 23)

	Main language	**Secondary language**	**Total number of speakers**	**Percentage of population**
English	82,349	3,443	85,792	98.4%
Jersey French	113	2,761	2,874	3.3%
Portuguese	4,002	3,303	7,305	8.4%
French	338	14,776	15,114	17.3%
Other languages	384	4,496	4,880	5.6%

fluently". But most of them (934 or 70.4%) are 65 or older. A further 3,438 people (5.7% of the total population) reported that they "speak Guernsey French a little" (Census of Guernsey 2001: 109). As for Sark (total population: 550) local estimates assume that 50 people still speak Sark French.

All present speakers of Norman French are bilingual, i.e. they are also speakers of English. They are local people who live mainly in the rural areas, where they typically work as farmers, growers, fishermen or craftsmen. Moreover, the use of the Norman French dialect is limited to family members, friends and neighbours of whom the speaker knows that they are able to understand the language. It is particularly in the case of older couples where both husband and wife are dialect speakers that Norman French is still the daily language at home.

Probably the most important reason for the decline of the dialects has been their low social prestige. They have generally been regarded as an uneducated, inferior tongue spoken by ordinary people in the country and, what is more, as a corrupt form of Standard French, which is commonly called "good French" in the Channel Islands. It is revealing that before the arrival of English it was not Norman French but Standard French which was preferred in public and official domains such as in the debates of the local parliaments (*States*), in the courts, in newspapers or in church.

2. Phonological features

As far as the phonological variation of English in the Channel Islands is concerned, the following three major aspects should be taken into account. (For a detailed description of phonological features to be found in Channel Island English, see Ramisch 1989: 164–178.) First of all, due to the language contact between English and the local Norman French dialects, one may expect to find features in English which can be attributed to an influence from Norman

French. In this context it is of particular interest to verify whether such features only occur with speakers of Norman French or whether they are also used by monolingual speakers of English. Secondly, Channel Island English is likely to include non-standard features that equally occur in other varieties of British English. These features may easily have arrived in the Channel Islands with the large number of immigrants from Britain. Thirdly, Channel Island English may be characterised, at least theoretically, by independent phonological developments with no influence from either Norman French or other varieties of English.

2.1. Vowels

Table 2. Vowel realisations in Channel Island English – summary

KIT	ɪ ~ ɪ̈	FLEECE	iː ~ ɪi	NEAR	ɪə ~ iə
DRESS	ɛ ~ ɛ̈	FACE	eɪ ~ e̞ɪ	SQUARE	ɛə ~ ɛː
TRAP	æ	PALM	ɑː ~ ɑ̹ː	START	ɑː ~ ɑ̹ː
LOT	ɒ ~ ɒ̈	THOUGHT	ɔː ~ oː	NORTH	ɔː ~ oː
STRUT	ɔ ~ ʌ	GOAT	ɔʊ ~ əʊ	FORCE	ɔː ~ oː
FOOT	ʊ	GOAL	ɔʊ ~ əʊ	CURE	jʊə
BATH	ɑː ~ ɑ̟ː	GOOSE	uː ~ ʉː	happY	i ~ iː
CLOTH	ɒ ~ ɒ̈	PRICE	ɒɪ ~ ɑɪ ~ ʌɪ	lettER	ə ~ œ
NURSE	ɜː ~ əː	CHOICE	ɔɪ ~ oɪ	horsES	ɪ ~ ɪ̈
		MOUTH	aʊ	commA	ə

Table 2 lists the typical vowel realisations in Channel Island English. Two prominent features will be discussed here in more detail, namely the realisations of the PRICE diphthong and the STRUT vowel.

PRICE

The starting point of the PRICE diphthong tends to be further back than in RP. Words such as *fight* or *buy* are pronounced [fɑɪt] and [bɑɪ]. Additionally, the first element of the glide may be rounded, resulting in [fɒɪt] and [bɒɪ]. The realisation of the PRICE diphthong as [ɑɪ] or [ɒɪ] is certainly not restricted to the Channel Islands, but commonly found in many other accents of English. It is particularly typical of the Cockney accent (London) and of urban areas in the south of England in general (cf. Wells 1982: 149, 308). Certain varieties of Irish English equally have [ɑɪ] or [ɒɪ] for the PRICE glide, which has led to the stereotype view in the United States that speakers of Irish English pronounce *nice time* as 'noice toime' (cf. Wells 1982: 425–426).

The question of whether the variable pronunciation of the PRICE diphthong in the Channel Islands may also be due to a influence from Norman French cannot be resolved conclusively. It cannot be a case of phone substitution, since the diphthong [aɪ] does exist in Channel Island French. But it is noteworthy that the diphthong [ɑɪ] is a typical and frequently occurring sound in the local French dialects. Verbs which end in *-er* in Standard French have the diphthong [ɑɪ] in the same position in Guernsey French, for example: [dunɑɪ] (Standard French *donner* 'give'). Similarly, the ending [ɑɪ] is used in the second person plural of the present tense [vu dunɑɪ] (Standard French *vous donnez*), in the imperative plural [dunɑɪ] (Standard French *donnez!*) and in the past participle forms of verbs [dunɑɪ] (Standard French *donné*).

Table 3. Realisation of the PRICE diphthong as [ɑɪ] or [ɒɪ] in Guernsey

informant group	**percentages**
MO	35.8
FO	21.0
MY	27.1
FY	12.2

Table 3 presents the results for the PRICE diphthong among 40 informants in Guernsey, divided into 4 different groups: MO = older (60+) male informants and speakers of Guernsey French; FO = older (60+) female informants and speakers of Guernsey French; MY = younger (19–32) male informants and monolingual speakers of English; FY = younger (19–32) female informants and monolingual speakers of English. The feature occurred most frequently with group MO. In slightly more than a third of all cases the glide was realized as [ɑɪ] or [ɒɪ]. The feature was quite common with the younger men (group MY) as well. Their percentage value is still above that of group FO. The younger women (group FY) clearly came closest to RP in their pronunciation of the PRICE glide.

STRUT

The STRUT vowel may be pronounced as [ɔ] in Channel Island English. Words such as *sun* or *duck* are locally realised as [sɔn] and [dɔk]. In comparison to the RP vowel [ɔ] is further back and above all, the vowel is rounded. Parallels to this feature in other varieties are rather difficult to find. In the data of the *Survey of English Dialects* (SED; Orton 1962–1971), [ɒ] is very occasionally used for the STRUT vowel. In the responses to question IV.6.14 ('ducks'), [ɒ] occurs three times in Kent, once in Essex and once in Hampshire. In question IX.2.3 ('sun'), [ɒ] was recorded twice in Kent, once in Wiltshire and once in the Isle of Man. An influence from Norman French seems more likely in this case. Channel Island French does not have a vowel sound comparable to English /ʌ/. One can therefore assume that a phone substitution takes place in English, replacing /ʌ/ by [ɔ]. This hypothesis is confirmed by the fact that the same phone substitution occurs in English loanwords in Channel Island French. Thus, the word *bus* is pronounced [la bɔs] in the local French dialects.

Table 4. Realisation of the STRUT vowel as [ɔ] in Guernsey

informant group	**percentages**
MO	19.6
FO	18.0
MY	8.7
FY	10.3

The results for the STRUT vowel among the same 40 informants in Guernsey equally lend support to the hypothesis. The quantitative analysis of the variable shows a generational difference. The older informants (and speakers of Guernsey French) scored about 10% higher than the younger informants (monolingual speakers of English).

2.2. Consonants

R (non-prevocalic /r/)

Channel Island English is variably rhotic, but only to a lesser degree. Thus, non-prevocalic /r/ may be pronounced in preconsonantal (e.g. *farm*) or in absolute final positions (e.g. *far*). The typical local realisation is a retroflex approximant, e.g. [fɑɻm], [fɑɻ]. The pronunciation of non-prevocalic /r/ in accents of British English is of a complex nature, involving both regional and social factors. In the traditional rural accents of England, three areas can generally be described as still preserving non-prevocalic /r/: Northumberland, Lancashire and a larger area in the south-west, ranging from Kent to Cornwall in the west and to Shropshire in the West Midlands (see Upton and Widdowson 1996: 30–31). In recent times, the rhotic areas have definitely become smaller.

The realization of non-prevocalic /r/ in the Channel Islands can certainly be attributed to an influence from other varieties of English. But on the other hand, an influence from Channel Island French seems equally possible. Speakers of the Norman French dialects are accustomed to pronouncing [r] (normally an apical type of *r*, pronounced with different degrees of vibration) both in preconsonantal (e.g. [parti], Standard French *parti* 'gone') and in absolute-final position (e.g. [vɛr] Standard French *vert* 'green'). Moreover, it is reasonable to assume that Norman French speakers of earlier periods who learnt English only at school tended to realize non-prevocalic /r/ under the influence of English orthography; in other words, their pronunciation of non-prevocalic /r/ would be based on a spelling pronunciation.

A clear indication that the realization of non-prevocalic /r/ is indeed influenced by Norman French becomes apparent in the ending *-er* in Guernsey English, which can be pronounced as [œr] (recall Table 2 above). Thus, the pronunciation of words such as *better* or *youngster* is ['betœr] and ['jʌŋstœr]. There is evidently an influence from Norman French here, the same ending [œr] also being used in Guernsey French as in [lə pɔrtœr] (Standard French *le porteur* 'carrier'). Another argument for the English ending *-er* being identified with the ending [œr] of Guernsey French is the fact that the latter is also found in English loanwords used in Guernsey French. In this way, the English words *shutter* and *mourner* have become [lə ʃɔtœr] and [lə mɔrnœr] in Guernsey French (Tomlinson 1981: 265, 325). The realisation of non-prevocalic /r/ was not very widespread among the 40 informants in Guernsey. The feature was mostly found in group MO at a rate of 9.2%. With the younger informants, it occurred only very occasionally, and solely in group MY. One can conclude, therefore, that the pronunciation of non-prevocalic /r/ is becoming increasingly rare in the Channel Islands as well.

H

H-dropping or the non-realisation of /h/ in initial position in stressed syllables before vowels (e.g. in *happy* ['æpi] or *hedge* [ɛdʒ]) is one of the best-known non-standard features of British English. It has achieved a high level of public awareness, is clearly stigmatized and commonly regarded as uneducated. For Wells (1982: 254) H-dropping is even "the single most powerful pronunciation shibboleth in England". Its presence in Channel Island English is hardly surprising. Moreover, there are individual items in which the initial position of /h/ is filled by a semivowel [j], as for example in *hear* [jɪə(ɹ) or *head* [jɛd], parallels of which can be found in English dialects, too (see SED questions VI.4.2 'hear', VI.1.1 'head'). It is an intriguing question to ask whether there possibly is an influence from Channel Island French on H-dropping. Nearly all varieties of French, including Standard French, do not realise initial /h/. But the Norman French dialects of the Channel Islands belong to the few varieties of French that have indeed preserved initial Germanic /h/, as e.g. in [haʃ] (Standard French *hache* 'axe') or [humar] (Standard French *homard* 'lobster'). Consequently, initial /h/ is a familiar sound for speakers of Norman French and should not lead to H-dropping in English. However, it has to be pointed out that the realisation of initial /h/ in Channel Island French is by no means categorical. Individual speakers may vary considerably in their use of initial /h/ and it appears likely that this variability has some effect on H-dropping in English.

NG

As in many other varieties of English, the pronunciation of the ending *-ing* in words such as *working* or *fishing* varies between velar [ɪŋ] and alveolar [ɪn], the latter form being more informal and possessing less social prestige than the former. There are no indications that an influence from Channel Island French has ever played a role in the realisation of *-ing*. The variable is well established and can be regarded as a general non-standard feature that has also found its way into Channel Island English.

2.3. Suprasegmentals

Channel Island English is characterised by features on the suprasegmental level (stress, intonation) which sound 'foreign' and which are either caused by an influence from Norman French or can at least be explained originally in terms of non-natives using English. Such features are most common with older people who are still regular speakers of Norman French. One may come across unusual stress patterns as for example in *Guernseyman* ['gɜːnzi'mæn], *educated* [edju'keɪtɪd] or *grandfather* [ˌgrænd'fɑːðə]. Alternatively, the difference between stressed and unstressed syllables may be less marked, with the use of secondary stresses on normally unstressed syllables as in *potatoes* ['pɔˌteɪˌtəʊz], *tomatoes* ['tɔˌmaˌtəʊz], *English* ['ɪŋˌglɪʃ].

3. The particle *eh*

This feature is strictly speaking a syntactic one, but it amply illustrates the interrelationship of different influences on Channel Island English also becoming apparent on the phonological level. *Eh* is a high-frequency particle in the Channel Islands (cf. Ramisch 1989: 103–113). Its normal phonological realisation is a diphthong [eɪ], but it can also be pronounced as a short [ĕ]. Three different modes of usage can be distinguished.

(1) *eh* is used as a request to repeat an utterance that the listener has not heard properly (rising tone on *eh*):
Interviewer: *What sort of trouble did you have there?*
Informant: *Eh?*

(2) *eh* is employed as a tag that is added to a statement to induce the listener to express his/her opinion on what is said by the speaker (rising tone on *eh*):
You grow your own stuff, eh - eh?

(3) *eh* is used as a phatic element which serves to establish or to maintain the contact between speaker and listener. It can occur repeatedly at relatively short intervals within one speech cycle, without giving the listener a real opportunity to voice his/her opinion. The aim of the speaker is merely to secure the listener's attention. The length of articulation of *eh* is often reduced, and the rising intonation which is typical of (1) and (2) is frequently omitted:

> *In the old days, you see, when we were children, there was no television eh, we had no electric* [sic] *anyway eh – yes a gramophone eh, that's all what we had you see, music eh, there was no wireless eh.*

Eh has indeed the status of a stereotype in the Channel Islands. People refer to it when they are asked about typical features of their local variety of English. It is certainly true that *eh* generally occurs in present-day English as an invariant tag question that invites the listener's response to a preceding statement (see e.g. Quirk et al. 1985: 814). But the question remains why *eh* occurs with such a high frequency in the Channel Islands. An influence from Norman French immediately suggests itself, because *eh* is equally common in the local French dialects and is employed in the same way as in English. Moreover, there is a tendency among older speakers to use a short [ĕ] for *eh* both in Norman French and in English.

4. Conclusion

Channel Island English is a variety that is characterised by a unique blend of features originating from different sources. On the one hand, one encounters non-standard features of British English that have arrived in the Channel Islands as a result of the close connections with Britain and because of the many British immigrants. This influence has existed for a long time and continues to be effective today. One can observe, for example, features such as T-glottalisation (the glottaling of intervocalic and word-final [t]) or TH-fronting (the use of [f] and [v] instead of [ð] and [θ]), especially in the speech of younger people in St. Helier (Jersey) and St. Peter Port (Guernsey). These features clearly are recent takeovers from British English. Yet on the other hand, Channel Island English comprises features that have their origin in Channel Island French. It is of particular relevance that they occur not only with speakers of Norman French but also with (younger) people who are monolingual speakers of English. Consequently, features of this type are not just transitional phenomena in the process of acquiring English. Some of the features have become an integral part of the local language variety and continue to exist even if the speakers themselves are no longer bilingual.

Our discussion of various phonological features has shown that in quite a number of cases the analysis is rather complex because both a Norman French influence and an influence from other varieties of English seem plausible. It can be confirmed that the same holds true for morphological and syntactic features (cf. Ramisch 1989: 91–163). If there is more than one explanation for a particular feature, these explanations should not necessarily be regarded as mutually exclusive; rather, it is reasonable to assume that there is a convergence of different sources of influence, reinforcing and complementing each other.

* I would like to thank my informants in the Channel Islands for their helpfulness and hospitality. The fieldwork in Guernsey and Jersey has always been a unique personal experience to me. I am particularly grateful to Michèle, Neil and Ross Tucker for their constant support and friendship over the years.

Exercises and study questions

1. In the audio samples there are two speakers from Guernsey who belong to different generations. Describe the generational differences between these speakers.
2. Find examples in the audio sample that can be characterised as recent adoptions from British English.
3. Examine the use of the particle *eh* in the Channel Islands and other varieties of English (for example, in Canadian English).
4. Give a detailed account of extralinguistic factors contributing to the rapid progress of English in the Channel Islands during the 20th century (cf. Ramisch 1989: 42–62).
5. Describe the social characteristics of bilingual (Norman French and English) speakers in the Channel Islands. Also consult the results of the local censuses published on the Internet.
6. Compare the Channel Islands to other communities of language contact (for example, Scottish English and Gaelic in Scotland) and identify parallels and differences.
7. The Channel Islands have gone through a process of 'language shift', which will most probably end in 'language death'. Outline the typical forces (both linguistic and extra-linguistic) in such a process (also cf. Jones 2002).

Selected references

Please consult the General references for titles mentioned in the text but not included in the references below. For a full bibliography see the accompanying CD-ROM.

Brasseur, Patrice
1980–1997
Atlas Linguistique et Ethnographique Normand. Paris: Editions du CNRS.

Census of the Channel Islands
1891 *Census 1891. Islands in the British Seas. Isle of Man, Jersey, Guernsey and Adjacent Islands*. London: Her Majesty's Stationery Office.

Census of Guernsey
2001 *2001 Guernsey Census. Report on the Census of Population and Households*. Guernsey: States of Guernsey.
Census of Jersey
2001 *Report on the 2001 Census*. Jersey: States of Jersey.
Gilliéron, Jules and Edmond Edmont
1902–1920 *Atlas Linguistique de la France*. Paris: Honoré Champion.
Guillot, Claude
1975 *Les Iles Anglo-Normandes*. Paris: Presses Universitaires de France.
Inglis, Henry
1844[4] *The Channel Islands*. London: Whittaker.
Jones, Mari C.
2001 *Jersey Norman French: Study of an Obsolescent Dialect*. Oxford: Blackwell.
Lemprière, Raoul
1974 *History of the Channel Islands*. London: Robert Hale.
Le Patourel, John
1937 *The Medieval Administration of the Channel Islands 1199–1399*. London: Oxford University Press.
Nicolle, E. Toulmin (ed.)
1893[3] *The Channel Islands*. London: Allen.
Quirk, Randolph, Sidney Greenbaum, Geoffrey Leech and Jan Svartvik
1985 *A Comprehensive Grammar of the English Language*. London: Longman.
Ramisch, Heinrich
1989 *The Variation of English in Guernsey/Channel Islands*. Frankfurt am Main: Lang.
Syvret, Marguerite and Joan Stevens
1998 *Balleine's History of Jersey*. West Sussex: Phillimore.
Tomlinson, Harry
1981 Le Guernesiais – Etude grammaticale et lexicale du parler Normand de l'Ile de Guernesey. Ph.D. dissertation, Edinburgh.
Tupper, Ferdinand B.
1876[2] *The History of Guernsey and its Bailiwick*. London: Simpkin and Marshall.
Upton, Clive and John D.A. Widdowson
1996 *An Atlas of English Dialects*. Oxford: Oxford University Press.

Received Pronunciation*

Clive Upton

1. Finding a model

Early in the twentieth century Daniel Jones described the model accent presented in *An English Pronouncing Dictionary* as

> that most usually heard in everyday speech in the families of Southern English persons whose men-folk have been educated at the great public [in the English sense of the word, i.e. private fee-paying] boarding-schools. This pronunciation is also used by a considerable proportion of those who do not come from the South of England, but who have been educated at these schools. The pronunciation may also be heard, to an extent which is considerable though difficult to specify, from persons of education in the South of England who have not been educated at these schools. It is probably accurate to say that a majority of those members of London society who have had a university education, use either this pronunciation or a pronunciation not differing very greatly from it. (Jones 1917: viii)

Jones's location of his model accent reflects social considerations of his time, with its reference to "men-folk" (then overwhelmingly the products of the public-school system) and the socially and economically dominant "London society", and emphasis on the normalizing force of *public school* education: indeed, so crucial is this element to his divination of his model that Jones initially calls it Public School Pronunciation, or PSP. Although non-Southerners might acquire the accent through privileged schooling, its possession is much more likely amongst educated Southerners.

Living in a hierarchical, south-east-focused and male-dominated world, Jones's stance on a model accent was understandable, and might be expected to have passed unquestioned in his day. Early twentieth-century assumptions are not necessarily ours, however: education is now more democratic in respect of both gender and class, and Southern England no longer holds a grip on linguistic prestige which it had on Britain a century ago. And to be fair to Jones, he himself was not completely locked into a narrow description of the accent. Despite the time-bound socio-cultural assumptions apparent in his description of his model, as the century progressed, although the essential prescription remained "public school" turned to "boarding school", "London society" became "Londoners", and by 1926 his label had become "Received Pronunciation" or RP (a term first used, though not as a specific label, by A.J. Ellis [1869: 23]). Further, he shows himself to be prepared to keep the boundaries of the accent and its speaker-base fuzzy, from the first noting "the delusion under which many lexicographers appear to have laboured, viz. that all educated speakers pronounce alike" (Jones 1917: viii).

If Jones could be open-minded about his model and its speakers, it is now time for us to be still more relaxed about the RP we acknowledge. The accent that has for a long time been regarded as a model in dictionaries and language-teaching texts is becoming much more widely based than it once was. There will always be a rearguard that deplores changes in the accent, as it will language change of any kind, and even some linguists out of touch with developments in England might misunderstand, but we should not on their behalf make the model too precious or confine its speaker-base to an elite.

Gimson makes the case for the acknowledgement of ongoing developments in the accent when, having outlined tendencies being shown by the accent in 1984, he writes:

> [I]f a different set of criteria for defining RP […] is adopted, together with a range of acceptable tolerances within the model, which will result in a somewhat diluted form of the traditional standard, the re-defined RP may be expected to fulfil a new and more extensive role in present-day British society. (Gimson 1984: 53)

That new role can most prominently be observed in the use of RP as the scarcely remarked-upon 'background' accent of the media newsreader. But despite Gimson's counsel, a commonly-held view persists that RP is a very narrow class-based and region-based variety of English pronunciation. This is in part the result of a peculiarly British attitude towards accent variety:

> The British are today particularly sensitive to variations in the pronunciation of their language. […] Such extreme sensitivity is apparently not paralleled in any other country or even in other parts of the English-speaking world. (Cruttenden 1994: 76)

Britons are indeed remarkably judgemental about all accents. That RP, when judged in the abstract, tends to be considered remote from the speech of most Britons suggests that a rarified version of the accent remains the target of people's perceptions, unsurprising if one considers the transcriptions which are frequently offered up, where the model lags behind Gimson's expectations.

The RP model with which native speakers and learners alike continue to be confronted is ultimately, of course, a matter of *sounds*: that is, phonetic realization of the phonemes of Received Pronunciation dictates the variety. But creating no little problem for the model is the choice of *symbols* by which those phonemes are described. The phonemic inventory of RP is often represented by a symbol set that was entirely appropriate when Jones began its description. Such have been the developments in the accent, however, that another transcription might now be thought more appropriate for some phonemes. Yet still the old description persists, a tradition of transcription being retained that fully supports Wells's description of the accent as "characteristic of the upper class and (to an extent) the upper-middle class" (Wells 1982: 10). The result is a situation in which traditionalists feel justified in insisting on the sounds transcribed, as if the symbols were phonetic rather than phonemic representations (while pragmatic users reproduce whatever sounds seem appropriate to them when they see the symbols).

Important to this chapter are transcription conventions first deployed in *The New Shorter Oxford English Dictionary* (1993) and subsequently in all the larger native-speaker dictionaries of Oxford University Press, and, alongside North American transcriptions, in *The Oxford Dictionary of Pronunciation for Current English* (Upton, Kretzschmar and Konopka 2001). These transcriptions are different in some small but significant particulars from those that might be encountered elsewhere in descriptions of Received Pronunciation, most notably as regards the TRAP, PRICE, and SQUARE vowels. They are descriptive of the reality of the kind of modern, "diluted" Received Pronunciation called for by Gimson twenty years ago.

2. RP and its lesser forms

There are, of course, various kinds of Received Pronunciation. A well-known classification aimed at making sense of this range is that devised by Wells (1982). There we find an upper-class accent labelled "U-RP", and a less marked form, taken in 1982 to be the most usual and unexceptionable variety, designated "mainstream RP". To these are added in close company "adoptive RP", "Near-RP", and "quasi-RP".

Simplification is sought in this chapter, with concentration on an accent that will not be the object of comment as regards elevated upbringing or social pretension. Furthermore, it is not to be associated with any one geographical region in England. This accent is simply labelled 'RP'. One stage removed from this is a variety that Ramsaran (1990: 179) calls "traditional" (here trad-RP). In most respects RP and trad-RP are identical. But they are different in important particulars that, since they are apparent to native British English speakers, should generally be made known to the speaker-learner who wishes to avoid being judged old-fashioned or affected. To trad-RP are consigned a range of sounds that many Britons are still wont to consider what is meant by "RP", leading them to think of it as "posh" (its almost universal pejorative label). Even further back in time and still more restricted socially than trad-RP is a version that does nevertheless continue to be heard as the accent of a few older speakers and as the affectation of some others. It also exists as a folk-memory in British society generally. Outmoded and, when heard (typically in old movies and newsreel commentaries), attracting amused comment, this is Cruttenden's "Refined RP" (1994: 80). The literature also abounds with speculation on possible innovations manifesting themselves in the speech of the young. Neither Refined RP nor speculative RP are treated specifically here, not because they are not interesting to debate, but because they do not belong in a purely descriptive setting, and for reasons of space.

3. The vowels of RP

There is an extensive literature in which a good deal of agreement, if not absolute unanimity, can be seen in the discussion of changes in RP. There is also, however, some disagreement about precisely how the accent is to be represented, because some commentators are more inclined to hold the line on the older transcriptional and realizational forms than others. (See for example Ramsaran's [1990: 180] critique of Bauer.) Given the fact of language change, there comes a time when certain sounds, conventionally labelled in a previous time, alter to such an extent that different symbols represent them more accurately: the phonetic symbols being absolutes, their interpretation cannot be altered to suit the new development, so that if anything is to change in the interests of accuracy and clarity it must be the label that is applied to the sound. This is especially important since transcriptions in dictionaries and English language teaching texts are invariably broadly phonemic, and if their users are to be properly served they need to be provided with transcriptions that correspond as honestly as possible to the sounds of the modern accent. The RP vowel inventory incorporates some judicious relabelling from that which is often to be seen. It contains nineteen stressed vowels, /ɪ, ɛ, a, ɑ, ʌ, ʊ, ɛː, iː, ɑː, ɔː, uː, əː, eɪ, ɔɪ, ʌɪ, aʊ, əʊ, ɪə, ʊə/ and two unstressed vowels, /i/ and /ə/.

RP and trad-RP share the same phonemic structure but differ in realizational (and hence labelling) particulars, and differ also occasionally in the lexical distribution of phonemes. Table 1 combines the accents in most of the lexical sets. Where there are differences, these are shown in separate columns.

It will be evident from Table 1 that RP and trad-RP coincide on KIT, LOT, STRUT, FOOT, FLEECE, FACE, PALM, THOUGHT, GOOSE, CHOICE, MOUTH,

NEAR, START, NORTH, FORCE, happY, lettER, and commA. NURSE shows only a slight difference, in which the RP transcription is indicative of a less restrictive rendering of the typical sound than is the trad-RP transcription. The BATH vowel coincides on [ɑː] in both varieties, with the addition of a further [a] variant in RP. CLOTH similarly coincides, though with a short vowel, in both varieties, with a long-vowel alternative in trad-RP. Both accents share [əʊ] in GOAT, with trad-RP having alternative [oʊ], and both share [ʊə] in CURE, with RP having alternative [ɔː]. Most significant developments have taken place, and so distinguish RP from trad-RP, in DRESS, TRAP, PRICE, and SQUARE.

Table 1. The vowels of RP and trad-RP

Vowel	**RP**	**shared RP/trad-RP**	**trad-RP**
KIT		ɪ	
DRESS	ɛ		e
TRAP	a		æ
LOT		ɒ	
STRUT		ʌ	
FOOT		ʊ	
BATH	ɑː ~ a		ɑː
CLOTH	ɒ		ɒ ~ ɔː
NURSE	əː		ɜː
FLEECE		ɪː	
FACE		eɪ	
PALM		ɑː	
THOUGHT		ɔː	
GOAT	əʊ		əʊ ~ oʊ
GOOSE		uː	
PRICE	ʌɪ		aɪ
CHOICE		ɔɪ	
MOUTH		aʊ	
NEAR		ɪə	
SQUARE	ɛː		ɛə
START		ɑː	

Table 1. (continued) The vowels of RP and trad-RP

Vowel	**RP**	**shared RP/trad-RP**	**trad-RP**
NORTH		ɔː	
FORCE		ɔː	
CURE	ʊə ~ ɔː		ʊə
happY		i	
lettER		ə	
commA		ə	

KIT

This is generally realized as half-close and retracted; one might expect a somewhat closer variant in some older speakers, although this is not a particular feature of trad-RP. The vowel is the norm in unstressed position in the morphemes *-ed*, *-es*, as in *hunted*, *faces*, and in such words as *minutes*, *David*. Elsewhere in unstressed syllables, reduction to [ə] is variably to be expected: vowel reduction is less likely in words where stressed [ɪ] is in the preceding syllable, as in *significant*, than when it is not, as in *horrible*, *happily*. Gimson (1984: 50–53) closely examines many of the details of this phenomenon.

DRESS

The RP vowel is half open front spread. Trad-RP has a raised variety that is best represented as /e/, although it does not typically reach the height of a half-closed vowel.

Recent change in this vowel is apparently part of a general lowering of the short front vowels, involving KIT and, most markedly, TRAP.

TRAP

Associated with the general tendency of the modern RP front vowels to lower articulation (see also KIT and DRESS), the movement by younger speakers from trad-RP [æ] to RP [a] is arguably one of the most striking changes that has taken place in the accent group in recent years. (This "classical" chain shift, it should be noted, is being recognized in the accents of some non-standard dialects too, as in Ashford, Kent, by Kerswill [2002: 201].) It is also undoubtedly a most controversial matter. This is seemingly at least in part because the newer form corresponds with what is perceived by many to be a 'Northern' sound (sometimes described rather curiously as "flat a"), on which see the discussion of the BATH vowel below.

Beyond this simple issue of regional prejudice, [a] is also a problematic sound for some Southern speakers, since, as Wells (1982: 291–292) explains, it is little different from a fronted version of their /ʌ/ ('their' since Northern accents do not possess this phoneme): with [a] and [ʌ] falling (close) together (see STRUT), distinctions between *fan* and *fun* blur or disappear in the perception of those used to the more obvious distinction between [æ] and [ʌ].

Although an issue for some, this trad-RP to RP change is a matter of which British English native-speakers are aware (mimicking trad-RP *bet* for *bat* and so on). It is also coming to be remarked upon in the usually conservative English Language Teaching field (Weiner and Upton 2000).

LOT

This is realized as a fully open to slightly raised rounded back vowel, whatever the variety of RP.

STRUT

The vowel is pronounced by many RP and by trad-RP speakers as a centralized and slightly lowered [ʌ]. For many speakers /ʌ/ is raised centralized [a]: the more central and lowered the vowel is, the more likelihood there is for confusion over RP [a] (see TRAP). There is an increasing appearance, however, of an innovation in which [ʌ] is raised and retracted from the centralized, towards (though not to) a half-close advanced position.

Variation in the STRUT vowel is a most prominent feature of north-south distinction in British English accents, and the recent RP raising development might be seen as a 'fudge' (Chambers and Trudgill 1998: 110–113) between the Northern [ʊ] and Southern [ʌ]. Interestingly, this feature was noted as the most usual form in the speech of mid-twentieth century traditional dialect speakers in the South and south Midlands (Orton 1962–1971; Upton 1995).

FOOT

Quite uncontroversially, this is realized as a half-close and advanced rounded vowel in all types of RP. The set gives rise to some of the most obvious and frequently-remarked hypercorrections amongst Northern STRUT [ʊ]-speakers striving to acquire RP when, aware that RP STRUT is invariably [ʌ], not [ʊ], they consciously change their FOOT vowel to [ʌ], producing [pʌt] *put*, [bʌtʃə] *butcher*.

BATH

The Received Pronunciation vowel is characteristically described as exclusively a long back spread vowel, its position being advanced from full retracted.

This is undoubtedly a correct description for the vowel of very many speakers. Two matters must be taken into account for a proper description of RP, however. Firstly, the long vowel is becoming both increasingly centralized and more shortened, while the more retracted sound is perceived by most native speakers now to be worthy of Refined RP caricature as being unacceptably 'plummy'. It would seem that the forward movement is being led by those words in the set where the vowel has a following nasal, as *chance*, *sample*.

This development might be connected with a second, the inclusion in the model adopted here of 'Northern short *a*' in the RP inventory. Many RP speakers, whose accent corresponds with that of other speakers on all other features, diverge particularly on this one variable, and might themselves use both [ɑː] and [a] variants interchangeably. (The other widespread Northern feature characterizing difference from the South, [ʊ] in the STRUT vowel, is, unlike this BATH-vowel feature, usually attended by other markers of northernness, such as long monophthongal FACE or GOAT vowels.) The use of BATH-[a] will essentially be because the RP speaker has Northern or north Midland origins, in the regional accents of which areas there is no TRAP/BATH distinction; the use of [ɑː] will either be because the speaker has Southern or south Midland origins, and so comes from an area with vernacular TRAP/BATH distinction, or because their speech is conditioned by trad-RP.

Wells's classification (1982: 297) of features as "Near-RP" on grounds of their not conforming to "phonemic oppositions found in RP" (of which [his] /æ ~ ɑː/ here is one) makes an assumption about RP structure supportable if one remains wedded to a south-centric view of the accent. Inclusion of BATH-vowel [a] in RP is on grounds already claimed: the accent is not to be thought of as an exclusively southern-British phenomenon (Upton, Kretzschmar and Konopka 2001: xii), and the inclusion of "a different set of criteria" resulting in "a somewhat diluted form of the traditional standard" (Gimson 1984: 53) is a description which well suits this move.

CLOTH

This vowel is in RP short, fully open, fully retracted and rounded. Trad-RP [ɔː] (a feature now more associated with Refined RP) is invariably judged risible by native British English speakers, RP and non-RP alike.

NURSE

There is some considerable variation in the realization of this central vowel, from half open to half close or slightly higher for some RP speakers. [əː] is chosen as the transcription here, reflecting the considerable variation apparent amongst speakers: it subsumes the more restrictive [ɜː] used by many transcribers of RP (also reducing by one the number of symbols in the transcription set).

FLEECE
In both varieties this is a long high front vowel, articulated with lips spread. The tongue is typically slightly lowered from the fully close position. Some slight gliding from the KIT-vowel position is usual, with [ɪi] being more usual than [iː].

FACE
This short upgliding diphthong shows little if any variability. Its startpoint is at or slightly below half-close front, from where movement is to the KIT vowel. Trad-RP speakers are likely to begin the diphthong high, at rather than below the half open position.

PALM
For both RP and trad-RP speakers, realization is as a fully open, advanced or centralized long spread vowel. The more retracted the form, the nearer it approaches that of Refined RP.

THOUGHT
This is [ɔː]. Compare this in all words in the set with the sounds applying at NORTH/FORCE below.

GOAT
Starting at a central position, this glide moves to or in the direction of RP /ʊ/, giving [əʊ]. Trad-RP has variant [oʊ], with a somewhat centralized startpoint, though by no means all speakers of that accent are characterized by its use.

GOOSE
In all forms this is a long high back vowel with lip rounding. The characteristic point of RP articulation is slightly relaxed from fully raised, and also somewhat advanced, with fronting becoming evident among many speakers, especially the young. A fully retracted form might be heard before [l], as in *pool*, *rule*, in all varieties (and in all positions in Refined RP). A short diphthong, [ʊu], is often to be heard word-finally, in such words as *sue*, *who*.

PRICE
RP starts this diphthong at a low central point, and moves in the direction of the KIT vowel /ɪ/. The startpoint is conventionally set at [a]. However, as the RP start-vowel can in fact be at any point from centralized front to centralized

back, and is raised from the fully open position, [ʌ] is most usefully to be identified for its description (see STRUT above). The RP transcription /ʌɪ/ was first used for the PRICE-vowel by MacCarthy (1978), and the [ʌ] startpoint is acknowledged as likely by Cruttenden (1994: 122). [aɪ], with just a slightly retracted startpoint, can be heard from some trad-RP speakers.

CHOICE
RP and trad-RP have a startpoint at a fully back half open position, the tongue moving in the direction of KIT.

MOUTH
The RP diphthong begins near the front open position, lips spread: some retraction is to be expected, although this is not considerable. The glide then proceeds towards, though not completely to, FOOT. Trad-RP sees a startpoint that is centralized rather than only retracted, and may encompass [ɑʊ] as well as [aʊ]. (The most retracted forms, accompanied by lengthening of the first element of the diphthong, are typical of Refined RP.)

NEAR
Beginning at KIT, the RP and trad-RP diphthong glides to a mid- to low-central position. (Refined RP characteristically places prominence on the second element, which might typically be rendered as [əː] or [ɑː]: these, and especially the latter, are, like [ɛʊ] for GOAT, likely to be singled out as features worthy of caricature.)

SQUARE
In RP this is a long monophthong at a front half-open position, articulated with lips spread: there might or might not be some slight off-gliding present, giving [ɛːᵊ ~ ɛː], but the dominant effect is of a single sound here. Trad-RP SQUARE is characterized by a centring diphthong [ɛə]. The monophthong-diphthong distinction between RP and trad-RP is, with TRAP-variation, one of the clearest that can be identified between the most modern and more dated varieties of the accent.

START
This vowel is essentially the same as that for BATH for those speakers who have a long vowel there. RP speakers with the short-vowel BATH variant have a long START vowel, but are likely to be among the speakers who have the most fronted versions.

NORTH/FORCE

RP and trad-RP vowels here are identical to that for THOUGHT, namely the half-open lip-rounded back vowel [ɔː].

CURE

A frequent realization of this phoneme is [ʊə], the centring diphthong starting at FOOT and gliding to a mid to open central position. This sound is to be heard from trad-RP speakers, and from many speakers of RP of the middle and older generations especially.

Increasingly occurring as a feature of RP, however, is long monophthongal [ɔː], explained by Cruttenden (1994: 134) as a stage further than the [ɔə] made possible for CURE by the loss of that sound as a feature of FORCE, where it was formerly heard: hence *Shaw*, *sure*, *shore*, formerly likely to be rendered in RP as /ʃɔː, ʃʊə, ʃɔə/ fall together for many present-day RP speakers as /ʃɔː/.

FIRE, POWER

These are most usually realized as triphthongs in RP, [ʌɪə] and [aʊə] respectively. "Smoothing" (Wells 1982: 286, 288, 292–293) of these to diphthongs [ʌə], [aə ~ ɑə] or to monophthongs [ʌː], [aː ~ ɑː] can readily be heard from all speakers in rapid speech (and especially from speakers of Refined RP in words in isolation).

happY

RP has a tense [i] for this unstressed vowel, where trad-RP has [ɪ]. RP [i] is sometimes attended by some, though not by full, length.

lettER

The mid-vowel [ə] is the realization for this in all RP varieties. Rhoticity is never a feature of RP, so that in final position no [r] is pronounced. However, [r] is used as a linking feature, when in speech a word ending in <r> is followed by another starting with a vowel. Thus *better or worse* is in RP [ˌbɛtər ɔː ˈwəːs].

commA

[ə] is the sound in all RP varieties, as with lettER. In the case of RP, [r] is used to create a link to a following word beginning with a vowel although, unlike with lettER, this is not supported by the orthography. This so-called intrusive <r>, although now "used freely in mainstream (native) RP" (Wells 1982: 284), is abhorred by many advocates of more restrictive varieties of the accent, and rarely features in its description in teaching texts or dictionary transcriptions.

4. The consonants of RP

RP and trad-RP correspond as regards their consonant phoneme inventory, and essentially in realization. Cruttenden (1994: 196) provides statistics for consonant frequencies in Received Pronunciation, based on the work of Fry (on "Southern English") and Perren, and these data introduce the twenty-four phonemes.

Table 2. Text frequencies of consonants in Received Pronunciation (Cruttenden 1994: 196)

	%		%
n	7.58	b	1.97
t	6.42	f	1.79
d	5.14	p	1.78
s	4.81	h	1.46
l	3.66	ŋ	1.15
ð	3.56	g	1.05
r	3.51	ʃ	0.96
m	3.22	j	0.88
k	3.09	dʒ	0.60
w	2.81	tʃ	0.41
z	2.46	θ	0.37
v	2.00	ʒ	0.10

Total all consonants: 60.78%

Some of these frequencies are, of course, structurally conditioned. Frequent occurrence of determiner *the* and pronouns in <th-, wh-> will account for comparatively high scores for [ð] and [w]. This aside, it is noteworthy that, as Cruttenden (1994: 196) observes, "the alveolar phonemes emerge as those which occur most frequently in English, this being a generalization which appears to be applicable to many languages". There is also some dominance of the voiceless over the voiced in sounds thus paired.

The phonology of the RP/trad-RP consonantal system is widely known and has been extensively discussed (see especially the seminal work begun by Gimson, manifested in Cruttenden 1994). The account below concentrates on particular *issues* in this area rather than on an account of each phoneme in turn.

Glottalisation

Existence of a glottal plosive in non-RP accents of English is well-known and much researched. It is often fondly supposed that this does not occur in RP. However, whilst it is true that, at least at present, [ʔ] does not occur in RP intervocalically within a word (Ramsaran 1990: 181), it is to be encountered elsewhere.

RP glottaling is most associated with /t/. Whilst it might be avoided in careful speech and is less likely to be heard in citation forms than in conversation, it is quite regularly to be expected in RP in syllable-final position preceding a non-syllabic consonant, as *rat trap*, *postbox*, *tentpeg*, *catflap*, *Rottweiler*. Like *Gatwick*, which regularly exhibits the glottal, another of London's airports, *Luton*, is also increasingly to be heard pronounced with [ʔ] preceding a syllabic /n/.

[ʔ] is frequently to be heard intervocalically at a syllable boundary, where the second syllable is stressed, giving [rɪˈʔɛntrənt] *re-entrant*, [dɪˈʔaktɪveɪt] *de-activate*. Trad-RP makes use of this device too in the break or hiatus created by the avoidance of intrusive /r/ (see below), as in *drawing*, *law and order*.

Linking and intrusive /r/

Linking /r/, retained historical post-vocalic word-final /r/ occurring before a vowel in the following word, is, as stated above at lettER, a normal feature of Received Pronunciation. In the most careful, mannered forms this might be avoided, rendering *far away* [fɑː ʔəˈweɪ] rather than [fɑːr ʔəˈweɪ]: it is unlikely that many speakers feel under special pressure to avoid such an hiatus now.

The insertion of a non-historical intrusive /r/, referred to in commA above, when following word-final /ə/, /ɑː/, or /ɔː/ before a word beginning with a vowel, has typically been proscribed for users of Received Pronunciation. This creates an hiatus between the adjacent vowel sounds or, alternatively, a glottal plosive might be interposed between them, giving [lɔː ənd ˈɔːdə] or [lɔː ʔənd ˈɔːdə] *law and order*. RP shows no such inhibitions, with intrusive /r/ being the norm: [lɔːr ənd ˈɔːdə], [ðɪ ʌɪˈdɪər əv ɪt] *the idea of it*. Similarly, intrusive /r/ occurs as the RP norm word-internally where the need is to avoid the hiatus, thus [ˈdrɔːrɪn] *drawing*.

Yod coalescence and yod deletion

Coalescence of /tj/, /dj/, /sj/, and /zj/ to /dʃ/, /dʒ/, /ʃ/, /ʒ/ is a general feature of Received Pronunciation (Ramsaran 1990: 187–188; Cruttenden 1994: 192), heard regularly for example in *attitude*, *residue*, *tissue*, *usual*. Coalesced forms are becoming increasingly apparent in all positions in RP, where they provide a less formal alternative to the more "careful" forms. The resistance to coalescence word-initially and before stressed vowels (*dune*, *reduce*) to which Ramsaran refers is more a feature of trad-RP speakers than of those of RP, although non-coalesced forms might be expected to be more regularly heard in their pronunciation of higher-level lexical items: for example *pendulate* is likely to be [ˈpɛndjʊleɪt] as well as [ˈpɛndʒʊleɪt].

It is usual in RP for the combination /luː/ to occur word-initially and following unaccented vowels in those words where historically /ljuː/ occurred and where it is in consequence found in Refined RP and some trad-RP. Thus RP *lute* and *loot* are homophonous.

Yod deletion is similarly characteristic word-initially in RP in such words as *super* and *suit*, where [sjuː] is found variably with [suː] in trad-RP.

<wh->

RP /w/ represented by the spelling <wh> in such words as *when*, *while*, *whistle* is invariably [w]. In trad-RP [w] is variable with [hw] (the regular form in Refined RP). In recent years "the use of /hw/ as a phoneme has declined rapidly (even though it is often taught as the correct form in verse-speaking)" (Cruttenden 1994: 195): the last part of this observation points to the somewhat rarified and self-conscious status now attaching to the feature.

Syllabic consonants

"The syllabic sound of a syllable is generally a vowel, but consonants may also be syllabic. The more sonorous consonants such as **n, l** often are so, as in the English words *people* ˈ**piːpl**, *little* ˈ**litl**, *button* ˈ**bʌtn**" (Jones 1969: paragraph 213). The morpheme *-ment* is typically [mn̩t].

It is normal for the syllabic consonant to be retained when a morpheme spelt with an initial vowel follows it, giving *littler* [ˈlɪtl̩], *buttoning* [ˈbʌtn̩ɪŋ]. (Jones uses the distinctive pair *lightening* [ˈlʌɪtn̩ɪŋ] and *lightning* [ˈlʌɪtnɪŋ] to illustrate this point.) It is frequently the case, however, that syllabicization does not occur before an unstressed vowel, especially in rapid connected speech, so that both RP *lightening* and *lightning* might be rendered as [ˈlʌɪtnɪŋ].

* I am most grateful to Dr Richard Matthews of the University of Freiburg for invaluable comments made on a draft of this paper. Any flaws remaining in its final form are to be laid entirely at my door, not his.

Exercises and study questions

1. Using the data in this chapter, identify some speakers (e.g. on film, in your community) who use RP, and others who have some trad-RP forms.
2. Analyze your own accent. What RP features do you have? Do you use any trad-RP sounds? Which of the speakers on the CD-ROM do you sound most like, and what evidence do you have for making this judgement? Which of your own sounds are entirely outside the range of Received Pronunciation?
3. The one feature that does tie RP to southern forms of British English of pronunciation is the STRUT/FOOT distinction, which is not found in northern regional accents. Find evidence of [ʊ] in a STRUT word in the recording of the speaker from the BBC Pronunciation Unit: what does this tell you about typical RP speakers? Find out all you can about the history and present career of the STRUT/FOOT split.
4. A north/south issue touched on in this chapter is the short-vs-long BATH-vowel distinction. What is the history of this regional difference? Discuss with others the judgement made here, that both sounds qualify for inclusion in RP.
5. Conduct a survey of attitudes to RP and some other accents of English, using semantic differential scaling (Fasold 1984: 150-151). You might investigate such attributes as ‘intelligence’, ‘friendliness’, and ‘honesty’ in this exercise.
6. Compare the ways in which RP is phonetically described in a range of dictionaries and/or English language teaching materials. To what extent can any differences be accounted for as transcriptional preferences only, and to what extent are they linguistically meaningful?
7. It is often said that Standard English can be spoken in any accent. Try to decide whether it is acceptable to call RP a ‘standard’ accent.

Selected references

Please consult the General references for titles mentioned in the text but not included in the references below. For a full bibliography see the accompanying CD-ROM.

Cruttenden, Alan
1994 *Gimson's Pronunciation of English*. 5th edition. London: Arnold.

Gimson, Alfred C.
1984 The RP accent. In: Trudgill (ed.), 32–44.

Jones, Daniel
1917 *An English Pronouncing Dictionary*. London: Dent.
1969 *An Outline of English Phonetics*. Cambridge: Heffer.

Kerswill, Paul
2002 Models of linguistic change and diffusion: new evidence from dialect leveling in British English. *Reading Working Papers in Linguistics* 6: 187–216.

MacCarthy, Peter
1978 *The Teaching of Pronunciation*. Cambridge: Cambridge University Press.

Ramsaran, Susan
1990 RP: fact and fiction. In: Susan Ramsaran (ed.), *Studies in the Pronunciation of English: A Commemorative Volume in Honour of A.C. Gimson*, 178–190. London: Routledge.

Upton, Clive
1995 Mixing and fudging in Midland and Southern dialects of England: the *cup* and *foot* vowels. In: Jack Windsor Lewis (ed.), *Studies in General and English Phonetics: Essays in Honour of Professor J.D. O'Connor*, 385–394. London: Routledge.

Upton, Clive, William A. Kretzschmar Jr. and Rafal Konopka
2001 *The Oxford Dictionary of Pronunciation for Current English*. Oxford: Oxford University Press.

Weiner, Edmund and Clive Upton
2000 [hat], [hæt], and all that. *English Today* 61: 44–46.

British Creole: phonology

Peter L. Patrick

1. Introduction

British Creole (BrC) is spoken by British-born people of Caribbean background whose parents, grandparents or great-grandparents migrated to Britain since 1948. It is an ethnic variety, rather than a regional or local one. BrC is the product of dialect contact between West Indian migrants, the largest group of whom during the period of critical formation (1950–1970) were Jamaican, and vernacular varieties of urban English English (EngE). I use *dialect contact* advisedly in view of the relative structural similarity between Caribbean English-lexicon Creoles (CarECs) and EngE, especially at the phonological level; the alternative, *language contact*, suggests the non-genetic relation between these varieties that most creolists assert, primarily on the basis of contrasts in morphology and syntax.

Because of the Jamaican input, most apparent at the lexical and grammatical level, BrC has been described as "a collection of local British varieties of J[amaican] C[reole]" (Sebba 1993: 139). This verdict derives from grammar-focused descriptions, however, which privilege the range of varieties most divergent from British English (BrE), and may not reflect the complexities of phonological variation and assimilation to British models, especially for UK-born speakers. Grammar-focused investigations of BrC (as most of them are) insist that "intermediate forms [...] [a]re sufficiently few in number to be excluded" from analysis (Edwards 1986: 50). This is not true of phonology. Moreover, as phonological markers of BrC are often the easiest to acquire, and present the weakest claim to British Black identity, as the range of speech including them is much wider than the range including only core grammatical features. Accordingly this chapter casts a wide net.

Languages brought by immigrant minorities to a new urban environment typically suffer one of two fates. They may die out as and when the immigrants or their descendants assimilate fully into the target society, and become native speakers of one of its existing varieties (often contributing a few loanwords, a grammatical construction or phonological pattern or two). They may be maintained as minority languages, serving the needs of an in-group which remains culturally distinct. This is the stance from which existing treatments of BrC are written: they emphasize its retention of Jamaican features, its systematic nature and distinctive properties. There are good social and pragmatic reasons for doing so in the case of discriminated languages and groups, quite apart from linguistic-theoretical imperatives.

Much more rarely, a deeper fusion of incoming and target languages occurs, wherein significant elements of language structure are retained, serving the social purposes of a group which becomes established on the local scene but never fully assimilates, often for reasons of oppression and discrimination. African American Vernacular English (AAVE), assuming its input languages included a (Caribbean or American) plantation Creole as well as African ancestral varieties, is a very relevant example. In such cases, analysis that focuses purely on retention of conservative features and systemic distinctness would miss much of what is most important. The description below presumes that a similar outcome (partial retention and incomplete assimilation) is possible for BrC, and deserves attention.

1.1. Input and diffusion

Linguistic variation among receiving communities in Britain, especially on the phonological level, is responsible for considerable diffuseness, so much so that it is incorrect to describe BrC as comprising a single accent. Indeed, BrC is found both north and south of England's principal dialect boundaries, and in all major dialect areas of the South of England. BrC speakers in Ipswich or Reading, with strong Barbadian input, or Dominican-ancestry speakers in Bradford, may differ systematically from London Jamaicans, whose speech contrasts with Dudley's Jamaican-derived population due to the West Midlands input in Dudley. Since Afro-Caribbeans, over time, moved beyond the initial entry points of migration to a range of urban areas (including Birmingham, Leicester, Manchester, Nottingham, Sheffield), and their children and descendants have become well-integrated into these speech communities (whose English dialect is their primary vernacular), such diffuseness in phonology may have increased rather than abated. Some authors (e.g. Sutcliffe and Figueroa 1992) describe BrC as a stable variety, meaning that it shows considerable continuity with Jamaican Creole (JamC). Indeed it does, but it is not known how far into the future this can be projected. Linguists can hardly focus only on how thoroughly Caribbean characteristics are retained, given the primacy of BrE for most UK-born speakers; investigation of a possibly-emerging, ethnically-distinctive dialect is an important research target.

With respect to ancestral Island Creoles (IslCs), i.e., source varieties of English-lexicon Creole spoken natively in the West Indies, and by Caribbean-born migrants overseas, BrC may be called a *post-native* variety. For its canonical speakers today it is a second or later variety, and their (other) first variety is not an Island Creole. It may occasionally be spoken indistinguishably from an Island Creole: Sutcliffe (1982: 132) notes that some British-born speakers in Bedford had essentially full native command of Jamaican Creole (JamC), while Tate (1984) describes Rastafarians of Dominican descent in Bradford whose accent passed for Jamaican among Jamaicans. BrC may also be acquired in childhood within the critical period: Sebba (1993: 37–40) reports that the age of acquisition varies (though studies of Afro-Caribbean child language socialisation into BrC are needed). Yet it seems clear that most speakers of BrC do not acquire it as a primary vernacular, and do not use it in preference to EngE, in a sustained fashion, across a wide range of domains. It is thus characteristic of BrC that, in any given community of speakers, a range of competence exists from token to full.

However, IslC input persists, via both earlier and current immigrants and family visits, as well as mass media (again largely Jamaica-focused). The presence of IslC speakers in British Afro-Caribbean communities ensures that adaptation, accommodation and acquisition remain a two-way street, with IslC speakers targeting EngE (and perhaps BrC) norms while BrC speakers are influenced by IslC norms. Although local British icons and exemplars have also arisen, BrC thus cannot be called normatively autonomous. As BrC serves different social purposes, Island JamC (Patrick, other volume) cannot reasonably be the touchstone for full competence. Given this, and the present focus on phonology (which shows perhaps greater assimilation to BrE norms than grammar), the description below attempts to avoid idealising BrC at its Creole extremity: not to police the distance between it and EngE, but to explore the linguistic space between that Creole pole and the possibly-now-emerging new dialect of BrE spoken by Caribbean-origin Britons.

BrC arose via the development of a generalised 'Black British' identity, partly externally imposed, as Caribbean people of many colours, ethnicities and class backgrounds found themselves viewed in Britain as *black, West Indian* and *working-class* (Gilroy 1987). Caribbean English (Island) Creoles are uniformly languages of ethnic and/or national identification; not so, BrC. Elements of BrC are used both between whites and blacks, as well as among white working-class (Rosen and Burgess 1980; Hewitt 1986) and Asian youth (Rampton 1995). Such 'crossing' indexes complex social meanings (like outgroup use of AAVE in the US), but appears both socially limited and grammatically restricted by comparison to British Afro-Caribbean community speech.

Little research exists on BrC; no sociolinguistic speech community survey has been performed in twenty years. The summary below, which follows earlier work by Sutcliffe (1982 in Bedford, 1992 in Dudley), Edwards (1986 in Dudley), and Sebba (1993 in London), must be considered tentative pending further investigation. However, it is not only lack of research that makes the picture more complex than most immigrant varieties. The principal causes can be identified, if their workings are not fully understood: (1) the structural relation between input varieties (CarECs and vernacular EngE), which is closer than for most genetically unrelated languages, yet further apart than that of many dialects; (2) the tangled history of language subordination, ideology and attitudes held by Caribbean peoples towards British English, and all it represents, as well as vice versa (Mühleisen 2002); and (3) the social and demographic factors relating to acquisition.

1.2. Forms of speech and social demographic factors

The forms of speech created by this contact situation are multiple, as are their labels, including Black London English, British Black English, London Jamaican, London/Jamaican, British/Jamaican Creole, and such less-discriminating terms as Patwa (~ Patois), Creole, 'dialect', West Indian English, Afro-Lingua, and Nation Language (which specify no particular source or British community). Such names for language varieties and people, though worthy of sociolinguistic study, cannot be explored here. An important research problem, only partially attempted to date (Sebba 1993: 10), is to identify, constrain and describe the major modes of BrC.

One might not wish to call all the forms of speech described below by the label BrC, but they exemplify the variety of language within the community:

(1)
   a. Use of partly-assimilated vernacular elements of British English into Island Creole (e.g. accent, lexicon);
   b. IslC that has undergone long-term accommodation to BrE, in face-to-face interactions by adult Caribbean immigrants (Wells 1973);
   c. use of IslC in code-switching with BrE by people who natively speak both;
   d. Creole-like speech learned young from native IslC-speaking family, by Afro-Caribbean native speakers of BrE;
   e. Creole-like speech learned later from IslC-speaking peers, by Afro-Caribbean native speakers of BrE;
   f. Creole-like speech learned late from non-native-IslC-speaking sources, and incorporated into BrE;

g. token elements of Creole speech, not sustained or sustainable, acquired unsystematically by Afro-Caribbean native speakers of BrE, or
h. …by non-Afro-Caribbean native speakers of BrE, and
i. emerging ethnically-distinctive varieties of BrE spoken primarily by Caribbean-origin Britons, incorporating various elements from Creole-like speech.

A range of factors combine in three major dimensions to shape these speech-forms: Caribbean family input (i.e. Jamaican/other English Creole/other Caribbean/none); community-type in Britain (i.e. urban South East England/other urban/rural, varying in degree of contact with London); and nativeness/degree of acquisition (i.e., acquisition from birth/before circa twelve years/afterwards; plus, generational status relative to immigration). While distinguishable in the abstract, these necessarily overlap in practice to produce the major modes of BrC, and are not exhaustive.

Little is known of linguistic variation according to classic sociolinguistic factors such as age, sex, and class, though it is clear that the great majority of BrC speakers are working-class, and that age has no simple relationship to generation of immigration. The complex role of ethnicity in acquisition has been explored mainly in terms of individual agency via "acts of identity" (LePage and Tabouret-Keller 1985), especially regarding assimilation into British nationhood and preservation of distinctive minority status. People of Caribbean heritage are of mixed background by definition, and mixing continues to occur in England across regional, social and racial lines. To the extent that "mixed-race" children represent linguistically heterogeneous family backgrounds, they will influence the development of BrC.

1.3. Linguistic convergence

Insofar as BrC possesses a stable phonological structure, it is the result of linguistic convergence between (i) JamC, as speakers perceive it; (ii) local vernacular BrE; and possibly (iii) another Caribbean English variety (though few traces of this type surface). The best-known variety, treated below, takes London Vernacular English (LonVE) as input (ii); other varieties are subject to some London influence as well. At the level of the phonological inventory, BrC as expected has the more numerous phonemic contrasts of LonVE, plus some phonetic realizations typical of JamC. Social pressures may also influence speakers to converge with "proper English" (as likely to be vernacular BrE as Received Pronunciation [RP]) in formal settings, producing a more

British-sounding result than conversational speech, as in the word-lists recorded.

2. Vowels and diphthongs

Nearly a dozen analyses of JamC vowel and diphthong systems exist, positing inventories from 8–17, and variously motivated by historical transparency (Cassidy 1961), symmetry (Devonish and Harry, Americas and the Caribbean volume) or phonetic accuracy (Beckford Wassink 1999). This last, the most detailed empirical analysis, describes JamC as a V-shaped, peripheral, symmetrical system with five front and five back vowels and two at the low apex, and demonstrates that contrasts often attributed to length alone, an important distinctive feature of JamC, are supported by systematic quality distinctions as well. BrC however relies primarily on vowel quality, and vowel length generally patterns with LonVE. Variants which might be contrastively associated with Standard Jamaican English (StJamE) are rare in BrC, where vernacular structures (both British and Jamaican) predominate, and are more often encountered in the speech of Caribbean-born migrants than later generations.

(2) Jamaican Creole vowel inventory (based on Beckford Wassink 1999)

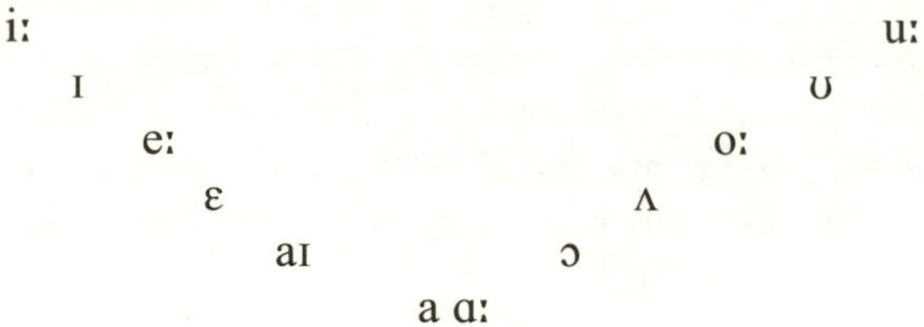

The inventory in (2) is fairly typical, except that it explicitly recognises quality distinctions as well as length in every sub-system. Analyses with fewer members inevitably dephonemicise some regular and salient distinctions; those with more typically admit debatable separate subclasses, such as rhotic vowels (Veatch 1991). Beckford Wassink concludes that /ɔ/ is not phonetically distinguishable for most speakers from /a/, as suggested in Patrick (1995), thus giving only five short vowels and six long ones or diphthongs.

Table 1. Variants in British Creole (South East England variety).

KIT	i ~ ɪ	FLEECE	iː ~ ɪi	NEAR	ier ~ iɛr > ɪə ~ iː
DRESS	ë ~ ɛ	FACE	ie ~ iɛ ~ eː ~ ɛɪ	SQUARE	ier ~ iɛr ~ eː ~ ɛː
TRAP	a ~ æ	PALM	aː ~ ɑː	START	aː ~ a̱ː > ɑː(r)
LOT	a ~ ɒ ~ ɔ	THOUGHT	aː ~ ɔː ~ oː	NORTH	aː ~ ɑː(r) ~ ɔː ~ oː
STRUT	ɔ ~ ɔ̈ ~ ɐ ~ ʌ	GOAT	uo ~ ʊo ~ ʊə ~ oː ~ əö	FORCE	uo ~ ʊo ~ öː(r) ~ ɔ̝ː
FOOT	u ~ ʊ	GOOSE	uː ~ üː ~ ʉː	CURE	jɔː ~ joː(r)
BATH	aː ~ äː ~ ɑː	PRICE	ai ~ aɪ ~ ɑɛ, ɑe	happY	ɪ ~ i
CLOTH	aː ~ ɑ ~ ɒ	CHOICE	ai ~ ɔɪ ~ ɔɛ	lettER	a ~ ɐ
NURSE	ɔ̈r ~ ɵ^{r} ~ ʉə ~ ɜː ~ ɜ^{r}ː	MOUTH	ɔʊ ~ aʊ ~ æə	horsES	ɪ
				commA	a ~ ɐ

Table 1 summarises the principal vowel variants; the general effect is a London-like system with a variably Jamaican-like sound. It is difficult, in the present state of knowledge, to make quantitative statements about preference, and it cannot be asserted (without premature idealisation) that all variants even belong to the same system, given such factors as variable rhoticity, vowel quality dispersion and overlap, alternation of centring glides with monophthongs with upglides in the same word-class, etc. Nevertheless, all variants may be encountered in the speech of Caribbean-origin Britons who claim to be using 'Patwa' or 'Creole'.

There are often differences, however, between speakers who were born and spent at least early childhood years in the Caribbean, and those born in Britain like Sally, the twenty-something speaker of the word-list sample on the accompanying CD-ROM. Though both Sally's parents are from Kingston, she identifies herself during the recording saying, "Yeah but I'm Cockney!" Her mother and Paulette, a British-born but Jamaica-raised woman a generation older, tease her saying "You fly the flag", and "You Londoner... Cockney". Sally's assimilated speech may represent the future of London Jamaican pronunciation, though the chart captures a range of variants (hers are generally rightmost, Paulette's to the left).

KIT, DRESS, FOOT, STRUT

For short non-low vowels, BrC realisations are often more peripheral and tenser than the London norm, accurately reflecting JamC. Most authors typically phonemicise the STRUT items as /o/ although they never reach [o]; however, they are relatively back and often rounded to [ɔ].

TRAP, LOT, BATH, PALM

Southern BrC is a "broad-BATH" dialect like its input varieties. Short-O (ME *ŏ*) and short-A (ME *ă*) merged in the formation of JamC, as the latter never raised from [a] to [æ] according to Cassidy and LePage (1980: xlix), so pronunciations with [æ] represent StJamE or, more probably, BrE influence. Again targeting basilectal JamC as reference variety, BrC may dramatically reduce vowel-quality contrasts among low vowels (Patrick 1999). Though their ranges do not entirely overlap, all four word-classes share front, open variants, sometimes centralised (e.g. Sally); for some speakers TRAP and LOT may be merged, though others retain rounding on the latter. However, length distinctions are robust and may even be exaggerated relative to London English (Beckford Wassink [1999: 186] finds a 1.6:1 ratio for long-to-short in JamC, typical of languages where quantity is the primary distinction). Some Jamaican-born speakers alternate [aː] and [ɑː] in succession, both long.

The possibly greater salience of quantity contrasts may account for the lengthening tendency observed in CLOTH words (normally short in South East England, Wells 1982) pronounced with front vowels; UK-born assimilated speakers tend to have short, backer vowels.

FLEECE, GOOSE

BrC long vowels appear to be only sporadically and lightly affected by the London Diphthong Shift, for UK-born speakers only (e.g. Sally has slightly centralised monophthongs such as [üː] for GOOSE); Jamaican-born ones generally follow both JamC and StJamE in having tense monophthongs. The fully centralised variants of /iː/ [əi] and /uː/ [əʉ] do not seem to co-occur with BrC grammar and lexis, even in code-switching. One wonders whether BrC, like AAVE (Labov 2001), might provide a locus for non-participation in predominant vowel-shifts.

PRICE, CHOICE, MOUTH

The PRICE/CHOICE merger, general in JamC (Thomas 2001: 163) but carefully distinguished by StJamE speakers, does not hold for BrC, where some back round diphthongs occur in CHOICE words. Use of /w/ to distinguish these (/bwai/ 'boy', as in JamC) from PRICE words is a salient marker of BrC, and may occur even where vowel quality makes it redundant. Both diphthongs contain strong glides; they may be more peripheral before unvoiced consonants. For UK-born speakers, both onset and target may be slightly retracted or lowered. However, Sutcliffe and Figueroa (1992: 98) observe a fronting and raising of the onset in Rastafarian-identified speakers in Dudley.

MOUTH generally does not show the [o] or [ʊ] starting point common in JamC but is lowered and/or fronted, converging with London realizations; the glide may be abbreviated to a centring one, targeting [ə]. Exceptions to this are lexicalized pronunciations of common words ending in a velar nasal, realised /ʌŋ/ in BrC, where LonVE has the MOUTH diphthong followed by /n/ or /nd/, as in *down* [dʌŋ ~ dɔ̈ŋ] *town*, *round*.

FACE, GOAT

These word-classes, among the most various and stigmatized in JamC, lend themselves to a host of realisations in BrC. They occur as down-gliding or, more commonly, in-gliding diphthongs, e.g. [guət], mid monophthongs, e.g. [goːt], or even London-like up-gliding diphthongs, e.g. [gəöt] (rarely as the high monophthongs occasionally found in Jamaica). They do not seem to participate in the London Diphthong Shift, which lowers the starting point for both right down to [a], since they rarely dip below [ɛ]. While Sally's FACE is London-like, her GOAT [gəöt] is a classic BrC hybrid: it has a central starting-point like many London speakers, but the [o] target is typical of JamC, with none of the fronting to [ɪ], [ʏ] found in recent years (Altendorf and Watt, this volume). Despite some l-vocalization, the vowel quality in GOAT ~ GOAL is similar.

Beckford Wassink (1999: 161) notes that [ie] is more prevalent and less stigmatised for FACE in urban Jamaican than [uo] is for GOAT; it is expected that frequency would be reversed in BrC, since what is not prestigious in Kingston may be a source of covert prestige or basilectal focussing in Britain. Lexical exceptions *mek* [mɛk] 'make, let' and *tek* [tɛk] 'take' are common markers of BrC, but do not vary as often with [miek] and [tiek] as in JamC.

happY, lettER, COMMA

The reduction vowel for weak syllables in JamC is generally closer to [ɐ] or even [a] in JamC than to schwa; /a/ is a plausible phoneme assignment. This has led some analysts to mistakenly posit /a/ as the target of all in-gliding and down-gliding diphthongs, as well, though there is no evidence that such glides ever terminate in [a]. It is common for native speakers of both JamC and StJamE to produce full, unreduced vowels in non-final environments where BrE varieties reduce them, but this is less true of BrC. HappY is occasionally lax for Jamaican-born speakers, whose open syllables regularly end in short lax vowels.

NEAR, SQUARE

JamC is variably (semi-)rhotic but BrC is less so. This may be due to the sociolinguistic confusion of values attached to rhoticity, which is more often present in StJamE than basilectal JamC, but less often present in both standard and vernacular varieties of South East England. Rhotic pronunciations may be interpreted as either basilectal or acrolectal in Jamaican contexts, depending on linguistic environment, but are non-local in London and thus not especially likely to surface in BrC, on either count. These two word-classes are salient environments for post-vocalic /r/ appearance in BrC, as it may coincide with basilectal in-glides [ier, iɛr], which are less stigmatised in this environment. However, both in BrC and basilectal JamC, non-pre-vocalic /r/ is generally limited to morpheme-final position. Wells (1973: 95–101), describing JamC adults undergoing long-term accommodation to BrE, gives frequencies of appearance before a variety of final consonants.

In BrC focused on basilectal JamC, the two word-classes may merge in NEAR with an in-glide, thus contrasting strongly with LonVE. For British-born speakers, the occasional acrolectal StJamE merging in SQUARE (in which *cheers* may be pronounced with a mid monophthong, as though it were *chairs*) is not typical of BrC, since the two word-classes may be distinguished on height, as [ɪː] and [ɛː], with or without a centring glide.

NURSE

This vowel is not normally a distinct one in JamC, being simply the STRUT vowel plus /r/. In BrC a range of somewhat higher, mid-central pronunciations also occur. In both varieties, rounding is common. R-coloration is most frequent morpheme-finally, but may occur before /rC/ combinations, especially /rt, rd/. With mid-central pronunciations it is less common, unlike the StJamE long monophthong, but does occur in BrC. Sutcliffe and Figueroa (1992: 103) record for Dudley a close central onset /ʉə/, “a new sound... not noted for JC formerly” in *wok* ‘work’, *tod* ‘third’, *church* ‘church’, etc.

START, NORTH, FORCE

As with TRAP etc., the START and NORTH vowels in BrC often merge in a front open vowel for JamC-focussed speakers, typically long and with no r-coloration [aː], though much backer and rounded pronunciations of NORTH words commonly occur for UK-born speakers (Sally has [öː]). FORCE is merged with NORTH in many dialects, including South Eeast English, but not in JamC or the Caribbean generally, which Thomas (2001: 47) calls "[p]erhaps the last stronghold of the /ɔr/ - /or/ distinction". Sutcliffe and Figueroa (1992: 102) hypothesise that this merger is underway in BrC, but in the London area they may still be distinguished, even in the most British-assimilated pronunciations, despite being frequently merged in RP and South East England: for Sally, FORCE remains /ɔː/ but NORTH is /oː/.

3. Consonants

t, k, g

In many BrE dialects including LonVE, syllable-final and word-medial /t/ are often subject to glottal substitution, glottal reinforcement, and other forms of glottalisation. This highly salient and stigmatised vernacular feature is not noticeable in JamC, but occurs regularly in BrC and is assimilated even by Caribbean-born adult migrants.

Straw (2001) examines glottal features in the Suffolk town of Ipswich, in the English of Caribbean-born speakers from Jamaica, Nevis and Barbados (it occurs natively in the last, uniquely in the West Indies [Roberts 1988], but in a pattern different from EngE). She finds different frequencies and environmental constraints among them, and between the accents of Caribbean and white Ipswich residents. Analysing spectrograms, Straw and Patrick (2007) observe that the Barbadians partly exhibit general configurations allegedly diffusing across England, partly resemble white Ipswich speakers (in a departure from known patterns of glottalisation elsewhere), and partly show distinctive features which may reflect IslC usage. Only the youngest Barbadian immigrants may have acquired local Ipswich patterns. T-glottalling is thus a candidate not only for incorporation into BrC, but also for phonological diversity within its varieties, and possibly for helping to distinguish a new ethnic dialect of BrE.

Palatalization of JamC /k, g/ and insertion of /j/ glides is studied in Patrick (1995) and Beckford Wassink (1999); nothing different has emerged in BrC. Initial consonant clusters, especially /sCC/, e.g. *spring, strong*, are more likely in BrC than JamC.

th-stopping

The most salient contrast with prestigious English accents is th-stopping, which uses alveolar stops [t, d] to correspond to dental fricatives [ɵ, ð]. This describes JamC and BrC; the stops themselves are sometimes fronted. This contrasts straightforwardly with LonVE, which instead substitutes [f, v], though only non-initially, for the voiced case. (Word-initial [ð]-stopping also occurs sometimes in LonVE; this environment is discounted below.) The [f] variant is more common; it is regularly assimilated by older Caribbean-born speakers, and surfaces unadapted, or misadapted (Sebba 1993: 53–56), in the BrC of the UK-born younger generation, in words such as *both, mouth, north* and *Samantha*. In a study of two London-born brothers whose parents were Jamaican-born, Knight (2001) found that David and Gary both avoided standard variants [θ, ð] entirely over several hours of speech (700 tokens). However, compared across three situations, David's use of the JamC/BrC variants ranged from 18% to 55%, while Gary's never surpassed 6%. Other variants were all LonVE forms, so both were highly vernacular speakers, but David was much more Creole-focussed, although even he used fewer such forms than the Dudley study found (Edwards [1986: 110] reports 41% to 100%). The pattern, confirmed with morphological data (plural-marking), suits their cultural styles: though close and involved in overlapping networks, the two contrast in their musical preferences, racial integration of football teams and school-friend networks, hair and clothing style, etc. In each case David's associations are more overtly Caribbean or Black British than Gary's. The family maintain strong contact with Jamaican culture, and neither boy is a 'lame' (Labov 1972): the language difference is down to individual agency, given joint exposure to varied resources.

As the likelihood of /v/ appearing intervocalically is bolstered by the [ð]-to-[v] rule, the old-fashioned occurrence of /b/-for-/v/ in JamC is not salient in BrC, though it happens for frequent forms such as *neba* 'never, not' or *beks* 'vexed'.

h-dropping

Except as a recessive feature in western dialects of the island, [h] is not contrastive in JamC but rather variably appears in syllable onsets, independent of historical or spelling patterns, to mark emphasis. It also signals social maneuvering in the style known as 'speaky-spoky' (Patrick 1997). In LonVE [h] also occurs noncontrastively to mark emphasis, a function it shares with glottal stops (Sivertsen 1960). Sebba (1993: 158) suggests that glottal stopping may be replacing h-dropping in this function for Creole-influenced LonVE. A possible motivation for this is that indiscriminate emphatic h-dropping invokes a "stereotype of rural, parental speech" for British-born black speakers (Sutcliffe and Figueroa 1992: 97), while glottal stopping retains local, covert prestige and is compatible with BrC norms. Regardless, Sutcliffe observes that younger British-born speakers seldom use emphatic h-dropping.

r, l
Rhoticity is slightly more frequent in JamC than in LonVE, where it only occurs post-vocalically in linking or intrusive mode. Wells (1982: 577) describes the variable occurrence of /r/ in historically r-ful words as semi-rhotic, noting that /r/ is lost more often before consonants in JamC than syllable-finally. It undergoes further attrition in BrC. While /r/ is retained most often in JamC for NURSE, NORTH and START words, no pattern has emerged in BrC.

In both JamC and StJamE, all laterals are clear including syllabics. Consequently there is no l-vocalization. This feature was notoriously not assimilated to EngE by the adult immigrant generation of Jamaicans (Wells 1973). They did alter the JamC rule for velarizing alveolar stops before syllabic /l/, adapting /bakl/ 'bottle', /niigl/ 'needle' to /batl/, /niidl/. Both pronunciations are found in the BrC of younger generations, who are not prestige-driven in the same way, and so produce basilect-focused tokens like *Ku kekl a kos pot* 'Look at the kettle cursing the pot' (Sutcliffe and Figueroa 1992: 83). There is some evidence for dark [ɫ] creeping into the speech of Jamaicans who came as children to London, where L-vocalization continues apace in LonVE: such speakers retain clear [l] in *chil(d)* but may have [ɫ] in *goal*, *ghoul*, and even vocalization in *old* and syllabic *fatal, beetle* (with /t/).

4. Prosody and intonation

The BrC prosodic system's interactive functions for turn-taking are studied by Local, Wells and Sebba (1985), who show that pitch characteristics of the final syllable of a syntactic unit help delimit turns in a way that contrasts with BrE.

Prosody and intonation are treated in depth for JamC and BrC by Sutcliffe and Figueroa (1992: 107–124), who regard them as syllable-timed tone languages with two contrastive tones, downstep and upstep. English word stress is most often associated with low tone, rather than high, resulting in English monolinguals' perception that stress is often oddly misplaced in BrC (they mistakenly interpret high pitch as stress). Sutcliffe records several cases where British-born speakers pointed explicitly to grammatical patterns differentiated by tone for his benefit. He outlines a number of patterns contrasting question types, consecutive verb constructions, relative clauses, conditionals and indicatives by consistent devices such as marked tones on subject pronoun and main verb. There is little doubt that such elements have carried over from JamC productively, and yet it is difficult to reconcile them with more assimilated aspects of BrC phonology, suggesting that not only is further research required, but fundamental alterations in the sound system of BrC may take place in rising generations.

* I thank David Sutcliffe for introducing me to the study of British Jamaican speech, and for discussion during the writing of this article; thanks also go to Michelle Straw and Pamela Knight, for allowing me to draw on their unpublished data and research, and contributing crucially to the fieldwork.

Exercises and study questions

1. Plan a small field study comparing word-list data from 4-6 speakers. Match individuals of Afro-Caribbean background and Anglo background from a single speech community. What are some of the social and socio-linguistic criteria you would need to take into account? Identify your ideal sample, and say why you would choose them.

2. Choose two phonological features to treat as linguistic variables: one consonantal, and one vocalic. Describe the phonetic variants that occur in BrC and in SE BrE (if needed, consult the chapter in this volume by Altendorf & Watt). What sociolinguistic hypotheses would you put forward for them? (e.g. concerning differential social distribution, changes in progress, etc.)

3. (a) Describe several aspects of BrC vowel realisations that may be traced to JamC.
   (b) Try to generalise your descriptions across sets or features of vowels.
   (c) Might these generalisations have any consequences for sound change among BrC speakers?

4. The use of glottal forms of consonants (/p/, /k/ but especially /t/), and the use of H-dropping, are two features that characterise many BrE dialects (including LonVE) as well as BrC. Describe the sociolinguistic patterns for LonVE and BrE briefly. What appears to be happening in BrC? Consult Foulkes & Docherty (1999), and other chapters of this volume, for comparisons to other urban BrE dialects.

5. What is the distribution of rhoticity in BrC? Compare this briefly to JamC and SE BrE. What effect do changes in rhoticity between JamC and BrC appear to have on the vowel system of BrC?

6. If one takes JamC as a source dialect, and an urban vernacular BrE dialect as the target, BrC might be treated as a transitional variety – i.e., a theatre for

sound changes in progress. Identify and discuss a split or merger that may be in process in BrC. Consult other chapters of this volume, and Foulkes & Docherty (1999), for comparisons to urban BrE dialects.

Selected references

Please consult the General references for titles mentioned in the text but not included in the references below. For a full bibliography see the accompanying CD-ROM.

Beckford Wassink, Alicia
1999 A sociophonetic analysis of Jamaican vowels. Ph.D. dissertation, University of Michigan, Ann Arbor.

Gilroy, Paul
1987 *There Ain't no Black in the Union Jack*. London: Hutchinson.

Knight, Pamela
2001 London/Jamaican in the speech of two subjects. B.A. thesis, Department of Language and Linguistics, University of Essex, Colchester.

Labov, William
1972 The linguistic consequences of being a lame. *Language in Society* 2: 81–115.

Local, John K., William H.G. Wells and Mark Sebba
1985 Phonology for conversation: phonetic aspects of turn delimitation in London Jamaican. *Journal of Pragmatics* 9: 309–330.

Patrick, Peter L.
1995 The urbanization of Creole phonology: variation and change in Jamaican (KYA). In: Guy, Baugh, Feagin and Schiffrin (eds.), 329–355.
1997 Style and register in Jamaican Patwa. In: Schneider (ed.) 1997b, 41–56.

Rosen, Harold and Tony Burgess
1980 *Languages and Dialects of London School Children*. London: Ward Lock Educational.

Sivertsen, Eva
1960 *Cockney Phonology*. Oslo: Oslo University Press.

Straw, Michelle
2001 Caribbeans in Ipswich – dialect contact and variation: a study of t-glottalisation. M.A. thesis, Department of Language and Linguistics, University of Essex, Colchester.

Straw, Michelle and Peter L. Patrick
2007 Dialect acquisition of glottal variation in /t/: Barbadians in Ipswich. In: Patrick Honeybone and Philip Carr (eds.), special double issue of *Language Sciences* 29 (2–3): 385–407.

Sutcliffe, David
1982 *British Black English*. Oxford: Blackwell.

Sutcliffe, David and John Figueroa
1992 *System in Black Language*. Clevedon: Multilingual Matters.
Tate, Shirley
1984 Jamaican Creole approximation by second generation Dominicans? The use of agreement tokens. M.A. thesis, Department of Language and Linguistics, University of York.
Thomas, Erik R.
2001 *An Acoustic Analysis of Vowel Variation in New World English*. Durham, NC: Duke University Press.
Veatch, Thomas C.
1991 English vowels: their surface phonology and phonetic implementation in vernacular dialects. Ph.D. dissertation, Department of Linguistics, University of Pennsylvania, Philadelphia.
Wells, John C.
1973 *Jamaican Pronunciation in London*. Oxford: Blackwell.

Synopsis: phonological variation in the British Isles

Clive Upton

1. Introduction

Drawn together here, in outline, is information central to the phonetic and phonological variation to be found in the varieties of English spoken in the British Isles, as described in detail in the chapters written by the contributors to this work. All varieties are taken to be the same in kind. However, whilst most are regional, two (British Creole and Received Pronunciation) are not in fact to be geographically placed, and some of those that are regional cover much larger territories than others. Treatment is inevitably 'broad brush', so that the summary is to be taken more as an introductory index to the descriptions than as a description in its own right. Where, as is for example especially the case for the national varieties of Scotland, Wales, and Ireland, there are marked internal differences to be taken account of, these are necessarily in large measure masked here. Readers should therefore take this summary as a starting point, and must refer to the relevant chapters themselves in order fully to appreciate the richness of present variation throughout the region.

Predictably, most phonological differences between varieties concern the vowel systems and realizations. As is quite customary for the British varieties, both qualitative and quantitative vowel distinctions are made, the quantitative ones resulting in the holding of categories of "short" and "long" vowels, along with diphthongs, and unstressed vowels. Each of these categories provides a major section of the summary: the convention of lexical sets, as employed in the chapters themselves to give order to vocalic variation, is maintained in this summary, and the keywords for those sets furnish the headings for the various sub-sections in which the vowels are discussed. Consonants, prosody and intonation will be discussed in the last two sections.

2. Short vowels

2.1. KIT

Widely throughout the British Isles, the realisation of this vowel is [ɪ]. This feature occurs in all varieties and is quite usual in all but Orkney and Shetland, where lowering and centralizing, heard variably also in Northern England and the Channel Islands, is to be expected. Lowering of the vowel to [e] is a feature of Urban Northern Irish, and this or an even lower and more retracted vowel is a feature of Urban Scots. A tense [i] is characteristic of the West Midlands, and may be heard in East Anglia and British Creole too.

2.2. DRESS

This vowel is rendered most widely as half open front, [ɛ], the only characteristic exception occurring in South-east England, where [e] is the norm: [e] can also be heard in the West Midlands and, retracted, in British Creole. Raising from [ɛ] is found in the Channel Islands, East Anglia, Urban Scots, and Orkney and Shetland, and lowering occurs in urban Northern Irish.

2.3. TRAP

Principal variants for TRAP are [a] and [æ], these serving to some extent as markers of north-south variation. [æ] is most characteristic of Ireland, East Anglia and the Channel Islands: it is also characteristic of Southern England, although [a] is becoming widespread in this area also. [a] is usual in Orkney and Shetland, in most of the accents of Scotland (where retraction is usual for Urban Scots), and the North of England, with the English Midlands showing some considerable [a]-[æ] variability. In the non-regional British Creole and RP accents, both [a] and [æ] occur: in RP, [æ] is traditional, whereas [a] is the usual modern realisation.

2.4. LOT, CLOTH

Quite considerable variability is to be heard with the LOT vowel, both between and within accent-types. [ɔ] is widely heard in Orkney, Shetland, Scotland, and Wales, and is a feature of Fashionable Dublin speech in Ireland, contrasting with a Colloquial Dublin (and Irish Rural Western) [a], a feature also of British Creole; [ɔ] might be found too in Creole, and in the West Midlands. [ɒ], the sound in RP, is also usual regionally throughout England outside the South-west and East Anglia, where [ɑ] is also reported, as it is across southern Ireland as a 'supraregional' form. Besides being found in Ireland, [a] can be heard in Creole too. The same distribution of variants exists essentially for CLOTH as for LOT: [ɔː], formerly widely heard before fricatives in Southern England, is still to be heard in the speech of older working-class East Anglians, and is a feature of the most conservative type of traditional RP. Creole exhibits variability in terms of length of [a], with CLOTH exhibiting length, and [ɑ] also occurs in CLOTH in this accent.

2.5. STRUT

This vowel exhibits a celebrated variation which is frequently offered as marking the distinction between the accents of Northern and Southern England: Northern English typically has [ʊ] (the FOOT vowel) here, whilst Southern and East Anglian English has somewhat fronted [ʌ] or the centralised [ɐ], this resulting in the North retaining what is the traditional five-vowel system of short vowels while the South has six. [ʌ] is typical of RP: an innovation here and in the accents of some English regional speakers towards a raised and retracted variant at or approaching [ɤ] may be seen as a move towards a compromise between the two extremes. Illustrative of its border status between North and South, the West Midlands have considerable variation in realisations of this vowel, tending however towards the Northern [ʊ] and 'compromise' [ɤ]. Elsewhere in the British Isles [ʌ], centralised in Ireland and Wales, is widespread, with [ɔ] occurring in Orkney and Shetland, the Channel Islands, and British Creole.

2.6. FOOT

[ʊ] is the very widespread British Isles realisation here, occurring in the varieties of all regions other than Orkney, Shetland and Scotland, and in Creole and RP. In Orkney, Shetland, and Scotland, a tensed [u] is heard, central or even fronted in Scotland according largely to the social profile of the speaker, with FOOT and GOOSE tending to fall together in these accents. The tensed central [u] is also found in British Creole, and in Northern Ireland, testimony to the close links of that area with Scotland. A fronted [ʏ] is heard in South-west England. Hypercorrection resulting from unease about the status of the STRUT [ʊ] seems to underlie realizations of FOOT as [ɤ] and [ə] in Northern and West Midland England.

3. Long vowels

3.1. FLEECE

The underlying quality of the FLEECE vowel is that of [i(:)] throughout the region. However, this is not always purely monophthongal, a frequent tendency being towards a short upgliding diphthong [ɪi]. In the North of England, the West Midlands and South-east England, wider diphthongs [əɪ] or [eɪ~ɛɪ] are found.

3.2. BATH

Like TRAP and STRUT, this vowel creates something of a marker of north-south distinction. Unlike the latter, however, there is little tendency for speakers to compromise in an attempt to move towards a perceived prestige. A consequence of this is the existence of RP variability which sees Southern speakers using [ɑː] while Northern speakers use [a] in an otherwise uniform system. [a] is, in fact, the principal form from Orkney and Shetland, through Scotland and Northern England into the West Midlands where, true to the transitional nature of that region, there is considerable mixing with the longer, backed South-eastern regional norm, [ɑː]. In South-west England [a] categorically has partial or full length, as it does characteristically in Southern Ireland and in Wales. In something of an inversion of the situation in England, however, Northern Ireland exhibits [ɑ], with variable length.

3.3. PALM, START

In South-east England and the Channel Islands, as in RP, the vowel of these sets is [ɑː], this being found variably with [aː] and [ɒː] in the North of England and with [ɒː] in the West Midlands. [aː] is the usual variant in South-west England and Wales (here with [ɑː]), and this or a retracted form is usual in East Anglia. Both [ɑː] and [aː] occur in British Creole and, with variable length, in Irish varieties. Scottish accents exhibit [a], sometimes retracted, in PALM, and [aː], sometimes retracted, or a close variety of [ɛː] in START, lengthening in the rhotic environment according to the 'Scottish Vowel Length Rule'.

3.4. GOOSE

The dominant realisation of the GOOSE vowel is essentially [u(ː)] everywhere in the region, with fronting in varying degrees being a very common tendency. [ʏ] can be found in Urban Scots and [ʏː] in more conservative rural speech in South-west England. A tendency towards short diphthongs exists in Northern England ([ʊu]), East Anglia and South-east England ([ʊʉ]), and the West Midlands ([ɔʊ~əu]).

3.5. THOUGHT, NORTH, FORCE

[ɔː] is a widespread realisation for these vowels, with a short vowel in THOUGHT in Scotland. [ɔː] is frequently diphthongised to [ɔə] in South-east England, where [oː] is otherwise usual, as it is in Scotland in FORCE and, variably, in NORTH. [ɔː] and [oː] co-occur in the Channel Islands and British Creole, and [ɔː] and [ɒː] in Northern England for all three vowels (with [aː] in THOUGHT and [oː] in NORTH and FORCE). NORTH and FORCE exhibit the characteristic if recessive feature of [ʊə] in North-east England.

There is marked variation within Irish accents. THOUGHT exhibits a range of rounded and unrounded back vowels and, in popular Dublin speech, [aː]; NORTH vowels similarly are [ɔː], [ɑː], [ɒː] and [aː]. FORCE exhibits predominantly [oː] and [ɔː], with [ɒː] in popular Dublin. An off-glide is not uncommon with non-rhotic accents.

3.6. NURSE

Considerable variability occurs in this vowel throughout the British Isles, though it may be very broadly summed up as consisting of [ɚ]in rhotic areas of Ireland and South-west England and [ɜː/əː] in the rest of the region, excluding Scotland. Most notable additions to this broad distinction are [ɔ], found in Orkney and Shetland, and a full NURSE/NORTH merger on this retracted form in the speech of some older speakers in North-east England, where a fronted variant [ø] has recently been identified in the speech of younger, mainly female, speakers. [œː] occurs in Wales and variably in the West Midlands. Rhotic Scottish accents exhibit [ʌ] (Scottish Standard English) and either [ʌ] or [ɛ] (Urban Scots).

NURSE and SQUARE also fall together for many speakers in Liverpool, with words from either set being pronounced with [ɜː] or [ɛː]. [ɛː] is also a feature of Hull and Teesside speech in Northern England, although SQUARE does not allow of [ɜː] in those places.

4. Diphthongs

4.1. FACE

The principal distinction here is between monophthongal realisations in the Northern British Isles and Ireland and diphthongal realisations from the Midlands southwards, though there is variability within this scheme. Whilst [e(ː)] is general in Scotland, Ireland, Wales, and the North of England, as well as being found in the speech of some speakers of British Creole, it occurs with [eɪ] in Shetland and, for some words in the set, in Wales. Diphthongal forms elsewhere range from [eɪ] in RP and the Channel Islands to [ɛɪ] in South-west and [ʌɪ] in South-east England, [ɛɪ/ʌɪ/æɪ] in the West Midlands, and [eɪ/æi] in East Anglia. To be compared with [ʊə] in GOAT, North-east England has a most distinctive diphthongal FACE vowel, in [ɪə].

4.2. PRICE

A wide range of open onsets can be identified for this diphthong, although, with the exception of British Creole with two diphthongs [ɑɛ/ɑe], end-points are at the front close position. [aɪ], typical of traditional RP, is recorded in Orkney and Shetland, Southern Ireland, Wales, Northern and Midland England: a higher onset, at [æ], occurs in the Rural West of Ireland, and yet higher, at [ɛ], in the Rural North of Ireland and for some North of England speakers. In Southern England and the Channel Islands, among younger East Anglian speakers, and in Fashionable Dublin speech, [ɑɪ], with a lip-spread back open onset, is heard. A lip-rounded back open position, [ɒ], is the start for the diphthong for some West Midland ([ɒɪ/ɔɪ]), Cockney (London), and Channel Island speakers, and is a stereotyped feature for South-west England.

Current RP, along with Standard Scottish English and some Channel Islands speech, has [ʌɪ]. The diphthong begins centrally, with [ɐ/ɜ/ə], for some speakers on Shetland, in Urban Scots, in Popular Dublin speech, and amongst older East Anglians. Monophthongal [aː] has been reported for Devon in South-west England, and [ɑː] is a feature of south and west Yorkshire (as well as the East Midlands immediately to the south of that area), while [iː] is characteristic of the pronunciation of some words in this set, such as *right* and *night* in Yorkshire and North-east England.

4.3. CHOICE

[ɔɪ] is very usual for this diphthong, being found in RP and (sometimes with a more tense high front end-point) in the accents of all areas other than Scotland, where [ɔe] occurs, and South-west England, which produces [oɪ]. [oɪ] can also be heard in Fashionable Dublin speech, in the English West Midlands, and in South-east England. Fully-open back onsets for the diphthongs, giving [ɒɪ/ɑɪ], are characteristic of a range of accents found in Southern and Western Ireland, in Northern and West Midland England, and in the Channel Islands. In East Anglia pronunciations across the range from [ɔi] to [ʊi] can be heard. British Creole, with [ɔɪ/ai], also exhibits [ɔɛ].

4.4. MOUTH

South of Scotland, MOUTH is generally represented by a glide from low front to high back, with an extreme range of [au], taking in onsets from [a] to [ɛ] and end-points from [ʊ] to [u] and [ʉ]. [aʊ] is the diphthong in RP, and is found in British Creole with [ɔʊ] and [æə]. Scotland has [ʌʉ], Shetland has [ʌʊ], and Orkney [əʊ], while all three share monophthongal [u(ː)] with northernmost Northern England. Also in the North of England, parts of west and south Yorkshire have [aː], while in the South London Cockney exhibits [æː].

4.5. GOAT

Somewhat in parallel with the situation in FACE, a basic distinction here is between monophthongal realisations in the North of the region and diphthongal realisations in the South. [o(ː)] occurs in Shetland, Scotland, (rural) Ireland, Wales, and the North of England (where innovative 'GOAT-fronting' to [ɵː] is occurring), and in British Creole. Orkney has [ɔ]. Besides monophthongal realisations, Ireland has the RP-like [əʊ] in Fashionable Dublin and supra-regional Southern accents, [ʌʊ] in Popular Dublin speech, and the traditional RP [oʊ] also across Southern accents: this is also a feature shared with many speakers in Northern and West Midland England, and in Wales. In Northern England, the North-east traditionally has [ʊə], to be compared to [ɪə] in FACE.

Principal vernacular diphthongs in Southern Britain are [ʌʊ] in the South-east, [ɔʊ] in the South-west and Channel Islands, and [oʊ/ɛʊ/aʊ/ʌʊ] in the West Midlands. East Anglia has [ɐu/ʊu], and British Creole narrow diphthongs in the range [uo/ʊə/əo].

4.6. NEAR

In most rhotic accents of the British Isles, those of Scotland, Ireland, and the South-west of England, the realisation of NEAR is typically as a high front monophthong, invariably of a tensed variety. Diphthongisation elsewhere is usually to [iə], with varying degrees of tenseness for the onset: a relaxed onset at [ɪ] is found in RP and one of the variants for British Creole (which also has available [ie(r)/iɛ(r)] in rhotic variants), while [eə/ɛə] also occur in the West Midlands. East Anglia has [eː/ɛː], creating a NEAR/SQUARE merger.

4.7. SQUARE

Rhoticity in Scotland and Ireland is typically on a lengthened half-closed monophthong, [e(ː)] SQUARE vowel, this co-existing with half-open [ɛ] in

Orkney and Shetland and Urban Scots, and being the norm in Popular Dublin speech. [ɛ(:)] is also the form in rhotic South-west England. The Irish Rural North differs from the South in having [ə(:)]. Rhoticity in British Creole is attended by diphthongs [ie/iɛ]. In other, non-rhotic, accents the most usual regional form is a centring diphthong with half-open front onset, or a long half-open monophthong, [ɛə/ɛː]. [ɛː] is found also in RP (as distinct from the traditional RP diphthongal [eə]) and, with [eː], in the absence of rhoticity in British Creole. Characteristic of Liverpool, and found more widely in the Lancashire area, is [ɜː] (compare NURSE), a similar sound being recorded slightly further south in the west Midlands too.

4.8. CURE

Rhotic accents of Scotland and Ireland and South-west England typically have [u(:)], with Orkney and Shetland showing [uə]. [uə/ʊə] is also usual over much of non-rhotic Britain, with a tendency to a disyllabic [(ɪ)uwə] in Wales. A comparatively recent innovation in RP for the CURE vowel is [ɔː], and this is also found in accents characteristic of Northern and West Midland England and, with [oː], in British Creole.

Unlike other accents of the British Isles, where the phenomenon of 'yod-deletion' (see section 7.3. below) has only limited application, the accent of East Anglia has no [j] before /uː/ after *any* consonant: this, together with a realisation of the CURE vowel as [ɜː/əː], results in such homophones as *cure/cur*.

5. Weak vowels

5.1. happY

Tense [i], in some cases with length, is a feature of most British English accents, and, having become the norm in RP (as distinct from traditional RP, where [ɪ] might sometimes be expected), is increasingly found in the North of England, where the slack vowel to and including [ɛ] has been a feature of vernacular speech. [e] is the vowel in Scotland and Rural Northern Ireland (in the latter alongside [ɪ]). Both [ɪ] and [i] are found in British Creole.

5.2. lettER

A central vowel, predominantly [ə], occurs in both non-rhotic and rhotic accents in the British Isles, exceptions being that some speakers of British Creole have [a] alongside [ɐ], and Scotland exhibits [ɪ/ʌ]. Alongside [ə], Wales has [ʌ] and the Channel Islands [œ].

5.3. horsES

The horsES vowel is mainly [ɪ] in the British Isles, though a central vowel is the norm in Shetland, Ireland and East Anglia, and both [ɪ] and [ə] can be expected in Northern England.

5.4. commA

The central vowel [ə] occurs throughout most of the British Isles for commA. An open central vowel [ɐ] is heard in Shetland and Popular Dublin, and sometimes in the North of England, in some cases fronted and lowered to [a] in Orkney and in British Creole. Scotland and Wales have [ʌ].

6. Vowel distribution

The Scottish Vowel Length Rule, describing lengthening of certain vowels before /r/, a voiced fricative, or a morpheme boundary, is explained in the chapter on Scottish phonology. That vowel length is environmentally determined rather than being intrinsic to the vowel results in the absence from transcriptions of the relevant varieties of that quantitative contrast which is customarily applied in the description of British English vowel sets. Although a slightly recessive feature, the Rule operates widely in Scotland itself, in Orkney and Shetland, and in the accents of England bordering Scotland. It is also a factor in some forms of Northern Irish English, but not in the English of the Irish Republic.

Undoubtedly the most marked absence of contrast in the British Isles vocalic system is that of TRAP and BATH in Scotland and Northern England, and in some instances of accents in Ireland, Wales, and Orkney and Shetland. Both are typically at the low front position, or slightly retracted from it: so distinct a marker of northernness is this feature that in Northern and northern West Midland England those speakers whose accent converges on RP are nevertheless most unlikely to abandon it, so that it is necessary to include BATH [a] in the RP inventory in order to avoid any judgement of Southern bias in what is in essence a regionless accent.

FOOT/GOOSE merger is a feature of Scotland, Orkney and Shetland, and of some Northern Irish accents associated with Scotland through settlement. The merger is also a feature of Northern and West Midland English accents outside the North-east, for a very limited set of lexical items and essentially amongst older speakers. LOT and THOUGHT also merge in Scotland, Orkney and Shetland, and this phenomenon can be found in some conservative Rural

Irish accents too. Some merger of LOT and STRUT on [ɒ] is encountered in the West Midlands.

In Northern England, homophony occurs between NURSE and SQUARE in Liverpool, where both sets can be rendered with [ɛː] or [ɜː], and, to the extent that NURSE is variably rendered [ɛː], in the Hull and Middlesbrough areas of the east of the region. Whilst NEAR and SQUARE are distinct sets in the south of the East Anglia area, they merge on [eː/ɛː] in the northern part, and they are at times homophonous in the West Midlands on [ɪə/ɛə].

7. Consonants

7.1. Stops: /P/T/K/ , /B/D/G

Word-initial voiceless stops are aspirated in the varieties of Ireland and England. There is some evidence that aspiration is weaker in Scotland. Strong aspiration approaching affrication is a feature in the whole of Wales, especially the north.

Glottalisation of intervocalic and word-final /t/ occurs everywhere in the British Isles, with considerable frequency: /p/ and /k/ are also glottalised, though not as regularly as is /t/.

/t/ and /d/ are generally dental in Shetland, and tend to have fronted or dental articulation in Scotland. This is also a feature of the English accents of mid and northern Wales.

Affrication of /t/ is reported as a special feature of Dublin speech in Ireland, and is, with affrication of /p/ and /k/, very prevalent in the Liverpool area of Northern England. Affrication of /k/ and /g/ before front vowels is also characteristic of accents of limited areas of Orkney and Shetland. Lenicisation of intervocalic /t/ is strongly evidenced in South-west England and is also found in Ireland and widely in the rest of England, while strong aspiration of /p, t, k/ is noted for the whole of Wales. A flap or tap, [ɾ], is part of a complex of allophones of /t/ in Ireland and Northern and Midland England, and of British Creole, though the sociolinguistics of this feature varies markedly between regions, as do other likely precise realisations.

There is a tendency towards unvoicing of word-final /d/ in the English of Wales where Welsh is spoken.

7.2. Fricatives: TH, F/V, S/Z, SH/ZH, H, CH, etc.

Initial Fricative Voicing, in which /f, θ, s, ʃ/ are realised as [v, ð, z, ʒ] word-initially, is a particular feature of South-west England, and is also to be found in southern, and especially south-western, Wales: it is a highly recessive element in the accents of both areas. TH-stopping, both voiced and voiceless, rendering *this thing* [dɪs tɪŋ], occurs in British Creole, and also as a highly stigmatised feature throughout Ireland: its occasionally reported presence in Glasgow might be as a result of influence from Ireland. Fronting of /ʃ/ is found in Shetland and Scotland.

Unvoicing of medial and word-final /z/ occurs in the English accents of those regions of Wales where Welsh is widely spoken. Interference from Welsh phonology is the cause.

Initial H-deletion is variable throughout Wales and England, generally taken as a feature of working-class speech. It is also found in the Channel Islands, in part perhaps as a result of influence from metropolitan French, and in British Creole, where, as a recessive feature, presence or absence of syllable-initial [h] can mark degrees of emphasis.

Characteristically Scottish /x/ in, for example, *loch*, is increasingly becoming [k] in Urban Scots, although [x] remains the widespread realisation otherwise in Scotland, and is also found in Northern Ireland.

Welsh <ll> and <ch> occur only occasionally in Welsh English outside the pronunciation of placenames, but, when they do, they may be expected to have their Welsh-language values of [ɬ] and [x] respectively.

7.3. Semi-vowels: W/WH, J

Word-initial WH realised by the voiceless labial-velar fricative [ʍ] is a recognised feature of Irish and Scottish speech, and of that of the most northerly parts of England. There is evidence that this is a recessive feature in all these accents, however. Its recessive nature in RP is signified by its status as a feature of the Refined and, variably, the traditional varieties of that accent only.

Apparently due to the influence of Welsh phonology, initial /w/ is occasionally dropped in Welsh English before close back rounded vowels.

Yod-dropping is one of the most distinctive characteristics of northern East Anglian speech, where /j/ is absent before /u:/ after all consonants. The feature is reported in more limited measure in Ireland, Wales, the West Midlands and the South of England.

7.4. Sonorants: N, L, R

In a feature known as 'velar nasal plus', velar nasal /ŋ/ is realised as [ŋg] in all words with <ng> spelling in the English West Midlands, this designation in this case covering an extended area stretching from Birmingham in the south to Liverpool and Sheffield in the north. The feature is by no means categorical, co-existing with both [ŋ] and, in <-ing>-morpheme representations, [n] realisation: the alveolar nasal [n] for /ŋ/ is widespread in Northern and West Midland English as a stigmatised feature. /n/ is fronted in Shetland, Scotland, and mid and northern Wales.

RP has clear [l] before a vowel and dark [ɫ] before a consonant or pause. Whilst this essential pattern might also be expected to occur in some regional varieties, considerable complexity does also occur in distributions of clear and dark /l/ regionally, with a general trend being a move from clear to dark as one moves from North to South within England, and post-vocalic /l/ frequently being vocalised in the South-east. The clear-to-dark trend is reversed in Wales, where [l] is more characteristic of the south and [ɫ] of the north in all positions. Dark [ɫ] is a feature of Scottish English, and vocalisation exists as both historically- and modern sociolinguistically-conditioned features.

There is an essential division between the principal rhotic areas of the British Isles, situated in Scotland, Ireland, South-west England and part of Northern England centred on southern Lancashire, and the non-rhotic areas of the majority of England and Wales. However, rhoticity is not categorical in rhotic regions; Northumberland in Northern England, the English of Welsh-speaking areas of Wales, parts of southern Wales with close cultural links with South-west England, and the Channel Islands also display the feature to varying degrees. Phonetic realisations of /r/ vary widely: in Scotland postalveolar [ɹ], retroflex [ɻ] and tap or flap [ɾ] are variably found, their presence determined by phonetic environments and sociolinguistics, and Ireland has [ɹ] and [ɻ]; /r/ in England is generally postalveolar or retroflex, with a characteristic uvular variety surviving in Northumberland; and uvular [ʁ] is also found as a rare form in north Wales. Intrusive /r/ is normal in non-rhotic areas.

8. Prosodic and intonational features

Distinctive in the area of East Anglia pronunciation is the tendency for stressed vowels to be lengthened, with any unstressed vowel being correspondingly reduced to [ə] or even disappearing. This is in marked contrast to the even syllable stressing which is characteristic of North-east England.

Especially amongst older Channel Islands speakers, stressing occurs which presents as being distinctly non-native: this might involve reversal of patterns typical of RP, or heavier syllable stressing than might otherwise be expected. Stress shifts are quite usual in polysyllabic verbs (only) in Irish English.

It is frequently remarked that Welsh English has a particularly lilting (or, more pejoratively, a 'sing-song') intonation pattern, an observation that is also made concerning Orkney speech. Recent observations on an apparent causal post-tonic rise in pitch in Welsh English ties the feature to a corresponding feature in Welsh. This high terminal intonation might also regularly be encountered in Ireland and in Northern and South-eastern England: the extent to which the high tone is rising or at a plateau is variable across accents, with that of North-eastern England being recorded as the latter and that of Glasgow as the former. In Scotland outside Glasgow, statements in most accents show a falling intonation. The extent to which the feature of terminal intonational raising is related across different regions is currently unclear.

Exercises and study questions

1. By consulting the synopsis, identify significant changes that have recently been taking place, to differentiate traditional and more modern pronunciations in British accents.

2. From the synopsis, discover ways in which it can be seen that the accents of the Celtic Englishes of Scotland, Ireland, and Wales are distinct from accents in England and the Channel Islands.

3. Compare what is said in the synopsis with the more detailed information to be found in one of the British English chapters. Do you agree that what has been extracted from the chapter for the synopsis represents the most important information?

4. Make what connections you can between the British English *regional* accents and either of the *non*-regional accents described in the synopsis, British Creole or Received Pronunciation. (You might go on to make connections between Creole or RP and other English accents around the world, using the interactive maps.)

5. Identify five consonantal features described in the synopsis that would enable you to locate a speaker as coming from a quite confined area of the British Isles.

6. Beginning with intuitions from the interactive maps, and using the synopsis for detail, identify those features which exemplify a north/south split in British English accents.

7. What accent features seem to be (a) universal or (b) near-universal to the English accents of Britain? Use both the interactive maps and the synopsis to decide this.

8. Identify instances where an area in the British Isles exhibits transitional status in its use of phonological variants. This might be through the use of an intermediate or 'fudged' variant, or through the use of two variants each of which is characteristic of the accent of a different neighbouring area. The interactive maps will help you especially with the second of these.

Morphology and Syntax

English spoken in Orkney and Shetland: morphology, syntax, and lexicon

Gunnel Melchers

1. Introduction

An account of the unique historical and linguistic background of the Northern Isles, which were ruled by Scandinavians until the latter half of the 15th century, is given in the phonology part of this volume (see Melchers, this volume). Today, the traditional dialects as spoken in the Northern Isles must be described as varieties of Scots, yet with a substantial component of Scandinavian features, manifested at all levels of language. This component differs from the Scandinavian linguistic heritage in other parts of Britain (possibly with the exception of Caithness), not only in size but also in structure and history. The Norse invaders of Yorkshire, for example, met a native Anglo-Saxon population with whom they – allegedly – could communicate. They influenced the Anglo-Saxon language and some of this influence has survived, mostly in the form of lexical borrowings. In Orkney and Shetland, on the other hand, we see the still powerful impact of a Scandinavian *substratum*, supported by positive – to the degree of romantic – feelings of affiliation with Scandinavia.

Orkney and Shetland can be characterized as bidialectal speech communities with access to a choice of two discrete, definable forms of speech – one a form of standard, basically Standard Scottish English, and the other what Wells (1982) calls traditional dialect. Orcadians and Shetlanders are generally aware of commanding two distinct varieties and they have names for these, e.g. "English" vs. "Shetland" or "Orcadian". Admittedly, age-related differences have been observed: on the one hand, young people are losing some of the traditional-dialect indexicals, on the other they often state explicitly that they do not wish to adapt to outsiders and tend to be scathing about islanders who do. It would, however, be difficult to find truly monolingual speakers of the traditional dialect today.

As for writing, it goes without saying that Shetlanders and Orcadians are in full command of Standard English, but there is a growing interest in maintaining written forms of the regional dialects as well, encouraged by schoolteachers and manifested in local publications as well as spontaneous notes, letters, scripts etc. The awareness of two varieties of language was demonstrated in the reading of the test passage for this handbook, *The North Wind and the Sun*, when a Shetland informant first read the text word for word and then spontaneously "translated" some words and phrases into a more Shetland version, e.g. *was arguin'* instead of *were disputing*, *what ane was stronger* instead of *which was the stronger*.

As varieties of Scots/Scottish English, Shetland and Orkney dialects naturally share a great many – if not the bulk – of the characteristics described in the chapter on the morphology and syntax of Scottish English (see Miller, this volume). This presentation should be seen as a complement to Miller's, exclusively drawing on examples from Orkney (O) and Shetland (S) data and highlighting some areas where language in the Northern Isles is particularly distinctive, often due to their Scandinavian substratum. As in the Scottish English chapter, the focus is on structures towards and at the Broad Scots end of the continuum, which in this case entails a sizeable component of Scandinavian features. Unlike the chapter on Scottish English, this presentation does not present morphology and syntax in distinctive sections. The main reason for this is that very little research has been carried out on the syntax of these varieties.

2. Research and data

Present-day language in the Northern Isles, especially Orkney, is indeed remarkably under-researched. With the exception of two dictionaries written in a popular style, *Orkney Wordbook* (Lamb 1988) and *The Orkney Dictionary* (Flaws and Lamb 1997), there has been no general study of Orcadian since Marwick's *The Orkney Norn* (1929), mainly a dictionary but with a useful, though extremely brief, general introduction to the language. Shetland dialect as spoken at the end of the 19th century was carefully documented in Jakob Jakobsen's monumental *An Etymological Dictionary of the Norn Language in Shetland* (1928–1932); as the title suggests, it obviously has a clear Scandinavian bias but provides some information about the language variety as a whole. As in Marwick's work, morphological and syntactic structures basically have to be worked out through the study of individual entries, however.

John Graham, a native Shetlander, English teacher, fictional writer and linguist, wrote *The Shetland Dictionary*, whose first edition appeared in the early 1970s. Although a slim contribution compared to Jakobsen's dictionary, it is very important in providing up-to-date knowledge about current usage as well as a wealth of authentic examples. With T.A. Robertson as co-author, Graham also wrote *Grammar and Usage of the Shetland Dialect* (1991), which has less than 50 pages but constitutes the only attempt so far at producing a comprehensive grammar of the dialect. For Orkney, we only have just over two pages in Marwick's introduction to his dictionary and a few comments in the more recent popular works.

Aspects of Shetland dialect syntax, with special reference to word order typology, are currently being investigated by Dianne Jonas (cf. e.g. Jonas 2002).

Extensive fieldwork on Shetland dialect was carried out in the 1980s by Melchers and Foldvik, described in several publications. A great deal of the data, including recordings featuring on the CD-ROM, derives from this project. *The Linguistic Survey of Scotland* (LSS) included various localities in Orkney and Shetland and provides useful information about the lexicon, but unlike the *Survey of English Dialects* (SED), its counterpart in England, unfortunately not on morphology and syntax. However, some unpublished LSS material in the form of slips containing answers to additional sections in the questionnaire eliciting aspects of grammar, e.g. negation, verb forms, and pronominal usage, has been consulted for the purpose of this chapter.

In addition to the above-mentioned recordings and material collected for this presentation in Orkney and Shetland during the summer of 2002, a great deal of material recorded for the purpose of oral history has been made available by the Orkney and Shetland Archives. This is particularly useful since the interviewers are mostly dialect speakers themselves, which means that the informants do not tend to adapt their language. Another source of information, reflecting present-day spoken language, is the extensive writing in local dialect, carried out in a variety of genres and encouraged in the schools (cf. Melchers 1999, which also contains some information about dialect writing in Orkney). The spelling used in the examples below is generally taken from local representations in writing, to some extent "standardized" in the widely circulated present-day dictionaries described above. Unless otherwise indicated, the presentation applies to Orkney as well as Shetland, although Shetland tends to dominate the description of characteristic features and hence the number of examples. There are two reasons for this imbalance:

- for historical and geographical reasons Shetland dialect has remained more distinct from other varieties of Scots and retained more of the Norse element;
- more linguistic research has been devoted to the present-day language situation in Shetland

It remains to be pointed out that some differences in Orkney and Shetland forms may be due to differences in the written tradition and that examples marked (O) or (S) do not necessarily signal that they are exclusive to Orkney or Shetland but mostly just state the origin of the data. "Unmarked" examples refer to both varieties.

3. Verbs

3.1. Some morphological characteristics

As pointed out by Miller (this volume), a given verb may be strong in Standard English but weak in Scots (cf. [1] below) and vice versa.

Regular verbs: Past tense and past participle endings are generally: a) *-ed* after vowels and voiced consonants other than plosives; b) *-it* (S)/*-id* (O) after plosives; c) *-t* after other voiceless consonants.

(1) *Somehoo he's never been da sam since he selled oot ta yon oil company* (S).

(2) *Kale and knockid corn* ('cabbage and crushed barley') (O).

(3) *He flipit* ('folded') *up his trousers* (S).

Irregular verbs include:

aet 'eat'	*öt*	*ötten/aeten*
brak 'break'	*brok/bruik*	*brakken/brokken*
cast 'cast'; 'dig peats'	*cöst/cuist*	*cassen*

(4) *Her man was cassen awa* 'lost at sea' (S).

geng 'go'	*göd* 'went'	*gien* 'gone'	*g(y)aan* 'going'

(5) *Der's a feerie* ('epidemic') *gyann aboot* (S).

gie 'give'	*gied* 'gave'	*gien* 'given' (i.e. a merger with the above)

There is further variation in the forms of the above two verbs in Shetland and Orkney dialects.

greet 'cry'	*gret/grat*	*grutten/gritten*
jump 'jump'	*jamp*	*juppm* (S)
rive 'tear'	*rave*	*riven*
shaer 'shear'	*shör*	*shorn* (S)
white 'quit'	*whet*	*whet*

(6) *Ah'm whet gaan tae the sea now* (O).

write	*wret/wrat*	*wret/written*

Data from Shetland demonstrate a great deal of regional – and probably idiolectal – variation in irregular verb forms, e.g. *jamp* (past tense of *jump*) and *skrivan* 'written' from Fair Isle, and *beuk* (past tense of *bake*) from some places as documented by LSS. Not surprisingly, there is also considerable overlap/

confusion between past and present participles: *skrivan* sometimes stands for 'writing', *gyann* for 'gone', and *pitten* could be either equivalent to 'putting' or the past participle form 'put', which may have played a part in the use of *be* as a perfective auxiliary (cf. section 3.3.).

In contrast with Standard English, a distinction in form is made between verbal adjectives/present participles on the one hand and verbal nouns on the other, as illustrated by the following Orkney examples:

(7) *Sheu's knittan.*

(8) *Sheu's deuan her knitteen.*

Substantial evidence of this distinction – though not in all localities – is found in the (unpublished) Shetland and Orkney answers to Question 190 in LSS, eliciting local forms of *he likes singing* and *he is aye singing.*

(9) *He laeks singeen; He's aye singin* (S).

Presumably by analogy, words like *lesson, pudding* are sometimes pronounced as '*lesseen*', '*puddeen*'.

The present indicative:

Not only in the third person singular but also in the second – at least after the informal *du* (S) and *thu*/*thoo* (O) – are *-s* endings used in Shetland and Orkney:

(10) *Thoo kens whit hid's like wi a hooseful o folk* (O).

(11) *Du minds* ('remind') *me aafil o dee grandfaider* (S).

In the historic present, *-s* endings are also used in the first person singular:

(12) *"So I grips and kerries her ta da hoose"* (Graham 1993: 12).

The present- and past-tense paradigms of the verbs *ta be* ('to be') and *ta hae* ('to have') in Shetland dialect are:

I am	*we ir*	*I wis*	*we wir*
du is	*you ir*	*du wis*	*you wir*
he is	*dey ir*	*he wis*	*dey wir*
I hae/hiv	*we hae/hiv*	*I hed*	*we hed*
du hes	*you hae*	*du hed*	*you hed*
he hes	*dey hae*	*he hed*	*dey hed*

3.2. Agreement

Plural subject nouns combine with verbs ending in *-s*, not just *is* and *was* (cf. section 3.1. in the Scottish English chapter). In the unpublished LSS material, Question 191, investigating dialect constructions corresponding to Standard English *these horses pull well* and *they pull well*, is accompanied by the following note:

> Shetland verbal usage is rather complicated, in some ways resembling Middle Scots. The third person plural present indicative has an *-s* ending if the subject is a noun or a pronoun separated from the verb: *Dem at comes oonbid sits oonsaired* ('Those who come uninvited get nothing').

Typical responses to the question in Shetland were:

(13) *dis (yon) horses pulls (poos) weel; dey pull (poo) weel*

Interestingly, an informant notes: "When we use *they*, *this* or *these* we are using English and would *never* say *these pulls* or *they pulls*".

The following story related in Graham (2002: 6) provides further illustration of the LSS observation on Shetland verbal usage:

> An owld Waas man commented: "We wir boarn ta help idders."
> Anidder character – a realist – said: "I winder what da idders wis boarn for?"
> (*Waas* 'Walls, a place in Shetland', *idders* 'others')

In Shetland dialect, *der* corresponds to 'there is' as well as 'there are' (cf. the use of *there* in examples [5–7] in the chapter on Scottish English and Orkney *thir* as exemplified below):

(14) *Der a boat hoose yonder.*

(15) *Der folk here fae Sweden and Norway.*

(16) *Der twa Women's Guilds been pitten aff da night.*

(17) *Thir a lock o fock here.*

This could be compared to the increasing use of grammaticalized *there is* in more standardlike varieties of English, as in *There's sheep and there's penguins* (Falkland English).

A "frozen" form is also used for the past tense, i.e. corresponding to 'there was', 'there were' in Orkney and Shetland dialect, viz. *they wir* (O), *dey wir* (S):

(18) *They wir a coo lowse in the byre.*

(19) *Dey wir no money dan.*

3.3. Tense

A remarkable feature unique to Orkney and Shetland is the use of *be* rather than *have* as a perfective auxiliary, not restricted to verbs of motion but categorically, as in:

(20) *I war paid him afore that* (O).

(21) *Hid'll lickly be been shoved in a draar someway*
'It will probably have been put in a drawer somewhere' (O).

(22) *I'm seen (heard) it* (S).

(23) *I'm been dere twartree* ('a couple of') *times* (S).

Although there is a parallel construction in one local dialect in Norway, this is probably not a Scandinavian feature. Jakobsen (1897: 113) characterizes it as a feature of "modern Shetlandic", which is difficult to prove owing to the non-existence of reliable early dialect texts. Recent data from Shetland show that the *be* construction belongs to the "Shetland code" rather than "Shetland English". It is possible that the use of *be* in Orkney and Shetland is due to ambiguity and confusion of expressions referring to transitivity vs. intransitivity and active vs. passive.

Another contributory factor might be that, at least in modern Shetland pronunciation, a realization of the participle form may often be identical with the gerund (cf. 3.1. above). In an example such as

(24) *Yun onkerry* ('carry on') *was pitten* ('put') *her in a aafil flickament*
('state of excitement'),

the pronunciation of the main verb would be identical with that of the form *putting*, which would be expected to be preceded by a form of *be*.

It is not unlikely that the general linguistic insecurity which must have resulted from the Norn/Scots contact situation, richly demonstrated in narrowing and extension of meaning in the lexicon and mergers in the phonological system, may have led to the overextended use of *be*. As Shetlanders were also exposed to Dutch and German influence from the Hanseatic period well into the 19th century, resulting in a number of lexical borrowings, types of constructions such as *ich bin gewesen*, *ik ben geweest* cannot be excluded from playing a part in the simplification pattern.

3.4. Modality

In contrast with other varieties of Scots/Scottish English, there appears to be no evidence of double modals in Shetland and Orkney, with the exception of structures containing *can* in the sense of 'be able to' in Orkney dialect, as in:

(25) *He'll no can deu that.*

Robertson and Graham (1991: 9) list the following modal verbs: *böst* 'had to, must' (*buist*, the corresponding Orkney word, appears to be obsolete); *man* 'must' (also found in Orkney); *may*; *sall* (the first person singular form is often contracted to *I's;* the past tense form is *sood*); *will*.

(26) *He böst til a come* ('must have come') *alang da banks*.

(27) *What man be man be* ('it is inevitable').

(28) *Shü* ('she') *sood a hed a lamb.*

(26) and (28) exemplify the use of *a* [æ], a form of *hae* 'have', after certain modal verb forms.

It is not clear why the Robertson-Graham handbook excludes *can* (which is used in much the same way as in Scottish English generally), *must*, and *have to*, now commonly used to express conclusions as well as obligation.

The subjunctive form *bees* is reported from Orkney:

(29) *Thoo'll git a sweetie if thoo bees good.*

(30) *We'll can stert cuttan the morn if hid bees dry.*
'We'll be able to start cutting tomorrow if it is dry'.

3.5. Negation

As in Scots/Scottish English generally, verbs tend to be negated by the independent word *no* or by the suffix *na(e)*, the latter typically found after modal verbs and *do*.

(31) *"Da fok fae sooth aye mention at dey canna understaand …"* (S)
'People from south (i.e. outsiders) always mention that they can't understand …'

(32) *Soodna we try dat?* (S)

(33) *A'm no ready yet.*

The last-mentioned example is taken from the Orkney and Shetland responses to Question 185 in the unpublished LSS material, eliciting 'I'm not ready yet' as well as 'I don't know'. Interestingly, the latter structure was realized as *I kenno/ken no/kno no/kjinna* by a number of Shetland informants. This structure was not elicited for Orkney but is mentioned by Flaws and Lamb (2001: 44) in connection with the intriguing entry *tae kenno* 'not to know'.

4. Nouns

4.1. Article usage

The indefinite article is always *a*, i.e. it is used before vowels as well as consonants (cf. also *a aafil* in [24] above):

(34) *a uncan* 'strange' *man* (S)

As in Scots generally, the definite article, which is realized as *da* in Shetland and *they* in Ronaldsey, Orkney, is used with a number of nouns with which it would not be used in Standard English. Typical categories of such nouns are names of seasons, meals, illnesses and institutions.

(35) *gaan tae the kirk/the skuil, makkan the dinner* (O)

(36) *da gulsa* 'jaundice', *da brunt-rift* 'heartburn', *da caald, dan cam da hairst* 'autumn' (S)

For 'today', 'tonight', 'tomorrow', 'tomorrow night' etc., Orkney and Shetland dialect has *the/da day, the/da nicht, the/da mo(a)rn, the/da moarn's nicht*. 'Yesterday evening' is *the/da streen*.

(37) *Da moarns night der a beetle drive in da Whiteness an Weisdale Haal* (Shetland radio script).

4.2. Plural forms

Irregular plural forms such as *breider* 'brothers', *een* 'eyes', *shön* 'shoes', *kye* 'cows' are still often heard, at least in Shetland dialect.

(38) *We riggat wiz athin wir Sunday suits in polished wir shön.*
'We put on our Sunday clothes and polished our shoes' (Alec Stout, Fair Isle).

An amusing example of cross-dialectal miscomprehension is reported from an incident during World War I, when the phrase *the kye, sir*, as said by a Shetlander, was interpreted as *the Kaiser* by an officer.

Horse and *beast* (S: *baess*) have unmarked plurality.

5. Pronouns

The subject, object, and possessive forms of the personal pronouns in Shetland dialect are:

I	*me*	*my/mi, mine(s)*
du (you)	*dee (you)*	*dy/di, dine(s) (your[s])*
he	*him*	*his*
shui/shö	*her*	*her(s)*
hit	*hit*	*hits*
we	*wis*	*wir(s)*
you	*you*	*your(s)*
dey	*dem*	*dir(s)*

Orkney dialect has a similar system, with certain realizational differences, such as *thu/thoo* and *hid*.

(39) *Come doon alang some nicht, lass, an tak dy sock.*
'Come along some evening, girl, and bring your knitting.' (S)

(40) *Whar's shoes is this? Mine's.*
'Whose shoes are these? Mine.' (O)

As shown in the table above, the second person singular can be realized either as *du/thu(thoo)* or *you*. The use of these forms is not random, but determined by subtle factors related to age, status, situation, familiarity, attitude etc. (cf. one of the Shetland recordings on the accompanying CD-ROM). This usage is reminiscent of the situation in Sweden and Norway, at least until quite recently. The significance of *you* as the formal variant is not quite clear, however, since its use may often simply be ascribed to the influence of Standard English.

The following results from an investigation of language attitudes carried out in the 1980s among 350 Shetland schoolchildren (cf. Melchers 1985) will illustrate some aspects of the *du/you* distinction:

- 7% of the children used *du* as the only form of address. This group was further characterized by their answers to other questions in the attitude questionnaire: they did not want to leave Shetland; if they moved to London,

they would go on speaking the way they did; their parents spoke dialect; they thought that in some situations it is not proper for a Shetlander to speak Standard English.
- Many informants used *du* to everybody except teachers and certain shopkeepers.
- Age is mentioned as the most important factor. Children of Shetland origin will use *du* to all their friends, including incomers, even if they say *you* to their parents.

A general impression from the survey as well as participant observation is that the *du-you* variation is very often a conscious code-switching phenomenon, not reflecting equality-inferiority so much as accommodation to speakers of different dialects.

Natural gender is very much alive in pronominal reference to certain noun categories: tools, for example, tend to be viewed as masculine, as are some natural phenomena such as the tide, whereas *lamp*, *fish*, *kirk*, *world* and some time expressions are feminine:

(41) *Da tide farder nort, he streams on da west side* (S).

(42) *Da millennium is comin, but shö ...* (S).

Of particular interest is the generic use of *he* referring to the weather. This may well be a substratum effect; there are similar constructions in some Norwegian dialects.

(43) *He's blowan ap* 'the wind is rising' (S).

Reflexive pronouns are often identical with the object forms of personal pronouns:

(44) *Set dee doon* (S).

(45) *He wis restin him* (S).

Although not exclusively found in Shetland and Orkney, the demonstrative pronoun *yon (yun)* is widely used and has come to signal foreignness and a special feeling of remoteness, e.g. with reference to the massive influence of the oil companies, a threat to traditional life (cf. Melchers 1997).

(44) *Yon oil company*; *yon muckle Concorde*; *yon Southfork* (Dallas ranch) (S).

(45) *Du's no telling me at a Shetlander biggit yon, is du?*

The demonstrative pronouns *this/dis* and *that/dat* are used in the plural as well as the singular:

(46) *This eens is better as that eens* (O).

The relative pronoun is always *at*. A frequently used indefinite pronoun is *twartree* 'two or three', 'several'.

6. Word order

The pioneering work by Jonas (2002) demonstrates that traces of an old Scandinavian type of word order in the negated verb phrase, still existing in Icelandic and to some extent in Faroese, can be found in traditional Shetland dialect. She draws on literary sources, mostly from the 19th century, but the structure she discusses was also elicited by the LSS (cf. *I kenno* under 3.5. above). Attention should also be drawn to the fact that Shetland dialect still may display inverted word order and lack of *do*-support (47) as well as overt-subject imperatives (48):

(47) *Sees du yon, boy?*

(48) *Geng du my boy!*

7. A note on the lexicon

The best-known dialect word in the Northern Isles, immediately picked up by incomers, is *peerie* (S)/*pidie* (O) for 'small', derived from French *petit*. It is not clear why this word rather than *wee* has come to be used in Orkney and Shetland.

Yet the most striking component of traditional Orkney and Shetland vocabulary is clearly the Scandinavian element. As in the case of other levels of language, it is more alive in Shetland. A detailed study of the vocabulary investigated by the *Linguistic Survey of Scotland* shows that Orkney retains about two thirds of the Scandinavian-based vocabulary elicited for Shetland.

Words relating to the Scandinavian substratum are generally close to everyday life on the Northern Isles, including semantic fields such as:

- flora and fauna: *arvi* 'chickweed'; *shalder* 'oyster-catcher', *scarf* 'cormorant'
- traditional tools: *tushkar* 'spade for cutting peats', *owskeri* 'scoop used for baling water out of a boat'
- weather terminology: *bonfrost* 'very severe frost'

- colours and characteristics pertaining to sheep: *sholmet* 'wearing a helmet', *moorit* 'light brown'
- emotive, characterizing adjectives: *döless* 'indolent', *inbigget* 'stubborn'

A recent investigation of young schoolchildren's knowledge of a selection of words representing the last category showed a remarkable competence in supplying Standard English synonyms.

8. Text samples

These texts have been included to add more flavour to the description of the unique traditional dialects in the Northern Isles.

Orkney:
A'm sheur thoo're haerd ower an ower again that the Orkney man is a paeceable quiet kind o' body, an' hid's been that aften said that feth the Orkney folk's beginnan tae believe 'id themsel's. Right enouf, wir no folk that carries things tae extremes, lik' sit doon strikes, or gaan merchan here an' there, gittan in folk's wey and livan aff o' the Nation for six or eight weeks. Na, wae cheust geung wir ain gate. (Costie 1976: 51)
(*feth* 'indeed', *merchan* 'marching', *cheust* 'just', *gate* 'way')

Shetland:
Du minds du said at du wid never ken ae yowe fae anidder? Weel, I tocht da sam until I wan among dem, an boy I learned different den. Hit wisna juist da colours ida yowes at dey spak aboot; hit wis der hale laekly, der ancestors an der relations, an aa der past deeds an misanters, an even da wye at dey lookit at dee. Whit wid du tink if some ane axed dee, "Did du see a muckle twa-bletted shaela yowe risin an lyin at da back ida nort crü styaggie?"? (Holbourn 1980: 7)
(*yowe* 'ewe', *hale* 'whole', *laekly* 'exact resemblance', *misanter* 'mishap', *muckle* 'big', *twa-bletted* 'two separate white patches on nose and forehead of sheep', *shaela* 'dark grey', *risin* 'getting up', *crü* 'sheep-fold', *styaggie* 'part of sheep-pen')

Exercises and study questions

1. What is meant by *substratum*?
2. Describe some differences between the Orkney and Shetland dialect.
3. Identify Shetland and Orkney features in the text samples.
4. Identify some differences between features described in this chapter and the chapter on Scottish English.
5. Why do you think the spelling is so variable in the examples and text samples?

Selected references

Please consult the General references for titles mentioned in the text but not included in the references below. For a full bibliography see the accompanying CD-ROM.

Costie, C.M.
1976 *The Collected Orkney Dialect Tales*. Kirkwall: The Kirkwall Press.

Flaws, Margaret and Gregor Lamb
1997 *The Orkney Dictionary*. Kirkwall: The Orcadian Ltd.
2001[2] *The Orkney Dictionary*. Kirkwall: The Orkney Language and Culture Group.

Graham, John J.
1993 *The Shetland Dictionary*. (Revised edition.) Lerwick: The Shetland Times Ltd.
2002 *Shetland Humour*. Lerwick: The Shetland Times Ltd.

Holbourn, Isobel
1980 Whit Laek an a Yowe wis Yon?. In: John J. Graham and Jim Tait (eds.), *Shetland Folk Book*, Volume 7, 7–11. Lerwick: The Shetland Times Ltd.

Jakobsen, Jakob
1897 *Det Norrøne Sprog På Shetland*. Copenhagen: Wilhelm Priors Hofboghandel.
1928 *An Etymological Dictionary of the Norn Language in Shetland*. Volumes 1–2. Copenhagen: Wilhelm Prior.

Jonas, Dianne
2002 Residual V-to-I. In: David Lightfoot (ed.), *Syntactic Effects of Morphological Change*, 251–270. Oxford: Oxford University Press.

Lamb, Gregor
1988 *Orkney Wordbook*. Birsay: Byrgisey.

Marwick, Hugh
1929 *The Orkney Norn*. Oxford: Oxford University Press.

Melchers, Gunnel
1985 'Knappin', 'Proper English', 'Modified Scottish' – some language attitudes in the Shetland Isles. In: Görlach (ed.), 87–100.
1997 *This, that, yon* – on 'three-dimensional' deictic systems. In: Cheshire and Stein (eds.), 83–92.
1999 Writing in Shetland Dialect. In: Irma Taavitsainen, Gunnel Melchers and Päivi Pahta (eds.), *Writing in Nonstandard English*, 331–345. Amsterdam/Philadelphia: Benjamins.

Robertson, T.A. and John J. Graham
1991 *Grammar and Usage of the Shetland Dialect*. Lerwick: The Shetland Times Ltd.

Scottish English: morphology and syntax

Jim Miller

1. Introduction

Speakers in Scotland use a range of syntactic structures varying from Broad Scots at one end of a continuum to Standard English at the other. Different speakers make different choices in different situations. This paper focuses on structures towards and at the Broad Scots end of the range. Broad Scots is essentially a spoken variety, and spontaneous spoken language has its own structures and properties. (See the references to the work of Blanche-Benveniste, Chafe, Crystal, Halliday, Sornicola, Zemskaja and others in Miller and Weinert [1998].) The structures and properties are found in all non-standard varieties of English, but also in spontaneous spoken Standard English (and other languages) and must be included in a compendium of structures used by speakers of Broad Scots. Properties of spontaneous spoken language apart, many (morpho-)syntactic structures used by Scottish speakers occur in other varieties. The structures are described here as Scots, which is not to be read as 'unique to Scots'.

The data is from various sources: a 220,000 word digitised body of conversations collected in Edinburgh and East Lothian (the Edinburgh Corpus of Spoken Scottish English or ECOSSE); a 12,000 word subset of a body of task-related dialogues produced by West of Scotland speakers – the Map Task corpus or MTC; data from Macaulay (1991), which analyses a set of narratives collected in Ayr; excerpts from narratives in Bennett (1992), excluding the narratives from Highland speakers; data in Häcker (1999); and data obtained by elicitation tests. Murray (1873), and Wilson (1915) were consulted for structures used or recognised by the oldest speakers. The audio tapes contain about 90 hours of conversation.

The paper steers clear of the question of literary Scots and focuses on current spoken language in the Central Lowlands. (Treating this as Scots is controversial but it is essential to avoid the myths and wishful thinking that vitiate some 'grammars of Scots'.) Examples from the Buchan area are excluded, as are examples from dialogue in nineteenth and early twentieth century novels set in various areas of Scotland. This approach yields a more coherent set of data than found in, e.g., Häcker (1999). Older constructions are cited from Murray

(1873) and Wilson (1915); they might still be used or recognised by the oldest speakers but are otherwise now extinct.

The structures described here are part of the everyday language of many speakers in Scotland but differ greatly from the structures of standard written English. They form a different system – see Häcker (1999: 11–12, 241) on this matter. Their survival is worth recording, their role in the construction of Scottish identity and the identity of individuals is central even if sadly neglected by researchers, and they bear directly on education, employment and social exclusion. (This point is ignored by politicians and many educators).

2. Morphology

2.1. Irregular verbs

A given verb may have different irregular (strong) forms in Scots and Standard English – *seen* (Scots) vs *saw* (Standard English). A given verb may be strong in Standard English but weak in Scots – compare *sold* (Standard English) and *sellt* (Scots). The following lists of words are illustrative, not exhaustive.

2.1.1. Past tense forms of verbs

brung 'brought'	*driv* 'drove'	*seen* 'saw'	*taen* 'took'
come 'came'	*killt* 'killed'	*sellt* 'sold'	*tellt* 'told'
done 'did'	*run* 'ran'	*sunk* 'sank'	*writ* 'wrote'

2.1.2. Past participles

beat 'beaten'	*feart* 'frightened'	*gave* 'given'	*saw* 'seen'
blew 'blown'	*fell* 'fallen'	*gotten* 'got'	*stole* 'stolen'
broke 'broken'	*forgot* 'forgotten'	*knew* 'known'	*took* 'taken'
came 'come'	*froze* 'frozen'	*rose* 'risen'	*went* 'gone'

Sellt and *tellt* indicate that irregular verbs can be made regular. *Sellt* is simply *sell* + *ed* (*ed* → *t* after *l* and *n*). *Went* occurs as a participle in Dunbar's poem *Celebrations* (late fifteenth century). *Gave* and *knew* are 'incomers'; the original verbs are *gie*, with past tense *gied* and past participle *gien*, and *ken*, with *kent* as past tense and past participle.

2.2. Plural nouns

Plural forms such as *een* ('eyes') or *shin* ('shoes') are vanishing. The author last heard *shin* in West Lothian in 1963, *een* can still be heard, and *treen* is long gone. Note the widely used *wifes*, *knifes*, *lifes*, *leafs*, *thiefs*, *dwarfs*, *loafs*, *wolfs*, all in a regular relationship with *wife*, etc.

2.3. Pronouns

Scots has a second person plural *yous* or *yous yins*, avoided by educated speakers. *Us* is informal but widespread instead of *me*, particularly with verbs such as *give*, *show*, and *lend* (e.g. *Can you lend us a quid?*). The possessive pronoun *mines* is analogous to *yours*, *his*, etc.; and *hisself* and *theirselves* are analogous to *yourself*, etc. In *me and Jimmy are on Monday our two selves* ('by ourselves'), *two* raises the question whether *myself*, etc. is one word or two.

2.4. Demonstrative adjectives

Scots has *thae* ('those') as in *thae cakes was awfy dear* ('awfully dear'). *Thae* is still alive but the most frequent form is now *them*: *them cakes was awfy dear*. Wilson (1915) gives *thir* as the plural of *this*. There is one occurrence in ECOSSE, from a young East Lothian speaker.

2.5. Adverbs

As in all Germanic languages (except Standard English), a given form can function as adjective and adverb: *they got on real good*, *drive slow* (on a sign at roadworks), *drive quick*. (With some exceptions, such as *fast*, Standard English adjectives and adverbs differ in form.)

3. Syntactic linkage

3.1. Number agreement

Plural subject nouns usually combine with *is* and *was*. Wilson (1915) gives *Ma glassiz iz broakun* ('My glasses are broken') and *Is they yours?* ('Are these yours?').

(1) *The windies wiz aw broken.*
'The windows were all broken.'

(2) *The lambs is oot the field.*
'The lambs are out of the field.'

We was is frequent. *We is* does not occur. Educated speakers avoid the structures in (1) and (2) but many use the existential construction in (3) and (4).

(3) *There's no bottles.*

(4) *Is there any biscuits left?*

Macafee (1983) cites *you was* and *goes* (and other verbs in *-s*) as a narrative form: *'Naw', I goes, near screaming, you know?* (Macafee 1983: 49–50). Macaulay (1991) gives examples of *there* ('there's') and *there were* ('there was'). Wilson (1915: 77) cites the example in (7), and *the're* (sic) is mentioned in passing in Grant and Main Dixon's 1921 *Manual of Modern Scots*.

(5) *There naebody going to force them.*

(6) *And there a gate just after you go ower the brig takes you intae this field.*

(7) *There no sic a thing hereaway.*

3.2. Measure phrases

Numerals from two upwards regularly combine with singular nouns: *five mile long*, *two foot high*, *weighs eight stone*, *two year old.* In Macaulay's data (1991: 110) forty-one out of ninety measure nouns are plural. *Minute*, *day*, *week*, *shilling*, *inch* and *yard* are always plural after numerals greater than 1. The percentage of inflected plurals for other nouns is *pound* – 89%, *month* – 86%, *year* – 68%, *ton* – 50%, *mile* – 17%. Wilson (1915: 62) cites *three gless o' whiskay*, *a guid wheen month* (*wheen* = 'few') and *five acre*, not to mention *broth*, *porridge* and *kail*, which were plural.

There is regularly no preposition between the measure nouns *bit* and *drop* and a following noun: *a bit paper*, *a bit steel*, *a drop water*. These constructions are typical Germanic. *Less* is normal with plural count nouns, as in *less cars*. Note too *much more cars* ('many more cars').

4. Syntax

4.1. Negation

In Scots verbs are negated by the independent words *no* and *not*, as in (8), or by the suffixes *-nae* and *-n't*, as in (9).

(8) a. *She's no leaving.*
b. *She's not leaving.*

(9) a. *She isnae leaving.*
b. *She isn't leaving.*

In ECOSSE *no* and *not* are most frequent with BE – *She's no 'phoned yet*, with *'ll* ('will') – *she'll no be coming to the party*, and with *'ve* ('have') – *I've no seen him the day*. The *no*/*not* construction is in fact the norm with BE, WILL and HAVE in Scots and Scottish English among all speakers. *Nae* is added to all the modal verbs and to *do* – *He doesnae help in the house*, *She cannae knit*. *Not* and *no* are the norm in negative interrogatives such as (10).

(10) *Are you not coming with us?*

The typical Scots tag question has *not* or *no*, as in (11). Educated speakers occasionally use *amn't*, as in (12).

(11) *That's miles away is it no?*

(12) *I'm coming with you amn't I?*

Nae is suffixed to modal verbs if *-nae* applies to the modal verb: *He cannae come to the party* ('he is unable…'). *No* and *not* do occur with modal verbs, but apply to the phrase following the modal: *will you not put too many on there in case they fall in the street please* (Macafee 1983: 47). *Not* applies to *put too many on there*. *Won't you put too many...* asks for too many to be put on.

Clauses without an auxiliary verb, as in *I got the job*, can be made negative with *didn't* or *didnae* but *never* is frequently used, as in (13).

(13) a. *...I could've got the job...but I telt them I couldnae leave till the end of May so I never got it.* [ECOSSE]
b. *I sat down to that tongue slips essay at 7 o'clock I never got it started till nine.* [ECOSSE]

Never is not emphatic. Speakers express the meaning 'at no time in general' with *never ever*. *Never* and *so* function as pro-verbs: *I added water and it fizzed I done it again and it never* ('didn't') (pupil to teacher); *You're not offended? – I am so!*; *you can't do that! – I can so!* (*I will so* and *I do so* are also frequent.)

There is an emphatic negative construction with *nane*, ('none') as in (14). The interpretation is that Rab is completely useless at singing.

(14) *Rab can sing nane.*

Finally, we turn to the relationship between *not*, *-n't*, etc. and the quantifiers *all*, *each* and *every*. Consider (15):

(15) a. *It is not democratic, because every member is not consulted on the decision.* [radio interview]
b. *We all don't have to be there.* [conversation]

In context, (15a) clearly meant that some members are consulted but not others; the written English version would be *Not every member is consulted....* (15b) was used as justification for not attending a meeting – colleagues of the speaker would be there. The corresponding standard constructions are *We don't all have to be there* and *Not all of us have to be there.*

4.2. Modal verbs

The system of modal verbs in Scots is massively different from that of Standard English.

(a) ECOSSE has no occurrences of *shall, may* and *ought*, though these modal verbs do occur in writing and in formal announcements, as in the notice *This shop shall be open on Monday* and in announcements such as *This train shall stop at Paisley Gilmour Street, Johnstone,...* The source of this usage may be legal.
In spoken Scots *will* marks future tense – *We will arrive in the morning*, promises – *You will have the money tomorrow* ('I promise you'), and occurs in interrogatives – *Will I open the window?* Permission is expressed by *can, get to* and *get* + gerund as in (16).

(16) a. *You can have this afternoon off.*
b. *The pupils get to come inside in rainy weather.*
c. *They got going to the match.*

Should and not *ought* is used, but *want* is frequent, as in (17), uttered by a judo instructor:

(17) *You want to come out and attack right away.*

(b) In Standard English *must* expresses conclusions, as in (18a), and obligation, as in (18b):

(18) a. *You must be exhausted.*
'I conclude from your appearance that…'
b. *You must be at the airport by nine or you will lose your seat.*
'It is necessary for you to be at the airport by nine.'

In ECOSSE *must* expresses only the conclusion meaning; obligation is expressed by *have to* and *need to*. Many speakers of Scots (and Scottish English) use *have got to* for external compulsion and *will have to* for milder compulsion, which can even be self-compulsion, as in (19).

(19) *I'll have to write to Carol because she wrote to us six months ago.*

Have to is less strong than *have got to*. It also expresses conclusions, as in (20).

(20) *That has to be their worst display ever.*

(c) *Need* behaves like a main verb – *Do you need to leave immediately* and *You don't need to leave immediately*, *They're needing to paint the windows*. It expresses obligation, and is equivalent to *have to*. (21a,b) are typical of answers produced by university undergraduates who were asked to complete the sentence *I must be back at midnight because* ____.

(21) a. *I must be back by midnight because I need to switch off my electric blanket.*
b. *I have to go to the library because I need to do my French essay today.*

Need can express external compulsion as in (22):

(22) *You'd need to go down there and collect her and drop her.* [ECOSSE]

In Scots *mustn't* expresses 'I conclude that not', as in (23). Some grammars of Standard English prescribe *can't*:

(23) a. *This mustn't be the place.*
b. *I mustn't have read the question properly.* [conversation]

Obligation is also expressed by *supposed to* or *meant to*, as in (24):

(24) a. *You're supposed to leave your coat in the cloakroom.*
b. *You're meant to fill in the form first.*

Meant to also occurs with the meaning 'It is said that': *The new player is meant to be real fast.*

(d) *Can't*, *cannot* and *cannae* all express 'not have permission to'. To express 'have permission not to', speakers of Scots use *don't need to*, *don't have to* and *are not allowed to*.

(e) Scots has double modals, as in (25):

(25) a. *He'll can help us the morn/tomorrow.*
b. *They might could be working in the shop.*
c. *She might can get away early.*
d. *Wi his sair foot he would never could climb yon stairs*. (Purves 1997: 57)

Note the acceptable interrogative *Will he can help us the morn/tomorrow?* and the unacceptable **Might they could be working in the shop?* There are grounds for supposing that *might* in (25b,c) is developing into an adverb, syntactically equivalent to *maybe*: note sentences such as *They maybe could be working in the shop*, with *maybe* in the same position as *might*.

Might occasionally combines with *should* and *would*, as in (26). Here again *might* is equivalent in meaning and position to *maybe*. Note too the parallel between (27a) and (27b).

(26) a. *You might would like to come with us.*
b. *You might should claim your expenses.* [both from informants from Prestonpans]

(27) a. *He might no could do it.*
b. *He maybe no could do it.*

The double modal sequence *will can* is relatively old – Wilson (1915) mentions it – but may be in decline. In her 1997 Edinburgh University Honours dissertation McIver found that in Orkney the over-60s used the construction but the under-25s neither used it nor recognised all the combinations. However, in a television interview (BBC Scotland, 22/01/2002) a woman in her mid-thirties, born and brought up in Fife, declared *once I started I wouldnae could stop*.

(f) Modal verbs occur after the infinitive marker *to*, as shown in (28):

(28) a. *You have to can drive a car to get that job.*
b. *I'd like to could do that.*

According to an informant born and brought up in Galloway, examples such as (29) are common:

(29) *Ah would uh could uh done it.*
'I would have been able to do it.'

Apart from the two instances of *uh* – presumably equivalent to *'ve* or *have*, the unusual feature is *could* preceded by *have*.

4.3. Tense and aspect

4.3.1. Progressive

Standard English stative verbs such as *know*, *like* or *want* do not occur in the Progressive.

(30) a. **Kirsty is knowing the answer.*
b. **Archie is liking this book.*

Know behaves in the same way in Scots but other stative verbs occur regularly in the Progressive, as in (31):

(31) a. *I wasnae liking it and the lassie I was going wi wasnae liking it.* [ECOSSE]
b. *We werenae really wanting to go last year but they sent us a lot of letters to come.* [ECOSSE]
c. *He's not understanding a single thing you say.* [TV programme]
d. *They're not intending opening the bottle tonight surely.* [informally recorded in conversation]

In Standard English *Soapy is washing the dishes* presents the action as in progress; *Soapy washes the dishes* presents the action as habitual or repeated. In Scots, younger speakers and writers use the Progressive where older speakers, including the author, use the simple aspect. The examples in (32) are from essays and examination answers by undergraduates at Edinburgh University. The author would have to use *learn* in (32a), and *forget* in (32b). We may be seeing the beginning of a process whereby the Progressive changes into an Imperfective (a change that has affected many languages).

(32) a. *Today, educational establishments are still trying to teach a standard. Many schoolchildren are not learning the standard outwith school.*
b. *The code is often changed and students are forgetting the new number.* [minutes of Liaison Committee, written by a student]

4.3.2. Past and Perfect

Combined with the Progressive, the Perfect refers to recent past time. *Kirsty has been working with the Royal Bank* is appropriate either if Kirsty is still working with the bank or was working with the bank until quite recently. Speakers of Scots can refer to a recent, completed event by the Past Progressive + *there*, as in (33):

(33) a. *I was (just) speaking to John there.*
b. *I was speaking to John on Friday there.*

Deictics such as *there* point to entities or locations visible to speaker and hearer. In (33a) the speaker presents the event of speaking to John as metaphorically visible to the listener and therefore close in time. The Friday referred to in (33b) is the Friday in the past closest to the time of utterance.

The Standard English *The electrician has just phoned* puts an event in the immediate past. In Scots the same effect is conveyed by *The electrician just phoned*, with the Simple Past and *just*. (34) exemplifies the same usage. The person addresses Bob immediately after the latter has bought a round of drinks (Macaulay 1991: 197–198).

(34) *And one of the men happened to comment he says "Bob" he says "you forgot the boy" "No" he says "I didnae forget the boy".*

In Standard English the Perfect can refer to an event which someone has experienced at some indefinite time in the past, as in *I have visited Prague*. In Scots the Simple Past with *ever* also conveys this experiential meaning, as in (35):

(35) *You said you enjoyed fishing – were you ever interested in football?* [ECOSSE]

The Perfect in Standard English conveys the result of a past action. In Scots, results of past actions are often expressed by constructions other than the Perfect which contain a resultative participle. (36) and (37) exemplify the resultative structure from which the Perfect is supposed to have developed.

(36) *You have access to a vein gained and a cardiac analysis done within one minute.* [radio discussion]

(37) I was wanting to borrow her hoover but she'll have it put away. [conversation]

A common structure is *there's* plus resultative participle:

(38) *There's something fallen down the sink.*

Speakers often report the completion of an action by referring to its result. The reverse cleft in (39), from A.L. Kennedy's 1994 novel *Looking for the Possible*

Dance, refers to properties assigned to the letters as the result of a writing event and a posting event.

(39) *That's the letters written and posted.*

Example (40), from Macaulay (1991), offers reverse clefts in which the noun phrase following *is* is the 'subject' of the action.

(40) a. *But that's me seen it.*
'I've seen it now.'
b. *And he says "That you left the school noo Andrew?"*
'...Have you left school now...?'

The equivalent of a pluperfect is in (41):

(41) *He just lay doon on the settee and turned over and that was him gone.*
'...he had gone.'

Resultative participles also occur in the construction in (42):

(42) a. *I need the car repaired by midday.* [conversation]
b. *She needs collected at four o'clock.* [conversation]

4.3.3. Pluperfect tense

The Pluperfect is rare in main clauses in Scots, and absent from certain subordinate clauses. The examples in (43) were written by secondary school pupils and 'corrected' to the Pluperfect by their teacher.

(43) a. *He said his mum had brought him the fireworks but she really didn't.* [hadn't]
b. *...he...was angry I didn't stay in the café.* [hadn't stayed]

4.3.4. Tense and aspect in conditional clauses

(44a,b) are typical of modern Scots:

(44) a. *If she would come to see things for herself...*
b. *If she would have come to see things for herself...*

Compare *If she came to see things for herself she would understand our difficulties* and *If she had come to see things for herself, she would have understood our difficulties*. Interestingly, (44) was a regular construction in Early Modern English and appears to be making a comeback, as in (45), from *The Times*:

(45) *Suppose further that all Conservative and Labour voters in England would have given the Alliance as their second choice...*

The Pluperfect is replaced with *had* + *'ve* ('have') in conditional clauses and in the complements of verbs such as *wish*. See (46a) and (46b):

(46) a. *I reckon I wouldnae have been able to dae it if I hadnae 've been able to read music.*
'…hadn't been able…'
b. *I wish he'd 've complimented me, Roger.*
'…had complimented…'

Häcker (1999) discusses how anteriority (one event preceding another) is expressed by means of *once* + Simple Past, as in *once her children left home, she got a job.*

4.4. Interrogatives

(a) Scots regularly uses *how* where Standard English uses *why*:

(47) a. A: *Susan, how's your ankle?*
B: *I can walk on it I think how?* '…why?'
b. *How did you not apply?*
'Why did you not apply?'

(b) *Whereabout* is used instead of *where* and is regularly split into *where* and *about*. *How* + *about* relates to quantity.

(48) a. *Whereabout did you see him?*
b. *Where does she stay about?*
c. *How old was he about?*

(c) *What time...at?* frequently replaces *when?*, as in *What time does it finish at?*

(d) In Standard English, *which book?* asks about one of a set of known books; *what book?* asks about one out of the set of all books. In Scots *what* fulfils both functions, as in (49):

(49) a. *What book have you been buying?* [addressee is carrying a book]
b. *What book is being published next year?*

(e) In writing, indirect questions have the constituent order of declarative clauses, as in (50):

(50) *The teacher asked what book they had read.* (cf. *What book have you read?*)

In Scots, indirect questions have the constituent order of direct questions, as in (51), which involved no hesitations or changes in intonation but were uttered as one chunk:

(51) a. *If they got an eight they had to decide where was the best place to put it.* [ECOSSE]
 b. *What happens in the last fifteen minutes depends on how keen are Rumania to win.* [football commentary]

(f) Scots has various tag-questions. Speakers use the same tags with repeated auxiliary, as in Standard English, as in (52).

(52) a. *John has left, has he no?*
 b. *John's no left, has he?*

They also use *e*, added to both positive and negative declarative clauses, as in (53a,b). Occasionally *e no* is added to positive clauses.

(53) a. *...we know him quite well by now e?*
 '... don't we' [recorded informally]
 b. *It's no too dear e?*
 *'It's not too d*ear, is it?' [recorded informally]

E occurs in imperatives, converting them to requests, even coaxing requests. In questions the tag asks the addressee to agree with the speaker's statement; in imperatives the tag asks the addressee to agree with (and act upon) the speaker's request, as in (54):

(54) a. *Let me tie my lace e! [conversation]*
 b. *Put it down there e!* [conversation]

When added to (54a,b) *won't you* makes a request sharper – *Let me tie my lace won't you*, *Put it down there won't you*, but *e* always makes a request less sharp and more polite. The author observed the following event in February 2002. A customer (male, over 50) came into a fish and chip shop in Leven, in Fife. The assistant asked what he would like; he replied *A mini fish supper e*? The *e* carried interrogative intonation and the Standard English equivalent is *Could I have a mini fish supper please?*, which is also an interrogative.

In July 2002 the author overheard a conversation in a barber's. The barber (male, 30ish) told his colleague he had gone to a particular pub at the weekend. He looked in the mirror at the author and said *I like Sambuca e?* The *eh* carried interrogative pitch but the barber could hardly have been asking about his own likes and dislikes. The utterance was interpreted by the author as equivalent to *I like Sambuca ken* ('you know', 'you see') or to *I like Sambuca* with the high rising terminal used by many speakers under 35. The author has heard the same usage from a male speaker in his forties and from a male speaker in his twenties. The latter was describing the location of a landfill site, saying that the Auchendinny to Penicuik road turned right at the bottom of a steep slope and that *I stay just opposite e?* Again the force of the utterance is *I stay opposite you know/you see* (and that's how I know all about the landfill site).

A positive clause can be followed by a positive tag, as in (55). The force of these tags in context seems to be that speakers expect a positive answer to their question.

(55) A: *Aye that's cos I didnae use to go.*
B: *Did you start skiving did you?* [ECOSSE]

Other tags available in Scots are illustrated in (56). (56f) is from Bennett (1992: 115), (56a,b,f) are from ECOSSE, and the others are from conversation:

(56) a. *You don't go for that sort, no?*
b. *You've mentioned this to him, yes?*
c. *They're not intending opening the bottle tonight surely?*
d. *He's not trying to make all of it, not really?*
e. *He's coming on Monday, right?*
f. *Have you not heard of rubber trees, no?*

(56a) expresses the speaker's strong confidence that the addressee does indeed not favour that sort of man. (56b) expresses the speaker's strong confidence that the addressee has mentioned 'it' to the other person. Particularly strong confidence is displayed by speakers who begin a declarative clause with *sure* or *e*, using interrogative intonation. Note that (57a,b) are not equivalent to 'Are you sure that Harry supports Celtic?' but 'I'm certain you can confirm my confident belief that Harry supports Celtic':

(57) a. *Sure Harry supports Celtic?*
b. *E Harry supports Celtic?*

4.5. The definite article and possessive pronouns

A well-known characteristic of Scots is the use of *the* with nouns denoting institutions, certain illnesses, certain periods of time, quantifiers such as *both*, *all*, *most* and *one*, games, family relatives and modes of travel. The examples in (58) are merely hints. There are many more examples in Miller (1993: 128), Macaulay (1991: 70–71) and Wilson (1915). Examples of possessive pronouns are given in (59):

(58) *the day* 'today'; *the morn* 'tomorrow'; *the now* 'now'; *have the flu*; *be at the school*; *through the post* 'by post'; *when the one supporter ran on the field*; *the both of them*

(59) a. *Look Cathy, I'm off for my dinner.* '...to have dinner'
b. *to get ready to go up to your work* '…to work'

4.6. Comparatives

What intervenes between *more than* and *as much as* and a following clause, as in (60):

(60) a. *more than what you'd think actually* [ECOSSE]
b. *You've as much on your coat as what you have in your mouth.* [conversation]

Macaulay (1991: 102) cites *and of coorse the traffic wasnae as strong as what it is noo* and gives two examples (uttered by his oldest speakers) with *nor* instead of than: *well it was better then nor what I think it is noo* and *you couldnae get any mair nor two pound.*

Comparative forms are used only before *than*: *Sue is bigger than Jane*. Elsewhere the superlative is used, as in *Who is biggest, Sue or Jane?*

4.7. Reflexives

The reflexive pronoun *myself* is frequently used in speech and writing where Standard English requires just *me* or *I*.

(61) a. *There wasn't one policeman on duty at the time and if it hadn't been for myself, no evidence either.* [radio discussion]
b. *Myself and Andy changed and ran onto the pitch.* [school essay]

4.8. Prepositions and adverbs

The prepositional system of Scots has yet to be studied in detail, but the following points can be made.

(a) The typical prepositions in passive clauses are *from*, *frae/fae* ('from'), *off* ('of') and *with*.

(62) a. *Heh, ah'm gonna get killt fae ma maw.* '…by my Mum'
b. *We were all petrified frae him.* [ECOSSE]
c. *Ah'd rather hae no job than bein beat frae pillar tae post aff a that man.* '…by that man' [radio interview 1992]
d. *I got helped with the midwife.* [radio interview 2001]

(b) *Off*, not *from*, generally expresses the source of something – *I got the book off Alec* – and occasionally cause, as in *I'm crapping myself off you* ('…because of you'), uttered sarcastically.

(c) *At*, *beside* and *next to* replace *by* in its location sense; *past* replaces *by* in its directional sense: *They drove past the house*. Elicitation examples such as *We went to Inverness* ____ *Stirling* elicited *via*.

(d) *In* and *out* are not followed by *to* or *of* after verbs of movement – *She ran in the living room*, *...because she's just walked out the shop with it*. Macaulay (1991: 111) gives similar examples.

(e) Likewise, *down* and *up* do not require *to* – *We're going down the town*, *go down the shops*. After verbs of location they do not require *at* – *One day I was down the beach*, *They were up the town yesterday*.

(f) *Outside* is followed by *of* – *outside of the school*.

(g) Miscellaneous examples: *shout on someone* ('to someone'), *over the phone* ('by phone'), *through the post* ('by post'), *wait on someone* ('for someone'), *fair on someone* ('to someone'), *married on someone* ('to someone'), *think on something* ('think of/about'). Macaulay (1991) gives examples with *to* – *He worked to Wilson of Troon*, *I'm labouring to a bricklayer*.

5. Clause constructions

5.1. Clause structure and function

Clause structure poses two major problems. One is that in written language clauses combine into sentences. *When Morag arrived at the house, she found it locked and empty* is one sentence consisting of two clauses; *Morag arrived at the house – She found it locked and empty* is clearly two sentences, each consisting of a single clause. The Scots data described in this paper is informal and spoken and the unit of analysis called the sentence has been abandoned by most analysts of spoken language (see the discussion and references in Miller and Weinert [1998], chapter 2).

Clause complexes bring us to the second problem. Clauses are organised into clause complexes, which typically lack the tight syntactic links found in written text. Their syntax is unintegrated (see discussion and references in Miller and Weinert [1998: 72–132]). This property is exemplified and discussed in relation to (63)–(64). Consider (63):

(63) *You have a little keypad down here* ***which you can use your mouse to click on the keys.*** [presentation at University of Edinburgh]

The clause in bold looks like a relative clause as it apparently modifies *keypad* and is introduced by *which*. The clause, however, has no gaps, contains a full set of subject, direct object and oblique object noun phrases. This particular clause is not embedded in a noun phrase although it could be; the central fact is that it contains no gaps or pronouns linking with *keypad*. (64) exemplifies another construction:

(64) *Everyone knows Helen Liddell how hard she works*. [radio discussion]

As the direct object of *knows*, *Helen Liddell* is central and salient in the clause complex. The clause *how hard she works* is syntactically optional but linked with *Helen Liddell* by *she*. A written text would have *Everyone knows how hard Helen Liddell works*. Another example is *I've been meaning to phone and ask about the new baby and Alan how they're getting on*.

The range of unintegrated constructions can be extended but the reader is invited to bear in mind Bernd Kortmann and Clive Upton's introduction (see Kortmann and Upton, this volume) and to read Miller and Weinert (1998: 105–121) on relative clauses, WH clefts and headless relative clauses in English and other languages.

5.2. Relative clauses

(a) Restrictive relative clauses are introduced by *that,* but also by *where*: *just about that other place where I started.* Relative clauses modifying time nouns such as *day*, *month*, etc. typically lack *that*, as in *the day she arrived* (which is the only construction in ECOSSE. Restrictive relative clauses in the Broad Scots of Glasgow are occasionally introduced by *what*: *like the other birds what takes Dexedrine*.)

(b) Event relative clauses are introduced by *which*, never by *that*, as in *my Dad came to an Elton John concert with us which at the time we thought was great*. What was thought great was the event of the speaker's father coming to the concert.

(c) Instead of *whose, that* + possessive pronoun is used: *the girl that her eighteenth birthday was on that day was stoned, couldnae stand up* (as opposed to *the girl whose eighteenth birthday was on that day*).

(d) Shadow pronouns are typical of complex relative clauses such as *the spikes that you stick in the ground and throw rings over them* [conversation] but also of simpler relative clauses such as *It's something that I keep returning to it* and *they're the ones that the teacher thinks they're going to misbehave* [both from radio discussions]. The possessive example in (c) is also an example of a shadow pronoun. The shadow pronoun construction is widespread in non-standard varieties throughout Europe.

(e) Prepositions always occur at the end of the relative clause (*the shop I bought it in*, not *the shop in which I bought it*) but are frequently omitted: *of course there's a rope that you can pull the seat back up* (*with* omitted) [ECOSSE] and *I haven't been to a party yet that I haven't got home the same night* (*from* omitted) [radio discussion].

(f) Existential constructions have no relative pronoun or conjunction; in writing, *that* or *who* would be in the square brackets in (65):

(65) a. *My friend's got a brother* [ ] *used to be in the school.*
b. *There's only one of us* [ ] *been on a chopper before.*

(g) Non-restrictive relative clauses are notably scarce. MTC and ECOSSE have no non-restrictive relative clauses with *who*. University undergraduates and 17-year-olds at an Edinburgh private school produced 19 non-restrictive relatives with *which*. Adults and 16–17-year-olds at state schools produced 3 such clauses. Macaulay (1991: 64) comments that in his middle-class interviews 20% of the relative clauses are non-restrictive, in the working class interviews 5%.

Instead of non-restrictive relative clauses, speakers of Scots use coordinate clauses: *the boy I was talking to last night – and he actually works in the yard – was saying it's going to be closed down* (not *the boy..., who actually works in the yard,...*).

The relative complementiser *that* is a conjunction which developed historically from a pronoun. *Which* is following the same path. Consider the second *which* in (66).

(66) *You can leave at Christmas if your birthday's in December to February which I think is wrong like my birthday's March and I have to stay on to May* ***which*** *when I'm 16 in March I could be looking for a job.*

The second *which*, in bold, does not link a relative clause to a noun but signals that the preceding chunk of text is connected to the following one. (This construction occurs in Dickens and in *Punch* throughout the nineteenth century.)

Finally in this section, we should note that shadow pronouns occur in another construction that can be heard on radio and television. Consider (67):

(67) a. *In New York on Manhattan Island there is a theatre* ***there*** *that...* [radio report]
b. *Out of the three questions we got two* ***of them.*** [conversation]

5.3. Complement clauses

In English generally some verbs take infinitives, as in (68a), while others take gerunds, as in (68b). Other verbs may take either an infinitive or a gerund, as in (69):

(68) a. *We hope to leave next week.* (not **we hope leaving...*)
b. *Archie resents spending money on books.* (not **Archie resents to spend...*)

(69) *The children started to quarrel/quarrelling.*

Verbs and adjectives that take either infinitives or gerunds in Scots are shown in (70).

(70) a. *It's difficult to know/knowing how to start this letter.*
b. *They always continue to work/working until the bell goes.*
c. *He started to talk/talking to his friend.*
d. *It was daft to leave/leaving the puppy in the house.*
e. *Try to eat less/eating less if you are putting on weight.*

Elicitation tests showed that for (70a–e) Scottish pupils had (statistically) significant numbers of gerunds while the English pupils did not. Some Scottish pupils used only gerunds. Teachers preferred infinitives, with English teachers showing a stronger preference than Scottish teachers.

In Scots the infinitive is regularly marked by *for to*. Macaulay (1991: 106) gives the examples in (71):

(71) a. *We had the clear road for to play on. [infinitive relative]*
b. *You don't need to faw ten thousand feet for to get killt.* [purpose/result]
c. *You werenae allowed at this time for to go and take another job on.* [verb complement]
d. *But my own brothers was all too old for to go.* [comparison]

His youngest working-class speakers have no *for to* infinitives, whereas the oldest two use them regularly. The construction may be in decline.

Some verbs are followed by *and* plus a verb phrase, as in (72):

(72) a. *Try and do your homework by tomorrow.*
'try to do...'
b. *Remember and bring her back by 12 o'clock.*
c. *She tells us to mind and dae what we're tellt.*
'...to remember...'

The television comedy show *Chewing the fat* uses the catchphrase *gonna no dae that*, which is probably a distortion of *go and no dae that*, the negative of *go and dae that (right the noo)*. Infinitives can follow *away*: *I'm away to the shops*, *I'm away to ask her to dance*.

5.4. Adverbial clauses

Adverbial clauses in general are less frequent (in speech) than relative and complement clauses. The following specific points are important.

(a) *Because* or *cause* clauses typically follow the main clause – *We lent them our car because the garage couldn't fix theirs right away*; in writing they both precede and follow the main clause – *Because the garage couldn't fix theirs right away we lent them our car*. Preceding *because* clauses act as signposts, whereas following the main clause they merely provide a reason (see the reference to Chafe in Miller and Weinert [1998]).

(b) Clauses of condition and time also tend to follow the main clause. In ECOSSE and MTC many *if* clauses are not straightforward adverbial clauses of condition but convey an instruction – *if you just draw the line 2 cms below the cave* – and constitute a complete discourse. Conversely, imperative clauses can express conditions: *tell a lie an they'll believe you* (Häcker 1999: 119).

(c) There are no concession clauses introduced by *although*. Speakers in ECOSSE concede points with *but* clauses or with clauses containing clause-final *though* – *They're not going to shut the factory – they're making a loss though*. Another construction for the conceding of points is exemplified in (73).

(73) *But eh customs is a' changed noo. You still see them in Glasgow right enough.* (Bennett 1992: 110–111)

(d) Consider *If Shona is coming to the party, I'm going to stay at home*. The *if* clause is starting point or theme and therefore prominent. Another common construction is *see if Shona is coming to the party – I'm going to stay at home* and *see when we get into the gardens, can we go up the tower?* This construction highlights the time or condition and breaks the integration of subordinate and main clause; the *if* and *when* clauses are complements of *see*.

(e) Adverbial clauses of time can be introduced by *frae* or *fae* ('from') instead of *since*, as in (74) from Macaulay (1991). The author has heard similar examples in West Lothian.

(74) a. *My it's a while fae I heard that.* '…since I heard that'
b. *The first time I ever was idle fae I left the school.* '…since I left the school'

(f) Time clauses can be introduced by tae ('to') instead of till, as in (75a), from Macaulay (1991). To or tae can also replace till as a preposition, as in (75b):

(75) a. *Wait here tae I come oot.* '...till I come out'
b. *Well you can hear her aw over the shop she just says you've nae right cos i cannae come in to this time.* [ECOSSE]

Häcker (1999: 172–173) suggests that adverbial time clauses introduced by *till* have a purposive meaning, as in (76):

(76) a. *Turn on the wireless till we hear the news.*
b. *An that wis wait till I think where that* [was].
'…wait so that I can think where that was.'

Wait in (76b) is an atelic verb and the *till* clause can be interpreted as a time clause setting a limit to a stretch of time. *Turn on* in (76a) is telic but has the interpretation 'turn on and leave turned on for a certain length of time' – note the (devised) example *they turned on the water till everyone got their buckets filled (and then they turned it off again)*. The purposive component of the interpretation can be seen as coming from a felicity condition on commands: the speaker(s) really want a situation to be brought about.

(g) Häcker (1999: 161, 192) comments on the use of gerunds introduced by *with* to express reason, manner or accompanying circumstances. (77) is from ECOSSE:

(77) *But he didnae like to take it* [a job] *with him being a friend.*

5.5. Non-finite main or adverbial clauses

Surprise, disappointment or a strong emotion can be expressed by non-finite clauses introduced by *and*: *He wouldn't help* ***and him a minister too!***, *She's taking in lodgers* ***and the house not even hers***, *He's gone off on holiday* ***and her still in the hospital***. It is unclear whether these clauses are main or adverbial.

6. Organisation of discourse

Scots has a range of devices for highlighting items. The devices belong to speech and many are not unique to Scots.

(a) Speakers often announce a new topic, possibly contrasting with another topic, by means of left-dislocation, a noun phrase followed by a complete clause. Left-dislocation is not primarily associated with planning problems; it occurs frequently with simple noun phrases with no pause between the noun phrase and the clause. The noun phrase may be introduced in an existential clause, as in (78c):

(78) a. *It's not bad –* ***ma Dad*** *he doesn't say a lot.* [ECOSSE]
b. *And* ***the minister****, ye just gave him five shillings. But on the way out we met a wee girl and we gave her the christening piece.* [Bennett 1992: 69–70]
c. *And* ***there's one girl*** *she's a real extrovert.* [ECOSSE]

The initial noun phrase can be quite complex – *well* ***another maths teacher that I dinnae get*** *he must've corrected my papers* – or may be separated from the main clause by a subordinate clause, as in (79):

(79) *But a lot of people,* ***although they didnae have a gift****, it was a coin that they would give them.* [Bennett 1992: 48]

(b) English possesses the IT cleft, WH cleft and reverse WH cleft constructions exemplified in (80):

(80) a. *It was Aongais that left. [IT cleft]*
b. *What I want is a large cup of coffee. [WH cleft]*
c. *That's what you should read.* [Reverse WH cleft]
d. *What he does is interrupt all the time.* [WH cleft]

The IT cleft picks out an entity from a set of possible candidates – Aongais as opposed to Ruaridh. The second clause, *that left*, is a relative clause.

There may be no complementiser, as in (81), from Macaulay (1991: 121).

(81) a. *It was* ***Jimmy Brown*** *was the fireman.*
b. *And it was* ***my mother*** *was daein it.*

77% of Macaulay's IT clefts are in the working class interviews. IT clefts in general are rare in ECOSSE and MTC but interrogative IT-clefts occur regularly in ECOSSE in WH questions, as in (82):

(82) a. *Where is it he works again?*
b. *Who is it that's been murdered?*
c. *Which part of Leith is it you're from?*
d. *What was it he did? Was doing law or something.*

The IT clefts both make the question less abrupt and highlight the WH word. (82a–d) are not contrastive, though other examples are, such as *Was that Malcolm that did it*? [ECOSSE]. One example is a YES-NO question – *Is that you skive skipping off this afternoon*? The construction awaits detailed investigation.

The most common WH cleft in the data has the structure of *What we're doing we're hanging them up to drouth* (= 'dry'). A headless relative clause – *what we're doing* is followed by a complete main clause *we're hanging them up to drouth*. In MTC WH clefts finish off a section of discussion and point forward. In ECOSSE WH clefts finish off a section of narrative and move it on to the next section.

Reverse WH clefts are frequent in MTC and occur in ECOSSE. They highlight some point that has been agreed and draw a line under a section of discussion but do not point forward. (For a detailed discussion of clefts see Weinert and Miller [1996] and Miller and Weinert [1998: 263–306].) Many discussions in MTC close with remarks such as *that's where you should go*. In Macaulay (1991: 78–79) sections of narrative are closed by reverse clefts introduced by *that* or *this* followed by a pronoun and a modifying phrase, as in (83):

(83) a. *So that was me on the rope-splicing.*
b. *That was him idle.* 'laid off work'
c. *And this was him landed with a broken leg.*

Macaulay (1991: 91) discusses right-dislocation but its discourse function is unclear and there seem to be two constructions. One is exemplified in (84):

(84) a. *In fact he offered me a job Mr Cunningham.*
b. *I was asking John if he ever heard of it Cabbies Kirk.*

In (84a–b) the right-dislocated noun phrases, *Mr Cunningham*, and *Cabbies Kirk*, appear to confirm the referents of pronouns inside the clause rather than highlight them. In the other construction, exemplified in (85), the right-dislocated noun phrase is a pronoun repeating a pronoun inside the clause. The referent is not only confirmed but reinforced and highlighted:

(85) a. *He was some man him.*
b. *But she was a harer her.*
c. *Oh it was a loss it.*

Right-dislocation is less frequent than left-dislocation and almost absent from Macaulay's middle-class interviews. Macaulay suggests that middle-class speakers are more likely to use emphatic stress than the repeated pronouns.

(c) Various focusing devices highlight items (or propositions) being introduced into the discourse. *See* in (86a) is close in meaning to the perception verb *see*, more distant in meaning in (86b):

(86) a. *See those old houses...this area was all houses like that right round.* [ECOSSE]
b. A: *There's a car park.*
B: *Aye – see I hate going in there.* [ECOSSE]

See highlights *those old houses* in (86a) and *I hate going in there* in (86b). In the MTC, examples such as *see the bridge below the forest* are always understood as questions: the reply is *uhuh* or *aye* or *right*. *See* does not normally occur in the imperative except in special phrases such as *see here! I've had enough of this nonsense!*

In the MTC speakers use *see* when they treat a landmark as given. *See* always takes a definite noun phrase: *see the fast-flowing river* but not **see a fast-flowing river*. Items treated as new are introduced by *a*, e.g. *Can you see a fast-flowing river?* or *Do you see a fast-flowing river? See* can also highlight entire clauses, as in 5.4.d. Example (87) is from the MTC.

(87) *See if you go straight down but not go straight to the aeroplane right see where the see where the pilot would go that wee bit.*

In the MTC, given items are introduced by means of interrogative clauses with *know*: *know the bridge across the fast-flowing river*. **Know a bridge*... is not possible. *Know* is equivalent to the Scots *ken* ('know'); you can *ken* someone and *ken* how to do something. *Ken* can highlight new items, including new topics of conversation:

(88) a. *Ken John Ewan – he breeds spaniels.* [conversation]
b. *The estate up at Macmerry – ken there's a big estate there – it's got a gamekeeper.* [ECOSSE]

Ken in (89) introduces a proposition by way of explanation.

(89) *She's on the machine until they can get another kidney for her – ken to have a transplant.* [ECOSSE]

Macaulay (1991: 160) says that *ken* often accompanies background or orientation clauses (as in 89) and marks interactional solidarity. That is, checking that your partner in conversation knows what you are talking about is a good way of bringing them into the conversation. Macaulay (1991: 145) notes that *you know* occurs at almost the same rate in the speech of his middle-class and working-class speakers.

The thing is and *thing is* highlight properties and propositions.

(90) a. *But the thing is – at our age what is there what sort of facilities can you provide.*
b. *Thing is he's watching the man he's not watching the ball.*
c. *The thing about school is that you can get them to relax.*

(d) There are two constructions with *like*, both discussed in detail in Miller and Weinert (1998). The older construction has *like* in clause-final position and is used by speakers to provide explanations and forestall objections as in (91):

(91) *You had a wooden spile – you bored on the top of the barrel...and then you had ready a spile, which was a wooden cone about that length... and a soft wood naturally was porous and it would help to get this froth to let it work down – you had to be very careful you didn't take it right down* ***like****/it went flat*. [ECOSSE]

The inference being countered by the *like* in (91) is "Surely the beer would go flat if you bored a hole in the top of the barrel?". The speaker points out that this inference is incorrect, because the operation was carried out very carefully, precisely to prevent the beer going flat. Similar *like*-final clauses are uttered by characters speaking non-standard English in Trollope's novels (1860 and 1870s) and in Dorothy Sayer's novels, set in East Anglia in the thirties.

Like occurs in interrogative clauses, as in (92):

(92) A1: *Got a bairn have you?*
B1: *Aye – Nicole's eh three.*
A2: *Three?*
B2: *Aye – I was married young.*
A3: *Aye – you must have been – how old are you **like?***

(92) has emphatic stress on *are*. A receives the surprising information that B's daughter is three and suddenly suspects that he has wrongly inferred B's age. Other examples of interrogatives with *like* can be paraphrased as IT clefts: *did you stick it down with Gloy like?* ('was it with Gloy that you stuck it down?').

ECOSSE has one occurrence of *likesae*, used by the research assistant's brother. Both were from north Edinburgh (not Leith itself but close to Leith). In his novel *Trainspotting* Irvine Welsh consistently uses the above construction with *likesae* instead of *like*.

In the second, more recent construction *like* occurs in any position except at the end of clauses.

(93) a. *I mean and **like** you've not got any obstacles here have you?* [MTC]
b. *To the lefthand side of East Lake? **Like** the very far end of East Lake?*

Like does not occur at pauses or where the speaker has planning problems. It is regularly equivalent to WH or IT clefts – note *what I want to ask is – you've not got any obstacles here?* and *is it the very far end of East Lake I go to? Like* regularly highlights items constituting an explanation, as in (94):

(94) *Like I knew I couldnae apply for Edinburgh because I didnae have an O level language so I just didnae do it.*

7. Conclusion

This paper has set out the major syntactic and discourse structures of modern Scots. Unfortunately there has been little study of Scots grammar since the late seventies. New bodies of data on computer, such as the SCOTS archive at the University of Glasgow, have to be exploited. The systematic collection of data by cassette recorder and elicitation techniques has yet to be undertaken. Map

Task dialogues help to build up our knowledge of structures currently in use but represent a different genre from spontaneous conversation. Some accounts of Scots are based on dialogues in novels; it is essential to determine which structures are peculiar to such dialogues and which are still in active use.

But in active use where? There are no detailed accounts of the morphology and syntax of current Buchan Scots nor about the grammatical differences between, say, the Scots spoken in Edinburgh and the Lothians, Glasgow, Ayrshire, the Borders, and Dumfries and Galloway. What is the linguistic situation in cities, towns and villages? How is grammar and discourse organisation affected by variation in setting and in topic and in the socio-economic status, age and gender of speakers? The participants in the ECOSSE conversations and the MTC are now approaching forty and thirty respectively. What is the spoken language of the 15–25 age group? What do people write in diaries, in personal letters, in work reports and so on? There is a small army of questions; where is the small army of researchers?

Exercises and study questions

1. In the following text pick out the structures that are typical of Scots or Scottish English. Analyse the discourse function of the structures that help to organise the contributions into a coherent discourse.

Katie1	are you no going to have a holiday?
Fiona1	aye but we'd like to borrow a car
Jeanie1	we were thinking that maybe Mary's Mum would lend us her Clio we were talking to her on Saturday there and she agreed it would be daft renting a car when the Clio was just sitting in the driveway
Fiona2	but see the Clio it's only a year old and Mary's scared she has an accident she's scared it gets dented off some other car she's no intending driving the Clio anywhere
Jeanie2:	but she's a good driver eh? she never said she wouldnae drive ken her Mum was trying to persuade her to take the car and she didnae say no
Katie2	there lots of parents wouldnae let their children near their car
Fiona3	aye but Mary's Mum and Dad trust her like and Mary never said she wouldnae take the car but it's no easy persuading Mary once she has her mind made up

2. The passage below is from the Education, Culture and Sport Comatee of the Scottish Parliament. 2nd Report, 2003, "Report on Inquiry intil the role o educational and cultural policy in uphaudin and bringin oot Gaelic, Scots and minority leids in Scotland". Analyse it and compare and contrast its vocabulary and grammar with the vocabulary and grammar of the conversation in (1) above.

   48 The feck o submissions in writing concentratit on the Scots leid. While mony submissions focussed on Scots and the education submission, it is clear that the weys that language is treatit inwith education an inwith culture is inextricably thirled. A want o awnin Scots in schuilswill lead tae bruckleness for the leid. Screivers o the future will tyne the ability tae communicate in Scots. Gin cultural resources in Scots isnae produced ony mair for an by theatre, literature or poetry, syne reference will be tint an there will be derth o teaching maitter.

   49 Clear fae the submissions wis concern that Scots is seen as inferior tae English. Aften quotit wis the example o a bairn getting checked either by parent or teacher for uisin Scots, getting tellt that this wis "slang" an no an acceptable wey tae speak. In mony submissions, the parallel wis drawn wi community leids whaur a body's first leid is tae aw intent smoored.

3. The examples below all contain relative clauses. The asterisks signal incorrect relative clause constructions (incorrect for present purposes). Write a description of the relative clauses. Pay attention to number agreement (not just in the verb).
   a. the wee laddies that was playing in the street came to look at the car
   b. *the wee laddies was playing in the street came to look at the car
   c. the books (that) we read was borrowed from the library
   d. the woman that her car was stolen was very annoyed
   e. the lassies that their skipping ropes was in a fankle thought Angus had done it
   f. the man that his dog ran off chased it up the High Street.
   g. my uncle had a dog was aye running away
   h. the box (that) the books are in is in the hall press
   i. *the box in which the books are is in the hall press
   j. the boy that they stole the bike from him phoned the police with his mobile

4. Obtain a copy of the report mentioned in (2) above. Email sp.info@scottish.parliament.uk or log on to www.scottish.parliament.uk. Discuss the language policies and practices recommended therein and whether they can be successfully implemented.

Selected references

Please consult the General references for titles mentioned in the text but not included in the references below. For a full bibliography see the accompanying CD-ROM.

Bennett, Margaret
1992 *Scottish Customs from the Cradle to the Grave*. Edinburgh: Polygon.

Grant, William and James M. Dixon
1921 *Manual of Modern Scots*. Cambridge: Cambridge University Press.

Häcker, Martina
1999 *Adverbial Clauses in Scots. A Semantic-Syntactic Study*. Berlin/New York: Mouton de Gruyter.

Macafee, Caroline
1983 *Glasgow*. Amsterdam/Philadelphia: Benjamins.

Macaulay, Ronald K.S.
1991 *Locating Dialect in Discourse*. Oxford/New York: Oxford University Press.

McIver, Mairi
1997 Modals in Orkney English. Honours thesis. Department of Linguistics. Edinburgh University.

Miller, Jim
1993 The grammar of Scottish English. In: Milroy and Milroy (eds.), 99–138.
2003 Syntax and discourse in modern Scots. In: John Corbett, Derrick J. McClure and Jane Stuart-Smith (eds.), *The Edinburgh Companion to Scots*, 72–109. Edinburgh: Edinburgh University Press.

Miller, Jim and Regina Weinert
1998 *Spontaneous Spoken Language: Syntax and Discourse*. Oxford: Clarendon Press.

Murray, James A.H.
1873 *The Dialect of the Southern Counties of Scotland*. London: Philological Society.

Purves, David
1997 *A Scots Grammar. Scots Grammar and Usage*. Edinburgh: The Saltire Society.

Weinert, Regina and Jim Miller
1996 Clefts in spoken discourse. *Journal of Pragmatics* 25: 173–202.

Wilson, James
1915 *Lowland Scotch, as Spoken in the Lower Strathearn District of Perthshire*. London: Oxford University Press.

Irish English: morphology and syntax

Markku Filppula

1. Introduction

The morphology and syntax of Irish English (IrE) follow in the main the patterns found in the other British Isles Englishes. This is particularly true of 'educated' IrE, which is not surprising considering that (British) Standard English has traditionally provided the principal norm for the teaching of English in Irish schools. However, the regional dialects and also urban working-class varieties present a very different picture. They contain many features which distinguish these varieties from most other regional or social dialects of British English (BrE). This is due to four main factors which have affected the development of both southern and northern IrE:

1. Conservatism, which means retention of some features of earlier 'mainstream' English, now mostly archaic or defunct in BrE;
2. dialect contact with other varieties of English spoken especially in the British Isles; of particular importance here is the diffusion of influences from the Scottish varieties of English to northern IrE (some of these are also found in the southern varieties);
3. contact influences from Irish, the indigenous language of Ireland, which is still spoken in some parts of Ireland and has for centuries exercised a considerable amount of 'substratal' influence upon IrE; though gradually fading away, the vestiges of this influence can still be heard even in the urban varieties of IrE but, naturally, they are better preserved in those dialects which are spoken in, or close to, the earlier and present-day Irish-speaking areas;
4. universal features associated with second-language acquisition in the kind of intense language shift conditions which existed in Ireland especially from the early nineteenth century onwards and which were characterised by a fairly rapid shift involving large numbers of speakers and general lack of formal schooling up until the latter part of the nineteenth century.

The combined effect of these factors makes IrE an interesting mixture of linguistic features derived from one or the other of the mentioned sources. As will be seen, the distinctive nature of IrE is much more visible in syntax than in morphology (which stands to reason in view of the relative poverty of English morphology).

The following discussion of the syntax and morphology of IrE is based on data drawn from a number of sources, all representing authentic speech recorded from Irishmen and Irishwomen in various parts of Ireland. The main source for what is here called 'southern' IrE consists of recordings made by myself and a number of other people in four different areas: Dublin City, Co. Wicklow, Co. Clare and Co. Kerry (for details of the corpus, see Filppula 1999, chapter 4). For the 'northern' IrE varieties, which comprise different varieties of Ulster English and Ulster Scots, I have relied on the so-called Northern Ireland Transcribed Corpus of Speech (henceforth 'NITCS' for short; see Kirk 1992 for details). In addition to these, previous studies of IrE, either spoken or written, and my own informal observations on language usage in Ireland over the years have provided useful data for the description undertaken below.

2. Tense-aspect-modality systems

The tense-aspect-modality (TMA for short) systems form an area which perhaps most clearly distinguishes IrE from the other British Isles Englishes. This is what could be expected, given the general cross-linguistic evidence from other varieties which have emerged in conditions of intense language contact and shift. The following discussion will focus on four TMA subsystems which all involve features deviating from Standard English (StE), and to varying degrees, from other varieties of English: perfective aspect, progressive aspect, habitual aspect, and imperatives.

2.1. Perfective aspect

The overall coding of tense-aspect distinctions in IrE is more complex than, for example, in StE. On the one hand, IrE makes prominent use of the present and past tenses for perfective aspect meanings which are in other dialects expressed by distinct forms such as the so-called periphrastic *have* perfect. On the other, IrE has developed, or preserves from earlier English, separate forms for some temporal and aspectual meanings; some of these forms are either not found or no longer used in other varieties.

One can distinguish as many as six different categories of IrE perfects, which are described and illustrated below with examples drawn from the above-mentioned databases. The localities and name of the database as well as speaker-initials are given in brackets after each example. Note further that curly brackets are here used to indicate questions or other contributions by the interviewer.

(i) the indefinite anterior perfect, which denotes events or states of affairs which take place at an unspecified point in a period leading up to the moment of utterance:

(1) ***Were*** *you ever in Kenmare?* (Kerry: J.F.)

'Have you ever been...?.'

(2) *{And do you go up to see it* [a car race]*?}*
I ***never went*** *till it yet*. (NITCS: CM119)

(ii) the *after* perfect, which typically refers to events or states in the (more or less) recent past:

(3) *You****'re after ruinin'*** *me*. (Dublin: M.L.)
'You have (just) ruined me.'

(4) *And when the bell goes at six you just think you* ***were only after going*** *over, and you get out and up again*. (NITCS: OM53)

(iii) the medial-object perfect, which focuses on the result, or resulting state, of an action rather than the action itself; verbs used in this way are typically dynamic and transitive, as in (5) from northern IrE, but occasional instances of other types also occur especially in the conservative rural varieties, such as the verb of 'inert perception' or 'intellectual activity' in (6):

(5) *Take your shoes off then {aye}, and go round the stations on your bare feet. And you... you eat nothing till you're,* ***have the stations made.*** (NITCS: OM51)

(6) *I* ***have it forgot***. (Wicklow: T.F.)
'I have forgotten it.'

(iv) the *be* perfect, which is the intransitive counterpart of the resultative medial-object perfect described above, and is used with verbs of motion or change such as *go*, *change*, *leave* or *die*:

(7) *I think the younger generations* ***are gone*** *idle over it*. (Kerry: M.C.)

(8) *...particularly the valley up the, mm, Cranagh road {mm},* ***is*** *drastically* ***changed****, and* ***improved*** *for the better*. (NITCS: JM51)

(9) *{How many brothers and sisters you have, and what they're all doing?}*
*They****'re*** *not* ***left*** *school yet*. (NITCS: EM20)

(v) the extended-now perfect, which refers to events or states initiated in the past but continuing at the moment of utterance:

(10) ***I'm not*** *in this* [caravan] *long... Only* ***have*** *this here a few year.* (Wicklow: D.M.)
'I haven't been/lived...'

(11) *{Well, how long are you* [have you been] *in here now?}*
*Oh, I'm in, I'****m*** *in here about four months.* (NITCS: I PT91)

(vi) the standard *have* perfect, which can express all of the above meanings and is so used in StE as well as in educated, especially written, IrE:

(12) *And we* ***haven't seen*** *one for years round here.* (Wicklow: J.N.)

Note that perfective aspect has here been understood as being based on both forms and meanings. Thus, although the indefinite anterior perfect, for example, assumes the form of the past tense, the kind of uses illustrated under (i) are here considered to belong to the category of perfects and perfective aspect on the basis of their meanings; there is that link between the present and the past which is normally considered a defining criterion for perfects. Similarly, the IrE extended-now perfect, although it formally coincides with the present tense, which in StE normally refers to present time, differs from the latter in that the extended-now perfect refers to some state of affairs or process which has been initiated in the past but which continues up to the present moment (or moment of utterance). The presence of a durative time adverbial further contributes to the perfective aspect reading.

Of the Irish English perfects, the *after* perfect is clearly the most stereotypical and is avoided by educated speakers at least in formal contexts; on the other hand, it is freely used in informal contexts and by working-class and rural speakers in all parts of the country. As regards its origins, it is more than likely modelled on the corresponding Irish *tar éis/tréis* construction. By contrast, both the indefinite anterior and the extended-now perfects are quite common even in educated speech, and occasionally occur even in writing, e.g. in newspapers. Both have Irish parallels but can also derive from similar perfects used in earlier English. In the written mode, the standard *have* perfect is of course the norm and is also used increasingly in present-day spoken 'common' or 'supraregional' IrE. Finally, the medial-object perfect and especially the *be* perfect are clearly recessive features; both are paralleled by Irish usages, but again may equally be retentions from early Modern English. (For further discussion, see Harris 1984a, 1993; Kallen 1989, 1994; Filppula 1999.)

2.2. Progressive aspect

Turning next to progressive aspect and the uses of the so-called progressive or *-ing* form (PF for short) in IrE, one is struck by the relative freedom with which the PF can be used in IrE dialects, both as a marker of progressivity (as in StE) and in a number of other contexts. Of the latter, the most striking is the use of the PF with stative verbs, such as those denoting 'intellectual states' (or 'cognition'), 'states of emotion or attitude', other states of 'being' and 'having' (so-called relational verbs), and 'stance'. These are illustrated in the following:

(i) intellectual states (or 'cognition'):

(13) *There was a lot about fairies long ago... but I'**m thinkin'** that most of 'em are vanished.* (Clare: M.R.)
'...but I think/believe that...'

(14) *They'**re not believin'** it.* (North Roscommon; cited in Henry 1957: 169)

(15) *I **was knowing** your face.* (North Roscommon; cited in Henry 1957: 169)

(ii) states of emotion or attitude:

(16) *Well, of course, Semperit is a, an Austrian firm... They **are not caring** about the Irish people, they are only looking after their own interest, ...* (Dublin: M.L.)

(17) *There was a school in Ballynew, and they were **wantin'** to build a new school.* (Clare: C.O'B.)

(iii) other states of being and having ('relational verbs'):

(18) *I think two of the lads was lost at sea during the War. They **were belonging** to the, them men here.* (Dublin: P.L.)

(19) *The money that they had saved they were actually waiting on it then... They **were depending** on it.* (NITCS: PT14)

(20) *I think they're more or less to blame themselves, because they'**re keeping** far too man(y), much stock.* (NITCS: BC24)

(iv) stance:

(21) [*They*] *call it the Golf Stream... And that'**s flowing** into the Atlantic. It **is flowing** into the Atlantic Ocean.* (Kerry: M.C.)

(22) *And it* [a road] ***is going*** *a way up...Up into the mountain. And it* ***is leading*** *up to this...old graveyard.* (Kerry: M.McG.)

Besides stative verbs, another important context of use of the PF is with inherently *dynamic* verbs in contexts where StE would use the simple present- or past-tense form or (in past-time contexts) *used to* + infinitive. The meaning in these is clearly one of *habitual* activity, as in (23) below.

(v) habitual activity (with dynamic verbs):

(23) *...but there, there's no bogland here now.*
{Yeah. And do people go up there to cut turf?}
They ***were going*** *there long ago but the roads got the, like everything else, they got a bit too-o rich and...* (Kerry: M.C.)

Thirdly, the PF is commonly found after the auxiliaries *would/'d/ used (to)* indicating habitual activity. In StE and in other regional varieties of English English (EngE), the simple infinitive is clearly preferred in these contexts. For example:

(24) *So, when the young lads**'d be going** to bathing, like, they'd have to go by his house, and they used to all...* (Clare: M.F.)

(25) *But they, I heard my father and uncle saying they* ***used be dancing*** *there long ago, like, you know.* (Clare: M.F.)

Fourthly, the PF is frequently used with other auxiliaries, such as *do/does* and *will/'ll*. The former usage is generally considered unique to IrE and will be discussed in greater detail in the next section. The latter, exemplified in (26), is a general vernacular feature found in other varieties, too.

(26) *...this fellow now, Jack Lynch, that's going to come into power now, that he'll,* ***he'll be forgetting*** *the North.* (Wicklow: M.K.)

Fifthly, in IrE – like in many other varieties of English today – , the PF is extremely common with verbs of saying and telling, especially in past-time contexts:

(27) *Ah, they were great old days. But now, anyhow, things went on, and I got wiser meself, and as I* ***was saying*** *you, I start selling for meself.* (Dublin: M.L.)

(28) *And that was his fault, and he went off then, I heard since that, I* ***wasn't talking*** *to him since. And he has bought two pups.* (Wicklow: J.F.)

The free use of the PF in IrE quite plausibly derives from Irish, which relies heavily on the so-called verbal noun construction in similar contexts; another factor promoting its use is the continually increasing use of the PF in English itself . The 'substratum' hypothesis gains further support from the fact that some Welsh English (WelE) and Scottish English dialects (ScE; especially those spoken in the Hebrides) display the same tendency, probably triggered by the same kind of substratum influence from Welsh and Scottish Gaelic.

2.3. Habitual aspect

Habitual aspect is here understood as a general concept, which subsumes under it iterative, frequentative, and generic states or activities. All involve situations which are viewed as being characteristic of an extended period of time rather than incidental properties of any given moment. Some means of expression of habitual aspect have already been touched on in the previous section, namely the use of the progressive form with dynamic verbs, the auxiliaries *would/'d/ used* [*to*] followed by the *-ing* form, and the auxiliary *do/does* used with the same form. An example of the last-mentioned is given in (29):

(29) *Yeah, that's, that's the camp. Military camp they call it... They* ***do be shooting*** *there couple of times a week or so*. (Wicklow: D.M.)

As noted above, this construction is one of the hallmarks of vernacular IrE and not found in other varieties spoken in the British Isles (it does occur, though, in some Caribbean varieties). Besides the *be* + V-*ing* pattern, as in (29), another common pattern consists of *do(es)* followed by the infinitive form of a lexical verb, as in (30), or by *be* + an adjective or a noun, as in (31):

(30) *Two lorries of them* [turf] *now in the year we* ***do burn***. (Kerry: M.C.)

(31) *They* ***does be*** *lonesome by night, the priest does, surely*. (Clare: M.R.)

All of these forms are highly stigmatised and carefully avoided in educated speech. Yet they can be regularly heard in the speech of urban working-class people and in southern rural dialects of IrE. Northern IrE dialects, including Ulster Scots, favour somewhat different constructions: *be* or *be's* (sometimes also spelt *bees*) followed either by the *-ing* form or by an adjective or a noun. As with the *do (be)* constructions, the meaning is habitual or generic (see Harris 1984b; Kallen 1989; Robinson 1997). Examples from the NITCS are:

(32) *{Where do they [tourists] stay, and what kind of pastimes do they have?} Well, they stay, some of them, in the forestry caravan sites. They bring caravans. They* ***be shooting****, and* ***fishing*** *out at the forestry lakes*. (NITCS: MC16)

(33) *{And who brings you in [to Mass]?}*
We get, Mrs Cullen to leave us in {ahah}. She ***be's going****, and she leaves us in, too.* (NITCS: EM70)

(34) *{And what do you do in your play centre? Do you think it's a good idea in the holidays?}*
It's better, because you ***be's*** *bored doing nothing {mm} at home.* (NITCS: KO121)

In both southern and northern IrE, the negated forms involve non-standard use of the auxiliary *do*, as can be seen from the following examples:

(35) *Well, it's* [*oats*] *generally cut, but sometimes it gets, it* ***doesn't be*** *up, to the mark, don't you know, it'd be bad, like oats, if you met a bad year...* (Wicklow: J.F.)

(36) *And they k(eep), they always keep the horse up above. It* ***doesn't*** *be usually down in the field now.* (NITCS: SM109)

While the southern IrE forms have by many scholars been ascribed to the influence of Irish (see especially Henry 1957; Bliss 1972), there is less agreement about the origins of the northern *be/bees* forms, with dialect diffusion from the Scottish dialects presenting itself as another possible source (for discussion, see e.g. Montgomery and Gregg 1997). Further parallels to the IrE patterns can be found in Welsh English and in some conservative south-western dialects of EngE, but in contrast to IrE, they generally involve the uninflected form of *do* followed by the infinitive. The possible Celtic influence on all of these varieties has long been a subject of debate but has turned out to be hard to substantiate (for discussion, see Filppula 1999, section 6.3.).

2.4. Imperatives

IrE dialects follow, with some exceptions, the 'mainstream' or standard patterns to express the imperative mood. The most salient feature of IrE in this category is the so-called overt subject imperative with inversion. This appears to be a special feature of northern IrE and especially Belfast English, as is shown by Henry (1995). Her examples include the following:

(37) ***Go you*** *there.* (Henry 1995: 52)

(38) ***Read you*** *that book.* (Henry 1995: 55)

As Henry notes, some northern IrE speakers accept only examples like (37), which involves an intransitive verb of motion, whereas others also find transitive examples such as (38) usable. This she explains by the existence of different 'grammars' with slightly different 'verb-raising' properties or 'settings' even within Belfast English.

Another noteworthy feature is the imperative construction with *let*. However, this is rare in present-day speech and, in fact, did not occur in my databases at all. Bliss (1972) discusses this feature, which he considers to be unique to IrE and most probably modelled on the corresponding Irish imperative paradigm. As an illustration, he provides examples like (39):

(39) ***Let ye listen*** *to what he said.* (Bliss 1972: 72)

Finally, mention should be made of the negative imperative construction involving the use of the auxiliary *do*, followed by *be* + V-*ing* (cf. the discussion on the auxiliary *do* above). As the following examples show, it occurs in both southern and northern IrE:

(40) *Whether it is Lutherarians or Protestant or Catholics, live up to it.* ***Don't be guessing****, or* ***don't be doubting****.* (Kerry: M.C.)

(41) *Oh, I enjoyed every minute of it. Lord, we used to have some times. Oh,* ***don't be talking*** *{LAUGHS}.* (NITCS: LD5)

3. Auxiliaries

The most distinctive feature of both north and south IrE in the modal auxiliary system is the almost complete non-occurrence of *shall* (and *shan't)* in vernacular forms of speech; even in educated speech *shall* occurs only rarely. Against this background, it was not surprising that there were no occurrences of *shall* in the NITCS and only one in the southern IrE corpus. This was to be expected on the basis of the previous studies of IrE, going back to the famous late nineteenth-century treatise by Dr. Molloy, entitled *The Irish Difficulty, Shall and Will* (Molloy 1897). The perennial problems faced by the Irish in the 'correct' use of these auxiliaries are also treated by P.W. Joyce ([1910] 1988), who mentions the Irish predilection for *will* even in interrogative phrases like *Will I sing you a song?* Joyce refers here to the similar American usage, which he considers to derive from the influence of the Irish immigrants to America (Joyce 1988: 77).

As a predictable corollary to the avoidance of *shall*, there is a clear preference for *would* at the expense of *should* in any other than the obligation meaning. Thus, instead of phrases like *I should think/say* most Irish people, north and south, would say *I would think/say*, as in the following example from the NITCS:

(42) *Well, they have table tennis, and they have bowls, and, eh, darts. That's the three main sports, I* ***would*** *think.* (NITCS: BC44)

In some northern IrE dialects the negation forms take the suffix *-nae* (*shouldnae/wouldnae* etc.), which will be discussed below in section 4.3.

Ought (to) is another auxiliary which is virtually non-existent in vernacular IrE dialects, including Ulster Scots (see Robinson 1997: 171 on the latter). No instances were found in the NITCS nor in my southern IrE materials, which suggests that *ought (to)* is confined to the more formal, written styles.

The so-called primary verbs *be*, *have*, and *do* also exhibit some features peculiar to the Irish dialects of English. *Be* and *do* have already been dealt with in the section on habitual aspect above. Of their other, main-verb uses, suffice it to mention here that IrE allows the interrogative form *amn't (I)* in tag questions. *Have* as a main verb is in conservative IrE often used on its own without *got*, and in interrogative or negative contexts, without the *do*-auxiliary, as in the following example from the NITCS where not even the interviewer's use of *do*-support prompts the informant to use the same pattern:

(43) *{What kind of farms do they have, mostly?} They* ***haven't*** *all that much. They just have cows, and...* (NITCS: SM99)

4. Negation

Three features can be singled out as ones which lend vernacular forms of IrE some distinctive flavour. The first is, in fact, the least distinctive, as it is shared by most non-standard varieties of English, namely multiple negation or 'negative concord', as it will be called here. By contrast, the two others are phenomena which have a much more restricted geographical distribution. One will here be labelled as 'failure of negative attraction'; as will be seen below, it probably has its roots in Irish. The other is something which testifies to the old linguistic connections between Scotland and Ireland and has to do with the northern IrE uses of the negative word or suffix *(-)nae*.

4.1. Negative concord

IrE dialects are no different from other non-standard varieties with respect to the use of negative concord. Thus, two or more negative items may occur in the same clause, as in the following examples drawn from the northern and southern dialects:

(44) *Och, I don't know just, they're just not the same,* ***nor never*** *will be like the old people.* (NITCS: LD77)

(45) *You've* ***not*** *heard of that* ***nothing****?* (Kerry: M.C.)

Rather than being a retention from the earlier stages of English, which allowed negative concord, or a result of transfer from Irish, this feature of IrE is best considered a general vernacular feature widespread in other varieties of English, too.

4.2. Failure of negative attraction

The term 'negative attraction' refers to a phenomenon of StE which concerns the behaviour of so-called non-assertive and universal pronouns or determiners such as *any(-body/-one/-thing* etc.) and *every(-body/-one/-thing* etc.) under negation: whenever such a pronoun/determiner is (part of) the subject of a clause (or sometimes even the object), the negation element is 'attracted' to it, instead of being left in its usual position after the verb. Thus, in StE negating a structure like *anyone goes* yields *no-one goes*, and not **anyone doesn't go*. The latter fails to observe the rule of negative attraction, hence the description of this phenomenon as "failure of negative attraction" (Harris 1984a: 305). Note that 'failure' is here used in a purely technical sense without any negative social or other implications.

Though not a particularly frequent phenomenon, failure of negative attraction occurs in both southern and northern varieties of IrE. Examples of non-assertive pronouns or determiners from the databases include the following:

(46) *There is great pity for this, what they call the students now, but I'd have no pity for them, because they're only howling for a good time, howling...* ***Any*** *country* ***couldn't*** *stand that.* (Kerry: M.C.)
'No country could stand that.'

(47) *Now, a,* ***anything*** *is* ***no*** *sin. But I think myself that the day's coming fast, in every one of us, when we'll know whether it is a sin or not.* (Kerry: M.C.)

(48) *Boxing, or football, something like that. But* ***anything*** *else I* ***wouldn't*** *lend it eyesight {mm}, you know. I like the boxing.* (NITCS: JM90)

Of the universal pronouns, *every* with its derivative forms seems the most liable to trigger this phenomenon; witness (49) and (50).

(49) *There seems, people seem to have a, a fair share of money, and getting on [...] Though, I say, you know, we don't, hmh, err, err, **everybody doesn't** use it to a good advantage, I s'pose.* (Wicklow: M.K.)
'...not everybody uses it...'

(50) ***Everybody hadn't** a hayshed, they talked about piking the hay.* (NITCS: IP57)

In my southern IrE database, most of the tokens of this feature occurred in the (south-)western dialects, which are generally conservative and retain many Irishisms. Indeed, an obvious explanation for the IrE usage is to be found in the similar behaviour of Irish expressions containing negation either with the indefinite determiner *aon* 'any' or its universal counterpart *gach aon* 'every'. The Irish negative particle *ní/níor* always stays in a position before the verb and is not attracted to an indefinite subject, as in English. Thus, the indefinite subject retains the same form in both affirmative and negative contexts, which is then carried over to conservative IrE (for further discussion, see Harris 1984a: 305).

It is interesting to note that failure of negative attraction occurs in some other varieties of the British Isles Englishes, too. It has been recorded, e.g., in Tyneside speech where it is possibly due to IrE influence, transmitted by the large-scale immigration of Irish people to the north-east of England starting in the nineteenth century. The same feature has also been observed for ScE, including the Gaelic-influenced varieties spoken in the Hebrides (see Filppula 1999, section 7.4., for further discussion and references).

4.3. Negation with *(-)nae*

The Scottish heritage in northern IrE manifests itself particularly clearly in the occasional use of negation forms with the originally Scots negation word *nae*, which can be used on its own as a negative determiner, as in (51), or as a suffix attached to the primary auxiliaries BE, HAVE, and DO, and to the modal auxiliaries SHALL/SHOULD, WILL/WOULD, CAN/COULD, as in (52)–(57):

(51) *Aye, there were **nae** motors, or...* (NITCS: JA4)

(52) *He **isnae** interested.* (NITCS: MC22)

(53) *No, I **havenae** got one* [a harvester] *yet.* (NITCS: JM25)

(54) *...but at the same time, at the back of your mind, you think that, maybe they **dinnae*** [do not] *want you at all, you know.* (NITCS: JM114)

(55) *Och, I **wouldnae** mind if she was good enough to me* [*as a wife*]. (NITCS: JM194)

(56) *..., and they **cannae** sell it* [an estate] *till she dies, know, she has her day o' it...so they **cannae** sell it.* (NITCS: JM181)

(57) *...my father maybe remembers it done, I **couldnae** say, he might have.* (NITCS: AM53)

The (colloquial) standard forms *isn't/haven't/doesn't* etc. and *shouldn't/ wouldn't/couldn't* etc. are by far the most common in northern IrE, too, but the usages illustrated above are preserved especially in areas where Ulster Scots is at its strongest (cf. Robinson 1997: 145).

5. Relativisation

Like many other non-standard varieties, IrE dialects north (including Ulster Scots) and south are known for their avoidance of the so-called WH-relatives (*who*, *whose*, *whom*, *which*). Instead, the most commonly used means of relativisation are *that*, the so-called zero relative construction (also known as the 'contact-clause'), and the conjunction *and*. The last-mentioned is particularly common in informal spoken language. It is sometimes labelled as a 'quasi-relative' construction, as it does not involve a 'proper' relative pronoun (see, e.g. Harris 1993: 149). The following examples illustrate the typical IrE usages:

(58) *They don't take in boys **that** haven't got the eleven plus*. (NITCS: MK76)

(59) *...there's older people Ø tell me that they were 13 different families Ø lived in it*. (NITCS: AM50)

(60) *There was this man **and** he lived, himself and his wife, they lived, and they had one only son*. (Clare: F.K.)

Of the WH-relatives, especially *whose* and *whom* are extremely rare in all dialects, while *who* and *which* are slightly more frequent. WH-forms do occur in written IrE, but even in that mode the Irish have a noticeable predilection for *that* at the expense of the WH-forms. Ulster Scots generally follows the same patterns as the other Irish dialects, with *at* (a shortened form of *that*; possessive form *ats*) or the zero-relative being the most common means of relativisation (Robinson 1997: 77–78).

Another noteworthy feature of IrE relative structures is the occasional use of so-called resumptive (or 'shadow') pronouns. These are 'additional' pronominal or other elements usually appearing at the end of the relative clause, especially in those contexts where StE would use a locative or possessive prepositional relative. Their function seems to be one of making sure that the point of reference becomes clear to the hearer. For example:

(61) *They jumped banks that time on the race-course that they wouldn't hunt over* ***them*** *today*. (Wicklow: D.M.)

The resumptive element can also be an adverb, as in the following example:

(62) *But the course was there in the sandhills of Lahinch, now, across from the golf-course, where the Sluagh hall is* ***there****, a grand flat, a grand, grand course*. (Clare: F.K.)

These kinds of structures have long been known to be part of IrE vernacular and are discussed, for example, by Joyce (1988: 52–53), Henry (1957: 209–210), Harris (1993: 150–151), and Filppula (1999, section 8.2.). Joyce ascribes them to the parallel structures in Irish, one of his illustrative examples being *there's a man that* ***his*** *wife leaves him whenever she pleases*. A similar usage is recorded by Robinson (1997: 78) from conservative Ulster Scots dialects. It is possible, indeed, that resumptive pronouns have been much more common in the past when the influence of Irish on IrE was at its strongest. Be that as it may, it is interesting to note that similar patterns are also found in some Welsh and Scottish English dialects, which gives further support for the Celtic hypothesis.

6. Complementation

6.1. *For to* - infinitives

A common feature shared by most vernacular forms of IrE is the use of *for to* instead of *to* or *in order to* in infinitival clauses expressing purpose. This usage is illustrated by the following examples from northern and southern IrE:

(63) *And there was always one man selected* ***for to*** *make the tea.* (NITCS: PM11)

(64) *I think it was a penny or halfpenny we used to bring to school* ***for to*** *see the Punch an' Judy Show*. (Dublin: P.L.)

While this construction is by no means unique to IrE because of its general occurrence in earlier forms of English and in other regional dialects, there are other usages especially in northern IrE dialects which appear to be peculiar to them. Such is, for example, the use of *for to* after an 'intentional' verb like *try*, as in (65):

(65) *And the father, he would try* ***for to*** *tell her, like,...* (NITCS: LM7)

Certain kinds of adjectives in predicate position can also lead to *for to* being used instead of *to*; witness (66):

(66) *It's very important, you know,* ***for to*** *have such a man {ahah} like him.* (NITCS: PL23)

A detailed description of the *for to* phenomena in northern IrE, and especially Belfast speech, is provided by Henry (1995), who distinguishes between 'weak' and 'strong' Belfast English varieties in this respect. Speakers representing the former variety restrict the use of *for to* to purpose clauses, whereas representatives of the latter group use it in a wider variety of contexts, including the usages exemplified in (65) and (66) above. To these, Henry (1995: 83–84) adds exclamations such as *For to tell her like that!*, infinitives in subject position, as in *For to stay here would be just as expensive*, and so-called object-control verbs, as in *I persuaded John for to go home.*

6.2. 'Narrative' infinitive with *to*

Other infinitival structures with *to* include the so-called narrative infinitive. This term was perhaps first used by Joyce (1988), who describes this construction as an Irishism, which usually occurs in responses to questions. One of Joyce's examples is as follows:

(67) *How did the mare get that hurt? – Oh Tom Cody* ***to leap*** *her over the garden wall yesterday, and she* ***to fall*** *on her knees on the stones.* (Joyce 1988: 45–46)

On the basis of the data from present-day IrE varieties, this feature is hardly used at all and can be considered old-fashioned and poetic. Henry (1957: 188–190) and Bliss (1984: 147–148) provide some examples from some conservative IrE dialects. Filppula (1999: 184) cites the following example from a nineteenth-century emigrant's letter:

(68) *I was very sorry to hear of you to let your old chapel to be chifted [shifted] to (Ballydafeen). O poor Derry* [the townland of Caheraderry in Co. Clare] *is gone and* ***to let*** *them grow over yea.* (*The Normile Letters*, No. 12, 1862; cited in Filppula 1999: 184)

6.3. Other features of complementation

Further under the heading of complementation, IrE displays some features which are less conspicuous but nevertheless characteristic of especially the present-day usage. The first concerns omission of *to* after certain verbs such as *be allowed* and *help*. IrE is not alone in this tendency, which seems to be on the increase in many other varieties of English, too. The same is true of another current trend, namely frequent omission of the preposition with originally prepositional verbs such as *agree*: one *agrees a deal*, instead of *agrees on a deal*, as in StE. Again, this is probably part of a more general process of 'transitivisation', which is under way in other varieties as well.

Finally, IrE speakers typically omit the reflexive pronoun with certain reflexive verbs. Hence, one *avails of something* instead of *avails oneself of something*, as in the following example from the NITCS where, interestingly, both the interviewer and the informant use the same non-standard expression:

(69) *{And do you find young people **avail of it**?}*
*Young people do **avail of it**, you know, ...* (NITCS: PP11)

7. Subordination

In complex sentences, one of the most distinctive features of conservative IrE is the use of the conjunction *and* to introduce a subordinate instead of the usual coordinate clause. The subordinate clause most often contains a subject noun or pronoun (either in the objective or nominative form) followed by the *-ing* form of a verb, as in (70) and (71):

(70) *I mind* [remember] *whenever* [when] *we were wee, **and my mother rearing us**, hey, she had to wash all with, just with a, steep them in a tub and...* (NITCS: JM201)

(71) *I only thought of him there **and I cooking** my dinner*. (Dublin: P.L.)
'...while I was cooking...'

A past participle form, an adjective, and even an adverbial phrase are also possible in this position, as is seen from the following examples:

(72) *I often got them [pheasants] dead out in the middle of the field **and they not torn up** or anything. There wasn' a fox got them.* (Wicklow: D.M.)

(73) *'Twas in harvest time **and the weather bad**.* (Clare: F.K.)

(74) *He said you could hear them* [strange noises] *yet, inside in his own house* ***and he in bed***. (Clare: M.R.)

The same construction type, often termed 'subordinating *and*', is also used in Ulster Scots:

(75) *Hè cum in* ***an me in thà middle o ma dinnèr***.
'He came in as I was eating my dinner.' (Ulster Scots; cited in Robinson 1997: 111)

Besides IrE, subordinating *and* is also found in Scottish dialects of English. It is plausible to assume that the origins of this feature are to be found in the parallel constructions in Irish and Scottish Gaelic (see Filppula 1999, section 8.3., for a detailed discussion).

A special feature of northern IrE and especially Ulster Scots is the use of *whenever* to refer to a single event or state in the past, instead of indicating 'indefinite frequency' as in StE. Montgomery and Gregg (1997: 610), who label this usage as 'punctual *whenever*', describe it as "something of a shibboleth for Ulster". According to them, it is of Scottish origin, though this is not generally recognised, as they point out (Montgomery and Gregg 1997: 610). A good example from the NITCS occurs in (70) above (*I mind* ***whenever*** *we were wee...*).

8. Subject-verb concord

Subject-verb concord is an area of English grammar which generally distinguishes non-standard varieties from StE, and IrE is no exception to this. A well-known feature of the northern IrE dialects is what Milroy (1981: 12–13) has labelled as the 'Singular Concord rule' or the 'SING-CON rule'. Other terms used in subsequent research on the same phenomenon (including various other English dialects) are 'Subject-Type Constraint' and 'Northern Subject Rule'. Briefly, this rule states that the verbal *-s* suffix can be used with plural noun subjects as well as with demonstrative pronoun subjects, but not with a plural personal pronoun, unless there are some other sentence elements between the subject and the verb. Thus, Milroy notes that sentences like *them eggs is cracked* can freely occur in Ulster speech alongside the standard *those eggs are cracked*. Even *them's cracked* is possible, because *them* is construed as the demonstrative 'those' rather than as a personal pronoun. By contrast, *they's cracked* is never used, as is predicted by the SING-CON rule. This rule, as Milroy points out, is in no way unique to Ulster speech but can be traced back to Middle Scots and even further back in history (Milroy 1981: 13). The Scottish influence on this feature of northern IrE is also confirmed by Montgomery and Gregg (1997: 610). In other recent research on northern IrE, Henry (1995) has studied subject-verb concord in Belfast English. She points out the optional nature of singular concord in Belfast English; in other words, a plural subject can also take the plural form of the verb.

As regards the southern IrE dialects, the picture is not at all so clear. Of the earliest writers on IrE (north and south), Hume (1878) is the only one who discusses S-V concord with plural subjects. He puts forward evidence which seems to confirm the existence of the Northern Subject Rule in what he subsumes under the general heading of 'the Irish dialect [of English]'. He states that "[t]he third person singular of verbs is invariably used, unless when immediately preceded by the pronoun *they*", adding that "[i]n the uneducated circles, the verb is invariably singular with nouns, whether one plural or several of the same or different numbers form the subject of the verb" (Hume 1878: 25–26). In his *Linguistic Survey of Ireland*, P.L. Henry briefly discusses the use of verbal *-s* but does not deal with the question of the historical or other background. His principal observation is that in Anglo-Irish dialects "-s is the common ending of the present pl." (Henry 1958: 130–131). He then provides examples of verbs taking the *-s* suffix with different types of subject. These include collective nouns, as in *people goes*, 'ordinary' plural nouns, as in *the wee things* [children] *catches*, and – what seems to work against the Northern Subject Rule – personal pronouns, as in *they learns it/we bakes it*. Existential *there*-sentences with plural NPs, such as *there is accidents*, form yet another category which exhibits the same feature.

My southern IrE data contain plenty of examples illustrating lack of standard concord with different types of plural noun or pronoun subjects. The following are the major categories:

Conjoined NP as subject:

(76) *Oh,* ***my mother and father was*** *born and reared in Dublin*. (Dublin M.L.)

*There*___NP:

(77) ***There was four boys of us,*** *and there's three of them dead*. (Wicklow: J.F.)

Collective NP as subject:

(78) *...and I think, at the pace* ***the people is going*** *they are not going to stick it*. (Wicklow: M.K.)

Other NP:

(79) *...but then,* ***sons of theirs comes*** *over here, an odd time* ***has*** *come.* (Wicklow: J.F.)

(80) *'Course he signed the Treaty, and* ***some was*** *for it and some again' it.* (Dublin: W.H.)

They:

(81) *Oh well, only,* ***they gets*** *pensions, you know and I get the old-age pension.* (Kerry: J.F.)

(82) *...when* ***they was*** *about three months old, or four, like, ...* (Clare: F.K.)

Them:

(83) ***Them is*** *all reclaimed* [land]. (Wicklow: D.M.)

(84) *And you know what wages* ***them was*** *getting that time in thirty-nine*? (Wicklow: J.F.)

Other personal pronoun:

(85) *We* ***keeps*** *about ten cows that way, you know, and few cattle.* (Kerry: J.F.)

(86) *...I happened to be, we* ***was*** *just getting our tea.* (Wicklow: J.F.)

However, these are counterbalanced by the even more frequent occurrence of standard S-V concord, which means that, all things considered, plural S-V concord in southern IrE represents a mixture of elements drawn from the 'northern', originally northern Middle English and Scots type, which follows the Northern Subject Rule, and from the 'southern' British type, which has 'universal *-s*' throughout the plural paradigm regardless of the type of subject. There may have been some influence from the concord system of Irish, which in this case would have promoted lack of concord with plural subjects and thus worked against the pressures from StE. As yet another factor explaining lack of concord, one should bear in mind the general trend in all kinds of Englishes to ignore concord especially in existential *there*-sentences.

9. Noun phrase structure

Perhaps the most notable feature of the IrE noun phrase is frequent use of the definite article in contexts where it is not used in StE. In this respect, IrE is very similar to ScE and also WelE. This feature has been known for long and is commented on, for example, in the early work by Joyce (1988: 82–83) and later works, such as Henry (1957: 117), Bliss (1984: 149) and Harris (1993: 144–145).

Non-standard uses tend to cluster around certain categories or groups of words and expressions. The major ones, and popularly the most widely known, include the following:

(i) names of languages and branches of learning:

(87) *And err, when I do be listen' to* ***the Irish*** *here, I do be sorry now, when you're in a local having a drink, nobody seems to understand it. Whoever is speaking* ***the Irish****, might as well be, as the saying says, speaking Dutch...* (Dublin: P.T.)

(88) *Oh,* ***the maths****,* ***the maths*** *nowadays seems to be complicated.* (NITCS: RF21)

(ii) (unpleasant) physical sensations or states:

(89) *I think Jim Larkin, Big Jim, err, brought it* [a ship] *here, called The Heir, with food ... for this, this is the poor people were starved with* ***the hunger***. (Dublin: W.H.)

(iii) names of diseases and ailments:

(90) *And that cured* ***the whooping cough****.... Some children does be terrible bad with it, whooping cough*. (Wicklow: T.F.)

(91) *But he's* ***the measles****, and he, he's off school for a while*. (NITCS: NK43)

(iv) names of social institutions:

(92) *I left* ***the school*** *in early age, nearly fourteen, you know*. (Dublin: W.H.)

(93) *...mm, best singer now, he's away in, in, the present time in* ***the hospital***. (NITCS: CM129)

(v) quantifying expressions involving *most*, *both*, *half* followed by a post-modifying *of* phrase:

(94) *Oh, well, down round Arboe* ***the most*** *of them was all small kind of farms,...* (NITCS: FC73)

(95) *I had more brothers, two more brothers there with 'im at the time. And* ***the both*** *of them is dead.* (Wicklow: J.F.)

(96) *Now Lough Melvin's a good salmon place. It's down here,* ***the half*** *of it's in, eh, Eire, you know, in the Free State.* (NITCS: JH80)

Less noticeable, but also characteristic of the vernacular forms of IrE, are the following categories:

(vi) names of festive days or seasons:

(97) *Yes. The wren, the wren, the King of all birds, Saint Stephen's day was caught in the bush. You see, they chased him up here* ***the Saint Stephen's Day,*** *the chap, boys.* (Wicklow: T.F.)

(vii) plural count nouns with generic reference:

(98) *Do they keep* ***the goats****?* (Kerry: D.B.)

(viii) non-count abstract nouns and concrete mass nouns:

(99) *I don' know when* ***the coffee*** *came. I s'pose it did, came later.* ***The tea, the tea, the tea*** *weren't there at all.* (Kerry: M.C.)

(ix) expressions involving reference to body parts:

(100) *Well, John Doolan cut a branch off it, and a crowd of birds come and they nearly took* ***the head*** *off him. They all collected round his head.* (Wicklow: T.F.)

(x) names of geographical areas and localities:

(101) *But I'm sure now, if you went out to Glendalough, you would get people that'd give you a good deal of the lowdown of* ***the County Wicklow****.* (Wicklow: M.K.)

Most of the usages described above have parallels in Irish and may have been transferred from there directly or at least reinforced by the Irish substratum in those cases in which there are similar earlier or dialectal English usages (for a detailed discussion of these, see Filppula 1999, section 5.2.).

10. Pronominal systems

10.1. Personal pronouns

Two features of IrE personal pronouns deserve to be mentioned here. The first is the frequent use of *them* as a determiner or 'demonstrative adjective' in colloquial speech, as in (102), or on its own as subject, as in (103) (see Harris 1993: 145). This feature is not, however, unique to IrE. Research on other varieties has shown that *them* in this function is one of the most commonly occurring features of non-standard British English dialects, both urban and rural.

(102) *...that time the people were rich that used to live in* ***them*** *houses.* (Dublin: J.O'B.)

(103) *{Mm. And those were cornstacks?}*
Them *was cornstacks...* (NITCS: WC15)

The distinction between singular *you* and plural *yous* (sometimes spelt *youse* or *yez/yiz*) is another well-known characteristic of IrE vernacular, and was already commented on in the early description by Hayden and Hartog (1909: 781). Interestingly, the same usage is also found in other varieties like Tyneside English, Scots, and Liverpool dialect, all of which have been influenced by the speech of the large numbers of Irish immigrants (see, for example Beal, this volume)

10.2. 'Absolute' uses of reflexive pronouns

It is a rule of StE that reflexive pronouns normally require the presence in the same clause or sentence of another nominal element, the so-called antecedent, with which they stand in a coreferential relation. In IrE dialects, however, reflexives can be used on their own, without such an antecedent. They can occur, for example, in subject position, in object position, or as prepositional complement in adverbial prepositional phrases. These types are illustrated by the following examples:

(104) *And by God, he said, ... he'd be the devil, if* ***himself*** *wouldn' make him laugh.* (Kerry: M.C.)

(105) *And d'you hear me, you didn't know the minute they'd burn* ***yourself*** *an' the house.* (Clare: J.N.)

(106) *... when Cromwell came over here... he was s'posed to say, he'd drive the Irish to hell or Connacht... The Irish used to say... the Irish went to Connacht and left hell* ***for himself****.* (Dublin: W.H.)

This IrE feature has attracted the attention of many scholars in the past. Thus, Hayden and Hartog (1909: 941) speak of the 'absolute' use of the reflexive pronouns, a term which they obviously adopt from the Latin grammatical tradition. Other commentators include Henry (1958: 92), who uses the same term,

Bliss (1979) and Harris (1993: 147). It is interesting to note that, although this feature is mainly found in vernacular and colloquial styles, occurrences can be spotted even in 'educated' varieties, including written language (see Filppula 1999: 81 for examples).

While the function of an absolute reflexive like *himself* is sometimes described as a polite form of reference to the 'man of the house', in actual usage there appear to be other functions, too. For instance, an absolute reflexive is often used with reference to that person or those persons who constitute the 'topic' of the conversation in some way or another. Of the examples cited above, this interpretation seems to suit the subject and prepositional complement reflexives in (104) and (106), though not so well the object reflexive in (105).

As regards the origins of absolute reflexives, it is hard to ascertain the exact source of the IrE usage because of parallels in both Irish and earlier English. Thus, Henry (1957: 120) points out that the Irish system of pronouns allows the same type of usage involving the emphatic pronoun *féin*. However, he implicitly notes the possibility of superstratal influence from earlier English by citing examples from Shakespeare's works to show that absolute reflexives occurred in earlier English, too (Henry 1957: 120–121; see also Hayden and Hartog 1909: 941; Harris 1993: 147).

11. Word order and information structure

11.1. Inverted word order in indirect questions

Along with Welsh and Scottish varieties of English, IrE dialects are well-known for their tendency to use inverted word order in indirect questions. This feature, which is here called 'embedded inversion', occurs in both Yes/No and WH- embedded questions in all regional varieties of IrE (see Bliss 1984; Henry 1995). The following examples illustrate the typical main-clause verbs triggering this phenomenon:

(107) *I don' know* ***was it*** *a priest or who went in there one time with a horse-collar put over his neck.* (Kerry: C.D.)

(108) *I wonder what is* ***he*** *like at all. The leprechaun. I don' know what* ***is it*** *at all.* (Clare: M.V.)

(109) *...oh, how long, wait till I see how long* ***would it be****?* (Dublin: P.L.)

(110) *...and the brogue was put in under somebody's knees this way, but you didn't... see where it was, and you could shuffle it on here to somebody else. And you were asked where* ***was the brogue.*** (NITCS: PH17)

(111) *{You know they had a roof, and they were square at the bottom, and they had a, they weren't...}*
Wonder ***were those*** *actually hay, or* ***was that*** *corn?* (NITCS: PH61)

It has long been thought that Irish substratal influence has been at work here. Thus, writing almost a century ago, Hayden and Hartog (1909: 938) note that "[t]he indirect question preceded by 'whether' or 'if' does not exist in Gaelic; and it is rare in the mouth of an Irishman, who will say 'I wondered was the horse well bred?'"

Indeed, it is true that Irish has no equivalent of the English conjunctions *if/ whether* but retains the interrogative word order in indirect questions just as IrE does. This also holds for the Irish counterparts of the WH-questions, although the parallelism is less obvious there because of the relative clause structure required by the Irish WH-questions. Though nowadays primarily a feature of informal spoken language, embedded inversion was a frequent phenomenon even in written texts in earlier IrE, as is shown by the following extract from a mid-nineteenth-century letter written by an Irishman to a Liverpool-based shipping agent:

(112) *Dear Sir i am writing to you to let you know that i am to embark on the 24th. day of september in which i hope your amiable Honour will be sure to keep room for me in the ship there is a friend of mine to be along with me that day a young Girl and she wants to know how much* ***will you charge*** *her from liverpool to newyork and herself to buy 1/2 provision please to write to me sir* ***will you keep*** *room for her in the ship. i am told that there are very sharp people in liverpool. i want to know how* ***will i know*** *them sir...* (*Grimshaw Papers*, 1865; National Library of Ireland MS 15,784)

Besides substratal influence, it is possible that embedded inversion is inherited from earlier English. Visser (1963–1973: 780–781) cites some parallels from Early Modern English texts but notes that "instances [of embedded inversion] do not seem to occur with great frequency before the eighteenth century". Others have suggested that embedded inversion is a phenomenon of 'learner English' or of colloquial, simplified fast speech regardless of the variety. Yet another, formal-syntactic and 'universalist', approach sees it as a reflex of the more general 'verb-second' (V2) properties of English and other Germanic languages. Despite their merits, these accounts fail to explain the geographical distribution of embedded inversion among the dialects of English spoken in the British Isles, and more specifically, its prominence in the western, north-western and northern varieties such as IrE, ScE, and WelE. Thus, it is hard to escape the conclusion that the Celtic substrate languages have had some role in promoting the use of embedded inversion in the said varieties (for further discussion, see Filppula 1999, section 7.3.).

11.2. Focusing devices

Focusing devices are so called because they serve to give emphasis or prominence to some element(s) of an utterance or a clause. In other words, some part or parts of an utterance, conceived of as a message purporting to convey the communicative intentions of the speaker, stand out from the rest as being more important than them. Prominence can in English (as in other languages) be achieved by various means, which include, first, prosodic ones: the speaker can highlight some word(s) by assigning it the primary sentence stress and thereby indicating the location of the main 'information focus' of his/her utterance. Secondly, various kinds of structural means can be used along with sentence stress to achieve the same effect. Such are, e.g. the so-called cleft construction (or 'clefting' for short), 'pseudo-clefting', and 'fronting' (sometimes also termed 'topicalisation'). These three can be exemplified by sentences such as *It was **the window** John broke* (not the door), *What John broke was **the window*** (not the door), and ***The window** John broke* (not the door), respectively (the information foci are emboldened).

Where IrE dialects clearly differ from StE and most other regional varieties is in their tendency to favour clefting and fronting over 'simple' sentence stress. This is particularly salient in those dialects which have been in closest contact with Irish as a living community language, and can be explained by the central role that clefting and fronting play in the grammatical system of Irish. Just like the other Celtic languages, Irish uses almost exclusively structural means such as clefting (often called the 'copula construction' in the Celtic grammatical tradition) or simple fronting instead of sentence stress for marking prominence, e.g. contrast or emphasis. Their functions are not, however, restricted to these special contexts: they are also used for introducing answers to specific questions, and more generally, for distinguishing between 'new' and 'old' information.

Besides frequencies of use, another factor speaking for Irish influence on IrE dialects is the special syntactic characteristics of clefting and, to some extent, fronting; these are either rare or not attested in other dialects of English. Thus, IrE (like Irish) allows part of a VP in the focus position of clefts (so-called VP-clefting), as in (113) from the southern IrE corpus. Similarly, subject complement adjectives and certain types of adverbial expressions such as those in (114) and (115), and 'absolute' reflexive pronouns, as in (116) from the NITCS, can occur in the same position in IrE vernacular. In StE, these would be at least odd, if not unacceptable even.

(113) *{Have many people left this area at all, or = or given up farming at all or?}*
Ah, very little's give up farming round this area. It's ***looking for more land*** *a lot of them are.* (Wicklow: J.N.)

(114) *It's* ***flat*** *it was.* (Henry 1957: 193)

(115) *It's* ***badly*** *she'd do it, now.* (Henry 1957: 193)

(116) *I don't know why it was now {I know}. I'll not say that it was {I know}* ***myself*** *was the cause of that...* (NITCS: PT86)

Clefting is also a common device in starting responses to questions, which is yet another reflex of the Irish tendency to front new information by means of the copula (cleft) construction. This is illustrated in (117) from the NITCS:

(117) *{And what kind of work do you do?}*
It's ***mostly missionary*** *work we do in the Mothers' Union.* (NITCS: HN38)

Simple fronting is slightly less common in IrE than clefting, but it is noteworthy that it can likewise be used in contexts in which StE would prefer 'straight' word order. Thus, in the following examples the primary motivation for the use of fronting seems to be highlighting the new information in the utterance rather than contrast or emphasis:

(118) *My brother that's over in England, ...when he was young,* ***a story*** *now he told me, when he was young.* (Kerry: M.McG.)

(119) *Indeed, I walked it myself when I young... all the way from here to Cahirciveen with cattle and with sheep. Oh,* ***about a distance of twenty and three or four miles*** *it were.* (Kerry: M.McG.)

As said above, both clefting and fronting are part of StE grammar but their syntactic and functional ranges are more limited there than in IrE dialects. It should also be noted that clefting is a relatively recent construction in English and had not fully developed until late in the Early Modern English period. A further factor suggesting Irish substratal influence on IrE dialects is the abundant use of similar focusing devices in the heavily Gaelic-influenced varieties of Hebridean English. Welsh English also has a predilection for structural means, but where IrE and Hebridean English use clefting, WelE prefers simple fronting, which can be explained by a parallel feature of Welsh (see Filppula 1999, chapter 10 for further discussion).

12. Prepositional usage

IrE abounds in turns of expression which involve prepositional usages which are not found in other regional dialects or in StE. Again, many of these can be explained by parallel expressions in Irish and, more generally, by the prominent role that prepositions play in Irish syntax: meanings which in other languages, including StE, are expressed by verbs, adjectives or adverbs, are often rendered by various types of prepositional phrases in Irish (see Henry 1957: 132; Harris 1993: 172).

The preposition *on* has been described as a "preposition-of-all-work" in IrE (Hayden and Hartog 1909: 939). Particularly well-known is its use in contexts which imply a disadvantage of some kind or another from the point of view of the speaker or some other person. This is illustrated in the following conversation where the informant describes how a fox managed to kill half of her flock of hens:

(120) *One year then he took the half of them* ***on me***. (Wicklow: Mrs. F.)

The same relation of disadvantage, often termed the 'dative of disadvantage', can also be conveyed by a combination of a verb + particle + preposition, as in (121):

(121) *But eh, there was some island, like, where there was a man living. And he was marooned, like, and there was no one in it but himself, like. And this day the fire went out* ***on him****, like*. (Clare: F.K.)

A second major function of *on* in IrE is its use to express various physical and mental sensations, states or processes. These are most often negative, as can be seen from (122):

(122) *...and Colonel Tottenham had a gamekeeper. Begor, the gamekeeper saw him huntin' an' he made after 'im. And they ran. And this blacksmith was runnin' too, and begor, the breath was gettin' short* ***on him***. (Clare: C.O'B.)
'...he was getting short of breath.'

Thirdly, *on* is used to express possession of an inherent physical or other property of a person or some other referent. It is usually of the 'inalienable' type, as in (123) and (124):

(123) *All the cattle had the horns* ***on them*** *that time*. (Kerry: C.D.)

(124) *There was another old lad used to clean windows. But I can't think the name that was* ***on him***. (Dublin: P.L.)

The preposition *in* has also developed several usages which are distinctive of IrE. Most of these involve the prepositional phrase *in it*, which has generally been considered a calque on the Irish *ann* (lit.) 'in it' or 'in existence' (see e.g. Henry 1957: 144–147). In the following example, *in it* clearly conveys the idea of existence in the general sense:

(125) *But she learned the deaf and dumb alphabet out of Moore's Almanac, that there used to be* ***in it*** *at the time, and...* (Clare: F.K.)

Like *on*, the preposition *in* can express some inherent quality or property of something, as in (126):

(126) *{Do you have to train them* [i.e. sheep-dogs] *especially for this purpose or?}*
Well, you do, ah, if it's in a dog he'll train himself, if the goodness is ***in 'im***. (Wicklow: C.C.)

The uses of the preposition *with* have also been moulded by contact effects. Thus, in conservative varieties of IrE, *with* can be used for the expression of the duration of a state or an activity. For instance, in (127) *with* has the temporal meaning 'for', 'for the duration of', or 'X time ago':

(127) *I didn't hear him playin'* ***with years an' years***. *Maybe he isn't able to play at all now*. (Clare: C.O'B.)
'I haven't heard him playing for years and years.'

The origin of the temporal meaning of *with*, which appears to be unique to the Irish dialects of English, lies in the corresponding Irish expressions involving the preposition *le* 'with; for the duration of' (Joyce 1988: 27).

Besides time, *with* is used to express agency in passive constructions. This usage, which has parallels in both earlier English and Irish, is illustrated in (128):

(128) *That was his ration, a trout and a half a day.*
{And the other half?}
Yeah, the other half would be, be ate, you see, ***with the monster or the serpent***. (Clare: F.K.)
'...by the monster or the serpent.'

Like the prepositions discussed so far, IrE *of* displays some special characteristics. Most of these are common to vernacular forms of speech throughout the British Isles, e.g. the temporal use in such expressions as *of a Saturday* 'on Saturday(s)', which has been recorded in a wide range of localities in Scotland, the north of England, the southwest and the east. Of greater interest in this connection is the intensifying construction known as 'attributive *of*', which is illustrated in (129) and (130):

(129) *And there was a young fella that, his father an' mother was buried, he was right orphaned and he was* ***a good hardy step of a boy****, and he was hurlin'*. (Clare: M.R.)

(130) *If it's there, it's there, and they'll* [sheep-dogs] *do the work with very little training. So they will. You get more* ***fools of dogs****, they are as useless... put sheep away on you, breaking, going through them, and...* (Wicklow: J.N.)

As Joyce (1988: 42) points out, idiomatic Irish parallels for these kinds of expressions exist in the form of constructions such as *amadán fir* 'a fool of a man' (where *fir* is the genitive form of *fear* 'man'). At the same time, he notes the existence of attributive *of* in EngE, which suggests two possible sources for the IrE attributive *of*.

Finally, the originally Scandinavian-derived preposition *till* in the directional sense 'to' can be mentioned as a feature which is still preserved in some northern IrE and especially Ulster Scots dialects, as is shown by (131) and (132) from the NITCS (cf. Joyce 1988: 84; Robinson 1997: 106):

(131) *I used to go down* ***till the aerodrome****, Ballykelly, the time the airport were down there,...* (NITCS: TF57)

(132) *...when I got up in years then, and went* ***till the dance****, I couldn't dance*. (NITCS: WC3)

13. Conclusion

As the foregoing discussion has shown, vernacular forms of IrE display a wide range of distinctive features in most areas of syntax, though much less in their morphology. Some of these features are shared with other regional or non-standard varieties of English and can thus be considered either retentions from earlier forms of English or 'general vernacular' patterns characteristic of most varieties spoken in the British Isles and Ireland. Then there are many others which have their origins in corresponding syntactic structures in Irish, which has over the last few centuries exercised considerable substratal influence on IrE. This influence, though clearly on the wane in the present-day urban varieties, is surprisingly persistent in some domains of syntax, such as the tense and aspect systems of IrE, and is still reflected to some extent even in educated informal speech; written IrE, on the other hand, mostly follows the StE norm. In rural dialects, both northern and southern, the presence of Irish-derived features is very noticeable, as can be predicted. Finally, the Scottish input to Ulster Scots and northern IrE in general forms yet another interesting strand in the linguistic make-up of IrE.

The writing of this article was supported by the Research Council for Culture and Society, Academy of Finland (Project no. 47424).

Exercises and study questions

1. Compare the IrE perfects with those of StE and try to identify the main areas of divergence and overlap in their coding of perfective aspect distinctions.
2. Identify and discuss at least 3 syntactic or morphological features which are shared by IrE and varieties of English spoken in Wales and/or Scotland. What do these similarities imply from the point of view of the origins of these features?
3. Discuss possible reasons for the preservation of many Scottish-derived syntactic or morphological features in especially the northern dialects of IrE. Could these have (had) other than linguistic implications?
4. Explain the syntactic significance, and discuss the linguistic background, of the italicised parts in the following examples drawn from spoken or written IrE sources:
   a. Well, I seen the time you'd buy a farm for five or six hundred [pounds]. Seen farms selling *and I young lad*. (Speaker from Co. Wicklow)
   b. Mr K. asked Ms A. what attitude Ms B. had to her during the week in the court building. Ms A. said she saw her brushing past. Ms B. said hello or recognised her. She had been a friend but she (Ms A.) would question the word friend at this point.
      Ms B. had been with *herself* and M.M. on many occasions and had sometimes gone to concerts with M.M. and *herself*. (From a newspaper report on a court case)
   c. *The most of the farms* were three cows and four. (Speaker from Co. Clare)

d. I *do be disputing* with my mother sometimes that I'll go to America and my mother gets angry with me for saying that I would go. (From a nineteenth-century letter)
e. … we'll go down over the wall. And *anybody won't know* where we, where we went, whether they'd see us or not. (Speaker from Co. Kerry)

5. What is meant by the term 'substratum', and how does it manifest itself in IrE syntax? Can IrE be considered a contact language or a creole?

Selected references

Please consult the General references for titles mentioned in the text but not included in the references below. For a full bibliography see the accompanying CD-ROM.

Bliss, Alan Joseph
1972 Languages in contact: some problems of Hiberno-English. *Proceedings of the Royal Irish Academy* 72: 63–82.
1984 English in the South of Ireland. In: Trudgill (ed.), 135–151.

Harris, John
1984a Syntactic variation and dialect divergence. *Journal of Linguistics* 20: 303–327.
1984b English in the North of Ireland. In: Trudgill (ed.), 115–134.
1993 The grammar of Irish English. In: Milroy and Milroy (eds.), 139–186.

Hayden, Mary and Marcus Hartog
1909 The Irish dialect of English: its origins and vocabulary. *Fortnightly Review* 85: 775–785, 933–947.

Henry, Alison
1995 *Belfast English and Standard English: Dialect variation and parameter setting*. Oxford: Oxford University Press.

Henry, Patrick L.
1957 *An Anglo-Irish Dialect of North Roscommon*. Dublin: University College.
1958 A linguistic survey of Ireland: preliminary report. *Lochlann* 1: 49–208.

Hume, A.
1878 *Remarks on the Irish Dialect of the English Language*. (From the Transactions of the Historic Society of Lancashire and Cheshire, Vol. XXX), Liverpool.

Joyce, Patrick Weston
1910 [1988] *English as We Speak It in Ireland*. Third edition. Dublin: Wolfhound Press.

Kallen, Jeffrey L.
1989 Tense and aspect categories in Irish English. *English World-Wide* 10: 1–39.
1994 English in Ireland. In: Burchfield (ed.), 148–196.

Kirk, John M.
1992 The Northern Ireland Transcribed Corpus of Speech. In: Leitner, Gerhard (ed.), *New Directions in Language Corpora*, 65–73. Berlin/New York: Mouton de Gruyter.

Molloy, Gerald
1897 *The Irish Difficulty, Shall and Will.* London: Blackie and Son.

Montgomery, Michael and Robert J. Gregg
1997 The Scots language in Ulster. In: Jones (ed.), 569–622.

Robinson, Philip
1997 *Ulster-Scots: A Grammar of the Traditional Written and Spoken Language.* Belfast: The Ullans Press.

Visser, Frederikus Th.
1963–1973 *A Historical Syntax of the English Language*. 4 Volumes. Leiden: E.J. Brill.

Welsh English: morphology and syntax

Robert Penhallurick

1. Introduction

This chapter describes the more notable and significant non-standard features of Welsh English morphology and syntax. It is divided into four sections: section 2 looks at features which seemingly arise as a result of Welsh-language influence; section 3 looks at influence on Welsh English grammar from non-standard English English; sections 4 and 5 consider phenomena worthy of highlighting, that is, predicate fronting, periphrastic verb phrases and periphrastic progressive verb phrases respectively, both already the subject of comparatively lengthy consideration in the scholarly literature on Welsh English.

The chief sources for the present chapter are as follows:

- Parry (1999), which is the most recent major publication of the *Survey of Anglo-Welsh Dialects* (SAWD), and which draws together data collected between 1968–1982 for Phase 1 of the *Survey*, on the English speech of the 60-plus age-group in rural Wales. Parry (1999) incorporates material from the other main SAWD and SAWD-associated publications, Parry (1977, 1979a) and Penhallurick (1991).
- Penhallurick (1994), which includes amongst its numerous historical sources pre- and early-SAWD material collected by David Parry and by Clive Upton in the 1960s.
- Penhallurick (1996), which adds to the data and findings published in Penhallurick (1991).
- Pitkänen (2003), which draws on her substantial doctoral research (University of Joensuu, in progress) into Welsh English syntax. Pitkänen uses four corpora in her apparent-time study, two of which she collected herself, in south-west Wales and north Wales during 1995–2000, and two from the SAWD archives (housed at the Department of English, University of Wales Swansea). Her SAWD material consists of, firstly, data from a selection of south-western and northern localities in the SAWD Phase 1 rural network, and, secondly, hitherto unpublished and indeed unused data from the intended urban Phase 2 of SAWD, for which fieldwork was carried out in Grangetown (Cardiff), Caernarfon, Wrexham, and Carmarthen during 1985–1987.

Unlike the rural informants, Phase 2 informants covered all age-groups, as also did Pitkänen's own informants.
- Williams (2000), which also includes the SAWD archives amongst its sources.

For an outline of the cultural and sociohistorical background to Welsh English, see the companion chapter on Welsh English phonology (Penhallurick, this volume).

2. Welsh-language influence in Welsh English grammar

Welsh-language influence, although not as pervasive as in Welsh English phonology, is prominently evident in some areas of Welsh English morphology and syntax. The discussions under 4 and 5 below, on predicate fronting and periphrastic and progressive verb phrases, also refer to Welsh-language influence.

2.1. Verbs

Generalized *isn't it* as a confirmatory interrogative tag, applying to the whole of a preceding statement, irrespective of the main verb, is common in Welsh English. Parry (1999: 115) states that it is "fairly widespread" throughout Wales, except for Monmouthshire. Penhallurick (1991: 204–205) records fourteen examples from the Welsh-speaking heartland of the north-west, including the following:

(1) *you have to rig him up in his clothes, isn't it*

(2) *I've heard the word, isn't it*

(3) *we say "clean under the grate", isn't it*

(4) *we saw some the other day, isn't it*

(5) *they had them in their hair, isn't it*

In these examples, pronunciation is frequently truncated to forms of the type [ɪnɪ] or [nɪ]. This tag no doubt arises as a result of the transfer of the Welsh generalized confirmatory interrogative *ydy fe?* 'isn't it?'. It should be noted, however, that *innit* forms are common in English English, including that of the south-west and south-east of England (see, for example, Anderwald, this volume), and it is entirely possible that this more general trend might have a reinforcing effect on Welsh English.

2.2. Adverbs

As Parry (1999: 120) reports, Standard English *how* + adjective as an introductory adverbial phrase in exclamations is commonly expressed in Welsh English by *there's* + adjective:

(6) *there's funny questions*

(7) *there's twp* ('stupid') *I've been*

(8) *there's nice to see you*

Although Parry has one example from north Wales, his others are all from south Wales, and this feature is associated more with southern Welsh English than with northern. It is to be heard frequently in the longer-anglicised regions of the south-east, but can be firmly linked with a corresponding formation in the Welsh language: *dyna* 'there is' + adjective.

2.3. Prepositions

Penhallurick (1991: 207) records several examples of *on* in the phrase *the name/term on* in north Wales (though not in the anglicised border region), such as:

(9) *I don't know the English term on that*

(10) *there's a special name on that*

(11) *there's a word on that*

Parry (1999: 119) records similar expressions mainly in mid-Wales. Like a good proportion of non-standard grammatical material in SAWD sources, these examples occurred in 'incidental material', that is, not as direct responses to any question in the SAWD questionnaire, so that any attempt to gauge the regional spread of such forms is, strictly speaking, tentative. However, it is noticeable that almost all of the instances in Parry (1999) and Penhallurick (1991) occur in traditional Welsh-speaking regions, which adds weight to the pretty clear connection with the Welsh syntagm *yr enw ar*, 'the name on'.

2.4. Indirect question word order

There are recorded instances in Parry (1999: 119) and Penhallurick (1991: 209–210) of indirect questions retaining the inversion of subject and verb characteristic of direct questions, for example:

(12) *I don't know what time is it*

(13) *I don't know what is that*

(14) *I'm not sure is it Caerleon or not* (Parry 1999: 119)

This appears to be a Welsh-influenced construction. In Welsh we find that the verb + immediately following form is identical in direct questions and their equivalent indirect ones. The SAWD examples come from incidental material and are few in number, but are almost exclusively from south-west Wales. Thomas (1985: 217) says that the elision of the conjunction (such as *if* or *whether*) in some examples is assisted by the practice in Welsh "of regularly eliding the corresponding conjunction (*a/os*) in similar environments in the vernacular". Filppula (1999: 167–172) notes the occurrence of such word orders in Hiberno-English (or Irish English), Scottish English, Hebridean English and Tyneside English, suggesting a general Celtic influence at work.

3. Non-standard English English influence in Welsh English grammar

In this section, a summary is provided of morphological and syntactic items recorded in Welsh English which seem to have travelled from the neighbouring dialects of English English. The traditional varieties of the borders, south Pembrokeshire, and the Gower Peninsula (i.e. areas subject to anglicization since the twelfth century and the aftermath of the Norman invasion of Wales) have been especially affected by this influence. Non-standard forms which illustrate less specific influence, such as double negation and demonstrative *them*, are not considered, although they may well indicate a more general 'vernacularization' of Welsh English, as Thomas (1985: 219) suggests. Parry (1999: 105–120) has a summary of such forms in SAWD data.

3.1. Pronouns

(15) *thee* – subjective and objective 2nd person singular personal pronoun;

(16) *thou* – subjective 2nd person singular personal pronoun;

(17) *a* – subjective 3rd person singular masculine personal pronoun, unstressed;

(18) *'en/un/n* – objective 3rd person singular masculine and neuter personal pronoun, unstressed;

(19) *thy* – 2nd person singular possessive adjective;

(20) *thine* – 2nd person singular possessive pronoun;

(21) *yourn* – 2nd person singular possessive pronoun;

(22) *ourn* – 1st person plural possessive pronoun;

(23) *theirn* – 3rd person plural possessive pronoun

These are forms recorded in SAWD and in material collected by David Parry in the early 1960s prior to SAWD (see Parry 1967, 1977, and 1999: 108–110), in the borders, south Pembrokeshire and the Gower Peninsula, and also attested widely in the *Survey of English Dialects* (SED) in the west and south-west of England. There is no doubt that they illustrate historical English English influence on Welsh English. However, in Welsh English most have a sporadic occurrence and the remainder are sporadic, and what is open to considerable doubt is whether they remain in current use.

Writing in 1979, Parry commented:

> *Thee* is still used among the older generation at Bishopston [Gower Peninsula, investigated by Parry in 1960, and again for SAWD in 1969], Middleton [Gower, investigated by Parry in 1960] and Llantwit [Vale of Glamorgan, investigated for SAWD in 1970]. But it is used only between equals and familiars. The form *a* (pronounced as in the first syllable of *about* [ə] is used for 'he' in unemphatic positions in the sentence at Bishopston and Middleton. And at these same localities, *un* (pronounced as in the first syllable of *untidy* [ən], as in *button*) may be used for the direct-object pronouns 'him' and 'it'. This is a reduced form of the Old English pronoun *hine* that meant 'him', and that was pronounced something like the word *inner* with an *h* added at the beginning. (Parry 1979a: 15)

He goes on to record that, in addition to these personal pronouns, the possessive forms *thy* and *thine* "survive amongst older-generation speakers" at Llangennith (Gower, investigated in 1969 for SAWD), Bishopston and Middleton, with their use again confined to equals and familiars. Elsewhere (Parry 1967: 135), he also records the personal pronoun *thou* as being in use in 1960 in Bishopston and Middleton. My own judgement, at least regarding the English of the Gower Peninsula, is that the late 1970s/early 1980s at best mark the dying moments of these forms. Indeed by that time they were probably little-used relics in the speech of the elderly generation. *Gowerland and its Language* (Penhallurick 1994) charts, through sources dating from the late seventeenth century to the late twentieth, the history of the traditional English dialect of the Gower Peninsula, a dialect having much in common in grammar, lexis and phonology with the dialects of the south-west of England. The coast of

England is visible across the Bristol Channel from Gower and it seems that there was significant settlement of south-west Englanders in Gower from the Norman invasion onwards. Throughout the history of scholarly investigation of this traditional Gower English, writers regularly declared it both an active variety and one on the verge of extinction. My conclusion in 1994 was that most of its historical characteristics had been swept away by the influx of a more general southern Welsh English. Certainly, the pronoun forms above are no longer current in Gower.

3.2. Verbs

Parry (1999: 112–118), summarizing information gathered by SAWD, records many instances of non-standard forms of *be*, *do* and *have* in Welsh English which can be connected with the traditional dialects of the west and south-west of England. Examples include:

(24) *I be/you am/thee art/thee bist/she be/we am/we be/they am/they be/them be*, all present tense, unstressed;

(25) *he do/he doth*, auxiliary, present tense, stressed;

(26) *he have/he hath*, auxiliary, present tense, stressed

Parry also records numerous examples of non-standard forms of other verbs, though these tend towards connections with a more general English English. With regard to the more specific west and south-west English English influence, as with 3.2. above it is the border, south Pembrokeshire, and Gower varieties of Welsh English that are affected, and, as above, there is the question of how current these forms are. Again, the example of the Gower Peninsula is arguably a useful indicator.

Penhallurick (1994: 165–168) presents a plethora of examples from traditional Gower English, including (27) to (32) from sources published between 1886 and 1957.

(27) *I be, art thee, yee binna* 'you be not';

(28) *thee casn't* 'you can't';

(29) *thee cust* 'you could';

(30) *it doth*;

(31) *I'th* 'I hath', *ye'th* 'you hath', *we hath*;

(32) *we makth*

In Parry (1977: 161–178, 1979a: 16–17), we find a fuller listing of such verb forms for Gower than in Parry (1999), and some commentary on their currency:

> In the present tense, forms such as *he goeth*, *he look'th* and *he cometh* were occasionally to be heard from older generation speakers at Middleton in 1960, when investigations were first carried out in that locality. Joseph Wright (*English Dialect Grammar*, section 435) said in 1905 that such forms were still used by elderly speakers in Somerset. (Parry 1979a: 16)

Research for *Gowerland and its Language* (Penhallurick 1994) indicated firmly that these south-west-English-English-derived verb forms were obsolescent by the 1960s and a disappearing folk-memory by the 1980s.

Ultimately, however, it would be a mistake to generalize too confidently from the Gower example. Gower English was rather isolated for centuries, bounded by a Welsh-speaking community in mainland south Wales. As that community became English-speaking, the grammar of Gower English, particularly during the twentieth century, merged with that of general southern Welsh English. South Pembrokeshire English is still bounded by a Welsh-speaking community, and Welsh English along the border has of course continually been in contact with west English English. With the exception of Gower English, the erosion (or not) of dialectal English English influence in varieties of Welsh English is a neglected topic of study.

3.3. Prepositions

The SAWD questionnaire elicited purposive *for to* 'in order to' as in (33) in south Pembrokeshire, Gower, and a couple of times in border localities.

(33) *I went to town for to see the doctor.*

SAWD incidental material provides a few more examples (see Parry 1999: 118, and Penhallurick 1991: 208), including, interestingly, one in Welsh-speaking north-west Wales (at Ynys, Gwynedd). Close inspection of the biographical details of the informant who provided this example (Penhallurick 1999: 16) shows that, whilst she was born locally, resident locally for most of her life, and had Welsh as her first language, she had lived in Dorset between the ages of 24–35. Dorset is one of the counties in which the SED records this syntagm. It is recorded widely across England by the SED, though its occurrence in Irish English should also be noted (Filppula 1999: 185).

4. Predicate fronting

Thomas (1985: 215) notes that "[o]ne of the more familiar distinctive features of sentence structure in Welsh English is the fronting of a constituent, when attention is focussed upon it: the fronted constituent is accompanied by emphatic stress". Examples of this feature are rare in SAWD data, because they are restricted to incidental material. Parry (1999: 119–120) records eight, under the heading *sentence-initial emphasis*, including:

(34) *A weed it is*

(35) *Coal they're getting out mostly*

(36) *A horse, 't was*

Thomas compares this Welsh English fronting with clefted and pseudo-clefted sentences in other varieties of English (in which clauses are divided into two separate sections), but argues that, in Welsh English, this feature is "best accounted for as an instance of interference from Welsh" (Thomas 1985: 216). In the Welsh language, 'clefting' is a simpler, blunter process than in English: any constituent of a sentence can be moved forward in a sentence (fronted) for emphasis. Tristram (2002) takes the case for Welsh influence further, arguing that clefting is one of a number of features exemplifying historical transference from Welsh to varieties of English.

Williams (2000) provides a detailed analysis of this phenomenon in Welsh English, which he terms *predicate fronting*. He detects two types of predicate fronting, distinguished according to the amount of new information contained in the fronted constituent. He argues that predicate fronting as it occurs in the now-English-speaking valley communities of south-east Wales "appears to be distinguished by a relatively small 'quantity' of new information appearing in the fronted constituent and consisting mainly of a reformulation of previous, immediately accessible textual material for modal purposes" (Williams 2000: 226). In his other data, however, collected in bilingual Llandeilo in west Wales, "The 'fronted' element is textually and situationally new, and there is no modal component" (Williams 2000: 227). Williams suggests that the first type is the more 'anglicised' kind of Welsh English predicate fronting, where a modal component has been added to a structure transferred from the Welsh language in which the "pragmatic function" (Williams 2000: 224) of the fronted constituent is merely to provide new information. It is a subtle but interesting distinction.

5. Periphrastic verb phrases and periphrastic progressive verb phrases

Here we have a fascinating area of variation in Welsh English syntax, in which there is, to an extent, competition between non-standard constructions caused by Welsh-language influence, non-standard constructions caused by dialectal English English influence, and Standard English constructions. The first type are periphrastic (that is, involving the use of separate words rather than inflections) progressive *be* verb phrases, and the second are periphrastic *do* verb phrases.

Taking the second type first, a periphrastic *do* verb phrase in Welsh English consists of unstressed and uninflected auxiliary *do* and the base form of a main verb. There is also a corresponding past tense structure: unstressed auxiliary *did* + base form of main verb. Ihalainen (1976) investigated and discussed such phrases in traditional East Somerset English, in which they are used to refer to repeated or habitual activity. The assumption has been that, where they occur in Welsh English, these *do* phrases are the result of influence from and contact with the dialects of the west and south-west of England. Klemola (2002) updates the discussion of periphrastic *do* in English English, and adds another perspective to Welsh and English contact in this matter, to which I will return shortly.

Unlike these *do* phrases, periphrastic progressive *be* verb phrases can be found in present-day British Standard English. Take, for example, the present progressive: unstressed and inflected auxiliary *be* + *-ing* form of main verb, which refers to an event or action in progress in present time; or the past progressive: unstressed and inflected past tense auxiliary *be* + *-ing* form of main verb, referring to an event or action in progress in past time. The 'nonstandardness' of such constructions in Welsh English arises because they can be used to express different (from standard) meanings, and it seems clear that the explanation for this lies in Welsh-language influence.

This area of Welsh English syntax is discussed in detail in Penhallurick (1996) and in Pitkänen (2003), but it was Thomas (1985) who set the template. Focusing on southern Welsh English, he identified the following "parallel occurrences" (1985: 214) in the present habitual:

(37) *He goes to the cinema every week* – inflected present (standard);

(38) *He do go to the cinema every week* – uninflected *do* (unstressed) + uninflected main verb;

(39) *He's going to the cinema every week* – inflected *be* (unstressed) + inflected main verb (*-ing* form)

Thomas's view (1985: 215) was that "the *do* pattern is characteristic of dialects which have a relatively long historical connection with the English dialects of the West Midlands – i.e. they fit into a dialect subcontinuum which reaches out from neighbouring English counties", whilst "the *be* pattern is characteristic of the speech of those who have a dominant Welsh-language influence". Thomas pointed out that there is a direct correlation of *be* forms with a present habitual construction in the Welsh language, for example in *Mae ef yn mynd i'r sinema bob wythnos*, which translates literally as 'He is going to the cinema every week'. The structure is: *bod* (realized as *mae*) 'be' + subject nominal (*ef* 'he') + linking *yn* + uninflected main verb (*mynd* 'go'), the truly literal translation thus being 'Is he in go to the cinema every week'. Thomas noted also (1985: 214) that there was a matching set of past habitual contrasts:

(40) *He went/used to go to the cinema every week*

(41) *He did go to the cinema every week*

(42) *He was going to the cinema every week*

SAWD data for south Wales, as summarized in Parry (1999: 110–112), shows *do* forms sporadically across the south: in south Pembrokeshire, the Gower Peninsula, and south-east Wales. The presence of these forms in south Pembrokeshire and Gower, on the face of it, implies that their point of origin should not be restricted to the West Midlands of England, but should encompass south-west England, too (though precisely how and when these forms arrived in these areas is open to debate). Klemola's maps (reproduced in 2002: 201–202) show that the geographical distribution of "unstressed periphrastic DO in affirmative statements" in traditional dialects, from the mid-nineteenth century to the mid-twentieth, encompasses all of the south-western corner of England, from Herefordshire to Dorset to Cornwall, with the exception of Devonshire. Klemola also makes a case, cautiously, for the idea that periphrastic *do* arose in English English as a result (or perhaps partly as a result) of Celtic influence: "the geographical distribution of periphrastic DO supports the conclusion that Celtic, especially Brythonic, contact influence may be a factor in explaining the origin of periphrastic DO in English" (Klemola 2002: 208). Klemola mentions (2002: 206) a Welsh construction "with a verb corresponding to periphrastic DO" attested before the late thirteenth century, the period when it seems that periphrastic DO appeared in English. This raises the intriguing but no doubt unprovable possibility that the *do* forms in Welsh English derive ultimately from Welsh influence. Pitkänen (2003) suggests the further possibility that auxiliary *gwneud* 'do' in Welsh might have reinforced (rather than caused) the use of periphrastic *do* in Welsh English.

Returning to SAWD data (Parry 1999: 110–111), and moving north in Wales, we see *do* forms petering out whilst periphrastic progressive *be* phrases become more common. The most complete listing of *be* constructions is in Penhallurick (1996), in which the data from northern Wales confirms the association of *be* forms with strong Welsh-language influence and reinforces Thomas's perception of the association of *do* forms with longerstanding anglicization. Penhallurick (1996) lists 112 examples: 110 instances of non-standard periphrastic progressive *be* phrases, and two of non-standard periphrastic *do* phrases. The overwhelming majority of *be* items were obtained in localities where the first language of the 60-plus age-group was Welsh, and indeed all but three of the 110 were obtained from first-language-Welsh informants. The northern Welsh English data exhibits considerable heterogeneity in the *be* forms, with the progressive tendency spreading beyond the habitual aspects (just as there is a present habitual construction in the Welsh language that can be translated into an English progressive construction, so are there similar types of construction in Welsh representing the past habitual, the present perfective and the future tense). Penhallurick (1996) presents a comprehensive classification of the *be* items, making use of five main semantic categories in addition to the present habitual and past habitual:

(i) *-ing* form of northern Welsh English verb corresponding to a Standard English base form: *you got to put this sharp side ... to cut the mouth ... to make it bleeding* (referring to breaking in a horse, using a special bit);
(ii) reference to future time: *if they don't receive the first time she's (h)avin' another chance* (referring to a cow not 'taking' to a bull);
(iii) state present, for example: *those that are keeping wild birds*;
(iv) present perfective, for example: *I have been using it myself*;
(v) state past, for example: *thirty years ago Lord Harlech was rearing them* (i.e. pheasants)

Pitkänen's work attempts to update the picture by assessing the frequency of occurrence of non-standard progressive forms in her south-west Wales, north Wales, and SAWD Phase 2 corpora compared with rural SAWD. What she finds overall is that the use of the progressive forms in their 'basic' non-standard habitual aspect remains pretty consistent throughout her corpora, but also that standard forms are used more in her newer corpora, apparently at the expense of progressive forms in the other semantic categories.

Exercises and study questions

1. Which general hypothesis is suggested concerning examples like the following?
   a. There's nice to see you.
   b. I don't know what is that.
   c. We saw some the other day, isn't it?
2. Check this hypothesis by consulting other varieties of English in the British Isles and elsewhere in the Anglophone world concerning the features in (1b) and (1c).
3. Give an account of how the habitual is marked in Welsh English, starting out from the example *He do go to the cinema every week.* What are other ways of habitual marking made use of in the British Isles?
4. Comment on an example like *A horse, 't was* from the point of view of the Celtic substrate hypothesis.
5. What can you say about the origins of the following Welsh English forms? In which parts of Wales, in particular, are they found?
   a. thee, thou, thy
   b. ourn, yourn, theirn
   c. he doth, he hath
   d. I went to town for to seek the doctor.
6. Identify three morphosyntactic features <u>each</u> for Irish English and Scottish English which they do not share with Welsh English.

Selected references

Please consult the General references for titles mentioned in the text but not included in the references below. For a full bibliography see the accompanying CD-ROM.

Ihalainen, Ossi
1976 Periphrastic *do* in affirmative sentences in the dialect of East Somerset. *Neuphilologische Mitteilungen* 77: 608–622.

Klemola, Juhani
2002 Periphrastic DO: dialectal distribution and origins. In: Markku Filppula, Juhani Klemola and Heli Pitkänen (eds.), *The Celtic Roots of English*, 199–210. Joensuu: Faculty of Humanities, University of Joensuu.

Parry, David
1967 Some features of Gower dialects. *The Anglo-Welsh Review* 16: 130–135.
1979a *Notes on the Glamorgan Dialects*. Swansea: privately published.
Parry, David (ed.)
1977 *The Survey of Anglo-Welsh Dialects, Volume 1: The South-East*. Swansea. privately published.
1979b *The Survey of Anglo-Welsh Dialects, Volume 2: The South-West*. Swansea. privately published.
1999 *A Grammar and Glossary of the Conservative Anglo-Welsh Dialects of Rural Wales*. Sheffield: National Centre for English Cultural Tradition.
Penhallurick, Robert J.
1991 *The Anglo-Welsh Dialects of North Wales: A Survey of Conservative Rural Spoken English in the Counties of Gwynedd and Clwyd*. Frankfurt am Main: Lang.
1994 *Gowerland and its Language: A History of the English Speech of the Gower Peninsula, South Wales*. Frankfurt am Main: Lang.
1996 The grammar of Northern Welsh English: progressive verb phrases. In: Juhani Klemola, Merja Kytö and Matti Rissanen (eds.), *Speech Past and Present: Studies in English Dialectology in Memory of Ossi Ihalainen*, 308–342. Frankfurt am Main: Lang.
Pitkänen, Heli
2003 Non-standard uses of the progressive form in Welsh English: an apparent time study. In: Tristram (ed.), 111–128.
Thomas, Alan
1985 Welsh English: a grammatical conspectus. In: Viereck (ed.), 213–221.
Tristram, Hildegard L.C.
2002 The politics of language: links between Modern Welsh and English. In: Katja Lenz and Ruth Möhlig (eds.), *Of Dyuersitie and Change of Langage: Essays Presented to Manfred Görlach on the Occasion of his 65th Birthday*, 257–275. Heidelberg: Winter.
Williams, Malcolm
2000 The pragmatics of predicate fronting in Welsh English. In: Tristram (ed.), 210–230.

English dialects in the North of England: morphology and syntax

Joan Beal

1. Introduction

Typologies of English dialects have tended to be based mainly on phonetic and phonological criteria. Both Wakelin (1983) and Trudgill (1999) classify dialects entirely according to phonological/phonetic criteria, whilst Ellis (1869), includes only one feature which might be considered morphological: the form of the definite article. In our chapter on the phonology of the dialects in the North (see Beal, this volume) we discussed the fact that only two phonological features, /ʊ/ in STRUT/FOOT, and short /a/ in BATH, unite the whole of the North (albeit including much of the Midlands as well). All other features discussed in that chapter differentiate part or parts of the North from others: for instance, /h/ retention is confined to the far Northeast and lack of /ŋ/ as a distinctive phoneme to the far South-west of the region.

As far as morphology and syntax are concerned, there are likewise very few features which both distinguish Northern dialects from those of the South and Midlands, and can be found throughout the North. With regard to morphology, syntax and lexis, the differences between Northern dialects are more transparently linked to the external histories of the regions and cities. In the far North, there is a continuum of morphological and syntactic features stretching from Tyneside to beyond the Scottish border, a testimony both to the shared history of these regions, formerly united in Anglo-Saxon Bernicia, and to continuing migration from the Central belt of Scotland to Tyneside (see Beal 1993, 1997). Further South, the "Scandinavian belt", stretching North-west to South-east from Cumbria to East Anglia, taking in all of Yorkshire and part of Durham, but excluding Northumberland, is evidenced in morphological features such as the *at* relative (Poussa 2002), and the presence of many lexical items of Scandinavian origin (e.g. *beck*, contrasting with Anglo-Saxon *burn* in Northumberland, *brook* in Lancashire and Cheshire). More recent evidence of contact can be found in the use of second plural *yous* in areas of high Irish immigration from the 19th century: Liverpool, Newcastle and inner-city Manchester within this area, as well as Glasgow, New York and urban Australia outside England.

Wherever possible, illustrative examples used in this chapter are taken from corpora of Northern English dialects, all collected within the second half of the 20th century. Two of these, the *Newcastle Electronic Corpus of Tyneside English (NECTE)* and the *Corpus of Sheffield Usage (CSU)* are currently being prepared for online access (www.ncl.ac.uk/necte, www.shef.ac.uk/english/natcect). The other corpora used here are those collected by Petyt (1985) in West Yorkshire, Cave (2001) in South Yorkshire and Shorrocks (1999) in Bolton, Greater Manchester. These corpora do not cover the whole of the North of England, but this is inevitable given the patchy nature of dialect studies carried out in this area. Anderwald (2002) acknowledges that the geographical coverage of the *British National Corpus* is likewise uneven. A more even distribution is provided by the *Survey of English Dialects* (SED) and by Cheshire, Edwards and Whittle (1993), but in both these cases the information on geographical distribution of non-standard features of syntax and morphology is obtained from questionnaire responses rather than actual utterances, and as such may reflect the speakers' passive knowledge of those features rather than actual usage. Reference will be made to the SED 'Basic Material' volumes (Orton and Halliday 1962), in order to illustrate patterns of usage in more 'traditional' and/or rural dialects, since all the corpora referred to above were collected in urban areas.

2. Morphology

2.1. Irregular verbs

Several verbs have different past tense and/or past participle forms in Northern dialects. The *-en* ending for the past participle is more common in Northern dialects than in Standard English. Examples of such forms are *getten*, *putten, and squozen* (compared to Standard English *got*, *put*, *squeezed*). Of these, *getten* and *putten* are attested in the North-east (McDonald 1981), and *putten* and *squozen* in Bolton (Shorrocks 1999: 135–148), but such forms could well be more widespread, given that these two studies are from opposite ends of the North. In a number of cases, the past tense and past participle forms are identical. Examples of this can be found in Table 1 below.

Table 1. Verbs with 'levelled' past tense and past participle forms in Northern English dialects

Base	**Past Tense**	**Past Participle**
bite	*bit*	*bit*
break	*broke*	*broke*
do	*done*	*done*
fall	*fell*	*fell*
freeze	*froze* / froːz /	*froze* / frɒz /
hang ('to execute')	*hung*	*hung*
go	*went*	*went*
ring	*rang/rung*	*rang/rung**
sing	*sang/sung*	*sang/sung**
speak	*spoke*	*spoke*
swim	*swam/swum*	*swam/swum**
take	*took*	*took*
write	*wrote*	*wrote*

* In all cases, the *a* forms are found in the North-east, and the *u* forms in Bolton. The same patterns would be found with *wring*.

In some cases, the same form is used for present tense, past tense and past participle: examples of this are *come* and *give*. The forms in Table 1 have either the past tense or the past participle form identical with that of Standard English. However, other verbs with 'levelled' paradigms have a non-standard form for both past tense and past participle in Northern English dialects. *Tret* for Standard English *treated* is found in Tyneside (Beal 1993), and West Yorkshire (Petyt 1985: 232), but not in Bolton (Shorrocks 1999). Others, such as *telled*, *selled* (pronounced / tɛlt, sɛlt / in the North-east, tɛld, sɛld / elsewhere), have 'regular' forms where the Standard English equivalent is irregular *told*, *sold*.

2.2. Nouns

2.2.1. Plural forms

A few instances of non-standard, irregular plural forms are found in Northern English dialects. *Childer* is found in both Bolton (Shorrocks 1999: 62) and West Yorkshire, but in the latter case, Petyt tells us that this was restricted to "two elderly Huddersfield informants" (1985: 231). In the North-east, the word *child* is less likely to be used by speakers of traditional dialect, who would use *bairn*. Shorrocks (1999: 63) also gives *een* and *shoon* for Standard English *eyes* and *shoes*. A more widespread pattern is the regularisation in Northern English dialects of the paradigm in which Standard English has an alternation between voiceless and voiced fricatives in singular and plural. Thus *knifes, roofs, wifes,* are found in contrast to Standard English *hooves*, *knives, wives*, and *wreaths* is pronounced /ri:θs/ as opposed to Standard English /ri:ðz/ (Shorrocks 1999: 60). After numerals, nouns of weight, measure and quantity, often lack the plural marker in Northern dialects, as in other non-standard dialects of British English. An example from the NECTE corpus is:

(1) *I lived in with my mother for not quite two year.*

2.2.2. Possessive forms

Plurals and proper nouns ending in *-s* take the possessive ending *'s* (pronounced /ɪz) in Northern English dialects. Thus the disinfectant is called *Jeyes's Fluid*, and *Marks and Spencer* is popularly referred to as *Marks's* in the North. An example of a plural with this form is *it's other folks's* (Shorrocks 1999: 64).

2.3. Pronouns

Personal pronouns in Northern dialects differ from those in Standard English at several points in the paradigm.

2.3.1. First person pronouns

The first person singular object form is often *us*, rather than *me*. In the North-east, *us* is used as both direct and indirect object, thus in the following examples from the NECTE corpus, the context makes it clear that the speaker is referring to herself in (2) and quoting a taxi-driver referring to himself in (3):

(2) *He telt us he was having a party, but he didn't tell us like… when.*

(3) *Oh, thanks pal. Thanks, you're the first person that's give us a tip.*

However, examples from Bolton and West Yorkshire show it only as indirect object: *Lend it us* (Shorrocks 1999: 76) and *give us a sweet* (Petyt 1985: 231).

Where the pronoun is conjoined with another pronoun or a noun, *me* is used throughout the North, thus:

(4) *So he says to me and our Jack (*Shorrocks 1999: 77)

(5) *They used to lock me and my mum in the top bedrooms*. (NECTE)

Me is also used throughout the North for the first person subject form when the pronoun is conjoined with another pronoun or a noun, thus:

(6) *Me and my mam and dad are going out for a meal.* (NECTE)

(7) *Him and me were there* (Shorrocks 1999: 78).

As shown in (7), this rule applies to all personal pronouns.

In the North-east, 'pronoun-exchange' occurs in the first person plural, with *we* /wə/ used for the object form, and, less frequently, *us* for the subject form. This contradicts the view stated in Ihalainen (1994: 231) that pronoun exchange is confined to western dialects of English. Examples are:

(8) *You can come with we to that as well.* (NECTE)

(9) *Us'll do it* (Macdonald 1980).

The first person plural possessive pronoun takes various forms in different Northern dialects. In the North-east, *wor* is found, as in:

(10) *Wor Thomas'll be fourteen on Christmas Day, and wor little Steven, that's the seventh; he'll be ten.* (NECTE)

This was formerly more widespread as Wright (1892) records it in Windhill, West Yorkshire. The most common form in West and South Yorkshire now is *us* as in:

(11) *We all take us cars to work nowadays* (Petyt 1985: 190).

2.3.2. Second person pronouns

In Northern dialects, two different strategies are used to retain the earlier English distinction between singular and plural in the second person.

In most of the North, excluding only Tyneside, Northumberland and Liverpool, singular *thou* and *thee* are retained in more traditional dialects. The subject/object distinction is often neutralised in /ða/, and use of *thou/thee* forms often depends on the addressee, as in Early Modern English. In South Yorkshire, the term *thee-ing and tha-ing* is used (cf. French *tutoyer*) to describe inappropriate use of the *thou* form, thus:

(12) *Thee thee and tha thyself and see how thou likes it.* (CSU)

Cave (2001) conducted an ethnographic study of the language of the former mining community in Barnsley, South Yorkshire. He found that use of *thou/thee* forms was confined to men in the corpus he collected, but that the wives of the former miners admitted to using these forms to their husbands in their homes. Shorrocks also finds *thou/thee* forms used for the second person singular in Bolton, and some evidence that *you* is still used as a polite form in the singular: "there are still sons in the Bolton area who appear to use only the *yo* form when addressing their fathers" (1999: 74).

In the North-east, *thou* is still used by older speakers as far north as county Durham, but not north of the Tyne. Northumberland lacked *thou* even in traditional dialects. Here *ye* was found for second person singular subject in the SED. This usage continues throughout the North-east today, as in:

(13) *Well ye haven't got any*. (NECTE)

In the Tyneside conurbation, as in Liverpool and inner-city Manchester, the plural form *yous* is used.

(14) *Yous'll have Thomas next year*. (referring to the whole class) (NECTE)

Cheshire, Edwards and Whittle (1993) demonstrate that plural *yous* appears to be diffusing from inner-city areas, but it would appear that the ultimate origin of this form is in Irish English. The *English Dialect Dictionary* (Wright 1898–1905) cites it as occurring in Ireland, the USA and Australia, but not in England or Scotland.

2.3.3. Third person pronouns

There is less variation both between Northern dialects and Standard English, and between dialects in the North, with regard to third person pronouns. The objective form is used for the subject when this is either conjoined (as in [7] above) or when it is separated from the verb or is emphatic, as in

(15) *I think she likes getting bathed her*. (NECTE)

(16) *Her and her son are still living there*. (NECTE)

(17) Y*ou-know, her that's always late*. (NECTE)

In other positions, North-eastern dialects have the subjective form, as in (15), but in Bolton, *her* is used here as well for the feminine form. The earlier form of this pronoun in Lancashire was *hoo*, but Shorrocks notes that this is now recessive (1999: 72–73).

2.3.4. Reflexive pronouns

Throughout the North, the paradigm of reflexives is regularised, so that all persons consist of the possessive + *-self/selves*. Thus, as well as *myself, yourself, thyself*, we have *hisself, theirselves. Self/selves* are realised as *-sel/sels*, or (mainly in Yorkshire.) *-sen/sens*. In Bolton, the objective form of the pronoun may also be used as a reflexive (see Shorrocks 1999: 91–94 for a full explanation of this). Examples from Shorrocks are:

(18) *they did it theirsel*

(19) *he codded 'issel* (= 'deceived')

(20) *he wouldn't shift 'im* (= 'move')

2.4. Demonstratives

The most common forms of the demonstrative throughout the North are *this, these, that and them*. Only the latter differs from Standard English. In the North-east, *they* is used (cf. Scots *thae*), but even here, *them* is more common. There are traces of the three-term deictic system in Northern dialects, the third term usually being *yon* or *yonder*. This is shown to be quite extensive in the SED, but Shorrocks (1999: 54) notes that *yon* refers, not to something distant, but to a 'known referent', so that *yon mon* may refer to a man not present, but known to all interlocutors, or easily identified from the preceding conversation. In this way, it is similar to Irish English *your man*. Emphasis can also be added by adding *here* to *this* and *there* to *that*, and, at least in Lancashire and Yorkshire *tother* is also used as a third deictic term.

2.5. Definite and indefinite articles

2.5.1. Reduction of the definite article

In the North-east, definite and indefinite articles have the same form as in Standard English. The syntactic constructions in which they are used differ from Standard English, but this will be discussed in 4.4.1. and 4.4.2. below. In the rest of the North, especially in Lancashire and Yorkshire, there is variation between full and reduced or zero forms of the definite and indefinite articles. Jones (2002: 325) notes that reduction of the definite article "is perhaps the most stereotypical feature of northern British English dialects, especially those of Yorkshire and Lancashire". The reduction may take the form of /t/, /ʔ/, /θ/ a preglottalised plosive, or zero. In the semi-phonetic spellings used in dialect literature and popular representations of Northern dialect, these are usually presented as *t'* or *th'* or the article is simply omitted. The distribution of these variants differs across dialects, age groups and social classes. Petyt (1985: 196–200) notes that the commonest reduced form in his data was the glottal stop, and that fricative forms were rare, confined to Huddersfield and part of Halifax (as opposed to Bradford) and only occurred prevocalically. Shorrocks gives a more detailed phonetic analysis of the variants in his Bolton corpus (1999: 23–31). Before consonants, the definite article is realised as a glottal stop or preglottalised consonant, depending on the phonetic environment, whilst before vowels, the /θ/ realisation is much more common than in Petyt's West Yorkshire data (which was collected at about the same time, in the early 1970s). Whilst this was a minority usage in Petyt's data, Shorrocks notes "there are no exceptions to the use of /θ/ before a vowel/diphthong" (1999: 29). In Bolton, zero forms of the definite article occur in certain phonetic contexts, notably after a fortis fricative, as in *across (the) road.* Zero forms are, however, more widely distributed in East Yorkshire, and Tagliamonte and Ito (2002: 245–246) report that the "zero definite article" is one of a number of dialect features "widely represented" in Tagliamonte's corpus of York English. Jones (2002: 342) suggests that this represents the final stage in a historical process of reduction from /θ/→ /t/→/ʔ/→ zero.

2.5.2. *Loss of the indefinite article*

The indefinite article may be realised as zero in some Northern dialects. I have not found any instances of this in the NECTE corpus, and would suspect that the geographical distribution of this is similar to that of reduced forms of the definite article discussed in 2.6.1. above. Shorrocks notes that "in the dialect of the Bolton area, the indefinite article is very often not used at all by comparison with S[tandard].E[nglish]. – or it frequently has a zero realisation. There is no rule to predict any individual case." (1999: 47). There are also instances of zero realisation in the CSU data, so we can conclude that this is found in Yorkshire as well as Lancashire. Examples are:

(21) *It were lovely summer* (Shorrocks 1999: 47).

(22) *Aye, but he were ironmonger* (Shorrocks 1999: 47).

(23) *I'd buy house there if I'd got t' money.* (CSU)

2.6. Adjectives

In Northern dialects, as in most non-Standard dialects of British English, comparative and superlative forms of adjectives may be doubly marked. Examples are:

(24) *Because you were more fitter* (Shorrocks 1999).

(25) *She's got the most loveliest clothes* (Beal 1993: 209).

2.7. Adverbs

Shorrocks notes that "a great many adverbs in the dialect have the same form as the adjective" (1999: 199). This also applies to adverbials used as degree modifiers. Examples (all from Shorrocks 1999) are:

(26) *I told thee confidential.*

(27) *Do it good.*

(28) *A high technical job.*

Tagliamonte and Ito (2002) report that this phenomenon is found in all dialects of British English (as well as many outside Britain), but that the constraints on variation between zero and *-ly* forms are more conservative in Northern dialects such as that of York.

3. Syntactic linkage

3.1. Number agreement

3.1.1. The 'Northern Subject Rule'

Traditionally, all Northern English dialects observe the 'Northern Subject Rule', according to which the verb takes *-s* in the plural where the subject is a noun or noun phrase, but not when it is a pronoun. Beal and Corrigan (2000) found that this rule still operates in Tyneside English with lexical verbs, though not with *be*. Examples from the NECTE corpus are:

(29) *Our young one's mates talks something like you.*

(30) *We visit her mam.*

The constraint against using the *-s* form after pronouns was particularly strong, but the use of *-s* after plural noun subjects was found to be more common after conjoined nouns, as in:

(31) *Aye, and your sister and your mam comes out.* (NECTE)

3.1.2. *Was/were*

With regard to the past tense of the verb *be*, Northern English dialects show a variety of patterns. Accounts of the traditional dialects of Yorkshire and Lancashire (Wright 1892; Ellis 1869–1889) suggest that the typical pattern in these areas was one in which *were* occurred with all subjects, singular and plural. Shorrocks (1999: 168) states that *were* is used throughout his Bolton corpus, but Petyt (1985: 196) finds this pattern confined to working-class speech in his corpus of West Yorkshire. Tagliamonte (1998) found that, in York, the tendency was for *was* to be used in positive clauses, and *were* in negative clauses, such as:

(32) *I was, weren't I?*

(33) *You was, weren't you?*

The more usual pattern in the North-east is for *was* to be used throughout, even with the pronouns *we*, *you*, *they* where the Northern Subject Rule would normally prohibit use of the *-s* forms. However, some examples of *were* with singular subjects have been found in the NECTE corpus. The following two examples are from the same informant:

(34) *When I were about fourteen... or fifteen.*

(35) *I was dropped in at the deep end.*

3.1.3. *Existentials*

Beal and Corrigan (2000) note that the use of the singular verb form after existential *there* is categorical for working-class males in the NECTE corpus, and becoming near categorical for working-class females. Examples from the corpus are:

(36) *There was quite a few mines.*

(37) *There is more women coming into bus driving.*

3.1.4. Relic forms

Apart from the patterns discussed above, there are a few non-standard patterns of agreement which can still be heard as 'relic' forms, mostly from older speakers. These include *thou art* in dialects which retain second person singular *thou* (see 2.3.2. above), i.e. South Lancashire and South-west Yorkshire. *I's* is found throughout the North in the SED material (Upton, Parry and Widdowson 1994: 494), but does not occur in any of the modern corpora used here. However, Shorrocks (1999: 116) notes the use of *-s* endings for first person singular "when describing habitual behaviour". Shorrocks also notes a few instances of plural *-en* in his Bolton corpus, but points out that "the use of these endings (which go back to Middle English) must now be accounted highly residual" (1999: 114).

4. Syntax

4.1. Negation

4.1.1. Auxiliary contraction

As in Scots, *have*, *be* and *will* (*'ll*) may be negated by uncontracted *not* in Northern dialects. In the North-east, *can* is also negated in this way, but the *not* is unstressed, so that the negated form is pronounced /'kanɪt/. In more conservative dialects of the North-east, the form /wɪnɪt/ or /wɪnət/ for *will* + *not* is also used. Trudgill (1984: 33) suggests that the frequency of this pattern of auxiliary contraction increases "the further north one goes" in Britain. However, Anderwald (2002: 75–78) notes that *be* favours auxiliary contraction in all dialects of British English. Her study, based on the *British National Corpus*, shows that auxiliary contraction is neither as common in Northern dialects, nor as restricted to the North, as Trudgill suggested. This may be due to the limitations of the *BNC* material, though, for, as the following examples from the NECTE corpus demonstrate, auxiliary contraction is found with a range of modal and auxiliary verbs in the North-east. Even here, though, as in (39), negative contraction is more common with *have*.

(38) *Neil's not letting you go.*

(39) *Definitely haven't got sea-legs like.*

Examples of other modal verbs with uncontracted *not*, all from the NECTE corpus are:

(40) *Yous'll not be in town this Saturday.*

(41) *We cannot let like a group of twelve lads in all at once.*

The modals *would* and *could* take negative contraction, as in:

(42) *Well you said we couldn't all come in at once.*

(43) *You wouldn't get one in there.*

In dialects of the 'lower north', notably Lancashire and Yorkshire, there is also a pattern of secondary contraction, where both the auxiliary and the negator are contacted. Here, forms such as *isn't*, *couldn't*, *shouldn't* are contracted to /ɪnt, kʊnt, ʃʊnt/ etc. and *hasn't/hadn't* become homophonous as /ant/. These forms are attested by both Petyt (1985: 179–189) and Shorrocks (1999: 153, 167, 172, 177).

In the North-east, the negative of *do* can be *divvent*, or *don't* for first and second person singular and all persons in the plural, with *doesn't* for third person singular. Examples from the NECTE corpus are:

(44) *Divvent get us confused.*

(45) *I don't know who.*

These two examples are consecutive utterances from the same speaker.

4.1.2. Negation in interrogatives

In some Northern English dialects, negation in interrogatives and tags shows systematic variation between forms with contracted and uncontracted negators. Shorrocks (1999: 180–181) states that, in the Bolton dialect, a negative tag following a positive proposition is contracted, but following a negative proposition is uncontracted, as in:

(46) *It rained, didn't it?*

(47) *It didn't rain, did it not?*

In the North-east, an even more complex pattern is found. A negative clause followed by auxiliary + subject + *not* is used when information is sought, as in:

(48) *She can't come, can she not?*

A negative clause followed by auxiliary + *n't* + subject + *not* is used when confirmation of the negative is sought, as in:

(49) *She can't come, can't she not?*

This pattern is also used in negative questions, where the speaker knows very well that the answer is *no*, but requires confirmation, possibly to settle a dispute with a third party. It is often used by children appealing to adult arbitration. An example would be:

(50) *Can't Jack not swim?*

Here, what is implied is that everybody knows that Jack can't swim, but Jack is denying this.

A similar contrast occurs between two patterns for negative tags following positive clauses, with auxiliary + subject + *not* used when asking for information, and auxiliary + *n't* + subject, when asking for confirmation. Examples of these would be:

(51) *She can come, can she not?*

(52) *She can come, can't she?*

Examples 49–52 are taken from McDonald and Beal (1987), but examples from the NECTE corpus are:

(53) *Had they not?*

(54) *Oh, will you not be nice to her for once?*

(55) *Did you not see the teeth?*

In all of these, there is an element of surprise or exasperation, suggesting that the uncontracted negative in an interrogative or tag has an emphatic force.

4.1.3. Multiple negation

Some of the patterns discussed in 4.1.2. involve multiple negation. This is generally assumed to be a feature of non-standard English which is common to all regional dialects. However, Cheshire, Edwards and Whittle (1993) and Anderwald (2002) find that, whilst multiple negation is indeed found in all dialects of British English, it is less frequent in the North. The exception to this pattern in Anderwald's study is the North-east, where the frequency of multiple negation is similar to that found in the South. Anderwald attributes this to the innovative nature of the dialect of Tyneside, but it is possible that the higher frequency in Tyneside could be in part due to patterns such as those in (49) and (50) above. Multiple negation is found in Bolton, in West Yorkshire, and in the North-east. Examples are:

(56) *I'm not never going to do nowt more for thee* (Shorrocks 1999: 193–194).

(57) *He couldn't get a job nowhere* (Petyt 1985: 238).

(58) *You're not getting none off me*. (NECTE)

4.1.4. Non-emphatic never

Throughout the North, *never* is used as a general negator, with reference to a single occasion. Examples are:

(59) *I never eat (ate) no dinner* (referring to one specific occasion) (Shorrocks 1999: 193).

(60) *He never dropped like a set... against anybody*. (referring to a specific tennis match) (NECTE)

As in Scots, *never ever* is used to express unambiguously the meaning 'at no time' as in:

(61) *They never ever talk about stuff like that...never*. (NECTE)

4.2. Modal verbs

The system of modal verbs in the North-east, especially Tyneside and Northumberland, is more like that of Scots than that of Standard English and English dialects in the South and Midlands. Some features of the modal system are shared by all northern dialects, but others are only found in the far North-east.

4.2.1. Shall, may *and* ought

These three modal verbs are hardly used at all in the North-east. *May* is rare in northern dialects generally (Shorrocks 1999: 154), but, whilst Shorrocks demonstrates (see examples 62 and 63) that both *shall* and *ought* are used in Bolton, albeit in dialectal forms, they are very rare in the NECTE corpus. In the North-east, *will* is used even in the one context in which it is compulsory for speakers of other English dialects, in first person questions, as in (64). Instead of *may*, *can* is used in the sense of 'permission' (65) and *might* in the sense of 'possibility' (66).

(62) *Theawst (= thou shalt) have one if we can manage it.*

(63) *He didn't ought to have done it.*

(64) *Will I put the kettle on?*

(65) *He's busy at the moment. Can I get him to call you later?*

(66) *Oh, well my spirit might be there but...guarantee I'll never get back in there*

4.2.2. Must, have to *and* (have) got to

In North-eastern dialects of English, *must* is used to express conclusions, not obligation. This applies to both positive and negative clauses. Examples are:

(67) *She was, she ... must have been drunk.* (NECTE)

(68) *The lift mustn't be working* (McDonald and Beal 1987).

Shorrocks (1999: 157) notes that *mustn't* to express conclusions is also 'permitted' in Bolton. There seems to be a North-South gradient here: in Scots and North-eastern English dialects, *must* is only used with the meaning of conclusion, in the 'middle North', both conclusion and obligation meanings are possible, and in the South (and Standard English), the 'conclusion' meaning is not permitted in the negative.

In North-eastern dialects, obligation is expressed by *have to* or *(have) got to*. In the negative, this gives *haven't got to* a different meaning from that of Standard English: in the North-east, this means 'you are obliged not to', i.e. *you mustn't*, whereas further South, it means 'you are not obliged to'.

(69) *They have to keep ... extending and-that. They keep building.* (NECTE)

(70) *We've got to stay awake.* (NECTE)

(71) *Well you played the game, you got to pay the consequences.* (NECTE)

4.2.3. Double modals

There is a 'rule' of Standard English that only one modal verb can appear in a single verb phrase. Thus, *He must be able to do it* is 'grammatical' whilst **He must can do it* is not. In North-eastern dialects of English, this rule does not apply so long as the second modal is *can* or *could*. Thus the asterisked sentence would be grammatical in these dialects. More combinations of modals are allowed in Scots than in North-eastern English dialects, and more are allowed in the dialect of rural Northumberland than in that of urban Tyneside. For instance, the combination of *would* and *could* only appears in the urban area if a negative is involved, but also appears in the positive in rural Northumberland. Examples from McDonald (1981: 186–187) are:

(72) *I can't play on a Friday. I work late. I might could get it changed, though.*

(73) *The girls usually make me some (toasted sandwiches) but they mustn't could have made any today.*

(74) *He wouldn't could've worked, even if you had asked him.* (Tyneside)

(75) *A good machine clipper would could do it in half a day.* (Northumberland)

Whilst these double modal constructions are found in Scots and in some dialects of the southern USA, the only area of England in which they occur is Northumberland and Tyneside. Even here, they are rare and probably recessive: the only example found in the NECTE corpus is:

(76) *You'll probably not can remember, but during the war there wasn't wool.*

The rarity of these constructions in corpora may be due to the fact that the need to use them only arises in certain circumstances. I have witnessed first-hand the consternation caused when my (Northumbrian) husband announced to a dinner-party of linguists *We might could do with some more potatoes up here*. However, elicitation tests do seem to confirm that double modals are recessive in the North-east of England. McDonald (1981) found that 15.42% of respondents from north of Durham found sentences with double modals were either wholly acceptable and normal or somewhere between. In a later survey, Beal and Corrigan (2000) found that only 9.37% of a sample of 16–17-year-olds from Bedlington, Northumberland, found the same sentences either 'natural' or 'familiar', whilst 90.63% found them 'alien'. The acceptability of the constructions was higher amongst working-class children, who may well still hear them used by their grandparents.

4.2.4. Can *and* could

We saw in 4.2.3. above, that in the 'double modal' constructions used in the North-east of England, the second verb is always *can* or *could*. These two verbs behave less like other modal verbs in other ways. In Standard English, certain adverbs are placed before main verbs but after modals, thus *I only swam two lengths* but *I could only swim two lengths*. In the North-east, these adverbs are placed before *can* and *could*, as in the following examples from McDonald (1981: 214):

(77) *That's what I say to people. If they only could walk a little, they should thank God.*

(78) *She just can reach the gate.*

These two verbs are also used in perfective constructions, where Standard English would require *be able to*:

(79) *He cannot get a job since he's left school.* (Standard English *hasn't been able to*)

(80) *I says it's a bit of a disappointment, nurse. I thought I could've brought it back again.* (Standard English 'would have been able to'; both examples from McDonald 1981: 215–216).

Even in Standard English, *can* and *could* are less 'modal' than the other modal verbs, since they are the only pair with a genuine present/past tense relationship. In North-eastern dialects, they are even less 'modal', which perhaps accounts for the survival of 'double modal' constructions only with these verbs in second place.

4.3. Interrogatives

Dialects of the North-east have certain interrogative constructions in common with Scots. There is no evidence in either Shorrocks (1999) or Petyt (1985) for these constructions occurring further south.

In both Scotland and the North-east of England *how* is used for Standard English *why*, so *how's that?* is a request for an explanation of a previous statement. In both these dialects, it is also common for indirect questions to have the same constituent order as direct questions, as in:

(81) *I asked him did he want some tea.*

In all Northern dialects, *what* is used more frequently than *which* in interrogatives, and prepositions are placed at the end of interrogative clauses. An example is:

(82) *What pit did t'work at?* (Standard English 'At which pit did you work?) (Shorrocks 1999: 55).

4.4. Non-standard distribution of articles and possessives

4.4.1. The definite article

In dialects of the North-east of England, as in Scots, the definite article is used with a range of nouns which would not take it in Standard English. These are names of institutions, illnesses, periods of time, games, relatives and even numerals. Examples from the NECTE corpus are:

(83) *Going over to the girlfriend's concert first though.*

(84) *So what are you doing in college the morrow?*

(85) *I think Karen and Kell are going down there the-night.*

(86) *So I never really started work 'til I was about the fifteen.*

(87) *Well, I've got a little laddie that gans to the Beacon Lough.* ('Beacon Lough' is the name of a school)

There is no mention of such uses of the definite article in Petyt (1985), but Shorrocks (1999: 31–42) gives examples in all the categories mentioned above. It would appear that such non-standard uses of the definite article are more widespread in the North of England than had been supposed, since they occur in the southern part of this region (Greater Manchester) as well as the far North.

4.4.2. The indefinite article

In the North-east, the indefinite article is used with *one*. In Standard English, this can occur if an adjective is interposed as in:

(88) *Would you like a drink? Yes, I'll have a small one.*

In dialects of the North-east of England, this constraint does not apply, thus:

(89) *Would you like a drink? Aye, I'll have a one.*

4.4.3. Possessives

It is common throughout the North to use the first person plural possessive pronoun with the names of, or nouns denoting, family members. Examples are:

(90) *Like wor lass wears a ring on that finger.* (NECTE)

(91) *Wor Thomas'll be fourteen on Christmas Day, and wor little Steven, that's the seventh; he'll be ten.* (NECTE)

Here, the Tyneside pronoun *wor* corresponds to *our* elsewhere in the North. A (younger) sibling will be referred to as *our kid*, especially in Liverpool and Lancashire, where this phrase is also used to address a close friend (cf. *brother/ sister* in African American Vernacular English).

As in Scots, possessive pronouns are used throughout the North to refer to anything very familiar. Examples from Shorrocks (1999: 49–50) are:

(92) *Oh aye, I mun go to my Bingo.*

(93) *They came to their tea.*

4.5. Prepositions

As Shorrocks (1999: 211) says, a full account of prepositional usage in Northern dialects would involve a large-scale investigation, such as has not yet been carried out even for individual dialects. Here, I can only point out a number of prepositions which are used differently in Northern English dialects. Where Standard English uses *by* to express agency, Northern dialects use *off* or *with*.

(94) *I won't do nothing unless I get paid for it. Not off my mam and dad anyway*. (NECTE)

(95) *Geet* (got) *taught with the teachers* (Shorrocks 1999: 197).

Off is also used where Standard English would use *from* as in the following examples from NECTE:

(96) *I got blood tablets off the doctor.*

(97) *Well, my father come off a hawking family.*

(98) *Aye, my sister tapes some canny songs off the charts like.*

In Yorkshire, *while* is used where Standard English and, indeed, other Northern dialects, would use *(un)til*. If you ask any service worker in Yorkshire about the opening hours of their workplace, the reply will be, e.g. *Nine while five*. Examples are:

(99) *eight in a morning while eight at night* (CSU)

(100) *I'm stopping while Monday* (Petyt 1985: 236).

Down is used immediately before place-names, where Standard English would require another preposition, such as *in* or *to*. Examples are:

(101) *I normally just stay down the Bigg Market now or gan* ('go') *down the Quay Side*. (NECTE)

(102) *He works down Manchester* (Shorrocks 1999: 218).

In the North-east, *bit* is followed immediately by a noun, without *of* as in *a bit cheese* (cf. German *Ein bisschen Käse*). As example from the NECTE corpus is:

(103) *I felt awful, because it was a bit lassie ye know; 'cos she was ower thin.*

5. Clause constructions

5.1. Relative clauses

Romaine (1982) argues that, in the history of English, the *wh*-relative markers (*who*, *whom*, *whose*, *which*) enter the written language from the 15th century onwards. They occur first in more formal (particularly Latinate) styles and the nominative type (*who*, *which*) is confined to formal usage for longer than the object or genitive types. Romaine goes on to assert that "infiltration of WH into the relative system [...] has not really affected the spoken language" (1982: 212). We might, therefore, expect to find little use of the *wh*-relatives in Northern dialects.

In the traditional dialects of the North of England, as exemplified in the SED, the '*wh*-relatives' (*who*, *which*) are not used at all where the antecedent is subject. The question designed to elicit subject relative constructions was: *The woman next door says: The work in this garden is getting me down. You say: Well, get some help in. I know a man ___ will do it for you*. In Northumberland, in five locations, the zero (Ø) strategy was used, i.e. 'a chap would do it'; in three *at* was used; and in one location *that* was used, whilst, elsewhere in the North, zero, *as*, *at* and *that* were all used, with a tendency for *at* to prevail in Yorkshire and *as* in Lancashire (Orton and Halliday 1963: 1083–1084). Considering the distribution of responses to this question throughout England, Poussa writes:

> [W]e might argue that the development from the OE *se* [...] the relative to the modern system in the spoken language has generally passed through a ZERO stage, and that these areas [the extreme north and south] are relicts of that development (1986: 101).

On the other hand, the SED responses to the question eliciting the genitive relative show some use of *whose*, especially in Northumberland and Durham. In response to the question *That man's uncle was drowned last week. In other words, you might say, that's the chap* ____, *wh-* in the form of /hwe:z/ or /wi:z/ was given in seven locations in Northumberland, *at his uncle was* ... in one location and *as his uncle was* ... in the remaining one location. Elsewhere in the North, informants tend to avoid the relativisation strategy altogether in answering this question. For instance, in the Sheffield area, informant 32 from Ecclesfield, then a village just outside Sheffield, uses the following circumlocution:

(104) *That's the chap thou knows, his uncle drowned hissen* (Orton and Halliday 1963: 1086).

The distribution of relative markers in traditional dialects thus seems to confirm Romaine's view, since *wh*-relatives are only used in the genitive. More recent studies of relativisation in Northern English dialects (Beal and Corrigan 2002) indicate that, whilst *wh*-forms are becoming more common, zero relatives are still used with subject antecedents throughout the North, as the following examples show:

(105) *There's about twenty of them are walking along*. (NECTE)

(106) *We have a coach comes down, he's very good* (Petyt 1985: 238).

(107) *He may know a friend works in a blacksmith's* (Shorrocks 1999: 97).

However, *who* was found in both the NECTE and CSU corpora:

(108) *There'll be a canny few six formers there who'll be starting the year anyway*. (NECTE)

(109) *Everybody who lived there did something towards it*. (CSU)

In the SED material, instances of *what* as a relative were confined to Lancashire and Yorkshire as far as the 'Northern Counties' are concerned (Upton, Parry and Widdowson 1994: 489). More recently, though, Cheshire, Edwards and Whittle found that, in a survey conducted in schools throughout Britain, *what* was reported "far more frequently than any of the other non-standard relative pronoun forms" and "was reported just as frequently in the North of England as in the South". They conclude that "*What* [...] appears to be the preferred relative pronoun in the urban centres of Britain today" (1993: 68). Shorrocks (1999: 101) finds the use of relative *what* in 'modified' (i.e. more standardised) speech, and Petyt (1985: 238) notes that it is used with both human and non-human antecedents in West Yorkshire. This suggests that the *what* relative has indeed become more common in Northern dialects in the second half of the 20th century. However, Beal and Corrigan (2002) demonstrate that, whilst *what* is, indeed, common in the CSU corpus, it is much rarer in NECTE. Examples from CSU are:

(110) *You know t' gully what goes down river what runs down Millinger Street?*

(111) *He was a German what run this shop what I worked for.*

Throughout North of England, *that* is used as a relative marker with both human and non-human antecedents. In Yorkshire, *that* appears to be taking over from traditional *at*. The only example found in a subsample of the CSU is:

(112) *Kelvin at my first husband came out of.*

At looks and sounds like a reduced form of *that*, but Wright (1892: 91) argues that it is an independent form of Norse origin. Petyt (1985: 201) notes that in his corpus of West Yorkshire speech "[ðət] occurred 1250 times altogether in conversational styles, while the non-standard [ət] and [əz] were heard 234 and 21 times respectively". In the NECTE corpus, there is a slight (52.1%) preference for *wh-* with animate antecedents in subject position, but in the CSU corpus, *that* is preferred even in this context. Examples from CSU are:

(113) *There were a schoolteacher that lived in here in this house.*

(114) *I've got two other sisters that are both working.*

Rather than *at* being a reduced form of *that*, it is more likely that, in the Danelaw, modern dialects have artificially 'restored' *that* in place of the Norse *at* under the influence of Standard English.

In Standard English, only *wh*-relatives can be used in non-restrictive relative clauses. Whilst the vast majority of non-restrictive relative clauses in both the NECTE and CSU corpora have *wh*-relatives, there are exceptions, suggesting that this rule is not categorical in Northern dialects. Examples are (115) to (117). The word *that* was not stressed in any of them.

(115) *The old grammar school on Durham Road, that was a co-educational school.* (NECTE)

(116) *This is Louise, that was meant to come.* (NECTE)

(117) *You know Mr. Hill, that you got down there.* (CSU)

Throughout the North, *which* is used as a sentential relative. In these constructions, a whole clause or sentence constitutes the antecedent of *which*. Examples are:

(118) *He said that...er...Anthony Eden was going the wrong way, which to me was ridiculous*. (NECTE)

(119) *They're busy wondering where their next meal's going to come in and stuff, which I think is really sad.* (NECTE)

(120) *If it's say like at Doncaster or wherever he goes, which he's got t' car so it's no problem*. (CSU)

Shorrocks also finds this use of *which* in his corpus. He writes of "a most remarkable and extensive use of *which* [...] whereby it may refer to an antecedent, often of clausal proportions [...] or predict a following predicate [...] in some cases, the referent can be so difficult to define, that *which* often appears simply to link clauses." (1999: 104)

Accounts of Standard English such as Quirk and Greenbaum (1973: 380) suggest that *where* is only used with antecedents of place. However, in both the CSU and NECTE corpora there are several examples in which *where* is used with antecedents other than those of place.

(121) *A mortgage where we'd be paying t' same for twenty years*. (CSU)

(122) *He's just going through a phase where his reports are absolutely lousy*. (CSU)

(123) *Perhaps when she reaches an age where she can differentiate and realise that there is a dialect, she can use it if she wants to*. (NECTE)

(124) *Apart from that it's, you-know, the cases where you're washing the car, or gardening or something*. (NECTE)

In all these cases, *where* fulfills the same function as 'preposition + *which*' in Standard English.

5.2. Complement clauses

In Northern English dialects, as in Scots, complement clauses can be introduced by *for to*. This is not reported everywhere in the North: Petyt (1985) does not mention having found this construction in West Yorkshire. It is, however, reported both in the far north of the region (NECTE) and the south (Bolton). Shorrocks (1999: 248) notes that "*for to* is used extensively in the dialect as an infinitive marker". He goes on to point out that there were a number of instances of *for to* in the Northern Region recorded in the Incidental Material of the SED. There are also several examples of *for to* in the NECTE corpus.

(125) *He used to say keep that for Bella that was for me for to get bread in for the bairns*. (NECTE)

(126) *When I moved it just didn't enter me head for to say I wonder what if it'll be different*. (NECTE)

(127) *We were glad for to get out* (Shorrocks 1999:248).

It is worth noting that, of these examples only in (125) does *for to* carry the meaning 'in order to'.

In the North-east, *need* and *want* take a past participle as complement, rather than a present participle or infinitive, as in *my hair needs cut, that referee wants shot* (meaning only that the speaker is extremely displeased with the referee!)

5.3. Order of direct and indirect object

Shorrocks explains the order of direct and indirect objects in Northern English dialects as follows: "With two noun objects, the indirect precedes the direct. When the direct and indirect objects are both pronouns, either one may precede the other" (1999: 80). He gives the examples:

(128) *He couldn't give him it.*

(129) *I tan* (= 'took') *it her back.*

Petyt (1985: 236) found two examples of non-standard ordering in his corpus:

(130) *I didn't show it Harry.*

(131) *Open me t' door.* (= Standard English 'Open the door for me')

This suggests that, where a clause contains a pronoun and a noun, the pronoun comes first. In both sets of examples, the preposition *to* or *for* is omitted in the Northern dialect. This would appear to be general throughout the North, as examples were also found in NECTE:

(132) *So she won't give us it.*

(133) *Thanks, you're the first person that's give us a tip.*

6. Organisation of discourse

6.1. Right- and left-dislocation

In Northern English dialects, right-dislocation is used mainly in constructions in which the referent is identical to that of a noun phrase or pronoun within

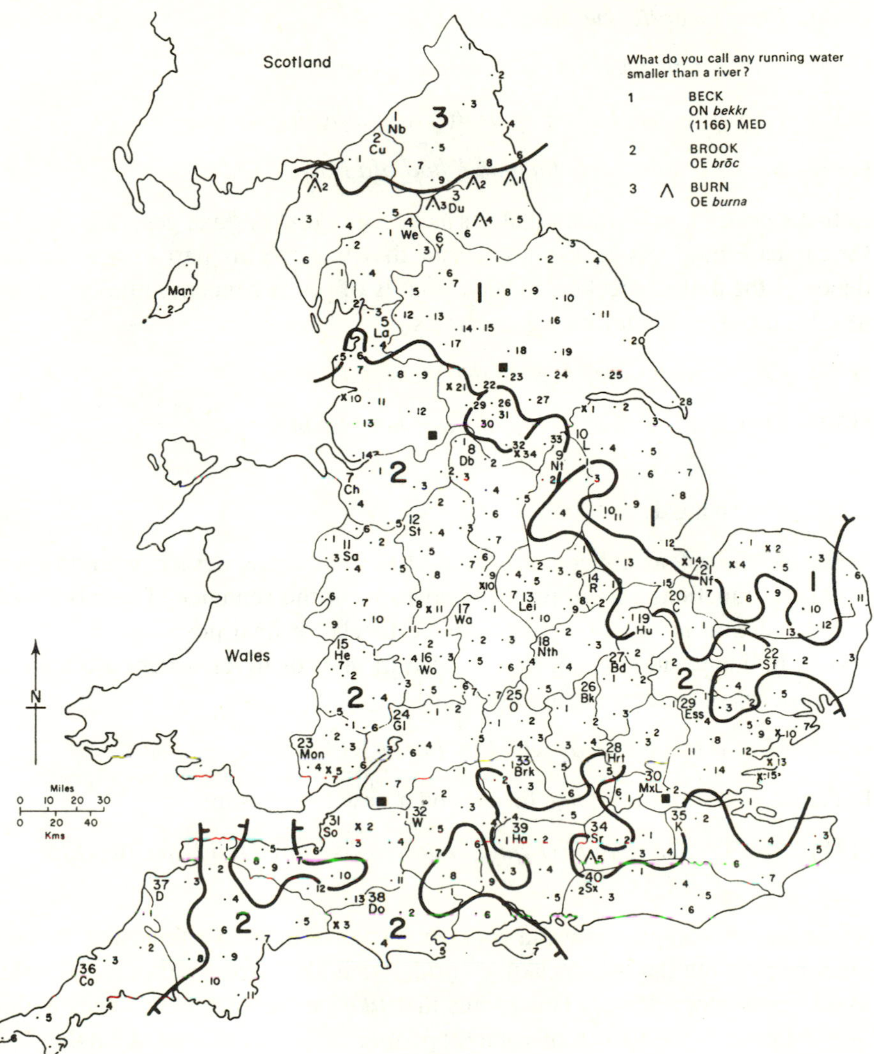

Map 1. Small River (Orton and Wright 1974: 87)

the clause. The constructions favoured for right-dislocation vary from one Northern dialect to another. In the North-east, typically only the noun phrase or pronoun is repeated, sometimes reinforced with *like* as in (134), whilst in Yorkshire, an auxiliary verb precedes it, as in (135). Shorrocks (1999: 85–86) reports both constructions in Bolton, as in (136) and (137).

(134) *I'm a Geordie, me, like.* (NECTE)

(135) *He's got his head screwed on, has Dave.*

(136) *They were like lightning, as they say,...his legs.*

(137) *Bet he'd done some laughing, had old Parr.*

Left-dislocation, in Northern dialects as in colloquial English generally, is used for topicalisation. Shorrocks points out that this "forms part of a wider tendency of the dialect speakers to state what is of prime concern initially" (1999: 88). He provides the following examples:

(138) *Coffee beans, they used to dry them outside.*

(139) *They'd no interest in you, the teachers hadn't.*

6.2. Focussing devices

In the North-east, as in Scots, *like* is used as a focussing device, with different discourse functions according to its position in the sentence. The most traditional function is as an emphatic device in clause-final position, as in (134) above. In this position it can also be used in interrogatives, where it often conveys a sense of interest or surprise as in:

(140) *How'd you get away with that like?* (NECTE)

In clause-initial position, *like* focuses on a new topic, as in:

(141) *Like for one round five quid, that was like three quid, like two-fifty each.* (NECTE)

As the above example shows, in younger speakers, in the North-east as in many other parts of the English-speaking world, *like* is also used within clauses, often as an explanatory device. This means that *like* can occur several times within one sentence in the speech of younger people in the North-east of England, as in (141) above. Another usage which adds to the ubiquity of *like* in this dialect is the recent (global) introduction of *like* as a quotative. In the NECTE corpus, the only speakers to use this were those born after 1974. An example of this, from a speaker born in 1977, is:

(142) *And they were like "Your .. best friend's going on holiday with your boyfriend?"*

7. Lexis

Dialects of English in the North of England are distinct both from dialects of other regions, and from each other, in terms of their lexicons as well as their phonologies and grammars. This is due largely to a number of historical factors. Most of the North (excluding the North-east) lies within the Danelaw, consequently dialects within the 'Scandinavian belt' retain a number of words of Norse origin. This is best illustrated in Map 1 below, showing the distribution of SED informants' responses to the question: *What do you call any stretch of running water smaller than a river?* In the far North-east, the Anglo-Saxon word *burn* is used, and in the area bordering on the North-west Midlands, another Anglo-Saxon word *brook* is found. However, in a 'belt' stretching north-west to south-east from Cumbria to Yorkshire, the word used is the Norse *beck*. These words are retained in place-names: *Troutbeck* in Cumbria, *Otterburn* in Northumberland, *Preston Brook* in Cheshire, and straw polls in class have revealed that they are still used by young speakers from these areas.

Some Norse words are found in North-eastern dialects: *lop* ('flea'), *garth* ('yard'), *gate* ('street'), the latter two found in street names such as *Garth Heads* in Newcastle, *Marygate* in Sheffield. However, a much greater number of Norse words is to be found in the dialects of Yorkshire, where words such as *lake* ('play'), *addled* ('earned') and *throng* ('busy') are found. Some words thought to be of Norse origin are used throughout the North. The most notable, because most frequently used, of these, are the affirmative and negative *aye* and *nay*. The NECTE corpus has numerous instances of the interviewer (born in Gateshead) using *aye* to encourage the informant to keep the floor, as in the interchange below in which I is the interviewer and S the informant:

(143) S *My father went to work in Clarkies.*
I *Did he? Aye there's a lot of people working there. There's a lot of people work in Clarkies.*
S *Aye in Clarkies, went to work in Clarkies…*
I *Aye.*

In other cases, Northern dialects retain words which have become archaic elsewhere. A good example of this is the retention of *lads* and *lasses* as colloquial alternatives for Standard English *boys* and *girls*. Examples from the NECTE corpus are:

(144) *I reckon lasses aren't as naive as they used to be.*

(145) *I've got three lads, no, four lads and three lasses.*

In (145), the informant is answering a question about how many children she has. When she refers to these children collectively, she uses the equally archaic northern word *bairns* as in (125) above.

Other influences are found in specific areas of the North. A number of Romani words occur in the North-east, many of which are still used, sometimes with developments in meaning, by young people on Tyneside. Examples are *cush* 'good'; *gadgie* 'old man' from Romani *gadgio* 'a non-Romani'; *radge/radgie* 'crazy/crazy person'; *charver* 'a disreputable working-class youth', from Romani *charvo* 'a boy'. The last of these has been adopted by young people on Tyneside to label a particular sub-group, known elsewhere in England as *townies*.

Speakers in the North of England use a range of terms of endearment, some of which are regionally distributed. These are often used in service encounters, and can cause misunderstandings when the addressee is a southerner, who believes that s/he is being patronised. The most widespread term is *love*, which I have observed in Sheffield being used by a male shop assistant and a male bus-driver, each addressing middle-aged male customers. This use of *love* between male peers has also been observed in Leeds, but elsewhere, even in the North, this would be unusual, as the normal pattern is for the terms to be used by older speakers to younger speakers and in male-female or female-male interactions. In the North-east *bonny lad* and *son* are used between males of the same age, and thus are equivalent to *mate* elsewhere. Regionally distributed terms of endearment are *pet* (North-east), *chuck* (Lancashire), *cock* (Lancashire and parts of Yorkshire), and *duck* (South Yorkshire). The latter three, like West Midlands *chick*, all refer to domestic fowl. *Son* is also used in the North-east as a term of address to dogs, so that a man in this region may address his wife as *pet* and his dog as *son*. *Man* is used in the North-east as a term of address to males or females (cf. US *guys*), often expressing annoyance or impatience. In the following example the speaker implies that the interviewer has asked her a stupid question, i.e. 'where do you go for holidays?':

(146) *I divn't gan for holidays man. I wish I could.*

A student in Newcastle reported to me that he had overheard an exasperated young man say to his partner 'Howay man, woman, man!'

One area of the lexicon to which little attention has hitherto been paid by dialectologists is the use of discourse markers, such as words and phrases used to gain the attention of an addressee, or to express surprise, annoyance, etc. These are worth noting, as they are often regionally distributed and highly salient. In the North of England, terms used to gain attention range from *ho-*

way in the North-east, to *ey up* in Lancashire and Yorkshire and *eck eck* in Liverpool.

8. Conclusion

This chapter has set out some of the distinctive morphological, syntactic and lexical features of northern dialects of English. It is apparent that, whilst some features, such as the 'Northern Subject Rule' (3.1.1.) and the regularised pattern of reflexives (2.3.4.) are found throughout the North of England, others, such as definite article reduction in Lancashire and Yorkshire (2.5.1.) and double modals in the North-east (4.2.3.) are restricted to particular regional dialects within the North. Examples used in this chapter have mostly been taken from four corpora collected in the second half of the 20th century, from Tyneside, Sheffield, Bolton and West Yorkshire. This leaves huge gaps in the geographical coverage, which need to be filled by the collection of new data from cities such as Carlisle, Lancaster, Liverpool and Manchester, and the processing of data already collected elsewhere. What is clear is that, whilst a sense of 'northernness' is felt by citizens of all these places, there are distinctive features of dialect which mark them off from each other.

Exercises and study questions

1. What features of Northern English syntax and/or morphology described in this chapter can also be found in dialects of Scottish English? Are these found only near the Scottish border, or are they more widespread throughout the North?

2. What features of Northern English syntax and/or morphology described in this chapter can also be found in Irish English? Is there any historical evidence for Irish settlement in the areas of England in which these features are found?

3. What evidence can be found in this chapter that the English dialects in the North of England can be divided into the 'far North' and the 'middle North'?

4. With reference to this chapter, and to the further reading recommended in the bibliography, discuss the extent to which English dialects in the North of England are losing their distinctive morphological and syntactic features under the influence of Standard English.

5. What evidence for variation between 'full' and 'reduced' forms of the definite article can you find in the recorded free passage on the CD-ROM? Can you discern any pattern to the variation? (Read Jones 2002).

6. What other features of Northern English dialect grammar and morphology can you find in the recorded passage?

Selected references

Please consult the General references for titles mentioned in the text but not included in the references below. For a full bibliography see the accompanying CD-ROM.

Beal, Joan
1993 The grammar of Tyneside and Northumbrian English. In: Milroy and Milroy (eds.), 187–242.
1997 Syntax and morphology. In: Jones (ed.), 335–377.

Beal, Joan and Karen Corrigan
2000 Comparing the present with the past to predict the future for Tyneside English. *Newcastle and Durham Working Papers in Linguistics* 6: 13–30.
2002 Relativisation in Tyneside and Northumbrian English. In: Patricia Poussa (ed.), *Relativisation on the North Sea Littoral*, 125–134. Berlin: Lincom Europa.

Cave, Andrew
2001 Language variety and communicative style as local and subcultural identity in a South Yorkshire coalmining community. Ph.D. dissertation, University of Sheffield.

Cheshire, Jenny, Vivian Edwards and Pam Whittle
1993 Non-standard English and dialect levelling. In: Milroy and Milroy (eds.), 53–96.

Ihalainen, Ossi
1994 The dialects of England since 1776. In: Burchfield (ed.), 197–274.

Jones, Mark
2002 The origin of definite article reduction in northern English dialects. *English Language and Linguistics* 6: 325–346.

McDonald, Christine
1981 Variation in the use of modal verbs with special reference to Tyneside English. Ph.D. dissertation, University of Newcastle.

McDonald, Christine and Joan Beal
1987 Modal verbs in Tyneside English. *Journal of the Atlantic Provinces Linguistic Association* 9: 42–55.

Orton, Harold and Wilfrid J. Halliday (eds.)
1962 *Survey of English Dialects: The Basic Material*, Volume 1, Parts 1, 2 and 3. Leeds: Arnold.

Orton, Harold and Natalia Wright
1974 *A Word Geography of England*. London/New York/San Francisco: Seminar Press.

Petyt, Malcolm K.
1985 *Dialect and Accent in Industrial West Yorkshire*. Amsterdam/Philadelphia: Benjamins.

Poussa, Patricia
1986 Historical implications of the distribution of the zero pronoun relative in Modern English dialects: looking backwards towards OE from Map S5 of the *Linguistic Atlas of England*. In: Sven Jacobson (ed.), *Papers from the Third Scandinavian Symposium on Syntactic Variation, Stockholm, May 11–12, 1985*, 99–117. Stockholm: Almqvist and Wiksell.

Poussa, Patricia (ed.)
2002 *Relativisation on the North Sea Littoral*. Berlin: Lincom Europa.

Quirk, Randolph and Sidney Greenbaum
1973 *A University Grammar of English*. Harlow: Longman.

Romaine, Suzanne
1982 *Socio-historical Linguistics: Its Status and Methodology*. Cambridge: Cambridge University Press.

Shorrocks, Graham
1999 *A Grammar of the Dialect of the Bolton Area*. Frankfurt am Main: Lang.

Tagliamonte, Sali
1998 *Was/were* variation across the generations: view from the city of York. *Language Variation and Change* 10: 153–191.

Tagliamonte, Sali and Rika Ito
2002 Think *really different*: continuity and specialisation in the English dual form adverbs. *Journal of Sociolinguistics* 6: 236–266.

Trudgill, Peter
1984 Standard English in England. In: Trudgill (ed.), 32–44.

Wakelin, Martyn
1983 The stability of English dialect boundaries. *English World-Wide* 4: 1–15.

Wright, Joseph
1892 *A Grammar of the Dialect of Windhill, in the West Riding of Yorkshire*. London: English Dialect Society.

The dialect of East Anglia: morphology and syntax

Peter Trudgill

1. Morphology

1.1. Present tense verb forms

1.1.1. Third-person singular zero

Probably the best-known morphological East Anglian dialect feature is third-person present-tense singular zero. East Anglian dialects have zero-marking for all persons of the verb in the present tense: *he go*, *she come*, *that say*. Of the localities investigated by the *Survey of English Dialects* (SED), this feature was found in all the Suffolk localities, in northeastern Essex, and in all of Norfolk except the Fens. Observations suggest that this geographical pattern is also valid for the Modern Dialects of the early twenty-first century. David Britain, an expert on the dialects of the Fens, confirms (personal communication) that the Cambridgeshire town of Wisbech and its Norfolk suburb of Emneth both have *-s*. Third-person singular zero is a social dialect feature (see Trudgill 1974). This has the consequence that a number of middle-class East Anglians do not use it at all, and that others use it variably.

One interesting question is why East Anglia is the only area of Britain to have this system. Other areas either have the Standard English system, or else have *-s* for all persons: *I goes*, *we likes* etc. My theory (see Trudgill 2002) about this is that it has to do with the "invasion" of Norwich in the 16th century by the remarkable group of people we now know as the Strangers. These were Protestants fleeing from religious persecution in the Low Countries – modern Belgium and Holland – at the hands of their Spanish Catholic rulers. They were mostly native speakers of Dutch (Flemish) but there was also a good proportion of speakers of French. People who are learning English as a foreign language often have trouble with the irregular third-person singular *-s* of Standard English. I hypothesize that the more or less simultaneous arrival into Norwich of the new *he likes* form from the north of England, and the *he like* forms from the foreigner English of the Strangers, both in competition with the old *he liketh* forms, led to a situation where there was competition between these three forms, *-th*, *-s*, and -Ø, in which the most regular form was the one which eventually won. It then subsequently spread outwards from Norwich, which was the second largest city in England at the time, to the whole of the area which it dominated culturally and economically, namely East Anglia (see Trudgill 2002).

1.1.2. To be

The present tense of the verb *to be* in Norfolk is identical with that in Standard English: *I am*, *he/she/it is*, *we/you/they are*. But there is one interesting exception. This concerns the phenomenon of *presentative be*. Speakers normally say *I am* but may nevertheless announce themselves, on arriving somewhere, by saying *Here I be!*. Similarly, if they are looking for someone and find him, they may exclaim *There he be!*. That is, *be* is used for all persons when the speaker is presenting themselves or someone or something they have found or come across. These forms probably reflect an earlier stage of the dialect when *be* was the normal present-tense form in all meanings, as in parts of the West Country where speakers still say *I be*, *you be* etc.

1.1.3. Have

Unless the next word begins with a vowel, the form *have* is most often pronounced without the final *v*: /(h)æ/, /(h)ɛ/ or /(h)ə/: *Ha'you got some?*

1.2. Past tense verb forms

1.2.1. Irregular verbs: past tense forms and past participles

The East Anglian dialect has a number of differences in verb-formation from Standard English. In some cases like *draw*, Standard English irregular verbs are regular. In other cases, Standard English regular verbs are irregular: for example, the past tense of *snow* is *snew*. In many other cases, partial regularisation has taken place, so that there are two forms instead of three, as with *break*, or one form instead of two, as with *come*. Typical East Anglian verb forms include:

Present	**Past**	**Past Participle**
begin	*begun*	*begun*
beat	*beat/bet*	*beat/bet*
become	*become*	*become*
bite	*bit*	*bit*
blow	*blew*	*blew*
break	*broke*	*broke*

(continued)

Present	Past	Past Participle
bring	*brung*	*brung/brought*
catch	*catched*	*catched*
choose	*chose*	*chose*
come	*come*	*come*
do	*done*	*done*
draw	*drawed*	*drawed*
drink	*drunk*	*drunk*
drive	*driv*	*driven*
forget	*forgot*	*forgot*
give	*give/gon*	*give(n)*
grow	*growed*	*growed*
know	*knowed*	*knowed*
mow	*mew*	*mown*
owe	*ewe*	*own*
ride	*rid*	*rid(den)*
rise	*ris*	*ris(en)*
ring	*rung*	*rung*
run	*run*	*run*
see	*see*	*see(n)*
shake	*shook*	*shook*
show	*shew*	*shown*
shriek	*shruck*	*shruck*
snow	*snew*	*snown*
speak	*spoke*	*spoke*
steal	*stole*	*stole*
stink	*stunk*	*stunk*
swim	*swum*	*swum*
take	*took*	*took*
thaw/thow	*thew*	*thew*
teach	*teached*	*teached*
tear	*tore*	*tore*
tread	*trod*	*trod*
wake	*woke*	*woke*
wear	*wore*	*wore*
wrap	*wrop*	*wrop*
write	*writ*	*writ*

Some of these forms are very archaic, especially *gon* and *wrop. Shew*, as the past tense of *show*, is, on the other hand, very widely used and is still very frequently found in the speech even of people whose English is not very dialectal. *Chose* and *choose* can be pronounced identically (see Trudgill, this volume).

1.2.2. Auxiliary and full verb do

As in most English dialects, in East Anglia, although the past tense of *do* is *done* rather than Standard English *did*, this is not true of the auxiliary verb *do*, where the past tense is *did*:

(1) *You done it, did you?*

1.2.3. The past tense of be

The past tense of *to be* is *wus* /wʊz/ for all persons in the positive, but *weren't* for all persons in the negative (see Anderwald 2002):

(2) a.

Singular	**Plural**
I wus	*we wus*
you wus	*you wus*
he/she/it wus	*they wus*

b.

Singular	**Plural**
I weren't	*we weren't*
you weren't	*you weren't*
he/she/it weren't	*they weren't*

The word *weren't* is pronounced in a number of different ways: /wɜːnt/, /waːnt/, /wɔːnt/, /wɒnt/. The older dialect, on the other hand, had *war* /waː/ for all persons in the positive.

1.2.4. Dare

The archaic English past tense form of the verb *to dare* was *durst.* In the East Anglian dialect, this has become the present tense as well:

(3) *You dursn't/dussn't.*
'You dare not.'

In less dialectal local speech, the Standard English negative present tense form of *dare*, *daren't*, is still distinctive in that it is pronounced as two syllables, rhyming with *parent*, unlike in the rest of the country where it is normally pronounced as a single syllable. This is true even of the speech of speakers who otherwise have few regional features in their pronunciation.

1.3. Present tense negative of *have* and *be*

Corresponding to the more geographically widespread *ain't*, the negative present tense form of *be* and of *have* in East Anglia is most often /ɛnt/ or /ɪnt/ for all persons:

(4) a. *I in't a-comen.*
'I'm not coming.'
b. *I in't done it yet.*
'I havent done it yet.'

1.4. Plurals

The older dialect had a number of archaic plurals:

(5) *house* *housen*
mouse *meece*

Forby (1830) also cites *cheesen* 'cheeses', and *closen* 'clothes'.

As in many other dialects, it is common for measurement nouns not to take a plural *-s* after numerals: *four foot*, *three mile.* In telling the time, *25* is generally *five and twenty*:

(6) a. *That leave at five and twenty to.*
'It leaves at twenty-five to.'
b. *Thass five and twenty past four.*
'It's twenty-five past four.'

1.5. The definite article

The normally appears in the form *th'* if the next word begins with a vowel: *th'old house, in th'oven.*

In the older dialect, the definite article could be omitted after prepositions of motion and before nouns denoting certain familiar domestic objects:

(7) a. *he walked into house*
b. *put th'apples into basket*
c. *she come out of barn*

1.6. Pronouns

1.6.1. Personal pronouns

Unstressed *I* is pronounced with the reduced vowel [ə], even at the end of a sentence, so that *can I?* is pronounced *can a?* rhyming with *banner*. Unstressed *they* is pronounced *thee: Where are thee?* Stressed *it* in Standard English corresponds to *that* in East Anglia:

(8) a. *Thass rainen.*
'It's raining.'
b. *Ah, that wus me what done it.*
'Yes, it was me that did it.'

In the older dialect, *thaself* was also found as the reflexive:

(9) *The dog hurt thaself.*

But now this has disappeared. In the older dialect, *that* also appeared as /tə/, often shown in dialect literature as *ta* or *t'*: *Ta fruz* 'it froze'. This has now also disappeared except in the concessive expression *t'is true* 'It's true'. In unstressed position, however, *it* occurs:

(10) *I don't like it, thass no good.*

It is not clear how we should explain this development of *that* as the stressed form of the pronoun. Poussa (1997) has argued that it goes back to the Danish of the Viking period: modern Scandinavian languages still have *det* meaning 'it'. This seems highly unlikely, however, since no other Danelaw area has it; Danish has not been spoken in East Anglia for a thousand years or so; and we have no record of it for East Anglia before Forby (1830). It seems much more likely to be the result of a perfectly normal grammaticalisation process: Diessel (2000) shows that demonstratives very frequently become third-person pronouns as a result of grammaticalisation. The fact that *it* is most usually pronounced as a possibly rather indistinct [əʔ] may have assisted this process.

You...together functions as a second person plural pronoun:

(11) a. *Where are you together?*
b. *Come you on together!*

The possessive pronouns *mine*, *yours*, *his*, *hers*, *ours*, *theirs* are used to refer to a place where somebody lives:

(12) *Less go round mine.*
'Let's go to my place.'

1.6.2. Pronoun substitution

In the southwest of England, the pronoun forms *he*, *she*, *we*, *they* can occur as grammatical objects, and *him*, *her*, *us* can occur as grammatical subjects. This feature, often known as *pronoun exchange*, has not yet been subjected to any definitive analysis, but it seems possible that what happens is that the Standard English subject pronouns occur as objects when the pronoun is emphasised, and object pronouns as subjects when the pronoun is not emphasised. Something similar occurs or occurred in southern East Anglia, although in this case we see only subject pronouns as objects. Charles Benham's *Essex Ballads*, first published in Colchester in the 1890s, contain a number of instances of this feature. Here is one example (italics are mine):

Tha's where they're gooin', are they? Pas' the mill,
Along the fiel' path leadin' tard the woods;
I'll give *he* what for some day, that I will,
For walkin' out 'ith that ere bit of goods.
J'yer hear him call "Good arternune" to me?
He think he's doin' of it there some tune.
Next time I ketch him out along o' *she*,
Blest if I don't give *he* "good arternune".

The evidence of these ballads and of the SED records suggests that in southern East Anglia the phenomenon was more restricted than in the southwest. The southwestern usage of *him*, *her*, *us* as subjects does not seem to have been a possibility; we witness merely the use of *he*, *she*, *we*, *they* as objects.

1.6.3. Relative pronouns

The relative pronoun is *what* for both animates and inanimates:

(13) a. *He's the one what done it.*
b. *A book what I read.*

1.6.4. Demonstrative pronouns

As in many other dialects, the distal plural form is not *those* but *them* e.g. *Eat you them carrots* 'Eat those carrots'. *Here* and *there* are often used as reinforcers:

(14) a. *this here book*
b. *them there books*

1.7. Prepositions

As in nonstandard dialects generally, there are many differences of preposition usage between the local dialects and Standard English. Distinctively East Anglian usages include:

(15) a. *Are you comen round John's?* (i.e. to John's [place])
b. *I was round John's*. (i.e. at John's [place])
c. *I'm goen down the city*. (i.e. to Norwich from the suburbs)
d. *I'm goen up the city*. (i.e. to Norwich from the country)

Standard English *of* is usually [ə] but is pronounced *on* when stressed:

(16) a. *What do you think on it?*
b. *There was a couple on 'em.*

Alonga, derived from *along with* or, more likely, *along of*, means 'together with':

(17) *Come you alonga me!*

1.8. Temporal adverbials

The traditional dialects of northern East Anglia not only had forms such as *t'night* and *t'day* but also *t'year*, *t'mornen*, *t'week*, meaning 'this year, this morning, this week'.

1.9. *Now*

An East Anglian feature found at most social levels is the use of *now* rather than *just* in expressions such as *I'm now coming.*

1.10. *Wholly*

Wholly, normally pronounced /hʊliː ~ hʊlə/ is widely used as an intensifier, e.g. *That wholly poured.*

2. Syntax

2.1. Conjunctions

2.1.1. Conjunction do

In the older dialects of East Anglia, the word *do* is used as conjunction which means something like 'otherwise'. The *English Dialect Dictionary* shows that this usage was once found in the dialects of Norfolk, Suffolk, Cambridgeshire and northern Essex.

This seems to be the result of grammaticalisation processes. Consider the following examples from local dialect literature:

(18) a. *Don't you take yours off, do you'll get rheumatism.*
b. *Don't you tell your Aunt Agatha about the coupons, do she'll mob me.*

In these examples, the insertion of *because if you* will provide forms readily comprehensible to speakers of all English dialects:

(19) *Don't take yours off,* [*because if you*] *do you'll get rheumatism.*

It seems, then, that the development of the conjunction *do* began with an initial stage in which speakers simply omitted phrases such as *because if you*. A second stage in the development of a more abstract meaning can be illustrated by the following:

(20) *Have the fox left? No that ain't, do Bailey would've let them went.*

Here the link between the two parts of the sentence is more abstract and complicated. The originally present-tense form *do* is being applied in a past-tense context, and *do* is used in spite of the fact that we would have to insert a form of *have*, not *do*, to get a full form of the sentence:

(21) *No that ain't, [because if that had] Bailey would've let them went.*

The third and final stage in the process is demonstrated in examples like:

(22) a. *That's a good job we come out of that there field, do he'd've had us!*
b. *We stabled them elephants right in the middle, do we should've capsized.*

Here present tense *do* is once again being used in past tense contexts, but it is also being used, in spite of the fact that it is a positive verb form, in a situation where a full form of the sentence would require a negative verb:

(23) *That's a good job we come out of that there field, [because if we hadn't] he'd've had us!*

This feature is also found in parts of the American South: it has been reported for North Carolina and northern Florida (see Trudgill 1997).

2.1.2. *Conjunction* time

The older East Anglian dialect employed *time* as a conjunction in the sense of Standard English 'while':

(24) *Go you and have a good wash time I git tea ready.*

We can assume that this is the result of grammaticalisation processes involving the deletion of phonological material such as [*during the*] *time.*

2.1.3. *Conjunction* (nor) yet

The form *yet* may function as a conjunction equivalent to *nor* in constructions such as (25):

(25) a. *There weren't no laburnum, yet no lilac.*
b. *There wouldn't be nothen nor yet nobody to start things off again.*

2.1.4. *Conjunction* more

The form (*no*) *more* can function as a conjunction or conjunct equivalent to *nor* or *neither*:

(26) *The fruit and vegetables weren't as big as last year, more weren't the taters and onions.*

2.2. Multiple negation

As in most nonstandard dialects of English, multiple negation is usual. However, East Anglian English extends this feature to include constructions with *hardly*:

(27) *I couldn't find hardly none on 'em.*

2.3. Imperatives

The second person pronoun is usually explicit in East Anglian imperatives:

(28) a. *Go you on!*
b. *Shut you up!*

This is true even when the imperative is strengthened by using the auxiliary verb do:

(29) *Do you sit down!*

2.4. *Ought*

Typical East Anglian forms of this verb, even in the speech of people who otherwise have used few dialect forms, involve negative and interrogative forms with the past tense auxiliary *did*:

(30) a. *You didn't ought to do that, did you?*
b. *Did you ought to do that?*

2.5. Progressive aspect

Older East Anglian dialect speakers sometimes uses non-progressive verb forms where other dialects would use the progressive forms with *-ing*:

(31) a. (*The*) *kittle bile!*
'The kettle's boiling!'
b. *I go to Norwich tomorra.*
'I'm going to Norwich tomorrow.'

2.6. *A*-verbing

As in many other dialects, it is usual in continuous aspect forms for participles in *-ing* (which is pronounced '-en' [ən]) to be preceded by *a-* [ə]:

(32) a. *I'm a-runnen* d. *we're a-runnen*
b. *you're a-runnen* e. *you're a-runnen*
c. *he's a-runnen* f. *they're a-runnen*

The history of participles as nominal forms can still be seen from the fact that such transitive verb forms are normally followed by *on* (which corresponds to Standard English *of* – see above):

(33) a. *He wus a-hitten on it.*
'He was hitting it.'
b. *I'm a-taken on em.*
'I'm taking them.'
c. *What are you a-doen on?*
'What are you doing?'

2.7. *Matter*

Standard English *It doesn't matter* is most usually *That don't matters*. The origin of this form with *-s* is not known.

2.8. Street names

Street names involving the names of saints typically omit the word *street*. Thus, in Norwich, *St Augustine's Street*, *St Giles' Street*, *St Benedict's Street*, *St George's Street*, are normally referred to as *St Augustine's*, *St Giles'*, *St Benedict's*, *St George's*. Note that this is only possible if the official street name actually includes the form *Street* rather than *Avenue*, *Crescent* etc. Thus, in Norwich *St Stephen's Road* has to be so called, and *St Stephen's* can refer only to *St Stephen's Street*.

Exercises and study questions

1. Identify and comment on the negation features in the following examples:
   a. He weren't there.
   b. I in't done it yet.
   c. I couldn't find hardly none on 'em.
2. Specify for each of the examples in (1) and the following examples whether it is a distinctly East Anglian feature (not or very rarely found elsewhere in the British Isles) or rather a feature frequently met with in the British Isles:
   a. I'll give he what for some day.
   b. That wus me what done it.
   c. Come you on together.
   d. You dursn't!
   e. She come out of barn.
   f. Norwich is only three mile away.
   g. Shut you up!

3. Which morphological feature of the East Anglian dialect is unique in the British Isles and rather characteristic of American dialects?
4. Comment on the following two examples:
   a. He wus a-hitten on it.
   b. What are you a-doen on?
5. Which conjunctions do the East Anglian dialects, especially the older varieties, use instead of Standard English *while*, *nor*, *otherwise*, or *else*? Comment on these East Anglian conjunctions from the point of grammaticalization.

Selected references

Please consult the General references for titles mentioned in the text but not included in the references below. For a full bibliography see the accompanying CD-ROM.

Diessel, Holger
2000 *Demonstratives: Form, Function and Grammaticalisation.* Amsterdam/Philadelphia: Benjamins.

Forby, Robert
1830 *The Vocabulary of East Anglia.* London: Nichols.

Poussa, Patricia
1997 Derivation of *it* from *that* in eastern dialects of British English. In: Raymond Hickey and Stanislaw Puppel (eds.), *Linguistic History and Linguistic Modelling: A Festschrift for Jacek Fisiak on his 60th Birthday*, 691–699. Berlin/New York: Mouton de Gruyter.

Trudgill, Peter
1997 British vernacular dialects in the formation of American English: the case of East Anglian *do*. In: Raymond Hickey and Stanislaw Puppel (eds.), *Linguistic History and Linguistic Modelling: A Festschrift for Jacek Fisiak on his 60th Birthday*, 749–758. Berlin/New York: Mouton de Gruyter.
2002 *Sociolinguistic Variation and Change.* Edinburgh: Edinburgh University Press.

English dialects in the Southwest: morphology and syntax

Susanne Wagner

1. Background

The Southwest or, to use a more traditional label, the West Country, has figured prominently in dialectological investigations for centuries. From a modern viewpoint, one can only guess at the reasons behind the considerable attention that has been attributed to West Country English, particularly in the 19th century. One of the major factors causing interest in the region certainly was its rural character and relative remoteness, which to a certain extent still survives to the present day. Traditionally, attributes such as "rustic" or "primitive" were associated with inhabitants of the West Country and their speech patterns.

No matter what reasons may have triggered the interest in West Country dialects, it resulted in an amount of studies, both professional (i.e. linguistic) and non-professional, that is almost unique in the field. Writers such as William Barnes or Thomas Hardy use vernacular speech in their poems and novels. Barnes also published a treatise on the grammar of his home country, Dorset, which shows a certain indebtedness to, for example, Frederic Elworthy's work on Somerset English (cf. Barnes [1844] 1994; Elworthy [1875] 1965a, [1877] 1965b).

Experts writing on West Country English list a wide array of peculiarities in the variety. Among those most widely known in pronunciation is the voicing of initial fricatives, which is also extensively used in Barnes' poetry and Hardy's novels. But in contrast with most other traditional as well as modern varieties, West Country dialect shows numerous morpho-syntactic idiosyncrasies as well. The sheer number of features and their occurrence in a relatively restricted area help further the claim that the West Country is unique as a dialect region.

For the sake of simplicity, "the West Country" or "the Southwest" will be considered as a homogeneous linguistic area here. The core of this area is constituted by the counties of Cornwall, Devon, Dorset, Somerset, and Wiltshire, while its boundaries are formed by parts of the adjoining counties of Gloucestershire, Oxfordshire, Worcestershire, and Herefordshire, which create a transition zone. Hampshire and Berkshire are not included; Berkshire is not often covered in studies of the Southwest, due to its "transitional nature"

(Ihalainen 1994: 211), while Hampshire shows a high degree of mixture of features from the Southwest and Southeast, justifying its exclusion (see also Altendorf and Watt, this volume.)

The following sections will mostly follow Rogers (1979), both in outline and content (grammatical features to be considered), whose *Wessex Dialect* to this day presents one of the most detailed accounts of the variety. Rogers' study will provide the background against which modern corpus data will be judged. Unless otherwise stated, all examples stem from the Freiburg English Dialect Corpus (FRED) compiled at Freiburg University (DFG research grant KO 1181/1-1–3). Additional material stems from the fieldworker notebooks of the Survey of English Dialects (SED). As with most other regions, the West Country exhibits a mixture of features that can be categorized according to their distribution (see section 9): a) exclusively Southwestern features; b) features also found in other (regional) dialects; and c) general features of spoken non-standard English. Sections 2 to 8 will first treat features irrespective of these categories.

2. Articles

The observed over-use of the definite article in certain environments in West Country dialects is a possible candidate for substrate influence from Celtic languages. While this feature has been researched in Irish English (see Filppula, this volume), there are to my knowledge no studies that link West Country dialects with other Celtic-influenced Englishes, although the connections are well-known. Non-standard uses occur for example with diseases (*the chicken pox*, *the arthritis*), quantifying expressions (e.g. *the both*, *the most*), holidays (*the Christmas*), geographical units and institutions (*the church*, *the county Devon*), etc.

The indefinite article, on the other hand, often occurs as *a* also before vowels, and in general in such a reduced form that the non-native might not even hear it at all – "but the intention to say it is there and if the speaker were asked to repeat slowly he would definitely include it" (Rogers 1979: 31). Modern examples from FRED include the ones in (1):

(1) a. [Interviewer: *Did you take any exam? For example, did you take a scholarship exam to the County School*?]
Yes, I took it two years following, and failed ***the both*** *of them.* (FRED Con_007)
b. *Well father couldn't drive* ***the both*** *engines* … (FRED Som_014)

c. *Going smashed the gate to pieces, broke* ***the both*** *shafts off old Harry's milk float.* (FRED Wil_003)
d. *...but I stayed on until* ***the Christmas***. (FRED Con_008)
e. *...we had to walk a mile to* ***the school*** *and back.* (FRED Som_012)
f. *…and naturally her father was* ***a older*** *man when she was a young girl, …* (FRED Con_009)
g. *…about three pound* ***a acre***. (FRED Som_031)
h. *A journeyman is* ***a apprentice*** *that has served his apprenticeship …* (FRED Dev_002)
i. *If* ***a end*** *comes off he automatically stops, see.* (FRED Wil_001)

3. Adjectives

Although the ending *-en* meaning 'made of' is also found in Standard English (StE), it is supposedly more productive and thus more frequent in the Southwest, yielding such phrases as *bricken bridge*, *dirten floor*, or *wheaten straw* (cf. Barnes 1994: 130; Rogers 1979: 33). In comparison, the synthetic strategy can be found also with multisyllabic adjectives; double comparison (analytic and synthetic strategy) is also common, a feature that is frequently encountered in other non-standard varieties as well (cf. Rogers 1979: 34; examples in 2). Note that examples (2a) and (2c) include instances of a dialectal comparison strategy (*than what*) which is generally not commented on in detail in the literature, but which seems common in a number of dialects (about 130 instances in FRED). No instances of *-en* adjectives could be found in the modern material.

(2) a. *I'd be* ***more happier*** *out there than what I should be haymaking.* (FRED Som_005)
b. ɪts ˈfɪftɪ ˈtɔɪmz **wɒsər**
'it's fifty times worse' (31 So 14, book VI)
c. ***More happier*** *then than what it is today I think.* (FRED Wil_022)

4. Nouns

In plural formation, West Country dialects at one time preferred the traditional *-en* ending over the StE *-s*, but have since adopted the StE strategy (cf. Barnes 1994: 129; Rogers 1979: 33). For some plurals, the distribution of allomorphs differs from that in StE in that dialects used [ɪz] as a means of consonant cluster simplification. Thus, one hears plural forms such as *ghostes* or *beastes* (cf. Rogers 1979: 33), a feature that settlers took with them to Newfoundland and which has been typical of Newfoundland dialect(s) ever since (see Clarke, Americas and Caribbean volume).

Another phenomenon widespread in most non-standard varieties of English is the absence of an overt plural marker on some measurement nouns and nouns after numerals. While a plural *-s* after such nouns as *pound*, *mile* or *year* would be the exception rather than the rule, Rogers (1979: 33; cf. also Barnes [1886[2]] 1970: 20) claims that the plural usually *is* marked on certain nouns belonging to the same respective family (or semantic field), namely *acre*, *ounce*, *inch*, *yard*, *hour*, *day* and *week*, a claim that essentially seems to hold for the modern corpus material as well. Examples of unmarked plurals abound; some typical ones are provided in (3).

(3)
a. *He used to have* ***four pound*** *of butter a week every week.* (FRED Con_005)
b. *If they had any money they did give you* ***a few pound*** … (FRED Som_031)
c. …*we were* ***three mile*** *away from Plymouth* … (FRED Dev_001)
d. …*'e was walkin'* ***six mile*** *a day to work mornin's an'* ***six mile*** *'ome* … (FRED Wil_004)

5. Pronouns

The pronominal system of West Country dialects is generally considered its most distinctive feature, as peculiarities cluster here. For example, Ihalainen (1994: 249–250) lists four features as typical of modern Southwestern dialect (voicing of initial fricatives, *bain't*, pronoun exchange, "gendered" pronouns), two of which can be found in the personal pronoun system (pronoun exchange, "gendered" pronouns; cf. also Trudgill and Chambers 1991). Phenomena that are unique to the Southwest can be found in the system of demonstrative and personal pronouns. It does not come as a surprise then that pronouns in general and personal pronouns in particular have drawn considerable attention over time. Nevertheless, two of the most interesting features have not yet been studied in detail: case assignment ("pronoun exchange"; section 5.1.1.) and gender assignment ("gendered pronouns", "gender diffusion", "animation"; section 5.1.2.).

5.1. Personal pronouns

5.1.1. Pronoun exchange

The generally agreed-upon label for the phenomenon illustrated in (4) is "pronoun exchange" (probably Ossi Ihalainen's term; Ihalainen 1991, based on a 1983 talk, but see also Wakelin 1981: 114). Pronoun exchange is defined as the use of a subject personal pronoun in an object position or all other positions that would normally require the use of an oblique (i.e. non-subject) form.

(4) a. *…they always called **I** 'Willie', see.* (FRED Som_009)
b. *…Uncle Willy, they used to call him, you remember **he**?* (FRED Con_006)
c. *…you couldn't put **she*** [= horse] *in a putt* … (FRED Som_005)
d. *I did give **she** a 'and and she did give **I** a 'and and we did 'elp one another.* (FRED Wil_011)
e. *Well, if I didn't know **they**, they knowed **I**.* (FRED Wil_009)
f. *…he never interfered with **I*** … (FRED Som_020)
g. *Never had no fault at all with **she**.* (FRED Som_005)
h. *Yeah, 'twere to **they** but 'twasn' to **I**.* (FRED Wil_018)

The most common explanation for this type of use found in the literature is that the subject forms are used when the respective form is emphasized, while the oblique forms are used in all other contexts (Elworthy 1965b: 35–38; Kruisinga 1905: 35–36; Wright 1905: 271). Rogers notes that the pressure of a rigid SVO word order in English might have contributed to "a certain amount of confusion over pronouns which followed verbs" (1979: 35), resulting in subject forms being restricted to pre-verbal contexts. This is reminiscent of the change in StE from *it's I* to *it's me*, which is presumably based on the same factors.

Utterances like the following are also found, although more restrictions apply to this type of use. The examples in (5) illustrate the reverse exchange scenario, namely oblique forms in subject contexts.

(5) a. ***'er's** shakin' up seventy.*
'She is almost seventy.' (37 D 1, book VII)
b. *Evercreech, what did **'em** call it?* (FRED Som_031)
c. ***Us** don' think naught about things like that.* (37 D 1, book III)
d. *We used to stook it off didn't **us**?* (FRED Som_027)

The extent to which these two patterns are applied differs from region to region. Rogers' (1979: 35) impression, for instance, is that the use of oblique forms in subject position (primarily *us* for *we* and *her* for *she*) is more restricted

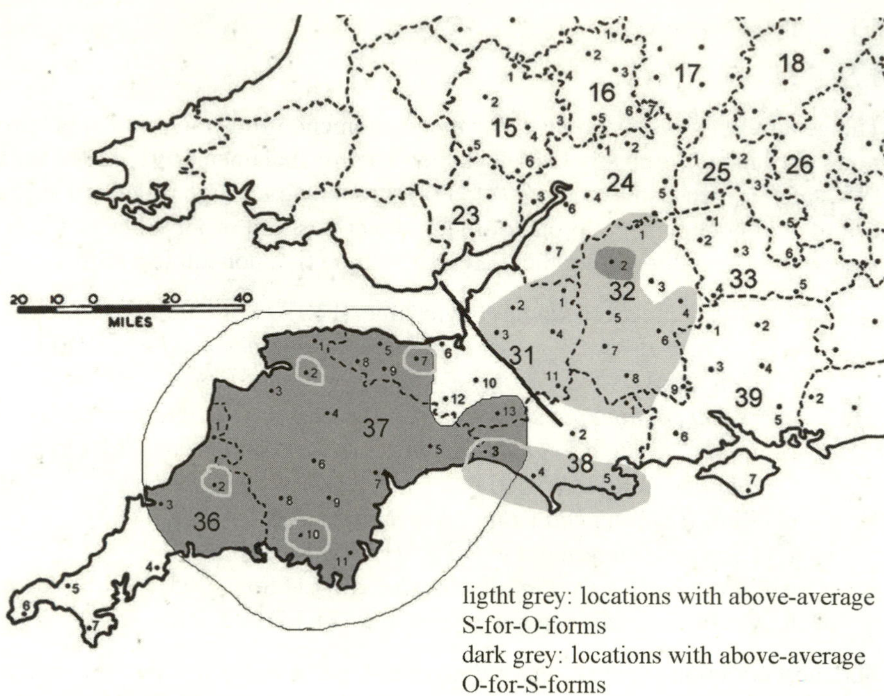

Map 1. Pronoun Exchange in the SED Basic Material

in Somerset, Wiltshire, Berkshire and Dorset than in Cornwall, Devon and Gloucestershire.

Overall, the factors that influence pronoun exchange are extremely complex. A detailed investigation of the phenomenon in the SED Basic Material and fieldworker notebooks revealed surprising distributional patterns from an areal point of view (cf. Map 1 and 2):

(i) Subject forms are used much more frequently in object slots than object forms in subject slots (55% to 20%).

(ii) Locations with a high degree of exchanged subject forms (i.e. subject forms used in oblique contexts) will almost certainly have a (very) low degree of exchanged object forms, and vice versa.

(iii) The West Country is split into two parts. Subject-for-object forms are typical of the eastern locations (particularly Wiltshire) rather than the West Country proper, where mainly object-for-subject forms are used. West Cornwall belongs to the East rather than the West.

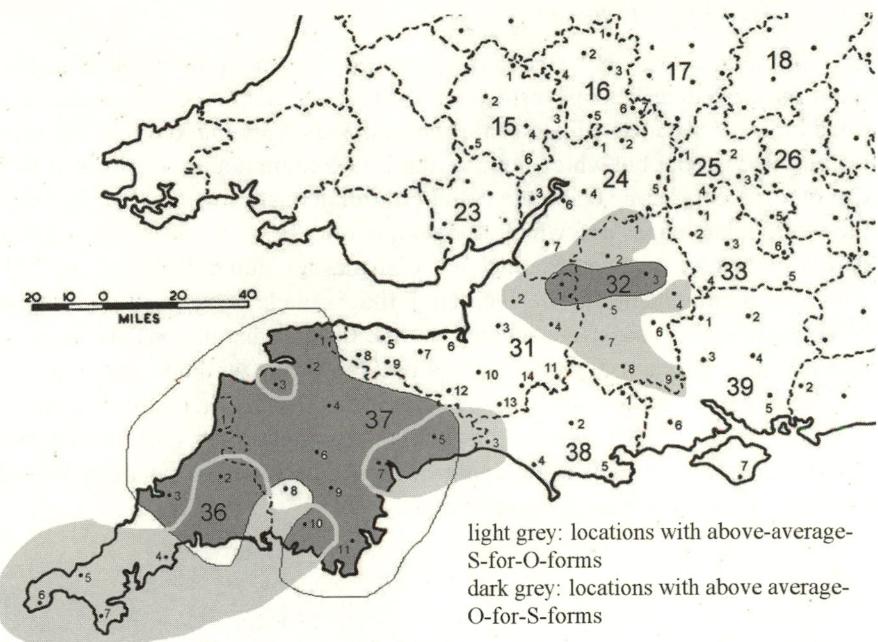

Map 2. Pronoun Exchange in the SED fieldworker notebooks

(iv) The comparison of the Basic and incidental SED material suggests that both areas are receding even within their original homelands. Somerset, which has already been split in the 19th century, seems to be on its way to losing pronoun exchange altogether, using very low percentages of "exchanged" forms in general.

(v) The use of subject-for-object forms seems to be spreading eastwards from West Cornwall. One possible explanation for this is a general tendency in colloquial English to use subject forms in non-subject functions, e.g. after prepositions (*between you and I*), which may help further such uses.

From a modern point of view, it has to be stated that pronoun exchange is rapidly receding. With a frequency of about 1% in the Southwest component of FRED, pronoun exchange seems to be all but dead in its former homelands.

5.1.2. *"Gendered" pronouns*

Like pronoun exchange, "gendered" pronouns are among the most frequently mentioned peculiarities of West Country dialects. "Gendered" pronouns as defined here are instances of personal pronouns which are marked for masculine or feminine gender but which refer to inanimate count nouns. Traditional West Country dialect uses an elaborate system of gender assignment which is rare in the world's languages and which to date has only been observed for non-standard varieties (see Pawley, Pacific and Australasia volume; Rohdenburg 2004: 343–348; Siemund 2002): The distinction that is made between different types of nouns is that of mass versus count nouns. Gender distinctions are based on that division, so that only count nouns use the forms we know as masculine and feminine, while mass nouns use neuter *it* exclusively. In reality, the system is much more complex. The factors influencing gender assignment in a number of varieties of English, including StE, are discussed in detail in Wagner (2004b). Illustrative material is provided in (6).

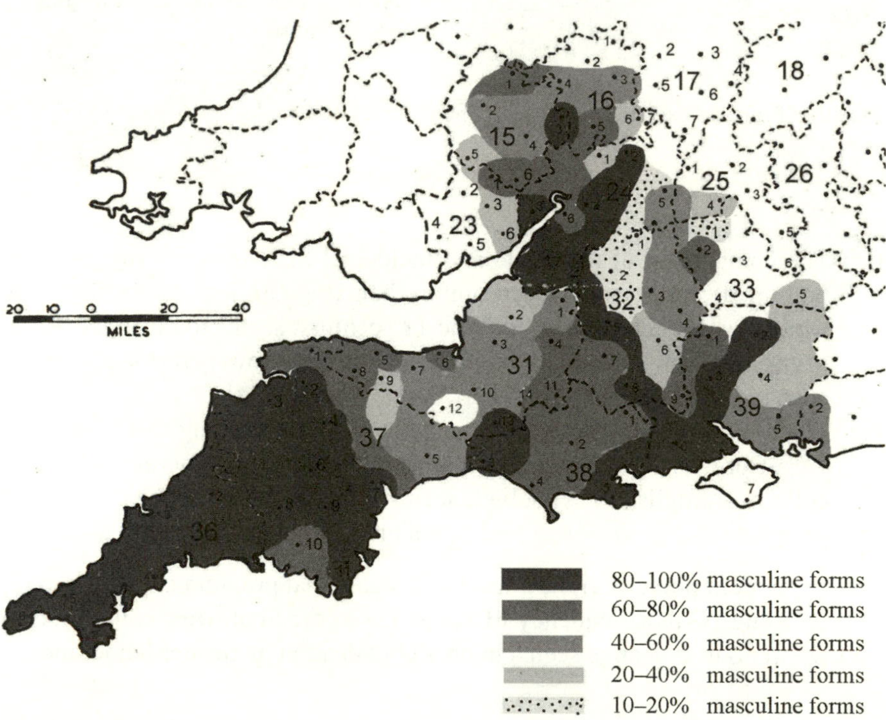

Map 3. Distribution of "gendered" pronouns in the SED Basic Material

(6) a. ˈɒɪ də ˈmɒɪnd ˈwʌn tɒɪm wɛn ðeː dɪd ˈkɔːɬ **n̩** ˈgaʳdn æʊs (38 Do 3, book V)
'I remember one time when we called it garden house.'
b. ˈʃʊt ðɪk ˈdɔər ðiːs ˈgɒt **n̩** ˈdʒarɪn
'Shut that door, thee hast got it jarring.' (31 So 14, book IX)
c. *That ball won' glance. If '**e**'s split '**e** won't.* (37 D 10, book VIII)
d. *I bet thee cansn' climb **he*** [= tree]. (32 W 9, book VIII)
e. ***He** do* [də] *go now. **He** 'ave been a good watch.* (31 So 11, book VII)

This section contains results from a study based on the responses to 10 SED questions possibly containing "gendered" pronouns. The questions and the respective referents that were used are: I.7.1 ("thing"), I.11.2 (cart), I.11.6 (cart), VIII.7.6 (bone), IX.2.6 (door), IX.2.8 (door), IX.3.1 (knife), IX.4.4 (spade), IX.8.2 (ball), IX.9.3 ("something"). Two things are noteworthy about the areal distribution of "gendered" pronouns in the Basic Material: First of all, the Southwest – once probably homogeneous regarding its use of "gendered" pronouns – appears to have given way to the system known from StE to different degrees in different regions. While the far West has been rather resistant to change, with percentages of "gendered" pronouns still between 80% and 100%, particularly Somerset shows figures much lower than some more eastern locations. Second, from the impression gained from the areal distribution of pronoun exchange, the figures for "gendered" pronouns, like pronoun exchange a traditional dialect feature, should be much lower in West Cornwall than they actually are. If due to its shorter history English in West Cornwall truly were closer to StE, we would expect "gendered" pronouns to be among the first features that disappear (if they ever existed in the first place). The impression of a surprisingly dialectal West Cornwall based on the Basic Material data is supported by the results from the fieldworker notebooks data.

Map 3 shows the percentages of masculine forms used in responses which would trigger a neuter pronoun in StE. Looking at the eastern belt of locations where "gendered" pronouns are still frequently used, one is forced to conclude that the "gendered" pronoun territory once covered an even larger area, extending both northwards and eastwards. When comparing Maps 2 and 3, parallels are obvious. The core territory of both pronoun exchange and "gendered" pronouns is Devon and the locations bordering it in the West (Cornwall) and Northeast (Somerset). With the NORM informants of the SED, pronoun exchange seems to have retreated from its original stronghold to a higher degree than "gendered" pronouns, which are still used frequently in a belt which nicely coincides with various proposed borders separating the Southwest from the Southeast.

Table 1. Frequency of "gendered" pronouns per county and location (SED field-worker notebooks)

county	no. of examples	no. of locations	examples per location	no. of speakers	examples per speaker
Cornwall	163	7	23.3	20	8.2
Dorset	40	5	8.0	8	5.0
Devon	126	11	11.5	26	4.8
Wiltshire	70	9	7.8	15	4.7
Somerset	88	13+1	6.3	28	3.1
Total	487	46	10.6	97	5.0

Columns 4 and 6 in Table 1 are of particular interest. Even on a very superficial level, the picture emerging could not be any clearer: Speakers from Cornwall produce most of the gendered pronouns by far and are responsible for almost exactly a third (163 out of 487; 33.5%) of all examples.

Speakers from Dorset, Devon and Wiltshire are close to the average of five forms per speaker, while once again Somerset lags behind. This overall picture does not change when looking at detailed distributions per location and per individual speaker. The order of counties is slightly different for examples per location – Devon and Dorset change places (see column 4). Examples per location range from two to 45. All but one of the Cornish locations are above the average of 10.6 examples per location, as are five out of nine in Wiltshire, six out of 11 in Devon, two out of five locations in Dorset, but only one out of 14 in Somerset (Montacute is not included in the Basic Material).

The order of counties stays the same when looking at the actual contributors of masculine forms: In Cornwall and Devon all informants do, while this is not so in the remaining counties. One of the nine Dorset informants (i.e. 11.1%) does not contribute, while this percentage climbs to 25% in Wiltshire (five of 20 speakers) and to 33.3% in Somerset (12 of 36 speakers, excluding Montacute).

Although the order of counties in the detailed distribution list changes to a certain extent, we cannot identify individual informants who might distort these figures. Contributions range between one and 24 per speaker, with an average of five. 70 speakers are below that average or conform to it, while 27 contribute more than their share. Those 27 (or 27.8% of speakers) contribute 295 forms, i.e. 60.6% of the total of 487.

The data presented here once more add to the already familiar impression: (West) Cornwall is much more dialectal than has generally been assumed, at least when it comes to the use of "gendered" pronouns. Somerset in the 1950s, on the other hand, does not seem to have much in common with the Somerset of Elworthy's times. While the gender system described in his studies can be considered the epitome of West Country dialect, the SED data show a system that is much closer to StE than to the 19th-century West Country one.

As with pronoun exchange, the situation of "gendered" pronouns in the modern FRED material is much more difficult to generalize. Although the feature is encountered more frequently than pronoun exchange, "gendered" pronouns are still rare. The only thing that can be safely said judging from the FRED examples is that the traditional system is by no means dead. Although the traditional dialects are influenced by StE and colloquial English, the level of dialect mixture has not (yet) reached a degree where West Country background can no longer be determined: Thus, while most non-standard varieties of English world-wide have extended feminine forms to inanimate (and also generic) referents (see e.g. Pawley, Pacific and Australasia volume), this task is still fulfilled by masculine forms in West Country speech, making it almost unique among English dialects.

5.2. Demonstrative pronouns

The system of demonstrative pronouns parallels that of personal pronouns in that they both distinguish count from non-count forms. Based on Rogers' description it looks as follows (Rogers 1979: 32; cf. also Barnes 1994: 130, 1970: 17–18; Elworthy 1965a: 23, 1965b: 29):

		West Country		**StE**
		count	**mass**	
close	singular	*theäse* or *thick* (*here*)	*this* (*here*)	*this*
	plural	*these* (*here*)		*these*
distant	singular	*thick, thicky* (*there*)	*that* (*there*)	*that*
	plural	*they, them* (*there*)		*those*

Although a close-distant-remote system has been postulated for Southwestern dialects in some modern studies (e.g. Trudgill 1999: 86; Harris 1991; Trudgill and Chambers 1991: 10), this assumption is supported neither by traditional accounts nor by data from the corpora, as examples of a threefold distinction are non-existent or at least difficult to find. Judging from the examples, the traditional system has declined, and the form *thick*(*y*) has all but died out, with a total of some 20 forms in FRED, some of which can be found in (7).

(7) a. *Well, like* ***thick*** *one what's in there now, ehr, for killing all* ***they*** *women*. (FRED Som_005)
b. *...they had* ***this here*** *place on the racecourse* ... (FRED Dev_004)
c. *...when you come to* ***that there*** *corner, that's called Tugrushen corner*. (FRED Som_014)
d. *That's what all* ***them*** *old buildings are*. (FRED Con_006)

5.3. Possessive pronouns

As in other areas of grammar, dialects prefer an analytic strategy in marking possession. Therefore, one would expect to find more examples of the type *the father of/on un* than *his father* (cf. Rogers 1979: 32; Barnes 1994: 129–130, 1970: 16; Elworthy 1965b: 13; Hancock 1994: 105; Wakelin 1986: 38; see also section 6 on prepositions for the status of *of* and *on*). Although some instances can be found in the modern material (see examples in 8a,b), speakers do not seem to avoid using possessive pronouns consciously. What they clearly *do* avoid, though, is the neuter possessive pronoun, *its*, once more preferring the analytic *of it* (see examples 8c–f), even if this results in two adjoining *of*-phrases, as in (8c).

(8) a. *And that was the end* ***of her***. (FRED Dev_002)
b. *...the owner* ***of her*** ... (FRED Som_028)
c. *I had an idea of the price* ***of it***. (FRED Con_009)
d. *...that car had carrier on the back* ***of it*** ... (FRED Som_029)
e. *Sherford was the name* ***of it****, that's right* ... (FRED Dev_001)
f. *...you couldn' really see the colour* ***of it*** ... (FRED Wil_002)

Rogers' claim (1979: 32) that *its* is substituted by the "gendered" alternatives *his* and *her* cannot be conclusively drawn from the data. In fact, the occurrence of "gendered" pronouns in the possessive is rather rare. A possible explanation for this could be seen in Ihalainen's accessibility hypothesis, according to which the standard forms invade the dialect system from the less accessible positions in the Noun Phrase Accessibility Hierarchy. The possessive slot would be one of the first to be taken over by StE forms (for a detailed account of Ihalainen's hypothesis, see Wagner 2004a). Furthermore, there is no evidence in the corpora that Southwest speakers use independent possessive forms usually associated with the Midlands, namely *hisn*, *hern*, *ourn*, *yourn*, *theirn.* It is likely that Rogers, as a native of Wiltshire, where possessives in *-n* are indeed found, overgeneralized from that observation. The feature is unknown further west, though. For the distribution of possessives in *-n*, see Trudgill (1999: 90 and his Map 20). Traditionally, it is assumed that these are formed in analogy with *mine* and *thine*.

5.4. Reflexive pronouns

Like many other non-standard varieties of English, West Country dialects have regularized the irregular StE system of reflexives by forming *hisself* and *theirselves* in analogy with the rest of the paradigm (possessive pronoun + *-self/-selves*, example 9a; cf. e.g. Barnes 1970: 20). In addition, the plural is not always marked on those reflexive pronouns whose first element clearly indicates plurality (thus: *ourself, theirself*, but not *yourself*, which would be singular only) – another common feature of English-based varieties, as illustrated in (9).

(9) a. *…everybody enjoyed* ***theirselves*** … (FRED Wil_007)
b. *Yes, we made that* ***ourself***. (FRED Som_004)
c. *…they call* ***theirself*** *A-1 Builders* … (FRED Dev_001)
d. *…the sort of food that we were having* ***ourself*** … (FRED Con_009)

5.5. Relative markers

What and to a restricted extent also *as* do duty as relative particles in West Country speech in addition to the relative pronouns *who, which* and *that* (examples 10a–c; see also Rogers 1979: 36; Elworthy 1965b: 41–42). Moreover, the division of tasks between the forms tends to differ from that found in StE. A general observation one can make is that dialects usually prefer uninflected and/or neutral forms which are unmarked for case and gender. This generalization holds for several areas of grammar. For relative particles, this means that we have a higher percentage of *that* with personal antecedents than in StE, as speakers tend to avoid the inflected *wh*-forms *whose* and *whom.* There is in fact not a single example of *whom* and there are only eight instances of *whose* in the FRED Southwest texts (ca. 500,000 words). We can also observe a preference for co-ordination rather than subordination – (10d) is a possible candidate for that tendency. The most striking difference from StE, however, is exemplified in (10e) to (10i). StE only allows gapping – a zero relative marker – in non-subject positions.

(10) a. *…we had a big churn* ***what'****d hold forty gallons* … (FRED Som_011)
b. …(gap 'name'), *you know* ***what*** *was boss* … (FRED Som_009)
c. *…my dear sister* ***as*** *is dead and gone* … (FRED Wil_005)
d. *…and there were a man in there* ***and he*** *were a dowser* … (FRED Wil_001)

e. *There's a pair of blocks down there* **Ø** *was made when I was apprentice.* (FRED Som_016)
f. *I know a man* **Ø***'ll do it for 'ee.* (36 Co 4, book IX)
g. *... you had a barrow* **Ø** *runs from there straight across like that ...* (FRED Som_001)
h. *... that's the last orchard* **Ø** *been done around here for years...* (FRED Som_002)
i. *You know anybody* **Ø** *wants some, he'll sell them.* (FRED Som_031)

When looking at relative clause formation, it becomes clear once more that analytic strategies take precedence over synthetic ones, a pervasive tendency in spontaneous English in general.

6. Prepositions

(11) a. *A lot of things you see in life if you'd only knowed* ***on it*** *were very interesting.* (FRED Wil_011)
b. *He eat eleven* ***on 'em***. (FRED Som_013)
c. *...give us half* ***on it*** (FRED Oxf_001)

An interesting feature in the use of prepositions is exemplified in (11). Rogers cites a possible explanation by Kjederqvist, who mentions a possible connection with Middle English where the two items in question were homophonous in certain contexts, but who rejects this idea at the same time. Rogers comments further that "*on* occurs in places where we might have expected 'of', mainly in front of the unstressed pronouns *'en* (him), *it* and *'em* (them)" (1979: 41). An extensive treatment of prepositional use can be found in Elworthy (1965b: 87–95).

Another interesting phenomenon is what Rogers calls "otiose *of*" (1979: 41), which is used before direct objects, but only after progressive verb forms. This use seems to have been extended to gerundial forms as well, resulting in utterances like (*the*) *doing of it* ('doing it'). (12a) to (12d) may be taken as illustrations from a total of about 60 instances in the corpora:

(12) a. *You couldn't afford to buy new ones so you had to keep* ***mending of 'em*** *didn't you*? (FRED Wil_009)
b. *I been* ***driving of her*** *for fifteen, sixteen years*. (FRED Som_014)
c. *I can't mind the* ***making of them***. (FRED Som_021)
d. *I don't mind* ***doing of it***. (FRED Som_002)

Last but not least, the substitution of certain prepositions with others is distinctive of the area. Rogers notes that *up, down* and *over* are used where StE would use *to* or *at*, the explanation behind it being a geographical one: *over* is used "for nearby towns and villages", while *up* and *down* follow the sun's path – East = *up*, West = *down* (cf. Rogers 1979: 41). This is a very frequent phenomenon (13a–c).

(13) a. *No, that was* [name] ***over*** *Downby, that was another* [name] *where* (gap 'indistinct') *is*. (FRED Som_020)
b. *Yes, there was one or two* ***down*** *Zennor. I can mind – now hold on a minute. They had one* ***down*** *Zennor, and when* [name]*'s brother* [name] *came over Treen to live – that's below the hotel here …* (FRED Con_005)
c. *…he went* ***up*** *Stroud district …* (FRED Wil_001)

7. Adverbs

The absence of the StE ending *-ly* in adverb marking is another feature that can be considered almost universal in spoken English. It is therefore not surprising that West Country dialects share it. In addition to a number of different intensifiers or boosters (Rogers [1979: 37] lists *main* "I do feel main bad" [14a] and *terriblish*), the Southwest probably used *real* in intensifying function at an earlier point in time than the varieties it is most commonly associated with nowadays (14b).

(14) a. *…she were* ***main*** *strict …* (FRED Wil_003)
b. *Oh yeah, they, in the end they was turning out* ***real*** *good furniture*. (FRED Dev_010)

Peculiar uses of *like* are known from a number of dialects, and have probably made their way into casual speech from there. Originally, *like* was used as a qualifying adjective in West Country speech, meaning *rather*. Thus, *He walks real quiet like* would correspond to StE *He walks rather quietly* (cf. Elworthy 1965a: 33, 1965b: 81–82; Barnes 1970: 34). Examples (15a–c) show this use and some others that are reminiscent of 1990s teenager speech, when *like* started to creep in as a discourse marker (cf. also Anderwald, this volume on *like* in Southeastern dialects).

(15) a. *'Course being silly* ***like****, I said …* (FRED Som_021)
b. *You had to tie your corn behind the strappers* ***like***. (FRED Som_006)
c. *…he used to pick it up* ***like****, you know, …* (FRED Con_004)

8. Verbs and the verb phrase

Apart from the pronominal system, the verbal paradigm of West Country English is the sub-system that is the most interesting to investigate. One should distinguish between antiquated traditional features that are no longer or only very rarely found today, and those features which may have become less frequent over the past decades, but which are alive and kicking nevertheless.

8.1. Antiquated traditional features

Rogers (1979: 37; cf. also Barnes 1994: 131; Elworthy 1965a: 21; Wakelin 1984: 82) describes an intricacy of traditional verbal morphology that has since been almost eradicated. Infinitives of transitive verbs that were used intransitively were marked by a *-y* ending. What we are dealing with here is a rather complex case of functional re-interpretation and extension at the same time: the Middle English infinitive ending was restricted to certain verbs, while it had nothing to do with transitivity. The modern Southwestern *-y*, on the other hand, can be added to all verbs, functioning as a marker of intransitivity. Thus, examples (16a,b) would constitute a type of minimal pair (from Rogers 1979: 37). While this form can still be found in the SED fieldworker notebooks (cf. 16c,d), it is absent from the comparatively modern corpus material. Note that (16c) supports the claim (cf. Rogers 1979: 37) that the *-y* is dropped before a vowel.

(16) a. *I do* ***dig*** *the garden.*
b. *Every day, I do diggy for three hours.*
c. aɪ gɒt ˈbɽe:v ɬɒt ˈdu: jənɔ: ˈpɪgz te:**me:t**_ ən ˈkæʊz tə ˈ**mɪɬki:**
'I've got a lot to do today, you know; pigs to mate and cows to milk.' (36 Co 4, book VIII)
d. wi: də ˈbɽɪŋ æʊɽ ˈʃi:p ɪn ˈ**ɬami**
'We bring our sheep in (to) lamb.' (36 Co 6, book I)

A feature that will only briefly be commented on is the use of (unsplit) *for to* or only *for* to introduce infinitival purpose clauses (17a–c; see Wakelin 1986: 38; Hancock 1994: 104). While *for to* is an old StE form and is still found quite frequently in the modern data, simple dialectal *for* seems to have died out.

(17) a. *I've got a one, but 'tis a job* ***for*** *keep up wi' 'em.* (36 Co 1, book VII)
b. wɒdˈɪv^{r}ɽ ˈɛɪɬd i: **və^{r}:** ˈdʊ ət
'whatever ailed you to do it' (36 Co 1, book VIII)
c. *Always the evenings* ***for to*** *get the men* ***for to*** *do it.* (FRED Som_025)

Another remnant of an earlier stage of English is the *a*-prefix found in present and past participles, including some unhistorical uses (cf. Barnes 1994: 132, 1970: 28; Elworthy 1965a: 9; Rogers 1979: 38; Wakelin 1984: 83, 1986: 36). It is ubiquitous in the SED data (18a), while only traces of it can be found in the modern material (18b,c).

(18) a. *'e's* ***a-waiting*** *for I* (24 Gl 4, book VIII)
b. *And he were down around Brown's farm* ***a-haulin'*** *pigs*. (FRED Wil_010)
c. *...if he'd* ***a-been*** *alive*. (FRED Som_032)

The forms *be* and in the plural also *am* (or *'m*) constituted the main part of the historical *be*-paradigm used in West Country speech. Thus, *I, you, he/she/it be, we'm, you'm* and *they'm* were frequently heard in traditional dialect (see Rogers 1979: 38; Wakelin 1986: 36). A study of the modern material indicates that interestingly the paradigm has since shifted towards that of modern West Country dialects, not that of StE. The present tense examples in (19a) and (19b) are therefore traditional, while the simple past forms in (19c) to (19e) can be considered modern. This shift in the *be*-paradigm is a rare example of a traditional system being substituted by another earlier standard (now non-standard) system.

(19) a. ***we'm*** *happy* ... (FRED Som_005)
b. *But* ***they'm*** *always giving them a bit of help* ... (FRED Con_005)
c. *I* ***were*** *very happy there*. (FRED Wil_008)
d. *If you* ***was*** *wrong, you* ***was*** *wrong* ... (FRED Con_009)
e. *...he* ***were*** *in the Navy*. (FRED Som_012)

Another agreement feature that to this day is said to be distinctive of Newfoundland English (see Clarke, Americas and Caribbean Volume) is discussed below. True West Country dialect is said to have distinguished the main verb from the auxiliary use of the primary verbs *do, have* and *be*. While the forms inflect as main verbs, taking *-s* in all persons, they do not in their auxiliary function(s), which use the base form. Instances exemplifying this contrast, as in (20), are rare, and it is probably safe to assume it does no longer exist in modern Southwestern dialects:

(20) a. [Interviewer: *It makes a messier cheese – was it now –*]
It ***do***. (FRED Som_025)
b. ... *and in they days the ladies didn't ride straddle like they* ***do's*** *today, they used to ride side-saddle*. (FRED Wil_001)

c. *...perhaps it might be a good idea if I* ***has*** *a bit of insight in case mother was taken ill ...* (FRED Som_011)

d. *...and they* ***has*** *these long trousers tucked up like this ...* (FRED Som_022)

8.2. Traditional features still in use

8.2.1. Regularization of irregular verbs

Two general tendencies can be observed in the irregular verb paradigms of basically all spoken varieties of English today: partial or complete regularization of the paradigm. For past tense and past participle formation, we are thus facing the following possibilities (Rogers 1979: 40–41; cf. also Barnes 1994: 125, 1970: 26–27):

(a) maintenance of irregular form(s), but reduction to one instead of two; for that purpose, either the simple past or the past participle form is extended to cover both these uses (e.g. *speak-spoke-spoke*; *break-broke-broke*; *do-done-done*, *come-come-come*; 21a–c)
(b) StE strong verbs receive an extra weak (i.e. regular) ending in addition to vowel gradation (e.g. *take-tooked; steal-stoled*)
(c) StE weak or mixed verbs become irregular (i.e. strong) in dialect (e.g. *creep-crope; scrape-scrope*)
(d) StE strong verbs are regularized (i.e. weakened) in dialect – probably the most frequent scenario (e.g. *know-knowed; see-seed; give-gived; blow-blowed; hurt-hurted* etc.; see 21d–f)

(21) a. *...he* ***done*** *odd jobs for farmers ...* (FRED Con_009)

b. *I* ***come*** *here in 1915 ...* (FRED Som_016)

c. *...you had to find out which one was* ***broke*** *and thread it through again ...* (FRED Wil_022)

d. *So, they went off one night, went up round and* ***catched*** *her 'bout six o'clock ...* (FRED Som_005)

e. *...he were* ***gived*** *the push ...* (FRED Wil_001)

f. *...you* ***knowed*** *this one ...* (FRED Con_006)

8.1.2. Double and multiple negation

Double (and multiple) negation is among the most wide-spread features of non-standard varieties and can also be found in the Southwestern dialects. The universal negator *ain't*, standing for all negated forms of *have* and *be*, is another form that is commonly found in non-standard varieties of English.

(22) a. *…he **wasn't no** rogue really*. (FRED Con_003)
b. *I mean you **couldn't** do **nothing** about it*. (FRED Oxf_001)
c. *We **never** went **no** more, did we*? (FRED Wil_017)
d. *So anyhow they **never** had **no**, **never** had **no** glasses **nor nothing** in them days, you know.* (FRED Con_006)
e. *No that **ain't no** use now*, … (FRED Dev_002)
f. *I **ain't** doing bad am I*? (FRED Wil_005)

8.1.3. Periphrastic do

The story of periphrastic *do* in the history of English is long and well-studied. Nevertheless, its modern unemphatic uses in some dialects and particularly in the Southwest continue to intrigue researchers. Klemola (1996) offers the most comprehensive account to date, using both historical and fairly modern traditional data for his investigation. The following account is for the most part based on Klemola's research and Rogers' summary of 19th-century analyses, which will be supported with examples from the modern corpora.

Scholars generally agree that unemphatic *do* (*do* [də], *did*) is most often used to express habituality, contrasting with the simple present and past tense forms, and as a tense carrier in affirmative sentences (cf. Klemola 1996: chapter 4; Kortmann 2004: 248–259). Rogers adds another form to the repertoire of what he calls "frequentative" forms, namely the *-s* ending. The distribution of the two forms is described as follows: "The stronghold of the 'do' forms is Dorsetshire but they are also found in Wiltshire (especially the western half), in Somerset and in parts of Gloucestershire. Devon prefers the *-s*-form with 'they' but the other reappears briefly in west Cornwall" (Rogers 1979: 39 and his map).

Judging from the modern corpus data (23), periphrastic *do* is omnipresent with some speakers, while others do not have it in their language system at all. Note that the previously mentioned rule of auxiliaries traditionally not inflecting for person is also valid for periphrastic *do*, thus generating the forms *he/she/it do* V.

(23) a. *As I **do** say to my niece, I say, you know, you're far better off, I said, than what we were, I said*. (FRED Wil_012)
b. *…and then I **did** cut 'em off as they **did** grow*, … (FRED Som_002)
c. *But it **do** get in the barrel and you **do** hear plop, plop, plop, you want to leave it alone*. (FRED Som_013)
d. *…she **did** do a lot of needlework*, … (FRED Wil_018)
e. *William, my son, **do** live down there*. (FRED Con_005)

f. *But they* ***did*** *work 'til quarter to six at night, that was their normal time and as I say, the hooter* ***did*** *blow at the finish and all machines* ***did*** *shut down they were gone within about five minutes. It didn't take long to do it. They* ***did*** *sweep round the machines before they left, they always do that when the machines are running*. (FRED Wil_006)

9. Summary and outlook

Table 2 summarizes which of the features listed here are found solely in the Southwest, and which ones can also be found in other varieties of English or are even features typical of present-day spoken English, in general. For other features that have not been mentioned explicitly here, see for example Cheshire, Edwards and Whittle (1989: 194–195).

The picture presented here is essentially that of the late 20th century, the time frame of the corpus material used. However, it should be noted that a comparison of 18th/19th-century features with those found in the modern material reveals surprisingly few changes. Of the features investigated here, Ihalainen (1994: 214) lists periphrastic *do*, pronoun exchange, "gendered" pronouns, otiose *of*, and uninflected *do/have* as morphological Southwestern dialect markers of the late 18th/early 19th century. With four of five features still alive and kicking, not *that* much seems to have changed, after all.

Table 2. Uniquely Southwest, regional and universal dialect features

Southwest	**universal**	**regional (British & overseas)**
– pronoun exchange	– no overt plural marking of some measurement nouns (after numerals)	– regularized reflexive pronouns (possessive pronoun + *-self/ -selves*)
– "gendered" pronouns	– plural demonstrative *them* (= StE *those*)	– irregular use (omission or insertion) of articles
– unemphatic periphrastic *do* as tense carrier	– no overt marking of adverbs derived from adjectives (no *-ly*)	– regularized *be*-paradigm (e.g. *was* vs *weren't* etc.)
– mass/count distinction in demonstrative pronouns (?)	– different inventory of relative pronouns (e.g. *as, what*) – gapping/zero relative also in subject position	

Table 2. (continued) Uniquely Southwest, regional and universal dialect features

Southwest	universal	regional (British & overseas)
– otiose *of* (?)	– multiple negation – *ain't* as invariant negative particle – reduced paradigm for irregular verbs (past tense = past participle form)	

The cut-off points between the second and third column, between universal and regional features, are often fuzzy. For the present author, regional features are those which can still be identified with certain regions, although these may be numerous. Universal features, on the other hand, occur in distributions that make it impossible to pinpoint their regional basis. Although the features in the two rightmost columns by far outnumber those unique to the region, the Southwest is one of the most distinctive dialect areas in the British Isles to this day, with a singular combination of traditional features (inherited from earlier stages of both StE and West Country dialect) and those features which even now, after more than a century of investigation, still defy (easy) classification.

Exercises and study questions

1. Name at least 4 distinctive morphosyntactic features of West Country dialects. Two features should come from the noun phrase domain, two from the verb phrase domain.

2. What is understood by "pronoun exchange"? Use the following examples to explain the phenomenon: *Her's almost 70. They stay open late, don't 'em? Us used to call it garden house. Give it to he, not I!*

3. What is interesting about "gendered" pronouns? Use the following examples in your discussion: *He won't let in any wetness* (about a roof). *Put it over the bucket and empty en out. He borrows he very often* (about a shovel). *That there milk's gone, he went to a crud. That's a main fog. I got lost in en.*

4. "The Southwest is a residual zone." – Discuss.

5. Name two West Country features each (6 in total) exhibiting the following distribution:
   - uniquely West Country
   - common in (some) other non-standard varieties
   - universal

Selected references

Please consult the General references for titles mentioned in the text but not included in the references below. For a full bibliography see the accompanying CD-ROM.

Barnes, William
1844
[1994] A dissertation on the Dorset dialect of the English language. In: Andrew Motion (ed.), *William Barnes: Selected Poems*, 117–138. Hardmondsworth: Penguin [originally published as part of *Poems of rural life in the Dorset dialect*].
1886[2]
[1970] *A Glossary of the Dorset Dialect with a Grammar*. Guernsey and St. Peter Port: Toucan Press.

Cheshire, Jenny, Viv Edwards and Pamela Whittle
1989 Urban British dialect grammar: The question of dialect levelling. *English World-Wide* 10: 185–225.

Elworthy, Frederic Thomas
1875
[1965a] *The Dialect of West Somerset*. (Publications of the English Dialect Society 7.) London: Trübner [Vaduz: Kraus Reprint Ltd.].
1877
[1965b] *An Outline of the Grammar of the Dialect of West Somerset*. (Publications of the English Dialect Society 19.) London: Trübner [Vaduz: Kraus Reprint Ltd.].

Hancock, Ian F.
1994 Componentiality and the creole matrix: the Southwest English contribution. In: Michael Montgomery (ed.), *The Crucible of Carolina. Essays in the Development of Gullah Language and Culture*, 95–114. Athens/London: University of Georgia Press.

Harris, Martin
1991 Demonstrative adjectives and pronouns in a Devonshire dialect. In: Trudgill and Chambers (eds.), 20–28.

Ihalainen, Ossi
1991 On grammatical diffusion in Somerset folk speech. In: Trudgill and Chambers (eds.), 104–119.
1994 The dialects of England since 1776. In: Burchfield (ed.), 197–274.

Klemola, K. Juhani
1996 Non-standard periphrastic DO: a study in variation and change. Ph.D. dissertation, Department of Language and Linguistics, University of Essex, Colchester.

Kortmann, Bernd
2002 New prospects for the study of dialect syntax: impetus from syntactic theory and language typology. In: Sjef Barbiers, Leonie Cornips and Susanne van der Kleij (eds.), *Syntactic Microvariation*, 185–213. Amsterdam: Meertens Institute http://www.meertens.nl/books/synmic/.
2004 *Do* as a tense and aspect marker in varieties of English. In: Kortmann (ed.), 245–275.

Kruisinga, Etsko
1905 *A Grammar of the Dialect of West Somersetshire: Descriptive and Historical*. Bonner Beiträge zur Anglistik, Heft 18. Bonn.

Rohdenburg, Günther
2004 Comparing grammatical variation in non-standard English and Low German dialects from a typological perspective. In: Kortmann (ed.), 335–366.

Rogers, Norman
1979 *Wessex Dialect*. Bradford-on-Avon: Moonraker Press.

Siemund, Peter
2002 Animate pronouns for inanimate objects: pronominal gender in English regional varieties. In: Dieter Kastovsky, Gunther Kaltenbröck and Susanne Reichl (eds.), *Anglistentag 2001 Wien – Proceedings*, 19–34. Trier: Wissenschaftlicher Verlag.

Trudgill, Peter and Jack K. Chambers
1991 Pronouns and pronominal systems in English dialects. In: Trudgill and Chambers (eds.), 7–10.

Wagner, Susanne
2004a “Gendered” pronouns in English dialects – a typological perspective. In: Kortmann (ed.), 479–496.
2004b Pronominal gender in varieties of English. In: Kortmann, Herrmann, Pietsch and Wagner.

Wakelin, Martyn F.
1984 Rural dialects in England. In: Trudgill (ed.), 70–93.
1986 *The Southwest of England*. Amsterdam/Philadelphia: Benjamins.

The varieties of English spoken in the Southeast of England: morphology and syntax

Lieselotte Anderwald

1. Introduction

Very little has so far been written about a distinctive dialect grammar of the Southeast of England. Although Standard English (StE) linguistically had its source in the dialect of the East Midlands, London (the seat of the court, of Chancery, of the printing presses) is the place where the standard evolved, and the Southeast of England in general has become inextricably linked with the concept of "Standard English", so much so that the language of the Southeast is apparently not deemed worthy of dialectological attention. In his historical survey of dialect studies, Ihalainen (1994: 252) expressly stresses that for lexicology, "the Home Counties do not emerge as a clearly focused area on the basis of lexical evidence, which can be accounted for by the close affinity to standard English". Similarly, Edwards (1993) states that "some observers have doubted whether a distinctively non-standard south-eastern speech actually exists" (Edwards 1993: 235). Indeed, perceived nearness to the standard may be a reason why non-standard speech in the Southeast is not seen as dialect, but simply as "incorrect standard".

Others have cited the fact that London was situated at the intersection of the three Old English kingdoms of Mercia, Wessex and Kent (Edwards 1993: 215); therefore no one distinctive dialect could be expected to continue into modern times and influence present-day dialects. In addition, in Early Modern English times, London was the destination of masses of in-migrants who brought their own dialects. Again, London as the melting pot could perhaps not be expected to evolve its own distinctive non-standard dialect apart from the standard language that arose from this dialect mixture and that was codified around the same time.

On the other hand, the fact that we find the Southeast not so very distinctive may be due to the fact that very few studies so far have dealt with the Southeast in any depth. Edwards and Weltens (1985) note in their survey not even a handful of studies concerned with this area, and twenty years later this situation has not changed greatly. The most important monograph to have appeared since then is Cheshire's study of adolescent non-standard speech in the town of

Reading west of London (Cheshire 1982), as well as a handful of articles based on the same material. Although Reading is situated on the border of what is considered here the Southeast and the Southwest, most features in Cheshire's description are paralleled by other accounts from the Southeast, which justifies its inclusion in this article. A little more recent is Viv Edwards' survey article "The grammar of southern British English" (Edwards 1993); however, this article does not include any original research, and does not systematically distinguish the Southwest and the Southeast. Also of interest is the Britain-wide school survey by Cheshire, Edwards and Whittle (1993) in the same collection, which finds practically all general non-standard features also for the Southeast, but also some unexpected quantitative differences between, very roughly, the South and the North. Newer material not so far explored for grammatical phenomena in depth is the COLT corpus (Bergen Corpus of London Teenage Language). Andersen (2001) is a first pragmatic analysis of invariant tags and the discourse marker *like* based on this material. The British National Corpus (Aston and Burnard 1998) also contains a sample of Southeastern speakers which has so far not been much explored (although parts of this material overlap with COLT). Finally, a new corpus at the University of Freiburg of English dialect speakers (FRED, financed by DFG grant no. Ko/1181/1-1 and 1181/1-2) is nearing conclusion so that some comparative work on dialect grammar is now becoming possible (cf. the contributions in Kortmann et al. 2005). FRED also contains material from the Southeast of England (from the counties of Kent, Middlesex and London), which has been exploited for this article and wherever possible, examples from FRED will be provided in the text.

Judging from what has been published so far, one could sum up that little has been found that is distinctive for the Southeast; instead we would expect to find many features that today mark non-standard speech in general. An overview of these general non-standard features is provided by Cheshire, Edwards and Whittle in the article mentioned above (Cheshire, Edwards and Whittle 1993). An interesting historical question would be to determine in how far the influential Southeast might have been the source for these developments, in particular as some non-standard features still seem to be spreading today.

1.1. Geographical delimitation

The Southeast of England is a relatively young dialect area in classificatory terms. A large area of what is now part of the Southeast – especially the counties directly south of London: Surrey, Sussex but even Kent – used to belong to the Southwest linguistically (cf. the description in Ihalainen 1994). Former general Southern features seem to have receded to the Southwest proper quite rapidly at least since the end of the nineteenth century. Today, the Southeast of England is clearly dominated – and influenced – by the metropolis London (see Altendorf and Watt, this volume, for phonetic and phonological evidence; whether this also holds for grammatical features remains to be seen). Based on Trudgill's modern dialect areas (Trudgill 1999: 65), the Southeast includes, for the purpose of this chapter, the metropolis itself and the Home Counties, i.e. those counties bordering London: Middlesex, Essex (where it does not belong to East Anglia), Hertfordshire, Bedfordshire, Buckinghamshire (where they do not belong to the South Midlands), Berkshire, Hampshire (where they do not belong to the Southwest), Surrey, Sussex and Kent.

2. Morphology

2.1. Pronouns

2.1.1. Possessive me

The use of *me* for *my*, i.e. doing double service both as the object form of the personal pronoun and as a possessive pronoun, is noted by all authors and is well attested in any material from the Southeast. Some examples from FRED are provided in (1a) to (1c).

(1) a. *... the fact was that* ***me*** *brother left home, you know.* (FRED LND_002)
b. *I sat down to have* ***me*** *tea as usual.* (FRED KEN_004)
c. *I think* ***me*** *memory's getting bad now, somehow.* (FRED MDX_001)

This is indeed a very frequent feature. Although wide-scale studies are not yet available, my pilot study of FRED material from the Southeast indicates that, on average, around thirty percent of possessive pronouns might be *me* rather than *my*. The use of possessive *me* also has repercussions throughout the reflexive pronoun system, as section 2.1.2. shows. Although this phenomenon is generally (synchronically) interpreted as an extension of the object form for the possessive form, it is plausible to regard *me* as a remnant of Middle English *mi/my* which, as a very frequent and unstressed form, may not have undergone the Great Vowel Shift. Unstressed *mi* would thus have fallen together with a weakened form of the object pronoun *me* /mi/ < ME /me:/, resulting synchronically in this apparently merged form (Krug 2003).

2.1.2. *Reflexive pronouns*

Generally, one can say that the paradigm of reflexive pronouns is regularized in the Southeast of England. In StE, the pattern is mixed: *myself*, *yourself*, *herself*, *ourselves*, and *yourselves* use the possessive case of the personal pronoun plus a form of *self*; *himself* and *themselves* on the other hand use the object case. *Self* inflects for number, such that the singular forms take *self*, the plural forms take *selves*. In the Southeast, however, we generally find the possessive case used throughout; thus we regularly encounter *hisself* as in (2a), and, as a consequence of possessive *me* discussed above, we also find *meself* used as a reflexive pronoun (see 2b). The plural forms are sometimes formed with *self* (*ourself*, *themself*) rather than *selves* (as in 2c to 2e), which indicates that *-self* has grammaticalized to a simple reflexive marker and is not perceived as indicating number any more. As a consequence, especially the third person plural shows a great deal of variation: StE *them* + non-StE *self*, non-StE *their* + StE *selves*, non-StE *their* + non-StE *self* as well as StE *themselves* are all attested, as examples in (2d) to (2g) show:

(2) a. [*He*] *put his hand to steady* ***hisself*** *on top of the winch.* (FRED LND_007)
b. *I had ten bob. Two bob for* ***meself*** *and eight bob for the board and lodging.* (FRED KEN_001)
c. [*We*] *used to have to stand in this copper and bath* ***ourself****, wash our hair and all.* (FRED LND_005)
d. *They wouldn't come round to make* ***theirself*** *a nuisance.* (FRED KEN_001)
e. *They would've never forgiven* ***themself*** *for allowing me out on the deck.* (FRED LND_006)
f. *They'd do it* ***theirselves****.* (FRED KEN_004)
g. *We used to say the fires just eh burnt* ***themselves*** *out.* (FRED MDX_002)

On the syntax of reflexive pronouns see also section 3.1. below.

2.1.3. *Subject* us

The StE object pronoun *us* is regularly found in subject position when followed by a noun phrase apposition, as in (3).

(3) a. ***Us kids*** *used to pinch the sweets like hell.* (FRED LND_005)
b. ***Us old boys*** *would be drinking beer, too.* (FRED KEN_002)

This feature seems to be restricted to the first person plural for several reasons. The equivalent third person plural form would be indistinguishable from demonstrative *them* (see section 2.1.5.) and *they* is not usually found in this construction anyway (cf. Quirk et al. 1985: 352–353). The second person has identical forms for subject and object pronouns (*you*), so that an exchange cannot be documented. With singular pronouns (except *you*) a combination with a noun phrase is probably not possible.

2.1.4. Singular us

As in most other dialect areas, the plural object form *us* can be used in place of the singular *me*. Although this phenomenon can be clearly documented, it is difficult to quantify, as extensive context is necessary to determine the exact reference. Some examples are given in (4).

(4) a. *He says, **Give us** a fiver for it, Ted, and you can have it.* (FRED KEN_002)
b. ***Show us** them boots!* (FRED LND_003)

As Edwards notes, "there are restrictions on the distribution of plural forms for reference to the singular. Thus, while it is possible to use *us* for *me*, the corresponding use of *we* for *I* does not occur" (Edwards 1993: 231). Even in the same context of requests, it seems unlikely that third person *them* would substitute *him* or *her*. Instead, this phenomenon seems to be specific to the first person, and to imperatives. Whether the use of *us* for *me* has its origin in being a mitigating factor in requests has not been investigated yet.

2.1.5. Them *as demonstrative pronoun*

The system of demonstrative pronouns is much the same in the Southeast as in StE: we find a two-way distinction between near and distant objects. However, as in many other dialect areas, for distant plural objects *them* is used rather than StE *those*:

(5) a. *I don't know if you've ever seen **them** old drinking horns, have you?* (FRED KEN_001)
b. *That was the way of life in **them** days.* (FRED LND_002)
c. *That bloke used to cut **them** willows.* (FRED MDX_002)

The use of *them* rather than *those* as the distal demonstrative pronoun is a highly frequent phenomenon; for example, FRED data from Kent has *them* rather than *those* in over seventy percent of all possible cases.

2.2. Past tense verb paradigms

As in other dialect areas, many speakers in the Southeast have verb paradigms different from the standard. Authors have tried to systematize the differences in various ways. It is clear that overall, irregular verb paradigms of the standard tend to be simpler than in StE. This concerns in particular StE strong verbs which have three-way paradigms (e.g. *know-knew-known*; *see-saw-seen*) and strong verbs with two-way paradigms (e.g. *run-ran-run*; *come-came-come*). While each verb undoubtedly has its own history, and many non-standard forms may be carry-overs from historical forms that did not make it into the standard, today non-standard grammar is often interpreted as simplifying the StE system. Thus, three-part paradigms are reduced to just two items – although it is not predictable whether the past tense form or the past participle is extended to the other function – and we also often find that two-part paradigms are reduced to just one form, as in the cases of *come* or *run*. Particularly frequent in previous accounts as well as my data from the Southeast seems to be the simplification of *come* to the past tense and the use of *done* for the past tense, as in (6) and (7).

(6) *I was standing looking at a chap working, and he* ***come*** *up to me and wanted to know* (FRED KEN_005)

(7) *He worked, but what he* ***done*** *for a living, I don't know.* (FRED LND_001)

In the case of (6), this results in a paradigm that today looks maximally simplified: it contains only the one form *come-come-come*, and past tense meaning is only inferable from the context (except in the third person singular, where it is also signalled by the absence of the present tense *-s*, as example [6] illustrates). Parallel to past tense *come* we also encounter past tense *become*. The past tenses of *give* and *run* also seem to follow this pattern fairly frequently. In the case of (7), the StE three-part paradigm *do-did-done* is reduced to the two-part paradigm *do-done-done*. This is a case of simplification, but not of regularization (*do* will be discussed in more detail in section 3.3.4.).

Cheshire (1982) distinguishes three classes of verbs: (a) verbs that are weak in the non-standard, but still strong in the standard, i.e. that have a non-standard past tense with *-ed* such as, in her data, *gived*, *holded*, *drawed*, *swinged*, *runned*, *blowed*, *fighted* and *waked*. (b) verbs where the StE past tense form is used for both the past tense and the (non-standard) past participle, as in *go*, *take*, *forget*, *run*, *break*, *throw*, *beat* and *see*. (c) In a third class, the reverse is the case, and the StE past participle is used for both the non-standard past tense and past participle, as for *come*, *become*, *run* and *do*. Particularly for the first three of these forms, however, present tense and past participle are identical in form, so that one could equally well speak of a maximally simplified system.

For some highly frequent verbs like *know*, *break*, *see* or *eat*, however, we find a variety of non-standard forms co-existing alongside each other, and indeed alongside the StE forms. (As most other dialect features today, the past tense/past participle forms are variable and co-exist with the corresponding StE forms.) In Cheshire's system, the same word can belong to several classes. This solution might however obscure the potentially interesting character of these verbs. Edwards for example draws attention to the fact that we find a number of different forms coexisting, which in her opinion "point[s] very clearly to a process of linguistic change which is still in progress" (Edwards 1993: 221). However, detailed studies of this change in progress are still missing, both in comparison with the historical switch of strong verbs to weak verbs, and in comparison with other dialect areas.

What is becoming obvious from the published accounts, though, is that those irregular paradigms of the standard which still consist of three different forms (present tense, past tense, past participle, e.g. *see-saw-seen* or *drive-drove-driven*) tend towards a paradigm that is differentiated only along two ways (a present tense form, and then identical past tense and past participle forms). In this regard, irregular verbs of the non-standard are becoming more similar to the regular verbs in *-ed* (of standard and non-standard): Even if they do not completely switch verb classes from strong verbs to weak verbs, they do follow the same pattern of not differentiating between past tense and past participle forms (cf. *see-seen-seen* parallel to *start-started-started*).

2.3. New modal verbs

Krug (2000) discusses the emergence of some new modal verbs, his "emerging modals" WANT TO, BE GOING TO, HAVE GOT TO and, more marginally, HAVE TO and NEED TO. Often, these occur as contracted forms, especially *wanna*, *gonna*, *gotta* and *hafta*. Interestingly, the contracted forms also tend to go together with a shift in meaning. *Wanna* for example seems to be on the path of becoming a modal, exhibiting the meaning of obligation, if not even a command, as in (8), *gonna* is becoming a simple future marker, and *gotta* has developed epistemic readings from the – still more frequent – deontic ones, as in (9).

(8) *You've got toothache? You* ***wanna*** *see a dentist!* (Krug 2000: 147)

(9) *And I think probably it's* ***got to*** *be her.* (Krug 2000: 94)

Although these forms can be found practically all over Great Britain today, quantitative differences based on regional comparisons from the BNC suggest that they may have had their source in the Southeast of England (cf. Krug 2000: 111–114, 185–192).

3. Syntax

3.1. Use of untriggered reflexive pronouns

In the Southeast of England, we encounter the use of *self*-forms that need no antecedent for their interpretation (so-called untriggered *self*-forms). What looks like a reflexive pronoun thus takes over the function of a simple pronoun. Untriggered *self*-forms are reported to appear especially in subject position, and especially in co-ordinated noun phrases (cf. Hernández 2002), and data from FRED supports this also for the Southeast of England, as examples (10) and (11) illustrate.

(10) *No, my younger brother and* ***myself*** *was his favourites.* (FRED LND_001)

(11) Interviewer: *How many of you were there?*
Informant: *There was* ***meself****, and me sister's four years younger than me. And then there's eh a brother of mine.* (FRED KEN_005)

3.2. Lack of plural *-s* with measurement nouns

It is widely reported that the Southeast permits the use of singular nouns after numbers or, put differently, generally has nouns of measurement in the singular, again as in many other dialects. Some examples are given in (12).

(12) a. *I had it made, cost thirteen* ***pound****, in nineteen twenty-six.* (FRED KEN_002)
b. *These people used to move the fence three* ***foot*** *every night.* (FRED MDX_002)
c. *We got five* ***mile*** *to walk.* (FRED KEN_006)

A careful analysis of a range of nouns of measurement paints a more differentiated picture, however. Not all nouns of measurement occur in the singular. *Ounces* and *yards* for example regularly appear in the plural in FRED with numbers larger than one, as do *days*, *weeks*, and *inches*. *Mile*, *pound* and *foot*, as in the examples in (12), on the other hand, are usually found in the singular.

Historically, these units of measurement were regularly used in the singular after numbers, as the Oxford English Dictionary (OED) documents. Plural use of these nouns (as measurement nouns) was introduced into the standard at different times for the individual lexemes, and indeed singular *foot* is still variably used even today in StE as a noun of measurement, while singular *pound* is still permitted in combinations (e.g. *two pound ten*), according to the OED (cf. OED, sub voce *foot*, *pound*, *mile*).

3.3. Subject-verb concord

3.3.1. BE was/were *variation*

In the Southeast of England, plural pronouns are extremely frequently used with the StE singular form *was*. Thus the combination of *we*, *you*, and *they* with *was* is almost categorical (around 80 percent in the data from FRED). Occasionally *was* is also used with full noun phrases, as examples (13d) and (13e) show (names have been anonymized by the use of the asterisk *; two asterisks represent two syllables).

(13) a. ***We was*** *never without food.* (FRED KEN_003)
b. *So* ***you was*** *a week on labour, a week off.* (FRED LND_006)
c. *They lost their mother when* ***they was*** *boys.* (FRED MDX_001)
d. *And that was where* ***the first aeroplanes was*** *built, over at Eastchurch.* (FRED KEN_006)
e. *Never out of work,* ***none of me brothers was*** *ever out of work, never.* (FRED LND_001)

(14) a. Interviewer: *Was it easy to get into trouble there?*
Informant: ***It were*** *easy. Yeah, very easy.* (FRED LND_001)
b. *He also worked for a very long time for Mr G**,* ***that were*** *young Mr F* G**, that had his building-yard up at D*'s Farm* (FRED MDX_001)

The reverse phenomenon, i.e. singular subjects occurring with the StE plural form *were*, also occurs in FRED, but only exceedingly rarely. In all three counties represented, relative frequencies are under or around the one percent mark for *were*-regularization. Two of the rare examples are provided in (14). The – far more usual – extension of *was* to plural subjects also holds for the negated forms, although confirmation is sometimes difficult as negation itself is quite rare (in data from FRED, one negative verb form occurs only per every sixteen positive verb forms). It is generally noted that negation plays an important role for this phenomenon, but for these particular dialect areas in FRED, relative frequencies for *was*-regularization are more than twice as high than for the negative equivalent, the use of plural pronouns with *wasn't*.

3.3.2. There + BE

Existential *there* is frequently used with the singular forms of BE, even if it refers to a plural subject. This is the case both for present and past tense forms of BE. Thus we regularly find *there is* and *there was* with reference to a following plural subject, as in (15).

(15) a. *There's no false ceiling, **there's** no columns*. (FRED LND_007)
b. ***There was** some papers wanted urgently.* (FRED LND_006)

At first glance, this might simply be another aspect of variation in forms of BE noted above. On the other hand, it might indicate a change in the status of *there* rather than be a feature of the verb *be*, as *there* seems to be treated as a normal singular pronoun. Whereas *was* with plural personal pronouns is a matter of variation, *there was* is as good as categorical: *we was* and *we were* exist side by side, whereas *there was* for many speakers is the only form attested. In addition, the singular form is also documented for the present tense with *there*, as in example (15a), whereas *is* with the plural personal pronouns, i.e. forms like *we is*, *they is*, is not attested at all for the Southeast of England.

3.3.3. HAVE *full verb vs. auxiliary*

Has, restricted in StE to the third person singular (*he has*, *she has*, *it has*), can also occur with other subjects in Reading English, according to Cheshire (1982: 32), as example (16) illustrates.

(16) a. ***We has** a muck around in there.*
b. ***You** just **has** to do what these teachers tell you.*

Interestingly, in Cheshire's Reading material, "the non-standard form never occurs when HAVE is an auxiliary verb" (Cheshire 1982: 32). No non-concord forms of HAVE could be detected in FRED, but this may be due to the overall rarity of *has* compared to the other primary verbs. (FRED only contains 29 instances of *has* for the Southeast, all of which are standard, i.e. occur with third person singular subjects.)

3.3.4. DO *full verb vs. auxiliary*

For present tense DO, Cheshire (1982) reports three non-standard forms: (a) Non-concord *does* [dʌz] is used with all persons, i.e. also with non-third-person singular subjects, especially when it is a full verb, as in examples (17a) and (17b). (b) Non-concord *do* is also used with all persons, especially with third-person singular subjects, when it is used as an auxiliary, as in (17c). (c) The non-standard form *dos* [du:z] is used mainly with third-person subjects, but only in full verb use, as in (17d). All examples in (17) are from Cheshire (1982: 35).

(17) a. *every time* ***we does*** *anything wrong*
b. *that's what* ***I does***
c. *it hurts my dad more than* ***it do*** *her*
d. ***one bloke*** *stays at home and* ***dos*** *the house-cleaning and all that.*

(18) *But nowadays* ***it don't*** *matter does it.* (FRED KEN_004)

Cheshire claims that the present distribution represents a change in progress, from the earlier main verb form *dos* [du:z] to the present day form *does* [dʌz] to the StE differentiation of *does* vs. *do* for third person singular – non-third person singular; on the other hand Cheshire postulates an earlier auxiliary verb form *do* (for all persons) which fell together with StE *does/do*. Although data from FRED do not support this distinction for the positive paradigm, in the negative paradigm *don't* is almost categorical, i.e. also used in the third person singular, as in (18). And indeed this would be the expected form from a former auxiliary *do*, as only the auxiliary can be negated by adding the negator *n't* (the full verb of course has to take *do*-support). The phenomenon of third-singular *don't* is discussed further in section 3.4.2.

In the past tense, full verb and auxiliary uses of DO are also distinguished. Cheshire (1982) claims a strict differentiation in Reading adolescent non-standard speech between DO used as a full verb and DO used as an auxiliary. Only full verb DO has the past tense and past participle form *done*, as in (19a). Auxiliary DO also has identical past tense and past participle forms, but here the form is *did*. A nice example that combines both uses of DO is example (19b) (both from Cheshire 1982: 48).

(19) a. *I* ***done*** *the most to him.*
b. *She* ***done*** *it,* ***didn't*** *she*?
c. *I don't know what they* ***done*** *with them.* (FRED KEN_002)
d. *but Mother used to take the bets, so* ***did*** *Dad.* (FRED LND_005)

As (19c) and (19d) illustrate, this distinction of full verb vs. auxiliary in the past tense of DO can also be observed in data from FRED, and can thus be confirmed as a feature of the wider Southeast.

3.3.5. Non-standard -s *with other verbs*

Many regular verbs sometimes occur with *-s* with subjects other than the third-person singular. It is not exactly clear what determines the use of this non-standard *-s*, as it is highly variable. Linguistic constraints (preceding environment, following environment) do not seem to play a decisive role. Style seems to be a more important feature. Cheshire for example finds the use of non-standard *-s* particularly frequent with "vernacular verbs", i.e. verbs which do not occur in StE at all, or that are used with a different meaning: "it can be seen that the use of a 'vernacular' verb acts as a lexical constraint on the form of the verb, strongly favouring the non-standard form" (Cheshire 1982: 43). Some of her examples are provided in (20).

(20) a. ***I goes**, oh clear off.*
b. ***We chins** them.*
c. ***We bunks** it.*

Especially in (20a), *I goes* functions as a – non-standard – quotative marker, i.e. a marker introducing (direct or reported) speech. Here *goes* rather than *go* seems obligatory. (On quotative markers see further section 3.9.) A more comprehensive database like FRED, which samples a wider range of texts than the speech of adolescents as in Cheshire's study, indicates that the historical present is not only used with vernacular verbs but also triggered in passages of increased involvement, and this is often marked by *-s*, as in (21).

(21) ***I goes** into the shelter.* (FRED LON_001)

Again, however, more detailed studies on this kind of non-concord *-s* are still missing. It is therefore difficult to judge in how far non-concord *-s* functions as a specific indicator of narratives, or whether it is a dialect feature that simply emerges more frequently when the speaker is emotionally involved.

3.4. Negation

3.4.1. Ain't

Ain't is probably the best-known indicator of non-standard grammar in North America and the UK. There are only very few exceptions, most notably Irish and Scottish English, where *ain't* is reported not to occur in the traditional dialects. It does occur in the Southeast of England, as in examples (22a) to (22c).

(22) a. *I asked him, and he said, Well, There* ***ain't*** *nothing you can do.* (FRED KEN_003)
b. *And he said no, I* ***ain't going****.* (FRED KEN_004)
c. *Him and I* ***ain't been fishing*** *for these last six weeks.* (FRED MDX_001)

Ain't is indeed part of the traditional dialect system of the Southeast (see data from the SED on the individual verb forms which also attest *ain't/en't/in't*, collected in Anderwald [2002: 122–123]). Although the history of this form still remains to be written, it must have been frequent enough by the early nineteenth century for Charles Dickens to use it as a regional stereotype which characterizes his working class characters from London, and it is still very popular there, as Wright notices: "People grumble about this widespread Cockney liking for *ain't*, but the thinking Cockney replies that he has to keep saying it, especially for asking questions, because it is so 'darned useful'" (Wright 1981: 120). And very useful it is indeed, as the one verb form *ain't* does service for all present tense forms of BE (*am*, *are*, *is*) as well as for all present tense forms of HAVE (*has*, *have*). While there is no differentiation in the use of *ain't* for BE (*ain't* can be used both for copula BE and auxiliary BE, as example [22a] and [22b] illustrate), it is generally held that only auxiliary (as opposed to full verb) HAVE can be substituted by *ain't*, as in (22c). It is thus not possible to have a form like **I ain't a clue*, e.g. according to Hughes and Trudgill (1996: 23).

For her Reading adolescent speakers, Cheshire notes a striking regularity in the use of *ain't* for these three verbs (auxiliary HAVE, copula BE, auxiliary BE): "Its occurrence follows a regular pattern, with *ain't* occurring most often as auxiliary HAVE, in the speech of all groups, and least often as auxiliary BE" (Cheshire 1982: 51). In my follow-up study based on about ten times as many tokens from the British National Corpus (BNC), I have not been able to substantiate this distribution (Anderwald 2002: 117, 135–139). There are however two robust trends across all regions in Britain: if one compares the two primary verbs, *ain't* is used much more frequently – in relative terms – for HAVE than for BE (copula and auxiliary uses taken together). Secondly, if we look inside the BE paradigm, there is an equally robust trend that *ain't* is used more frequently for auxiliary BE than for copula BE. An underlying reason for both distributions might be the fact that BE is much more frequent than HAVE (at a ratio of about three to one), and that copular BE is much more frequent than the auxiliary (at a ratio of about five or six to one). In both cases, the less frequent member of the pair in absolute terms (HAVE < BE; aux BE < cop BE) is simplified to *ain't* much more often – a typical pattern for simplification strategies, which tend to affect high frequency items last. Another possible generalization is that *ain't* is used far more frequently for the negation of an auxiliary (HAVE or BE) than for negating a full verb.

In his jocular account, Wright already points to the fact that *ain't* might be particularly frequent in interrogatives (Wright 1981). The data support this, especially if one takes into account the different phonetic forms that *ain't* can take (in particular, /eɪnt/ /ɪnt/ and /ent/, usually transcribed as *ain't*, *in't* and *en't*). As Cheshire has noted, "tag questions strongly favour the use of a non-standard form" (Cheshire 1982: 55), and in particular *in't* occurs almost exclusively in tag questions. From here it is only a short step to the highly contracted tag question *innit*, which will be dealt with in section 3.7.1.

3.4.2. *Third person singular* don't

The negative form of present tense DO is *don't* across the whole of the Southeast, as in (23). This is possibly an independent development from positive third person singular *do* mentioned above, but could also be plausibly interpreted as a relic of an earlier, more widespread auxiliary *do* used for all persons.

(23) a. *That's funny,* ***He don't*** *live in there.* (FRED LND_005)
b. *They say, What* ***the eye don't*** *see,* ***the heart don't*** *grieve.* (FRED LND_004)

Although *don't* is almost categorical in data from FRED, absolute figures are so low that quantitative analyses do not seem feasible for this phenomenon. Again, this is a feature that is not restricted to the Southeast of England.

3.4.3. *Multiple negation/negative concord*

Cheshire, Edwards and Whittle (1993) have very tentatively suggested that – contrary to every expectation – multiple negation (or negative concord) seems to be more frequent in their data from the South than it is in the Midlands or in the North. Although they do not provide any statistical analyses as to whether these differences are significant, and if so at what level, their figures look interesting enough to merit further examination. In Anderwald (2002: 109–114) I have investigated this possibility in data from the BNC, and significant differences between the South and the North did indeed emerge. More detailed preliminary studies based on FRED corroborate that there is in fact a robust quantitative difference between the North and the South, such that negative concord is far more frequent in the South, and relatively infrequent in the North. Data from FRED suggests a ratio of around 36 percent negative concord for the three Southeastern counties included, as against just over 11 percent for the North, with the Midlands patterning in between. In other words, negative concord in the Southeast is more than three times as likely as in the North – a striking regional distribution that has not been investigated in detail yet.

Structurally, negative concord usually consists of the sentence negator *not* as the first element, combined with other negative elements, as in (24).

(24) a. *He* ***wouldn't*** *give me* ***nothing***. (FRED LND_001)
b. *I* ***didn't*** *know* ***nothing*** *what to say to 'em.* (FRED KEN_004)

Other frequent first elements are *never*, as in (22), and, more marginally, *no-one.*

(25) a. *He* ***never*** *got* ***no*** *supper.* (FRED MDX_002)
b. *He* ***never*** *done* ***nothing***. (FRED LND_001)
c. ***No-one*** *would* ***never*** *take much offence.* (FRED KEN_003)

(On the use of *never* in past tense contexts see section 3.4.4. below.) What Labov (1972) has called NEG concord to pre-verbal position does occur as well, if only marginally so. This feature has sometimes been adduced as distinguishing African American Vernacular English from other dialects of English, but a careful study of dialect data shows that NEG concord to pre-verbal position is also systematically possible in at least some British English dialects as well, as example (26) shows.

(26) *Yes, and* ***no*** *people* ***didn't*** *trouble about gas stoves then.* (FRED KEN_005)

3.4.4. Never *as a past tense negator*

Cheshire (1982: 67–71) stresses that in Reading, *never* can act as the sole negator in past tense contexts with the specific meaning 'not on a specific occasion'. In example (27), *never went* is thus equivalent to StE *didn't go.*

(27) *I* ***never went*** *to school today.* (Cheshire 1982: 67)

This is relatively difficult to verify quantitatively, as the meaning is extremely context–dependent, and even a large context is not always sufficient to disambiguate between the standard meaning of *never* ('not on any occasion') and the non-standard meaning ('not on a specific occasion'). Some clear cases however can be found in the transcribed material from FRED, and one example is (28):

(28) *and, uh, he, he never done a lot of schooling. And he come running out of a, his house one day. And a kid swore black and blue he's nicked a ten bob note off him. He was gonna get some errands. They turned him over, the boy,* ***never*** *found no ten bob note. And then when they f- the school report, that was it. It convicted him.* (FRED LND_004)

Again, this is a feature not unique to the Southeast, but one that qualifies as a widespread non-standard feature in Cheshire's, Edwards' and Whittle's list (1993: 64).

3.5. Adverbs = adjectives

In the Southeast of England, as probably in most other dialect areas, adverbs often have the same form as the corresponding adjectives. This holds particularly for the very frequent adverbs. Again this is a feature already included by Cheshire, Edwards and Whittle (1993) in their questionnaire, and especially the form *quick* as an adverb is common currency across the Southeast, as in example (29). Other adverbs however are also found in this form, as examples (30a) to (30e) show.

(29) *I swum me way out of it* ***quick***. (FRED LND_006)

(30) a. *They fussed him up* ***terrible***. (FRED LND_001)
b. *that used to last you a week* ***easy*** (FRED KEN_005)
c. *That is* ***honest*** *true, that is.* (FRED LND_004)
d. *If you got* ***proper*** *disabled.* (FRED KEN_005)
e. *And he'll have his own Sam Browne* [belt] *off, and he'd give them so many straps, real strap,* ***real*** *hard.* (FRED LND_001)

On the other hand, a large number of adverbs never occur without *-ly*, e.g. *actually, generally, particularly, recently, suddenly*. The distinction is not quite clear, but it does not so much seem a function of the etymology of the stem (for example, Romance origin vs. Germanic), but of their syntactic function. Only the prototypical adverbials, with the adverb modifying an adjective or the verb phrase, seem to occur without *-ly*, while adverbials like *actually* appear in their full form. Again, there are no detailed studies on the constraints of this interesting phenomenon to date.

3.6. Subordination

3.6.1. Subject zero relatives

According to Wright (1981: 117) and Edwards (1993: 229), it is possible to use zero to introduce subject relative clauses in the Southeast of England, whereas the standard only permits this construction for the object (and oblique) position. These subject contact clauses occur quite regularly and seem to be particularly frequent in the existential construction, i.e. after existential *there is/there was*, as the examples in (31) demonstrate:

(31) a. *There was no nurse Ø came.* (FRED LND_006)
b. *There's one single house Ø stands right against the school gates.* (FRED MDX_001)

Indeed, Quirk et al. claim that in this context (existentials, cleft sentences) we are not dealing with a typical adnominal relative clause, because the left hand portion is obligatory (Quirk et al. 1985: 1250). As they do not offer an alternative analysis, however, I have retained general dialectological practice and referred to these constructions also as subject zero relatives. This is an extension of a standard strategy to a position where the standard does not permit it, which results in a non-standard construction. Unfortunately, no detailed regional or indeed cross-dialectal studies are available yet for this phenomenon, leaving much scope for further research.

3.6.2. What as a relative pronoun

As in many other dialects, *what* can be used as a relative pronoun; according to Wright (1981: 116) and Edwards (1993: 228), *what* is doing service for *who, whom* and *which*, and data from FRED confirm this, as example (32) illustrates.

(32) a. *Anybody* ***what*** [=StE *who*] *been away from them, there, well, this last twenty years wouldn't know it.* (FRED KEN_006)
b. *the stuff* ***what*** [=StE *which*] *came from the gas corroded the cable.* (FRED MDX_001)

In contrast to zero as a relative marker in subject position mentioned above, the relative pronoun *what* is not permitted in the standard in any position. We are thus dealing here with a non-standard feature that has no parallel in the standard. First results from dialect-comparative work indicate that the origin of *what* as a relative marker may very well lie in the Southeast, from where it seems to be spreading (Herrmann 2003: 88).

3.6.3. *Relative* as

Another non-standard relative marker mentioned for Cockney in Wright (1981) is *as*. The relative marker *as* does not seem to be nearly as frequent as *what* above, and there are some indications that *as* is an older form that is receding from dialect speech (Herrmann 2003: 88). An example from Wright (1981) – also indicating *h*-dropping – is given in (33a), perhaps the only equivalent from FRED is given in (33b).

(33) a. *That noise* ***as*** *you 'eard.*
b. *He ... was a chap* ***as*** *got a living anyhow.* (FRED KEN_002)

Although this is a very infrequent phenomenon, the regional spread of relative *as* does seem to reach at least beyond London, as the example from FRED (Kent) indicates. Edwards likewise still reports the use of *as* "in some parts of the region" (Edwards 1993: 228).

Again, however, non-standard relative markers (both *what* and *as*) have not been examined in detail until very recently (cf. Herrmann 2003, who unfortunately only includes data from East Anglia, not the wider Southeast in her study), so that regional comparisons must still remain tentative.

3.7. Tag questions

3.7.1. Innit

A feature typical of adolescent London speech is the invariant tag question *innit*. This has clearly grammaticalized from *isn't it*, although a derivation from *ain't it* is also possible (cf. the discussion in Andersen 2001: 168–179). Today, *innit* is used with all persons and verbs as an non-canonical tag, as Andersen (2001: 97–208) shows on the basis of data from COLT. Some examples are provided in (34).

(34) a. *He gets upset quick* ***innit****?* (for *doesn't he?*) (Andersen 2001: 105)
b. *you can go with your Mum then,* ***innit*** (for *can't you*) (Andersen 2001: 171)

Andersen (2001: 113–114) traces the history of this invariant *non-canonical* tag to the multilingual community of London, in particular the Jamaican community from which it may have originated. The non-standard tag *innit* certainly seems to be on the spread; indeed Andersen states that "it is used by both genders and by young and older adults alike, suggesting that *innit* is fairly well established as a non-standard tag in London English generally" (Andersen 2001: 109), but in the speech of adults today *innit* always corresponds to *isn't it*, i.e.

it is not used as an invariant tag, but as a non-standard canonical tag with third-person singular neuter subjects. Whether the use of *innit* as a non-canonical tag will spread out from the adolescent population, or whether it will remain a feature characteristic of adolescent speech and thus be subject to age-grading, remains to be seen.

3.7.2. Aggressive tags

Cheshire already reports the use of what she calls "unconventional tags" (Cheshire 1982: 57–60) in her adolescent material, especially in the context of (verbal or indeed nonverbal) fights, as in (35).

(35) *You're a fucking hard nut, **in't you**?* (Cheshire 1982: 58)

Although the form of these tag questions is not necessarily non-standard, the function certainly is. They are intended to convey assertion or even aggression, rather than seek confirmation. Similar uses can also be confirmed for the FRED material and are thus not a feature of adolescent language exclusively, as example (36) shows.

(36) a. *I was playing up the wall and all of a sudden, something's hit me in the bleeding head, **hasn't it**.* (FRED LON_001)
b. *'Course we had a fight there, **don't we**.* (FRED LON_001)

Wright similarly notices that "the oddest thing about Cockney tag questions is their use to ask a listener things he or she cannot possibly know, especially in recounting incidents" (Wright 1981: 121).

3.8. Conjunctions

3.8.1. Without *as a conjunction*

The use of *without* as a conjunction introducing finite clauses has not been documented before for the Southeast of England, but the examples from FRED in (37) are unambiguous. In StE, an equivalent construction would have to contain a non-finite clause with *-ing* (… *without having to sit on the floor*), as *without* in StE can only introduce non-finite or verbless clauses (Quirk et al. 1985: 704). Similar to comparative *as* and *than* discussed below, *without* can be strengthened by *that*, as in (37b), yielding a non-standard complex conjunction.

(37) a. *Because my old man couldn't walk from here to the corner* ***without*** *he had to sit on the floor.* (FRED LND_004)

b. *He was a very nice man. Wouldn't let you go in his place* ***without that*** *you, you (pause) cleaned your shoes before you come in the door.* (FRED LND_004)

Unfortunately, there are no further examples available for the Southeast, so that this interesting phenomenon remains to be investigated in more detail in the future. A cursory look across FRED suggests however that this use of *without* is not restricted to the Southeast, but occurs in all dialect areas across Great Britain. The OED supplies evidence that *without* and *without that* as conjunctions introducing finite clauses were in use in StE until the end of the nineteenth century (OED, sub voce *without*). (At least some) non-standard varieties of English here seem to have maintained the historical construction.

3.8.2. *Comparative* as, than

In the Southeast of England, *what* can be added to the comparatives *as* and *than* and thus form a complex conjunction, as in (38) and (39).

(38) *Well, Mum was as bad* ***as what*** *he was.* (FRED LND_002)

(39) *So he's about eight years younger* ***than what*** *I am.* (FRED KEN_005)

Again, this is a frequent strategy that has not been investigated in any depth yet. It does not seem to have historical predecessors in the standard, as the OED only refers to it as "dialectal" (OED, sub voce *what*), in contradistinction to *without (that)* above.

3.9. Pragmatic marker *like*

While non-canonical *innit* discussed above seems to have its origin in London (Andersen 2001: 97–208), the discourse marker *like* seems to be an imported feature from the U.S. (Andersen 2001: 216). Like *innit*, the pragmatic marker *like* is used almost exclusively by adolescents and young adults – Andersen states that in his material, "83 percent of the tokens of the pragmatic marker *like* are uttered by speakers aged 41 or lower" (2001: 225). The pragmatic marker *like* has a wide range of functions: it is used in "ad hoc concept construction", i.e. for purposes of approximation and exemplification, as in (40a) and (40b); *like* is used to construct a metalinguistic focus, as in (40c), it is used as a quotative after BE (as in 40d), and, very frequently, it is a hesitational device or a discourse link (Andersen 2001: 209–299).

(40) a. *It's just* ***like*** *all sticking out all over the place.* (Andersen 2001: 237)
b. *You know what I mean it's* ***like*** *all plotted.* (Andersen 2001: 237)
c. *It's* ***like*** *one day developing, right* (Andersen 2001: 242)
d. *I was* ***like****, he should come and speak to me* (Andersen 2001: 250)
e. *I know and* ***like*** *... on Friday yeah ...* (Andersen 2001: 255)

Not surprisingly, given its recency, this pragmatic *like* is not found in the FRED material, which dates from the 1970s and 1980s and contains the speech of mostly older speakers. What can be corroborated, though, is the use of a distinct, "traditional" dialectal *like* for the Southeast of England as well, supporting Andersen's hunch that this dialectal *like* is not exclusively a northern phenomenon, as examples (41) from FRED show.

(41) a. *but they 're dead and gone now* ***like****. And eh, I went out with eh, ...* (FRED LND_003)
b. *Used to come down here* ***like*** *and have the day* (FRED KEN_001)

This older *like* is used "parenthetically to qualify a preceding statement" (Andersen 2001: 206, quoting from the OED), quite distinct from the new uses as recorded in COLT by Andersen. It is not implausible however that London is the source for the outward spread of these new – imported – uses of *like*, especially – perhaps most notably – of quotative *like* which is currently being recorded all over Great Britain (cf. Macaulay 2001).

4. Conclusion

Most of the features presented and discussed here are not used in the Southeast of England exclusively. However, even if features may have a more widespread geographical distribution, quantitative differences may be hiding behind qualitative similarity, opening up interesting research questions that only larger-scale comparative dialect studies will be able to answer. In the absence of more detailed dialect studies of this overlooked area of England, as well as larger comparative studies that include the Southeast, much of the material presented here must remain speculative for the moment. Nevertheless, I have attempted to document some aspects of the grammar of the Southeast of England, hoping that this may serve as an impetus for future research on this surprisingly neglected dialect area.

Exercises and study questions

1. From one of the standard histories of the English language, determine the source of migration into London in the 16th and 17th centuries. Which arguments do you find to support or contradict the claim that Standard English originated in the (linguistic) Southeast?

2. Discuss the proposed explanations of possessive *me*. From the literature, what is the accepted position in dialectology? Do you find the historical explanation plausible? Are there other words that did not undergo the Great Vowel Shift?

3. "The paradigm of reflexive pronouns is regularized". Draw up a table that illustrates graphically that the non-standard system is more regular than Standard English.

4. Consider again the fact that in the Southeast, *do* seems to have undergone a functional split in the past tense/past participle paradigm. Can you find a cognitive explanation for this development? Can you imagine why we do not find this split in the Standard?

5. From a comparison of other contributions in this volume, determine the regional spread of the relative particle *what*. Compare this to the relative particle *as*.

6. Trace the development of *innit* from the respective full forms. Say for each step which linguistic processes apply, and where. Distinguish canonical and non-canonical tags.

Selected references

Please consult the General references for titles mentioned in the text but not included in the references below. For a full bibliography see the accompanying CD-ROM.

Andersen, Gisle
2001 *Pragmatic Markers and Sociolinguistic Variation*. (Pragmatics and Beyond 84.) Amsterdam/Philadelphia: Benjamins.

Aston, Guy and Lou Burnard
1998 *The BNC Handbook: Exploring the British National Corpus with SARA*. Edinburgh: Edinburgh University Press.

Cheshire, Jenny
1982 *Variation in an English Dialect: A Sociolinguistic Study*. (Cambridge Studies in Linguistics 37.) Cambridge: Cambridge University Press.
Cheshire, Jenny, Viv Edwards and Pamela Whittle
1993 Non-StE and dialect levelling. In: Milroy and Milroy (eds.), 52–96.
Edwards, Viv
1993 The grammar of southern British English. In: Milroy and Milroy (eds.), 214–238.
Edwards, Viv and Bert Weltens
1985 Research on non-standard dialects of British English: progress and prospects (1). In: Viereck (ed.), 97–139.
Hernández, Nuria
2002 A context hierarchy of untriggered *self*-forms in English. *Zeitschrift für Anglistik und Amerikanistik. Special Issue: Reflexives and Intensifiers: The Use of self-Forms in English*: 269–284.
Herrmann, Tanja
2003 Relative clauses in dialects of English: a typological approach. Ph.D. dissertation, English Department, Albert-Ludwigs-Universität, Freiburg. http://www.freidok.uni-freiburg.de/volltexte/830.
Ihalainen, Ossi
1994 The dialects of England since 1776. In: Burchfield (ed.), 197–274.
Krug, Manfred G.
2000 *Emerging English Modals: A Corpus-based Study of Grammaticalization*. (Topics in English Linguistics 32.) Berlin/New York: Mouton de Gruyter.
2003 (Great) Vowel Shifts Present and Past: Meeting Ground for Structural and Natural Phonologists. Penn Working Papers 9.2.: Selected papers from 11 NWAVE at Stanford, CA, USA, 107–122.
Labov, William
1972 Negative attraction and negative concord in English grammar. *Language* 48: 773–818.
Macaulay, Ronald K.S.
2001 You're like 'Why not?': the quotative expressions of Glasgow adolescents. *Journal of Sociolinguistics* 5: 3–21.
Quirk, Randolph, Sidney Greenbaum, Geoffrey Leech and Jan Svartvik
1985 *A Comprehensive Grammar of the English Language*. Harlow: Longman.
Wright, Peter
1981 *Cockney Dialect and Slang*. London: Batsford.

British Creole: morphology and syntax

Mark Sebba

1. Introduction

1.1. General description of British Creole

British Creole, as explained by Peter Patrick in his chapter on its phonology (see Patrick, this volume), is the product of dialect contact between the Creole language varieties of migrants from the Caribbean (the largest group of whom were Jamaican), and vernacular varieties of urban English English (EngE) (Patrick 1999). Speakers of British Creole (who usually call the language *Patois* or *Patwa*), from the second generation onwards, are all bilinguals or multilinguals. At a very early age, they acquire a local variety of British English; at school if not earlier, they will be exposed to Standard English as well. In the second and later generations, code-switching in private conversations is common, with local EngE predominating over Creole. Although grammatical, phonological and lexical evidence indicates clearly that British Creole is based on Jamaican Creole (JamC), its speakers are not confined to the descendents of Jamaicans. They include people whose heritage is Caribbean but not Jamaican, and, on a smaller scale, others who have no Caribbean connections at all (Sebba 1993; Hewitt 1986). As mentioned by Patrick in his introduction, there is a range of fluency in British Creole, from passive knowledge (with only token productive capability) to competence comparable with a Caribbean island-born speaker of Creole.

In Britain, Caribbeans were immersed in local varieties of British English and in the second and third generations have become dominant in those varieties. Edwards (1986: 100) describes the competence of some second-generation speakers of Creole as "highly reminiscent of that of second language learners." Sebba (1993: 39) argues that the speakers he studied are more like 'new dialect learners' (Trudgill 1986) in that they acquire, sequentially, a new variety (Creole) which is similar in grammar, phonology and lexis to their first (London English).

Creoles within the Caribbean have long been a source of interest to linguists because of their high degree of variability, a variability often modelled as a 'post-creole' continuum in which two distinct and mutually unintelligible varieties – the *basilect* or 'broadest' Creole and the *acrolect* or local Standard English – are linked in 'a continuous spectrum of speech varieties' (DeCamp 1971: 350). The great syntactic variability of British Creole cannot be explained by a continuum model alone, being due on the one hand to the existence of both Creole-like and standard-like variants for many linguistic forms, and on the other to the frequent mixing of distinctively Creole forms with distinctively EngE forms, sometimes as part of a conversational strategy of code-switching and sometimes, apparently, as a result of incomplete fluency in the Creole. There is evidence that less fluent second-variety Creole speakers 'create' Creole by adapting British English forms to make them seem Creole-like. From time to time hybrid linguistic forms appear which can only be explained this way. For example:

(1) *What time did unu* (*you*-plural) *reach home?*
'What time did you get home?'

This utterance, marked as Creole by pronunciation (throughout) and pronoun forms (*unu*), would not be uttered by a first-language speaker of Creole in Jamaica, because JamC has no subject-auxiliary inversion in questions. The 'normal' JamC form for this question would be

(1') *What time unu* (*you*-plural) *did* (or *en*, or ∅) *reach home*?

The existence of forms like this suggests a strategy of 'dressing up' a basically London English sentence (e.g. *Did he give you what you were looking for?*) as Creole by adding Creole phonology, lexis and grammar. The results sound Creole enough to count as Creole for the purposes of the interaction, but would not pass for Creole in Jamaica. For these speakers 'Patois' is produced by a strategy of systematically 'adapting' their first language variety to produce utterances which conform, at least superficially, to the grammar of Creole. As a result their Creole intermittently shows some or all of the following (Sebba 1993: 52):

(a) incomplete adaptation: insufficiently salient features of JamC 'slip through' and fail to be adapted;
(b) inconsistency: due to possible learning or memory constraints, some adaptations are made sporadically, so that the same item might appear sometimes in its London English variant, sometimes in its JamC form;
(c) misadaptation: where the systems differ in such a way that adapting correctly requires recognising a contrast that exists in JamC but not in London English, speakers occasionally create forms which are neither the target (JamC) nor London English

For many British-born speakers, the use of Creole in conversation is largely symbolic: purely communicative functions can all be carried out through the medium of English. The symbolism of Creole as a marker of group identity is powerful even for those speakers who have limited fluency in it. A broad range of speech styles or language varieties might count as 'British Creole' for different purposes. For the purposes of symbolising group membership, the token use of a few lexical items with a high symbolic load (e.g. forms of address, greetings, swear words) might suffice for the speaker to be considered as talking 'Black' or 'chattin' Patois'. At the other end of the scale, some utterances of some speakers may be identical to basilectal Creole utterances produced by Jamaican speakers.

To summarise, British Creole is very poorly served by models of language which emphasise the separateness of different varieties and the regularities of differences between them. Variability in British Creole results from several different processes: variation with its historical origins in the Caribbean, code-switching, and second dialect acquisition strategies. Patrick (1999: 171) points out that for JamC "*a priori* categorical statements equating form and meaning are misleading". Creole languages have inspired innovative models of both language variation and language contact, and 'British Creole' (even the label begs many questions) exhibits complexities of both types.

For the purposes of this chapter, the morphosyntax of Standard English and JamC as described by Beryl Loftman Bailey (1966) and Peter Patrick (America and Caribbean volume) are used as reference varieties.

1.2. Sources of data on British Creole

The examples contained in this chapter are drawn from the following sources:

1. A corpus of informal conversations among British-born Caribbean adolescents recorded by the author in London in the early 1980s. This data reflects mainly the usage of adolescent second-generation speakers and would not necessarily be typical of the third or subsequent generations who are by now adolescents themselves.
2. The Corpus of Written British Creole (CWBC) (Sebba, Kedge and Dray 1999), which contains texts in a range of genres produced in Britain by writers of Caribbean heritage. Although all the writers of the texts were based in Britain as adults, the language of the texts does not necessarily reflect specifically British, as opposed to Caribbean, usages. Most of the Creole in the corpus is actually a representation of speech (e.g. dialogue). More information is available at http://www.ling.lancs.ac.uk/staff/mark/cwbc/cwbcman.htm.

1.3. Orthography

Cassidy developed an orthography for JamC which is used in Cassidy and Le Page ([1967] 1980) and is widely used by academic linguists but little used elsewhere (see Sebba 1998 for a discussion of Creole spelling practices). Orthography in this article is that of the original source for most citations, elsewhere it is Cassidy orthography (for grammatical citation forms etc.).

2. Verbal syntax and morphology

2.1. Verbal morphology: invariance of forms

Basilectal JamC is characterised, in common with other Creoles, by invariance of forms. There is a general reduction or absence of morphological processes which commonly serve grammatical functions in Standard English, such as affixation, vowel changes, and suppletion. The corollaries of this, detailed further below, include a lack of person/number agreement, invariance of pronoun forms irrespective of grammatical function, absence of morphological plural marking and invariant verb forms.

Even where JamC appears to have morphological marking of verbs, the reality is otherwise. For a few common verbs the base form of the JamC verb derives historically from an English past tense. Examples are *brok* ('break/broke'), *lef* ('leave/left'). These forms are used invariantly in JamC for both present and past.

As with other features of basilectal JamC, 'invariance' in British Creole is found variably. In other words, we can often find forms which show a lack of morphological marking alongside other forms, even in the same utterance, which display morphological marking in accordance with Standard English norms. Examples can be seen below in sections 2.2. (example 6) and 6.1. (examples 35 and 36).

2.2. Agreement

Agreement for person and number is absent in basilectal JamC. Generally this is also the case in British Creole, e.g.

(2) *She **look** pretty though, and **favour** you too.* (CWBC, fiction)

However, in British Creole we sometimes find agreement, even in a sentence where there is a lack of agreement elsewhere:

(3) *It **seems** like young Zukie **want** Paradise fe himself!* (CWBC, fiction)

Although the copula appears in different forms, these do not usually reflect person or number agreement:

(4) *OK, star, we know say **you is** a top soldier down ah Yard.*
'OK, star [a friendly term of address], we know that you are a top soldier down at the Yard.' (CWBC, fiction)

(5) *I **is** a very expensive man right now.* (CWBC, fiction)

(6) *Me and my spars dem **was** coming from a club in Dalston.* (CWBC, school writing)

2.3. Tense – aspect – modality systems

Unlike the Standard English system of verbal tense and aspect, which relies on affixation, morphological change, and the auxiliaries *be* and *have*, the JamC basilectal tense/aspect system is usually described in terms of a system of invariant preverbal particles, which allow for a set of contrasts different from those available in Standard English.

According to Bailey (1966: 45–46), the particle system comprises a 'tense indicator' *en* and an 'aspect marker' *a*. The third member of this system is zero, the absence of a marker. The following examples show how the tense and aspect markers may combine (the Standard English glosses are approximate):

Function	**Morpheme**	**Example**	**Gloss**
habitual, anterior	∅	*Mi ron*	'I run' (habitually); 'I ran'
progressive	*a*	*Mi a ron*	'I am running'
anterior	*en*	*Mi en ron*	'I have run'; 'I had run'
anterior progressive	*ena* (*en*+*a*)	*Mi ena ron*	'I was running'

The tense marker which Bailey cites as *en* does not usually appear in that form in British Creole. It occasionally appears as *bin*, but much more frequently as *did*.

Examples below show unmarked anterior or past tense (7), progressive aspect marking *a* (8), anterior tense marking with *did* (only) (9), and combined aspect and tense marking (10).

(7) *Is wha appen Sharon, unnu reach already?*
'What happened Sharon, are you there already?' (CWBC, scripted dialogue)

(8) *Check wah' de bwoy* ***ah do****.*
'Check what the boy is doing.' (CWBC, fiction)

(9) *Him* ***did sing*** *pure lovers rock tune.*
'He sang only 'Lover's Rock' tunes.' (CWBC, school writing)

(10) *de sun* ***did a shine*** *same way*
'the sun was shining the same way' (CWBC, poetry)

Example (11) below shows that the sequence of tenses also differs from that of Standard English: the anterior marker *did* occurs only once, at the beginning of a sequence where all the verbs are preceded by the aspect marker *a*.

(11) *Mi* ***did a stan up*** *inna di miggle a di road an mi* ***a*** *flag dung di bus fi stop an nun a di bus* ***naah stop*** *a nuh time at all.*
'I was standing in the middle of the road and I was flagging down the buses to stop and none of the buses ever stopped at all.' (CWBC, scripted dialogue)

In decreolisation, morphemes of non-standard appearance may be replaced by others which *resemble* morphemes of Standard English, but do not necessarily have the same function. In this context we may note that an important site for this is in the tense/aspect marking system. Thus basilectal *ben* or *en* may be replaced by *did*, while the preverbal 'aspect marker' *a* may be replaced by a suffix /in/ (modelled on the Standard English *-ing* ending), with or without a preverbal /iz/ modelled on English *is*. The first of these changes is almost categorical in British Creole, but the second occurs variably, cf. examples (12) and (13).

(12) *Mi* ***did*** *really* ***glad*** *fi see them.* (CWBC, school writing)

(13) *We movin in a single file.* (CWBC, poetry)

2.4. Auxiliaries, modal verbs and infinitives

2.4.1. Infinitive marking

The English infinitive marker *to* is most often translated by *fi* in JamC. In the Caribbean *fi* is considered to be a marker of extremely broad Creole; many otherwise broad Creole speakers will use *tu* (English *to*) in preference (see Bailey 1966: 122–124 for a description of the use of *fi*).

(14) *Me want a permanent stamp* ***fe go*** *ah New York City.* (CWBC, fiction)

In some cases infinitive marking is optional in Creole where it is obligatory in English (e.g. after *want* and *start*):

(15) *Mi nose* ***start run*** *wid misery*. (CWBC, poetry)

(16) *I* ***waan*** *yuh* ***play*** *a record for me idren.*
'I want you to play a record for my brothers.' (CWBC, fiction)

2.5. The copula

In Standard English the verb *to be* is used in a number of different functions:

(a) As an auxiliary verb to form different verb tenses: *I am writing*, etc.
(b) As an equative verb: *I am a teacher* etc.
(c) As a locative verb: *We are in London* etc.
(d) As a copular verb with a predicate adjective: *This book is old* etc.

Basilectal JamC uses a different expression for each of these:

(a') Auxiliary verbs are not used to form tenses or aspects of the verb in JamC (see 2.3. above): this is done by using invariant particles.
(b') The JamC equative verb *a* "regularly connects two nominals" (Bailey 1966: 32):

(17) *Den him know sey dat dem a duppy.*
'Then he knew that they were ghosts.' (CWBC, school writing)

(c') JamC has a separate locative verb *de*:

(18) *Him* ***deh*** *ah jail.*
'He is in jail.' (CWBC, fiction)

(19) *Me* ***deh*** *pon some serious business.*
'I am on some serious business.' (CWBC, fiction)

Sometimes the copula is omitted altogether in locatives:

(20) *"The bathroom upstairs," Joseph said.* (CWBC, fiction)

(d') With true predicate adjectives in JamC, no copula is required, the predicate adjective functioning like a stative verb:

(21) *Di place* ***clean*** *and di food* ***nice***. (CWBC, humour)

(22) *De night* ***did cold***. (CWBC, school writing)

British Creole speakers may use /iz/ as a substitute for *a* and/or *de*, obscuring some of the grammatical differences between JamC and Standard English.

2.6. Negation

The main negator is preverbal *no*, as in:

(23) *Perhaps she have a secret man and* ***nuh*** *tell we*. (CWBC, fiction)

No can also combine with the aspect marker *a* to produce *naa* (*no+a*):

(24) *Mi* ***naah*** *bak affa she.*
'I'm not barking at her.' (CWBC, fiction)

Other possible negators are *never* and *don't*.

'Double negatives' are used with quantitatives in basilectal JamC, and are frequently found in British Creole, where their distribution is similar to that in most non-standard British varieties of English:

(25) ***Nothing don't*** *seriously wrong wid him*. (CWBC, fiction)

Ain't is also a common negator (=BE+*not*) though it may be better to consider it as British English rather than British Creole:

(26) *I* ***in't*** *taking nothing from none of them*. (CWBC, fiction)

2.7. Adjectives and stative verbs

As mentioned in the section on the copula, predicate adjectives in JamC show behaviour similar to stative verbs. A number of words which in Standard English would be classed as adjectives are in fact verbs in JamC (e.g. *dead*), and vice versa (e.g. [*be*] *born,* [*be*] *named*).

(27) *One man from de Village* ***did dead***. (CWBC, school writing)

(28) *That boy* ***born*** *and look exactly like you people*. (CWBC, fiction)

(29) *She sey she* ***name*** *Mervalin*. (CWBC, school writing)

3. The pronoun system

The JamC 'basilectal' pronominal system has only seven terms, as follows:

person	singular	plural
1	mi	wi
2	yu	unu
3	im (m/f) i (n)	dem

Mesolectal varieties would differentiate *im* (masculine) and *shi* (feminine) in the third person. These forms are used in subject, object and possessive functions.

An alternative construction, *fi* + PRONOUN, e.g. *fi-mi*, is available for the possessive:

(30) *That a* ***fe yuh*** *business.*
'That's your business.' (CWBC, fiction)

British Creole speakers variably use pronoun forms modelled on Standard English alongside the Jamaican forms, where these are different. Thus while *mi* (for first person subject pronoun) is less standard-like and therefore has more symbolic potential as a group marker, we also often find *I* (and this particular pronoun has special significance for Rastafarians, see section 8 below).

In British Creole, the strict distinction between *yu* (singular) and *unu* (plural) may have been lost for some speakers who use *yu* for the plural, in analogy with Standard English.

4. Noun syntax and morphology

4.1. Plural marking

Basilectal JamC does not mark the plural of nouns, except in the case of animate nouns, which may be followed by the suffix *-dem*. In mesolectal varieties the Standard English suffix *-s* may co-occur with the JamC suffix *dem*, and this is also commonly found in British Creole, with animate and sometimes also inanimate nouns:

(31) *Look how me make yuh* ***dumplin's dem*** *fresh and crispy*. (CWBC, fiction)

4.2. Possessives

In basilectal JamC, in keeping with the principle of invariance of form and lack of nominal morphology, possession is expressed simply by juxtaposition, with the possessor preceding the possessed. The effect is that the ordering of nouns is as in Standard English, but there is no possessive marker (')*s*: thus *di bwai niem* 'the boy's name'.

This structure applies to common nouns but also to pronouns, so we find *mi buk* 'my book', *unu kyaa* 'your car' etc., although alternative forms *fi-mi buk*, *fi-unu kyaa* are possible.

(32) *Nuh tell me seh, you nuh recognise* ***yuh husband sister****!*
'Don't tell me you don't recognize your husband's sister!' (CWBC, fiction)

In British Creole, the possessive'*s* of Standard English may appear variably.

5. Complementation: the complementiser *seh*

A number of the Atlantic Creoles, including JamC, and many African languages, have a complementiser which in function is similar to *that* but which in form is similar to a verb meaning *to say*. According to Cassidy and LePage (1980: 396), in JamC *seh* [sɛ] is used, "after verbs such as *think*, *know*, *believe*, *suppose*, *see* or others involving communication, as, *tell*, *hear*, *promise*, introducing the object clause: virtually equivalent to *that*. (Sometimes *that* is used redundantly after it.)"
Although *seh* is equivalent to Standard English *that* in some contexts, the rules governing the use of *seh* are different from those which apply to *that*: in fact *seh* occurs as a complementiser in much more restricted contexts than *that*. In British Creole, *seh* is common as a complementiser especially after *know*, *think* and *tell*, and can even be found in the English of British-born speakers (see Sebba 1993: 62).

(33) *You must* ***t'ink seh*** *me turn English girl.*
'You must think I've become an English girl.' (CWBC, fiction)

(34) *Phone Lefty,* ***tell*** *him* ***seh*** *we ready fe him now.*
'… tell him that we're ready for him now.' (CWBC, fiction)

6. Word order and information structure

6.1. Question structure

The process of subject/auxiliary inversion which characterises some kinds of question in written and formal Standard English is absent in basilectal JamC, so the word order of a question is the same as the order of the corresponding statement, e.g.

(35) *So how Ethel's been doing?* (CWBC, fiction)

(36) *You heard about Fluxy?* (CWBC, fiction)

British speakers of Creole sometimes produce hybrid forms which appear to have subject/auxiliary inversion, e.g.

(37) *Did him give you what you a look for?*
'Did he give you what you were looking for?' (Conversational data, London, 1980s)

Here, the corresponding JamC form would have the same word order as the declarative: *him did give…*?

Did him seems to be a case of direct transfer from English, but is strictly speaking neither English (which requires *did he*) nor JamC. Since Creole *did* is not an auxiliary, but an invariant particle, and therefore cannot undergo 'subject/auxiliary inversion', the best way to analyse this part of the utterance seems to be as an English string which has been adapted by changing the subject pronoun into its Jamaican form (cf. 1.1. above) while leaving the English grammar intact.

6.2. Topicalizing constructions

6.2.1. Clefts

Clefts are constructions which involve fronting a nominal element. Cleft constructions are introduced by a topic marker or 'highlighter' which in JamC takes the form of the copula *a* (alternatively: *is*) or zero in positive clefts, and copula *a+no* in negatives. While in Standard English clefts seem to be uncommon and slightly awkward in questions (cf. *Who is it that you're looking for* vs. *Who are you looking for?*), in JamC they commonly occur in *wh*-questions with *what*, *when*, *where* and *who*.

(38) ***A who** dat?*
'Who's that?' (CWBC, fiction)

(39) *"**Is what area** dis, star?" he asked.* (CWBC, fiction)

(40) *So **is weh** de load deh?*
'So where is the load?' (CWBC, fiction)

More rarely cleft constructions can be found in non-questions.

(41) *Skeets seh **is one ki** you bring, weh de rest deh?*
'Skeets said you brought one key [kilo of drugs], where's the rest?' (CWBC, fiction)

(42) *We see sey **a mini cab** him inna.*
'We saw it was a minicab he was inside.' (CWBC, school writing)

6.2.2. Predicate clefts

Predicate clefts are constructions which involve fronting and repeating the main verb (or predicate adjective) for emphasis or contrast. They are introduced by a topic marker or 'highlighter' similar to the one used in a (nominal) cleft construction. Predicate cleft constructions are characteristic of some Atlantic Creoles, including JamC, and some West African languages (Holm 1988: 179).

In JamC the topicaliser takes the form of the copula *a* (alternatively: *is*) or zero in positive clefts, and copula *a+no* in negatives.

(43) *Work?! Where? Here? **Joke** you **a joke**, man!* (CWBC, fiction)

(44) *A no **play** we **a play**.*
'We're not playing!' (CWBC, poetry)

Predicate clefts are rare in British Creole.

6.3. Verb chaining

Verbs in JamC may be combined in ways which are not possible in English. One set of possibilities involves the motion verbs *go* and *come* immediately followed by another verb, e.g.

(45) *Prettyboy, **go bring** you gran'uncle something to drink.* (CWBC, fiction)

A second possibility is where the motion verb follows a main verb with lexical content, e.g.

(46) *Weh you ah **rush go** so?* (CWBC, drama)

Other combinations of verbs in this kind of construction are sometimes found both in JamC and in British Creole. Verbal constructions of this type resemble serial verb constructions which are characteristic of some West African languages and certain Atlantic Creoles (see Sebba 1987).

7. Prepositions

The preposition *a* has a wide range of uses corresponding to some uses of Standard English *in*, *at* or *to*.

(47) *Me go **a** de airport.* (CWBC, fiction)

(48) *Me lef' Jamaica an' come **ah** England!* (CWBC, fiction)

Other common prepositions which differ from Standard English are *ina* ('in') and *pan* ('on'). In written form there are numerous variant spellings of these.

(49) *Why should I let you* ***inna*** *me house?* (CWBC, fiction)

(50) *Him saddle up* ***'pon*** *bicycle an' t'ing.*
'He's saddled up on a bicycle and stuff.' (CWBC, fiction)

8. The lexicon of British Creole

The lexicon of JamC as spoken in the Caribbean is derived from a variety of sources including various languages of West Africa, languages of indigenous Caribbean peoples such as the Arawak, and colonizer groups such as the Spanish and Portuguese. However, the great majority of the vocabulary of JamC is identifiably of English origin and is recognisably similar to Standard English (LePage and DeCamp 1960, Cassidy 1961, Cassidy and LePage 1980). Some of the JamC vocabulary which is not shared with other varieties relates to species of flora and fauna which are not found in Britain; these words are therefore largely redundant in Britain and may well not be known to second and subsequent generations. Some words relating to widespread Jamaican cultural practices and beliefs such as *obiah* ('magic') and *duppy* ('ghost') seem to be well-known to second generation speakers but are probably used mainly with reference to events in the Caribbean.

In the British context, as British Creole functions largely as a youth language, there are many new coinages which are short-lived and restricted to users of a particular age group: hence a popular perception that 'Black English' is actually a type of slang. Since at least the 1970s there has been a movement of vocabulary from Creole to the 'local multiracial vernacular' of adolescents (Hewitt 1986) in cities with large Caribbean minorities like London. Hewitt (1986) mentions finding at least 30 items of Creole origin in the speech of young whites. The trend may well have accelerated since then. However, it is likely that the movement is not just in one direction, and that Creole as used by young second and third generation Caribbeans contains new words of British (not necessarily *English*) origin. The degree of cultural and linguistic contact between Creole and other British language varieties makes the origin of new terms difficult to pinpoint. The work of Rampton (1995, 1999) has shown that adolescents from different ethnic backgrounds in London are able to make use of each other's 'ethnic' languages to some extent.

One source of lexical innovation for British Creole is the Rastafarian religious movement, which has developed its own vocabulary for Rastafarian cultural practices and beliefs (Pollard 1994). Much of this vocabulary would also be used in the Caribbean. A distinctive Rastafarian linguistic practice which serves to make common lexical items incomprehensible to outsiders is to replace the first syllable of a word with *I* /ai/, as in *Idrin* (< *bredrin* 'brethren, fellow Rastafarians'), *ital* (<*vital* 'vegetarian food'), *iration* (< *generation*). Another practice is to replace 'negative' morphemes with their 'positive' counterparts, e.g. *overstand* < *understand.* Some of this vocabulary is occasionally used by non-Rastafarians.

Exercises and study questions

1. Look in detail at each element of the sentence below, noting its form and grammatical function, and characterise it as either London English (= same as Standard English in this case), British Creole, or potentially either.
   OK, star, we know say you is a top soldier down ah Yard. (= ex. 4 above)
2. It could be argued that the sentence in (1) is wholly in British Creole, or in a mixture of London English and British Creole. On what basis would you make each of these arguments? If it is a mixture of the two varieties, which parts of the sentence are in which variety?
3. Sebba (1993) recorded a London informant saying the following:
   (h)e wouldn't even be around /wen ai asli:p/ ('He wouldn't even be around when I'm asleep/sleeping')
   The utterance /wen ai asli:p/ has non-Standard English syntax so it was considered to be Creole (/wen mi asli:p/ would be even more clearly Creole). However, it is grammatically ambiguous within Creole.
   (a) What is the ambiguity (hint: see sections 2.3 and 2.5)?
   (b) What problems does this ambiguity pose for someone transcribing the utterance?

   Note:
   This example is discussed as a transcription issue in the *LIDES Coding Manual: A Document for Preparing and Analysing Language Interaction Data*, a special issue of the *International Journal of Bilingualism* (issue 4:2, 2000, pp. 131–270).
   'In this example, *I a sleep* could be *I* (subject pronoun – a form found in both London English and Jamaican Creole, although the Creole more typically would have *me* as the subject pronoun) followed by a Creole construction *a* (continuous aspect marker) + *sleep* (verb); or it could be *I* + *asleep*

(adjective), a construction consisting of two *English* lexical items combined in a characteristically Creole predicate adjective construction, which lacks the copula which the English construction requires (*am* in this case). In this transcription, the transcriber has taken the position that it is actually the first of these, and has represented it as three words rather than two.' (LIDES manual 2000:141)

4. The embedded clause of sentence (29): *She sey she name Mervalin* is in fact ambiguous, having two translations into Standard English:
   (i) She is called Mervalin
   (ii) Her name is Mervalin (with omission of the copula in this case)
   (a) Show how this ambiguity arises (i.e. show the syntax of each of the alternative readings).
   (b) How would you decide which of these was the actual syntactic structure of the sentence as used by the speaker? (Note that this is not the same as deciding which is the better translation in context!)

Selected references

Please consult the General references for titles mentioned in the text but not included in the references below. For a full bibliography see the accompanying CD-ROM.

DeCamp, David
1971 Towards a generative analysis of a post-creole speech continuum. In: Hymes (ed.), 349–370.

LePage, Robert B. and David DeCamp
1960 *Creole Studies I: Jamaican Creole*. London: Macmillan.

Pollard, Velma
1994 *Dread Talk*. Kingston: Canoe Press.

Rampton, Ben
1999 *Deutsch* in inner London and the animation of an instructed foreign language. *Journal of Sociolinguistics* 3: 480–504.

Sebba, Mark
1987 *The Syntax of Serial Verbs: An Investigation into Serialization in Sranan and Other Languages*. Amsterdam/Philadelphia: Benjamins.
1998 Phonology meets ideology: the meaning of orthographic practices in British Creole. *Language Problems and Language Planning* 22: 19–47.

Sebba, Mark, Sally Kedge and Susan Dray
1999 *The Corpus of Written British Creole: A User's Guide*. http://www.ling.lancs.ac.uk/staff/mark/cwbc/cwbcman.htm.

Synopsis: morphological and syntactic variation in the British Isles

Bernd Kortmann

1. Introduction

With the exception of British Creole, all varieties or regional groups of varieties spoken in the British Isles covered in this volume are L1 varieties, which makes the British Isles the second major L1 region in the Anglophone world, besides North America. Since this is, from the present-day perspective, the most distinctive characteristic of this world region, this synopsis will largely confine itself to these eight varieties or groups of varieties. More exactly, the focus will be on (the distribution of) the most salient properties and patterns of the so-called Celtic Englishes (IrE, ScE, WelE) as well as of the non-standard varieties spoken in the Orkney and Shetland Isles, in East Anglia, in the North, the Southwest, and the Southeast of England. Of these, IrE and the dialects in the North of England exhibit the largest number of non-standard morphosyntactic features, while the Orkney and Shetland dialects are the least non-standard of all British Isles varieties covered here.

British Creole (BrC) is the only Creole spoken in the British Isles and exhibits typical Creole properties like preverbal tense and aspect particles (e.g. the progressive marker *a* or the anterior marker *did*), *no* as a preverbal negator, deletion of *be*, and a *say*-based complementizer, as in *tell him* ***seh*** *we ready fe him* (Sebba, this volume). These properties are not attested in other varieties in the British Isles and not found in L1 varieties of English in general (cf. the Global Synopsis by Kortmann and Szmrecsanyi, 2004). Moreover, as pointed out by Sebba (this volume), giving an adequate account of BrC is even more complex than for Jamaican Creole, on which it is based, since variability in BrC also results from code-switching and L2 acquisition strategies. This makes the grammar of BrC even less suitable for inclusion in the present synopsis, as for most areas of morphosyntax special comments would be necessary setting BrC apart from all other, exclusively L1, varieties in this world region.

A synopsis is necessarily subject to severe constraints concerning the breadth and depth of coverage. As a consequence it may give the impression of a much higher degree of homogeneity and pervasiveness than is appropriate, especially for regional groups of varieties like the dialects of North England, where in a number of respects the dialects of the Far North(east) behave differently from those in the Central North (especially in Lancashire and Yorkshire). Below only the most remarkable features, patterns and tendencies will be addressed, based on the 76-features catalogue which forms the basis of the interactive maps on the CD-ROM (for an in-depth account cf. Kortmann and Szmrecsanyi, 2004) and the individual chapters in this volume, to which the reader is referred for detailed information. For easier reference, the number code of those features which are part of this catalogue is specified in square brackets. All examples are taken from the chapters unless indicated otherwise.

2. Tense, aspect and modality

Especially when compared with the L1 varieties in the US, the varieties of the British Isles, seen as a whole, do not exhibit many non-standard tense and aspect features, even if interesting (combinations of) properties may be attested in individual varieties.

The two most widely attested tense and aspect features, found in five varieties each, are the levelling of the difference between the **Present Perfect** and the Simple Past [25], which is especially pronounced in ScE, IrE, and the Southwest, and the use of *be* as a perfect auxiliary [26]. The conservative Germanic *be*-perfect is a typical northern feature (Orkney and Shetland, IrE, ScE, North), but also attested in the Southeast. In the Orkney and Shetland Isles the *be*-perfect has even taken over the entire territory of perfect marking, i.e. to the exclusion of *have*, as in *I'm seen it.* IrE makes use of both features and is, in general, that variety with the broadest array of perfect markers and constructions in the British Isles. Besides the *be*-perfect for mutative verbs and the use of medial objects (for resultative uses of the perfect, as in *And you eat nothing till you're, have the stations made*), both of which are recessive features, witness the use of the Simple Past for the experiential perfect (*Were you ever in Kenmare*?), of the Simple Present for the continuative perfect (*I'm in here about four months*), and of the clearly substratal (and most stereotypically Irish) *after*-perfect [33] for events in the recent past, as in *And when the bell goes at six you just think you were only after going over.* The medial-object perfect is also attested in ScE. Other special uses in ScE corresponding to the Present Perfect in StE include *there* with (a) the past participle in resultative contexts (*There's something fallen down the sink*) and (b) the Past Progressive for events in the recent past, as in *I was speaking to John on Friday there.*

For many non-standard varieties of English across the world (and spontaneous spoken English, in general) it has been observed that the **Progressive** is used with a wider range of verbs and displays a wider range of uses. This has resulted in suggestions that the English Progressive may indeed be on its way, or having developed already, into a general Imperfective (Gachelin 1997: 34-36, 43-44). This tendency is less pronounced in the British Isles, where we find a kind of north-south divide (see section 11 for more details of this divide). In the southern varieties (Southwest, Southeast, East Anglia) a widening use of the Progressive [21] is not reported. In fact, in traditional East Anglian dialect the simple form sometimes does service for *be* + V*ing* as a progressive marker, as in (*The*) *kittle bile*! ('The kettle's boiling!'). On the other hand, in ScE, the Northern dialects, and especially in IrE and the Orkney and Shetland Isles, the tendency for the Progressive to conquer further territory is confirmed. Beyond the widespread habitual use of the Progressive in WelE (*He's going to the cinema every week*), special meanings of the Progressive are attested mostly in the northern parts of Wales for older speakers with Welsh as their first language, suggesting Welsh influence on WelE. Concerning constructions coding progressive aspect, WelE, IrE, and the dialects of Northern England share a feature which is found only very rarely outside the British Isles, namely *was sat* and *was stood* with progressive meaning [32], as in *when you're stood there* 'when you are standing there' (which in IrE is the less frequent of the two).

Special markers of **habituality** are characteristic of the SW, WelE and IrE. Relevant markers are *do* [23] (*As I* ***do*** *say to my niece, I say,...*; SW), *be('s)* [22] especially in Northern Irish dialects and Ulster Scots (*It's better, because you* ***be's*** *bored doing nothing at home*), and *do be* [24], as in (*They* ***does be*** *lonesome by night...*; IrE). *Be(s)* and *do be* can be used both with the simple and progressive forms of the verb. In IrE habitual marking involving *do* is typical of urban working-class people and southern rural dialects.

Beyond the domain of habituality, IrE, WelE and the dialects of the SW share the use of *do* as a tense and aspect marker [27]. In WelE, for example, special progressive constructions involving *do* are attested, and in both WelE and, especially, the SW we find the use of unstressed *do* as an analytic tense marker, as in *She* ***did*** *do a lot of needlework*. The use of (forms of) *do* as tense and aspect markers is also attested for BrC and in many non-standard varieties outside the British Isles, especially in Pidgins and Creoles (cf. Kortmann 2004).

In the domain of **modality**, clear examples of **double modals** [34], as in *They might could be working in the shop*, are attested only in ScE and, as the only dialect area in England, in the Northeast, i.e. Northumberland and Tyneside. More combinations of modals are possible in ScE than in the Northeast, where the second element always needs to be *can* or *could* and where, in general, this feature is recessive. In general, the Northeast modals system resembles ScE much more than StE. In Orkney dialect only *can* 'be able to' is found in double modal constructions (e.g. *He'll no can deu that*). Another noteworthy modals feature which only these three northernmost British varieties share is that they categorically make use of **epistemic *mustn't*** [35], i.e. *mustn't* generally (in ScE indeed *must* generally) has the conclusion meaning, as in *This mustn't be the place*. This use is also found in IrE and the Southeast of England, but is categorical in neither of these two varieties. What applies to all non-standard varieties in the British Isles is the absence or very rare use of the StE modals *shall, should, may,* and *ought to*. In some varieties (e.g. ScE, North), for example, *will* is used instead of *shall* even in questions, as in *Will I open the window?*, and *can* is regularly used with permission sense, as in *You can have this afternoon off.* **Special (uses of) modal verbs or constructions** include *böst* 'had to, must' (Shetland), *man* 'must' (Orkney and Shetland), archaic past tense forms of *dare* (*dursn't/dussn't* 'dare not' in East Anglia), *want* meaning 'should' (ScE), and constructions with *need* or *want* combining with the past participle, as in *your hair needs cut* (North). Surprisingly rare, or at least rarely commented on, in the British Isles is the use of *would* in *if*-clauses [31] (attested only in ScE and the Southeast).

3. Verb morphology

For **non-finite forms** the most widely and pervasively attested morphological feature in the British Isles is the levelling of the morphological distinction between preterite and past participle forms. In seven out of eight varieties this is due to the use of either unmarked forms [37], as in … *and he come up to me and wanted to know*, or preterite forms also serving as past participles [38] (e.g. *you had to find out which one was broke*). The sole exception is WelE, which appears to make use of neither of these strategies, preferring the regularization of irregular verb forms [36], which indeed is the third levelling strategy used in Orkney/Shetland, the North, East Anglia, the Southwest and the Southeast. This strategy is not found in ScE and IrE, though.

Only the southern varieties (East Anglia, Southwest, Southeast) and WelE have *a*-prefixing on present participles [41] (e.g. *I'm a-runnen*). *For to* is regularly used as an infinitive marker in ScE (and BrC), whereas in more varieties it is used in infinitival purpose clauses [70] (see section 6 below).

With regard to **finite forms**, East Anglia is unique in the British Isles in that it categorically uses zero marking for the third person singular in the Present Tense [53] (*he go*, *she come*, *that say*), a pervasive feature in almost all other regions of the English-speaking world. In East Anglia, invariant present tense forms are found even for *be*, if only in a specific context, namely the so-called presentative invariant *be*, as in *Here I be*! Otherwise there is a wide array of variety-specific inflected forms of *be* (non-negated as well as negated) in all tenses, such as *bees* for the Present subjunctive in Orkney and Shetland. Attested in a number of varieties, especially in the Southeast, is the morphological distinction in the Past Tense between full verb and auxiliary for *do*, namely *done* full verb vs. *did* auxiliary, as in *She done it, didn't she?*. For the Southeast, more exactly Reading, something similar has been reported for *have*: only for the full verb is *has* used as the invariant Present Tense form for all persons in singular and plural, as in *We has a muck around here*.

4. Agreement

There is a pervasive tendency in non-standard varieties of English to do away with the last remnants of subject-verb agreement which we still find in StE (cf. also Hudson 1999). The most pervasive features in the British Isles in this respect are the following three. By far most widely attested is **existential/presentational *there's*,** *there is, there was* with plural subjects [55], which appears to be categorical in all eight varieties investigated (e.g. *There's no columns*, *There was quite a few mines*), and which may indeed be considered to have crossed the threshold of spontaneous spoken StE. Attested in six varieties (not in the Southwest and Orkney/Shetland) is the **generalization of past tense *be*-forms** [59], i.e. either *was* for all persons in the singular and plural (*You was thirsty and they was thirsty, too*) or *were* for all persons in the singular and plural (*I were thirsty and he were thirsty, too*), closely followed by **invariant present tense forms** due to the generalization of third person singular *-s* [54], which is found in five varieties (but not in ScE, Orkney and Shetland, the northern dialects of IrE, and East Anglia). East Anglia does not exhibit the latter feature because, as the only variety in the British Isles, it uses just the opposite strategy for creating invariant present tense forms, namely zero marking of third person singular *-s* [53]. In only two varieties has each of the two following non-agreement features been observed: in East Anglia and Orkney/Shetland the use of **variant forms of dummy subjects in existential clauses** [56] (e.g. in the Orkney dialect *der* 'there is/are' and *they/dey wir* 'they was/were', as in *They wir a coo lowse in the byre*), and in (northern conservative) IrE and the North of England the so-called **Northern Subject Rule** [60], which can roughly be formulated as follows: every verb in the present tense can take an *s*-ending (as in *Aye, and your sister and your mam comes out*) unless its subject is an immediately adjacent simple pronoun. (Third person singular verbs always take the *s*-ending, as in StE.) In other words, the Northern Subject Rule involves a type-of-subject constraint (pronoun vs. common/proper noun) and a position constraint (+/- immediate adjacency of pronominal subject to verb); for a comprehensive analysis of the Northern Subject Rule compare Pietsch (2005). Something related to this feature is attested for the Shetland dialect where plural subject nouns often combine with verbs ending in *-s*, as in *dis horses poos weel* 'these horses pull well' or *Dem at comes oonbid* 'those who come uninvited'.

5. Negation

The two by far most pervasive negation features in the British Isles, attested everywhere except for the Orkney and Shetland Isles, are **multiple negation** [44], as in *I couldn't find hardly none on 'em*, and unstressed ***never* as preverbal past tense negator** [49], as in *He never dropped like a set… against anybody* (referring to a specific tennis match). Multiple negation is far more frequently used in the South than in the North of England (see section 11 below). Two other stereotypical negation features in non-standard varieties are *ain't* and invariant *don't*. These two are, however, found in far fewer varieties (and with more restrictions) than in the other world regions of English investigated in the companion volumes. Both features are not attested in the two northernmost varieties of the British Isles (ScE, Orkney and Shetland). ***Ain't*** is primarily a southern phenomenon: as the negated form of *have* [46], as in *Him and I ain't been fishing for these last six weeks*, it is found only in the Southwest, the Southeast and East Anglia; as the negated form of *be* [45] (*He ain't heavy, he's my brother*) it is found in these three varieties as well as in WelE and IrE. Across all regions, *ain't* for negated forms of *have* is used much more frequently than for negated forms of *be*. **Invariant *don't*** [48] is a pervasive feature in WelE, East Anglia and the Southeast, but also attested in the dialects of North England. Interestingly, the Orkney and Shetland dialects exhibit none (!) of the nine non-standard negation features in our 76-features catalogue.

In East Anglia, the Southeast and the North we find an interesting phenomenon which has been observed in few other non-standard varieties of English around the world, namely the ***was-weren't* split** [51], as in *You was, weren't you?*. These varieties use *was* for all persons in the singular and (!) plural in affirmative sentences, while using *weren't* for all persons in singular (!) and plural in negative sentences, thus remorphologizing the number distinction of StE as a polarity distinction. What we have here is a showcase example of iconicity: a maximal difference in form (*was* vs. *weren't*) codes a maximal semantic and cognitive difference (affirmation vs. negation). The relevant non-standard varieties of English have clearly developed a more iconic polarity pattern than StE has.

Special negative markers are used in individual varieties. Best known is *nae,* which is a bound form in ScE (*They cannae sell it now, He isnae interested*), a free form in Orkney and Shetland (also *na*), and used both as a free and bound form in northern IrE. Also well known from these varieties in the northern parts of the British Isles is the use of *no* instead of *not* (most frequently with *be* and *have*), as in *She's no leaving* and *I've no seen him the day*.

Invariant concord tags of the type *innit/in't it/isn't it* [52] are a phenomenon typical of the three southern varieties (Southwest, Southeast, East Anglia). Otherwise an invariant tag particle is reported only for ScE, namely the agreement-seeking particle *e*, as in *He's coming, e?* or *He hadnae gone, e?* Other non-standard varieties have **tag systems** differing in interesting ways from the one of StE. In Tyneside English, for example, the tag system seems to be organized on the basis of the difference between questions seeking information and questions seeking confirmation. A special characteristic of IrE is that it allows *amn't* in tag questions (*I'm here, amn't I?*).

6. Subordination

The two most important domains to be discussed in this section are relativization and complementation. The most widely found **relativization strategies** in the British Isles are the following three (cf. also Herrmann 2005). First of all, across all regions, the use of **relative particles** (e.g. *that, what, as, at*) is much preferred over the use of relative (*wh-*) pronouns; moreover these relative particles are used in restrictive and non-restrictive contexts alike [62]. Of the non-standard relative particles, *what* [61] has the widest distribution and is indeed spreading: it is found everywhere in the British Isles except in the northern varieties (i.e. not in Orkney/Shetland, ScE, IrE; it is very rare, too, in Northumberland and Tyneside). Also found in five varieties (ScE, North, WelE, SW, SE) are **analytic possessive forms** (e.g. *that his, that's, what his, what's*) instead of *whose* [65], and (in IrE, North, East Anglia, Southeast, Southwest) **gapping** (or: zero-relativization) in subject position [66], as in *My friend's got a brother used to be in the school* and especially in existential and cleft constructions like *There was a parson went away from the village here*. In four varieties **resumptive (or: shadow) pronouns** [67] are regularly used, especially in IrE and the North, but also in the Southwest and ScE (e.g. *Out of the three questions we got two of them*). Regionally most restricted in the British Isles is the use of the **relative particles *as* and *at***, both of which are recessive. *As* [63] is found both in the North and the South (Southeast and Southwest), e.g. in *my dear sister as is dead and gone*, while *at* [64] is exclusively a northern feature attested only in the (middle) North of England (e.g. *Kelvin at my first husband came out of*), Ulster Scots (here also *ats* 'whose'), and Orkney and Shetland. Another non-standard property of relative clauses which does not seem to have a wide regional reach is the omission of prepositions attested in ScE (e.g. *of course there's a rope that you can pull the seat back up* [*with* omitted]).

For **complement clauses**, the two most pervasive features in the British Isles are **inverted word order in indirect questions** [69], as in *He asked me had I seen her*, and **unsplit *for to*** in infinitival purpose clauses [70], as in *there was always one man selected for to make the tea*. The former feature is found in all varieties except Orkney and Shetland, East Anglia and the Southeast. The only variety where unsplit *for to* is not attested is East Anglia. In ScE the infinitive is regularly marked by *for to*, also in non-purposive contexts like *You werenae allowed at this time for to go and take another job on*. ScE also offers many examples, which upon closer examination may as well be observed in other varieties, of different verb complementation patterns than in StE, e.g. verbs taking both infinitives and gerunds as complements where StE allows only one of the two, or verbs taking the infinitive where StE takes the gerund and vice versa. In ScE, young speakers, in particular, seem to prefer gerunds over infinitives. For certain verbs taking infinitival complements individual non-standard varieties omit the *to* (e.g. IrE for the verbs *order, compel, allow* and *help*).

The most pervasive and (near-) categorical subordination feature in the British Isles is to be found neither among relative nor complement clauses, but for **comparative clauses**, namely the use of ***as what / than what*** [71] (*He's older than what he looks, more than what you'd think*). Only in the Orkney and Shetland Isles is this feature not attested, otherwise it may be considered one of the top candidates for a non-standard feature on the brink of becoming part of the (informal) spoken standard.

For other types of subordinate clauses, notably **adverbial clauses**, many variety-specific connectives and uses of subordinators different from StE can be observed. Consider, for example, IrE *from* 'since' and *what time* 'when', or in traditional dialects of East Anglia the subordinating conjunctions *time* ('while' in *Go you and have a good wash time I git tea ready*) and, perhaps most strikingly, *do* ('otherwise, or else', as in *Don't you take yours off, do you'll get rheumatism*). Among special uses made of conjunctions known from StE we find, for example, IrE *whenever* 'when' (single occasion) or *while* 'until' in the Northern dialects, as in *Come home, see your horses, work while six o'clock*. One feature which has reached fame in the Celtic substrate debate is subordinating *and* in IrE (e.g. *I only thought of him there and* ['while'] *I cooking my* *dinner*) and, with restrictions also known from spontaneous spoken English, in ScE, where it is also used as an element introducing non-restrictive relative clauses. In ScE, Tyneside, and East Anglia we also find a special use of the StE coordinator *but*, namely as a sentence-final conjunctional adverb equivalent to *though,* as in *Well I warn't so very old but.*

7. Pronouns

The **most pervasive pronominal features** in the British Isles are the following three: *me* instead of *I* in coordinate subjects [10], as in *Me and my mam and dad are going out for a meal*, is pervasive in all eight varieties. Pervasive everywhere except in the Orkney and Shetland dialects is the use of *them* instead of demonstrative *those* [1], as in *Eat you them carrots*. Pervasive in all varieties except for ScE and Orkney/Shetland is *me* instead of possessive *my* [2] (*me mum, me brother)*. Another distinctive pronominal property of the British Isles varieties is **the use of *us***. In no other world region are there so many varieties which use *us* in functions different from those in StE [11]: this applies to all varieties apart from WelE and, again, Orkney and Shetland. Widest currency has singular *us* 'me' (*show us, give us a kiss, you're the first person that's give us a tip*), which is the only non-standard use of *us* in IrE and East Anglia, but frequent is also plural *us* 'we' in expressions like *us kids*. Of all varieties in the British Isles, the Northern dialects exhibit the widest functional range of *us*, notably possessive *us*, as in *We like us town*, which is largely restricted to the North. In the North we also find *us* in subject function (*Us'll do it*), which is part of a broader phenomenon known as **pronoun exchange** and documented only in the North, the Southwest and southern East Anglia: non-coordinated object forms are used in subject position [13] and, much more frequently (in East Anglia as the only option of the two), non-coordinated subject forms in object position [12], as in *Uncle Willy, they used to call him, you remember he*? The latter scenario is restricted to the first person plural in the North (*He got we out of bed*). Possibly, emphasis offers the key to understanding pronoun exchange (see Trudgill, this volume): subject pronouns occur as objects when they are emphasized, object pronouns as subjects when they are not emphasized. In East Anglia, emphasis (i.e. stress) also plays a role in the choice between *it* (only unstressed) and *that* (for stressed *it*), as in *Thass rainen* vs. *Ah, that wus me what done it*, on the one hand, and *they* vs. *thee*, on the other hand (*they* when stressed, *thee* when unstressed 'they', as in *Where are thee*?). These two features are not attested anywhere else in the British Isles.

Attested in more varieties, but nevertheless much more rarely in the British Isles than in non-standard varieties in other parts of the English-speaking world are **special forms or phrases for the second person plural pronoun** [3]: this feature is found pervasively in IrE and the Northern dialects, less so in ScE and East Anglia. The following pronominal forms are used: *yous(e)* is used in IrE (also *yez/yiz*), ScE (also *yins*) and Tyneside English (as well other areas in the North heavily influenced by Irish immigrants, such as Liverpool and inner-city Manchester). An analytic form can be found in East Anglia (*you... together*, as in *Where are you together*?). For the second person singular pronoun, we find in these (and other) dialects *you* or the conservative forms *ye, thou/thee*. In the Orkney and Shetland dialects *du/you* variation corresponds to ***thou/thee* variation** in the more traditional dialects of the North (especially in the Central North, like southern Yorkshire) and is an accommodation phenomenon.

In Orkney and Shetland, the Southwest and IrE we find a phenomenon which in the recent literature has come to be known as **pronominal gender,** gender animation or "gendered" pronouns (e.g. Wagner 2004, 2005). *She/her* is used for inanimate referents [7], as in *She was burning good* [about a house]. In Shetland English, for example, *lamp*, *fish*, *kirk*, *world* and some time expressions are feminine (*Da millennium is comin, but shö ...*). In IrE this usage seems to be largely restricted to cars and bikes. Much rarer, and a prominent feature only in the Southwest, is generic *he/his* for all genders [8], as in *I bet thee cansn' climb he* [about a tree]. This pronominal feature is also attested in Orkney and Shetland for tools and natural phenomena such as tide and (perhaps due to Norwegian substratum) weather, but in general much less pervasively than in the SW.

As for **reflexive pronouns**, regularized reflexives paradigms [4], as in *they did it theirself/-ves*, are attested everywhere in the British Isles except for WelE as well as Orkney and Shetland. In IrE this regularization does not include *hisself*. In five varieties (but not in ScE, WelE, and East Anglia), object pronoun forms may, additionally or alternatively to feature [4], be chosen as the base for reflexives [5], e.g. *meself*. In Orkney/Shetland the object pronoun forms by themselves may even serve as reflexives (e.g. *him* 'himself'). Besides these two properties of reflexives, three varieties exhibit a third one, namely a lack of number distinction in reflexives [6] (plural *-self*; IrE, Southeast, Southwest). Another relatively frequently found reflexives feature across the British Isles (attested in five varieties) is the use of *myself/meself* in a non-reflexive function [9], as in *this is me husband and meself*. By contrast, the absolute use of reflexives seems to be restricted to very few varieties, and is particularly prominent in IrE (e.g. *And by God, he said, ... he'd be the devil, if himself wouldn't make him laugh*) where it can interpreted as a kind of 'topic' marker.

Special **demonstratives** exhibiting remnants of the original three-term (close-distant-remote) system known from Middle English and traditional dialects of ScE and IrE are reported only for the dialects of the North, Orkney and Shetland (*yon* or *yonder* indicating remoteness). Moreover in a number of dialects (e.g. in the North, the Southwest and East Anglia), *this* and *that* are reinforced by *here* and *there* respectively, yielding *this here/that there*.

8. Noun phrase structure

The **two pervasive properties** which the British Isles varieties exhibit in the noun phrase are the absence of plural marking after measure nouns [14] (e.g. *four foot*, *three mile*) and the irregular use of articles [17]. Unusual uses of the definite article are reported for Orkney and Shetland, the North and in the Celtic Englishes, e.g. in IrE *the maths nowadays seems to be complicated*, or *poor people were starved with the hunger*. On the other hand, in some northern dialects (especially in Lancashire and Yorkshire) the reduction (e.g. to /t/ or a glottal stop) or even deletion of the definite article (especially in East Yorkshire) or indefinite article can be regularly observed. In Orkney and Shetland we find the invariant form *a* for the indefinite article, regardless whether the following noun begins with a consonant or a vowel.

The only varieties where **group plurals** [15] (e.g. *two Secretary of States*) and **group genitives** [16] (e.g. *the man I met's girlfriend*) are not reported are the northernmost variety (Orkney/Shetland) and the two southernmost varieties, i.e. the Southwest and the Southeast. For individual nouns many irregular plural forms could be reported (e.g. *knifes* or *wifes* in the Northern English dialects); similarly, for possessive forms, in the dialects of the North plurals and proper nouns ending in *-s* nevertheless take the possessive *-s* ending, yielding *Marks's* (for *Marks and Spencer*), *Joyce's* or *other folks's*.

With regard to **adjectives**, the two pervasive features in the British Isles, again with the exception of the Orkney and Shetland dialects, are the use of double comparatives and superlatives [19], as in *I'd be more happier out there than what I should be haymaking*, and regularized comparison strategies [20] (e.g. *one of the most pretty sunsets*, or *the regularest kind of person*), with restrictions in some varieties on the latter (e.g. in IrE *most pretty*, but not *regularest*).

9. Adverbs and prepositions

As in almost all non-standard varieties of English around the world, there is no formal distinction between adverbs and adjectives in the British Isles varieties, i.e. adverbs have the same form as adjectives. For example, this is a pervasive and exceptionless property for **manner adverbs** (*he came quick*) [42]; only for East Anglia it seems as if **adverbs used as degree modifiers** [43] keep their adverb ending *-ly*, different from the vast majority of non-standard varieties of English in the world (e.g. *a high technical job*).

Prepositional usage in non-standard varieties is certainly a field which merits systematic investigation, not least from a cognitive semantic perspective. However, no larger regional patterns can be identified in the British Isles. Interesting examples of prepositional usage in individual varieties include the following from Northern dialects: *down* instead of *in/to* (*He works down Manchester*), *off* or *with* instead of agentive *by* (*I won't do nothing unless I get paid for it. Not off my mam and dad anyway*), *off* instead of *from* in *my sister tapes some canny songs off the charts like*, and the omission of the prepositions *to* and *of* in double object constructions, as in *So, she won't give us it* (see also section 10). In Yorkshire *while* is used instead of *(un)til* (e.g. *working nine while five*), not only as a preposition but also as a subordinating conjunction (see section 6 above). In East Anglia, for example, StE *of* is pronounced *on*, as in *What do you think on it?* In other varieties *on* does service not only for StE *of* but also StE *for*, as in the WelE expressions *the name on* or *the term on* (e.g. *there's a word on that*).

10. Discourse organization and word order

Two syntactic features which are pervasive among the non-standard varieties in all other anglophone world regions are surprisingly rarely attested in the British Isles: the **lack of inversion or lack of auxiliaries in *wh*-questions** [73] (*What you doing?*) and the **lack of inversion in main clause *yes/no* questions** [74] (*You get the point?*), both of which can be considered a firmly established part of spontaneous spoken English. If these two features are reported at all in the British Isles then in the northern varieties (ScE, IrE, North of England; not in Orkney and Shetland). The varieties in the South of England (East Anglia, Southeast, Southwest) do not seem to exhibit them at all, and in WelE only [74] is attested.

By contrast, the **presence of the subject in imperatives**, as in *Go you there!*, is widely found. In **double object constructions**, either order of direct and indirect object is possible in northern dialects in the case of two pronominal objects (*He couldn't give him it*; *I tan* ['took'] *it her back*); if only one of the objects is a pronoun, then the pronominal object precedes the non-pronominal one (e.g. *Open me t'door*).

A characteristic property of the Celtic Englishes (and a likely case of Celtic substrate influence) is a predilection for **clefting and fronting**, with the former being slightly more common in IrE (*It's looking for more land a lot of them are;* cf. also reverse clefts in ScE, such as *And this was him landed with a broken leg*) and the latter in WelE (e.g. *Coal they're getting out mostly*). Of course, typical spontaneous spoken structures like **left-dislocation** (*Joan, she's an angel*) and, less frequently, **right-dislocation** (*He was some man him, He's got his head screwed on, has Dave*) are recurrently reported for many varieties.

As a focussing device, almost all non-standard varieties of the British Isles, especially those in the North (except for Orkney and Shetland) and the Celtic Englishes, employ ***like*** **as a focussing device** [75]. The dialects in the North of England exhibit a particularly broad range of uses of *like* in this function: clause-finally as a reinforcing element of right-dislocation (*I'm a Geordie, me, like*) or as an element indicating interest or surprise (*How'd you get away with that like?*), clause-initially as an element introducing a new topic (*Like for one round five quid, that was like three quid, like two-fifty each*). Especially in the speech of young people, ***like*** **is pervasive as a quotative particle** [76], as in *And she was like "what do you mean?"*.

11. Conclusion

Perhaps the most interesting result of the comparative study of the morphology and syntax of the non-standard varieties of the British Isles is a recurrent regional pattern. What emerges when viewing together the information in the volume chapters and in the large-scale comparative analysis of the British Isles varieties based on the 76-features catalogue investigated worldwide is a **north-south divide** for a range of morphosyntactic properties, with the core of the north constituted by ScE, Orkney/Shetland and the dialects of North England, and the south constituted by the Southwest, the Southeast, and East Anglia. For most of the relevant features, IrE (not least due to northern IrE) patterns with the varieties in the north, and WelE with those in the south. Table 1 illustrates those features which are exclusively or almost exclusively found in the varieties of the north, Table 2 the corresponding set for the south:

Table 1. North-South divide I: Morphosyntactic features exclusively or predominantly found in the northern parts of the British Isles

	NORTH					SOUTH		
	O/S	ScE	N	IrE	WelE	SW	SE	EA
3		✓	!	!				✓
21	!	✓	✓	!				
26	!	✓	✓	!		✓		
34	!	!	!					
35	!	!	!	✓			✓	
67		✓	!	!		✓		
73		✓	!	!				
74		✓	!	!	!			

✓ attested, but not frequently used
! pervasive

3 special forms or phrases for the second person plural pronoun (e.g. *youse, y'all, aay', yufela, you ... together, all of you, you ones/'uns, you guys, you people*)
21 wider range of uses of the Progressive (e.g. *I'm liking this, What are you wanting?*)
26 *be* as perfect auxiliary (e.g. *They're not left school yet*)
34 double modals (e.g. *I tell you what we might should do*)
35 epistemic *mustn't* ('can't, it is concluded that… not'; e.g. *This mustn't be true*)
67 resumptive / shadow pronouns (e.g. *This is the house which I painted it yesterday*)
73 lack of inversion / lack of auxiliaries in *wh*-questions (e.g. *What you doing?*)
74 lack of inversion in main clause *yes/no* questions (e.g. *You get the point?*)

To these we may add the Northern Subject Rule [60], found exclusively in northern IrE and the North of England, as well as the relative particle *at* [64] in the North of England as well as Orkney and Shetland.

Table 2. North-South divide II: Morphosyntactic features exclusively or predominantly found in the southern parts of the British Isles

	NORTH					SOUTH		
	O/S	ScE	N	IrE	WelE	SW	SE	EA
41					✓	✓	✓	!
45				✓	✓	✓	✓	!
46						✓	✓	!
52		✓			!	✓	✓	
61			!		✓	✓	✓	!

✓ attested, but not frequently used
! pervasive

41 *a*-prefixing on *ing*-forms (e.g. *They wasn't a-doin' nothin' wrong*)
45 *ain't* as the negated form of *be* (e.g. *They're all in there, ain't they?*)
46 *ain't* as the negated form of *have* (e.g. *I ain't had a look at them yet*)
52 invariant non-concord tags (e.g. *innit/in't it/isn't* in *They had them in their hair, innit?*)
61 relative particle *what* (e.g. *This is the man what painted my house*)

Another syntactic feature supporting this north-south divide is multiple negation (or: negative concord), as in *I've **never** been to market to buy **no** heifers*. As in most regions of the English-speaking world, multiple negation [44] is widely attested, too, in the British Isles, with the sole exception of the Orkney and Shetland dialects. However, a most surprising and as yet undocumented regional skewing is reported in Anderwald (this volume, 2005) for England, Scotland and Wales. In analyzing (a) the spoken subsample of the British National Corpus and (b) the data in the Freiburg English Dialect corpus (FRED), Lieselotte Anderwald found a clear south-north cline, with rough proportions of multiple negation usage of 40-45% in the South of England, 30% in the Midlands, and around 10% in the North of England, Scotland and Wales.

Beyond this major north-south divide, which has not been observed before and needs to be explored further, two points seem worthwhile mentioning. The first of these relates to the varieties in the North of the British Isles. Although the grammar of the Orkney and Shetland dialects is allegedly closely modelled onto the grammar of ScE, more parallels can be found between the grammars of ScE and the dialects of the North (especially Northeast) of England than between those of ScE and the Orkney and Shetland dialects. Of the 76-features catalogue investigated worldwide, five features attested in Orkney and Shetland are not attested in ScE, and 24 morphosyntactic features attested in ScE are not documented for the Orkney and Shetland dialects. In general, the Orkney and Shetland dialects exhibit the by far smallest number of non-standard morphosyntactic features in the British Isles. Secondly, it is in the tense and aspect domain that IrE and WelE, often joined by the dialects in the Southwest of England, exhibit properties not or hardly found in other varieties. Relevant features are the use of special habitual markers and constructions, and *was sat/stood* with progressive meaning.

Finally, this comparative analysis allows us to identify **the most and the least widely attested morphosyntactic features** in the non-standard L1 varieties of the British Isles. Of the 76 features investigated in the non-standard varieties of English around the globe (see Kortmann and Szmrecsanyi, 2004), the following are attested in only one or at most two varieties in the British Isles. Four features are attested in only **one variety**: generic *he/his* for all genders [8] in the Southwest, habitual *be* [22] in (especially Northern) IrE, the *after*-Perfect [33] in IrE, and invariant present tense forms due to zero marking for the third person singular [53] in East Anglia. Attested in no more than **two varieties** are, for example, non-coordinated subject pronoun forms in object function [12] and, vice versa, non-coordinated object pronoun forms in subject function [13] in the North and Southwest, *would* in *if*-clauses [31] in ScE and the Southeast, variant forms of dummy subjects in existential clauses [56] in East Anglia as well as Orkney and Shetland, the Northern Subject Rule in northern IrE and the North of England, and the relative particle *at* [64] in the dialects of the North as well as the Orkney and Shetland Isles. On the other hand, we can also pinpoint the most pervasive grammatical properties in the British Isles. In **all eight non-standard L1 varieties** do we find existential/presentational *there's, there is, there was* with plural subjects [55], *me* instead of *I* in coordinate subjects [10], adverbs (other than degree modifiers) derived from adjectives lack *-ly* [42], and the absence of plural marking after measure nouns [14]. Attested in at least **seven varieties** are *them* instead of demonstrative *those* [1], the irregular use of articles [17], double comparatives and superlatives [19], levelling the distinction between preterite forms and past participles via the use of unmarked forms [37] or via preterite forms replacing the past participle [38], degree modifier adverbs lacking *-ly* [43], multiple negation/negative concord [44], *never* as preverbal past tense negator [49], *as what / than what* in comparative clauses [71], and *like* as a focussing device [75].

Whether the top British Isles features are equally pervasive, and the rarest features in the British Isles equally rare, in the other world regions covered in the three companion paperback volumes has been explored in the Global Synopsis (Kortmann and Szmrecsanyi, 2004). It is there, too, that the regional distribution of the 76 morphosyntactic features in the appendix has been put in perspective against a comparison of the structural properties of non-standard L1 varieties, L2 varieties, and Pidgins and Creoles.

Exercises and study questions

1. Of which group of varieties in the British Isles are the following examples characteristic?
   a) *It's looking for more land a lot of them are*
   b) *Joan, she's an angel*
   c) *He's got his head screwed on, has Dave*
   d) *How'd you get away with that like?*
   e) *And she was like "what do you mean?"*

2. Draw up a list of the various types of present perfect constructions and check which of the individual British Isles varieties make(s) use of them.

3. Which of the following negation phenomena is/are untypical of L1 varieties in the British Isles?

a) *I couldn't find hardly none on 'em.*
b) *He never dropped like a set... against anybody* (referring to a specific tennis match)
c) *Him and I ain't been fishing for these last six weeks.*
d) *He don't live in there.*
e) *You was, weren't you?*
f) *Perhaps she have a secret man and nuh tell we.* (CWBC, fiction)

4. In what way(s) are the dialects of Orkney and Shetland different from all other British Isles varieties discussed in this volume?

5. Review the relative particles used in the British Isles, commenting especially on the degree of regional spread and their spreading or diminishing frequency of use.

6. Identify five features found in several British Isles varieties which represent conservatisms (i.e. remnants of previous periods of English).

7. Select any three domains of morphosyntactic variation in the British Isles and check whether the non-standard varieties exhibit a higher degree of regularity and/or consistency than Standard English does.

8. What are the most striking parallels and, especially, differences concerning pervasive morphosyntactic features in the L1 varieties of the British Isles and those of North America? Is it possible to identify individual (groups of) British Isles varieties which are particularly close to the American and Canadian L1 varieties?

References

Anderwald, Lieselotte
2004 Local markedness as a heuristic tool in dialectology: The case of *amn't*. In: Kortmann (ed.), 47–67.
2005 Unexpected regional distributions: Multiple negation in FRED. In: Yoko Iyeiri (ed.), *Aspects of Negation*. Kyoto: Kyoto University Press.

Gachelin, Jean-Marc
1997 The progressive and habitual aspects in non-standard Englishes. In: Schneider (ed.), 33–46.

Herrmann, Tanja
2005 Relative clauses in English dialects of the British Isles. In: Kortmann, Herrmann, Pietsch and Wagner, 21–123.

Hudson, Richard
1999 Subject-verb agreement in English. *English Language and Linguistics* 3: 173–207.

Kortmann, Bernd
2004 *Do* as a tense and aspect marker in varieties of English. In: Kortmann (ed.), 245–275.

Kortmann, Bernd and Benedikt Szmrecsanyi
2004 Global synopsis: morphological and syntactic variation in English. In: Kortmann, Burridge, Mesthrie, Schneider and Upton (eds.). 2 Volumes, 1111–1117 (Volume 1), 1142–1202 (Volume 2).

Pietsch, Lukas
2005 *"Some do and some doesn't"*: Verbal concord variation in the north of the British Isles. In: Kortmann, Herrmann, Pietsch and Wagner, 125–209.

Wagner, Susanne
2004 "Gendered" pronouns in English dialects – A typological perspective. In: Kortmann (ed.), 479–496.
2005 Gendered pronouns in the Southwest of England. In: Kortmann, Herrmann, Pietsch and Wagner, 211–367.

Index of subjects

D

M

N

Q

R

T

Index of varieties and languages

P

R

S

U

W